Your Hidden Face:
Projection in the Horoscope

Tim Lyons

Copyright 2014 by Tim Lyons

No part of this book may be reproduced or transcribed in any form or by any means, electronic or mechanical, including photocopying or recording or by any information storage and retrieval system without written permission from the author and publisher, except in the case of brief quotations embodied in critical reviews and articles. Requests and inquiries may be mailed to: American Federation of Astrologers, Inc., 6535 S. Rural Road, Tempe, AZ 85283.

ISBN-10: 0-86690-653-3
ISBN-13: 978-0-86690-653-1

Cover Design: Jack Cipolla

Published by:
American Federation of Astrologers, Inc.
6535 S. Rural Road
Tempe, AZ 85283

www.astrologers.com

Printed in the United States of America

Preface: Some Words About Words

Unless otherwise noted, the gendered pronoun "he" refers to a person of either gender. "He or she" seems unduly cumbersome, particularly when used continually throughout an entire book, and "s/he" seems graceless; "she" could easily induce readers to think that I wish to make a point related to gender when I have no such point in mind.[1] In England, one might feel perfectly comfortable using "one," but to readers from this side of the pond, such usage often sounds stilted, so one should think twice before presenting it to American audiences. In the chapters on gender-related projections, the gender-related pronouns will have more specific meanings, of course.

I use the word *psychic* in the Jungian sense: not to denote "psychic abilities," but merely to indicate that the material has its primary locus in the mind.[1]

---

[1] Judith Jarvis Thomson, *The Realm of Rights* (Cambridge: Harvard University Press, 1990), 3.

Table of Contents

Chapter I. Projection: The Basic Pattern	1
Chapter II. Gender-Based Projections I	23
Chapter III. Gender-Based Projections II: The Moons of Men	57
Chapter IV. Gender-Based Projections III: Other Gender-Based Projections	85
Chapter V. Aspects and Projection	125
Chapter VI. Houses as Indicators of Projections	147
Chapter VII. Perception, Projection and the Signs	169
Chapter VIII. The Foci of Security: Saurn and the Moon	207
Chapter IX. Collective Projection	243
Chapter X. Projection and United States Foreign Policy	275
Chapter XI. Perception and "Reality"	319
Chapter XII. Truth-Seeking 101: An Epilogue of Sorts	349
Appendix I. Polarity Therapy: The Six-sign Zodiac	357
Appendix II. Chart Data	371
Bibliography	385
Index	389

Chapter I

Projection: The Basic Pattern

I. Projection

Swiss psychologist Carl G. Jung referred to projection as "an unconscious, that is, unperceived and unintentional, transfer of subjective psychic elements onto an outer object."[1] If a person projects such "subjective psychic elements" onto an outer object, he will not see that outer object accurately. Rather, he will see some mixture of the outer object with the "subjective psychic elements" and thus not see the object objectively. In looking at the world and relating to it, a person will see, not the world "as it really is," but as a mixture of his own (generally unconscious) psychic contents with external elements. In other words, what we generally refer to as "observation" often doesn't qualify as such, for most (perhaps all) of our observations involve a lot more unconscious shaping, interpreting, and deciding than simple observing. This statement doesn't refer solely or primarily to after-the-fact conceptualizing, but to something that happens unconsciously—and apparently automatically—in our interactions with the world.

To some extent, Jung developed his ideas about projection from Freud's ideas about transference (though Jung used the latter term as well). When Freud spoke of transference, he meant both the transfer of early-life parental images from patient to analyst in the process of psychoanalysis *and* something more general. In *An Autobiographical Study*, he wrote:

> It must not be supposed…that transference is created by analysis and does not occur apart from it. Transference is merely uncovered and isolated by analysis. It is a universal

---
[1] Marie Louise von Franz, *Projection and Re-collection in Jungian Psychology* (London: Open Court, 1987), 3.

phenomenon of the human mind; it decides the success of all medical influence, and in fact dominates the whole of each person's relations to his human environment.[2]

Further, Freud said, the transference "is used…to induce the patient to perform a piece of psychical work—the overcoming of his transference-resistance—which involves a permanent alteration in his mental economy."[3] We can probably agree that much unconscious material, and thus much projection, involves early life or even infantile material related to the parents, even if we sometimes disagree with Freud about the emphasis we give to that material.[4]

Freud and Jung recognized that much of a person's experience of the world, even if the person takes it as "objective," has an ongoing connection to unconscious contents that we transfer to, or project upon, the world around us. That unconscious material constantly arises through and in the events of a world we see as an objective conglomeration of some sort, and it permeates not only what Freud called "the whole of each person's relations to his human environment," but each person's relations with the non-human environment as well, for we can cast our projections onto institutions, collective developments, and even elements of the material world, just as we do onto individuals.

Some would say that it's neither possible nor desirable to stop the process entirely; let's put off until a later chapter our discussion of this issue. For practical purposes, we can talk of understanding the process more fully so that we can reduce the suffering that arises when we become blinded, and even dragged or driven about, by projections, that series of ongoing and largely unseen or unacknowledged links that bind together mind (generally the unconscious elements), individual perception,[5] and the phenomenal world as a whole. These links appear through projections that on the one hand form a series of bridges that we cross to encounter other people and the world, and that on the other hand obstruct our relationship *to* and understanding *of* that world. We generally remain unaware of our projections, taking them as part of "normal" existence. In short, we take our projections as reality. As Jung put it,

> …every normal person of our time, who is not reflective beyond the average, is bound to his environment by a whole system of projections. So long as all goes well, he is totally unaware of the compulsive, i.e., "magical" or "mystical" character of these re-

---

[2] Sigmund Freud, *The Freud Reader*. Edited by Peter Gay. (New York: W.W. Norton and Company, 1989), 26.
[3] Freud, 26.
[4] In his natal horoscope, Freud has Mars retrograde in Libra as the handle of a bucket configuration; he also has Uranus and Mercury (and the Sun, though more loosely) square the Midheaven-Nadir axis. Surely he had his own issues to resolve regarding repression and parental images. This doesn't mean that we should see his ideas as merely reflecting his own psychology—his own transference, writ large as psychological theory—but we needn't insist on them with the Taurean firmness that Freud did. We might also note his Mercury-Uranus conjunction as pointing directly to his revolutionary insights, for surely he had many.
[5] As we will see, this apparently simply term masks some complexity. In a later chapter, we will divide it into its parts; for now, let's just consider "perception" as a process by which we link mind, perceptual organs, and the perceived phenomena.

lationships…So long as the libido can use these projections as agreeable and convenient bridges to the world, they will alleviate life in a positive way. But as soon as the libido wants to strike out on another path, and for this purpose begins running back along the previous bridges of projection, they will work as the greatest hindrances it is possible to imagine, for they effectively prevent any real detachment from the former object. We then witness the characteristic phenomenon of a person trying to devalue the former object as much as possible in order to detach his libido from it.[6]

This doesn't mean, of course, that the individual can't prevent himself from projecting or that he *must* project in order to maintain proper function. That someone takes a process to be part of "normal existence" doesn't mean that the process must remain in its current state or that the person can have no influence over it. We know, for example, of organs in the human body that developed as "part of normal existence" but that we no longer need—and that in some cases can cause great difficulties, even death.[7] Nevertheless, it seems that people *do* use their projections as a way to make contact with the world around them: in myriad ways, they make that connection through the mind, by adopting various versions of the world and the people in it. Our problems arise, it seems, not because we have such versions of the world, but because we become attached to them and because they often don't correspond very closely to the world itself.[8]

Much evidence suggests that people can to a large extent free themselves from the bindings and blindings of projection. The degree to which they do so depends largely on their moral courage, their inquisitiveness, and the efficacy of the means they employ in their attempts to liberate themselves. If a person can free himself from his projections, he will surely see the world more accurately. But it probably does us less good to ask questions about "people in general," or even about particular others, than to ask similar questions about ourselves, at least at first. If we find ourselves making judgments about others, we should ask ourselves whether we might judge more accurately if we did so without the filter of our own projections, or whether, when free of such projections, we would wish to judge at all.

Jung felt that we shouldn't consider projection *per se* as a problem. As he pointed out, one generally recognizes a projection *as* projection only when the projection hinders or blocks one's adaptation to the world. Marie Louise von Franz explains:

> To be precise, we could in practice speak of projection only "when the need to dissolve the identity with the object has already arisen," or, in other words, when the identity [between perceiver and perceived, between subject and object] begins to have a

---

[6]Carl Jung, "General Aspects of Dream Psychology," GW 8, para. 507; qtd. in Von Franz, 8.
[7]Despite its alarming connotations, the comparison doesn't seem inapt. It seems that some particularly virulent projections—and many collective ones—can have enough power to harm or even kill. In a later chapter, we will return to a discussion of these matters.
[8]This noun phrase—*the world itself*—needs more examination. We will undertake that examination in later chapters, particularly chapters XI and XII.

disturbing effect and exerts a negative influence on the adaptation to the outer world. At this point the identity of the inner image with the outer object becomes perceptible and the object of criticism, whether it be our own or that of other people.[9]

When someone projects inner psychic material onto someone else, the receiver of the projection "becomes an *image* or a *carrier of symbols*."[10] The projector generally doesn't see this; rather, he sees the projection as identical with the material or person projected upon: he assumes that he perceives accurately. Jung called this the "archaic identity of subject and object," so called because the projector does not differentiate between the projected material, which belongs to him, and the projected-upon object, and because people have done this for, it seems, a very long time, and because the process seemed integrated into archaic cultures. Jung notes that we can observe this process quite clearly in so-called primitive peoples and children, just as we can observe it in so-called non-primitives like ourselves. According to Ms. von Franz, in such situations "the unconscious is merged with the outer world" so that "it is not yet possible to speak of an ego-environment relation, because an ego, as we understand it, hardly exists."[11] We purported non-primitives may assume that our egos have more clear boundaries, but closer examination will lead us to question such an assumption, and perhaps to conclude that in many situations we respond rather like so-called primitives, for like them, we find ourselves immersed "in a stream of events in which the outer and the inner world are not differentiated, or very indistinctly so."[12] And, like so-called primitives, we generally do not recognize the process, probably because though we have concepts about the boundary between internal and external worlds, we often fail to notice the permeable qualities of that boundary—or that it sometimes seems to dissolve altogether.

Though we may assume that we can distinguish clearly between perception and environment, with some sort of this-person-over-here objectively observing some set of those-things-or-people-over-there, if we look more closely we will see that this kind of dualism becomes quite tenuous—and when we have the willingness to acknowledge ourselves fully, we can see this tenuousness even in our most ordinary relationships. So while we may think that for us the unconscious "has become perceptible and an object of criticism" through a differentiation of consciousness, we possibly overestimate the degree to which such differentiation occurs.

For most of us most of the time, what we call "reality" arises so imbued with projections that we should probably question whether we should use the term "reality" at all, a matter to which we will return in later chapters. Most of the time, most of us remain mostly unaware of the dynamics of projection. Even when we strive to cut through the projection-making process, we often find our habit patterns persistent and apparently intransigent. We will explore some of this apparent intransigence in later chapters; here, we need note only that projection, while pervasive or nearly

---

[9]Von Franz, 9.
[10]Von Franz, 6.
[11]Von Franz, 7.
[12]Carl Jung, *Letters*, I, p. 549; qtd in Von Franz, 7.

so, and while not necessarily pathological or unnatural, leads every day, in both personal situations and international politics, to misunderstandings and misjudgments of all sorts, and that, as a result, people don't deal with the world as well as they might. At the same time, to very loosely paraphrase Ms von Franz, when we're engaged in everyday life, projection doesn't seem to be a problem until it becomes a problem.

In most cases, the projected characteristics appear in both the subject and the object, but the subject remains largely and habitually unaware of those characteristics in himself, seeing them primarily in the object. But this matter of seeing the projected characteristics in the object needs further investigation. It's not that the object doesn't possess those characteristics at all, for as Jung said, the outer object serves as a "hook" upon which the projector hangs the projection much as one hangs a coat upon a hook. However, the outer object or person does not possess those characteristics to the degree or in the unalterable way perceived by the subject. Thus the subject does not see the world—or himself—accurately. Jung puts the matter this way:

> Just as we tend to assume that the world is as we see it, we naively suppose that people are as we imagine them to be. In this latter case, unfortunately, there is no scientific test that would prove the discrepancy between perception and reality. Although the possibility of gross deception is infinitely greater here than in our perception of the physical world, we still go on naively projecting our own psychology into our fellow human beings. In this way everyone creates for himself a series of more or less imaginary relationships based essentially on projection.[13]

Generally speaking, the subject sees somewhat accurately and somewhat inaccurately, the degree of accuracy or inaccuracy varying according to many factors, and as we will see, we can trace many of these factors through natal, transiting, progressed, and directed factors in a horoscope. Jung's remarks about the "hook" upon which one "hangs" a projection suggest that we take projection-making as a matter of course, as part of what we experience as normal life; surely this occurs at least partly because, as Ms. Von Franz writes, "…seldom, if ever, is nothing of what is projected present in the object."[14] The projection therefore doesn't seem to delude; it forms part of what we take as "the real world." However, as the discrepancy between hook and projection grows, the projection can—and, hopefully, will—become more visible, more readily a subject of analysis, investigation, and curiosity.

The projections of a so-called psychotic seem to follow the same pattern as those of a purportedly sane person, but the former's hooks generally look more doubtful to others than do those of the latter. Those we call "psychotics" often hang enormous and, to the projector, opaque projec-

---

[13]Carl Jung, "General Aspects of Dream Psychology," *The Structure and Dynamics of the Psyche*, CW 8, para. 507; qtd.in Von Franz, 6.
[14]Von Franz, 3.

tions onto the smallest of hooks, whereas most purportedly sane people hang less enormous and less opaque projections onto much more reasonably sized hooks. If I project anger onto you, and if I and others take that projection as fitting, then quite likely you will appear angry, and quite likely I and others will refer to you as "an angry person" and find what we will take as "evidence" to support our conclusion. At the same time, those others and I will likely see me as a sane and non-angry person who has dealings with a sane and angry one. If I habitually make this kind of projection, I will habitually gravitate toward people generally considered "angry," and I will feel an odd kind of comfort in relating with such people. If I project my anger onto such people, I will find it easier to ignore it in myself, a result I might find provisionally pleasant, as I probably find the anger *un*pleasant when experienced as part of *me*; quite likely I do the projecting in large part *because* of this unpleasant feeling. I might even say to myself that I "am not an angry person," but that I "have learned to deal" with such people. If I project my anger onto "an angry person," the projection will seem to fit: many people will find my response sane and reasonable.

The so-called psychotic, on the other hand, may experience the same purportedly angry person as some sort of tyrant or evil monster, perhaps even as the devil himself or the embodiment of Adolph Hitler. The process of the so-called psychotic parallels that of the purportedly sane person, the two situations differing in degree but probably not in kind.[15] Whether we label a person as psychotic or sane, he will often defend himself rigorously against insight into his projections. Jung points out that if a person does accept correction, he falls into a depression.[16] It seems that the resistance to insight, here, forms part of ego's ongoing defense-mechanism: if a person sees through his projections, he will see through many of the ways that he props up his identity and maintains a convenient, though not necessarily wholesome and happy, adaptation to the world. He may realize, suddenly or in flashes, that his own solidity and reliability—his self-conception—have a rather mysterious relationship with his ongoing attempt to have a solid and reliable relationship with what he takes as the world "out there." Ego feels threatened, at least partly because ego describes itself in terms that exclude the "unacceptable" material that ego projects onto others. So, if ego begins to withdraw its projections, it will have to acknowledge psychological and behavioral factors it has heretofore rejected. This process seems integral to the discovery of what Jung called the *self*.

We generally project, whether onto individuals or into the environment in general, psychic material that we find unacceptable. In Jung's words, whatever is not integrated into the self appears in the world as an event. Ms. Von Franz summarizes this view, distinguishing it from the one held by Freud:

> In Freud's view, projection is a matter of a neurotic person's ridding himself of an emotional conflict by shifting it onto something else as the intended object...In Jung's

---
[15] Possibly, too, the psychotic more readily connects to the unconscious mind of the projected-upon person. The former may either pick up different data, so to speak, or more readily absorb the data he picks up; he may not let the rational mind intrude so much, or he may not harness the rational mind to what we might call "useful purposes." Thus he finds himself unable to make his projections appear "reasonable."
[16] Von Franz, 3.

view, however, this is only one of many possibilities. According to Jung, all psychic contents of which we are not yet conscious appear in projected form as the supposed properties of outer objects.[17]

Because so many projections arise from our rejection of certain parts of ourselves, the path begins with a more complete self-acceptance, though we will probably find it useful to consider that self acceptance more as a *process* than as a solid state of being. Similarly with investigating our projections: we engage a process that throws us back on ourselves.

If I project my anger onto Harriet, I can see Harriet as angry and myself as patient. But if I withdraw this projection to myself, I must recognize that *I* feel angry and must, as Jung put it, "call myself to order."[18] I can defend myself against this insight if I keep the projection quite solid, projecting into the world, and particularly onto Harriet, what *I* find unacceptable in myself. Conflict will result—probably more conflict than would arise were I to examine myself instead of merely coming to conclusions about Harriet. In doing so, I should remember that self-examination does not always and everywhere lead to peace, and that I shouldn't expect everything to go smoothly if I withdraw my projections. Still, if I *can* withdraw them, at least in part, I can begin to see where Harriet and I can at least have a more *useful* conflict or disagreement.

We may wish to see this process as "spiritual" because as we withdraw our projections, we cultivate compassion, both to ourselves and to others. We cultivate compassion to ourselves by cultivating self-acceptance, by acknowledging ourselves more fully. We cultivate compassion to others not only by trying to see them accurately, but also by attempting to stop a problematic kind of energy transfer. As we will see later, if I project my anger onto Harriet, I do her an unkindness in more than one way: not only do I misjudge her, but I also hand over to her some of the energy that I have "negativized" in myself. I have devalued this energy, found it unacceptable, and then projected this "unacceptable" energy onto Harriet. She will be hit by the projection and possibly be wounded by it – because, as Marie Louise von Franz says, "When one becomes the target of another person's negative projection, one often experiences that hatred almost physically as a projectile."[19]

Ms. Von Franz's remarks suggest the possibility of an actual transfer of energy, though of a kind that we would find difficult or impossible to measure. In any case, Harriet will surely *seem* to take in some of my anger, and if she does so unconsciously, her actions may reflect and in some sense *carry* my anger as well as her own, particularly when we find ourselves together. So not only do our projections make others seem more negative or disagreeable to us, they may also affect those people in what may appear as organic ways.

If, on the other hand, I withdraw my projections, Harriet will probably feel better—and our relationship will have more space in which to develop. This doesn't mean that the relationship will flourish. After all, once I own my own feelings, I may recognize how angry I feel towards Harriet,

---

[17] Marie Louise Von Franz, "Projection," *Psychotherapy* (Boston: Shambhala, 1993), 256.
[18] Carl Jung, *Modern Man in Search of a Soul* (New York: Harcourt Brace Jovanovich, 1933), 203.
[19] Von Franz, *Projection and Re-collection in Jungian Psychology*, 21.

or perhaps toward people in general, or perhaps at times toward the entire cosmos! As long as Harriet serves as a hook for my anger (or some other psychic content), I may preserve some elements of a cherished self-image, but my relationships will hardly flourish if I continue to deny my own tendencies, energies, and potentials. Withdrawing my projections may lead to depression at first, but if it also leads to a more sober self-understanding, it may engender all sorts of changes that will prove helpful in the long run. To the degree that Harriet has carried some of my psychic energy, *she* will feel a great release of pressure as well. We will explore this kind of energy-transfer in succeeding chapters.

To the degree that I project, to that same degree I refuse to accept myself in all of my complexity. If I refuse to see myself accurately, how will I expect others to do so; and how will I see others accurately? And if I don't see others accurately, how will I find satisfaction in my interactions with them?

Some of this may seem to ignore Jung's claim that the subject projects positive qualities as well as negative ones. Though we could easily find examples of people projecting those qualities, we should also remember that some qualities, though seeming positive from an "objective" point of view, may seem less positive to the person who has them. In general, a person will tend to project qualities that he feels do not accord with his self-image, with some set of cherished and probably not-entirely-conscious convictions about himself. For example, a person may see himself as a meek or retiring person. He may reject – and therefore project into the world—his own ability to have authority or to rule or take charge. He may have significant and unacknowledged abilities in this area, and these abilities might, if put to use, produce much good in the world. But his cherished self-image, even if it produces suffering, will not admit these qualities.[20] He will likely project them, experiencing them through authority figures with whom he has difficulties; meanwhile, the inner authority, the capacity for authoritative action, goes unacknowledged. The people onto whom he projects these qualities will probably appear—to him, and when he finds himself in their presence—excessively authoritative.

Furthermore, to the individual, these "positive" qualities will often appear in problematic form in the world precisely because the person has "negativized" them in his own mind, though not necessarily consciously. Thus even apparently positive qualities may, when they appear as projections, seem negative, or at least problematic. Some people experience these "positive" qualities through rather negative projections; others experience them through longing: through situations in which the positive qualities appear in what one takes as positive qualities in others.

So a person's attachment to cherished notions about himself—cherished and habitual notions that have helped him form and maintain a coherent view of himself—discourage him from with-

---

[20] When we investigate the personal history in such cases, we will often find a strong influence from the early family environment. In a horoscope, they will often arise in connection with the twelfth house, the Moon, Saturn, and the fourth and tenth houses. See chapters III, VI, and VIII.

drawing his projections. If he withdraws his projections, he alters his image of himself and must undergo what Ms Von Franz calls a "moral integration" of the projected material:

> What is known as integration in modern psychology is thus a remarkable and complicated process, in which a hitherto unconscious psychic content is brought repeatedly into the view of the conscious ego and recognized as belonging to its own personality.[21]

It takes inner strength to integrate these unacceptable contents. Without inner strength and confidence, the person may feel inundated with hitherto unconscious material that will seem to drown the personality. However, if the person can summon enough inner strength to accept his own contradictions and conundrums, enough to undergo the moral integration described above, he may experience depression. If he gets through this process, he develops even more strength, feels less afraid of his mind or of depression. If he accepts what he sees as his limitations, he feels less limited.

So to withdraw projections will not necessarily strengthen the ego in the usual sense, for that "usual sense" depends on blindness and self-conceit. Ego maintains itself not only by internally-held convictions about itself, but also by a series of projections that serve, in various ways, to anchor it in the world, to give it some sense of stability. We could probably define ego as, in part, the process by which we hold onto these convictions while remaining blind to these projections and their results. As one begins to see more clearly, one sees the hollowness of the whole process and thus feels insecure, seeing the inaccuracy of many cherished notions about the world, including one's interpretation of other people and situations. In other words, as ego begins to see projections *as* projections, ego feels threatened. Feeling threatened, it will throw up all sorts of defenses both subtle and not-so-subtle. But if one brings the material "repeatedly into the view of the conscious ego," as in some forms of counseling, one can make progress, gaining insight while retaining a firm and authentic sense of strength, presence, and confidence. Paradoxically, one gains this confidence by constantly undermining one's psychological security.

II. Using Astrology to Illuminate and Elucidate Projections

Let's start with a hypothetical case. Consider a well-educated, highly aware, creative woman (later we will describe analogous situations for a man[22]) who feels that her partner "is getting restless," feels that he has all sorts of "new interests" (perhaps, either in her imagination or in the extensional realm,[23] including a new relationship or affair), wants to stray, wants "more space," doesn't want to commit, wants to see other women or explore other relationships (intimate or otherwise), wants to engage himself in some sort of new work or enterprise—and so forth. We all probably

---

[21]Von Franz, *Projection and Re-collection in Jungian Psychology*, 11.
[22]At least for now, let's not get bogged down by asking what "highly aware" means.
[23]I have borrowed this term—*the extensional realm*—from S.I. Hayakawa's *Language in Thought and Action*. It refers to the world that goes on outside of our heads, purportedly (and according to most) independent of our ideas about it—matters to which we will return. Hayakawa uses *intensional* to refer to operations taking place in the mind (i.e. thoughts, evaluations, conclusions, etc.). See *Language in Thought and Action*, chapter four.

know the story, with its attendant insecurity, lack of self-esteem, impotent anger, and so on. Of course, the woman may misinterpret the situation, but quite likely her version contains at least *some* truth. The partner, the hook for the projection, may well feel some of what the woman feels certain that he feels, though probably not to the same degree, at least not at first.

If we looked at the partner's horoscope, we might well find some corroborating evidence: some transit or progression involving Uranus, or even Neptune; something involving what we generally call the "relationship points" (Moon, Venus, Ascendant, or even the Sun or Mars); in some cases developments involving horoscope factors related to creative work (or, in many cases, claims about creative work purportedly to get done, for as we will see when we look more carefully at Uranus, the person may resist bringing that work to fruition). We might say, then, that the woman's fears "are justified," that the man "really" feels what she feels so convinced that he feels. Perhaps he would even say, were we to ask him, that his partner's fears have some basis in fact, that he really *does* want more freedom or is interested in another woman, some new work, more space, and so forth.

Even if the woman's version of things has some basis in what we can verify about the man's reactions, we should look more closely. Astrologers will note that we don't need the man's horoscope to deduce much of what we see; we can deduce a good deal of it, at least the general outlines of the situation and sometimes considerably more than that, from the *woman's* horoscope, the evidence from the man's horoscope serving only to corroborate what we see in the woman's. This should give us pause. What, after all, can we say about the relationship between her horoscope and her experience? We could also put the question this way: what connection can we discern between her inner world and the developments taking place in her life? What connection can we see between developments in *her* horoscope and *his* actions or state of mind?

It might seem strange—though when you've seen it often enough it doesn't seem strange at all—that we can deduce much of one person's feelings and actions from another person's horoscope, particularly the horoscope of a close partner. Theoretically, a person's horoscope tells us about that person alone, not about other people or about the world in general; the birth-data, after all, applies to a person, not to the larger world. So much for theory. In the scenario sketched above, you can bet your broken down, ragged Ford[24] that you'd find, in the woman's horoscope, a challenging transit, direction, or natal aspect involving Uranus, Saturn, the Sun, or Mars; and if you wanted to win your bet, you'd probably place your bets on Uranus—bringer of revolution and freedom, a planet with no liking for premature commitments, or for any commitments at all, a planet loathe to give up his freedom, insisting as he does that one should remain free to create one's life day-to day—whose symbolism seems in this case to describe the man's behavior more than the woman's. In many cases, we will find in the woman's horoscope an afflicted Uranus, or Uranus in the seventh house, or "difficulties" with some of the above-named planets, probably activated by transit, direction, or progression.

---

[24]Thanks to Chuck Berry for providing the phrase.

Let's put aside for now questions about whether human beings "are inherently non-monogamous"; let's also put aside questions about the morality involved in such situations and about whether men (or women) who stray "are immature *puers*" (or *puellas*).[25] Instead, let's concern ourselves first with the demonstrable fact that we can see in the various astrological factors of a person's horoscope many situations that seem external to that person, for the horoscope will often describe not only a person's character, but his experience as well, including the people or institutions that contribute to that experience, reminding us of Marc Edmund Jones' remark about character being destiny. The same applies to the horoscopes of nations and other collectivities, where, not surprisingly, the process seems more mechanical and therefore more predictable. (See chapters IX and X.) Once we see this connection, we should inquire about its causal factors, and once we do that, we might ask how we can alleviate the suffering so often associated with it.

Astrologers have surely seen again and again that one person's behavior arises in someone else's horoscope. Still, the pattern should seem stranger to us than it apparently does. That we expect to see this doesn't mean we should take it for granted or leave it unexamined. The pattern suggests something rather odd or mysterious about the world—and about horoscopes. If in theory my horoscope, drawn from *my* birth data, gives information about *me*, then why should some factors in my horoscope arise through others? Why should my horoscope predict, often with great precision, the behavior of those other people, and even tell me something of their inner worlds? If my horoscope tells us about *my* mind, should we conclude that my mind and the phenomenal world (including, it seems, the minds of others) have an ongoing and intimate involvement? Should we conclude that we can't really distinguish between the two? Perhaps, but let's leave this kind of question until later in our investigation and begin, instead, with the observations noted above: that when astrologers examine someone's horoscope, they see, again and again, symbolic representations of the people and events in that someone's life—and not only intimate partners, but also children, sometimes friends, bosses, coworkers, or employees.

Furthermore—and here we come to the *raison d'etre* for this book—we can trace many of the operant psychological factors by referring to specific astrological ones and by utilizing standard and much-tested astrological techniques, some of which extend back through many hundreds of years. Even if the astrologer relies only on very traditional tools in examining a person's horoscope (or nation's, or other collectivity's), he can see not only those qualities or energies that the person will experience as creative subjectivity, but also those qualities or energies that the person will tend to reject and therefore experience as projections. For example, the astrologer knows and has been taught that if you want information about the spouse, you look to the seventh house; if you want information about the first child, look in the fifth house; if you want information about a person's "hidden enemies," look in the twelfth house; and so forth. In various ways, then, astrologers have for centuries assumed as a matter of ordinary praxis that the horoscope describes a person's projec-

---

[25] *Puer Aeternus*: an eternal youth. Puella Aeternus: an eternal maiden. Many have connected these terms to the so-called Peter Pan Complex. Interested readers can consult Marie Louise von Franz's *Puer Aeternus*. (See bibliography.)

tions, though they did not use that terminology until comparatively recently and did not use the language of analytical psychology to describe the process.

If we investigate this whole matter of projections further, we will find ourselves asking provocative questions about what we so blithely call "reality." If we say that the horoscope describes not only the person's psychology and behavior, but also the world with which the person finds him or herself interacting, then we will find ourselves with questions about that world and its relation to mind. As we will see, the horoscope does this in many more ways and much more pervasively than we might have supposed.

Jung felt that whatever a person does not accept as a part of the self, whatever one relegates to the unconscious, or whatever has simply remained unconscious, appears in the world either as an event, or as the properties of purportedly outer objects.[26] Because a horoscope can tell us a lot about what a person will bring to consciousness, relegate to the unconscious, or have difficulty bringing to consciousness (or what a person has never brought to consciousness), it can tell us a lot about a person's projections.

If a woman has a challenging transit from Uranus to her natal Moon, her partner's (or partners', for the aspect suggests a pattern of behavior traceable through different relationships) resistance to commitment will reflect a process that has its locus somewhere within the woman herself. We might expect that if she withdrew all of her projections under such an influence, *she* would resist commitment, Uranus suggesting a desire for freedom and the Moon suggesting the emotions and security patterns, the combination suggesting a desire to have more freedom in emotional matters. If, though, we find her seeking commitment, and especially if she clings to the commitments she has, we might find it troubling that Uranus so often appears through others, not through her, at least in intimate relationships. We would expect—we would perhaps *want*—her to embrace the energy and potential that we describe astrologically as "Uranus." If she did this, she would recognize the personal limitations of a perhaps overstated security-orientation, and she would find renewal by living every moment as a fresh experience. She would see more clearly that some situations become claustrophobic if she doesn't establish and express her need for freedom in whatever form that takes. She might also see that the more she emphasizes security, generally a lunar matter, the more Uranus will arise through people apparently intent on resisting any security on offer.

Of course, this insistence on living by one's ideas, by one's own truth, may itself threaten the security of a relationship. Whether the Moon acquiesces or not, Uranus will generally insist on living by ideas—sometimes by rather *fixed* ideas—often by ideas that threaten the status quo, for Uranus has a great fondness for the new and untried and a great impatience with what people call the *tried and true*. Uranus sometimes assumes that truth cannot arise except in new forms, and

---

[26]Von Franz, *Psychotherapy*, 256.

that the *tried*, coming as it so often does coupled with habitual blindness, will never qualify as *true*. In extreme cases, Uranus will claim that something qualifies as true because it *hasn't* been tried or that something cannot qualify as true *if* it's been tried. We might call this "The Jack Kerouac Approach to Reality," for one of Kerouac's character's (Dean Moriarty, if I remember correctly) once declared, 'We don't know where we're going, but we're going. We don't know what it's like there, but it's not here, and we've been *here*, and we don't like it.' (Not surprisingly, Kerouac had a strongly placed Uranus: on his descendant, square his Mars and opposed his Moon, making Uranus part of a t-square to Mars that included the angles of the horoscope. Perhaps he sometimes projected *his* Uranus onto Mr. Moriarty!)

III. Working with Projections

The mythic Uranus lives primarily by his ideas; he decides that his children "are too ugly" and so tries to bury them back into the mother, the tale reminding us, among other things, of Uranus' difficulty dealing with matters-feminine. Any Uranus-Moon interaction brings a demand that one learn how to combine drives so different that most people find it difficult to combine them fruitfully—so the lesson-plan generally proves difficult! This remains true even if what we might call "the available evidence" suggests that, when brought together, these energies can bear much valuable fruit. For example, because the Moon symbolizes habit patterns taken from childhood, Uranus' interactions with the Moon can prompt one to break free of old and counterproductive patterns of behavior. A transit from Uranus to the natal Moon, or any insistence on living by one's ideas, may or may not bring a relationship to an end, but it will threaten any security bought with the rather painful coin of self-denial. If such a transit *does* bring a relationship to an end, we would hypothesize that something in the structure of the relationship has discouraged the people in it from expressing some vital energy or potential.

But if the person ignores this need for freedom—if she refuses to express it, or if she devalues it or tries to pretend that it doesn't exist, attempting to banish it to some psychological netherworld—it will likely appear as a projection. Because ego generally, and apparently by definition, likes security and clings to the security of the status quo, it will often reject anything that threatens that status quo. First the woman will reject it within herself; then she will reject it as it appears "out there" in situations that force her to confront an energy that, despite being born within her, now appears as something external. To work effectively with that situation, she will have to withdraw the projection, to "re-collect"[27] facets of herself from the world "out there." She may do so in fragments at first, and she will certainly find that the process demands reevaluation of her own needs and her own creative potential.

We might call this process *self-discovery*, or perhaps self-*recovery*, as it suggests the bringing back to awareness of something relegated to the shadows. As we know, the self seems comprised not

---

[27]Marie Louise von Franz, *Projection and Re-collection in Jungian Psychology*. Here and elsewhere, I have drawn a good deal on Ms. Von Franz's writings—and, of course, those of Jung.

only of elements easily available to consciousness, but also of elements not so easily available, and many of these latter will arise as projections. As Jung wrote, referring not only to individuals, but to groups as well, the psyche is generally to be found not only "in here" but also "out there" in the phenomenal world:

> …the psyche is not always and everywhere to be found on the inner side. It is to be found on the outside in whole races or periods of history which take no account of psychic life as such.[28]

Much empirical evidence, not all of a piece but nonetheless convincing, suggests that a woman having a transit from Uranus to her natal Moon will tend to play the role of the Moon and to project Uranus onto men. A man having a similar transit may well play the role of Uranus, the archetypally male planet in the pairing, and project his Moon, his capacity for feeling, onto women in general or one woman in particular. In that case, he will appear to want freedom instead of security; he will apparently deal with the world through his ideas instead of through his feelings. Though much will always depend on factors in the individual horoscope, the principles remain the same: whatever a person rejects from his or her own consciousness or self-concept will appear in the world as an event, as a person, or as an ongoing pattern. We can use the horoscope to help us see how the external world in some sense contains or reflects energies properly belonging (so to speak) to the individual, and to make helpful hypotheses about the psychological and phenomenological patterns involved.

In succeeding chapters we can explore some of the natal or transiting factors often associated with projection. This exploration will give us helpful information not only about our relationships or about astrological methodology, but also about the world itself, about phenomena and their relation to mind and consciousness. Though we will not deal explicitly with these larger questions until later chapters, we should keep them in mind as a background to the discussions in the earlier chapters. We might find something mysterious in even the most intimate of matters, or about the processes we call *perception* and *relationship*—and surely about this practice we call *horoscope interpretation*! Perhaps, after all, we often don't perceive the world and the people in it as accurately as we might; by implication, we perhaps don't always experience ourselves accurately either.

Quantum theory suggests that we might not *ever* perceive the world with complete accuracy. (Heisenberg once wrote that we cannot know the world in all its particulars. See chapters XI and XII.) Perhaps the world exists and arises in an ongoing relationship with the perceiver and his or her awareness. Even if our emotions and habitual patterns seem to insist that the "external world" has a definite nature distinct from our perception of it, much empirical evidence suggests that the interaction between mind/perception and the so-called "external world" provides the basis for a

---

[28] C.G., *Modern Man in Search of a Soul* (New York: Harcourt Brace Jovanovich, 1933), 201-202.

kind of magic that pervades even ordinary experience. As astrologers, we should look at these matters carefully and insistently, not only because in doing so we can help our clients (and ourselves), but also because in doing so we gaze into one of life's great mysteries: the relationship between awareness and phenomena. When we discuss matters related to personal relationships, we should have as a goal not merely to "solve relationship problems," but to understand both the world in which we live *and* this entity each of us calls "me," insofar as we can distinguish one from the other. Of course, we might categorize these mind-world matters as "relationship issues" in the larger sense, as we would like to solve the "problems" that arise in our relationship with the phenomenal world as a whole.

In the scenario described above, as in any situation involving a good deal of projection (i.e. most of our experience[29]), the woman cannot really do much about the man's behavior if she considers the problem merely as an external situation with which she must cope. The man acts freely, it seems, and, and coerce him as she might, or as she might *try,* she probably cannot control him if he doesn't want that to happen. She will probably find that the more she tries to control his behavior or convince him that he should commit to her or do what she wants—the more, we might say, that she plays the lunar role, seeking security and providing emotional sustenance—the more resistance he will likely put up, for she has not recognized the projection. That she hasn't recognized the projection means that she hasn't fully recognized and accepted *herself,* for she has "farmed out"[30] some of her own capacities to the man. The more she tries to influence him to acquiesce to her lunar demands, the more she ignores the personal needs and urges symbolized by Uranus. (See chapter II.) If she doesn't admit these into her own sense of self, she will continue to experience them through someone else. In such a situation, the more she tries to coerce him, the more freedom he will seem to want. We've all seen or found ourselves involved in analogous scenarios.

However, though she can't control the person onto whom she's projected her own energies, she can do a great deal about her *own* behavior, and, more importantly, about her own attitudes and evaluations, her own awareness, and the about the assumptions she habitually makes about herself and her experience, particularly those elements connected to her lunar behavior As she goes further, she will have to investigate not only conscious attitudes, but also unconscious dispositions and those habit patterns that seem to lie on the borderline between the conscious and unconscious elements of mind: dispositions and habit patterns that appear, however obliquely, through her experience. She should try to find out why she rejects the Uranus energy, and she should find ways

---

[29]Some would say all of it, a matter to which we will return.

[30]The term comes from baseball. To "farm someone out" means to send him to the minor leagues. The image fits in many ways. For example, a player who has been farmed out has been in some sense rejected; however, he can still be brought back to the major leagues (that is, to consciousness). The minor leagues, of course, are considered inferior (to the major leagues), yet when a player goes to the minors, he gets work that often enables him to play a helpful role in the major leagues at some future date. The general manager of the major league team may "bring someone up from the minors" if he thinks that someone can solve a persistent problem—or, interestingly, when the team finds itself out of the pennant race, so that relaxation sets in.

to bring that energy into her life in some way. If her horoscope shows a strong influence from Uranus (e.g. a natal aspect between Uranus and the Moon, or a transit or progression involving both planets), she will probably find that, whatever the situation with the man, she herself feels restless, "in need of"[31] more space, chary about commitment, not entirely sure that she wants to commit herself completely and forever to this man, and so forth; and she may find it easier to access these feelings when by herself. Perhaps she will have to challenge her own patterns of denial. But in any case, she needs to find a place in her life for an *active* Uranus, not a *re*active one, for a Uranus that emerges from her volition, not from her fear.[32]

All of which doesn't necessarily mean that she couldn't love this man, wouldn't be willing to stay with him, cherish him, love him with all his contradictions, putting up with his foibles as she enjoys his creative spirit. It simply means that to the degree that the man appears intransigent in his desire for freedom, space, and non-commitment, to that degree (we can hypothesize) the woman continues to project much of the Uranus energy onto him and fails to recognize her own "need" for freedom, space, latitude, and openness. In what we might call "classic cases," the man will then act out these "needs," quite likely in what will seem, certainly to the woman and perhaps to others, an egregious fashion.

The situation will feel quite painful to *both* parties, for as we will see, in such a situation, both people will find themselves powerfully affected: just as the man must in some sense carry the woman's Uranus energy, so the woman may find herself carrying the man's lunar energies, for a man prone to (or asked to, however unconsciously) play the Uranian role may find little room to express the lunar side of his personality—and many men have difficulty doing that under any circumstances. In situations rife with projection, both people feel incomplete. All of this suggests that the investigation of projections has moral implications.

By withdrawing projections (see below), we do not magically siphon all pain and suffering from the world or from ourselves, but we can reduce much *needless* pain. That phrase touches on a big subject, for we suffer many types of pain, some of which seem inescapable and omnipresent (what Buddhists refer to as birth, old age, sickness, and death), some of which seem to arise from longstanding habit or cultural prejudice, and some of which seem to arise because the person hasn't

---

[31] I've enclosed this phrase with quotation-marks because we probably don't really need much of what we say we "need." When I say, "I need more space," I probably mean that I'll feel badly if someone doesn't let me alone a bit more, or that I want to engage in some different activities, or something along those lines. I may also mean that, if I project current interaction patterns forward through time, I anticipate that I will feel so claustrophobic that I will see the relationship as "unworkable." We can say something similar about other phrases that I've put into quotations. Consider "makes me feel," used a few paragraphs below. No-one can make anyone feel alone. Sally might leave me to go off and live with an acrobat, but we should distinguish that extensional action from my intensional reaction: my feelings, whether about aloneness or anything else.

[32] Again, similar things might be said for all projections, whether the subject be a man or a woman, prosperous or poor, confident or timid, and so forth. As we will see, sometimes a person has an easier time "re-collecting" a projection through behavior first and then through attitudes: through first behaving in, say, a Uranian manner, and through this behavior accessing the too-often-denied energy.

explored his inner world as completely as he might. If we work to withdraw our projections, we can probably do something to alleviate, mitigate, decrease, and maybe eradicate this last kind of pain, and probably much of the second type.

Ignorance has much to do with fear, for we all seem to fear complete self-knowledge; in the words of T.S. Eliot, "human kind cannot bear very much reality."[33] However, we should probably consider ignorance as a *process* rather than a *thing*: as something we *do* rather than something we must confront or with which we must cope, even though when it arises through projection, it appears solid and thing-like. We often ignore what we would do better *not* to ignore, so instead of trying to "get rid of ignorance" the way we get rid of garbage, we should probably start by not ignoring ourselves. We generally fear to acknowledge ourselves fully and thus ignore what we know. When we succumb to this fear, we refuse to acknowledge or accept specific facets of ourselves; we then project those facets of ourselves into the world. Sooner or later, the projected energy comes back to haunt us, seeming to attack us or undermine our lives, our security, and our self-esteem; typically it does this in the guise of other people and their actions.

We have the ability to see the dynamic clearly; we can investigate the fear that lies at the root of projection-patterns; we can see how often these patterns come from habit. From this point of view, fear becomes a kind of beacon that can lead us forward, for only by investigating fear and seeing the fear-process accurately—which means seeing it *as* a process, not as some sort of solid block—will we find a way to withdraw our projections. And only by withdrawing our projections will we begin to see the world clearly. Such clear seeing will obviously not alleviate all pain, and it may actually increase *some* pain, as the phenomenal world seems characterized by suffering; however, it may alleviate much *unnecessary* pain, enabling us to distinguish between the pain and suffering that seem an inescapable part of human existence, and the pain and suffering that arise from fear, neurosis, and attachment.[34]

So the woman in our example will probably not escape pain. She may actually discover a new kind of pain: the kind that comes from self-acknowledgment, from full acceptance of herself. If she acknowledges that she needs more space, more freedom—if she acknowledges that she feels claustrophobia—she risks losing her relationship, or at least the relationship that exists in her mind, the relationship she thinks that she wants; she will have to abandon some elements of a habitual self-conception, particularly those elements that seem inaccurate. Further, if she loves the man or has convinced herself that she does, losing the relationship will surely feel quite painful. She may need to abandon the assumption that "love" and life-long commitment must arise together.

---

[33] T.S. Eliot: "Burnt Norton" (from *The Four Quartets*).
[34] This section relies heavily on some Buddhist ideas about suffering. Buddhists texts speak of three types of suffering or pain: all-pervading pain; the pain of alteration; the pain of pain. The first refers to the ongoing pain that we feel because of aloneness and the pervasive dissatisfaction that comes with being alive. The second refers to the pain that we feel because of ongoing change, as from happiness to suffering, from sanity to insanity, and so forth. The third refers to the pain we feel when we try to get away from pain; by doing that, we constantly create more pain and suffering. (I have followed, here, the presentation of Chogyam Trungpa in *The Myth of Freedom*. See pp.7-12.)

Honesty will not always get rewarded, at least not immediately or in easily recognizable ways: for her honesty, the honest person often must pay the price, at least temporarily, of perhaps-necessary aloneness. But quite likely the woman in our example already feels alone; for if she feels, even with her Uranus-Moon interaction, that she wants life-long commitment, then the man's resistance, which we might see as at least partly her *own* resistance, will "make her feel" alone. Acknowledging her feelings openly will not change that: it will neither assuage nor confirm her pre-existing feeling of loneliness. It may even make it more palpable.

We get no guarantees other than what may seem the rather dubious guarantee of honesty with and about ourselves, apparently a necessary ground for all relationship. We can, at least, move toward that honesty. The material in this book has much to do with finding honest and satisfying, though not necessarily painless, relationship with others (not just with our lovers or spouses) and the world in general; it also has to do with considering relatedness as *path* instead of as *fruition*. We won't find satisfaction unless we first get honest with ourselves; certainly no relationship (and thus no *experience*, for much of our experience involves self-other connections, broadly speaking) will feel satisfying if a person avoids being fully present within it, with all faculties engaged and in touch (so to speak) with his or her complete potential. So the evidence suggests that we will, after all, find some satisfaction from withdrawing our projections from the world even if in going through that process we confront the dissatisfaction that we so often feel about many of our experiences, and even if by doing so we move from an experience of unnecessary suffering to an experience of another sort.

We needn't start with all-or-nothing statements. We may think, "I must withdraw all my projections and be totally real in the world." But projections apparently serve as our bridge to the world altogether. If they do, we might do better to work with them than to reject them. In other words, we'll do well to bring our projections into the light as much as possible, recognizing that they needn't generate fear and that they arise from completely natural processes. Human beings project, apparently. If we reject the fact that we do this, we reject part of ourselves. Whatever we do to deal with our projections, we must begin by acting kindly toward ourselves, not considering ourselves as a set of quasi-objective problems, but rather as a series of subjective processes that we can sometimes understand objectively—and should, at least insofar as such an approach yields insight.

So we begin, paradoxically enough, by accepting ourselves and our projection-pattern or projection-tendency precisely as we experience them. We can then develop curiosity about them. As the *Tao Te Ching* says, "The journey of a thousand leagues begins with what was under the feet."[35] This one begins with non-violence, particularly to ourselves. Many people experience this as one of the great benefits of astrology: that it tells them the truth about themselves in a non-judgmental way. Dane Rudhyar once said that the horoscope symbolizes what the universe needed at the time and place of a person's birth. Whether or not we accept the idea that the universe has *needs*, we can at

---

[35] Arthur Waley (trans.), *The Way and Its Power: A Study of the Tao Te Ching and Its Place in Chinese Thought*. (New York: Grove Press, 1958), 221.

least see how the natal horoscope offers us not a series of judgments but a series of interwoven facts that link inner and outer worlds in pervasive and mysterious ways. Before we judge that woven pattern, we should first try to understand it.

IV. Withdrawing Projections

The path just described demands awareness, perception, and self-acceptance. In her *Projection and Re-Collection in Jungian Psychology*, Marie Louise von Franz outlines, through a case study, five stages in the withdrawal of projections:

> …Jung refers to the case of a Nigerian soldier who heard a voice calling to him from a tree, whereupon he tried to break out of the barracks in order to go to the tree. When interrogated, the soldier stated that everyone who bore the name of this tree heard its voice from time to time. To us this is a case of the above-mentioned archaic identity, because, for the soldier, the tree and the voice were obviously identical. A separation of the idea of the tree from that of the voice or of a tree-demon (as the ethnologist might put it, in this case) is actually a secondary phenomenon, corresponding to the next stage of consciousness, since a *differentiation* has now taken place. A third stage would arise with the need for a *moral evaluation* of the phenomenon of the voice, which would be seen as the manifestation of an evil or good spirit. A fourth stage would go still one step further in the process of elucidation. At this stage the existence of spirits would be denied altogether and the experience written off as an *illusion*. At the next, or fifth stage, one would have to reflect on how such an overpowering, extremely real, and awesome experience could suddenly become nothing but self-deception. Even if one must perhaps assume that trees do not talk in human speech and that no spirit inhabits the tree itself or even that, looked at objectively, no "spirit" at all was heard by the soldier, this perception of a spirit must nevertheless have been a phenomenon pushing upward out of his unconscious, whose *psychic* existence cannot be denied unless one denies the reality of the psyche altogether. If we do not do this, today we would describe the spirit in the tree as a projection, which does not, however, imply an illusion but rather a psychic reality of the highest order.[36]

The initial stage (identity between subject and object) describes the experience of many people before they begin to question or investigate their projections. At this stage, people tend to describe their experience, and to describe others, through a variety of "is" propositions. One might say, "Joe Schmidt *is* such-and-such" (or, in Jung's example, that the tree "is" a spirit) because one has not asked whether some of what one perceives in Joe might belong more properly to oneself. One has oversimplified Joe even as one has denied or ignored one's unconscious participation via one's own devalued qualities. We should note, here, the importance of judgment, one that the projector does not even know he has made: that such-and-such *is* such-and-such. The projector has attributed

---

[36] Von Franz, *Projection and Re-Collection*, 9-10.

qualities to the external world that perhaps belong more properly to his inner world.[37]

The moral evaluation (third stage) has to do with what we mentioned above: that each person must take responsibility for his or her own mental contents,[38] even the unconscious ones that appear via projection. Each person must accept him or herself completely, without rejecting those qualities one would like to ignore or that one has found unacceptable, the rejection encouraging or making possible the projection of those qualities onto someone (or some*thing*) else. And it seems that one must also accept contents that have never reached consciousness in the first place but that still pervade some projections (connected to what Jung called the *collective unconscious*).

Third, though some might say that in the example "there is no spirit in the tree" and that the notion that there *is* such a spirit "is completely misguided," in most projections we find in the object some of the projected material—or at least something very much like it.[39] Putting aside for now the question of whether we could find a spirit in the tree, we will still probably acknowledge that in our daily experience, because we generally project psychic material onto other people (and organizations, etc.) instead of onto objects, we generally "see" some sort of "spirit" in other people. In evaluating this process, we probably shouldn't conclude either that our perception "is an illusion" or that it "is not an illusion," even though our language might deceive us into thinking that we have only those two alternatives.

While we might not want to offer an opinion on whether there "really is" a spirit in the tree—or whether, for example, there "really is" some "anger" in someone else—we should acknowledge, as noted above, that we generally find, in the object of our projections, what Jung called a *hook* on which to hang the projections. At the same time, we should acknowledge that other people prob-

---

[37]Certain language forms obviously play a crucial role here If, instead of saying that Joe "is" such and such, I say merely that I "find" Joe such and such, I have encouraged myself to look more directly at my own evaluations. Perhaps I say, "My girlfriend is impatient (etc.)," but I can help myself to see more clearly by recognizing how I get trapped in my conclusions. If I say, instead, that I feel upset when my girlfriend does such-and-such, I can begin to see how I have attributed some quality, however vague, to the world/girlfriend, assuming that the quality belongs there instead of inside of me (so to speak). We will look more closely at these matters as we proceed. The statement about my alleged girlfriend's alleged impatience uses the is-of-predication: noun or pronoun/to-be/modifier. The is-of-identity (noun or pronoun/to-be//noun or pronoun) subsumed into the term girlfriend—as in, "That person is my girlfriend" – also presents problems, but let's put such discussions off until a later chapter. These language-structures suggest Saturn at work, for he has much to do with structures of all sorts. (These ideas about language – though not the astrological correspondences—derive from the work of Alfred Korzybski.)

[38]These contents include "conceptual" and "emotional" elements, two areas with rather vague boundaries, as most (perhaps all) concepts have an emotional quality and most (perhaps all) feelings have conceptual content. We will discuss these matters in later chapters.

[39]Perhaps not always. As we will see, language can encourage us to think we see some quality in someone else—perhaps the impatience mentioned in an earlier footnote—when the question at issue doesn't have to do with that quality at all. For example, if someone says that his or her partner "is an idiot," the speaker probably intends no evaluation or judgment of the partner's intelligence at all! But if one continues to say that someone "is an idiot," one may begin to think that one actually perceives the unperceivable idiotness. A Buddhist teacher once said that the world arises as it does for us because of the way we label it.

ably *do* have some kind of spirits (psychic energies) in them, some of which may arrive (so to speak) via projection. And we might remind ourselves that, as Ms von Franz puts it, we find ourselves dealing, here, with "a psychic reality of the highest order." Perhaps, too, we experience, in these matters, something akin to the creation of the world, or at least some aspect of it: psychic energy arises from the unconscious, which Jung felt was difficult to distinguish from the material world itself, to appear as what we call "reality." We name the world; we attribute qualities to it; we go on with our version of things.

If we try to understand this process and withdraw from the world those projections that cause suffering, we must apparently go through these stages. First, we get caught up in the projection: we accept without question our description of reality. Then, for whatever reason of awareness or circumstance, we experience some separation: we distinguish between our projected version of the world and "the world itself," even if we don't quite know what the latter consists of. This generally occurs because we sense something not quite accurate in our relationship with that world; we feel somehow haunted. Then we make a moral evaluation: we recognize that some of what we have perceived really belongs to us, and we acknowledge that we haven't taken responsibility for our own psychic material. Perhaps we begin to suspect that "the world itself" hasn't yet appeared to us and that we can't verify the reliability of what we have perceived. Finally, we reflect, perhaps discovering something somewhat astounding about our experience in this world: that we can't (as Heisenberg put it) know the world in all its particulars, that we can't seem to pin down "the world" as an objective something-or-other existing apart from the perceiver.

In ensuing chapters, in describing projections by using astrological terminology, I will loosely follow Ms Von Franz's (and Jung's) schema. For each projection, we will start with a description of how phenomena appear at the stage of archaic identity, how one will experience "other" when one gets completely caught up in the projection of a specific astrological factor. Then we will look at how things might appear after some differentiation has taken place: using astrological terminology, we will describe the projected energy, differentiating it from the object of the projection. In particular, we will distinguish between the energy as it appears in others and the energy as it might arise in oneself. We will discuss how one might honor that energy in oneself, for, after all, one's dishonoring of that energy apparently sets the whole process in motion. We will try to describe the illusions in which we might get caught, illusions describable by reference to the astrological symbolism. And finally, we will explore the kinds of reflections that might prove valuable as we try to understand the projection-pattern in question.

———————

In discussing projection, we probably shouldn't say merely that one sees one's own *version* of the world. The word "version" suggests conscious intent even as it suggests a verifiable reality underneath the version. (Webster's New World Dictionary defines *version* as "an account showing one point of view; [a] particular description or report given by one person or group [the two *ver*sions of the accident]") Though we generally do not, when projecting psychic contents, have a conscious intention of giving our own version of things, we should still assume that we see a world mysteriously imbued with our own unconscious contents: not the world as it *is*, but a world that *appears* in a certain way to *us* because of unacknowledged psychic material. And, as we will explore further, we often see a world created by our language, first because of the way we shape the propositions that shape perception, and second because each language seems to contain its own metaphysics, its own version of reality.[40]

Most of what we call *experience* arises imbued with projected material. Perhaps we would say that we "don't experience reality," but because that question leads us into either-or thinking (either we experience reality or we don't), we might do better to say that what we call "reality" includes at least *some* projected material. Let's leave up in the air for now the question of whether it may contain something else as well. Until we investigate, we probably shouldn't make hard-and-fast statements. We *can* verify that the projected version of reality ends up having power: it includes verifiable causes that lead to verifiable effects, so even though we might say that "it's not ultimately real," it functions as if it's real (having its own logic, generally following accepted physical laws and so forth). We will see this process quite clearly when we consider collective projections (chapter IX); though we might describe Adolf Hitler, for example, as a collective projection, he obviously had an enormous effect on the world. We will call "relative truth" that "truth" that we accept as such, that "truth" that, consistent in itself, we haven't yet examined.[41] When we *do* examine that relative truth, we find a deeper, more reliable truth. We might say, in general, that experience arises imbued, saturated, and generally inundated with projections of all kinds—as far, at least, as we can see in our so-called natural state of being. With effort, a person can begin to see through these projections. In the following chapters, we will have more to say about this "seeing."

---

[40]I have borrowed this idea from the linguist Edward Sapir. See his "The Status of Linguistics as a Science," reprinted in *Selected Writings in Language, Culture and Personality* (Berkeley: University of California Press, 1963). See also Arthur Waley's introduction to The Way and It's Power, particularly pp. 64ff (Grove Press, 1958 edition). I explore these matters further in later chapters.

[41]Students of the Buddhist Madyamika teachings will recognize this way of describing relative truth and relating it to what I have called "a deeper, more reliable truth." In Tibetan, the two operant terms are *kundzop* (relative truth, something that is "all dressed up") and *dondam* (absolute truth, sometimes described as what a master sees after examining and investigating kundzop, kundzop being, by definition, unexamined; for according to the teachings, kundzop, when examined fully and with the proper methods, no longer arises).

Chapter II

Gender-Based Projections I

In investigating gender-based projections, we should proceed with some caution. Though I will argue in this chapter that women often project Uranus onto men, we could find not only women who don't do so or who do so only minimally, but also men who do so quite readily. Furthermore, we all project Uranus into the environment to some extent; Uranus appears there as all sorts of ground-breaking, rule-breaking, iconoclastic, revolutionary, or cutting edge activities. In the next chapter, when discussing men and their tendency to project the Moon onto women, we will say something similar: not all men project the Moon onto women; some women project the Moon onto men; for all of us, the Moon appears in the environment, sometimes through women, sometimes through the natural world (the "sub-lunar realm"). I therefore do not wish to say that men always do X and women always do Y. Nevertheless, the hypotheses in the next three chapters may serve all of us well as we attempt to see both intensional and extensional realms more clearly and to act more compassionately toward ourselves and others.

Let's begin with some hypotheses borne out by experience: men will tend to project the Moon, Venus, and sometimes Pluto onto women; women will tend to project Uranus, the Sun, and sometimes Mars onto men. If you're playing the percentages, go with those, at least at first. Furthermore, though everyone to some extent projects Saturn onto others, women seem to do so more often and more problematically than men do (though probably not by much), and though everyone to some extent projects Neptune, men seem to do so more often and more problematically than do women (though, again, probably not by much). Women seem to project Mercury and Jupiter onto men a bit more than men project them onto women, and though it may seem to complicate matters overmuch, everyone, to a greater or lesser extent, projects Uranus, Neptune, and Pluto onto either specific people or into the world in general. We will look at all of these in succeeding chapters.

We will find gender-based projections most prevalent within intimate relationships or in relationships that have intimate (though not necessarily sexual) qualities or areas. In other life areas, the projections may not appear very readily or at all. For example, if a woman works in the computer industry or with some other form of new technology, or if she does some sort of radical political work—or if, in general, she works independently, trusts her intellectual insight, and uses her "individual genius"[1] in some way—we should probably conclude that she embodies and works actively with her Uranus in those arenas. Similarly, if a man finds a life-work that enables him to nurture others or to express his emotions in some way (e.g. as a counselor, musician, or poet), we should probably conclude that he embodies and works actively with his Moon in those activities. Yet in intimate relationships, women often project Uranus onto men, while men often project the Moon onto women.[2]

Obviously and as always, we must take all horoscope factors into consideration. For example, a woman with important placements in Cancer, Taurus, or Scorpio (signs associated in various ways with security in relationship) may project Uranus more readily or predictably than will a woman with important placements in Aquarius, Aries, or Gemini.[3] Similarly, men with important placements in Cancer, Taurus, or Scorpio may project the Moon less readily, while many men with important placements in Aquarius, Aries, Gemini, or even Leo will often do so more readily. We will investigate some of these factors as we proceed, remembering as we do that we cannot use horoscope factors alone to determine the level of awareness—and awareness seems like the crucial factor any time we attempt to determine how projected material will arise or if a person will project specific psychic material in the first place.

As we proceed, we should try to get beyond the dictates of political correctness. In the politically correct world, women all own or embrace their own freedom of thought and action, while men own or embrace their own feelings and security needs. But though we might hope for, or even work toward, a world in which people make conscious use of their own potentials all the time, if we look at how people actually behave, we find that many women often project Uranus onto men, that many men often project the Moon onto women, and that the women and men who do so do not necessarily, or even often, qualify as unaware, un-astute, or un-perceptive. Though we will find many variations, some of them generational, we should see these variations *as* variations.

---

[1]Dane Rudhyar's term for Uranus. I believe it comes from *The Astrology of Personality*.
[2]What of same-gender sexual relationships? My observations strongly suggest that the same projection and role-playing patterns emerge: one partner will tend to play the role of Uranus, for example, while the other plays the role of the Moon. The people involved may trade off roles more frequently, perhaps because genetic factors don't reinforce socially defined roles. From what I've been able to see, people who identify themselves as trans-gender also find themselves involved in these projections, though, again, the gender-related symbolism may vary from case to case.
[3]In many cases, of course, we will find a mix. A woman might have her Sun in Leo and a Taurus ascendant. And she might have Venus, ruler of that Ascendant and therefore extremely important, in Cancer. The independence of the Leo Sun finds itself at odds with the demands of Venus in Cancer. So, as always, we must take all horoscope factors into consideration.

Women (and the Rest of Us) and Uranus

Everyone projects Uranus sometimes. Uranus symbolizes revolutionary change that challenges ego. On some level, ego wants to protect itself, to find security, to maintain the psychological or social status quo. So ego will generally have a hard time with Uranus simply because ego doesn't want to change. Ego attempts to hold onto things, ideas, and notions of self-identity. Uranus brings new ideas that frequently upset anyone holding on to any status quo. Uranus also brings circumstances that disrupt, that show us how or in what ways or areas the flow of life has stagnated. When we find ourselves stuck, we often need reminding that this has occurred, and we generally find Uranus more than willing to do the reminding, often not gently.

However, though Uranus generally challenges ego, ego sometimes enlists Uranus for ego-driven purposes, particularly when Uranus manifests through new ideas, particularly in technical fields. We can see this enlistment (some would prefer the term *co-option*) around us every day as computers and electronic technology further the interests of people intent on maintaining some elements of the status quo. Governments make extensive use of high technology every day, probably far more pervasively (e.g. in the NSA) than does any individual, and the individual ego often uses insight to solidify its position.[4] Astronomical factors suggest this cooption: if a person knows where to look, she can sometimes see Uranus, just as she can see all the planets within Uranus' orbit. This suggests that the conscious ego can bring Uranus into ego's bureaucracy. A person may say, and quite accurately, that he (i.e. ego) *wants* more freedom, less responsibility, more latitude, and so forth. Uranus' demands then arise as ego's stated "needs."

On the other hand, ego generally has difficulty controlling Uranus' energy: though we can see Uranus some of the time, most of the time he remains hidden (i.e. unconscious). You have to know where and when to look.[5] This suggests that the conscious ego can use Uranus to further ego's ends only at specific times and in specific ways. We can say that Uranus symbolizes factors that remain unconscious most of the time; we can also say that though we may often sense our "need" for freedom, we will more often remain blind to how this "need" serves to further ego's claustrophobia.

---

[4]Notably, when we articulate these insights, we often use the verb *to be* (a mark of Saturn, as we will see). For example, I might have an insight about what I call "my need for freedom." I might say, "I am a person who needs more freedom. I am not a person who likes to be tied down." We can easily get into linguistic traps, using the language of freedom to cement limiting ideas about ourselves. When we limit ourselves in this way, we generally don't state the limitations explicitly; however, because these propositions state that we "are" such and such, they limit implicitly. Saturn, Uranus' mythic son, has to do with the way we structure our world (to borrow Robert Hand's phrase), and we do this partly, perhaps *largely*, through language-structures in which we describe ourselves and the world through self-limiting is-propositions and *should*-propositions. The myth suggests that Uranian insight too often results in or leads to a reiteration of the limitation against which Uranus would like to rebel. We will return to this matter in chapter XI.

[5]We can see Uranus during his geocentric opposition to the Sun. The sun's light shines on him directly at this point, and he is closer to earth than at any other point in his orbit. That takes care of the "when." "Where?" Approximately one hundred and eighty degrees from the sun. And make sure you have good eyesight, some sense of what to look for, and a clear night on which to do the looking from a smog-free area.

Because ego finds Uranus' energy difficult to co-opt, both men and women will sometimes project it into the environment; however, it seems that men usually feel more comfortable with Uranus than women do and so will enlist Uranus more often than women will, though not necessarily more wisely. It seems that in close relationships, women usually have more difficulties with Uranus than men do. Cultural factors surely play an important role in this. In the somewhat disreputable court of popular opinion, Uranian men have an easier time than do Uranian women. Men often receive applause, and women castigation, for trying to find more freedom in their lives or for espousing new or unpopular ideas.[6] When men stray from their wives, people often say that such actions "are typical of men," suggesting that people see men as to some extent Uranian all the time. When a woman strays from her husband, on the other hand, we don't often say that she does so because of something purportedly in her "nature"; quite the contrary, as many people will say that she's acted contrary to her "nature" as a mother or as a woman. Furthermore, men receive more encouragement to work to work in Uranian fields (high technology, science, inventing, and so forth) than women do. Certainly men have continually tested higher in these fields than have women, though scientists have not detected a physiological basis for these results.

While acknowledging that cultural factors play a significant role here, we shouldn't exclude the possibility that biological factors may make Uranus-integration an easier path for men than for women. Women bear children, a lunar activity, and mothers generally find it much easier to nurture their children—and the children seem to thrive better—in an environment characterized by stable patterns of behavior (Moon) rather than in a situation fraught with constant change or upheaval (Uranus). In addition, inventiveness doesn't play as helpful a role in nurturing as it does in procuring, and the body of a woman works in harmony with rhythmic currents symbolized by the Moon, the disruption of which often presages major changes in a woman's health or life-stage. When women go through menopause, these patterns no longer recur, suggesting a Uranian break from lunar patterns; that this happens around the mid-life opposition from transiting Uranus to natal Uranus surely seems suggestive. Jung felt that in the second half of life, women show more masculine traits while men show more feminine ones, a view that seems in harmony with the astrological material just mentioned.[7]

In the first few years of a child's life, the father may range far and wide either in search of food or of the wherewithal to purchase it, while the mother often stays in a secure environment and nurses the child—or, we might say, doing so generally promotes health in the children, as suggested by abundant evidence pointing to the importance of breast-feeding for infants. Very young children

---

[6]Though not a supporter of Hillary Clinton, I think that the 2008 Democratic presidential primaries showed quite clearly how women get treated when they show even the slightest signs of independence.
[7]We can see menopause as a Uranian break from a lunar pattern and hence as a move toward the masculine. Though men also experience Uranian breaks, they usually break from a Saturnian pattern rather than a lunar one. Finally, we should acknowledge that men, too, have their lunar cycles. They generally experience these cycles first through the feelings instead of through the body. However, if you follow the transiting Moon in a man's chart, you will detect emotional patterning.

obviously cannot protect or feed themselves very well, so the mother generally does so; children cannot gather their own food, so the father generally does so. The father's role involves more freedom of movement than does the mother's.

Many will find it hopelessly politically incorrect to suggest that women will project their Uranus energy onto men; they may find it even less politically correct to suggest that the operant factors may have a biological basis. If Uranus symbolizes freedom, emancipation, insight, and a willingness to follow the so-called beat of one's own drum, should we conclude that women have less inclination or ability to engage these potentials than do men? Certainly millions of women exercise their freedom, offer their insights, and express their individuality, freeing themselves from cultural stereotypes and making important contributions to society; certainly, too, women espouse radical political views as readily as do men (perhaps *more* readily, as men in our society often assume Saturn-defined roles). These facts certainly suggest that in myriad circumstances, women incorporate Uranus into their lives instead of projecting it onto men. However, that a woman brings Uranus into her activity in professional or intellectual ways does not tell us how she will deal with Uranus in her intimate relationships.[8] The empirical evidence suggests that in such relationships, even "Uranian women" will often project Uranus onto men, though, again, we will find many exceptions. That we find these observations uncomfortable doesn't mean we should reject them.

I should point out that though my client data base may not qualify as representative of the larger population, my woman clients include acupuncturists, psychotherapists, writers, teachers, people who work with computer or high technology or people's finances, massage therapists, lawyers, and so forth. I think that from any objective viewpoint they would be viewed as women who find a use for their insight, who insist on personal and creative freedom, and who have in many ways broken free of stultifying tradition. But *in their intimate relationships*, many of them still project Uranus onto men, at least through their childbearing years.

As already noted, we will find variations depending on sign-placement. I've had the opportunity over the past few years to do horoscope-readings for some women with Uranus in Scorpio. These women did not seem to project Uranus nearly to the degree that I have come to expect. Perhaps women with Uranus in Scorpio access the Uranus energy more easily, for not only does Uranus have his exaltation in Scorpio, but Scorpio also has a close connection to the great mother energies, to sexuality and power, suggesting that women in this Uranus generation may often channel the Uranus energy through sexual and psychological power, to feel the power of the mothers arising most readily when they free themselves of cultural constriction.

---

[8] Hillary Clinton again seems to provide a ready example. Though her ambition reflects Saturn more than Uranus, her break from the usual "First Lady" role surely suggests Uranus. Ms. Clinton has Uranus square Moon, and though her Uranus may tell us of her break with tradition, it also seems to characterize her husband's behavior, at least in matters related to intimacy. (Astrologers have suggested different birth times for Ms. Clinton. Some of these place Uranus on the Ascendant. In the Astrodatabank collection, Ms. Clinton has Saturn square the Ascendant and Uranus in the eighth house.)

None of this means that men will not sometimes project Uranus as well. They will, and with just as painful results. As noted, much here will depend on other horoscope factors. For example, if the man's horoscope suggests a strong desire for stability, he may have difficulty dealing with Uranus in his close relationships, while a woman whose horoscope suggests a strong desire for freedom may not have such a difficult time. But if a man's chart and a woman's chart show equivalent tendencies (so to speak) toward freedom and emotional security, bet on the man to act out the need for the former while the woman demands the latter. But whatever we might or might not find through statistical studies (and we would have a hard time doing a reliable statistical study about *desires*!), the projection of Uranus demonstrates not an unalterable fate, but unnecessary suffering that a person can do something about.

In the most characteristic scenarios of a Uranus-projection, the man onto whom Uranus is projected (the man who receives the projection) will want more freedom or will act in what we might call a non-status-quo manner, threatening the security of the relationship and seeming cool or detached about emotional matters or intimacy. The man will often act out the more problematic characteristics of Uranus; the woman has already "negativized" [9] Uranus within herself and so projects out that negativized version. If she does this, she will have difficulty relating positively to someone onto whom she projects, and in whom she perceives, the "negativized" quality. So though we might feel tempted to blame the man, the woman should look first to herself.

Uranus as a projection often appears as someone (often an intimate partner) making what someone else sees as a strong, probably overstated, generally overly-detached movement toward greater "freedom." This person will often appear aloof, not only from the relationship, but also from his own feelings. He will seem to act on an idea, not a feeling. He will seem to be involved in his own ideas: ideas about his alleged "freedom," his "creative spirit," "cutting-edge notions," the need to "cut ties," and so forth. On the other side of the coin, if a woman projects her Uranus onto men, she may find herself interested in Uranian men, men who use their brilliance or seem in some way on the real or imagined cutting edge of something (though sometimes that *something*, when viewed objectively, will seem more banal than brilliant); men who seem willing to play the rake, the rebel, the malcontent, the misunderstood genius, the wanderer from customary paths, the wunderkind not quite adjusted to adulthood or women; men who say they "don't want to be tied down" even to the responsibilities of their own creative gifts; men who live by convictions instead of emotional connections; men more than willing to say, along with Jake Moriarity, "We don't know where we're going but we're going. We don't know what it's like there, but it's not here, and we've been here, and we don't like it."[10]

---

[9] Let us coin this verb: to *negativize*: to see some person, thing, action, attitude, or quality in a negative light, not necessarily because the person, thing, action, attitude, or quality "is" inherently bad, but because of factors in the negativizer's attitude. Much evidence suggests that the verb should also mean, "To transfer one's own negative attitude into the purportedly negative behavior of the person or thing onto whom or which one projects the energy-in-question," for it seems that when a person projects, a transfer of energy takes place. See below.

[10] Jack Kerouac: *On the Road* (quoted from memory). Perhaps notable here: Jack Kerouac's Uranus conjoins his descen-

Mythic Implications

In the Greek creation myth, Uranus (Ouranus), the great sky god, fathers many children in Gaia, the earth goddess. In one version of the myth, Uranus finds his children too ugly and tries to bury them back into the mother (or, in other versions, tries to confine them to Tartarus). Gaea, understandably upset, conspires with Saturn (Kronos) to fashion a sickle that he uses to castrate his father. Because of this act, Saturn gets a bad reputation, and understandably; however, the problem starts with his father, and the nature of the problem reminds us of the astrological Uranus. The mythic Uranus acts on an idea—he finds his children "too ugly"—and tries to escape from the karmic chain. Without apparent connection to the emotional qualities of the situation or to the prerogatives of the feminine, he tries to bury his children back into the mother. In acting as he does, he tries to bury his own creative issue, refusing to let them see the light of day, a mythic pattern with obvious implications for the so-called "creative freedom" of the Uranian person.

A man receiving the projection of Uranus will often act like the mythic Uranus. Interestingly, though, he will often find himself *re*acting instead of acting, concerned more with the feeling of claustrophobia he wishes to escape than with a creative inspiration for which he feels compelled to find a form; if the woman has negativized her Uranian energy, she will more often than not encounter and feel drawn to men who manifest the problematic side of Uranus, often men who act out the problematic elements of the myth, among which we can number a distrust of and resistance to form, organic (Moon) or otherwise (Saturn), a tendency to avoid any commitment to formal demands, including those commitments necessary to bring a creative impulse to a formal conclusion. We see in the myth Uranus' resistance to form (as he tries to bury Saturn/Kronos, the Lord of Form, away and out of sight) and his insistence on freedom from the karmic principle of cause and effect.[11]

Thus the receiver of the projection may, like the mythic Uranus, reject the form principle, attempting to bury it away just as Uranus tries to bury his children—most notably Saturn (Cronus), symbolizing form, duration, and karmic result—back into the mother. The man who serves as a hook for the projection receives an already negativized energy and may talk a lot about creativity yet resist the effort and discipline needed to put that work into form. Just as the mythic Uranus resists karma, not wanting to deal with the effects of his actions and even wanting to reverse the flow of time (Saturn has to do with time; Uranus tries to put the children back into the mother),

---

dant, opposes his Moon, and squares his Mars, participating in the t-square to Mars. The Uranus-Moon opposition suggests that he experienced an either-or relationship between his drive for security and his drive for freedom; we might say that he would play the Uranian role (leaving the lunar role for his mother or his partners), though with Uranus on the Descendant, he would have a contrary tendency to experience Uranus through others (perhaps the mythic Moriarity). Mars squares both planets from Sagittarius, accounting for his gypsy mentality. The empty leg falls right at the Midheaven, so he made a profession from his wanderlust.

[11] These implications should give us pause as we enter an aeon ruled by Saturn and Uranus. We see around us the problematic karmic results of human ideas. Saturn, the other ruler of Aquarius and known as the Lord of Karma, will surely exact a price for humanity's tendency to re-enact the myth on a collective scale.

so the one receiving a Uranus projection may, even before he has come to serve as a hook for someone's projection, put more emphasis on the creative *idea* than on the effort, discipline, and learned technique needed to give definite *form* to that idea.

Gaea, the Earth, has a close connection to the Moon, ruler of the sub-lunar realm of organic life on our planet. In giving birth, she threatens Uranus' freedom. Uranus' attempt to bury his children back into the mother certainly qualifies as a violation of the feminine principle of organic growth and development. Uranus' actions perhaps show us why women have such difficulty integrating Uranus into their intimate relationships, for Uranus will often see relationships as entanglements instead of opportunities. If they do not fit with his ideas about creative freedom, he will more than likely reject them. Though he represents an energy in all of us that remains wary of commitment, he presents a particular problem to the organic principle that brings forth new life out of relationship, for not only do human beings come into existence through relationship, but all other organic forms do as well, though the relating elements differ.

We often see strongly Uranian people (people taken up with Uranus) following a pattern similar to the one enacted in the myth: they have creative ideas, but once they attempt to put those ideas into form, they find the form unacceptable in some way, not "up to" the original conception—and this despite the connection between conception and birth, a connection suggesting that though we may think of ideas and concepts as masculine in nature, they take on form because of interaction with the feminine. (Thus we may *brood* over an idea that we have *conceived*.) If we ignore the importance of the feminine in our creative ideas, we will find ourselves prone to act like Uranus, thinking that the form through we promulgate an idea *never* measures up to the original notion and never serves as an adequate vehicle for its expression. Form always limits, after all! Uranus resists such limits, but the myth suggests not only that form must result from ideas (just as Saturn results from Uranus), but also that those forms consist of a combination of free insight and organic imperatives (Gaea, the Earth). The formal elements consist of what the Western tradition calls *spirit* and *matter*, and ideas naturally emerge as and through form (if for no other reason than that we express ideas in symbolic languages of various sorts).[12] However, though Uranus tries to bury Saturn away, apparently hoping to be done with the demands of form, Uranian people benefit from an engagement with the very forms that they resist so strenuously. Thus they have many of the qualities of the *puer aeternus*, and they may benefit from hefty doses of both Saturn and the Moon. Marie Louise von Franz writes of the *puer*,

---

[12]Some will see the idea and the form as inseparable. This seems reasonable, as we perhaps don't have ideas until they emerge in some form (e.g. language). On the other hand, it seems that in idea and form we see two stages in a process, and some evidence suggests that ideas arise before we clothe them in form. It seems, for example, that Helen Keller had ideas even before she learned language. Perhaps some of Saturn's penchant for form came through his father (and not only through his mother, as we might at first assume). If Uranus rejected his own potential to give form to his ideas, he perhaps experienced that potential via projections that emerged through his son. And, of course, he felt drawn to the Earth Mother, who surely has a lot to do with form and whom we should perhaps consider a representative of Uranus' animus! (See next chapter.)

> The *puer aeternus* has to learn to carry on with the work he does not like, rather than only with the work where he is carried away by great enthusiasm, which is something that everybody can do…The work which is the cure for the puer aeternus is where he has to kick himself out of bed on a dreary morning and again and again take up the boring job—through sheer will power.[13]

This is not to say that the person marked by Uranus does not have legitimate gifts, spiritual aspirations, or inspired notions. Often he does. However, when acting through the projections of others, such a person will often manifest the more problematic side of Uranus. If a woman has in some sense *given* her Uranus to the man, the man will feel doubly Uranian (see below), and some of that energy will have the qualities just described.[14] But just as the man feels compelled to act out the Uranian impulse, so the woman will feel constrained to act out the non-Uranian one (often connected to the Moon). The man, perhaps having lost touch (at least when he's with the woman[15]) with his own feelings and security needs, overstates his need for freedom, or makes that statement spasmodically, at least partly as a way to avoid dealing with states of being that astrologers will recognize as lunar—states in which he is in touch with his security needs, for example.

But though it may seem accurate to say that the man has a compulsive need for freedom and that when under that compulsion he will ignore his emotional and security needs, the woman probably won't get far by trying to change him, even if she feels that she gets stuck dealing with what partly belongs to the man, just as Gaea would have ended up with the children again had Uranus gotten his way. The woman should, in such cases, begin by looking at the reason she has projected Uranus in the first place. That a woman projects Uranus onto a man suggests that, at least in her connection with him, she has devalued the Uranian energy. Quite likely, she has split her ideas from her feelings, her intellectual needs from her emotional ones, her desire for freedom from her desire for security, her genius from her vulnerability. The same kind of split occurs with men, but whereas the men will generally (at least in intimate relationships) align themselves with the Uranian side of things, women will generally do the opposite, and so they will project Uranus onto men. Instead of asking why the man doesn't want to commit or make a close emotional connection, the woman should probably ask, "Have I assumed that I can't have an intimate relationship if I remain a free agent in my own right? Have I assumed that being in a relationship means giving up my brilliance, my ideas, my creative inspiration, or my need to be part of a bigger world?" In other words, she should ask whether she has devalued in herself the energy astrologers symbolize as Uranus.

---

[13] Marie Louise von Franz, Puer Aeternus (Sigo Press, 1981), 43.
[14] I refer to them as "problematic" because they ignore cause-and-effect, apparently an integral part of our lives.
[15] As we will see in the next chapter, many men often do not know quite what they feel when they are in the presence of their intimate female partners. They may, however, know exactly what they feel at other times. The presence of the woman apparently incites or constellates the projection of the Moon.

What, in the myth discussed above, shall we make of Saturn's castration of his father, and the fact that he performed this gruesome act with a sickle fashioned with the help of his mother? The testicles fall into the ocean where they mix with the sea-foam and emerge as Aphrodite (Venus). The blood falls and transforms into the furies, the spirits of vengeance (who seem to have a close connection to Mars). The story reflects Uranus' lack of connection with matters-feminine and to the form-principle generally, the former appearing in his resistance to organic processes such as birth, the latter in his treatment of Saturn, whom astrologers associate with the demands of non-organic or created form. Uranus prefers to remain in the realm of ideas; he refuses to accept the karmic situation, the results of his actions (i.e. his children). He rebels against and tries to reverse the organic process that yields what he sees as inadequate results, a judgment coming from ideas instead of feeling. We see here Uranus' connection with Aquarius, a fixed air sign associated with fixed thinking-patterns. Aquarius, known to astrologers as a barren sign, has to do with fixed ideas that can separate a person from the flow of organic life. (This does not mean, of course, that those ideas cannot also have great importance to progressive social movements.)

We can discern here, Uranus' difficulties with Saturn, Aquarius' other ruler. As Uranus' child, Saturn demands of Uranus a responsibility that Uranus does not wish to take on, preferring as he does the freedom of his ideas to the demands of fatherhood, which he apparently sees as a limiting form. His children (forms) simply don't measure up to his ideas: Uranus finds them too ugly. Reacting to these ideas, Uranus ignores and tries to escape from the karmic situation, and the story suggests that if we take this approach—if we insist on finding our freedom somewhere outside of what we see as limitations, if we try to live by disembodied ideas instead of by using our insight to penetrate *into* the situation-at-hand—we lose the life-giving power of our insight.

The mythic story also suggests that if we can lose that life-giving power in another way: if we don't accept the demands placed on us by our own creations or our creative inspiration. The demands, here, generally involve bringing our inspirations into form. Saturn/Kronos, one of Uranus' children, symbolizes form, particularly the type created by humans. Such forms emerge from inspiration and insight, just as the mythic Uranus fathers Saturn. Yet just as the mythic Uranus resists the formal and earthy results of his creative urges, so the astrological Uranus often points to an arena in which a person will resist putting things into definite form. Certainly if a woman projects Uranus onto men, she will often end up in the lunar role, the role of the earth mother (Gaia), for if Uranus gets his way, the children end up back with the mother. In such cases, the woman often has to take on some of the Saturnian role as well, for she has to function as the responsible party as regards the children, giving form and structure to their lives because an absent father will not. Uranus, meanwhile, won't readily accept either the maternal role or the paternal one, for he doesn't seem to like roles at all! The myth also suggests that if a person acts out the problematic side of Uranus, he will resist giving form to his creative inspiration and will seek freedom *from* responsibility instead of freedom *for* creative expression, for the latter generally brings him into the realm of form. Again we find ourselves looking at the *puer* energy.

The Moon rules the sub-lunar realm of organic life and thus has a close connection to Gaia, the Earth Mother. In the myth, Gaia conspires with Cronus (Saturn) to castrate Uranus. Saturn and the Moon symbolize two sides of the karmic situation, Saturn representing (in part) responsibility and the demands that come from our commitment to human society; the Moon representing (in part) the natural processes of life that bring the most omnipresent and inescapable manifestation of karma. We might also say that Saturn and the Moon symbolize fundamental elements in the karmic process: the Moon symbolizes organic process, which we might call the seed of karma (at least from the point of view of a single lifetime); Saturn symbolizes the development of commitments, structures, venues, situations, and attitudes—and the fears that give birth to them—through which we carry the karmic process forward through time. Those fears have a close link to security needs, a category that includes not only the emotional security associated with the Moon, and not only the lunar securities associated with the home, and not only with situational security (e.g. "job security") associated with Saturn, but also security in one's own identity, with who one "is," a matter clearly associated with Saturn, yet also with lunar elements insofar as identity gets bound up with patterns of emotional security. And, it seems, not only in the myth but in our experience, Uranus takes a dim view of all that. In doing so, he runs the risk of losing the power of insight simply because he has divorced that insight from lived experience.[16]

Though the mythic Uranus surely reacts to Saturn, he reacts first to Gaia, the Earth Mother, a figure with obvious connections to the Moon, as we can see from very old notions about the "sub-lunar realm." Uranus sees lunar processes as threatening to his ideas, as a web that discourages the free expression of those ideas, a realm in which ideas must always suffer some constriction from the formal demands of matter. Uranus symbolizes a freedom that we gain through ideas, through our attempt to be like the gods themselves, whereas the Moon represents our most ordinary humanness, the way our lives develop in rhythmic, cyclical patterns that cannot be separated from the patterns of the earth itself. Uranus' difficult relationship with the Moon appears clearly in the ecological situation we face now as we enter the Age of Aquarius, a period partly-ruled by Uranus.[17] Certainly the discovery of Uranus ushered in a period markedly destructive to the ecosystem, largely as a result of new technologies (associated with Uranus). More personally, we can see in Uranus' attitudes an assumption that emerges when Uranus loses his connection to earth: that to have value, ideas must function without limitation or confinement. The myth suggests that the assumption leads to all sorts of difficulties.

That we discern in the myth an apparently ancient antipathy doesn't mean that people can't work with Uranus-Moon combinations or that strongly lunar people (not only women, but also

---

[16]Perhaps not coincidentally, Saturn and the Moon have some astronomical connections, as Saturn goes through the signs in 29.49 years, while the Moon goes through its synodic cycle in 29.53 days (and its rotational cycle in 27.32 days).
[17]In the traditional astrological system, Saturn rules Aquarius. Since the discovery of Uranus in the late 18th century, most astrologers have seen him as the new ruler or co-ruler of that sign.

men with a strongly placed natal Moon or other Moon-related factors; and all of us insofar as we occupy the sub-lunar realm) cannot work effectively with Uranus. However, we should first recognize that we have to do, here, with a basic human conundrum. As we will see, the early Jungians apparently saw this conundrum as one of the most basic elements of our psychology; thus Marie Louise von Franz refers to the *anima* and *animus*, energetic factors with clear connections to the Moon and Uranus, as "the great mediating daemons." Like most basic conundrums, this one appears in our most ordinary experiences: we all sense, for example, the creative power of the mind and the cyclic patterning of the body and the myriad ways in which these sometimes seem to diverge. The elemental nature of the conundrum explains why so many people struggle to bring the Uranian and Lunar energies together in ways that feel healthy and that don't do violence to or overly restrict either one. Women may feel the lunar elements of the conundrum more personally and in ways more obviously painful (men's pain in this kind of situation often remaining less obvious, as we will see) simply because the lunar elements in their lives play a more evident role. Though to a man the Moon may seem to arise "only" as the feelings, for a woman the lunar elements arise in obvious ways through her physiology.[18]

None of this means that women can't access potentials symbolized by Uranus. Many women obviously *do* access that energy. But the myth seems to suggest that a woman's physiology (that is, biological factors) play a role in her tendency to project Uranus onto men. Although both men and women project Uranus for psychological reasons (because Uranus threatens ego's stability), a woman's projection of Uranus may express biological elements as well. Or, we might say, her projection involves more obvious biological elements. Most men also require some stability, though, in order to function effectively, and this tendency may reflect biological elements as well.[19]

---

[18] We might note here, at least in passing, that the Uranus myth seems to tell us something about "original sin." Kronos, here, seems very similar to Saturn/Satan. Saturn resents Uranus' freedom, or least Uranus' way of expressing it. In Genesis, the original sin also had to do with freedom, though Satan (Saturn) seemed to be the one promoting the idea! We might speculate that Satan, who had been kicked out of Heaven, resented the preternatural freedom of Adam and Eve, a freedom untrammeled by the demands we often associate with Saturn. Though Satan advertised freedom, he knowingly promulgated bondage to karma: he probably knew that if his temptation succeeded, Adam and Even would find themselves in a world shaped by cause-and-effect. Adam and Eve then acted because they desired (that is, had an idea about) emancipation and found themselves in the world of birth and death. Uranus generated Saturn even in Eden! Thus the Greek and Hebrew myths have interesting parallels. Small wonder, then, that as we approach the Uranus-ruled Aquarian Age, many people look askance at the Garden of Eden myth. The Biblical version faults Eve for seeking freedom - for valuing or seeking to embody Uranus. Many still fault women for being too liberated (Uranus)! But Aquarius is co-ruled by Saturn (Kronos), the Lord of Time and Karma, so as we proceed into the new aeon, we may find ourselves seeking freedom through our ideas yet bound to karmic situations that we can't really escape. In the Bible, of course, Eve seems to bring the demand of freedom to Adam. She may think that she represents Uranus, but she really brings the word of Saturn/Satan and of the earth (Gaea) with its demands. Many women in our culture find Uranus through Saturn: they find a kind of freedom by participating in the structures of the status quo, their bondage having been previously defined, in part, by their exclusion from those structured opportunities. But if Aquarius represents our need for wider social participation, we shouldn't feel surprised that women (and men!) who seek such participation should find it marked by both Saturn and Uranus, not merely the latter.

[19] I don't mean that we can find some sort of anti-Uranian or pro-lunar gene. Specific genes apparently do not determine complex behaviors.

We might ask why a woman projects Uranus so readily in her relationships even if in other areas and activities she will more often embody that energy. Perhaps when a woman enters a relationship, some part of her, some part of her feminine daemon, will connect that relationship either to the procreative process or to instincts related to the protection of organic life. If she does this, she will naturally play the lunar role, and so the man will often find himself in the Uranian one. This bit of psychic trading may often explain why so many women cease to project Uranus after they go through menopause. After that point, a woman may find herself agreeing with Malkah, the wise, wily, and sensual grandmother in Marge Piercy's *He, She, and It*, seeing love as "mostly nonsense and self-hypnosis" and men as "by and large fine to work with and fun in bed," even if in dealing with them women should "never expect much otherwise."[20] That the woman nurses the child while the man builds the external structure and defines boundaries suggests that the woman projects Saturn as well, at least at certain times; that the woman seeks security while the man seeks freedom suggests that the woman projects Uranus, though not always and not in all circumstances.

When a woman experiences Uranus as a projection, she might conclude that the problem lies in the man or in men-in-general. We may hear her saying, "Men are such-and-such-and-such." But though we all know that men do not often behave like angels, they don't seem to act with complete deviltry either—at least not always! In any case, from a purely practical point of view, when a woman deals with Uranus, she will deal most effectively if she looks at her own attitudes instead of at the man's behavior. If a woman experiences the man as constantly resisting commitment, she has possibly disowned or devalued her own Uranus, her own desire for freedom within relationships, her desire for space there, her desire to go her own way and yet be intimately involved with someone. We might say that the woman has done this for understandable—even good—reasons; however, she will still feel more whole if she takes responsibility for the energy astrologers symbolize as Uranus, even if doing so seems to threaten not only her self-conception but also her relationship. She may even find that as she takes this step, her relationship improves, for not only does she take responsibility for her own energy, she also takes from the man the burden of two Uranus energies, his own and hers. As she acts in a more Uranian way, he will often feel less compelled to do so.

Uranus and the Animus

We can come to terms with a projected Uranus by looking into the relationship between Uranus and what Jung called the *animus*. He wrote that each woman is "compensated by a masculine element" and that therefore "her unconscious has, so to speak, a masculine imprint,"[21] which he called the *animus*, meaning "mind" or "spirit." Part of Jung's description of the animus sounds very much

---

[20] p.38. Interestingly, Malkah shocks Shira, her granddaughter, who has a strong personal and erotic attraction to the android Yod, by telling her that she (Malkah) has greatly enjoyed her sexual experiences with him. If we take Yod as a Uranian character (and not unreasonably, considering his nature!), we would say that the grandmother, now long past her childbearing years, has found great satisfaction integrating the Uranian energy with her own—and not surprisingly, as she has played a major role in programming Yod's social conditioning. See the discussion of Emily Dickenson below. (See the bibliography for publication information about *He, She, and It*.)

[21] C.G. Jung, *Aion* (Princeton: Princeton University Press, 1959), 14.

like a description of Uranus—and sometimes like a description of Uranus-ruled Aquarius as well: the animus, he wrote, "…consists of opinions instead of reflections, and by *opinions* I mean *a priori* assumptions that lay claim to absolute truth."[22] Uranus-ruled Aquarius, as a fixed air sign, has to do with fixed ideas,[23] while Uranus symbolizes the new, the revolutionary, and the groundbreaking. As we have seen, his mythic background suggests that he does not like to change his mind and that he prefers to live by his ideas instead of by his feelings, for ideas can remain fixed even as feelings and structures change. The myth suggests that though Uranus' ideas have to do with emancipation, sometimes those ideas get twisted slightly, detaching us from responsibility and the demands of the present moment—or even the demands of form generally. Uranus also has to do with new ideas that bring absolutist convictions, and though we can deceive ourselves when these insights arise (Uranus leads to Neptune[24]), the flash of insight itself seems to express something fundamental about human awareness. However, despite Uranus' connection with fundamental insight, when he arises as a projection, the projecting person will often experience it as a movement toward detachment (from relationship, from empirical evidence, from emotional tone, etc.) expressed by others.

Having much in common with "the divine *puer aeternus,*"[25] Uranus includes in his purview not only rebellion and youth, but also any person who refuses to accept the dictates of the status quo and who, at least from the perspective of that status quo, refuses to grow up. At the same time, like Uranus, the animus can appear "as a creative spirit who can inspire a woman to undertake her own spiritual achievements."[26] According to Ms von Franz, this spirit "is a spirit of love, that is, of her own living inner mystery, which comes into realization in the Eros between man and woman." She adds that the animus lures the woman "away from reality now and again." These observations bring us back to Uranus' actions in the myth: his attempt to avoid what I have called "the karmic situation." When Uranus functions unconsciously, he tends to draw us out of tangible, lived experience and into the realm of disembodied ideas. We may think that we see this most clearly in psychotics, but the pattern appears to some extent in every person for whom concepts mediate access to the world—in other words, probably in all of us. We can see why some astrologers have associated Uranus with aberrant behavior, for though Uranus can emancipate, he can also detach to such a degree that the mind loses its anchor in consensus reality.

Uranus provides insight that enables us to cut through the karmic chain as long as we apply that insight into our lives directly, as a means to greater and more insightful participation in the world of tangible things, responsibility, and human relations (Saturn as Uranus' child). However, the

---

[22] Jung, 15.

[23] Most astrologers agree that Uranus rules Aquarius. Some hold that Uranus has his exaltation in Scorpio, another fixed sign. Though many non-astrologers tend to see Aquarius as a sign connected with revolution and ongoing change, astrologers know that though the sign has a progressive side, it also gravitates toward fixed ideas, perhaps even obsessions. Saturn also rules it, so Aquarius' conundrum often arises as tension between progressive and conservative notions.

[24] Uranus leads to Neptune not only in the order of the planets, but also historically: unexplained perturbations in Uranus' orbit led to the discovery of Neptune.

[25] Marie Louise von Franz, *Projection and Recollection in Jungian Psychology*, 134.

[26] Von Franz, 135.

myth suggests what experience demonstrates: that we will often use Uranus to attempt an escape from the karmic situation, to avoid dealing with that situation either through seeking what we naïvely imagine as "greater freedom," or through an escape into ideas (which may, of course, prompt the naïve seeking just mentioned). In short, Uranus often urges us toward escapist action through which we ignore our responsibilities both to others and to ourselves. Uranus lives by the creative idea, but he resists those processes by which we give form to those ideas. The hook for a Uranus projection will often seem to have at least some of these characteristics.

All of this recalls Ms. von Franz' remark that the animus often arises as a spirit of death (suggesting Uranus' exaltation in Scorpio), which we might take as either a desire to escape karma or as an impetus toward true transcendence, a mediating spirit pointing the way toward spiritual development. Von Franz points out that whereas a man's *anima* produces "projections that bind the man to objects," the animus "produces…projections that tend to cut the woman off from the world of objects" (as, for example, a man who will not remain with her). These projections may arise as "absolute convictions," but when a woman projects Uranus, she can get carried away by the *man's* convictions, spiritual or otherwise; and often the man will eventually cut the woman off from his idea-driven pursuit. The "absolute conviction" associated with the *animus* can also arise through a *puer* figure who is "absolutely convinced" of something-or-other; in extreme cases, the woman will also adopt these convictions and live vicariously through them. That the cutting appears to begin with the man doesn't mean that the woman has no involvement. Whatever the (apparently) external situation suggests, the woman must begin her process of re-collection by looking at herself.

Similarly, a Uranian figure will resist the woman's efforts to tie him to a specific situation or obligation. In some cases, he will refuse all responsibility, particularly to the woman. To the woman, such a person (usually a man) may seem guided (metaphorically speaking) by a star, but the woman deludes herself in relation to him if she shows an unshakable conviction in her tie to him. While the person may in some way represent, in projected form, the woman's impetus toward spiritual development, the woman will probably do better to feel that impetus within, as an inner drive rather than an external partner with such qualities. And if she *does* feel the quality through the partner, she should attain certainty that the person acts as a true mediator to the realms of spirit (as, for example, a reliable spiritual teacher will do) instead of as just an unavailable *puer*.

In her *Animus and Anima*, Emma Jung discusses a section from Goethe's *Faust* in which Faust translates from the Gospel of John the passage normally rendered as, "In the beginning was the Word," or *Logos*, sometimes referred to in the western tradition as the gateway to the spirit. Faust wonders whether the passage might not read better as, "In the beginning was the Power," or, "In the beginning was Meaning," or, "In the beginning was the Deed." Ms. Jung feels that in these four expressions, meant to explain, or unpack, the Greek *logos*, "the quintessence of the masculine principle seems to be expressed." She feels, further, that these terms present a sequence, with "each stage having its representative in life as well as in the development of the animus." The first stage, she says, corresponds to Power, and "the deed follows, then the word, and finally, as the last stage, meaning."[27] These terms correspond fairly closely to the planets that women most readily project onto men: Mars (Power, or what Ms. Jung calls "directed power"), Mars-Saturn (Deed), Uranus (Word, Idea, Meaning).[28] But when they arise through the anima, these ideas often appear in ways that separate a person from ordinary truth and ordinary life.

Admittedly, Uranus often manifests not only as fixed ideas about absolute truth, but as sudden flashes of insight—insight, perhaps, into a vaster truth or more encompassing view; or, perhaps, what ego takes as absolute truth. These insights can impel a person to break free of psychic imprisonment, undue restriction, or narrow view. But, as noted, they sometimes separate a person from ordinary experience. Ms. Jung writes:

> Often it is very difficult to realize that a thought or opinion has been dictated by the animus and is not one's own most particular conviction, because the animus has at its command a sort of aggressive authority and power of suggestion. It derives this authority from its connection with the universal mind, but the force of suggestion it exercises is due to woman's own passivity in thinking and her corresponding lack of critical ability. Such opinions or concepts, usually brought out with great aplomb, are especially characteristic of the *animus*. They are characteristic in that, corresponding to the principle of the *logos*, they are generally valid concepts or truths which, though they may be quite true in themselves, do not fit in the given instance because they fail to consider what is individual and specific in a situation. Ready-made, incontrovertibly valid judgments of this kind are really only [sic] applicable in mathematics, where two times two is always four. But in life they do not apply for there they do violence, either to the subject under discussion or to the person being addressed, or even to the woman herself who delivers a final judgment without having taken all of her own reactions into account.[29]

Though we needn't take these remarks as a universal truth about how women's minds work in all situations, Ms. Jung does describe a psychological situation that many women find particularly challenging, and one that Ms. Jung herself no doubt found particularly challenging, given the intellectual status of her husband. The connection between the animus and the universal mind suggests a woman's latent power of intellect, what we might call the feminine aspect of intellect, as two of

---

[27] Emma Jung, *Anima and Animus: Two Essays by Emma Jung* (Dallas: Spring Publications, 1957), 2-3.
[28] Some might argue that I should include Pluto here. Surely Pluto has a connection with these matters, but I've not included him because he—or she, for Pluto embodies the feminine as much as the masculine—does not represent an energy that women project more readily than do men. Rather, we all project Pluto, and women do not project it onto men more readily than men do onto women. Pluto symbolizes, among other potentials, the transformative element of the intellect and perception. Pluto occupies a central place in any discussion of projection, both as the focus of specific projections and as connected to the making of projections per se. See chapters XI and XII. Mercury also plays a role here, but I discuss that influence at length in the same chapters.
[29] Emma Jung, 14-15.

the primary symbols for the intellect, Mercury and Pluto, both have hermaphroditic qualities. To the degree that a woman projects this power onto men, it will remain latent in the woman herself. The astrological symbolism suggests that for many women, projections involving the intellect will remain difficult to discern and therefore difficult to recall or re-collect, for they will often arise as an apparently immutable conviction instead of simply as an obstacle to one's realization. The same could be said of any projection, but those of the animus seem to have a particularly hypnotic effect, perhaps because of their connection to universal ideas.

Like the animus, Uranus has a "connection with the universal mind," and like the animus, Uranus will often ignore the subtleties of a situation, preferring an absolutist position to an engaged one. This facet of Uranus arises more virulently when Uranus appears as a projection: the person onto whom the Uranus-projection falls will often ignore the personal element in a situation simply because he appears driven by absolutist ideas; thus he serves a similar function as does the woman's animus. And of course, the two manifestations can co-exist: the woman may tend to state absolutist positions herself *and* to develop associations with men who have many such positions to offer.

In re-collecting her projection of Uranus, a woman may at first threaten her own self-conception, particularly if she sees herself only or primarily as faithful, supportive, accepting, and nurturing. She may often act in faithful, supportive, accepting, and nurturing ways, and she may feel comfortable in doing so, but if she identifies with these qualities to the exclusion of others, she will find herself confronted by projections that serve as warning signs of an unbalanced view in which she sees herself in either-or terms: she may think that, in the realm of intimate relationships, she can either take on the role of the faithful nurturer or the role of one following her own insight—either one but not both. Here we will often find the nub of the problem; the woman will need to see that she can act in one way at one time and in another way at another time, without contradiction—and that she can combine both potentials in myriad actions. (The astrological symbolism can help her to see this, of course, for it reminds us that no-one "is" just one "thing." The planets symbolize the many facets of a person's being. We exercise these capacities in various ways at various times.) At one time, she may emphasize her faithfulness; at another, she may emphasize her desire for interpersonal and creative freedom.

That the Uranus' story comes from an ancient creation myth suggests that Uranus symbolizes something basic about human nature and about how we create our own worlds (to the extent that we do, of course). In the story, Uranus may seem antithetical to the Moon and Saturn, for Uranus seeks freedom instead of security, ideas instead of feeling, and often looks out into the world instead of back toward home, hearth, or hierarchy. He prefers untrammeled latitude to discipline or responsibility. Thus, though we may say that a woman needs both freedom and faithfulness, she may find it difficult to combine these demands, difficult to fulfill one potential without denying the other. She finds herself dealing with what seems a basic human conundrum that resists facile solutions—though, of course, the difficulty may tell us more about the way we structure our thinking than about "human nature." (Men deal with a similar conundrum; however, as we will see, they come at it from a different angle.) Whether she chooses one to the exclusion of the other or tries to combine both behaviors, she will experience some discomfort. Since we all have both the Moon and Uranus in our horoscopes, we might surmise that such conundrums, because unavoidable, provide conditions ensuring that life will always involve some degree of anxiety.

Still, the woman in this case first needs to honor the energy of Uranus. She can certainly begin this process by engaging in activities—ways of acting or ways of being—marked by Uranus. She might want to work more independently, or to study a new subject, or to learn a new technology or technique. At work, she might strive to honor her own capacity for innovation and her own rebellious tendencies. Such approaches can be particularly helpful for women who've largely denied the importance of Uranus in their lives. But even if a woman gets this far, even if she manifests Uranus in her profession or public life as so many do, she'll still have to apply Uranus *within* her relationship, not only outside of it and certainly not primarily as a way to be free from it. The tendency or willingness to apply Uranus outside of one's relationships doesn't necessarily indicate a similar tendency or willingness to apply Uranus *inside* those relationships. To do the latter will entail challenging many social taboos and perhaps some instinctual patterns as well.

Uranus has a fairly well-documented connection with infidelity: as far as we know, he has never loved structure, containment, or commitment.[30] To cultivate Uranus within a relationship does not mean that one must seek other partners, or even other friendships. But the woman should not fall prey to false dilemmas (which often come from the structure of our *ideas,* as noted). To put the matter in astrological terms, she needn't think that she must "be like" either Uranus or the Moon. She will have to honor both, even if she initially experiences them as antithetical; perhaps she needs to honor them both *because* she finds them antithetical. If Uranus asks that a woman do things by herself sometimes, that she have her own circle of friends (men or women), or that she go out dancing and so forth—fine. But no matter what she *does,* she'll have to recognize and honor her feelings

---

[30]However, because Uranus will usually challenge any prevailing status quo, if that status quo involves an ongoing tendency to avoid long-term commitment, as we saw during the first Uranus cycle for many who have Uranus in Cancer, then a transit from Uranus (such as the mid-life Uranus-Uranus opposition for the Uranus in Cancer generation) can stimulate a desire for precisely those commitments one has heretofore avoided. Of course, this shift brings no assurance that the relationships will last. It merely suggests that the person will attempt to break free of an established pattern.

[31]Intimate same-sex relationships in our culture seem marked by Uranus partly because such relationships are not honored by the status quo and partly because they don't lead to the same karmic results (i.e. children) as do opposite-sex relationships. Many people in our culture seem to consider intimate same-sex relationships as outré, unusual, sometimes even immoral. In different cultural contexts (e.g. ancient Greece), contexts in which people had different attitudes, we might find same-sex relationships marked by Saturn as much as by Uranus. (They would still retain some connection to Uranus, though, because they do not lead to the same kinds of karmic consequences, as noted.). Full discussion of this matter would take us too far afield, but I agree, with provisos, with those who link homosexuality to Uranus, though only for the reasons offered above and not, for example, because homosexuality is an aberration. Hopefully, we can link an activity to Uranus without saying that it is unhealthy! Otherwise, we'd have to describe as unhealthy all revolutionary activity, all improvisational art, and all creative activity that breaks timeworn codes. But if Uranus symbolizes that which rebels against the status quo, his manifestations will vary depending on the status quo available. As long as same-sex intimate relationships run counter to the prevailing status quo, they will carry the mark of Uranus.

of claustrophobia, her interests in or involving other men (or other women),[31] or her feeling that one marriage or one partner will never really meet all of her needs and that such a situation needn't cause great concern. However, we should remember that, as a partial representative of the animus, Uranus symbolizes an *inner* mediating figure, an energy arising *within*. Though we should hesitate to make facile distinctions between inner and outer worlds, the woman herself will sense whether she has made a merely external accommodation or whether she feels Uranus' energy arising within.

We can see from all this that a projection of Uranus can threaten a woman's primary relationship. Such a threat may arise whether the woman re-calls (or *re-collects*) the projection or not, for Uranus tends to threaten any stability that doesn't promote freedom. Uranus seems particularly disruptive of relationships based on some kind of unconscious contract. For a woman, this contract often suggests that she should spend all her time fulfilling the traditional woman's role as homemaker, child-rearer, and faithful companion—ignoring, the while, her Uranian needs—while the man fulfills, perhaps because *some*one must act the Uranian role in this situation, what some will cynically call *his* traditional role as untrustworthy companion, as seeker after other women, while ignoring his lunar needs (as discussed in the next chapter). If a relationship depends too much on the woman seeing herself as the one who keeps or demands the security and seeing the man as the one prone to rebel, then the relationship will probably change dramatically when the woman begins to acknowledge and express her Uranian energies and finds an inner connection to Uranus. In the latter (probably preferable) case, if the women starts to "go against the program" of the relationship, the man will often feel threatened or insecure. Quite likely he'll rediscover, somewhat painfully, his connection to his anima. (See the next chapter). We can't predict what he'll do in these circumstances, for he might act in a "lunar" manner or, as a reaction, further ignore the lunar side of his nature. In any case, once the woman begins to act more freely, things will change, Uranus having a long-standing dislike for the status quo.

If the man finds himself relating to his lunar energy—his security needs, his feelings, and so forth—he may feel threatened; and both people will probably benefit from the shift. If both he and the woman experience *both* the Moon and Uranus as elements of their own psychology, they will probably relate to each other more honestly. In the end, the couple's chances for a long-term relationship probably improve more with such a scenario than with the one in which the man acts out the Uranus energy while the woman opts for the lunar position. We should tread warily even here, however, because though the Moon will value duration, Uranus will not. To say, "This relationship is good because it lasts" may reflect a lunar bias. So if the woman thinks that by re-collecting her Uranus she can "make her relationships last," she should look carefully within herself for hidden biases. The Moon wants its changes to take place within a rhythmic container, and Uranus generally wants its changes to take place outside of available containers, particularly when the people involved value the container more than what it contains. He may err, though, in thinking that he can have the contents without the container.

Sometimes, of course, people will prefer, though not necessarily consciously, to remain in the world created by their projections rather than to move toward more awareness. Perhaps people do this (*when* they do) because they sense that if they re-collect their projections and see a relationship more accurately, they will have to admit some painful truths about it. In such cases, projections can at least provide the illusion of a connection.

Nature and Nurture? Culture and Biology?

It's somewhat difficult, in a discussion of projection, to separate cultural factors from biological ones. As noted above, that we find our behavior reflected in the ancient Greek myth suggests that the behavior has roots that go deeper than current custom. On the other hand, we know that in our society and in many others, women don't receive much encouragement to emphasize their own independence, either in their lives in general or their close relationships in particular. Some might argue that women of our time receive less negative feedback than did women of other eras, that they will therefore rebel more often against traditional roles, and that they will therefore project Uranus less often and less automatically.

However, though some women are less tied to traditional maternal roles, they often move into Saturnian positions rather than Uranian ones (this last term perhaps qualifying as an oxymoron), following the pattern of the Greek myth in which Uranus leads to Saturn. Sometimes this will seem completely appropriate, for Uranus apparently *must* generate Saturn. Much depends on circumstance and motive, however, and we should not assume that a woman taking up a profession has thereby successfully taken on the role of Uranus. She must ensure that the form serves to express the idea as fully as possible, for sometimes we accept overly rigid forms simply because we fear our own freedom and insight. That an action liberates a person from social limitation does not necessarily mean it has the same effect psychologically.

Certainly women these days enter professions previously dominated by men, but the roads often remain rough and muddy in that neck of the woods: rough due not only to overt sexism, but to numerous more covert varieties; muddy because one has to deal with men's emotions and security needs, matters long ignored and hence somewhat hard to get off one's shoes. Still, we certainly find many women doctors, women lawyers, women college professors, and so forth. Not, as just noted, that the professions themselves reflect Uranus, for the professional realm has a strong connection to Saturn; but by entering them a woman plays a Uranian role insofar as doing so constitutes a break from some personal pattern of restriction or a challenge to the larger status quo. A woman may make a change for what we call Uranian reasons and yet end up in a position characterized by Saturn—and this should not surprise us, for the reasons given above.

On the surface, then, we have a paradox: making the break, the woman embodies Uranus; having done so, though, she often finds herself with Saturnian restrictions of a new type and apparently integral to many professions, for just as in previous eras Saturn arose as law and custom restricting a woman's choice of roles largely to the lunar one, now Saturn will often arise as a commitment to a position characterized by Saturn. Though for some women (and men!), such a development will often have a liberating effect, Saturn, lover of shadows, can come back in through the back door and exert control from the back rooms. In any case, the Saturn-Uranus dynamic often emphasizes evident social patterns rather than shadowy psychological ones.[32]

The presence of both cultural and biological factors here does not at all indicate that women can't withdraw at least some—even most—of the relevant projections. Though the presence of a primordial element in all of this (and in a man's anima-related projections, as we will see) may indicate, as Jung put it, that "nature is conservative and does not easily allow her courses to be altered" or that nature "defends in the most stubborn way the inviolability of the preserves where anima and animus roam,"[33] we nevertheless see women withdrawing these projections, and not only in the latter part of life when lunar demands recede. We should, though, heed Jung's warning (if we can call it that), for we should consider the animus and the anima as archetypes, as functions that "filter the contents of the collective unconscious through to the conscious mind."[34] We cannot, Jung felt, integrate the archetypes themselves, but only their contents; the archetypes themselves Jung considered "foundation stones of the psychic structure, which in its totality exceeds the limits of consciousness and therefore can never become the object of direct cognition."[35] Though we shouldn't say that Uranus "is an archetype," Uranus symbolizes energy with a close connection to the archetype that Jung called the animus. Sometimes we see this energy working through our projections or habitual mental patterns. We can integrate some of those contents, but we may never get at the factor that creates them.

On a more practical level, we can probably admit that a woman will find it difficult to engage in front-line revolutionary activity (Uranus, probably with an admixture of Mars) while nursing an infant, and that single mothers (or single fathers) won't find it easy to nurture their children, make a living, *and* express unique creative talents unrelated to these two functions. In other words, on that practical level a woman will face evident challenges if she attempts to re-collect a projected Uranus and to act as an embodiment of that energy, and she may never fully integrate the energy of the creative sky god, the first and primordial father of Greek myth. She can still work with the contents of the projection, though, re-collecting the elements of her potential that she experiences vicariously. Social circumstances may hinder the full *expression* of Uranus, but each person can recognize Uranus as an integral element of a personal potential.

---

[32]Saturn and Uranus co-rule Aquarius, a sign associated with groups and with social value or structure. Until the discovery of Uranus in 1781, Saturn seemed the predominant planet in all social systems. Opposite to Leo, Aquarius symbolizes a field in which personal self-expression operates. Uranus' discovery brought not only technical developments that aide in social coherence, but also revolution. Despite Uranus' revolutionary insistence, however, and despite the myriad ways in which high technology has infiltrated even the most reactionary of social bureaucracies and hierarchies, Saturn still seems to rule the most visible roosts. Thus when anyone moves into society, he must deal with Saturn first of all. A person may state his or her freedom from restrictive circumstance by "getting a job" or contributing to society in some way, but he or she must always remain watchful lest Saturn restrict unduly. As a trickster, he often makes promises that he has no intention of keeping.
[33]C.G. Jung, *Aion*, 17.
[34]C.G. Jung, 20.
[35]C.G. Jung, 20.

When projections proliferate, prompted either by social factors or biological ones, or even the psychological ones that seem connected with both, one must begin by questioning the solidity of the external situation—or, the solidity of one's *version* of it. In working with Uranus, a woman may conclude that a specific man has acted irresponsibly, or she may conclude that the good economic cards always seem to end up in someone else's hand; she can consider these as messages from the world and with a strong connection to her own Uranus. She can opt to take advantage of her psychological freedom first of all. Uranus has much to do with ideas, after all, particularly the ones that enable her to understand her experience more clearly. Then she can decide how to give form to those ideas, to make a better go of the Uranus-Saturn connection than did the ancient gods.

The Football Analogy

That may seem an odd section-title to use in a discussion of the animus, but the analogy can help explain some of the energy-exchanges that seem to take place when we project. In the situation outlined above, we might say that each partner has a Uranian football and the woman hands hers over to the man, so that now he has two and therefore feels rather obsessed about his "freedom"—while the woman now has no Uranian football at all.[36] In such a situation, the woman won't consciously feel the Uranian urge to freedom, the drive to free herself of roles. Uranus rebels against role playing, particularly when the role one plays doesn't promote free expression. When a woman sees that she must free herself from mental slavery[37] before she can free herself from any other kind, she can begin to differentiate the particular man from the projections she casts on him. Thus freed, she can make a moral evaluation of the situation, deciding to move toward the human energy that astrologers describe as "Uranus." She frees herself from a situation in which she maintains a more-or-less illusory relationship with the man and with herself. And the more she says that the man "is" such-and-such (e.g. "is" incapable of commitment), the more she should question, investigate, and re-collect.

The irresponsibility that she perceives in the hooks upon which she hangs the Uranus projection reminds us again of the darker side of the mythic Uranus: Uranus doesn't want to take responsibility for his own creations, and so he suffers castration. This suggests, on the one hand, that the men who serve as or allow themselves to serve as hooks for these projections may not escape unscathed: if they play the irresponsible *puer* blindly, they ignore legitimate responsibilities, not only to the women involved but to themselves as well, to the creative daimon within. So they may lose the life-giving power of their insight. A man might ignore the inner daemon that drives him to do the work he feels, at other times, driven to do. He prefers—or finds himself preferring—a directionless and reactive kind of freedom. Though he may see this as his own choice, he may not know how he came to have two Uranian footballs instead of one—and no lunar one at all, for he often finds that

---

[36]For the uninitiated: if you want to carry two footballs, you probably need to use two hands, for though you can perhaps handle two with one hand, you would find yourself prone to fumble one of them; if you carry one with each hand, or under each arm, you couldn't carry much else.
[37]Bob Marley: "Redemption Song," from *Bob Marley's Greatest Hits*.

he has handed his lunar football to the woman, so that just as he acts "doubly Uranian," so she acts "doubly lunar." In other words, the projections often seem to involve not merely mistaken perception, but an actual transfer of energy—the handing over of a Uranian or lunar football.

Further, because the woman has already "negativized" one of her Uranian footballs, the man receives the negativized energy; so he feels strangely impelled toward the directionless freedom described above, acting out the negative or devalued side of the Uranian demand, acting irresponsibly, trying to ignore or to escape from the karmic situation, acting the puer, perhaps even ignoring his own creative inspiration, preferring freedom *from* claustrophobia to freedom *for* creative endeavor, preferring to remain content with inspiration instead of putting that inspiration into form. None of this means that we shouldn't hold the man accountable for his own behavior, but the people involved will probably not make progress until they acknowledge that they've made an exchange. The project*or* can begin the process by withdrawing his or her projection, by re-collecting parts of oneself from the hooks of the world.

On the other hand, the woman may act out her *own* negativized Uranus: she may seem irresponsible, escapist, directionless, failing to bring her freedom to creative fruition. We can expect for her the same consequences we described above in connection to the man: a loss of the life-giving power of her insight, an emphasis on freedom *from* restriction instead of freedom *for* creative development. For people of either sex, a healthy Uranus symbolizes the seed of creative insight along with the responsibility to plant that seed where it will grow to help oneself and others become free of fear and its resultant restrictions.

Saturn, symbolizing both fear and form, is Uranus' offspring, suggesting that insight gives birth to both fear and responsibility. This seems workable enough, yet we often experience Uranus not as the father *of* Saturn but as a reaction *to* Saturn: when we feel beset by what we feel as obdurate responsibility, we often yearn for freedom. Yet the myth suggests something quite different: forms should grow *from* our ideas; creative *work* should develop from our inspirations even if we fear rejection coming from Saturnian "authorities" either within or without. We see the mythic pattern in artistic creation: the artist begins with an idea, something not yet formed (and perhaps coming from a vague feeling: Neptune), and then works to bring that idea into form. The mythic Uranus fathers children: his actions lead to forms, to creative issue. Insight should do likewise. When we engage the psychological energy we call "Uranus," we should seek not merely to escape from limitation, but to understand limitation more fully, more spaciously and more freely, to see possibility within the limits, for apparently it doesn't exist outside of them.

The mythic Uranus prefers potentiality to actuality; he prefers ideas-about-reality to lived-reality itself. When he views his creative issue—his creative potency given form—he tries to bury it back into the earth. We see this myth brought to life when a person with creative gifts doesn't bring them forth into the light of day, when he looks at his creative issue and finds them unacceptable. Creative ideas naturally gravitate toward forms (Uranus fathers Saturn) that express the idea even if the forms seem to limit it, for the limitation serves as a necessary right-of-passage for anyone wishing to do creative work. Too often, though, we do as Uranus did: we say that our creative children should be buried back into the earth. That Uranus thought this true of his children doesn't mean we should act as he did. Part of the creative process involves seeing that our ideas about what we wish to create will not emerge fully embodied in the actual creation; we will almost always go through some disillusionment as our ideas emerge into form. William Faulkner, with Saturn and Uranus closely conjoined in Scorpio, once described *The Sound and the Fury* as four separate failures. Fortunately, he did not bury the child back into the earth.

The Midlife Uranus Opposition

Many women seem more willing to play the Uranian role after the midlife Uranus-Uranus opposition.[38] By contrast, many men seem less willing to play that role after that transit—or, at least, less willing to play it blindly. We can think of many reasons for the change in women, the most obvious having to do with the fact that as they enter their fourth decade, many women move beyond their child-bearing years. However, though this development surely makes some women less desirous of having a stable home environment, the biological changes by themselves don't seem sufficient reason for the developments that occur. Any opposition aspect can produce a more objective awareness about the factors involved. During the midlife Uranus-Uranus opposition, we all have the opportunity to develop more objective awareness about the ways that Uranus has functioned in our lives, our habit patterns related to that planetary energy, and the ways we might want to develop Uranus' energies in the future.

If a woman has habitually projected Uranus onto men, the midlife transit provides a splendid opportunity to see the pattern more clearly and, as we might expect from a Uranus transit, break free from it by developing greater insight. This doesn't seem like just a theory, as many women do precisely what I've just described, acting more freely within relationships, developing an increasingly integrated connection to social causes, and generally concerning themselves more with the wider world of political movements. This doesn't mean that women suddenly take to the streets, though some do, but that they turn their attention outward toward the non-personal, applying their insight and developing a wider sense of empathy.

Meanwhile, men often have a very different experience of the transit. From what I've seen, many men become more lunar in orientation. They, too, develop greater awareness of how Uranus has functioned in their lives, but they often see that they've so emphasized Uranus that they've forgotten the lunar imperatives that all of us feel, however much we habitually project the lunar energy out into the world. I have also seen men develop more Saturnian qualities—or, I should say, approach Saturn from a different direction. Early in life, we often approach Saturn via Jupiter, seeking security through social position by gaining more authority, either as indicated by social position or as indicated by knowledge and understanding. After the midlife opposition, however, we often want to develop structures and disciplines that grow out of a sense of individuality. In

---

[38]Uranus goes through the zodiac in about 84 years, so he opposes his natal position around the forty-second birthday.

other words, we want to make a contribution dictated not by a sense of social participation, but by a sense of individual genius.[39] Women often show a similar pattern, though from what I've seen, their connection with Uranus often has to do with relationship or related*ness*. In *The Stages of Life,* Carl Jung writes,

> We might compare masculinity and femininity with their psychic components to a particular store of substances of which, in the first half of life, unequal use is made. A man consumes his large supply of masculine substance and has left over only the smaller amount of feminine substance, which he must now put to use. It is the other way around with a woman; she allows her unused supply of masculinity to become active.
>
> This transformation weighs more heavily still in the psychic realm than in the physical. How often it happens that a man of forty or fifty years winds up his business, and that his wife then dons the trousers and opens a little shop where he sometimes performs the duties of a handyman. There are many women who only awake to social responsibility and to social consciousness after their fortieth year.[40]

And:

> …we cannot live the afternoon of life according to the programme of life's morning—for what was great in the morning will be little at evening, and what in the morning was true at evening will have become a lie. I have given psychological treatment to too many people of advancing years, and have looked too often into the secret chambers of their souls, not to be moved by this fundamental truth.[41]

In the second half of life, Jung says, an "inexorable inner process forces the contraction of life" and that for an aging person "it is a duty and a necessity to give serious attention to himself."[42]

These remarks accord well with the astrological patterns, in particular those patterns indicated by the midlife Uranus-Uranus opposition and Neptune-Neptune square. Whereas the latter asks us to develop a structure in which to give tangible expression to the spiritual and/or artistic yearning (some would call them *instincts*), the former asks us to develop more objectivity about our use of insight and about the inner drive to rebel in the service of truth. In relationships, if a man has too often let Uranus separate him from Eros, the midlife transit can induce him to use his insight to bring himself further into the life of the flesh and of simple communion. On the other hand, if a woman has too often projected Uranus onto men, the midlife transit can encourage her to experience Uranus as an integral element of her own selfhood, not merely in professional matters, but in intimate ones as well.

---

[39] Rudhyar's term, as noted.
[40] C.G. Jung, *The Stages of Life, Modern Man in Search of a Soul* (New York: Harcourt Brace Jovanovich, 1933), 107-8.
[41] C.G. Jung, 108.
[42] C.G. Jung, 109.

Case Study: Emily Dickinson[43]

Emily Dickinson stands as a good example of how in intimate matters even a highly creative woman might project Uranus onto men even if Uranus contributes to her creative work in obvious ways. Her twelfth house Libra Moon suggests not only her propriety and concern with social form (Libra) but also her seclusion and reticence, her tendency, as biographer Alfred Habegger puts it, to shrink from the public gaze.[44] If we accept the 5:00 AM birth-time, the Moon rules the ninth, suggesting that Dickinson published (ninth) about a very personal privacy and propriety (Moon in Libra in the twelfth). Her Uranus, intercepted[45] in Aquarius in the third house, along with her Mars-Pluto conjunction in Aries in the fifth, which Uranus sextiles, gives quite a different message: one about powerful, assertive, iconoclastic speech or writing (third house). An interception would indicate that the iconoclasm would gather power as it incubated over many years. The north node closely quincunxes both ends of the sextile, and Saturn does so more loosely, so we have at least a loose yod that would also indicate a period of incubation.[46] That Uranus semi-squares her Mercury, septiles her Venus, and bi-septiles her Moon (which septiles Venus) suggests the importance of rebelliousness to her life as a whole. That the Moon squares a Jupiter-Neptune conjunction in Capricorn, also in the third, suggests that she found her recluseness markedly at odds with more outgoing qualities seeking expression through some form of speech (third house).

What evidence can we cite that Dickinson projected Uranus onto men instead of, or sometimes in addition to, experiencing it as part of her own capacity? Consider her relationship with Samuel Bowles, a friend of the Dickinson family who served as co-editor of the *Republican*, a literary magazine coming out of the Amherst area. Much evidence suggests that Dickinson played a much more

---

[43] According to Alfred Habegger's biography (*My Wars are Laid Away in Books: The Life of Emily Dickinson*, New York: Modern Library, 2002), Emily's father noted in the family Bible a birth-time of "5. o'clock A.M." I have cast the chart for that time. I consider it inexact, but not far off. Habegger's biographical information certainly lends credence the 5 AM birth-time, for many of his remarks strongly suggest that Dickinson had her Moon in the twelfth house. Further, his account of Dickinson's life strongly suggests that we accept the 5:00 AM Midheaven or something close to it. Of course, even if we move the birth-time by a few, or even many, minutes either way, the planet-to-planet aspects would remain unchanged. As will become clear, I have drawn many biographical details from Habegger's book.

[44] Habegger, 390

[45] Considering the uncertainty of the birth-time, we should take this interception with a grain of salt. If we move the birth-time backwards a few minutes, Ms. Dickenson would have Aquarius, not Pisces, on the fourth house cusp—and she would not have Uranus intercepted. We should save a few salt-grains for some of the house-positions, though we can use smaller grains. I think that some of the house-positions "make sense," so I suspect that we have a reasonably accurate birth-time.

[46] An intercepted planet often indicates an energy that will incubate for many years because it doesn't find a ready outlet into the world. Yods, with their strong quincunxes, indicate something similar though the etiology differs in the two cases. An intercepted planet incubates because something in the immediate environment (i.e. something related to the houses) discourages the expression of the planet's energy. The expression of a yod may not emerge for many years not because of environmental factors, but because the energies themselves seem subtly out-of-synch with each other, so the person often must mature before she can put the energies together effectively. We might say that yods have difficulty working in the world and that intercepted signs have difficulty because of that world.

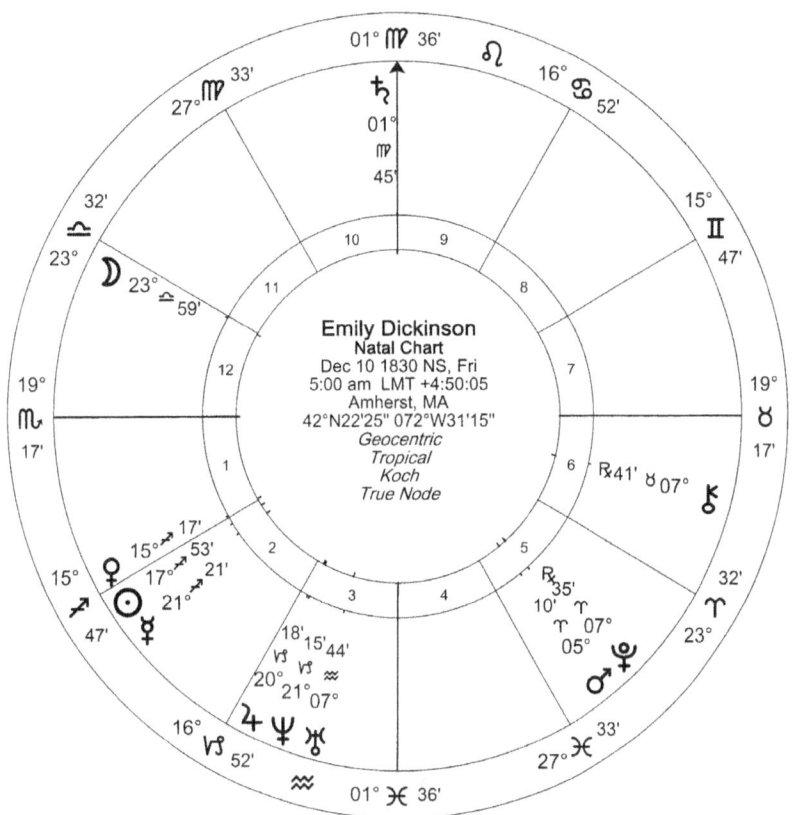

conservative role in the relationship than did Bowles, for though Bowles again and again advocated for a more public presentation and open consideration of literature written by women, Dickinson apparently felt a bit intimidated by him:

> Well ahead of current opinion, [Bowles] realized about 1860 that women's civic freedom and functions had to be drastically enlarged, if only for the good of society. His progressivism seems to have made Dickinson all the more sensitive about her "small," "old fashioned," fugitive side. He is the only known recipient for the defensive "Perhaps you think me *stooping*!" (Fr273A) She was well aware of how little she had in common with the modern women Bowles admired.[47]

Until at least 1859, Dickinson was "still very afar from seeing how a female pen could aspire to greatness."[48] Around that time, though she encountered the works of Elizabeth Barrett Browning, George Eliot, and others, and though she hinted in a letter to a woman friend that even a woman

---

[47]Habegger, 382-3.
[48]Habegger, 386.

might decide "to be distinguished," she still felt herself, as Habegger puts it, "at odds with Bowles' enlightened advocacy of a greater public role for women." At the same time, though, she was "emphatically…staking everything on a bold claim to greatness," a contradiction to which Bowles, "whether on purpose or not," called her attention.

Habegger also feels that Bowles would probably have published Dickinson's lyrics had she given him the opportunity, which she didn't, and that though she shared Bowles' progressivism on religious matters, she couldn't, at first, keep up with his ideas on women's literature. This interpretation suggests that Dickinson had owned her Uranus (progressive ideas) in arenas having nothing to do with gender, but that in gender-related matters, she at that point still left Uranus to others, particularly Bowles. This accords well with assertions made earlier in this chapter: that many women will play the role of Uranus in some areas of life yet still project it onto men—or, often, onto a particular man—in more intimate matters. Something like this seems to have happened with Dickinson in her relation to Bowles, as we can see from a letter she wrote to him after a conversation in which they had had a disagreement on an issue involving "women." In her apology-letter, Dickinson says that she feels "much ashamed," that she "misbehaved" and would like "to sit in dust." She writes that her friends "are very few," that she can "count them" upon her fingers" and "besides, have fingers to spare."[49] She asks his forgiveness. The signs of Uranus appear throughout, but not as part of Dickinson herself.

In 1859, as transiting Uranus trined his natal position and transiting Saturn moved toward his return (which took place the next year), probably in the tenth house, Dickinson began to create structures (Saturn) appropriate to her creative gifts: she began to experience her Saturn not as the order presented to her, but as the order she wished to create. At the same time, she began, through her reading, to experience her own independence and literary genius—at least in seed form. During that year she came in contact with *Aurora Leigh*, by Elizabeth Barrett Browning, "a female epic tracing the growth of a woman writer and dealing with women's special burdens and capacities."[50] That apparently led to the line about how she "in the dining room decided to be distinguished." The same period saw Dickinson's exposure to Fanny Kemble, an actress who "had left her southern slaveholding husband and was making a career reading Shakespeare's plays." She offered a series of twelve performances in Boston in December of 1859, the same month as the above-named letter, a letter that "records Dickinson's dissent from the Homestead's reigning authority," disagreeing with her father's view that Kemble was "an animal," as she wryly noted that "zoology has few such instances."[51] Notably, Jupiter was also moving through her ninth house and toward her Midheaven: she contemplated expanding her horizons and the scope of her ideas. The solar arc (SA) Moon had moved to 22+ Scorpio, over the 5:00 AM Ascendant, suggesting feminine influences and an emergence from limitations imposed by the early environment.

---

[49]Habegger, 391.
[50]Habegger, 386.
[51]Habegger, 388.

After her Saturn return in 1860, with transiting Saturn quite likely in her tenth house, and with transiting Jupiter approaching that tenth and then moving through it, Dickinson entered into a period of enormous productivity, writing many hundreds of poems. Perhaps most significantly, transiting Pluto squared Dickinson's natal Uranus from 1859 through 1861, apparently giving re-birth to that energy in full strength, bringing out the dormant power of the natal sextile (not to mention the latent power of natal Pluto's conjunction with Mars) and possibly the intercepted energy as well. This "upper" sextile (with Uranus sixty degrees behind the slower moving Pluto) has an eleventh house flavor,[52] reiterating the theme of social independence; Dickinson began to see herself and her work in a larger social context.

Not that Dickinson's genius became completely public, for she remained, with her twelfth house Moon, very much out of any available limelight. But her genius found powerful (Pluto) forms (square) as she witnessed the wounds (transiting Pluto conjoined natal Chiron) of the world (wounds including those of the Civil War). She began to develop a powerful personal voice. As Habegger puts it, her poems "articulate a very real personal effort," what Dickinson called a "tug for life."[53] And, as Habegger further notes, "the subject is, first and last, desire," clearly pointing to the Mars-Pluto conjunction in Aries, "and when the topic shifts to heaven, that is because it is the only place where earth's broken conversations can be completed."[54] Habegger seems to speak again of Mars-Pluto, however unwittingly, when he concludes his discussion of this period of Dickinson's life, and of her line about "[t]he smitten Rock that gushes," by saying that just as Moses brought forth water for the Israelites "by striking a rock with his rod," so that rod "was on Dickinson now, and the one pressing question was whether blood or literature would flow."[55]

Thus much evidence suggests that Dickinson clearly projected Uranus early in life, and that, in the early 1860s, she reclaimed some of that energy. It emerged through Pluto (which, if we accept the 5:00 AM birth-time or anything close to it, co-rules the Scorpio Ascendant): through desire and power. And yet, though she had reclaimed Uranus in her work, she had more difficulty doing so in her life, for she remained in the seclusion indicated by the Moon and continued to develop relationships with men who clearly carry the symbolism of Uranus. In scores of poems, she casts herself in the role of the ignored offerer of affection, friendship, and love. Habegger quotes the following lyric, in which Dickinson is the neglected lovebird bleeding to death as her blood bubbles up:

> Stab the Bird—that built in your bosom—
> Oh, could you catch her last Refrain—
> Bubble! "forgive"—"Some better"—Bubble!
> "Carol for Him—when I am gone"![56]

---

[52] As do all upper sextiles, the faster moving planet having now moved 300 degrees (10 complete signs) ahead of the slower-moving one.
[53] Habegger, 406.
[54] Habegger, 406.
[55] Habegger, 393.
[56] Habegger, 408.

Many of these poems remained in manuscript books; her rebellion did not drive her from her solitude. Included in these poems we find the series of love-lyrics, apparently written in 1861-2, in which the beloved remains longed for but distant, and in which the speaker constantly reiterates her faithfulness; the speaker plays the lunar role, while the lover plays the Uranian one. So, again, though we see Uranus in the brilliance of the poetry, we do not see it yet in the personal life.

Scholars have had difficulty in trying to link these poems to specific events in Dickinson's life. Astrologers might note that Dickinson's Moon squares Neptune, suggesting that fantasy could have played an important role here—and with Jupiter conjoining that Neptune, the imagination was big and publishable, on the one hand, and both dramatic and self-sacrificing on the other.[57] Thus we have this lyric:

> …the Prayer
> I knew so perfect—yesterday—
> That scalding one—Sabacthini—
> Recited fluent—here—[58]

Some have speculated that the mysterious male of these poems was the Reverend Charles Wadsworth. It doesn't really matter to our study; what matters, rather, is how the events affected Dickinson herself. Habegger writes:

> There was a man, probably a minister; he was married and in other ways out of reach and unsuitable; his feelings for her had little in common with hers for him; and she knew little about him and began to project her powerful desires and fantasies on him; their correspondence became increasingly troubling for her; they met, perhaps in 1860, perhaps only once, parting in a way that may have looked quite ordinary to a bystander; and in the poems she wrote afterward, she returned again and again to this impossible relationship, developing its latent elements in fantastic ways.
>
> Whether or not Wadsworth was the man, this romantic crisis was the necessary and climactic phase of Dickinson's long-delayed maturity and of the huge demands she made on intimates. This was the first event that forced her to think about the satisfactions she could reasonably expect in life and the compensatory goals she might plausibly achieve. By 1863, when she wrote in passing of "the Heart I former wore" (Fr757), she had come to regard the crisis as her life's transforming event.[59]

---

[57]If we accept the 5:00 AM birth-time, Cancer occupies the ninth house cusp. Thus her privacy (Moon in the twelfth house) did indeed take publishable form (ninth house), particularly if we consider Jupiter as the exalted ruler of Cancer, with Jupiter in the third house (writing) in Capricorn (ambition) and conjoined Neptune (imagination). In the 5:00 AM horoscope, Jupiter also rules the fifth house (Pisces on the cusp), and for any Dickenson horoscope, it would disposit her three conjoined planets in Sagittarius (Venus-Sun-Mercury).
[58]Habegger, 409.
[59]Habegger, 421.

The astrological evidence supports the idea that Dickinson developed a strong attachment to an unavailable man, that this connection would, through writing, serve as a vehicle for her passion and creative brilliance (Uranus sextiles Mars-Pluto, probably from the third to the fifth), and that in this relationship (even if, as some critics have suggested, totally imagined)[60] Dickinson would play the role of security-keeper and holder of emotions. The following seems to support such an interpretation:

> Oh, Signor, Thine, the Amber Hand—
> And mine—the distant Sea—
> Obedient to the least command
> Thine eye impose on me—[61]

As does this, perhaps even more powerfully:

> Rearrange a "Wife's" Affection
> When they dislocate my brain!
> Amputate my freckled Bosom
> Make me bearded like a man!
>
> Blush, my spirit, in thy fastness—
> Blush, my unacknowledged clay—
> Seven years of troth have taught thee
> More than Wifehood ever may!
>
> Love that never leaped its socket—
> Trust intrenched in narrow pain—
> Constancy thro' fire—awarded—
> Anguish—bare of anodyne!
>
> Burden—borne so far triumphant—
> None suspect me of the crown,
> For I wear the "Thorns" 'til Sunset—
> Then—my Diadem put on.
>
> Big my Secret but it's bandaged—
> It will never get away
> Till the Day its Weary Keeper
> Leads it through the Grave to thee.[62]

These lyrics and many others like them (sometimes referred to as the "Master" poems) come from what many critics acknowledge as Dickinson's most fertile creative period, a period of four

---

[60]Habegger doesn't accept this argument. He feels that the available evidence suggests, though by no means unambiguously, a relationship with Reverend Wadsworth.
[61]Habegger, 410.
[62]Habegger, 414.

years in which she wrote, by some reckonings, over seven hundred poems. We should not attribute this creative explosion only to this unrequited passion—for, after all, these years span the Civil War, and though Dickinson remained largely sequestered physically, her work shows that did not remain that way intellectually or psychologically—but passion surely plays an important role. Dickinson herself seems to acknowledge, obliquely as usual, that it served a transformative role in her life. The passion of her work seemed to take a quantum leap forward, and she expressed this passion in direct, even shocking, images, some of them suggesting, in their references to martyrdom, her Moon-Neptune square, yet at the same time pointing to a breakthrough surely connected to Uranus.[63]

The astrological evidence from this period, evidence consisting of transits, progressions, and directions, surely corroborates what we read in her biography: that she went through a creative upheaval. As we have seen, not only did Dickinson have Pluto transiting square the all-important Uranus in the third (iconoclastic views; unusual and brilliant writing), but she went through her Saturn Return, had the solar arc Ascendant conjoin both her Sun and her Mercury, had the solar arc Sun and Mercury conjoin the Jupiter-Neptune conjunction and square the Moon, had solar arc Mars also square Uranus, and, perhaps most tellingly, had solar arc Saturn oppose the natal Mars-Pluto conjunction. This last aspect suggests, on the one hand, that someone with an established position would reject Dickinson's passion; it could also suggest the discovery of a different form (Saturn) for that passion, the discovery taking place as she looked out into the world.

We see here, among other developments, the awakening of Uranus, the moving out, though partly via projection,[64] from a largely lunar world of parental enclosure into a world in which she developed her own voice and developed forms more appropriate to her genius. All of this emerged through the vehicle of frustrated desire (solar arc Saturn to Mars-Pluto[65]) and the creation of a literary world—a world of great imaginings (Jupiter-Neptune, conjoined by solar arc Sun-Mercury, plus the pervasive influence of the third house). Corroboration comes from secondary progressed Venus' conjunction with natal Neptune (imaginary lover or relationship?) in 1859, secondary progressed Mars' slow square with natal Jupiter then Neptune, and secondary progressed Mercury's conjunction with natal Uranus the next year (suggesting brilliant writing). It seems that we have sufficient astrological evidence for the claim that during that period Emily begin to reclaim Uranus in her writing even if she found it difficult to reclaim in her life! We see in Dickinson a striking example of the patterns under discussion here: she played the lunar role and, in her relationships,

---

[63]The Moon-Neptune aspect manifested in many ways. Most obviously, it emerged through this sense of martyrdom (Moon in the twelfth house) in emotionally based (Moon) relationship (Libra). Jupiter participates, so we see a curious combination of self-effacement and self-confidence. Despite her isolation, Dickenson shows at times that she knew the value of her work. Throughout her life, Moon-Neptune emerges in her "predilection for fiction, fantasy, secrecy" (412). In connection to one of her lyrics, Habegger speaks of Dickenson making an "infantile proposition" yet with "an energetic fullness of expression that is nothing less than…masterly" (417). Some will see obsessive self-sacrifice also in her Mars-Pluto conjunction in Aries, a sign associated with sacrificial lambs, even if Mars-Pluto gives the lamb enormous chutzpa!
[64]Recall Jung's idea that projections serve as a bridge to the world.
[65]And, probably, the Mars-Pluto conjunction itself, particularly for a person of her era in rural Massachusetts, and particularly for a woman.

projected Uranus readily and constantly onto men even as she developed that Uranus through her work.

Finally, we might ask whether as she got older Dickinson began to own that Uranus-energy not only in her writing but in her relationships as well. Her relationship with Otis Philips Lord suggests that she did exactly that. Lord, a man eighteen years Dickinson's senior and thus perhaps closer to her father's generation than to her own (reflecting, it seems, Dickinson's powerful Saturn: in the tenth, conjoined her North Node, possibly conjoining the Midheaven), had a quasi-legendary status as a courtroom lawyer. His Whig stances set him apart from the purported liberalism of his time and area (he felt, as had Dickinson's father, that the Union should win the war, but not free the slaves, whom he saw as the lawful property of southern landowners). Still, in his private life, he had a reputation for geniality and kindness.[66] Apparently the friendship began in earnest in the mid-1870's, though they had probably had an acquaintance since the 1860s. The evidence here comes largely from letters, and though some of them have been destroyed (by Emily's request) and others edited (via scissors), they suggest that the friendship bloomed into a love affair somewhere in the 1880s. The suggestive letters come from 1882, the year that Charles Wadsworth died. Otis Lord's wife died in 1878; Lord visited Amherst in 1880. In some letters from that period, Emily refers to Lord as her father's "best friend."

We see in Emily's letters, that she no longer played the meek suppliant. If anything, she played the role of Uranus, though in some combination with the Moon. In her letters, she shows a "kind of unleashed, over-the-top playfulness now that the 'soul' is in its native country."[67] We find much "play of language," for she knew that she

> was writing to a highly literate man, and the pleasures she enjoyed were in part those of a shared imaginative and linguistic romp—what she had called in a tormented letter to Master two decades earlier, "the prank of the Heart at play on the Heart."[68]

Some letters strongly suggest that she now played the role of the hard-to-get, though with promise and not harshness:

> Don't you know you are happiest while I withhold and not confer—don't you know that 'No' is the wildest word we consign to Language?
>
> You do, for you know all things.

Here, she "both confessed her desire and insisted on her freedom." Further, "she dares to speak of their shared nights and her vagrant proclivities. She also appears to assume the 'no' is not 'no' but a basis for additional play, intimacy, confession. Of course, we can't be sure that the letter was

---

[66]Habegger, 585.
[67]Habegger, 589.
[68]Habegger, 589.

actually sent."[69] It dates, apparently, from 1882:

> I am a restive sleeper and often should journey from your Arms through the happy Night, but you will lift me back, wont you, for only there I ask to be.[70]

If we read these letters from an astrological point of view, we will find evidence for the claim that Emily now plays the role of Uranus and that Lord, the older man, plays the role of Saturn. That she does the former reminds us of what we have said: that many women withdraw the projection of Uranus more and more as they get older. That she still perhaps projects Saturn suggests interesting investigations into her psychology, but those lie beyond the scope of this chapter.

---

[69] Habegger, 590.
[70] Habegger, 590.

Chapter III

Gender-Based Projections II: The Moons of Men

What shall we say about men and their Moons? We hear much talk, these days, about men "accessing their feelings," or "getting in touch with their vulnerabilities"; we see men taking on the role of nurturer for their children, men functioning effectively as nurturing counselors, teachers, and friends; we see men create artistic works of great feeling and depth. Yet the evidence suggests that in intimate relationships one man after another will project his Moon onto a woman, and that on the whole, men do so perhaps more consistently than women project Uranus. And just as even a woman who manifests Uranus in her professional life will still find herself projecting it in her intimate relationships, so a man may manifest lunar qualities at work and in various areas of life and yet project his lunar capacities and difficulties onto his closest female partner.

We will find it difficult to find reliable data for men's projection or integration of lunar energy—more difficult, at any rate, than to find evidence about women and Uranus. To some extent, we can measure a woman's rebellion against status quo arrangements by looking into the world, for Uranus often appears in behavior of a more quantifiable type than does the Moon. When we ask ourselves whether women access Uranus through their professional activities, we can look to two types of activity amenable to quantification: we can measure how many women enter the workforce, and we can note what occupations they enter once they do. We have already discussed the first, interpreting it as a Uranian break from traditional roles and toward Saturn's world of hierarchy, vocation, or organized relations; though a woman achieving a position of eminence surely shows Saturn at work, and though the position itself may have Saturnian elements, and though a woman will have to manifest Saturnian qualities in order to achieve such a position, the initial break from routine and expectation carries the mark of Uranus. We can gather statistics on how many women make this move, one we can see as Uranian insofar as it constitutes a break from the status quo. Beyond that, we can quantify how many women enter specific professions, particularly those marked to a significant extent by Uranus.[1] In either case, Uranus appears in ways susceptible to the statisticians methods.

The Moon, by contrast, seems much more difficult to quantify, for the statistician has no reliable way to quantify feeling or emotion. Though we consider some professions as markedly lunar, the Moon more often describes a general attitude *toward* one's work than it does the work itself. So whereas Uranus often describes either a definitive break from the norm or a more-or-less specific *type* of work, the Moon, a symbol of the inner emotions and sensitivities, more often describes internal processes. As we know, Uranus describes professional activity involving high technology, innovation, communications, and the cutting edge generally; it also can describe self-employment, for a strong Uranus will not readily take orders from others, and it brings about an iconoclastic approach that, because it constitutes a break from the norm, lends itself to clear identification. By contrast, though the Moon does describe some specific professions, its energies often emerge in professions that we would not describe as lunar *per se*. Consider, in this light, teaching, counseling, public relations, administration—professions we would not consider lunar in themselves, yet professions to which one can bring a lunar approach. Admittedly, one can also bring a "Uranian" approach, but too much Uranus will drive one right out of many professions, whereas lunar energies lead more readily to inclusion. Uranus resists containment; the Moon promotes it.

Furthermore, unless they emerge as or through violent actions, the "emotional blockages" of men don't generally become headline items, and if they *do* emerge through headline items, those headlines generally bear the mark of either Mars or Pluto, not the Moon. By contrast, fluctuations in the employment rate for women often emerge through statistics announced on the evening news. Many will measure advances in "women's liberation" by referring to statistics related to the job market and women's employment; if a woman wishes to be more independent, she may also wish to have her own income, not to mention her own goals, ideas, and creative freedom. Even if she takes on a profession not specifically Uranian, her actions carry the mark of Uranus insofar as she breaks with the tradition that would have her remain as wife and helpmate. On the other hand, if a man wishes to be more in touch with his feelings, he may disappear from our statistical analyses. We can observe independent action; we may miss "getting in touch with feeling" completely, for though we have developed many devices to measure the former, we have few to measure the latter.

---

[1] Some astrologers will assign specific professions to specific planets – military profession to Mars or Saturn, childcare to the Moon or Mercury, executive positions to Jupiter and Saturn, and so forth—and with some justification. However, just as no complex activity will fit completely into any of the houses of the horoscope, so no complex activity such as those we find in the vocations will come completely under the auspices of any planet. We will find many planets marking any complex activity, though some planets have a particularly close connection to specific lines of work or activities.

Further still, lunar issues, dealing as they do with the emotions, don't lend themselves to easy articulation. We can more readily identify a Uranian action because it will involve a break from an established order of some sort, but a lunar action may fly below the available public radar—and it may do so for the reasons given above: because we find it difficult to describe or quantify emotional reactions. Uranian energies project themselves into the environment in definite ways; lunar energies appear in indirect, sometimes shadowy ways. Uranus, after all, rules an air sign, the Moon a water sign; Aquarius has much to do with society and social trend, Cancer with remaining hidden (appropriately enough, considering that constellation's dimness in the night sky). In the moonlight, we know things by their shadows instead of simply by their outlines. Not surprisingly, men don't seem to talk as readily or as clearly about lunar matters as women seem to about Uranian ones. We might wish to attribute this pattern to the "fact" that men "can't talk about their feelings very well"; however, that "fact" may not tell us very much (and, of course, may not qualify as a *fact* at all), for feelings seem to resist clear articulation in a way that employment statistics do not. That so much of our artistic expression deals with matters related to feeling instead of to facts should certainly tell us something! Of course, perhaps many men haven't articulated the problem very clearly to themselves, and very few social forces or media organs even tell them that they have a problem.[2] As we will see, when a man projects his Moon onto a woman, he often won't know quite what he feels, which brings us to the nub of the problem.

Certainly many demands put on men in our society don't encourage them to undertake the lunar journey, for that journey usually takes a person inward, not outward into the affairs of the world. Astrologers would describe these affairs as Saturnian, having to do with professional position and development, with providing for one's family a tangible structure (e.g. a home) and for oneself an inner scaffolding upon which to build a world-view or a career. Matters related to men's feelings come less often into the public eye and often don't appear clearly to the conscious eye of the men themselves. Circumstances often encourage—some would say impel—men to look in other directions; and men often do so, at least in the social framework prevalent in the West. If a man works eight to ten hours a day to support his family, he may not feel, at the end of such a day, that he wants to explore his feelings! In astrological terms, we might say that his connection to lunar matters remains simple and external: he comes home to his home.

Checking Out

Some will say that many men seem to "check out" psychologically when lunar issues come up. Let's accept that as at least partially true, particularly when the man finds himself around women, and particularly when around his primary partner. Whether biological factors impel or social factors predispose them in this direction (whether the behavior results from biological "necessity" or social training), the resulting dynamic generally leads to difficulties. As the man "checks out," the

---

[2] Current difficulties related to the most "masculine" professions such as the military may bring changes in this area. When we consider the number of military men who commit suicide these days, we suspect a problem related to the devaluation of the lunar principal.

woman relating to him may seem or act extremely or "excessively" emotional. Using our football analogy from the previous chapter, we would say that the man hands his emotional (lunar) football over to the women; the woman, with a lunar football of her own, thus ends up with two. At the same time, as we saw in the previous chapter, the man, meanwhile, quite possibly has two Uranian footballs, one of which rightfully belongs to the woman; so, like Uranus in the myth, he may say that he doesn't want to deal with the immediate (lunar) situation: the woman's feelings or his own. Small wonder, then, that to the man the woman may seem "overly emotional." Small wonder, too, that while the man will seem divorced from his own feelings, the woman will feel distanced from the man—distanced, surely, from the man's feelings, which he will not give up on demand, perhaps because he doesn't know them *if* someone demands them of him. He doesn't know them because at that moment he in some sense doesn't *have* them; *she* has them, having accepted them (under the table, so to speak) from the man.

Quite likely, the man will not initially feel lonely, frustrated, angry, hurt, or insecure when interacting with the woman; and if he *does* have these feelings, he may try to ignore his reactions and try to solve what he sees as the presenting problem: the woman's "overly emotional" state of being. The appearances (the behavior) may mislead us about what lurks beneath or behind those appearances, for Moon-created shadows serve as great hiding places, as anyone knows from having walked beneath a Full Moon.

The observations lead to a hypothesis: that the woman acts out the man's emotions for him, at least and especially when the two people find themselves together. However, when they find themselves apart, and particularly if they have permanently concluded their intimacy, the man will very often, and perhaps usually, experience the full flood of his emotions, generally quite unexpectedly. Quite likely, he won't feel the flood coming until, rising suddenly out of the sea of his unconscious, it inundates him. He may also experience this flood after the woman has fallen peacefully asleep, perhaps after having had an "emotional blow up." While the woman falls asleep, a flood of feelings carries the man away, for, asleep, the woman does not serve as a very effective hook for the man's projection. As we know, floods may leave fertile silt behind, but they may also destroy situations (e.g. homes) that bring security. Some people, preferring not to experience them anymore, may move to what they see as higher ground, a kind of intellectual position, as if to get away from the danger of floods altogether.[3]

When the woman no longer serves as the hook for the projection of lunar energies, the man discovers the enormous and unruly ocean on which he sails every day—not unruly by nature, perhaps, but because pent up for so long. If we follow our hypothesis, we would not take as coincidence the fact that the man makes this discovery just when he has no available hook. For as long

---

[3]Though some dams serve as part of irrigation systems (often with less-than-wonderful consequences, it seems), others serve as part of flood control systems. The United States has had a particular penchant, some would say obsession or compulsion, to build dams in order to generate hydroelectric power and power for large corporations, obstructing the natural flow of nature for purportedly civilized purposes. We can perhaps find a metaphor in these developments.

as the woman remains available and active as a hook for the man's emotions, the man will appeal successfully to reason; he will try to apply insight and fresh ideas (Uranus) to the situation, the while experiencing his emotions vicariously through the woman. During that time, to know what he feels, he will often have to experience what *she* feels, for she will often state his feelings as her own, or in combination with her own: he will see in her the quality and power of his own emotions, even if the content differs.

Her feelings will represent his only partly, of course. For the most part, they will represent that aspect of feeling that he finds hard to accept. Insofar as he relates to conscious feelings, he will probably feel somewhat noble, perhaps compassionate or uplifted: feelings amenable to order and reason instead of leading to chaos. He may feel, and quite sincerely, that he must solve a problem, one belonging not to him but to the woman—who will often seem to him rather loony (because doubly lunar). And he will probably feel that he must deal with the problem by distancing himself from his own emotions. Often he will feel frozen, as if unable to express himself, seeing the woman as "too emotional" or "beyond reason," not amenable to his "insight" (Uranus). However, by distancing himself from his own emotions, he probably distances himself from his partner, at least as long as she acts out his emotions for him.

Lunacy originally meant that one had contact with the lunar goddess; the word *moon* comes from the Indo-European *manas*, or mind.[4] These etymological connections surely suggest that if a man distances himself from the "overly emotional woman," he may lose an element of mind that he would do better to welcome. Plutarch noted an important distinction between solar and lunar drives when he said, "The effects of the moon are similar to the effects of reason and wisdom, whereas those of the sun appear to be brought about by physical force and violence."[5] We find corroborating evidence for Plutarch's remarks in the development of solar cults coinciding, five millennia ago, with the development of the military class and of state-organized warfare. And, of course, in many spiritual teachings (e.g. those of Zen), the moon symbolizes enlightenment. *Mania*, derived from *manas*, the root for our *moon* and *mind*, originally mean ecstatic revelation.[6] Lunar energies apparently play an integral role in what we call *sanity* and in our understanding of spirituality.

The connection of the moon with mind, or at least with some aspects of it, recalls to us the notion that one can have a lunar intelligence possibly distinct from other types. Lunar intelligence has to do with the feelings, the instincts, the blood-power, and the life-force within all organic life. Thus when a woman receiving a man's lunar projection seems "overly emotional" or even "out of her mind," the man should probably consider that part of his own mind has travelled away from him and found a place in his projection, so that though the woman appears "out of her mind," he should consider her behavior as having emerged at least partly out of his *own* mind—or, we might

---

[4]Barbara Walker, *The Woman's Encyclopedia of Myths and Secrets* (San Francisco: HarperSanFrancisco, 1983), 670.
[5]Qtd. in Walker, 670.
[6]Walker, 670.

say, he should consider not that the woman "is out of her mind," but that his *own* mind is out of *him*! Try as he might to reason his way out of the situation, or to resolve it through the kinds of reason not associated with the Moon, he will probably end up making the situation increasingly polarized. One cannot subdue one's projections without first making friends with them and recognizing (i.e. knowing again) those inner elements that one has misplaced.

If this hypothesis has merit, the situation involves an exchange: the man gives his Moon over to the woman (while, as noted, she probably gives her Uranus to him). The woman will carry and express his emotions. She now has two metaphorical footballs—or, two Moonballs: her own and the man's. The man, having none, will probably feel that he has no feelings relevant to the "problem" at hand.[7] Typically, the man will feel unseen while the woman feels exposed; and we can easily see why, for the woman will expose her feelings while the man will keep his hidden, often from himself as much as from anyone else. The man's projection encourages the woman to express feelings, and while the content of the feelings she expresses will belong at least partly to her, she will express them with an energy fed by the hidden exchange, the man having handed his feelings—his lunar energy—to the woman. Thus we can see why "lunacy" has often been associated with women. Though we shouldn't blame the man for the woman's difficulties or absolve the woman of responsibility, we should at least acknowledge that in many situations the woman will act "loony" to the degree that she becomes the hook for the man's projections. Further, because men will often feel drawn to women who serve as appropriate hooks for their lunar projections, even the *content* of the woman's emotions may feel strangely familiar to the man, should he stop to consider the situation honestly. If Joe has his Pisces Moon square Neptune, his partner's sense of emotional martyrdom will resonate with something within Joe even if Joe remains unaware of such tendencies in himself, or unwilling to accept such feelings as his own.

The man's feelings have power, whether they appear through a woman or through his own sensitivities, for those feelings have probably percolated in the shadows for a long time; to the degree that they have also remained unexamined, they will also seem to him irrational, as will the woman who expresses them. The woman will express the man's inchoate feelings (while he, as noted in the last chapter, expresses ideas). Further, insofar as the woman insists that "connection" involves only the emotions (perhaps because she has projected her Uranus onto the man), she will feel disconnected from the man, who at the time expresses ideas or notions instead of feelings. Insofar as he projects his lunar energy onto the woman, he won't relate to his own feelings of dependency, or even of tenderness or closeness; he will seem emotionally unavailable, though he may seek emotional connection out of a sense of duty, driven by an idea. The woman, meanwhile, will seem obsessed with the emotional gap yawning between them.

---

[7] According to Joseph P. Shipley (*Shipley's Dictionary of Word Origins*; New York: The Philosophical Library, 1945), *problem* comes from Greek roots referring to *something thrown in front of one*. When one has a problem related to a *projection*, the thrower and the one dealing with the problem seem identical, even if it seems that one's partner does the throwing.

We may feel tempted, here, to say, "Relationship is, after all, a matter of emotional closeness" and to blame the man for the problem. But who can speak authoritatively about what relationship "is"? Instead of asking what relationship purportedly "is," we should ask questions about people's thoughts, feelings, and reactions (etc.) in actual relationships.[8] If a woman has accepted a man's lunar projection, she will probably not feel comfortable unless the man makes what she interprets as an "emotional connection" with her; but how will he make such a connection if he projects his Moon onto the woman—and if she accepts the projection? At the same time, if the man seeks a connection based in Uranus, he may expect the women to discuss ideas or behave in ways he deems rational, but as long as he accepts her projection of Uranus, she probably will not act in the ways he thinks he wants.

She will probably find herself prone to accept the man's lunar energy. In many cases, women find themselves thinking that "women are more emotional than men." She may then take the situation—in which she accepts the man's projection and in which he accepts her Uranus projection—as natural, as a reflection of the way things "are." (Note again the "to be" propositions: the situation *is* natural; things *are* such-and-such a way, matters to which we will return in chapter VIII and XI.) She may even feel, in an odd sort of way, comfortable with it—comfortable in the way people can feel comfortable with what they see as their own discomfort. And aren't men "supposed to be" objective? The man may see himself as quite available, but unless he works to withdraw the projection, he'll act as if available only for the giving of insight (Uranus), not for the sharing of feeling (Moon); and the more she demands feeling, the less he feels relevant. He will tend to strive for objectivity, making what he takes as reasonable and objective remarks about the emotions then in play, perhaps feeling that the situation demands objectivity—that is, that it requires him to deal with people as if they were objects, so that his emotion becomes detached. This scenario depends, of course, on the woman's engagement; if she disengages, he will probably *feel* more.

The woman will not necessarily or always express the man's emotional *content*. Sometimes she might do so, but she will more usually express his emotional *energy*, his emotional charge, through her own emotional *contents*, generally magnified. Even if she *does* express the man's emotional content, it will appear mixed with her own. She will feel her own feelings, but probably with increased intensity and confusion; meanwhile, *he* will express her need for rationality and "objectivity."

If the woman projects her Uranus onto the man, she will experience difficulty when trying to feel emancipated or detached (Uranian qualities, at least in part). The man, carrying the woman's Uranus, will then act strangely, even spookily detached, for he will carry both Uranus energies to the degree that the woman carries both lunar ones. This doesn't mean that he will leave the relationship, for the lunar pull will remain strong even if he remains unaware of it: he does, after all, feel drawn toward security, even if unconsciously. That feeling will likely remain hidden unless the

---

[8]We should probably take care in using these terms. Most thoughts have a feeling-component, most feelings have a thinking-component, and most reactions have some of each. Alfred Korzybski (*Science and Sanity*; Englewood: International Society for General Semantics, 1933) recommended hyphenated terms (e.g. thought-feelings) to overcome the limitations, and see through the illusions, suggested by language.

man makes an effort to reclaim his Moon. In the meantime, the woman cries and emotes; the man backs off (psychologically anyway) and takes a rational stance; a kind of feedback loop results, for the more "irrationally emotional" she appears, the more irrationally reasonable *he* appears. The two will feel increasingly alienated both from each other and from themselves, yet attracted at the same time, partly because of the natural attraction between the sexes, and partly because each partner carries or has unconsciously commandeered some of the partner's energy. It will seem to them that they must relate to each other to get that energy back; however, if the man relates only "objectively and rationally" while the woman does so "subjectively and emotionally," both will feel curiously empty.

The people involved obviously do not appreciate themselves accurately. The man considers his detached state as an accurate version of his real state of being; the woman feels *her* emotional state as *her* real feelings about the matter. If they've been through this scenario enough times, they may convince themselves that "this is the way we are together," or even that "this is the way men and women act; this is the way they are." The man has not recognized and accepted his own lunar qualities; he may not know what he feels, or he may "know" it only very reasonably, objectively, for he has made himself an object to himself, not something felt fully and directly. The woman, by contrast, feeling swamped by her feelings, appears and feels unstable. The situation may bring harm even to the man, for he misplaces, temporarily but perhaps as the result of deeply ingrained habit, his capacity for intimacy. If we consider the Moon to symbolize "soul," he will feel soulless. Though many may conclude that men do not suffer in such situations (because, after all, they can ""be free"), or, at least, that they don't suffer to the extent that women do (a view I've heard many women express), the astrological evidence suggests otherwise.

As noted above, men's inner reactions generally remain more hidden. Many men seem to talk about their feelings less often than do women. Furthermore, just as we find social taboos against women "becoming" too Uranian, so we find tenacious taboos about men "becoming" too lunar. When men *do* talk about lunar matters, they often offer insights (Uranus) about them instead expressing the feelings themselves (Moon). And while men's groups encourage men to "get in touch with their feelings," this doesn't seem to solve the problem, for a man must learn to stay in touch with those feelings when connected to a woman, not when separate from her. (The men in such groups will not serve so readily as hooks for the lunar projection, so the projection will probably not constellate and the man will not have to deal with it. Similarly for women trying to deal with Uranus in women's groups.) When by himself or with other men (and sometimes when with women with whom he has a more objectified, generally non-intimate, relationship), the man may know exactly what he feels, though the mentioned inundation may consist of negative feelings, the ones he's projected onto the woman. But the man needs to experience those feelings when *with* the woman. The journey must involve emotional inter*action*, not merely emotion. Marie Louise von Franz writes that "without a close and living relationship with a counter-sexual partner, one almost never picks up the trail" of the anima.[9]

---

[9]Marie Louise von Franz, *Projection and Re-collection in Jungian Psychology* (London: Open Court, 1980) 123.

In any case, because the Moon symbolizes a person's inner feeling-state, a man's efforts to understand his Moon often go unnoticed. Yet if men continue to "run the show" in the collective (a kind of activity related in many ways to Saturn), their lunar projections will have a great deal to do with how they see the world that they attempt to "run"—what they accept or reject in that world. For example, we might interpret the ongoing attempt to gut the welfare system and other safety-net programs as indications that the men in power have lost touch with their own lunar capacities. Having negativized the lunar drive, they see lunar matters in a decidedly negative light. So, they see a certain class of women first as "welfare mothers," then as "welfare queens"; then they perceive that class as a huge social problem. We've all heard the rhetoric: that welfare mothers are too dependent, too irrational, too strident, and so forth. Because the Moon also has to do with working with or before the public—"the public" here having to the unconscious contents of the men in question—these men influence the public's view even as they fall victim to their own projections.

But though the *results* of men's projections often arise as public concerns, the men doing the projecting must undertake a very private journey in order to work these matters out. They confront a paradox: each man's *private* journey will generally go further if he undertakes it *with* a woman with whom he has an intimate tie. Though his two Uranus footballs might urge him to undertake the journey independently, he will usually get further if he gives one of those footballs back to its rightful owner.

Anima and Moon

Here we tread again on the ground that Jung called the *anima* and the *animus*. Marie Louise Von Franz refers to these as the "great mediating daemons," for they have enormous power to influence behavior. Just as a woman's Uranus seems to have a strong connection to her *animus*, a man's Moon seems to have a strong connection to his *anima*. Though we would not say that the Moon "is" the anima, for Venus, Pluto, and even Neptune all play roles, as do the Moon's sign and aspects, it certainly has a pervasive connection to a man's view of the feminine. In a passage partly quoted above, Ms. Von Franz notes that Jung used the term *anima* to indicate what she describes as

> ...the feminine aspect of a man's psyche that is first embodied in the mother-imago and rejuvenated in the image of the beloved or the wife. *She* is *par excellence* the fate-spinning core of the unconscious psyche in a man, which is why in the East she is called Maya—the world-spinner, or the dancer who creates the illusion of the real world. Those projections woven not by the shadow but by *this* factor are much more difficult to recognize; without a close and living relationship with a countersexual partner one almost never picks up the trail. It is actually the power that stands behind all love entanglements and behind most marital conflicts. The anima appears as an irrational sort of temperament, or disposition, of which the man himself is deeply unconscious, or as a stimulus to life that drives him to this woman and not to that one and inclines him to this life-style and not to that one, that disposes his feelings to warmth and *joie de vivre*

or to a cold and lackluster outlook, that fills him with enthusiasm or revulsion, seduces him to lust and "sin," and also finally brings him an awakening to himself.[10]

The man will project much or all of his anima onto women, particularly onto the woman or women with whom he becomes emotionally involved—women who alternately inspire him in this or that direction, or who bring him "down" from the lofty heights of achievement or ideation into the realm of immediate pleasure or pain, who stimulate in him reactions both neurotic and inspired.[11]

Much of this suggests the Moon. The Moon symbolizes "the mother imago" and we could certainly say that it "is rejuvenated in the image of the beloved or the wife," for a man will often find himself drawn to women whose horoscopes show a close relationship with his Moon (and its sign and aspects)[12]—which often means women similar to his mother in important ways, though the similarities may prove hard to discern. Or, we might say, the man will find himself drawn to women with whom he has experiences that recall, even if unconsciously or in uncanny ways, his experiences with his mother. If we examine the relevant horoscopes, we will generally see why the projections occur, and why they remain so opaque (if they do, of course).

So, in general, a man will find himself drawn to women on whom he can conveniently hang the projections indicated by his natal Moon and its aspects. At certain periods, he may also find himself drawn to women on whom he can hang (so to speak) projections reflecting important transits or directions involving lunar factors (e.g. to or from the Moon, or, less often, involving the fourth house or Cancer). Such a woman brings or draws a man "down to earth"; he finds that he must descend from the Uranian realm of ideas into the realm of lived experience, of birth and death (symbolic or otherwise), perhaps into parenthood and its responsibilities, or in some other way. Yet, as Ms. Von Franz notes, the *anima* may appear "as an irrational sort of temperament" that can drive the man to distraction, though sometimes he gets distracted from an overly intellectual

---

[10]Von Franz, 123-4. Ms. Von Franz's description here may seem to have a closer connection to Neptune than to the Moon; however, we shouldn't underestimate the power of habit to influence our perception of the world and our conclusions regarding what "is real." In the Mind Only School of Buddhism (the Yogachara School), the texts call the world of ordinary experience the "imaginary"; they say, further, that we experience the imagery, distinguished from "the real," because of mind under the influence of or dependent on habit.

[11]We shouldn't lay at the feet of the anima all of a man's neurosis, though. Some of it belongs to the shadow. From the Eastern point of view, much of it reflects karma. We might also say that it reflects the general human resistance to becoming fully aware.

[12]This doesn't necessarily mean that a man will marry a woman who has, for example, the same sign position as his Moon. It may mean instead that she has similar lunar aspects (say, a square from the Moon to Saturn), or that her aspects reflect his lunar sign (the Moon-Saturn square reflecting a man's Capricorn Moon, for example). Sometimes one of the woman's important planets or angles will make a close aspect to the man's Moon. A man with a Moon-Neptune square may feel drawn to a woman with a Sun-Neptune square; a man with a Moon-Saturn affliction may feel drawn to a woman with Moon-Pluto issues or some other "lunar difficulty." Sometimes we see a connection through a woman's twelfth house planets. The particulars vary, and other factors also play a role. For example, a man deficient in water signs may feel drawn to a woman with important planets in Cancer, Pisces, or Scorpio.

approach to life and into a possibly-necessary irrationality of feeling. The man will generally remain unconscious of the process; such consciousness as he attains will often arise first as notions instead of emotions, ideas instead of feelings.

Consider a hypothetical situation in which a man, receiving a strong transit involving lunar elements, perceives the energies associated with that transit arising through his wife or girlfriend. Let us say, too, that the woman has some sort of corroborating transit or progression. She will serve as a ready hook for the man's projection not only because she has a close relationship to him, but also because her own feelings correspond in some way to the ones we associate with the man's transit. Thus the two people don't question the situation, for everything seems to accord with common sense. However, if they don't question, problems may well escalate, for the man may well ignore important inner promptings, taking them as part of the woman's process instead of his own. As we have seen, if he hands his lunar football to the woman, she will seem increasingly loony, and he will feel that he must supply the requisite rationality. If the people don't re-collect their projections, their interactions will likely involve more mistaken perception and inadequate interpretation than valid understanding.

When the woman is not in the man's presence, she will serve less well as a hook for the man's projections, so the feelings associated with the transit will generally reconnect to their source within the man himself, though the man will still probably experience the woman through his projections. Thus we can see at least two reasons for each person to withdraw temporarily from the other: first, as the man carries the woman's Uranus, his withdrawal will help her to re-collect that energy and allow or encourage him to feel less claustrophobic, for his feeling of claustrophobia will increase when he carries the woman's Uranus; second, as the woman carries the man's Moon, his withdrawal may help him reconnect with his own lunar energy. But if this withdrawal goes on too long, the man will likely lose the trail of the anima, for the anima serves as a *mediating* daemon, as a way to make reliable contact with the feminine elements of the psyche and of the phenomenal world. Even if the man feels more connected to his on-the-spot feelings when the woman goes away, he must eventually learn to access those feelings with the woman present. In other words, he should learn to experience them on the spot, not merely after-the-fact. He can't run away from his Moon, so he might as well make friends with it – and with those women who serve as hooks for his lunar projections. In doing this, he should always distinguish his version of the woman, his experience of her, from the woman as she exists apart from his notions or assumptions. Though we can't completely divorce ourselves from ourselves, we can at least remind ourselves of the pervasiveness of projection, thus encouraging ourselves to investigate further.

Curiously, even a purportedly objective observer might acknowledge that the man's description of the woman often coincides nicely with her behavior, which may suggest to us either that the woman has accepted the man's projection (the man's football, in our analogy) and so acts out the man's unacknowledged feeling-nature, or that the man has sought, probably unconsciously, a relationship with someone whose behavior coincides in this curious way with his own projection-tendencies; in many cases, we see a combination of these. On the other hand, we might suggest that the man's descriptions of the woman do not resemble her as much as they do the lunar elements of the man himself, however unacknowledged. In addition, because the Moon has much to do with a person's emotional connection to the world generally, the man's description of the woman and his connection to her tell us much about the man's general emotional state and his feeling-connection to the world.

If the man has attained to a reasonable degree of sane consciousness—if, we can say, his projections bear some reasonable resemblance to consensus reality[13]—the woman on whom he projects his lunar energy will serve as an appropriate hook for that energy. Quite likely, he will feel attraction to women who most people will see as "such-and-such type of person."[14] Often he will form close bonds with such women, though perhaps he should ask himself whether he has formed close bonds with a *type* or with a *person*. As a result, his projections will often seem to adhere fairly closely to consensus reality. If his Moon is in Gemini, he will likely feel drawn to women who act out that energy—perhaps to women with the Sun or other important placements in Gemini, or with a prominent Mercury-placement. If a man has a Moon-Saturn square, he will likely feel drawn to women who in some way resonate with that energy: women with Moon-Saturn aspects, or the Moon in Capricorn or the tenth house, or other Saturn/Capricorn energies or lunar challenges. But if the man has "negativized" his lunar energies, he will likely draw and feel drawn to women who seem to him to display (perhaps encouraged by the dynamic described above) the more problematic aspects of the astrological symbolism. So the Moon-Saturn projection will emerge through a woman who appears emotionally restricted or fearful, perhaps a woman who didn't receive much nurturance as a child, rather than through someone with the kind of vigorous independence sometimes indicated by Moon-Saturn aspects.[15] In short, a man with what we might call Moon-Saturn difficulties will feel drawn to, and will often establish close connections with, women who seem to manifest the difficult qualities of the astrological material. He may decide that he should reform or help such a person, though he will probably do better to reform himself.

---

[13]The people referred to as psychotics seem to have projections that bear very little resemblance to consensus reality; therein we see a defining difference between those we call sane and those we call insane. A so-called psychotic person may see someone as the devil incarnate, whereas a non-psychotic would see merely a troublesome person. But the psychotic's situation differs from the purportedly sane person's situation in degree and not in kind. Both people project constantly, but the former's projections don't adhere as closely to consensus reality as do the latter's. From the perspective of the enlightened, both people might well appear deluded. Alfred Korzybski often referred to the so-called normal state of mind of most people as *unsane*, though for somewhat different reasons than the ones that concern us here.
[14]So, for example, if a man projects onto women his Moon-Mars square, he will find himself drawn to women who most people will take to be angry, willful, or impetuous.
[15]Moon-Saturn interactions, even the hard aspects, can suggest emotional independence. However, we see this independence more often in older people than in younger. The former have, of course, gone through more transits from Saturn to the Moon and the Moon to Saturn, so they have had many opportunities to learn how to work with the energy. We might change an old fable slightly to suggest that one with a Moon-Saturn aspect learns that the world will not feed him, so he learns to feed himself.

Though we will often find the expected astrological signatures behind someone's lunar projections—challenging aspects to the Moon, particularly from Saturn and the outer planets, but also from Mars; any aspect or position suggesting that the man has difficulty integrating his lunar energies—even men with benign lunar aspects will sometimes project lunar energies onto women, though usually not with such problematic results. Because the hard aspects suggest that the man finds lunar energies difficult to integrate, they also suggest a greater propensity for projections that the man will have difficulty integrating with the rest of his life. When people project the easier aspects, the projections may prove more difficult to track down simply because they don't disrupt the man's life. For example, a man with a Moon-Jupiter trine might project that onto a woman who manifests the uplifted qualities of that aspect: such a woman might be quite easy to get along with, so the man might not be prompted to recognize Moon-Jupiter in himself; or the woman might act confidently in social situations while the man may have more difficulties. If the aspect "alleviates life in a positive way," or if "all goes well" so that the man "is totally unaware of the compulsive, i.e., 'magical' or 'mystical' character" of projections indicated by the aspect, the man, not feeling an acute need to recognize the projection, may leave it unexamined.[16]

Challenging lunar aspects, on the other hand, bring experiences of a different type. Consider the afflictions between the Moon and Saturn. These aspects usually appear through repeatedly painful experiences that can prompt or impel one toward inner search and examination. The original experiences often involve women who appear "cold," or who seem to find security only in work, or who seem constantly in emotional pain. To re-collect his projection, the man must focus on his own emotional habit patterns, patterns probably connected to his early experience with the mother and often beyond the reach of conscious memory. Because such experiences took place so early in life, the man will contact them largely by the traces they leave in his world: in his attitudes, in the way he structures his world emotionally, situationally, psychologically, and through the women to whom he feels drawn and with whom he forms intimate bonds. Obviously, the man will generally experience such situations as problematic. Others may also interpret them as problematic, but the external problem will resist solution until the man looks at the part of himself symbolized by the Moon in his natal chart, a part he has rejected in whole or in part.

Instead of judging the woman or automatically withdrawing, he should follow the five steps in the withdrawal of projections,[17] beginning with what Jung called "archaic identity," the stage in which a person unquestioningly identifies his own energy, his own feeling-response to the world, with the woman. He must first separate the projection from the external event or person. In other words, he must differentiate. Then he must make "a moral evaluation" of the projection. Though the man will hopefully not refer to the woman as an evil spirit, when caught in the flood of his own projections he will nonetheless experience her as problematic, as a force that creates difficulties for him. If he intends to recall the projection, he must begin to honor the feeling-energies that rightly

---

[16] Jung: "General Aspects of Dream Psychology," *Collected Works*, 8, para.507. (Qtd. in Von Franz, 8.)
[17] See chapter I of this book. The five steps come from Marie Louise von Franz (*Projection and Re-collection in Jungian Psychology*, 9ff).

belong to him. Then he must question (in the fourth stage) whether he had perceived the situation correctly in the first place. He might not consider the *entire* situation as an illusion, but he should at least recognize that his assumptions about and reaction to the situation (perhaps to the woman's purported over-emotionality) and his description of it reflect an inaccurate perception not only of the woman but of himself as well. He might then reflect on the emotional exchange that has taken place and one how the entire situation came about. At this stage, he must sink further back into himself, not only to come into fuller contact with his own necessarily-non-rational feelings, pleasant or otherwise, but also to discern how he has subtly arranged the situation so as to encourage just such a projection as he's experienced.

Just as a woman must stop blaming the man for accepting her projection of Uranus, so the man must stop blaming the woman for accepting his lunar projection. He must accept responsibility for his own feelings, his own security-related reactions, his own need for relationship and caring, and his own experience generally. To say that the woman "is doing this to me" misses the point; in any case, it probably won't get the man very far toward a solution, toward feeling any better, or toward any useful understanding either of himself or others. He must retain, and perhaps recover, responsibility for his own world, his own experience. To accept this responsibility may feel like taking the blame for something; or it may feel like becoming more whole, less fragmented, less alone, even when he's "alone with his feelings."

Though he may find that temporary withdrawal helps him to regain contact with himself, he should also remember that a woman will constellate the projection for him; she will, we might say, place the projection in front of him so he can see it more clearly—or more "objectively," because it appears to arise outside of him. He may have to withdraw in order to acknowledge that he sees his own feelings thus projected, but he will also have to step forward in order to deal with the projections as they arise, considering the projections as partners, not as enemies.

According to Emma Jung, a man's anima "represents the feminine personality components of the man and at the same time the image which he has of feminine nature in general, in other words, the archetype of the feminine."[18] She connects the anima with the nymphs, swan maidens, undines, and fairies from myth and legend, figures "of enticing beauty but only half human" and about which we find "a taboo…that must not be broken."[19] We can see this taboo partly reflected in the reluctance, seen in so many men, to talk about their feelings; we can also see it in the tendency, as in some barroom chat, to see women as objects, for one can control objects much more easily than one can control swan maidens or undines! The man will attempt to objectify and give conceptual form to the anima. We see a similar pattern in some mythic stories, where an anima figure from the non-human realm becomes human for (or sometimes after) a certain period, usually as a result of

---

[18] Emma Jung, *Anima and Animus: Two Essays* by Emma Jung (Dallas: Spring Publications, 1957), 45.
[19] Emma Jung, 46.

the man having met certain conditions. Similarly, if the man develops sufficient awareness, he can see through his projections to the human person who carries his anima.

At the very least, the anima threatens the naïve integrity of a man's life, for like the mythic figures mentioned above, feelings, and the relationships that seem to bring them up, often "lure a man into their realm, where he disappears forever" though they may also "bind the man in love, that they may live in this world with him." In some stories, the anima figure inspires the man to go to battle or to engage in some other sort of striving, suggesting, as Ms. Jung writes, that "the yearning, the desire for new undertakings, makes itself felt first in the unconscious-feminine. Before coming clearly to consciousness, the striving for something new and different usually expresses itself in the form of an emotional stirring, a vague impulse or unexplained mood."[20]

Just as anima figures, with something other-worldly about them, do not easily inhabit the world of consensus reality, so lunar issues prove difficult to track in the visible world, difficult to measure statistically or discuss with what we call "rationality." Situations involving the anima will resist logical or intellectual analysis; and in any case a man cannot liberate himself by analysis alone. If an *animus* figure has much to do with power, and with the speech and language that confers such power (the power, in part, to control the world via conscious intellect and language-based concept), an *anima* figure's power lies elsewhere. Ms. Jung relates the story of Pururavas and Urvasi in which Pururavas can maintain his connection with Urvasi only if he observes certain conditions, one being that he must not let her see him naked. When, due to the machinations of the Gandarvas, Pururavas breaks this taboo, Urvasi is taken away from him. He searches for her until he discovers her among the swan people and eventually, after meeting other conditions set by the gods, leaves this world to join her. Ms. Jung notes that a son has resulted from their union, suggesting that "apparently something with a place in the human realm results from their union, but one learns nothing more about it."[21] She continues:

> In this relation the attitudes of Pururavas and the heavenly nymph are markedly different; he, with human feeling, laments the loss of his beloved, he tries to find her again and wants to speak with her, but her words, when she says that women have the hearts of hyenas, are the expression of a soulless elemental being passing judgment on itself.[22]

Ms. Jung points out that anima figures often have a mist-like, hard-to-pin down quality; we see something similar in a man's difficulty pinning down the constantly changing elements represented by his Moon—and the purportedly constantly changing behavior of women. (Men often say that women change constantly, but the anima may influence such remarks, which reflect the views of the men who make them and may not accord with the women's experience of themselves.) We should probably question whether the "soulless" quality arises in the woman herself, as it seems connected with the man's rejection of his own lunar energy, which remains elemental despite all of

---

[20]Emma Jung, 52-3.
[21]Emma Jung, 48.
[22]Emma Jung, 48.

his attempts to understand it rationally. Men today may find this elemental quality even harder to pin down, for contemporary conditions seem to encourage a rationalistic, rather than empathetic, approach to relationship. Further, if women find themselves as housewives or "faithful partners," they may ignore parts of themselves that seem to reflect the mythic qualities associated with *anima* figures. (Of course, if a woman, in trying to please the partner or fulfill some obscurely-understood social role, ignores the elemental in herself, she may encourage the partner to seek it elsewhere.) The mythic material suggests that men will project onto women this hard-to-pin-down quality, this elemental and soul-less quality, but it seems that the projection of lunar elements results in a loss of soul.[23]

Form: Lunar and Saturnian

The Moon symbolizes how, probably because of instinct, we give form to the world, but the forms created by the Moon differ from those of Saturn. Saturn symbolizes how we give *structural* form to the world—how we build forms derived not from instinct or emotion but from what we see as the demands of consensus reality and our decisions either about what is or is not "real," or about what we "are" or "should be." Saturn's boundaries have to do with commitments and borderlines of various sorts, matters often decided or accepted, purportedly via rational consideration, via the structures of language, unlike the Moon's forms, which resist our attempts to define them rationally. Saturn's boundaries operate partly on the surface of things, though they have their roots deep within the psyche; though Saturn's forms may have their origin in the unconscious, they generally find expression in definitive statements about what one finds reliable, useful, or called upon in the world—and they have much to do with how one acts. So one the one hand, we have Saturnian structures, particularly non-organic forms that humans have built (e.g. buildings, scaffoldings, firm convictions, thought-structures). On the other hand, we have lunar structures: usually organic forms that have developed through organic processes (as in the forms of plants or other parts of the "sub-lunar realm").[24]

We could also say that we have two ways of cocooning ourselves: we can do so by structuring our activities and thinking according to what we see as true or necessary; or we can do so via emotional habit patterns taken from childhood. Whereas humans *make* many of the structures of Saturn (though often driven by unconscious impulses), humans generally *find themselves involved* with

---

[23]As we will see in chapter IV, men also tend to project Pluto onto women. Pluto adds to the elemental quality of the anima projection. Though Greco-Roman myths depict the underworld ruler as male, other myths from other cultures depict this figure as female.

[24]We also have the skeleton, an organic structure usually associated with Saturn but with a close connection to the Moon. Like Saturnian structures, it supports and has a rigid quality; like lunar structures, it grows and develops. It supports lunar developments and thus has some similarity to buildings in which organic creatures work creatively. Here, as so often in astrology, we should realize that world-elements with complex origins (e.g. skeletons) generally have more than one astrological correspondence. Astrologers should therefore consider opting for statements like, "X rules Y insofar as Y does Z." Saturn rules the skeleton insofar as the skeleton serves as a scaffolding and structural support, but the Moon rules Saturn insofar as the skeleton emerges from the sublunar realm.

the forms created by the Moon; most humans see Saturn's structures as somehow separate from the self and the Moon's structures as intimately connected to the self.[25] And whereas straight lines characterize many of Saturn's structures, we find few straight lines in nature; with the former, we find matters rationally conceived, whereas with the latter we find matters organically interwoven. Just as the ongoing patterns of the sub-lunar realm arise as the organic forms of life on this planet, so the flux of feeling, whether manifest in the ongoing lunar cycle or in the repeating behavior patterns that reflect a person's very early life, gives to each person's experience a form both unique and all-pervasive, both extremely personal and so encompassing that we often remain unaware of its existence.

These modes of structuring don't operate independently of each other—at least not completely! In mammals, the skeletal structure (Saturn) has a close connection to the kinds of organic structures (the organs, muscles, and so forth) that develop. Our thought-structures influence our emotional habit patterns, and the thought-structures of our parents have influenced our early-life patterning, just as a child's natural development will influence the parents' thought-structures. Laws influence how we feel; human feeling has influenced how humans have made laws. The laws of an era influence how children grow and develop; how children grow and develop, and particularly their connection to their own sensitivities, in turn influences the legal system. Saturn and the Moon have their detriment in each other's sign, and between them they rule one of the six bi-polar signs in the zodiac.[26]

Women experience the monthly menstrual cycle that reminds them of their ongoing connection to biological forms and to transpersonal demands that give an ongoing form to life. Men don't have this advantage, at least not in such obvious physiological patterns. However, if a man chooses to look into the effects of the transiting Moon (or any transiting planet, but the Moon most obviously) as it moves through the houses of his horoscope, he will find that he also lives in a cyclic pattern.[27] But a man must usually use his intellect to see it, whereas a woman can more easily experience it physically. Of course, many men spend a lot of time trying to escape the demands of their lunar energies. To contemporary men, such an ongoing connection may remain mysterious. Many will feel glad to escape it even if the escape doesn't yield much satisfaction.

The anima also seems to retain a connection to the weaving of fate and the foretelling of the

---

[25]Some will object, reasonably enough, that we often "find ourselves involved" in Saturnian structures such as government. True, but we can often decide to accept or reject such structures, and in any case we know that they have resulted from human decisions and judgments. You can reject the IRS in a way that you cannot reject your flesh. As noted, though, Saturn also rules skeletal structures, so we shouldn't see the dividing line as a hard-and-fast one in all cases. See previous footnote.
[26]See Appendix.
[27]We can characterize astrology as a feminine art insofar as it helps us to see, experience, and find harmony with these rhythmic forms symbolized and measured by the many planetary cycles.

Your Hidden Face: Projection in the Horoscope

future. In many cultures, women served as prophetesses, sibyls, witches, or seers. That we find this quality in a man's anima suggests a similar capability in *him*, but one that will not arise so readily. It often seems that men must contact these energies through the rational intellect, and they must take care, in doing so, not to sacrifice their natural fey qualities and project them onto women, where they will see it as something much more questionable, even pathological, perhaps as "irrational mood swings" or some such. (The rational connection to such capacities may account for the number of men who write about such matters.) On the other hand, some men can draw on these qualities for inspiration. As Emma Jung points out:

> Because the anima, as the feminine aspect of man, possesses this receptivity and absence of prejudice toward the irrational, she is designated the mediator between consciousness and the unconscious. In the creative man, especially, this feminine attitude plays an important role. It is not without cause that we speak of the conception of a work, of carrying out a thought, delivering oneself of it, or brooding over it.[28]

Despite its value and importance, many men will try to reject this inner capacity. We might think that a man with an afflicted Moon might do so more readily and more steadfastly, but experience shows that many men with close lunar afflictions feel compelled to come to a deeper and more empathetic understanding of the energy-pattern they represent. To ignore the problem means to ignore the potential, for they arise together; if one projects blindly, one ignores both, whereas if one re-collects the projected elements, one gains potency, redeeming the rejected material via more intimate contact with it. The process begins with a re-valuation—a re-*e*valuation—of the lunar potential. Ms. Jung notes that the being who appears as a swan in many fairy tales and legends (the anima figure) was not originally a swan:

> …the swan form is not an original condition, but secondary, like a dress hiding the princess. Behind the animal form is concealed a higher being which must be redeemed and with which the hero will eventually unite.[29]

It seems, then, that a man's connection to his lunar side has a spiritual quality or consequence. The process leads him to undiscovered territory, as through the anima the man enters a psychic area of autonomous power. Jung saw this autonomous power as "compensatory," in part because it compensates for an overly rationalistic view concentrated on the extensional realm. It seems to accrue more power to the degree that we ignore it, and modern conditions may encourage us to do just that. Jung writes:

> It is only under ideal conditions, when life is still simple and unconscious enough to follow the serpentine path of instinct without hesitation or misgiving, that the compensation works with entire success. The more civilized, the more conscious and complicated a man is, the less he is able to follow his instincts. His complicated living conditions and the influence of his environment are so strong that they drown the quiet voice

---

[28] Emma Jung, 56.
[29] Emma Jung, 57.

of nature. Opinions, beliefs, theories, and collective tendencies appear in its stead and back up all the aberrations of the conscious mind. Deliberate attention should then be given to the unconscious so that the compensation can set to work. Hence it is especially important to picture the archetypes of the unconscious not as a rushing phantasmagoria of fugitive images but as constant, autonomous factors, which indeed they are.[30]

That modern man lives so far from nature, in a manner so divorced from the rhythms of the natural world, may both symbolize and indicate a man's distance from his anima. It seems that in so-called primitive cultures, the energies that we customarily associate with the Moon were directed not only or primarily toward individual women but towards the feminine as a whole. Men propitiated that power; they apparently found it in nature as much as they found it in women; and it seems that they didn't make the kinds of distinctions we do between individual women and the powers of nature.

We find examples of this in Native American rhetoric. Native American spokesmen spoke often, readily, and eloquently about their connection to Mother Earth. It seems that whatever emotional energy flowed into their intimate relationships, they also directed a powerful flow of emotion toward the earth itself. It seems that men (and women) today also need this connection, though people find it harder and harder to find as our connection to the natural world becomes more and more tenuous. If we try to channel the enormous current of our emotional energy only into our relationships, we endanger those relationships much as we endanger a fuse through which we try to put too much electrical current. And the earth rebels.

Because I discussed these matters years ago in *Astrology Beyond Ego*,[31] I won't go into them in depth again here, merely noting that if a man wishes to withdraw or recollect his anima-related projections, he may need to do more than deal with his feelings for a particular woman or set of women (e.g. those with whom he has had close relationships). He also may need to reconnect to the earth principle as a whole, not only to a particular woman but to the feminine in general. This principle has a close connection to the earth itself, but "earth" here may be understood in different ways, some of them psychological rather than ecological. The lunar principle, connected with the earth and the sub-lunar realm, has to do with acceptance,[32] beginning with *self*-acceptance. The lunar principle does not make the kind of judgments made by the solar principle or the intellect; the earth doesn't accept one quality of being and reject another. All forms of organic life seem equal in the earth's eyes (so to speak). So, one must have the same attitude toward oneself and one's experience: to develop a kind of equanimity. Part of the man's journey, here, will usually take place alone

---

[30] C.G. Jung, *Aion* (Princeton: Princeton University Press, 1959), 20-21.
[31] Tim Lyons, *Astrology Beyond Ego* (Tempe: The American Federation of Astrologers, 2010), 69-88.
[32] According to Emma Jung (55), Carl Jung felt that in general woman "is more open to the unconscious than man. Receptivity is a feminine attitude, presupposing openness and emptiness, wherefore Jung has termed it the great secret of femininity."

and will take him inward instead of outward. Unlike Native Americans of two hundred years ago, men today find themselves part of a culture that seldom honors earth or any emotional connection to it; and if they look for practical reward, they probably court disappointment.

The process involves care and kindness to oneself, first of all; we might call it self-nurturing. A person who respects or has a deep connection to nature respects natural processes. He doesn't decide that he likes one natural process and doesn't like another, for the processes depend on each other and seem separate from one another only to the rational, categorizing mind. He realizes that winter prepares for spring, that wet and dry weather both have their places, and that the entire living world arises with such inter-dependence that one should probably not facilely reject one part and accept another. This same kind of acceptance—the acceptance of inter-dependence[33] that recognizes all natural processes as sacred—must be applied to oneself, to one's habitual mind, to one's "security needs," to one's most natural way of making oneself comfortable in the world, to one's automatic sensitivities—lunar matters all.

This kind of self-acceptance runs counter to the ways many men see themselves and their lives. It seems that something in our culture teaches men to emphasize what they *should*[34] do (get a job, be successful, etc.) instead of to sink into what they *feel*. To decide what one should do, one generally excludes from one's attention whatever one has decided one should *not* do; and if one emphasizes what one *should do,* one will tend to emphasize and value those parts of the world that aid one in the doing. The term *should* both implies and encourages this kind of dualistic viewpoint. Furthermore, in a capitalistic economy, one finds oneself encouraged to look at the world as a place where one sets oneself against others. Though we needn't completely reject such an attitude (for rejecting runs counter to the principle-in-question), and though sometimes, even if only for practical reasons, we would do well to *take* such an attitude (e.g. rejecting the over-use of fossil fuels), we shouldn't do so to the exclusion of the view that the two approaches comprise two sides of a larger whole. In some so-called primitive societies, hunters would on the one hand develop effective hunting techniques, considering the external world as something they must work with effectively, while on the other hand they would consider the prey as part of larger pattern that they apparently regarded as sacred.

As we know, the Moon symbolizes habit patterns taken from childhood, patterns through which a person seeks emotional security in the world; it also symbolizes a person's most natural way of reacting to the world, moment-to-moment and day-to-day. The Moon symbolizes how a person reacts to experience and digests it. It has much to do with creature comforts and caring; at the same time, it has much to do with how a person acts most naturally in the world he finds himself in. It is this simple, habitual, ongoing pattern of being, a habitual pattern of mind, that a person must

---

[33] I am not using *interdependence* in the Buddhist sense here. I mean simply that all organic processes interweave. In Buddhist teachings, the understanding of interdependence goes beyond the merely organic to include the entire karmic process.
[34] As we will see in chapter VIII, both *should* and *to be* generally indicate Saturn at work.

accept and get to know. Doing so, a person finds himself moving into an undiscovered country characterized by non-dualism—a state of mind in which one finds oneself dropping dualistic reference points.

A Buddhist teacher once cited "self-hatred" as one of the main blockages Western students of the Buddhist teachings encounter. Buddhists define *aggression* as any attitude that wishes things different than the way they arise naturally. In practice, a student begins with *maitri*, kindness to oneself. Through formal meditation, one practices the acceptance and equanimity mentioned above. That one accepts oneself unconditionally doesn't mean that one cannot tell right from wrong or the helpful from the harmful. It means, rather, that in dealing with one's state of mind, one must begin by *becoming familiar* with one's mind rather than by picking and choosing among mental states (for, as many Buddhist teachers have pointed out, *dhyana*, the Sanskrit word generally translated as "meditation" really has a meaning closer to "familiarization"). One takes a simple, precise, direct approach, looking at one's state of mind and coming to know it more accurately. To do this, one must eschew the tendency to reject some states of mind and to accept others, for if one takes such an approach, one will not come to know the complete mind. Those who want to withdraw anima-related projections must take a similar attitude in dealing with whatever arises.

Archetypally, a mother exemplifies these lunar qualities: she has unconditional acceptance of her child, yet she distinguishes harmful actions from beneficial ones; she offers a love not conditioned or altered by the child's behavior; she bases her actions on empathy, not merely on rational or judgmental considerations. Lunar energies reflect our instinct to connect unconditionally to the world, to embrace the world as we would our child (a metaphor with a peculiar aptness, for, as we will see in a later chapter, if the world of experience consists largely of our projections, then we give birth to it moment-by-moment). This unconditional approach enables a man to approach the domains of the anima. Without it, he finds himself rejecting his lunar qualities again and again, falling back into intellectual categories instead of stepping forward into empathy and acceptance.

The Real Moon

The Moon has a diameter approximately one fourth that of the Earth; no other moon-planet relationship in our solar system comes anywhere close to this ratio.[35] This fact reminds us of the Moon's powerful influence upon us, an influence permeating all matter on earth. We have a conscious experience of the tides, but we may not experience the Moon's effect on the cells of our bodies, on the organic life that surrounds us, or even on inorganic structures, the molecules of which respond to the Moon's gravitation. If we think merely in terms of the symbolism involved, we

---

[35]Some will see Pluto-Charon as an exception, though many astronomers don't categorize Charon as Pluto's Moon. However, that we see this similarity between Sun-Moon and Pluto-Charon suggests something important about Pluto for people who live on Earth. We find another connection between the Moon and Pluto in ancient notions connecting the moon with death and the after-death states, matters that modern astrologers will often associate with Pluto. If we take the Moon as connected to mind, as noted earlier in this chapter, we would see a further connection with Pluto, a planet associated with the projective power of mind and the connection between perception and concept. See chapter XI.

would say that habitual patterns of response have enormous control over each of us, giving to our lives a form that we only occasionally bring to consciousness. However, given the powerful gravitational effect of the Moon, we might suspect that lunar issues have some causal elements. Because for many eons humans have responded to the gravitational pull of the moon, we would expect the moon to have a pervasive influence on human behavior. In *The Night Sky*, Richard Grossinger describes this influence:

> The engagement of these two [the Earth and the Moon] is carried out in the one way possible for bodies in space: gravitationally. Our surface seas, biological waters, and molten metals are tugged back and forth by the Moon. Inanimate materials record this force through their own mammoth structures on the earth, transposing lunar rhythms into grand topographies, selenean grottoes and palaces. Caves are hollowed out by the Moon's tides, and sediments are built up in lunar cycles. Glaciers accumulate the icy tides. Animate materials "remember" the Moon and store it in cellular and psychic phases that go on for the lives of organisms and the histories of species even when these are broken from the rhythm of the actual Moon. Inanimate tides can only respond to the Moon as it is. Living things can record the lunar music, dance to it in other phases, and pass it on through chromosomes to their remote descendants, so that they will embody both the ancient Moon and the Moon of their own moment in time.[36]

Because of this physical influence, we should perhaps put the Moon into a category different from the other planets (and astrologers *do*, of course, referring to the Moon as one of the two "lights"), for with the others we discern no significant and readily observable causal connection. The gravitational connection suggests that the Moon has a profound affect on the body and that this may account for some (though probably not all) of what we call the "lunar influence."[37] This connection with the physical world suggests, in turn, a method of dealing with lunar issues. We know that to withdraw any projection, one must first honor the energy of the planet-in-question. How, then, to honor the Moon? One might begin by honoring the body, not by initiating a Spartan regimen, but through a more lunar approach: by nurturing the body, by finding what simply feels good physically and emotionally. Each person must find what feels nurturing for him: for some it will mean getting massages; for others it will mean getting to bed early and reading elaborate and wonderful science fiction novels; for others it will mean taking oneself out for a good meal; for others it will mean buying a fine bottle of Scotch and listening to music—or even howling at the big, round, white thing in the night sky!

I would recommend this self-nurturing for everyone in our culture all the time, but particularly the men, and particularly during transits or directions from Saturn to the natal Moon. After all, it

---

[36] Richard Grossinger, *The Night Sky* (New York: Random House, 1983), 205-6.

[37] Lunar progressions and directions, for example, do not involve physical bodies. Furthermore, any transit from the Moon to a natal position does not affect a physical thing; it has symbolic importance but no apparent physical quality, for though the transiting Moon itself has material substance, the horoscope symbol does not, as far as we can tell with our present scientific instruments. That symbol refers, after all, to a planetary position from long ago.

seems that Saturn dominates the Moon for just about everyone in our culture these days; people generally put Saturnian matters before lunar ones, perhaps because they feel that they have to, the world outside of them working along what we might call Saturnian lines, and partly because they receive more evident rewards for doing so. People often put work, demand, responsibility, and life's apparently-endless series of *should's* ahead of the Moon's non-socially-conditioned drives. People tend to emphasize their position in the social hierarchy instead of their relation to their own feelings. Therefore, and particularly during Saturn-Moon interactions, they benefit from getting off of whatever track they find themselves on and offering themselves some creature comforts. Life often leaves us, as D.H. Lawrence put it, "slurred over,"[38] so we all need to get off our tracks periodically and give something back to ourselves, to reestablish our connection to the lunar principle. The Moon symbolizes the offering; Saturn suggests that we must make it in an organized way, as part of our daily schedule.

Certainly social conditions prod men to put more emphasis on the Saturn principle than on the lunar one. Many people expect a man to get a job, support the family, take care of practical affairs, and do all sorts of Saturn-related things, thus leaving the lunar-related matters to the woman. Though this seems less true now than it did sixty years ago, statistics suggest that the pattern still dominates. Because men find themselves under such pressure, they would do well to take some time for lunar activities even if they do so via Saturn (by scheduling). If they leave the matter to chance, lunar matters will probably remain on the always-available back burner. And if one doesn't know what would feel nurturing, he should schedule in some time (Saturn principle) to find out.

One final note on this: though various actions such as taking care of the kids or cooking dinner fall into the "lunar category," men should, for the most part, find activities divorced from responsibility. For example, though in taking care of the kids one may take on the lunar role and enjoy it, the activity can rather quickly get mixed in with Saturn-matters: one may feel that one is "responsible for" taking care of the kids; in taking care of the kids, one finds oneself involved in all sorts of Saturnian demands, some apparently unique to our culture. The Saturnian element can dominate even here simply because one finds oneself feeling beset again by *should's*. So though taking care of the kids may help one to feel the lunar element in oneself, one might also engage in activities in which one does not have to accomplish much of anything. Anything related to nature will generally serve well—activities ranging from hikes in the forest to planting the garden to lying in whatever fields of flowers present themselves.

Whereas a woman's attempt to recollect her animus involves cultivating *logos*, the side of her that arises through ideas and that leads her out into the world, a man's attempt to recollect his anima involves cultivating *eros*, the side of him that arises through feeling and that arises from something within. Though in the long run a man's attempt to recollect his anima will enrich his relationships with women, in the short run, because of habitual tendencies to experience *eros* through women (and *logos* through himself), the man might consider cultivating the lunar principle in periodic

---

[38] If I remember correctly, the quotation comes from *Sons and Lovers*.

solitude, at least until he cuts through the tendency to immediately and automatically seek that principle in women. In the ongoing quest for self-completion, it seems that the hero must often go through a withdrawal-and-return pattern.

We may think that the lunar principle will lead the man back to ordinariness. Thinking that, we might conclude that whereas a woman's work with Uranus involves the recollection of an allegedly "transcendental" or "transformative" energy, a man's work with the Moon involves the recollection of a decidedly non-transformative energy. Yet the Moon symbolizes that which constantly changes, so it has to do with transformation as part of everyday experience. In working with his Moon, the man will discover that "spirituality" arises most often in ordinary situations.

Finally, just as many women seem to integrate Uranus later in life, so many men seem to integrate the Moon after midlife, and particularly after the second Saturn return, when Saturnian demands recede. Midlife seems to bring about a reversal in which, as Jung said, men begin to develop the feminine element. However, in our culture, with the retirement age now set beyond the sixtieth year, men may feel that they have to pay attention to Saturnian matters for many years after the midlife transits. This doesn't seem healthy, and it may account for some of the particular forms of malaise that older men experience.

Case Study: William Butler Yeats

Just as in Emily Dickinson we have a woman who we would expect to manifest Uranus in her behavior but who nonetheless projected it onto men for much of her early life, so in William Butler Yeats we have a man whom we would expect to manifest the Moon in his behavior but who nonetheless projected it onto women for much of his early life. Also, though we have another questionable birth-time, we can still analyze Yeats' Moon along with its sign and aspects.[39] Even a cursory examination of Yeats' horoscope shows that the Moon makes powerful aspects: it opposes Mars and squares his Venus-Pluto conjunction, so that Yeats has a t-square to that conjunction; it also trines Saturn and the Sun, forming a grand trine in air signs; the addition of Jupiter, sextile the Moon and opposing the Sun from Sagittarius, turns the grand trine into a kite.

Though the first projection of Moon-Pluto went to his somewhat fey mother, Yeats later developed a strong attraction for, one might even say obsession about (Moon square Pluto; Venus conjoined Pluto), Maud Gonne, who some called the most beautiful woman in Ireland, an ardent revolutionary and nationalist as well as an actress of wide acclaim. She helped organize Irish brigades who stood against the British in the South African War; later, she was active in the 1916 uprisings in Ireland, activity for which she was imprisoned.[40] (Her husband, fellow-revolutionary John Mac-

---

[39]June 13, 1865, 10:40 PM, Dunsink, Dublin. Source: Lois H. Rodden's *The American Book of Charts* (San Diego: Astro Computing Services, 1980). Ms. Rodden considered the data accurate ("A," in her system of evaluation). The evidence suggests that, at the very least, the 10:40 birthtime comes extremely close.

[40]All of this suggests, of course, that Yeats also projected his seventh house Mars onto Gonne. Though we generally categorize Mars as a masculine planet, we consider the seventh house as one carrying projections. (See chapter VI.) We can see why Yeats, with Mars closely aspecting Venus-Pluto, often projected that male energy onto women.

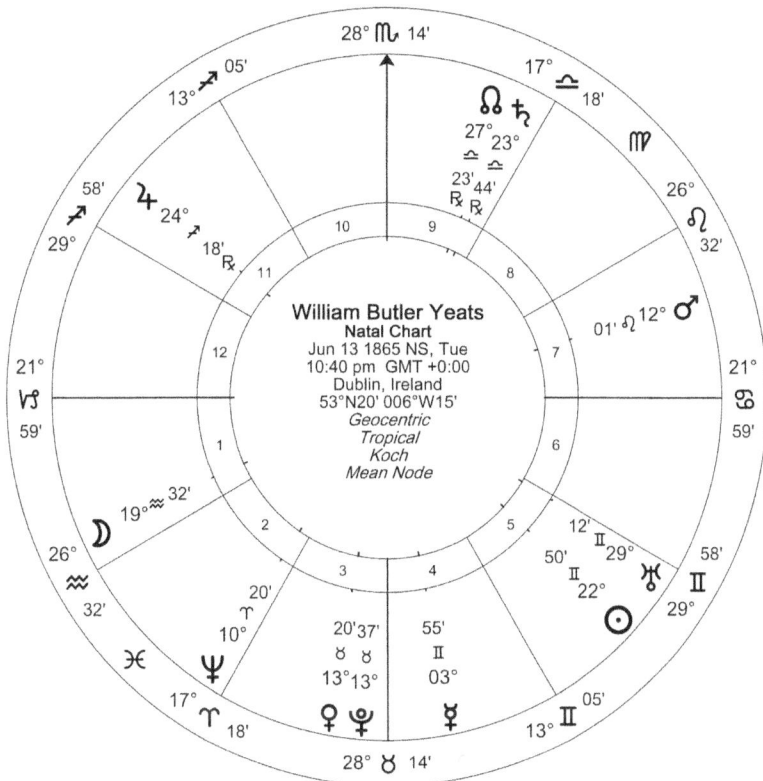

Bride, was shot. Their son Sean later became Prime Minister of Ireland.) She also achieved fame on the Irish stage, and Yeats wrote *Cathleen ni Houlihan* with her in mind for the lead role.[41] But in 1903, she accepted the marriage proposal from MacBride.[42]

Certainly she provided a ready hook for Yeats' Moon-Mars opposition; we can discern her dramatism in the Moon-Pluto aspect and her dramatic self-assertiveness in Mars. Not that Yeats didn't have the political concerns we might associate with an Aquarius Moon and a Sun-Uranus conjunction; and not that these concerns didn't inform his public life, as we might expect from the grand trine including Saturn above the horizon and with Jupiter, ruler of the Midheaen and in its own sign, forming the kite from the eleventh house. He had great sympathies with the Irish cause, writing about it in several important poems, though always from a point apart. But Maud Gonne apparently lived too dynamic a life for Yeats. We might attribute this to projection of the Moon-

---

[41] Richard Ellman, *Yeats: The Man and the Masks* (New York: E.P. Dutton and Company, 1948), 159.

[42] In the year previous, when Yeats had felt some hope that she would marry him, his solar arc Moon squared Jupiter; in the year she married, that solar arc Moon had moved away from Jupiter and started to move toward a square with natal Uranus. Essentially, Yeats had a temporary t-square to his solar arc Moon from natal Jupiter and Uranus. The obsession continued: solar arc Venus-Pluto moved over his Sun just about the time that solar arc Moon squared Uranus.

Your Hidden Face: Projection in the Horoscope

Mars opposition, for it lies in angular houses and thus has to do with direct action. Though here we will focus on the Moon, we find Mars in the seventh, a house symbolizing what we often project onto others regardless of sex, and clearly Maud Gonne, with her penchant for confrontation and dramatic action (Mars in Leo), served as a good hook for that projection, or even for the Moon-Mars opposition altogether, with Yeats projecting the Moon for gender-related reasons and Mars for house-related reasons. And if we include Venus-Pluto, we find Yeats playing the role of an obsessed but unrequited lover, and Gonne, also taking on at least some of that Venus-Pluto energy (and not surprisingly, as both planets often align with the feminine), as a dramatic, powerful, active woman, and one who would, in her role as the Moon, feel drawn to Mars-like men (e.g. John MacBride). Yeats realized this, seeing, correctly as it turned out, that Maude Gonne sought a man of action, that she longed "for some impossible life, for some unwearying land, like that of the heroine of my play."[43]

In his biography of Yeats (*Yeats: The Man and The Masks*), Richard Ellman writes of a split in Yeats' personality: on the one side, a person of action; on the other, a dreamer. When he was young, he seemed to project Moon-Mars rather constantly onto Maud Gonne, even though, much later in life, he involved himself in politics, thus taking on the role of a man of at least some action. (Earlier, he had organized the Irish theatre in Dublin, activity suggesting Saturn as much as Moon-Mars.) But early on, we can see a split between a kind of persona Yeats longed to embody, and a sense of identity that he more clearly *did* embody. We can see the dreamer in Yeats' strong air signs: in the grand trine in air, plus Mercury, dispositor of the Gemini Sun, also in Gemini and unaspected. That last stands as a good symbol for someone whose constant stream of ideas—whose dreaming into writing, we might say—did not on its own connect to everyday reality, a tendency exacerbated by the air trine, for air trines sometimes indicate a tendency to cycle through patterns of thought constantly. And to *this* grand trine we add Jupiter in Sagittarius making it into a kite, something that can fly off, particularly when in contact with air. Jupiter in Sagittarius surely stands as a good symbol for a mind wrapped in—and rapt *by*—myth. Saturn helps to ground this sometimes-wayward grand trine: near the top of the horoscope, it strongly suggests that the ideas found form in ways that furthered his vocation; he found a structure for his mythic leanings and love of language.[44]

In 1917, Yeats finally married. Ellman writes of this experience,

---

[43]William Butler Yeats, "The Land of Heart's Desire," qtd. in Ellman, 108. Yeats' horoscope even seems to suggest the death of Gonne's husband. Mars in the seventh closely squares Venus-Pluto, suggesting the death of a lover as a result of a struggle to transform. So Yeats' chart offers us some details about the woman onto whom he projected so much of his energy for so long.

[44]On the cusp of the ninth, Saturn suggests formal approaches to philosophy. Surely this interpretation fits Yeats nicely, as he seemed fond of systems and models. (See, for example, *A Vision*.) The aspect also suggests Yeats' feeling of intellectual inferiority. Though we might find this odd in one so renowned for works redolent with ideas, Yeats apparently felt a deep mistrust of his own intellect, at least partly because of his father, a well-known artist known for his vast intellectual range. I have heard that once when someone asked the senior Yeats if he were 'the father of the Great Yeats,' he puffed himself up and let the questioner know that he himself was "the Great Yeats." His son William perhaps spoke of himself when he said that "the best lack all conviction."

Marriage to Georgie Hyde-Lees released his energies like a spring. He fell deeply in love with his wife and knew for the first time the happiness of a relatively uncomplicated relationship with another person. He was astonished to find himself playing the role of husband and, after February 1919, of father, without feeling that it was a role at all. 'The marriage bed, he wrote later, 'is the symbol of the solved antinomy.' Certainly it was so for him…A great serenity came over Yeats as he emerged from the isolation and eccentricity of bachelorhood into peace and harmony. His wife was kind and self-sacrificing; she understood his strange mixture of arrogance and diffidence and behind the pose which he put on before strangers found him deeply human. For his part, Yeats kept no more diaries of his mental difficulties, wept no more over a barren passion, and no longer thought of himself as shut out from common experience.[45]

And then there was his wife's automatic writing. Surely it suggests Yeats' Venus-Pluto conjunction in Taurus and the Moon-Pluto square: we see, in other words, another iteration of the projection of the Moon. Nevertheless, though we still see projection, it seems that Yeats had come a long way to integrate this energy, for he found in it a tremendous grounding: the voice that came through told him that it spoke in order to give him images for his poetry.[46] Notably, at this time, solar arc Mercury had moved to square Yeat's Saturn, and possibly to conjoin the descendant, so we see new structures in Yeats' poetry, a new grounding and a new resonance. He seemed ready to take on the masculine role of his seventh house Mars, and though he continued to experience some of his Moon through his wife, we see after this time that he speaks more confidently in his own voice. He gave voice to his feelings with new confidence. Ellman writes:

> A newly acquired sense of strength enabled him now to write lyric after lyric in which he spoke, with fresh confidence, in his own person. He would say a few years later in a letter to Tagore that as husband and father he felt 'more knitted into life.'[47]

Certainly this "knitting" suggests not only a grounding of the intellect, but a willingness to live in the ordinary emotions symbolized by the Moon.

So we see with Yeats a pattern similar to the one we saw with Emily Dickinson. First, just as Dickinson projected her Uranus onto men, so Yeats projected his Moon onto a woman. In both cases, because the vigor of the projections suggests that Dickinson and Yeats had rejected parts of themselves, the personal longings went unrequited. Yet in both cases we see that, as they got older, Dickinson and Yeats apparently made peace with that projected energy, which meant making peace with themselves, and found satisfying relationships as they integrated the projected material into their lives. We see in both cases, too, that the blind tendency to project either Uranus or the Moon onto an intimate partner does not at all indicate a lack of creative vitality, though it does seem to point to some degree of personal anguish.

---

[45]Ellman, 221.
[46]See Yeats' *A Vision*.
[47]Ellman, 221.

Chapter IV

Gender Based Projections III: Other Gender-Based Projections

In the mythic story referred to earlier, Uranus' actions remind us of the astrological Uranus, while Gaia's approach reminds us of the astrological Moon: Uranus wants freedom from karmic entanglement, wants to deal with the world largely through ideas related to and in support of that freedom; Gaia acts possessively and instinctually. Uranus attempts to escape from karmic entanglement; the Moon presents the straightforward demands *of* karmic entanglement, reminding us that actions have consequences, not only in the psyche but in the physical world as well, and that we can't escape the physical world no matter how much we insist on ideas related to emancipation. Uranus' actions suggest cool detachment; the Moon's suggest an instinctual involvement. Uranus can either spark an enlightened detachment or drive one to use concepts as a shield against reality; the Moon can bring either the wisdom of lived and embodied experience or the blindness that comes from unexamined living.

That these figures appear in an ancient myth depicting the creation of the world suggests that they have much to do with something basic in the way human beings create their experience. (Thus, it seems, Jung's views about the primordial nature of the anima and animus.) That the myth deals with the creation of the world reminds us not only of the fundamental importance of gender to the continuance of organic life, but also of the way gender-related assumptions permeate our perception moment-to-moment, serving as potent filters through which we experience the world. Not only would we not even *have* a world without gender, but we apparently have a deeply-rooted tendency to perceive the world in dualistic terms. Of all the world's dualities, the male-female duality seems to occupy our attention most consistently—and it mirrors a perhaps even more basic duality, which we will discuss more fully in a later chapter: the duality of perceiver-perceived, the notion or assumption that the perceived world has some sort of definite existence outside of the mind of the perceiver.

Though the Saturn-Uranus-Gaia myth seems to have much to do with the *anima* and *animus* projections related to the Moon and Uranus respectively, projections that may have some basis in genetics or instinct, some gender-related projections seem to reflect cultural factors at least as much as genetic or instinctual ones. As with projections related to the Moon and Uranus, these projections relate to specific astrological factors, and, as above, we can start with some working hypotheses: that women tend to project the Sun and Mars onto men; that men tend to project Venus onto women; that both men and women project Saturn onto each other, or onto restrictive factors in society generally, though women seem a bit more prone to this projection than do men. (Though both men and women project Saturn, they apparently do so for different reasons, as we will see.) Finally, though both men and women tend to project Neptune and Pluto onto others or into the environment generally, men seem to have more difficulty integrating these energies than do women.[1] That the list for women contains more planets than the one for men may suggest that the prevailing cultural framework discourages women's self-expression more than it does that of men. The tendency of women to project the Sun more than men do strongly suggests, among other things, that women have fewer opportunities for confident self-creation.

As with the rest of the material presented in this book, consider these ideas as hypotheses, not as self-evident truths. We should always take all horoscope factors into consideration in any analysis, and in any case we should seek to help the client, not simply to predict behavior. Before concluding that a woman will project the Sun or Uranus onto a man, the astrologer should see how those two planets function in her horoscope (and similarly for a man's Moon and Venus). If Uranus makes challenging aspects to personal planets, for example, or if the Sun is in the seventh or twelfth house, then the woman will probably project those planets more readily.[2] And, here as elsewhere, we should avoid two-valued thinking: instead of asking whether a person will or will not project a specific planet, we could ask how often, or under what conditions, or to what degree that person will project a specific planetary energy. Gender-based projections reflect proclivities based on gender, but they do not force a person to act in one way or another. The astrological symbols point to tendencies, not to mechanical processes.

---

[1] Everyone, to a greater or lesser degree, seems to project Saturn, Uranus, Neptune, and Pluto—and not only onto intimate partners. Millions of people project these planets into the collective. In a later chapter, we can investigate collective projections by using the symbolism of these planets. When I say, then, that women tend to project Saturn onto men or that men tend to project Pluto onto women, I mean that we can observe, in addition to the ongoing collective projections, these more personal ones.
[2] See chapters V and VI for a discussion of aspects and houses.

Women and the Sun

A hundred years or so ago, many astrologers would have interpreted a woman's Sun-placement as representing the man that the woman would marry. Thus in 1847, W.J. Simmonite wrote in his section on "Women's Marriages" that

> [t]he Sun is to be taken and considered in all respects the same as the Moon in the man's nativity...Should the Sun be posited between fourth and first, or between the tenth and seventh, women will marry either in their own youth, or to men younger than themselves; but if the Sun be met in the other quadrants, they will either marry late in life, or to men who have passed their prime, or some years their senior.[3]

We should direct our attention, here, not to the particulars of Simmonite's predictions, but to the fact that he makes predictions at all and that he assumes that the woman's Sun gives us information about the man or men that the woman will marry. He assumes, apparently as a matter of accepted procedure, that women would project the Sun onto men, particularly onto the man or men to whom she felt a particular tie. (We can see, too, that the astrologer would have made a similar assumption about the man's Moon.[4]) This practice has deep roots, and even today it sometimes yields accurate predictions. However, if we adopt this practice without inquiring into the reasons that it works (when it does so, of course), we will miss a chance to gain some insight into both psychological processes and the restrictive assumptions of society both now and in the past.

The astrological Sun symbolizes the conscious, creative vitality of the self. Unless denied expression, the Sun will tell us, by sign and aspect, how a person will express herself[5] and how she will throw light onto other personality factors. The Sun tells us how a person finds a personal, creative, independent reference point within the ongoing flux of emotional involvement and social demand. It tells us much about the kind of path that the person will likely follow if she seeks self-completion. It also tells us how a person rules his or her world, the sun having a long connection to kingship, to the central principle around which a collectivity—in this case, the collectivity of personal indicators: the planets—forms. Psychologically, the Sun represents the central reference point of the self, though when operating blindly, the Sun often functions as a central reference point only for ego.

Only to the degree that a person decides to seek self-completion and lives a life actualized by internal inspiration instead of external coercion, obvious or subtle, will the Sun and its sign give us an accurate list of easily visible personality traits. If, on the other hand, a person habitually de-

---

[3] W.J. Simmonite, *Arcana of Astrology* (North Hollywood: Symbols and Signs, 1979), 124.
[4] See pages 122-124 of the same text, where Simmonite says, referring to the "quality" of a man's wives,
Mark the planet to which the Moon first applies, by aspect: if to Uranus, there will be little domestic comfort...and the wife will be of hasty temper, yet fond of science....If Saturn receives the Moon's application..., the wives whom he provides are morose and grave. (122)
[5] Or *himself*, of course, though this section deals mostly with women.

nies her own need for self-completion—if, for example, she finds herself believing, consciously or unconsciously, that she will find self-completion only through the creative work of a partner, or through partnership generally, or through men who play the solar role—then the qualities of the Sun, both in itself and by sign or aspect, will likely appear at least partly through the partner. The woman will often feel disappointment to the degree that the man doesn't demonstrate the qualities indicated by her Sun in combination with its sign and aspects. To the extent that she seeks to live vicariously through the partner, the Sun will appear more clearly through that partner and less clearly in the woman herself. Her own personality, in such cases, will often seem reflected in the Moon, Venus, and the Ascendant.

Of course, even for men the Sun does not always appear clearly and forthrightly. A man may act like his ascendant, or even like his Moon, particularly if he has challenging aspects to the Sun or if has it in the twelfth house or in some other challenging position; furthermore, many people find that they grow into the Sun (so to speak). Still, though creative self-actualization never comes easily for anyone, men in our era generally find more cultural support for the process than do women. And, obviously, a woman who bears a child will find that during her pregnancy and in the years after that, she will often express her creative inspirations at least partly through lunar activities related to mothering rather than though solar activities related to radiation. Our society generally seems to reward the latter more readily and more evidently than it rewards the former.[6]

The Sun gives light, conscious awareness, and a sense of centrality and energetic reference point. The creative nature of our conscious reference point seems to distinguish us from most (perhaps all) animals and enables us to take part in the adventure of creative living. We might even say that consciousness itself creates both the world and the adventure, a matter we will explore in later chapters. In any case we know that a solar figure in myth often has a deity for one parent or seems to emerge in some way from a trans-human realm. The solar child often doesn't know his true parents, but he has a sense of destiny. This sense of destiny expresses itself through a conscious reference point, a sense that one's creative light emerges or emanates from a central point. Though we may see this notion as an illusion from the ultimate point of view, from a relative point of view we can see how the creative reference point leads, often inexorably, to a sense of destiny.

Some astrologers associate the Sun with the ego, claiming somewhat facilely that the Sun "is" the ego. It seems more precise to say that though the Sun clearly has a connection to ego, it does not symbolize ego per se; if we equate the two, we ignore not only the complexity of the ongoing process of ego creation, but also the inherent limitations of the thing purportedly created. The Sun symbolizes ego only insofar as ego arises through conscious, creative development, and insofar as or when the person sees him or herself as something solid and enduring situated at center of his or her world. Ego, though, doesn't result entirely, or even mostly, from conscious processes; it results

---

[6] I consider current "austerity" programs, both in the United States and abroad, as attempts to ignore lunar or quasi-lunar imperatives; the assault on welfare seems like a case in point. We see a similar emphasis in the myriad initiatives, again both here and abroad, that emphasize "development" while ignoring the environment in which such development occurs.

just as much from unconscious, automatic, reactive processes that constantly repeat and provide an illusion of solidity.[7] The Sun-sign may symbolize the way a person expresses her completeness (or, of course, her blindness), and we know that if she doesn't express that sign completely, she will feel some dissatisfaction. The Sun symbolizes a seed that can give rise either to ego or egolessness, to ignorance or to wisdom. Through greater awareness, we shed light on the world; then we react to that light.

We know that the sun gives light to all the other planets and that without the solar light those planets would remain cold and lifeless. Symbolically, then, the Sun represents the potential for warmth and conscious living; through its radiance, it sheds light on diversified interactions and activities, making those activities possible (though the Sun, in itself, does not generally symbolize the interactions or activities themselves). The planets (including the Moon) in some sense distribute this energy, making it available for the creative activities symbolized by those bodies. At the same time, the Sun's sign-position colors or lends its energetic style to all of those activities.[8] Thus, a Venus-Jupiter aspect doesn't mean the same thing for a Scorpio as it does for a Libra; Mars in Sagittarius may manifest in one way when combined with a Cancer Sun, and in quite another way when combined with an Aries Sun; and so forth.

If a woman projects her Sun entirely onto men, we can often see her Sun-sign, along with its aspects and house-position, in the men to whom she feels attracted. In this, a woman's projection of her Sun has much in common with her projection of Uranus, but the former seems to yield connections of a more stable sort, not only because Uranus symbolizes revolution while the Sun symbolizes radiation from a central point, but also because a woman's projection of the Sun doesn't seem to involve the *negativization* process described above in connection with projections of Uranus—and even when a woman does to some extent *negativize* her solar energy, she doesn't usually do so completely. Still, we can find abundant support for the claim that women often experience the Sun's energy at least partly by projecting it into the world. The astrological indicators will vary. If a woman has her Sun in Capricorn, she may feel drawn to men not only to Capricorn men, but also to men with a strong tenth house or important aspects to Saturn; if a woman has a Sun-Neptune square, she may feel drawn not only to Piscean men, but also to men with the Sun in the twelfth or in aspect to Neptune; a woman with her Sun in Scorpio may feel drawn not only to Scorpio men, but also to men who have Pluto in high emphasis.[9] We often find that unconscious or only-vaguely conscious psychic factors in the woman will attract unconscious or vaguely-conscious elements in the man. Though in theory the woman's horoscope tells us more about her *experience* of the men than it does about the men themselves, if the projection has enough strength (if the solar

---

[7]The question of ego and ego-maintenance has occupied philosophers, particularly Buddhist ones, for centuries. To discuss the matter here would take us too far afield. See chapter VIII and the Appendix of my *Astrology Beyond Ego* (see bibliography) for a discussion of the astrological indicators of ego-formation.
[8]I have borrowed from Antero Ali the use of "style" to describe energies related to the Sun. See his *Astrologik* (Berkeley: The Vertical Pool, 1990).
[9]We should distinguish, in such cases, between a Scorpio woman feeling attraction to a Scorpio man, and a non-Scorpio woman, say a Gemini, with a close opposition to Pluto, especially but not exclusively from the Moon or Venus.

energy remains firmly unconscious), the Sun will also seem to provide a good description of the men. (This will hold true as long as the woman remains sane in most people's eyes, *sanity* meaning that her perceptions accord with those of consensus reality.)

From what I have seen and among the women I know either as friends or clients, the Sun, along with its situation in the natal chart, arises *both* through the woman's own character and through the men to whom she feels drawn, though I have found the Sun a less reliable indicator in this area than Uranus. Furthermore, I have not found completely accurate the old adage about women appearing to be more like the Moon-sign than like the Sun-sign, though often a woman's Moon will appear more clearly in her behavior than a man's Moon does in his. Even if the woman's Moon has more prominence than her Sun, the latter will be visible in some way even though mixed with the former. Still, most women project the Sun onto men some of the time even as they retain it some of the time; at other times, they merely seek a connection to it generated via conscious values instead of via unconsciously-generated magnetism.

Much of this suggests that these women make conscious, creative use of the Sun-sign and that they see themselves as creative agents unless the solar energy gets constellated in a man. When this occurs, solar projections will recur. Such a situation (in which the woman projects some solar contents onto men some of the time, yet at others seems to possess those qualities herself) seems to have a close connection to what Jung called the *wanderings of projections*:

> [That the *whole* content of the projected image will not become conscious] is in fact generally the case with archetypal contents, because such contents cannot be integrated by ego-consciousness. Consequently a phenomenon occurs that could be described as the *wanderings of projections*: the unconscious content is in part recognized as subjective and thereby differentiated from the object in which it hitherto appeared as a projection; its still-unrecognized aspect, however, appears again projected onto another object after a period of latency in the unconscious. Or it may appear in another medium, which now becomes the new bearer of the projection. If one wants to prevent such a renewal of the projection, the content must be recognized as *psychically real*, though not as a part of the subject but rather as an *autonomous power*.[10]

Why, though, do women project the solar energy onto men—that is, *when* they do so? At least partly, I suspect, because of the cultural factors mentioned above. They do so (as men also do sometimes) when they fail to see themselves in a central role as creators, as people who create their own worlds or as creators of specific works. For some hundreds of years in so-called Western culture, women have often expected and generally been expected to accept the world of their husbands and to see those husbands as the creative element in the relationship, with the woman playing a reactive role, reflecting the husband's light even as the moon reflects the sun's. Even today, the woman generally goes off to live with the man instead of the other way around,[11] and the man's social class

---
[10] Von Franz, 13.
[11] We find different practices in some other cultures.

and income often shapes the woman's world just as it shapes the man's. Certainly millions of people see women as the satellites and supports of men; they see woman circulating around the man as he defines or delineates what "is important" and what should have priority in the marriage and the life derived from it.[12]

Biological factors may play a role as well. A woman finds herself linked to biological cycles connected in obvious ways to the moon; if she bears children, she develops an acute awareness of the earthy quality of human life. Because she has such a personal experience of earth and of the cyclic patterns of life, she may have more difficulty embodying the solar energy, involving as it does a destiny that purportedly transcends, and may seem to ignore, the biological imperatives of which a woman has such a powerful ongoing experience. The hero may believe that he comes from afar, but the mother knows that the child came from *her;* the mother feels close to the child not because she feels that the child has a special destiny as the world understands that phrase, but because the child has lived within her for so many months—and, it seems, because she often has a different referent for "special destiny" than do others.

If the Sun in a woman's horoscope receives challenging aspects, particularly from the outer planets, a woman will probably project it more readily—and when she does so, she will often project the aspected planets with it (as occurs with most other projections). Thus a woman with a challenging Sun-Pluto aspect may project it onto "Scorpionic men" of various types (e.g. Sun in Scorpio, Sun in close aspect to Pluto, a strong eighth house). This doesn't necessarily mean that a well-aspected Sun won't end up in a projection as well; the pleasant aspects don't force themselves into awareness in the way that challenging aspects often do, so a well-aspected Sun may indicate a harmonious relationship with a male partner. Much depends, here as always, on a person's level of awareness, a factor that, though it doesn't appear in the horoscope, seems the most important ingredient in the mix.

We might also say that the woman's animus shapes the man—or shapes the way he expresses himself in the world, shapes the way he "gives shape" to the woman's world. That animus appears at least partly through the woman's Sun along with its signs, aspects, and house position. A woman often wants to find in a man some of the qualities of her Sun-sign. A Gemini woman will often seek a man of sharp intellect; a Libra woman will often want a man who has some sort of social grace. Of course, Libra women have a documented propensity to try to shape their men in some way, to "get them in shape" socially; however, if a woman's Sun-sign tells us something about her animus, and if the animus has a propensity for "shaping," we would expect even non-Libran women to be unconsciously shaping "their men" so that those men conform to the demands of the women's Sun-signs.[13] The people involved often don't have complete awareness of these processes, so the

---

[12] Interested readers might look at "Moments of Discontent: University Women and the Gender Status Quo," by Dorothy C. Hollard and Margaret A. Eisenhart, from *Anthropology and Education Quarterly*, 19;2, 1992. (An abridgement appears in *Schooling the Symbolic Animal: Social and Cultural Dimensions of Education*, edited by Bradley A.U. Levinson et. al.)
[13] Something similar occurs with men and their Moons.

processes may go unexamined. The woman may feel quite frustrated if the man doesn't come up to snuff in the desired area—if, for example, he doesn't go in for sharpening his intellect in the way the woman wishes or for developing more adept social skills—and if the woman doesn't bring the matter to consciousness, she will probably experience it as some sort of nagging difficulty (as will, quite likely, the man). But because the animus possesses an idea of how things "should be," the woman will often attempt to shape the man and will feel justified in doing so, often living with the frustration.[14]

We should note, though, an important difference between projections related to the Sun and projections related to Uranus. When a woman (or anyone) projects Uranus onto others, those others will often seem to use their ideas not as a way to enter life more fully, but as a way to escape from life or live only provisionally. As we have seen, the same pattern appears in the myth, where Uranus uses an idea (that his children are too ugly) as a way to escape from the karmic situation and from cause-and-effect altogether (i.e. he tries to bury his children back into the mother). As we have seen, Uranus has a close connection to puer figures of all sorts. A projection of the Sun, on the other hand, does not so directly involve ideas. Neither the Sun nor the Moon gives themselves up to language or concept, for they remain elemental. The Sun has to do with radiant energy, confidence, light, and strength, whether articulated through ideas or not. Further, projections of the Sun do not generally, or even usually, appear through people who seem to detach themselves from life. The solar energy does not necessarily resist organic processes; rather, it often participates in and emerges through them. The Sun distributes energy to the different planets, and those planets serve as modes through which the person integrates into the world. Whereas the negative side of Uranus has to do with idea-driven detachment, the negative side of the Sun has to do with arrogance or overbearing self-concern and often appears in men who will seem intricately integrated into the world and deem themselves essential to it.

Whatever the external situation, the woman will search for meaning at least partly through the masculine side of her personality, whether that side expresses itself through a creative confidence or activity, or through projection onto someone who serves as a hook for either. The word *create* derives from the same roots as *Creole*, a word first applied to West Indians with white fathers. *Creole* "in a way is the father's admission of his paternity."[15] Thus our word *create* seems to have a relationship to the masculine—oddly enough, perhaps, considering woman's role in giving birth. But *create* comes from roots meaning "to form out of nothing,"[16] such as gods purportedly do, not to create out of some already existing substance. As ruler of Leo, the polar-opposite of Aquarius, ruled by

---

[14] We can see, slightly hidden here, part of the reason why astrologers of previous eras saw the Sun arising through the husband. A Libran woman will find it easier to shape a Libran man in Libran ways than to shape a Scorpio man in the same direction. More generally, she will probably find fire and air signs more amenable to Libran shaping than she will earth and water signs. So, perhaps, she will gravitate toward men with these signs emphasized in their horoscopes. On the other hand, opposite charges attract, so she may draw and find herself drawn to men whose energy-charge differs markedly from hers.

[15] Joseph T. Shipley, *Dictionary of Word Origins* (New York: The Philosophical Library, 1945), 100.

[16] Glynnis Chantrell, ed., *The Oxford Dictionary of Word Histories* (Oxford: Oxford University Press, 2002), 126.

Uranus, the Sun serves as a complement to that most iconoclastic of planets. It suggests the radiant, embodied, creative potential of a person's insight, the radiant energy of the creative idea.

The Sun seems closely related to the first and last of the four animus-manifestations mentioned by Emma Jung: power and meaning. Certainly the astronomical sun empowers the earth altogether, and though Mars (see below) seems a more apt symbol for "directed power,"[17] the Sun gives power to all of the other planets to direct as they will. Further, though Uranus seems an apt symbol for *ideas*, the Sun, through its connection to basic radiant energy, has a pervasive connection with *meaning*. We can see this quite readily in the ways the different signs find meaning, for what gives meaning to a Libra may not have much importance for a Cancer, and vice-versa. Thus meaning arises not simply through verbal formulations or through suddenly-arising ideas, but also through the ongoing energetic interaction between each person and the world. After all, meaning doesn't come into existence on its own; each person brings it into existence—and in a unique way. Through its connection to this ongoing energetic creation of meaning, the Sun has a close connection to the animus.

Women (and Men) and Mars

Numerous social historians have told us that the ideal woman of centuries past would certainly not raise her voice, remonstrate, ridicule, become randy, act robust, or in any way demonstrate any but the most subservient of temperaments. Such a woman would not express her own desires; even if she knew quite well that she had them, she would observe propriety and keep the desires to herself. We have been told that people expected her to identify with her male partner and his prowess, and if she had prowess of her own, she generally did well not to demonstrate it, as the witches of New England certainly discovered. For a woman to identify with her own actions instead of her husband's brought suspicion onto her, and though in the American fable, Polly Ann drove steel like a man, she was clearly the exception to the rule. Perhaps she would have had more difficulties if she had written or spoken independently; perhaps, too, her steel-driving abilities scared off more than one person thinking of challenging her when she picked up her hammer! Notably, in the song, she didn't drive steel like a man until John Henry, clearly an animus figure, had died. This fact may suggest that even Polly Ann had animus projections that she had a hard time recollecting until her husband, apparently a fine hook for those projections, had laid down his hammer and died beside the steam drill.[18]

Clearly, some men expected women to at least partly resemble shrinking violets and never to turn purple with rage; and many men with no love or lust for shrinking violets still want women to have some obeisance as regards men. But just as clearly, contemporary society has found more to fear from, and has become more concerned about, men's Mars-energy than women's: consider the prevalence of rape, serial or mass murder, assault, and ongoing aggression in our world—most

---

[17] Emma Jung, 3.
[18] These assumptions about women and their role played a major role in life of Alice B. Sheldon, who wrote under the penname James T. Tiptree, Jr. See the discussion at the end of this chapter.

of it coming from men. So it seems that just as women now get more permission to manifest Mars in the world (e.g. notice how many women have entered professions that require the expression of the Mars-energy), so men apparently get *less,* at least outside of sanctioned activities like sports, military service, and politics. If we inquire into the reasons for this situation, we will find many people saying that men do more harm with their Mars energy than women do with theirs.

We hear many people say, quite simply, "Men are more aggressive than women," and one could cite some impressive evidence in support of that claim: armies generally consist primarily of men, the leadership of such armies almost entirely so; until recently, all "fighting sports" invited men and excluded women; many will say that little boys fight amongst themselves, at least physically, a lot more than little girls do; and if you think of someone coming to your rescue, you'll probably think of that someone as male rather than female. Men "are explosive," "are dangerous," and so forth. But Mars doesn't symbolize aggression only; as the ruler of Aries, he also symbolizes focused action and self-assertion generally. He symbolizes the kind of action with which a person has a high degree of identification. Further, as the exalted ruler of Capricorn, he has a particular affinity for activities with practical ends or taking place within clear social structures, as within teams or military organizations. Thus Mars has a close connection not only to the animus' manifestation through "directed action," but also to its manifestation through "the deed"[19] (a term closely connected to Saturn as well: see chapter VII).

This facet of the anima seems not so closely connected with instinct, so we see many women who have brought it effectively into action. Emma Jung writes:

> …there are also women in whom this aspect [the stage of power and deed] is already harmoniously coordinated with the feminine principle and lending it effective aid. These are the active, energetic, brave, and forceful women. But also there are those in whom the integration has failed, in whom masculine behavior has overrun and suppressed the feminine principle. These are the over-energetic, ruthless, brutal, men-women, the Xantippes who are not only active but aggressive. In many women, this primitive masculinity is also expressed in their erotic life…On the whole, however, it can be assumed that the more primitive forms of masculinity have already been assimilated by women. Generally speaking, they have long ago found their applications in the feminine way of life, and there have long been women whose strength of will, purposefulness, activity, and energy serve as helpful forces in their otherwise quite feminine lives.[20]

These remarks speak to what I said above: that women project Mars much less often than they project Uranus.

Astrologers know Mars as the "lesser malefic," the second word suggesting that the expression of this energy often involves danger. At the same time, Mars symbolizes an energy vital to life, the energy that pushes back against the world, not just against particular enemies, but against the

---
[19] See Emma Jung, 3
[20] Emma Jung, 4.

pressure of the atmosphere, understood literally and figuratively. Thus Mars has much to do with integrity, for without it, each of us would wilt under pressure from the world and thus fail to contribute anything worthwhile.

All of us express Mars all the time as we automatically push back against the intense atmospheric or social energy of the world around us. Nevertheless, it seems that millions of women still project some Martian elements onto men. Though biology and culture probably both participate, and though we might spend a long time trying understand the influenced of either, it seems that the projection of Mars involves at least as many social factors as biological ones. As the lesser malefic, Mars certainly causes a host of problems currently besetting our society; the evidence appears around us almost every day: jails full of men who have acted violently toward others, particularly toward women or toward the archetypally feminine (the earth, the family, the sub-lunar realm as a whole, the feelings); bureaucratic aggression that destroys the environment; organized aggression that drives millions from their homes; and so on.

Though that evidence may suggest that "men are the problem," or that male aggression is, we must look more deeply to get at the root of the problem. Quite possibly many of these problems involve an un-integrated Mars in both men *and* women: many men act out the Mars and many women find the Mars-energy "coming at them" via projection. It seems that, other things being equal, women still project their Mars-energy onto men more readily than men do onto women,[21] but if what we have said above in the football analogy about energy transfer has merit, both men *and* women will have to take some responsibility for the situation. Each person can do so by owning the Mars energy, or trying to, so that he or she doesn't project it into an environment that seems to have more than enough un-integrated aggression and narrow self-identification.

If you wager that a woman will project her Mars more than the man will, you'll probably win your bet more often than not, though you shouldn't see that bet as a sure thing. Though women still project Mars onto men, they apparently don't do so nearly as often or as predictably as they did a hundred years ago. Women often show their anger quite as readily as men do these days, and as for rage, women often find themselves with more permission than men to show it, male rage having garnered for itself a rather bad reputation, both domestically and internationally. In domestic situations, many women express Mars quite freely, perhaps more freely than men do. The social climate has shifted, and along with it the permissions, often unstated or unacknowledged, given to men and women.

Further, we now see women in the military, women as Secretaries of State[22] who further United States' international aggression, women in various sports (even boxing), and women in Congress

---

[21] Of course, "other things" are often not equal. If the man has Mars in the twelfth house and Libra rising, for example, he may gravitate toward partners he experiences as aggressive and self-focused (Libra rising equals Aries on the Descendant; the descendant symbolizes that which a person projects onto others). Anyone strongly Libran will probably have difficulty with Mars, as will many Cancerian men. The difficulty increases if the man's Mars has challenging aspects or a difficult house position.

[22] Consider Madeline Albright, Condoleezza Rice, and Hillary Clinton: hardly wilting violets. Many will see one or more

forcefully stating their views. Historically, people have witnessed women's aggression primarily as it arises in various defensive postures: a woman would defend her children or her home; in many such instances, we will interpret the woman's actions as a way of defending lunar priorities. It seems, though, that women now have more permission to utilize Mars for non-lunar priorities as well. Often these priorities have to do with solar drives, for a woman might act assertively in order to free some space for creative self-expression or the pursuit of a particular solar vision, all of this despite social pressure to act differently.

Though particular cultural or personal factors in a man's background may encourage him to see anger as unacceptable,[23] men still have a physiology that suits them for going out into whatever version of the hunt they can find. Women still go through a monthly menstrual cycle, which periodically makes that kind of vigorous action difficult; and when infant children enter the picture, many women find themselves more in demand in the home than on hunts, metaphorical or otherwise. In the sexual act, men often act more centrifugally, going out from a center, while women often act more centripetally (taking energy in).

We find a wonderful metaphorical description of the centrifugal nature of the masculine and the centripetal energy of the feminine in Frank Waters' description of the Pueblo Indian Deer Dance in *The Man Who Killed the Deer*. In this dance, the males (dressed as animals) attempt, again and again, to get away, to escape from "that inexorable power which held unbroken the circle of sobbing, defiant animals." Waters makes the gender symbolism clear as he describes the male animals' reaction to the Deer Mother:

> They gave way before her as the male ever gives way to the female imperative. They tried to break free of the circle only to be irresistibly pulled back as man in his wild lunges for freedom is ever drawn back by the perpetual, feminine blood-power from which he can never quite break free. And all the time they uttered their strange, low cries, the deep, universal male horror at their submission. Out of them it welled in shuddering sobs of disgust, of loathing and despair, and still they answered the call. On all fours, as the undomesticated, untamed, archaic, wild forces they represented, impelled

---

of these figures as almost pathological in her aggression. Of course, we might see these women as standing up for lunar priorities, as they perhaps see themselves as defending something Cancerian: the United States, with Sun, Mercury, Venus, and Jupiter in Cancer. (See chapter X.)

[23]It seems to me that men who reached maturity during the '60s deny their own Mars-energy rather often. Many of these men witnessed Vietnam and all sorts of U.S. government aggression. Their fathers had fought in World War II, and many of those fathers, and the sons who fought in Vietnam, seem to have suffered from some sort of post-traumatic stress disorder. By and large, men growing up in the 60's don't seem to have a very positive view of Mars, the sexual revolution notwithstanding. Furthermore, many of them have Neptune in Libra, so they may idealize harmony. Those with Neptune in Libra on an angle or in aspect to important natal planets find themselves particularly prone to act harmoniously even when disruption seems required. Perhaps not coincidentally, this "flower child generation" has produced or helped to elect leaders who have markedly increased United States aggression throughout the world.

to follow her in obedience to that spiritual cosmic principle which must exist to preserve and perpetuate even their resentment.[24]

It seems that the "feminine blood power" has a hold on all of us, for each of us will die; we will all experience the limits of earth and the flesh, no matter what ideas we have or how we assert ourselves. The Pueblo Indians apparently saw self-assertion, an archetypally male energy found in both men and women, as a natural part of a larger pattern, as part of the fabric of the cosmos, yet an energy best held within the circle of human society and empathy by what Waters calls "the female imperative." By contrast, male aggression has earned itself a bad name in contemporary times, at times seeming to have escaped that circle to run amok in all sorts of ways, perhaps because the female imperative has weakened, or at least remained in the background because of a *male* imperative that goes largely unquestioned on the level of national and international politics.[25] Perhaps as a result of this bad name, many men find themselves less willing to own up to or express their own aggression or anger; however, if we don't "own" the Mars energy, we help to ensure that will appear more problematically via projection.

As the ballyhooed pig-headedness of men gets a lot of press, men may find themselves less willing to own up to or accept their own blindness, a blindness often indicated in the astrology chart by Mars, whose position will sometimes tell us where a person will act like a racehorse wearing blinders, where a person will plunge forward and look neither to the right nor to the left. Male aggression has gotten its bad name largely because it has assaulted that which participates in the feminine imperative: assaulted women themselves, or assaulted homes or settled countries, or assaulted the earth itself. Thus if a woman feels understandable anger at having been abused, she may feel that her anger, aggression, and self-identification are fully called for, acceptable, even necessary and laudable; she may find, in such circumstances and somewhat paradoxically, that she can free her Mars while the man loses a healthy connection to his. If the Pueblo people have it right, the male energy loses its way when it escapes—or, perhaps, convinces itself that it has escaped—from the female imperative.

It often seems that women today will own up to their Mars more readily than will men;[26] in daily interactions, many women seem as Mars-like as do men in their emotional statements. On the other hand, I still see as many women drawn to men who somehow exemplify the qualities of their Mars as women drawn to men who exemplify their solar qualities. Most typically, we still see women drawn to men whose Mars energy activates Venus or Moon, so that he plays the Mars role and she the Lunar or Venusian one, at least in sexual situations, and we probably shouldn't see the situation as problematic as long as the woman finds a ready outlet for Mars.

---

[24] Frank Waters, *The Man Who Killed the Deer* (New York: Washington Square Press, 1942), page 174.
[25] Of course, the rising threat of climate change seems to suggest that the feminine imperative will have its say at last, reminding us all of its power, insisting on obedience to the "spiritual cosmic principle" Waters mentions.
[26] My data-base here consists mostly of people in the so-called educated classes. We might see a different picture in different social classes or different countries.

Of course, some projections of Mars lead to clearly unfortunate consequences. We find, in many of these cases, the expected horoscope factors: Mars with difficult aspects; Mars in the seventh or twelfth or (though less obviously) ruling those houses; sometimes Mars in a sign that does not encourage straightforward self-expression.[27] For example, if a woman has Mars in hard aspect to Saturn and Pluto, the projected energy may arise through assault and rape more often than it arises through disciplined and transformative action, at least early in life or until the woman develops a healthy connection to her Mars-Saturn or Mars-Pluto potentials. Until she does that, she will often experience the entire aspect as a projection, often finding for a hook someone who feels powerless and thus seeks power over others. In such cases, Mars-Saturn will arise more often through harsh authority figures than through healthy ambition, while Mars-Pluto will arise less often through the woman's powerful action and more often through obscurely powerful men who, paradoxically, themselves feel powerless and thus want power over others.[28] Mars in or ruling the uncongenial (at least for Mars) seventh will often arise initially through angry or aggressive partners instead of through the woman's own assertiveness in partnership; Mars in or ruling the twelfth will often arise through men who are uncertain about their sexuality or their capacity for self-assertion, instead of through the woman's work for the defeated. As always, though, the woman can intervene in these patterns, initially by looking at psychological habit patterns.

Whether the projection of Mars represents biological factors or cultural ones, the process begins with the woman dishonoring or failing to accept her own drive toward self-identification or identified action, her ability to defend herself, her own integrity-of-action; her own assertiveness, aggression, desire, or focus; her drive for survival or her instinct for self-preservation. When a woman projects Mars onto a man, the man will often, even usually, manifest the undesirable side of some or many of these traits. He may be inappropriately aggressive; he may think only of his old war-stories; he may hit his children; he may lift weights all day and walk around in some sort of blind self-adoration; he may always react as if his survival or his male dignity has been offended. Depending on aspects to the woman's Mars, the man may seem passive-aggressive (often signified by Mars-Neptune), or he may assert himself through manipulation and control with an edge of violence in it (Mars-Pluto), or he may simply spend all of his time trying to "get ahead" (Mars-Saturn).

In such cases, the woman must begin not by deciding what the man "is," but by honoring her own Mars-energy. She will generally accomplish this best, at least initially, through some sort of action instead of with purely psychological exercises. That is, rather than simply sitting at home and engaging in some sort of inner work to re-establish contact with an inner warrior, the woman

---

[27] We should not see difficult positions as malefic, for they encourage valuable kinds of human development. However, they don't encourage the planet to express itself blindly, and Mars loves to do precisely that. For example, Mars in Libra must assert itself not blindly or in self defense or in order to demonstrate any kind of prowess, but within social situations and with an eye toward maintaining some degree of harmony.

[28] Mars-Uranus will arise more often through willful men who accept no limitations on their freedom than through the woman's own iconoclasm; Mars-Neptune will probably arise at least as often through dissipated men or men who seem in some sense victimized by their own inspirations as through compassionate action.

would do well to do something Martian, even if that means only getting angry when anger seems appropriate, working out regularly if she has the inclination, or finding find ways to assert herself at work and elsewhere. She needs to find out what she wants and to act in order to get it; if she approaches the matter this way, she will move toward the root of the problem. Depending on aspects to Mars, she may take up yoga, or she may want to be assertive as part of an effort to help others (Mars-Neptune),[29] as a way or giving new life to moribund situations (Mars-Pluto), in work connected with politics or new technologies (Mars-Uranus), or in simple ambition, administration, or authority (Mars-Saturn). Though she should accompany any of these with psychological work, the woman will often do well to start with action, for Mars has much to do with the muscle system and the assertive will. But more fundamentally, Mars connects her to how and on behalf of what she wishes to assert herself (the muscle system serving as the means to accomplish this).

We should remember, too, that some of these projections have long since worked themselves into the prevailing cultural framework. Men have gone out on the hunt; men have protected; men strike forth and take on the world; men go off to work while the woman stays home. As noted earlier, though some of these cultural patterns may (or may not) reflect biological factors, we shouldn't conclude that Mars belongs to men. That women behave differently than men doesn't mean they can't or shouldn't act through Mars. The differences make it all the more imperative that they do so.

Mars has much to do with what a person identifies with. We generally identify, to some extent, with the body; but we also can identify with action, with projects, with our efforts to make a mark in the world. Mars' exaltation in Capricorn suggests that we will often identify with our social roles. (We see this identification reflected in our language: a person will say, "I *am* a lawyer," or "I *am* a mother.") Thus women often re-collect the projection of Mars by identifying with their own vocational efforts instead of the vocational efforts of male partners. So though the process of re-collection must involve in-depth *acceptance* of the Mars energy within the psyche, it seems that it benefits from an ongoing *expression* of the Mars energy in the extensional world.

Men and Venus

When men project Venus onto women, the projection generally seems less virulent, pervasive, and opaque than does their projection of the Moon. Still, I have seen so many cases of transits to a man's Venus arising through the actions of the woman with whom he has an intimate connection, and so many men who describe their intimate partners in terms reflecting their own Venus-placements (Venus' sign, house, and aspects), that I tend to think men project Venus onto their

---

[29]Some will argue that yoga has more affinities with Neptune than with Mars. I think, though, that most activities involve many different planetary energies depending on the person's attitude toward that activity. Yoga reflects Mars because yoga uses muscles and deals with the physical vessel; it reflects Neptune when a person emphasizes the spiritual component, Pluto when a person emphasizes the transformative component, Uranus if the activity involves (for that person) an iconoclastic statement or seems like a break with the past (as seemed true for many who took up yoga in the sixties, when yoga, despite its ancient roots in India, appeared as part of the "new age movement" in this part of the world), Saturn if one emphasizes discipline or takes up yoga because of ambition.

lovers or wives rather often.[30] For example, if transiting Uranus forms a challenging aspect to a man's Venus, a woman in a man's life may demand more freedom, or the man may feel drawn to "freer" women, though perhaps irresponsible ones as well. If natal Venus and natal Uranus form a challenging aspect with each other, a man influenced by Uranus will often feel drawn toward such women, even if they prove unfaithful—or perhaps *because*, or *only if* they prove so, though the man may have mixed feelings about the "unfaithfulness," and though, as always, we should take the whole horoscope into consideration in any analysis. In general, if we look at a man's Venus, including its sign and aspects, we will often find much information about the women to whom he feels attraction, about how those women approach relationship and self-value, *and* about how he describes those women. Sometimes we will not see very much of a man's Venus placement in his values or behavior, at least early in life, for men seem to grow into their Venus placements just as they do with their lunar ones—and just as women do with their animus-related placements. We should remember, though, that this information tells us, first and foremost, about how the man *experiences* the woman, not necessarily about "the woman herself"; Venus tells us much about the man's animus, and thus about something within.

When projected, Venus arises through the underlying and unexamined values that imbue the man's perception, particularly his perception of women. The man will most readily perceive, among all the qualities in the women to whom he feels drawn, from whom he feels he may choose, or whom he feels he must evaluate, those qualities that reflect his natal Venus and its aspects, or that reflect his natal Moon. For example, if he has Venus in Gemini, he will not only feel attracted to Gemininian or Mercurial women and value Gemini or Mercurial traits and tendencies, but will also perceive in women Gemini traits more readily than he will perceive other traits. He may also feel indifferent, at least sexually, to women who do *not* seem to him to have these qualities. The same principles apply with the other Venus placements.

We will find many exceptions, of course. If a man has his Venus in Libra and most other planetary placements in air or fire, he may feel drawn to earthy or watery women (women with many planets in earth and/or water signs), for opposites, in elements as in genders, often seem to attract, sometimes apparently irresistibly. In such a case, he might feel more strongly attracted to women who seem very different from what his Venus placement would suggest than to women who seem to reflect that placement. However, we would probably want to distinguish between what one wants and what one purportedly needs,[31] between what one feels drawn to and what brings more energetic fulfillment. We may often feel drawn to those whose energy differs markedly from our

---

[30]Sometimes, though, a man will project his Moon onto his wife, seeing her as a homemaker, and seek his Venus through other women. This tension within the man's anima seems to reflect the fact that Venus and the Moon rules signs, Libra and Cancer respectively, that square each other. That the Moon has her exaltation in Venus' other rulership (Taurus) suggests harmony in combination with the tension. How a person experiences this tension obviously depends on factors from the individual horoscope.

[31]Thanks to a certain Robert Zimmerman for the line. It comes from "Stuck Inside of Mobile with the Memphis Blues Again" (from *Blonde On Blonde*) and reads, in full, "Your debutante just knows what you want, but I know what you *need*."

own, but we may have difficulty settling with one of those people, particularly if the element-differences pervade the synastry.

Similarly, a man with an afflicted Venus may have difficulties with women who resonate with that Venus. This doesn't necessarily mean that that he won't feel an attraction, for often (and, sometimes it seems, more often than not) such a man will feel an extremely strong attraction to such a women, particularly if he has *close* afflictive aspects. Also, sometimes the man will feel drawn not to the Venus energy itself, but to the planet afflicting that Venus: a man with a Venus-Neptune square may feel drawn to Piscean women or to women with Neptune strongly placed. Though it would seem logical that a man would think he discerns something wrong or amiss in a woman reflecting his afflicted aspect, this sense of wrongness doesn't generally arise until after the relationship has progressed a bit. Then we often find the man devaluing the previously valued object (for in some sense he will often make her into an object), so the situation has the marks that Jung describes (in a passage quoted earlier) as running back over bridges in order to separate oneself from the previously valued person—one to whom one has developed an attachment via one's projections.

Obviously enough, that a man feels drawn to women who stimulate his Venus does not mean that the man will experience contentment as a result. A man with Venus in Cancer may feel drawn to Cancerian women even if he often experiences them as overly clingy, overly self-protective, overly concerned with security—and not enough concerned with adventure, intellectual or otherwise; this will occur particularly if he has rejected those personal capacities symbolized by Venus in Cancer. He may find this clinginess particularly irksome if he has a strongly placed Uranus, particularly one aspecting his natal Venus, but the most important problems arise if the man sacrifices his own capacities by projecting them onto a woman—if, in other words, the man has negativized his own Venus. For a man with Venus in Cancer, these capacities will have a Cancerian imperative and may emerge (problematically) as clinginess; a man with Venus in Aries, he may find himself with women who cannot or will not, as he sees the matter, settle themselves into grounded patterns of social contribution; a man with Venus in Libra may find himself with women always doubting their own beauty or attractiveness.

As with projections involving the Moon, planetary aspects to the projected planet play an important role in the interpretation. If a man's Venus squares his Saturn, he will tend to perceive the woman onto whom he projects his Venus as cold, demanding, and in search of long-term commitment to the exclusion of or in place of emotional closeness, women whom he sees as preferring the trappings of closeness to real closeness. We might find something similar for a man with Venus in Capricorn. At the same time, he will actually value Venus-Saturn qualities in women.[32] For example, he may value tradition or have rather traditional values but not want to acknowledge this, forcing (so to speak) these value to arise through the woman. He may value women who success-

---

[32]This may sound odd. Why should a man value what he perceives to be coldness in a woman? This occurs because the alleged coldness remains tied to something within the man himself. The difficulties he encounters arise, it seems, because of the man's difficulties with his own capacities.

fully take their place in society, though if he has devalued the Venus-Saturn energy, he may have difficulty making connections with such women.[33] The house-placement will also play a role: if we find a Venus-Saturn conjunction in the tenth, for example, the man may find himself attracted to women who seem ambitious or much concerned with career; if we find Venus in Capricorn in the twelfth, he might be drawn to women who seem ambitious yet seem to need help in some way.

When a man does not acknowledge his need or desire for relationship, he will generally project Venus onto a woman who seems to desire that relationship overmuch, possibly to the detriment of her own creative self-expression. The man may play the role of creator (Sun) while the woman plays the role of "the woman who wants more attention" (reflecting Venus, a planet connected with personal magnetism and often concerned with magnetizing attention), the man apparently having more concern with various creative ventures. Again, we see an exchange of energy: in giving to the woman his own Venusian energy, the man asks her to act in a doubly-Venusian way; and the woman gives to the man her Solar or Martian energy, so that the man sees himself as wanting to live a creative and vital life. If, as we often see, the woman projects her Uranus *and* Sun onto the man even as he projects his Venus and Moon onto the woman, the man will seem possessed by his drive for independent creativity while she seems possessed by her desire for relationship, commitment, and seduction.

As the man begins to honor his own Venus and thus to withdraw the projection, he will, instead of insisting that the woman carry his Venus-potential, allow her more space to undertake self-development within relationship. At the same time, he encourages himself to explore his desire and need for relationship and his own aesthetic capacities. The qualities of a projected Venus have some similarity to qualities of a projected Moon, and whether or to what degree they give an accurate description of the woman involved will depend on many factors in both the man and the woman. To the man, an unintegrated Venus manifests through a woman whom he takes as overly concerned with her own Venusian qualities: much concerned with appearance to the detriment of other personality factors, obsessively (as he sees it) concerned with form and aesthetic order, constantly seductive, concerned with relationship or the trappings of it, instead of with her own (or the man's) personal development within that relationship. He may see her as one who finds creativity threatening; and, quite likely, she will see *him* as one who finds relationship claustrophobic. Because these projections affect the phenomenal world, a woman who resonates with them will feel drawn into the man's orbit, where she will manifest these tendencies more and more.

The tendencies represent, first and foremost, the man's devaluing of his own Venus; only secondarily should we take them as characteristics of the woman. If we take *do* them as characteristics of the woman, we would want to know how she acts when away from the man; we would ask whether her own self-creative drives kick in when she no longer carries the man's projection (or, as in our analogy above, to carry the man's Venus-football). Obviously enough, if the woman at the

---

[33]This statement may apply to Venus in a Saturn-ruled sign (Capricorn, Libra) if natal Saturn has difficulties in the natal horoscope.

same time projects her Uranus and Sun onto the man, the man will gravitate toward independent, self-actualizing activities while the woman gravitates toward supportive and seductive ones. The woman will suffer in evident ways as she loses track of the healthy *logos* that she projects onto the man (who appears to her as project-oriented); the man suffers less evidently as he loses track of the healthy *eros* that he projects onto the woman (who appears to him as concerned only with "closeness").[34]

What, then, must the man cultivate or acknowledge? He must cultivate his own aesthetic, surely, and his own capacity for artistry altogether. He must acknowledge his need for relationship, partnership, intimacy; he must acknowledge and cultivate some sense of his own beauty and charm, his capacity to magnetize energy and people. Charm? Of course, Venus symbolizes more than charm: though a person might use charm to magnetize others, or though he might magnetize charming people, he might also develop a firm sense of inner value and thereby magnetize others, and he might then magnetize people with a similar sense of inner value. Though Venus symbolizes marriage or "love," she symbolizes much else besides, so much so that we should probably see "marriage" and "love" as derivative connections. As others have pointed, out, the mythology of Venus has as much to do with harlotry as with marriage, as much to do with independence as with the dependent position a woman's relationship seems to require in many cultures. Though Venus rules Libra and Taurus, and though both of these signs may desire stability in relationships, Venus herself doesn't always demand this from her relationships. Certainly she doesn't do so as readily as does the Moon, and she doesn't necessarily see stability as a necessary sanction *for* relationship. Though we say that love and marriage "go together like a horse and carriage," we might often find that Venus, planet of love, wants to ride bareback and leave care of the carriage to others.[35]

Marriage has at least as much to do with the Moon and Saturn as with Venus, a planet connected with magnetism, with the drawing together of different energies because of mutual valuation, not primarily because of rules, regulations, and responsibilities. In other words, Venus has to do with the drawing-together itself, not with the societal regulations about what "should" happen once people find themselves drawn! Though Saturn has his exaltation in Venus' sign, Venus does not have her exaltation in Saturn's. The former suggests that our human sense of order has much to do with social values and that the sense of order or durability expresses itself well through commitments between equals. The latter suggests that love has no particular connection to duration, and Venus' exaltation in Pisces suggests that her concerns go far beyond those connected with social order. Saturn's exaltation in Libra suggests that our sense of order finds exaltation through partnership; that Venus does not have her exaltation in Capricorn suggests that she doesn't find exaltation in order and hierarchy (such as the hierarchy sanctioned in many marriages); Venus' exaltation in

---

[34]Some of this may reflect or result from social divisions that occurred millennia ago, when human beings began to settle in villages and to work the land. Women, freed from taking part in the hunt, developed into the keepers of the hearth and home. Though eventually a split developed between the farmers and the villagers, within village culture itself, the functions of women diverged increasingly from those of men.

[35]Though both Libra and Taurus will sometimes seek stability in relationship, they do so for different reasons. Libra often seeks stability in relationship in order to find balance within the status quo (Saturn's exaltation).

Pisces suggests that love finds fulfillment in boundarilessness and through a connection to wider or deeper truths. The man who projects his Venus must re-collect his sense of love, of eros, of the desire for what Robert Hand once called "non-coercive bonding."

That Venus has her exaltation in Pisces suggests that love truly knows no bounds. Just as a king may rule a nation, but the nation does not rule the king, so love may rule over a marriage without having the marriage rule over or love. That Venus is exalted in Pisces suggests that value-based connections or bonds have unlimited potential or universality, that love flourishes most when operating without socially sanctioned limits, and that individual love and magnetism (Venus) has a close connection to permeability and compassion. The various sign positions of Venus tell us what sorts of prejudices or imposed limitations a person sets on Venus, often unconsciously; men will often project these limitations onto their female partners. Quite commonly during relationship difficulties, a man's evaluation of his partner will contain at least some of the more problematic elements symbolized in his own natal Venus placement.

Consider a man who has Venus in Cancer. He will probably see value, relationship, and aesthetic through the lens provided by Cancer. This position often indicates confusion between lunar and Venusian energies, and the position of the man's Moon will influence Venus (which it disposits). If that Moon squares Saturn, the man may well find himself in relationship with women he finds judgmental or who seem to him concerned more with form than with what he sees as heart, all combined with what he sees as her emphasis on security. Venus in Cancer may feel that love must be tied to or must arise in dependence on emotional security. If a man with Venus in Cancer projects this energy onto women, he will not only seek women who seem to him to link love and dependency, but will also unconsciously select from (and notice *in*!) the woman's behavior or habitual tendencies those elements that move in that direction. He will generally think that the problem lies outside of himself. The Saturn aspect suggests that he will find himself drawn to women whom he sees as emotionally restricted once they have drawn him into his orbit, women he sees as in need of care and nurturing and perhaps unable to give much in return. These women will not necessarily or usually have Venus in Cancer; they may have Cancer rising, possibly afflicted, or one of the lights in Cancer, again possibly afflicted, or some other challenge involving the Venus and Saturn complexes of symbols.[36]

As Jung would say, these women will probably serve as appropriate "hooks" for the man's Venus in Cancer, along with its aspects. Such women will then appear in a Cancerian light—but a troubled Cancerian light; and in each case the man will think that the trouble comes from the woman, not from him. All of this, then, to the extent that the man denies the challenges associated with his Venus. He will have difficulty seeing that his own love-energy has gotten tied up, probably in early

---

[36]The Venus complex of symbols includes Venus, Libra, Taurus, the second house, and the seventh house. It may also include Pisces (Venus' exaltation). The Saturn complex surely includes Saturn, Capricorn, and the tenth house; it may also include Aquarius and the eleventh (which Saturn rules in the traditional system). It may also include Libra, the sign of Saturn's exaltation, particularly if the man has a Venus-Saturn aspect or some other Venus-Saturn connection (e.g. mutual reception).

childhood, with security issues; he may not see, or not see clearly, that he has linked his own eroticism with ideas about home, security, faithfulness, and emotional support. And all of this seems to come *at* him from women, not from his own heart or experience. If the man projects this energy onto the woman, she will find herself acting, and perhaps thinking or assuming, in ways shaped by the man's unconscious, unacknowledged, and unexamined assumptions. Or, we might say, she will feel a hard-to-pin-down tendency to conform to the man's often-unconscious expectations, acting out some qualities of the man's anima, where we find, as Jung says, the man's *eros*. Again, this will occur to the extent that the man has not acknowledged or examined that eros—has not recognized and integrated a change of attitude toward the feminine.[37]

A man with Venus in Gemini will be drawn toward women who manifest that energy. For him, the erotic, the beautiful, and the magnetic will seem ineluctably connected with movement, change, ideas, and ongoing communication. If he projects this energy onto a woman, he has probably to some extent negativized it within himself, so the energy will emerge in a negativized form in the woman: to him, she will often appear flighty, irresponsible, dilettantish, unable to stay still, and concerned only with play (perhaps flirtation, for example, and not only with him) that he may judge as irresponsible – and yet the man will find her fascinating. She probably has within her some "hook" upon which the man hangs his projection.[38]

A man's biology may[39] predispose him to reject, and therefore project, the Moon, but the projection of Venus seems to have much to do with social custom, though not necessarily to the exclusion of biological factors. We might find it curious that in Western culture women have been expected to *appear* beautiful, whereas men have been expected to *express* the beautiful or create works of art that appear beautiful. Hence, throughout our history, the male artist paints the female model or sculpts the female figure; the male poet writes of the beauty of nature or of his love, often invoking the (female) muse. Yet in other cultures, we see men adorning themselves for dance and posturing, and in birds we often see that the male's feathers outshine the female's (often for survival-related

---

[37] See Emma Jung, 87. As always in such matters, that we must take all horoscope factors into account. A man with his Sun in Leo and Venus in Cancer will probably tend to reject Venus more summarily than will someone with, say, the Sun in Taurus. The United States has Venus in Cancer, and so we see a strong emphasis on "family values," even though the U.S. seems prone to attack countries that really promote family values, perhaps through adherence to tradition. (Native Americans come to mind, here, as do the Vietnamese people.) It seems that no candidate can get elected if he doesn't speak of these values. This should come as no surprise, as Venus conjoins Jupiter in Cancer, joining the Sun and Mercury there. That Venus and Jupiter rule the two most self-assertive angles (the ascendant and midheaven) points to the public display associated with these two planets. However, because Venus and Cancer often present such divergent demands, we can expect tension from this national assumption, a tension perhaps evident in the emphases we find in our advertising and in the strength of the pornography industry. See chapter X.

[38] We should distinguish, here, between the draw toward Gemini indicated when a man has his Venus in Gemini, and the draw toward Gemini or other earth signs when a man's horoscope has few air placements. Quite commonly, we feel drawn toward that which we do not possess—at least in our horoscopes. Quite commonly, too, we feel drawn to that which we do possess, but in a contra-sexual form (i.e. as either anima or animus, symbolized at least partly by the gendered placements in the horoscope).

[39] As always, "may" also means "may not." We should let the jury remain out on the dictates of biology.

reasons). We shouldn't assume that our cultural trappings reflect biological imperatives.

Venus' glyph suggests completeness (the circle) rising out of the cross of matter, from the world of duality. By dealing with or giving oneself to the world of duality, one finds completeness. Thus Venus has much to do with finding wholeness through partnership, through relationship, and through sexuality—through any activity that emphasizes polarities. Venus magnetizes divergent energies, energies that complete each other or bring wholeness (the circle) in a world characterized by limitation (the cross of matter). Venus has a close connection to the world of earth and carnality; her path begins in this world of opposed complements. Venus seeks balance, and she finds it in the world of relative truth, of relationship. She has less to do with ultimate or absolute values than with relative ones, but she opens the door *to* absolute values, as suggested by her exaltation in Pisces. Marie von Franz writes,

> According to Jung, the anima is the projection-creating factor par excellence: she weaves the hidden pattern of a man's fate but she also builds a bridge to an experience of God within his own psyche.[40]

The anima reminds us to relate directly with duality and by doing that to find a wholeness that seems to give meaning and value to one's life, arising naturally from experience instead of as something granted from above. Venus brings a man out of the world of conceptions and into the life lived in the flesh and feelings.

Venus seeks to create wholeness out of duality. If marriage furthers this purpose, Venus encourages marriage; if it does not, expect her to look elsewhere. She has no major objection to security except when that security runs counter to the wholeness that she seeks above all and that motivates her famous magnetism. Some will say that Venus "needs" relationship, but we would do better to say that Venus creates an atmosphere that leads to or engenders relationship, an atmosphere that magnetizes potentially complementary energies and thus makes relationship arise naturally. Also, within relationship, she finds integral self-value, the wholeness that arises from duality. Though Venus wants to create wholeness out of duality, she chooses various means to achieve her goal.[41]

We know, of course, that Libra, one of Venus' dignities, emphasizes social structure, the status quo, "socially accepted standard weight,"[42] and a general drive to be accepted in a social context. We know, too, that Taurus, Venus' other dignity, emphasizes stability, emotional security, and rootedness—but also a longing for heaven that seems another manifestation of Venus' longing to find wholeness by working with magnetic polarities (genders, the earth's poles, the magnetic currents within the planet). Both Libra and Taurus get their desire for stability through their exalted rulers: Libra gets a desire for stability and her connection to the status quo largely from Saturn, and Taurus gets a desire for emotional security and rootedness largely from the Moon. When we see Venus

---

[40] Von Franz, 127.
[41] Compare this with Mars, whose glyph shows the cross of matter arising from the circle: from a sense of integral wholeness, one strikes forth into the world. In Venus' end, we find Mars beginning—and vice-versa.
[42] Dane Rudhyar, *Astrological Signs: The Pulse of Life* (Boulder: Shambhala, 1978), 85.

working within a stable, emotionally secure, and socially sanctioned marriage, we can detect the underlying polarity of Saturn and the Moon (rulers of Capricorn and Cancer respectively, situated directly across the zodiac from each other). We can ask, in such cases, whether, in order to achieve her purpose (having unity develop from duality), Venus has allowed herself to operate within the demands of Libra. Beauty, magnetization, allure, and sexuality should, it seems, rule over marriage and manifest as its defining characteristics. This kind of situation seems quite different from the kind that prevails in many societies today, where the prevailing hierarchy (Saturn) insists that love manifest only within the limits defined by the social order. Rather than saying that one can have Venus only *in* marriage, we should say that marriage remains viable if—and, it seems, *only* if—Venus remains the dynamic ruler *of* that marriage.[43]

Certainly Venus will sometimes seek or desire stability, but she generally does so as she seeks value and valuation, accepting or seeking stability only insofar as it promotes value—at least optimally! But this value, this wholeness, arises from the world of duality. Venus finds wholeness through interaction, not as a prelude to it. By contrast, Mars' wholeness becomes a stimulus for action that may or may not involve *inter*action. Mars acts out of wholeness, but he moves into a world of duality in which he may consider others as objects, not subjects in their own right; Venus acts out of an acute sense of duality and moves into the world seeking wholeness by considering others as equals, each with his or her own objectivity. Mars symbolizes wholeness extending out into the world of duality through action. Mars feels a sense of identity and from that sense of identity strikes out into the world; Venus lives in the world of duality and from that play creates or develops a sense of wholeness.

Thus in projecting Venus onto women, men may largely forsake the path in which they find wholeness through relationship. If they do so, they will too often ignore the fact that such a path has validity for them, seeing it as the prerogative of women. Women, meanwhile, if they project Mars onto men, forsake the path in which, feeling a preexisting wholeness, they act effectively on the world. When enveloped in these projections, women will find themselves constantly seeking a self via interaction, while the men find themselves interacting from an assumed sense of self. That the two approaches seem to complement each other doesn't mean we should ignore the projections arising from each.

Venus' glyph suggests wholeness as fruition, not as cause. In the world of duality, we form relationships, whether between people or between elements in an artistic creation; Venus symbolizes a profoundly relational energy. When a man projects this energy into the world, he has generally, by disowning it in himself, disowned his capacity to discover wholeness through interaction. He may feel that he can discover this wholeness only in solitude (as in the idea of "finding oneself"), yet to fully "own" his Venus and to withdraw the projections related to it, he will have to see how

---

[43]We should remember, though, that in Alice Bailey's occult system, Venus rules not only Gemini (see below), but also Capricorn. The latter suggests that in terms of spiritual development, we find wholeness through discipline and work endured for a long time—not a social discipline so much as an inner one.

wholeness arises from and within interactions with others and how it cannot take place outside of a social setting. As Ms. Von Franz once said, a man will have a difficult time integrating the animus without a counter-sexual partner; more generally, we can say that without interactions in a world of polarities, our ideas about "self" remain abstractions.

If we look into Venus' archaic connections, we see that the temple harlot promoted and encouraged a man's wholeness not primarily by initiating him into social sanction, but by enabling him to find wholeness through interaction, by serving as a balance for the man's tendency to see his wholeness as a preexisting thing in itself that decides to enter the world of duality. Venus enables the man to see that *self*, at least as a lived reality, arises only within the dualistic world.[44] The harlot promotes this sense of wholeness-through-interaction not because she seeks or needs security as a result of her interactions, but because she knows that the world arises through the interplay of opposites and that opposites arise from one another. (Interestingly, these ancient customs gave these representatives of Venus a clear social place related to the sacred, whereas in our society, women who act in any way similarly find themselves shunned and excluded from social sanction.[45]) Thus Mars symbolizes independence moving into duality; by making this move, he encounters Venus, mistress of duality, and so rediscovers wholeness. Without Venus, Mars gets lost in the conflicts that seem essential to, not to mention endemic *in*, the dualistic world; without Mars, Venus' wholeness lacks expressive power, serving as result instead of as cause. In the end, Venus gives wholeness to the world of duality, to people trapped in that world. Thus in Alice Bailey's occult system, Venus rules Gemini: Venus reminds us that wholeness arises naturally within and inseparable from the duality that seems its opposite.

Moving within the orbit of Saturn, both Venus and Mars tend to get lost in the polarities of our world and to forget to search for wholeness. Though Mars' glyph symbolizes the way people can act in the world even after they've come to a sense of self-completion, too often an emphasized Mars indicates action that has lost its connection to self-awareness and that has become an end in itself: people act for ego-centric reasons, not because of the needs of the self. Sometimes Mars acts like an aggressive version of Venus, as people act aggressively in order to "find themselves." Similarly, though Venus' glyph suggests the way people can find wholeness through interaction, too often an emphasized Venus acts like a misguided Mars: a person initiates and engages in a never-ending search for interaction, forgetting what she seeks.

In American society—and, it seems, in many others—many women somehow end up think-

---

[44] Mars' glyph, the opposite of Venus' suggests this drive: one starts from a sense of unitary completion (the circle) and extends out into the world of duality. A person desires, and then acts centrifugally, moving out from center, out from a sense of unitary completion into the dualistic world. That is, one desires something outside of oneself. Mars moves toward separation and ego-distinction in a polarized world; Venus moves from that polarized world toward wholeness. Thus Venus has been considered benefic and Mars malefic: it has been considered that wholeness is preferable to polarization, connection to separation. The former is generally felt as more pleasurable than the latter. But of course, even this judgment comes from the assumption that polarization is undesirable, a cross that we perhaps must bear.

[45] This may change, of course. I heard recently on the radio that prostitutes in New Zealand have unionized.

ing that they should *reflect* wholeness rather than seek it; they somehow decide or accept that they should reflect and support the partner's wholeness instead of displaying their own. Many social institutions other than our schools teach, even if indirectly, that women should display only those qualities that will attract a man through whom the woman will supposedly become complete even as *she* helps to complete the man. That is, women learn to be Venusian and Lunar in ways beyond the biological. They may end up thinking that in order to "find completion," they must attract something complete from the external world. In Venus' glyph, the woman often plays the role of the cross as the man plays the role of the circle. (Similarly with Mars: the "other" the man seeks is a woman, or something female. Hence a man may desire to conquer the archetypally feminine earth or anything that serves as container: to take over homelands, to subdue either nature or more women, or to find the muse.)

Much social custom encourages women to magnetize energy from outside themselves, to go through the Venusian process (if not to achieve what we might call Venusian fruition). It often seems that men have either concluded or been taught that they must act on the basis of a sense of completion, however little they may actually feel it. Social custom often teaches them to conquer phenomena and to leave the magnetization to women. Thus they tend, often compulsively, to project Venus onto women. This can mean that they reject the process by which relationship leads to completion, to reject the aesthetic, and to reject the need to work with phenomena entirely. Acting this way, they may ignore the path to wholeness in a world seemingly characterized by duality and polarity.

In sum, then, a man's projection of Venus might be said to consist of two parts, one collective and one personal. The collective element consists of those Venusian elements that all men tend to project onto all women: seeing women as objects of desire, as the makers of the aesthetic within any relationship, as the voice of earth (Taurus) and social sanction (Libra). The personal elements appear in the man's Venus sign-placement and aspect-situation. For example, if the man's Venus squares or otherwise connects with his Neptune, he will seek out and feel drawn to Venus-Neptune qualities; he will tend to see in his partners mystical or quasi-mystical leanings, confusion, lack of discrimination, Dionysian wildness, Hollywood ideals, and so forth.[46] If Venus makes a challenging aspect to or has other connections with natal Uranus, he will seek and tend to see Venus-Uranus qualities in his female partners. Analogous statements apply to connections between Venus and Saturn, Mars, Pluto, or any of the other planets.

The road to integration for the man will demand that he integrate Venusian qualities into himself. This means that he must honor those elements of life ruled by Venus as well as those qualities connected to Venus' situation in his horoscope (symbolized by Venus' sign position, house position, and aspects). On a very ordinary level, the man must develop his own aesthetic appreciation, pay some attention to his own appearance, to his own attractiveness, and so forth. But he must also learn, through experience and not merely intellectually, the importance of magnetizing energy generally—and he must learn to find wholeness through and within relationship, interaction, and

---

[46]Some of this will apply to the entire Neptune in (Venus-ruled) Libra generation.

artistry. He must engage in relationship not only as a socially sanctioned process through which he asserts himself, but as a spiritual process through which he might find his hidden face. He should strive to develop his own artistry even if he thinks that artistry comes at the expense of what he feels to be his male drives; and he needs to admit his need for partnership, not only for emotional reasons or because he feels lonely, but in order to walk the Venusian path altogether.

The path to integration for a woman must include an insistence on one's own integrity, not in a moral sense so much as in a behavioral one: feeling an integral sense of self and potency, she will act on the world, not in order to receive sanction from that world or in order to gain position, but simply from an inner conviction. Probably she will not feel unshakeable in this conviction at first (any more than a man will immediately and easily sense how one might find completion through relationship), so the path may involve a good deal of experimentation (Uranus). In a sense, she will seek something already present and obvious, though covered by custom and habit: satisfaction through completely embodied action, the satisfaction arising not from results but from integrated action itself.

Partial-Family Lineages and Their Psychological Implications

Venus results (so to speak) from Saturn's (Cronus') rage against his father, Uranus. As we have seen, Saturn castrates his father, and the testicles fall into the ocean, mix with the sea foam, and emerge as Aphrodite, or Venus. She doesn't have a proper mother, though one might argue that testicles falling into the sea symbolize sperm falling into the mother.[47] We can take the sea as part of the earth, Gaia, Uranus' wife and mother of the Titans, a group that includes Saturn. We can therefore interpret Venus as a rather unusual child of Uranus and Gaea and a half-sister to Saturn and the other Titans (for in some sense she has the same father). This interpretation makes astrological sense, for the sea suggests Pisces, the sign of Venus' exaltation, and astrologers recognize the link between Venus and Saturn by assigning them both to a dignity in Libra. Still, though we can see Gaea as Venus' symbolic mother, Venus has no biological mother. She has come into existence largely because of two males, Uranus and Saturn, while Gaea, though having hatched the plot with her son, remains in the background. Venus, we might say, is not of Gaia's flesh. So just as Venus, a primary feminine symbol, has no biological mother, so Mars has no biological father, for though clearly the son of Hera, he comes into being when she, infuriated at Zeus for having given birth parthenogenetically to Pallas Athena, decides to give birth to her own parthenogenetic child. The Venus-Uranus myth may also suggest that Venus arises from unresolved father-son issues, or that men in the grip of such unresolved conflicts may seek Venus as a compensation, either through relationships with markedly Venusian women or through art and aesthetics.

These family matters—Venus having no biological mother, Mars no biological father—suggest that Venus, coming from a male lineage, partakes of the rational, cerebral, symbol-making element of our humanness, while Mars, coming from a female lineage, partakes of the non-rational, non-

---

[47]In French, *mere* means "mother" and *mer* means "sea."

cerebral, non-symbol-making element.[48] Venus comes into being as a result of Uranus' resistance to the feminine power; Mars comes into being as a result of Hera's resistance to—or, as Liz Greene suggests, desire for revenge against—the masculine power (Zeus) who "has created a female child of the spirit (wisdom) without her," and so "generates a son-phallus of her own who will fight for her."[49] Uranus wishes to escape karma and live in a world of ideas, but his wish eventually leads to the "birth" of Venus: an impulse to live in a realm of ideas leads to the birth of a decidedly physical entity, yet one possessed of her own set of ideas; independence, taken to its ultimate extreme, gives birth to the most relational of all energies (Venus), suggesting that from independence arises relationship. Mars' mother, Hera, angry because Zeus has usurped the power of the mothers, gives birth to Mars, probably the least rational of all planets. We see again a conversion into the opposite: from the concern about relationship—from anger because of a birth not involving relationship—comes an expression of separation. These conversions suggest the close relationship of Venus and Mars to anima and animus respectively, particularly in the sense that a man's anima can also have its own animus and thus express the unformed ideas that Emma Jung and her husband connect to the animus energy generally, and in the sense that a woman's animus can have its own anima and thus express itself non-rationally.

The mythic relations appear in the planetary energies. Though a "feminine" planet, Venus manifests a rationality that we generally associate with the masculine; though a "masculine" planet, Mars manifests an instinctual insistence that we might generally associate with the feminine. Venus, particularly through her Libran side, can act with cool detachment, giving balanced judgment and objectivity; Mars, particularly through his Arien side, expresses the blind, instinctual desire for self-preservation. The contra-sexual sides of these planets suggest that it is easier for men to recall a projection of Venus than to recall a projection of the Moon, for Venus has in her an important "masculine" element, and that it is easier for women to recall a projection of Mars than to recall a projection of Uranus, for Mars has a strong "feminine" element. We can find evidence for these propositions by observing people's behavior. When involved in any kind of aesthetic work, a man will be working actively with Venus; and women will be distinctively Mars-like when defending a child or the security upon which that child depends. The mythic material suggests that the resulting projections will not seem as opaque as those involving the Moon and Uranus and that insight into the projection will come more easily.

And Neptune?

We all have many questions about Neptune, at least partly because Neptune so often dissolves those boundaries and limits that we impose on experience in order to, we hope, understand and deal with our lives more effectively. Because Neptune dissolves coherence, and because ego generally likes even the most delusory feelings of coherence, we will all tend to project Neptune into the

---

[48]Some of this material owes an obvious debt to Liz Greene. See *The Inner Planets* (York Beach, Maine: Samuel Weiser, 1993), 184ff.
[49]Greene, 185.

world around us. Furthermore, because Neptune will dissolve the boundary between self and other and between self and projection, it can induce what C.G. Jung called the *archaic identity of subject and object* and that Claude Levi-Bruhl called "participation mystique."[50] If the boundary between consciousness and object, perceiver and perceived, dissolves, then one may experience either ecstatic rapture or delusional abjection, either exaltation or inundation—and one may have difficulty distinguishing the one from the other, for they cover much of the same ground!

On a more mundane level, men have certainly received encouragement both explicit and implicit to idealize women, to put them on some sort of pedestal even as they consider them as somehow inferior. And women have apparently received encouragement, again both explicit and otherwise, to idealize the social participation to which men purportedly have easier access than women do. Insofar as we don't question these kinds of encouragement, we will have gender-related projections related to Neptune. As so often when dealing with the outer planets, we must cultivate the antidote: a sense of critical understanding. We must understand *critical* here in the sense that we use it when we speak of much literary criticism or social criticism, for much of the work in those fields has to do not with evaluations per se, but with helping readers to come to a deeper understanding of the matters under investigation. If men come to a deeper understanding of women, they will feel much less prone to idealize them, and similarly for women's understanding of the social roles from which they feel excluded.

Despite much evidence to the contrary, many people still feel that women have more psychic susceptibility or receptivity than do men. Further, it seems that in our culture, we ask that men maintain coherence and that women go in quite a different direction. If, along with many astrologers, we consider Neptune as the "higher vibration" of the Moon, and if we consider women more "loony" than men, we would expect to find men projecting Neptune onto women rather often. Further still, if we consider the connection between Neptune, the sea, and the French words *mer* and *mere*, we would expect women to carry the Neptune energy more often than not, serving as the hook for men's Neptune projections more often than men serve as hooks for women's Neptune projections.

However, because we probably won't ever collect statistics on such matters, we can let the jury remain out on whether men project Neptune more often than women do, or the other way around. In the Greco-Roman mythology that has played such a role in our culture, Neptune appears as a male deity, and if he also serves as a symbol for mystical understanding, then we would expect men to carry the projection rather often. This doesn't mean that men have more mystical understanding than women do, for we have to do, here, with projection, not clear seeing. Most of the major spiritual and religious traditions current in our culture, and in many others, have more men than women serving as gurus, priests, or spokespeople for religious or spiritual principles. These projections surely have a lot of Saturn in them, particularly if we talk about religion as distinguished from spirituality, but Neptune just as surely plays a role. I tend to think that those occupying authorita-

---

[50]Von Franz, 7.

tive positions in religious organizations have as much Saturn in them as Neptune, though, so we can turn our attention to spirituality and both its legitimate spokespeople and its bogus ones.

Neptune has a lot to do with either, of course, as he (or she) has a lot to do with deception generally, for Neptune symbolizes, on the one hand, our yearning for what of its very nature lies beyond our grasp, and, on the other, our delusions regarding that whole grasping process. We will tend to project Neptune onto those who delude us and onto those who serve as guides on any path that requires (so to speak) the dissolving of ego, the permeability of boundaries, and the attempt to pierce through passion, aggression, and ignorance.[51] I suspect that we see social conditioning in our tendency to project Neptune onto male figures who either offer spiritual guidance or delude us into thinking that they do: I see no reason why women can't perform either operation equally well, but my anecdotal observations suggest that men serve as hooks in this area more often than women do (with, again, Saturn playing a significant role). On the other hand, because we often consider operations like participation, union, and emotional absorption as archetypally feminine, and because we too often devalue these approaches to spirituality (and to economic enterprise!), I suspect that men often deal with related gender-specific projections related to Neptune. We can recognize the hooks by the way they lead us, for good or ill, through ecstasy, rapture, or hysteria, this third term referring to activities in which the boundaries between self and other dissolve to the extent that one has difficulty distinguishing one's own contents from someone else's.

In general, people project Neptune onto spiritual leaders and gurus, alcoholics and addicts, and onto people involved in illusions ranging from outright trickery (e.g. embezzlers, though Pluto plays a role there, too) to trickery under another name (e.g. politicians) to those involved in creating illusions for artistic purposes (a group including, but not limited to, movie stars). Anyone who stands as a symbol for another's yearning for what of its nature remains beyond one's grasp can serve as a hook for a Neptune projection, and we seem particularly prone to such projections when we become cemented into a particular social role or a particular view of ourselves (marks of Saturn) that exclude (Saturn again) the powerful human capacity symbolized by Neptune.

Of course, to accept this capacity as part of oneself does not mean that one submits to the manipulations of others. Neptune needn't make a person wishy-washy or overly accommodating. Much depends, as always, on other factors in the horoscope: a strong Saturn, Mars, or Sun certainly aids in one's efforts to work constructively with Neptune.[52] We would all like to grasp the ungraspable, and a projection of Neptune may make the ungraspable seem graspable. However, it seems vital that we accept the basic anxiety that comes with Neptune, accepting that basic suffering that apparently comes naturally to beings with perishable bodies yet with minds capable of an awareness extending beyond the perishable. In the old saying, heaven seems linked to the various ways

---

[51]These three terms describe what Buddhist calls the three "poisons" symbolized at the center of the Wheel of Life: the three main drivers of human delusion, and the three main potentials, once fully understood, that enable us to transcend delusion (for Buddhists speak of transforming delusion into ignorance, not of simply replacing the latter with the former).

[52]If women project these energies onto men, we would suspect that women would act in ways more recognizably Neptunian than would men.

in which reaches must exceed grasps, but we delude ourselves if we think we can find heaven on earth merely by adopting a few new concepts. It seems that our only hope of experiencing anything heavenly lies in our capacity to dissolve boundaries, particularly the one we think we see between heaven and earth.

Everyone and Pluto

As we will see in chapters X1 and XII, Pluto has much to do with overcoming the dualistic fixation that lies at the root of many (probably *most*, perhaps *all*) of our projections. However, this double planet also arises in specific gender-related projections, where, despite its connection to the mother lineages, it often arises through activities we associate with masculine imperatives. This bit of cosmic subterfuge need not surprise us: when Pluto (Greek: Hades) went into the world, he/she wore a helmet conferring invisibility. Furthermore, Greek myth has cloaked some of Pluto's more important characteristics, for in Greek myths, the underworld ruler manifests in male form.

Liz Greene has often called astrologers' attention to the fact that in many pre-Greek cultures, feminine figures ruled the underworld. The mythology parallels the experience of many people, for whom the underworld arises most evidently as feelings not rationally understood. The mythic material also accords well with astrological tradition in which the Moon, which clearly has a connection to some qualities of the unconscious or habitual mind, symbolizes a feminine energy, for certain elements of the feminine energy clearly run in cycles. Archetypally, the feminine seems to have connections with the underworld, and thus to all projections, regardless of the projecting person's gender. This feminine energy has to do with the source of life, with hidden powers and taboos. These two—*the source of life* and *hidden powers and taboos*—have a close connection, as humans have developed many taboos about looking directly into the face of great power, so that some sort of taboo often stands at the doorway to the chambers in which such power lies coiled.

Men, at least in our culture, tend to project Pluto onto women precisely because Pluto seems non-rational and beyond conscious control or logical appeal. On the other hand, women will tend to project Pluto onto men because Pluto has so much to do with the kinds of apparently rational social power (however problematic) that women (and the rest of us!) have been taught belongs to the masculine. When we think of plutocrats, we generally think of men; when we ask who rules the evident plutonic powers of our world, such as we find in plutonium and wealth, we will probably agree that men do—and we will probably acknowledge this even if we see those men as dominated by psychic elements we see as archetypally feminine! None of which means that the plutonic powers "are masculine," but merely that unless we look deeply into things, it will seem that males have proprietary interests in such power and may think that they control them. None of this means that women "are *per se* non-rational," for as we will see, Pluto has a side closely connected to rationality, though not of the everyday sort. Furthermore, men find themselves encouraged by society to play the rational role (so to speak), however non-rational the activities themselves (as for example the activities of the political realm or the control of nuclear weapons), and so to project non-rational energies onto women. Women, meanwhile, find themselves encouraged by society to emphasize the non-rational elements in their psyches and so to project the rational onto men, at least in the public sphere. To these observations, we can add one more: that we find social conditions lying behind or beneath such projections does not mean that we could not also find instinctual drives lurking about.

Two-valued thinking lurks in many discussions about these matters, for such discussions often focus on two terms: *emotional* and *rational*. Equipped with these two terms, we interpret experience terms of the stated dichotomy, seeing women as connected primarily to the former and men to the latter. However, in dealing with Pluto, we can get quite confused by thinking in such terms, for at its most basic level Pluto symbolizes a profoundly non-dualistic energy that fuses opposites together. We can speak of "emotional reactions" and "rational actions" as if those two terms have distinct and self-evident referents, but if we do, we may create a verbal map with little relation to a territory in which emotions affect the rational intellect, and ideas or notions affect the emotions. Though we must use abstractions to discuss experience, we should bear these provisos in mind as we proceed.

Many—perhaps all—of our projections arise from two-valued thinking of some sort. Such thinking lies beneath our assumption that we can locate an external world distinct from the perceiving mind; such thinking also emerges in the way ego sees some types of energy as acceptable and some as unacceptable. We can withdraw the resulting projections by changing the way we think, or by observing the way we think in the first place, matters to which we will return in chapter XI. This principle holds even for projections that carry a powerful emotional current.

Initially, many women will want to withdraw or re-collect the projection of rational and manipulative power from men; initially, many men will want to withdraw or re-collect the projection of non-rational power from women. A woman projecting Pluto will generally find as a hook someone who seems shadowy, who on the surface seems intent on rationally ordered control but whose control very much derives from unacknowledged feeling, someone who manipulates through a kind of collective power (money, status: generally a power that arises through and because of either social position, sexuality, or both), but who, on second look, seems driven largely by unconscious or collective forces, unable to relate to the healing power of his own emotion. A man projecting Pluto onto women generally finds as a hook someone who seems intent on thrashing about, powerless, in her own underworld of conflicting emotions driven by obsessive ideas—women who seem powerless because apparently controlled by their own feeling nature, unable to bring rational insight to bear. The woman will often perceive the plutonic man as exerting control for what he takes as rational reasons even if others see him as driven by unconscious and non-rational forces (e.g. the so-called power instinct); the man will often perceive the plutonic woman as out of control yet having some sort of dimly perceived desire for control exerted through an appearance of powerlessness. But because all the people involved find themselves in the grip of projections, we should not take one person's descriptions of the other person (the hook for and receiver of the projection) as an accurate character-description.

Because Pluto "is" neither masculine nor feminine and so may appear as either, both men and women project this energy. But those who project it will find that they perceive power as residing outside, not inside: the other person will often appear to have power in the situation, even if the power arises as social or emotional manipulation and even if the power masquerades as social or emotional powerlessness. Men often learn, through a culture's educational setup and other venues, to value a kind of freedom characterized by untrammeled latitude in behavior and emancipation from biological factors (Uranus). Women often learn from an early age—and possibly from bodily cycles more than from imposed education—about the power of biological factors to shape one's life, to draw a person inward (so to speak) toward life's mysteries. Thus when a man projects Pluto onto a woman, he will often have disowned his connection to his own power to transform through feeling, and he will likely disavow any connection with non-rational powers that manifest as cycles beyond his control. But that he disavows such cycles doesn't mean they don't have power over him or work their power from beneath him. The transiting Moon's movements through his horoscope, or the aspects from the transiting Moon to important planets in his horoscope, will generally reveal the disavowed psychic material, though often as projection. To the degree that the man disavows these powers, he will project Pluto (and the Moon, as discussed earlier) onto women.

When a woman projects Pluto onto a man, a different set of causes—most often socially-induced ones—apparently do the work. As noted, men hold most social power in most areas on the planet, surely in Europe and the United States. Generally, this power involves some degree of manipulation; furthermore, it almost always involves power *over* someone, even when exercised benevolently, and it often involves money. Thus women will often project Pluto onto men who hold social, financial, or coercive power. But as astrologers know, Pluto, through its connection to both Scorpio and the eighth house, has to do not only with money, but also with sexuality. Thus some women will project Pluto onto a man who, she will come to feel, has some kind of sexual power as well, though with social power and money often in the mix, even if that social power has no evident social sanction. The person serving as a hook for the projection will generally seem to have the power to release the woman (or others) from some kind of anguish or some kind of powerlessness, from the person's own underworld, for now the underworld appears outside, projected onto the hook. Thus the feeling of powerlessness on the part of the person doing the projecting; thus, too, the anguish that arises when the projection dissolves (often because of abandonment).

These kinds of control have their root in the mind as much as in the world. No doubt men have social and financial power of various sorts, but just as certainly, the control generally arises through a person's thoughts rather than through overt action.[53] In general, then, a man who projects Pluto

---

[53]The exceptions to this principle generally include a hefty dose of Saturn, and perhaps of Mars. Thus challenging Pluto aspects in a natal chart do not, by themselves, generally indicate physical sexual abuse by the parent. When we see physical abuse, we generally find Saturn and/or Mars participating with Pluto. When Pluto alone indicates abuse, we generally find psychological abuse rather than physical, and what some have called psychological incest rather than physical incest. Challenging Moon-Pluto aspects, for example, seem to have a connection to such incest, particularly in a man's horoscope.

onto a women will perceive that woman as psychologically manipulative but in what he will take as a subversive way not easily perceived by others. A woman who projects Pluto onto a man will often perceive that man either as psychologically manipulative, though in a manner more easily recognizable to others, or as powerless in personal ways even if powerful socially. The man projects a power that purportedly lies beyond the reach of intellect, while the woman projects a power purportedly rational and visible to all. But in general, a projection of Pluto arises through any power that controls or any power perceived as controlling. This occurs, at least partly and probably in large part, because power has to do with change and ego doesn't like change; power and transformation, so often and so facilely associated with Pluto, often mean the same thing. Ego takes a dim view of either, resisting changes that threaten its illusory hegemony.

Some astrologers, pointing to the fact that female figures have functioned as underworld rulers, have interpreted Pluto as a feminine energy. From that point of view, the Greek Hades and the Roman Pluto seem like aberrations reflecting the so-called male-dominated societies from which they arose. I think, though, that we should not entirely reject the masculine manifestation of Pluto. As a non-dualistic energy, Pluto has both masculine *and* feminine qualities—and they often seem inseparable. We know that astronomers recognize Pluto as a double planet, so it makes sense that Pluto would have a double nature. In a later chapter, we will explore what this suggests about perception; here, we should recognize that Pluto-in-the-world generally takes a masculine form, at least in the political goings-on of the present era. Male dictators often carry the Pluto energy for us, as do plutocrats, and though we might say that both derive their power from the feminine, the *manifestation* of that power includes elements taken as rational by the dictator-in-question and the subjects-under-dictation (so to speak). The so-called civilized world has tended to see power as something that arises from the intellect and that people exert over visible phenomena, even if, since the advent of depth psychology, many people dimly recognize that power has its roots in the underworld.

As a symbol of power, Pluto has to do with whatever brings about change—what astrologers call "transformation" or "death and rebirth experiences"—and this kind of change must include something beyond intellectual understanding; as Jung said, psychological transformation does not occur without a powerful emotional element. What we call *transformation* occurs as part of the natural ongoingness of a world characterized by change, and that natural pattern includes both rational and non-rational elements fused together. On the one hand, people can transform their world via intellect and penetrating understanding; on the other hand, even our intellectual categories have unconscious roots.

We think we know that the masculine intellect has unleashed the destructive power of plutonium into the world. This historical record tells us that many scientific processes necessary to this power developed rapidly around the time of Pluto's discovery. However, because we also can observe how much power the rational intellect has to effect positive transformation, we should not conclude that the feminine rules all helpful transformation. If transformation pervades the world as we experience it, we would expect it to have a masculine component linked with processes we see as feminine. Thus we would expect women to project Pluto onto men as often as men project Pluto onto women, even if different psychological factors lie behind the projections. In the end, Pluto's transformation directs us beyond those realms in which facile gender distinctions seem helpful. Though these distinctions might help us to effect that transformation, the process itself seems to annihilate the distinctions in question. These observations may prove helpful even in the apparently dualistic world of relations in which we all find ourselves.

Sample Horoscope: James T. Tiptree, Jr.[54]

Science fiction fans will recognize "James T. Tiptree, Jr." as the best-known pen-name for Alice Bradley Sheldon, who, after her work in photo reconnaissance during WWII (as the first woman to enter that field), her later stint with the CIA, her many years as a painter, her work as an experimental psychologist (the field in which she took her doctorate and had a brief teaching career, also publishing a paper in a respectable journal[55]), her studies in perception and art, and her work managing a poultry farm, took to writing science fiction under a male pen-name, part of which, she says, she took from a jar of marmalade she saw in a local supermarket. By all accounts, she completely fooled all of her readers, even such people as Ursula LeGuin and Joanna Russ, with whom she corresponded regularly, and once received praise for her "masculine writing style."

The "B" in Ms. Sheldon's name stands for "Bradley," her family-of-origin name. Mary Bradley, her mother, wrote voluminously, achieving some notoriety for her fiction and travel writing, the latter emerging from the family's trips to Africa during Alice's early years—trips that prompted Alli[56] to say that she had travelled hundreds of miles from the nearest roads in Africa years before she had a playmate of her own age. She described her mother as

> …a dazzling and formidable little person, a "queen bee" with two adoring males in addition to her husband. (In our Victorian culture they were Father's best friends.) She was gifted, beautiful, emotional, accomplished; a linguist, writer, spell-binding conversationalist—and a superb shot and brave endurer of considerable real hardships…She didn't provide a model for me, she provided an impossibility.

Alli also wrote of her mother's "dazzling looks," adding, "I am still approached by doddering wrecks, extinguished Scandinavian savants or what have you who want to tell me about mother as a young woman." The mother's dramatic bent, worldliness, and love of center-stage seems indicated in her

---

[54]Biographical details on Alice Sheldon (James T. Tiptree, Jr.) come from Julie Phillips' excellent biography (*James T. Tiptree, Jr.: The Double Life of Alice B. Sheldon*; New York: St. Martin's Press, 2006).

[55]"Preference for Familiar Versus Novel Stimuli as a function of the Familiarity of the Environment," by Alice B. Sheldon, in *Journal of Comparative and Physiological Psychology*, vol. 67, no. 4, April, 1969. She also published articles in *Mademoiselle* ("I am a WAAC," June 1943, under the name Alice Bradley Davey, her name during her first marriage) and New Yorker ("The Lucky Ones," November 16, 1946, under the name Alice Bradley).

[56]Following Julie Phillips' lead, I will refer to Ms. Sheldon as Alli, the name she apparently preferred through most of her life. The quoted material comes from page 4 of Phillips' book.

daughter's opposition from the Moon in Aquarius to Venus in Leo experienced via projection early in life. Certainly Mary Bradley cast a long creative shadow that her daughter would have to find her way out of; also, as some astrologers have suggested, a Moon-Venus affliction can suggest an overly close connection to the mother.

Her father worked as a lawyer, and Alice experienced him as a person who worked out of the limelight cast on her mother, as somewhat hidden yet extremely effective. He served as the organizing force behind the family's several safaris in Africa and supported the family admirably through much of Alice's life. Her description of his efforts during one of the family's African safaris seems to point to her own Virgo Sun, experienced, particularly early in life, as a projection:

> …the official non-intellectual of the party. […] a sweet, silent, sensitive, compulsive man of action. His action took the form of […] holding everything together all the time, and required truly heroic exertions. Father got us through by dint of ceaseless vigilance, activity, versatility (he even learned to fill teeth!), checking and double-checking; ridden with malaria, burning with fever, he was the one who went back for a final check and found the medicine box, or the ammo cans, discarded and about to be lost.[57]

If her mother seemed like a force of nature, her father functioned in the less dramatic ways demanded by the exigencies of life, whether back home in Chicago or as the organizing force behind a troupe of the first white people some African villagers had ever seen.[58]

Alice Sheldon's horoscope also serves as a lesson in yod-dynamics, for it has an important, even dominant yod to Uranus from the Mercury-Saturn sextile, with the Mars-Pluto conjunction participating via Mars' loose conjunction with Saturn. Yods often take many years, even decades, before they manifest fully, and despite her precocious brilliance as a child and the numerous signs of creative gifts (particularly as a painter), Alli didn't find her niche in the world for decades. The niche she found certainly qualifies as non-traditional, as befits someone with Uranus as the focal planet of a yod. That placement suggests that she would refuse to accept the standard feminine roles presented to her, which she surely did, not only regarding social position, but regarding sexual orientation altogether, as she clearly had powerful sexual attractions to many women. The Mercury-Uranus quincunx suggests a brilliant mind that would have difficulty finding its proper application; it also suggests as do many Mercury-Uranus connections, that her mind worked extremely quickly, so that what seemed to her like simple logic seemed to others like wild leaps of intuition. Rudolf Arnheim, a mentor for Alli in her psychology work and a friend via letter for many years, once reminded her that "…you think 99% faster than the rest of humanity, and therefore you better write with one nostril closed like that fairy tale giant who was always about to blow the whole landscape to pieces."[59] (The ability to blow landscapes to pieces may also include some Mars-Pluto, particularly for someone with such a close conjunction.)

---

[57] Qtd. in Phillips, 32.
[58] Phillips, 32.
[59] Phillips, 249.

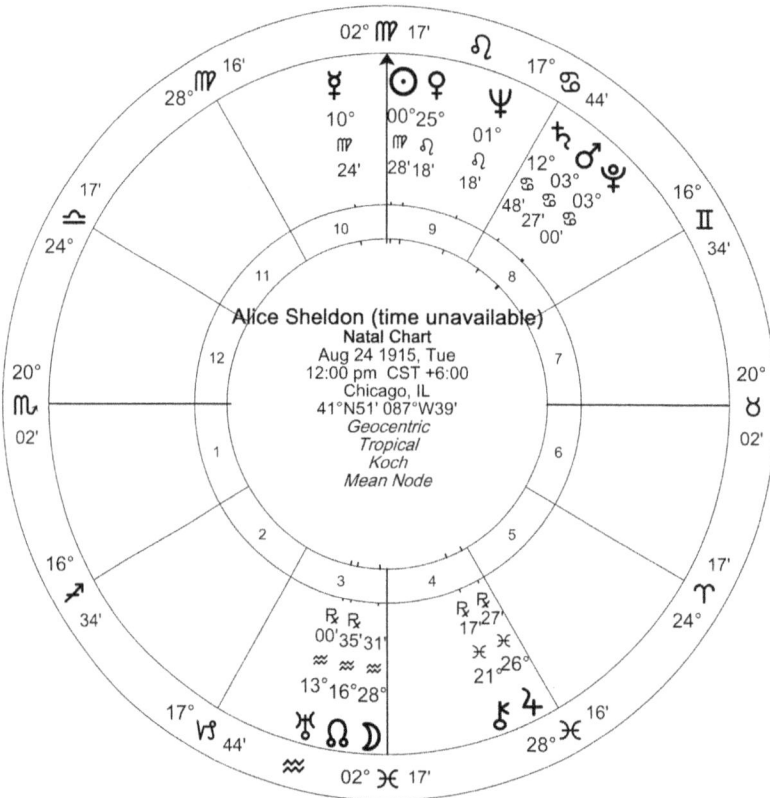

When the quincunx finally found appropriate applications, they had the mark of Mercury-Uranus: first as an experimental psychologist with unusual ideas; later as a science fiction writer of even more unusual ideas. As to the former, though, she didn't have the patience to continue in academic channels; though a Mercury-Uranus quincunx might love a ritual in which one creates knowledge by doing experiments, neither that aspect nor the adjacent Saturn-Uranus quincunx took well to the established and rigid hierarchies of academe. As to the latter, Tiptree's fiction surely qualified as iconoclastic, not only because of the way it presented male-female relations (not always, strictly speaking, between humans!), but also because of the way it delved into human relationship and the human connection to technology. Saturn entered the science fiction through the way Tiptree used some rather traditional science-fiction motifs, complete with references to rocket ships, ray guns, and aliens of all sorts. Within the structure of the genre, her iconoclastic tendencies found a means of expression. The powerful Uranus statement also manifested in her connection to the women's movement, for though she supported it, she did so on her own terms.[60]

---

[60] A full explanation of this assessment would take us too far afield. Interested readers can consult Phillip's biography for details. In lieu of that, let these two remarks suffice, the first by Alli as herself, speaking of her plan for a scientific book

Though the Moon-Venus aspect emerged first through the mother, Sheldon later came to own it herself, when, as Tiptree, she presented women in dramatic ways through which they shed social accoutrements. The Mars-Pluto aspect, linked fairly closely to Saturn, emerged sometimes as a personal trait and sometimes through men. Both of her husbands served as hooks for Mars-Pluto, the first through abusive behavior, the second through sexual frustration—and, as a CIA employee, through secret action, though Alli/Tiptree clearly had her own secret activities! As perhaps befits someone with an Aquarius Moon, however, Sheldon's emotions seemed connected to her need for friendship, which Ting, her second husband, definitely provided. Though she included Ting (Huntington Denton Sheldon) when she said, "I'm fond of a hundred people who no more know 'me' than they know the landscape of Antarctica," she also said of him, "Since the last ten years, we are so as one it's ridiculous. Without agreeing on how to do the simplest thing, like open a jar, we arrive at the same basic life-conclusions and perceptions."[61] Notably for someone with an Aquarius Moon, she found security through shared ideas.

However, we see her sexual frustrations in the Mars-Pluto conjunction, which loosely conjoins Saturn, all in Cancer. Alli wrote to feminist science-fiction writer Joanna Russ that "'platonic marriage' with a really solid male friend has good points…I should know."[62] Further, in Tiptree's stories, one searches long and hard to find indications of satisfying sexual connections—or even, it seems, satisfying communication! By all indications, her first marriage didn't provide any more satisfying physical sexuality than did her second, and it brought violence and abuse in addition. We can interpret the first husband's violence as a projection of Alli's inner drives as well as a characteristic of the husband himself (William Davey). Thus the Mars-Pluto-Saturn material appears continually in her life, not only in her husbands and many other intimate male partners, but also in her own difficulty having orgasms.

But Mars-Pluto didn't restrict itself to her sexuality. We would expect a good deal of secrecy in one with such an aspect, particularly when it appears in Cancer, and though as Tiptree she carried on a voluminous correspondence, suggesting her Aquarius Moon and its opposition to Venus,

---

to be titled *The Human Male*, the second by Tiptree in a letter to Joanna Russ. Describing her proposed book, she wrote that "evolutionary concepts are still the best tool we have in thinking about sex differences," a view that set her at odds with those who emphasized social factors—who argued as Joanna Russ did in a letter to Tiptree, that humans had no biological cues to maternal behavior at all, only "customs, traditions, learning, illusions, myths, power politics…There is no human biology." (See page 293. I can't resist adding the following passage, written by Alli as herself, though the passage doesn't seem germane to the discussion in this footnote: "Consider how odd it would be if all we knew about elephants had been written by elephants. Would we recognize one? What elephant author would describe—or perhaps even perceive—the features which are common to all elephants…So when the human male describes his world he maps its distances from his unspoken natural center of reference, himself. He calls a swamp 'impenetrable,' a dog 'loyal,' and a woman 'short.'" See page 291.) Second, she rejected any idealism about women. In a letter to Russ, Tiptree wrote (regarding a task they had both taken on: to write a story for an anthology with *Beyond Equality* as the working title), "Equality is necessary, but it isn't sufficient; you still have people. When they come to get me—if we achieve equality first—I can see just as many ferocious mindless grins coming at me on female faces, right along with the males." (See page 304.)
[61] Phillips, 248.
[62] Phillips, 247.

she guarded her secret carefully, to the extent that she gave Tiptree a post-office box and a bank account. Interestingly, the aspect also seems to have manifested through a kind of male magnetism, as at least one female correspondent seems to have become smitten with Tiptree and tried to entice him into a meeting. (Considering Alli's earlier assertions that she felt like a man trapped in a woman's body, we perhaps should not find her male magnetism all that surprising! Nor should we feel surprised at such sexual fusion in one with a Mars-Pluto conjunction.) Of course, in true Mars-Pluto-Cancer fashion, Tiptree remained secretive and dimly lit, refusing all offers of personal meetings or invitations to conferences. In one case, before Tiptree had his post office box, David Gerrold, an admirer and fellow science-fiction writer, found his way to Alli's door, finding there a woman who "couldn't help" him locate the mysterious Mr. Tiptree. Apparently Alli, taken by surprise on that occasion, simply told him "the first lie she could think of." Shortly after that, Tiptree began receiving his mail at the post office.[63]

We might see her CIA work as further indicating Mars-Pluto, though that work didn't go on for long, Tiptree's hints to the contrary notwithstanding. Ting, however, worked for the CIA for many years, and thus seems to have continued to receive some of Alli's Mars-Pluto energy. Of course, the aspect hints of a more pervasive secrecy, one dealing not with place of employment but with name, gender, and identity. Though we might see Mars-Pluto mostly in Ting, it seems that by her fifties, Alli had gone quite far to owning the aspect herself, doing so by flying so far under the available radar that she found the underworld ruler in one of his male manifestations! As the urbane, often witty, genial, apparently celibate, and surely reclusive and secretive Tiptree, she could speak effectively of matters generally considered taboo to women, and many of his stories surely qualify as plutonic excursions even as they manifest the three planets in her yod.

Of course, Mars-Saturn-Pluto has a documented connection to sexual assault and to forbidden modes of self-assertion, sexual and otherwise. As noted, her first husband abused her; as also noted, she experienced life-long sexual frustration. Also, it seems that her mother once tried to seduce her (when the pair shared the same cabin on a return trip from Europe), and throughout her life Alli had a powerful sexual attraction to women. Further, several Tiptree stories present a joining of sexuality and brutality. The aspect also seems an apt marker for the depression Alli experienced throughout her life and for the severe migraines that she experienced for many years. Finally, the aspect appears in her ongoing contemplations about self-destruction and in her eventual planned suicide: having made a suicide pact with Ting, she eventually kept her promise. The two bodies were found lying side-by-side in their home, holding hands.

A final point about her Virgo Sun. As we have seen, it appeared first through her father. Yet later, she began to shows signs of successful integration: first she managed a chicken farm, a job that required extensive attention to detail and a skill-set that enabled her to deal with matters ranging from sick chickens to inventory to budget-balancing. Later still, she showed great attention to detail and great analytical precision as an experimental psychologist. Further, she dearly loved her

---

[63]Phillips, 243.

routine as a writer and correspondent. Julie Phillips writes that though Alli loved the time she spent with Ting during vacations in the Yucatan (vacations that apparently gave her material for *Tales of the Quintana Roo*, one of Tiptree's more unusual efforts—and that's saying something!), she also "missed her house, her garden, and her office." One suspects that any self-respecting Virgo would want some degree of efficiency, but in Yucatan Alli found that "[s]upplies such as typewriter ribbons and even paper were hard to come by there in the mangrove swamps, and she was cut off from Tiptree's medium, the mail."[64] So on the one hand, like many Virgos of both genders, she seemed to have struggled for years to coordinate her many talents into one life-path, going from painting, to writing, to her work in the WAC, to photo-reconnaissance, to chicken farming, to experimental psychology, to teaching, to "academic" writing in psychology, to, at last, writing again, now in the science fiction genre under an assumed name. On the other hand, she apparently possessed not only Virgo's documented sexual magnetism, but also a typically Virgoian attention to detail and access to hidden realms.

I think it fair to see Alice Sheldon as somewhat unbalanced, as long as we consider that as a description and not an evaluation. Like many artists, she seemed somewhat unbalanced from the perspective of the workaday world. As Tiptree, she signed her letters "Tip," suggesting some lack of balance! Her horoscope, an off-kilter see-saw chart with a number of important dissociate aspects (all major aspects to Neptune, the opposition from the Sun to the Moon), suggests this interpretation. But we should, particularly when speaking of someone with such a strong Uranus, and even more particularly one linked to Mercury and Saturn, see it as a brilliant kind of unbalance that eventually found the necessary form. She saw things from a different perspective than many others, and once the yod activated, she put her brilliance forth into the world. The Saturn-Uranus quincunx that makes up one side of the yod points to her difficulties finding a place in society where she could manifest her brilliant iconoclasm; the Mercury-Uranus quincunx suggests that the venue, once developed, would involve intellectual brilliance. Once she found the venues, through psychology and science fiction, with one persona for each venue, she surely made her mark on the world. She remains a unique figure in 20th century science fiction, and certainly one of the most respected, one of the few to have an award named after her (The James T. Tiptree Award). Her (his?) work so impressed Philip K. Dick that he inquired about writing collaboratively. Harlan Ellison once said in a letter to Tiptree that he was "the single most important new writer in science fiction today" and that "[n]obody touches you! Not me, not Delany, not Blish, not Budrys, not Disch, not Dick…none of us." This kind of praise suggests not only that the yod had found its proper venue, but that Alli Sheldon had, through Tiptree, harnessed much energy that earlier in life she had projected.

In many ways we see in Alice Sheldon's life a pattern with some points in common with the one

---

[64]Phillips, 247.

we saw in Emily Dickinson's life: great difficulty, early on, integrating her projections of archetypally male energies symbolized by Uranus, the Sun, and Mars, but a more successful integration later in life, both professionally and interpersonally, as she found appropriate and creative outlets for the energies in question.

Chapter V

Aspects and Projection

A challenging aspect often indicates that the person will either project one of the planets onto others, as commonly occurs with the opposition, or will project the entire aspect into the environment as a situational challenge requiring a new venue or life-structure through which to bring together the two planetary energies, as commonly occurs with the square. Sometimes, too, when a person projects an entire aspect onto another person, gender-issues play a role, as they apparently do in the Moon-Mars opposition in William Butler Yeats' horoscope, as discussed in chapter III. Gender-roles also play a role in the projections of infants, for when very young, we all tend to project various aspects onto our parents; an infant with a Moon-Saturn square will generally project the whole aspect onto the mother, or the father, or the aspect may arise through the general environment in the early home.[1]

When interpreting aspects in terms of projection, the astrologer should take all relevant factors into consideration. For example:

1. Particularly with the opposition, and as long as gender-related factors do not play a role, one will tend to project the outermost planet of the pair onto another and to experience the inner planet as part of oneself.

---

[1] Many people with Moon-Saturn afflictions experience some limitation in nurturance. Sometimes this experience tells us something about the mother's character, perhaps that she doesn't feel comfortable in the nurturing role; sometimes it will tell us something about the mother's circumstances, for perhaps she had to get a job and thus cannot nurse her child regularly. It may also tell us that the mother feels judged by her husband, her father, or both, though the aspect alone doesn't always enable us to distinguish the mother's external circumstance from her inner disposition. Sometimes the mother herself didn't get properly nurtured and so has difficulty nurturing her child; sometimes the child experiences some privation in the early years.

2. Particularly with the square, one may project the entire aspect onto someone else, some recurring type of situation, or a series of people who present the same or similar challenges.

3. In any aspect, one will tend to play the role of the gender-friendly planet and project out the non-gender friendly planet. (Perhaps surprisingly, this sometimes occurs even with conjunctions.)

4. Much depends on the planets involved: though even the challenging aspects between Venus and Jupiter may present some problems, they don't present the daunting challenges that Venus-Saturn aspects do. Furthermore, ego doesn't always reject challenging Venus-Jupiter aspects, as ego often experiences them as supportive, an adjective most would not apply to the experiences associated with Venus-Saturn.

5. House-positions matter. Though in the next chapter we will have more to say about house-placements *per se*, those placements have relevance here as well, as they will influence the interpretation of any aspect.

6. Challenging aspects often prod a person toward creative response, though the typical response varies from aspect to aspect, the opposition generally prodding one toward a more objective awareness or understanding, and the square generally prodding one to create a new life-venue through which to express the challenging aspect.

7. These factors arise in combination and sometimes give a mixed message that the astrologer should not ignore, for they can indicate conundrums prompting creative response.

As in other sections of this book, take these suggestions as hypotheses, not hard-and-fast rules to follow blindly regardless of the vicissitudes of individual character. If we hypothesize that a woman will play the lunar role and project Uranus onto men, we should, with that hypothesis in hand, investigate the actual situation, letting our hypothesis inform our observations without blinding us to actual developments, for just as a pick-pocket, when he sees a holy man, generally sees only the man's pockets,[2] so the astrologer who lets the symbols blind him will see only the categories provided by astrological methodology, thereby perhaps missing the living person.

The Opposition

In *Horoscope Symbols*, Robert Hand writes:

> Whatever energies are linked by the opposition, they are combined in such a way that they produce instability and change through conflict. If one examines the conflict, it is seen to arise between an aspect of oneself that has been projected outward and an aspect of oneself that is experienced inwardly. Put more concretely, the opposition signifies a conflict between an external factor and an internal one, and the external factor is the result of an inward energy that one does not as yet understand to be within the self.[3]

---

[2] I think this saying comes from an old Sufi text.
[3] Robert Hand, *Horoscope Symbols* (Rockport: Para Research, 1981), 124.

Though oppositions tend to manifest in the way Hand describes, keep at least three provisos in mind: first, aspects other than the oppositions sometimes split just as an opposition does, for both squares and conjunctions can also function this way, though they do so less often, less predictably, and with less consistent results than does the opposition); second, the opposition itself may not *always* manifest this way (for example, many Moon-Venus oppositions in women's charts or Sun-Jupiter oppositions in men's do not reliably indicate projection[4]); third, the process does not proceed mechanically, for much depends, here as elsewhere, on the person's level of awareness and willingness to accept critique – and the horoscope does not give us reliable information about level of awareness; as Liz Green has pointed out, the horoscope we examine could easily belong to a dog! Further, one must look at the relationship of the opposed planets to other factors in the horoscope.

In some horoscopes, oppositions almost always seem to produce projections. For example, in the charts of collectivities (e.g. nations; see chapter X), oppositions almost always arise that way, probably because collectivities have a difficult time doing the inner work necessary to recall projections of any sort, having no awareness as we usually understand that term and no consciousness through which to effect change.[5] Similarly, when we see an opposition in the horoscopes of so-called world leaders, we can predict fairly reliably that one end of that aspect will appear as a projection, perhaps because these so-called leaders get so completely engaged with the external world that they don't engage in much self-reflection; if the external world seems so compelling, the inner world perhaps gets short shrift. Further, many such leaders get so identified with national interests that they ignore anything not connected with those interests.

During specific periods, both rulers and ruled in specific countries seem to project planets in the nation's horoscope onto particular foreign leaders or foreign countries. This seems to have occurred continually in United States history; consider, for example, the United States' projection of its natal Pluto onto Native Americans, African slaves, the Soviet Union, the Vietnamese, and later onto Iraq. At other periods, certain groups of people may "own" astrological factors previously projected and at the same time serve as hooks for the projections of other groups: young adults during the late 1960s both acted out and served as conduits for the Uranus-Pluto conjunction then taking place, and at the same time served as the hook for other groups who remained identified with the status quo (a status quo indicated in the U.S. horoscope by the square from the Sun in Cancer to Saturn in Libra in the tenth). For a while, transiting Saturn opposed the Uranus-Pluto conjunction, further symbolizing the split that took place in the collective: those who identified with Saturn projected Uranus-Pluto onto the best available hook (e.g. demonstrators; yippies and hippies; so-called radicals; Vietnamese freedom fighters; etc.); those who identified or found themselves acting out the energy of Uranus-Pluto projected Saturn onto the best available hook (e.g. the

---

[4]Consider, as an example of the former, the Moon-Venus opposition in Alice Sheldon's horoscope, discussed in the previous chapter. Though the aspect sometimes split, in early life Ms. Sheldon apparently projected the entire aspect onto her mother. Later in life, the aspect appeared in Ms. Sheldon's own behavior.
[5]See chapter X for a discussion of the projections in the horoscopes of nations or collectivities, and more particularly for a discussion of the horoscopes for the United States and other nations.

government, the police, the National Guard). Certainly the U.S. government projected Uranus-Pluto onto many people in the younger generation (and, it seems, the Vietcong and others), for governments generally don't like powerful revolutionary forces, whether domestic (e.g. '60s "radicals") or otherwise (Vietnamese people rebelling against U.S. domination). Furthermore (and as we will see in chapter X), the United States tends to project both Uranus and Pluto onto others most of the time, so those representing the status quo interpreted many radical acts as anti-American. Small wonder, then, that those who served as hooks for the government's projection had projectiles hurled at them: students were shot at Kent State; Vietnamese and Cambodians were bombed and killed with impunity.[6] Small wonder, too, that policemen had bottles hurled at them. When we find this kind of polarization in the collective, we will generally find projection at work.

We arrive, then, at the principle stated above: oppositions often arise through projections, through situations in which a person projects one end of the opposition—one planetary energy or group of energies, one's rejected capacities—out into the world, generally onto another person but sometimes onto institutions or impersonal situations. People generally play the role of the planet closest to the Sun and project into the world the energy of the planet farthest from the Sun,[7] though sometimes a person will play the role of the gender-friendly planet and project out the less-gender-friendly planet. In either case, the person acts out the energy of the *owned* planet, the energy that ego finds most congenial, and projects out the *disowned* planet, the energy that ego finds uncongenial, whether for gender-related reasons or not.

As we move further from the Sun, the planets symbolize increasingly non-personal or no-cop-opt-able elements of experience, with important transitions between Mars and Jupiter (self-assertion and social integration) and Saturn and Uranus (the status quo and the revolutionaries beyond the walls). Ego generally interprets the outermost planets as threats, for they demand developments and symbolize potentials that ego usually finds difficult to encompass—and because ego, of its very nature, generally resists change (for ego wants to maintain itself). Even the two planets associated with social integration and form (Jupiter and Saturn) sometimes represent processes that seem beyond ego's direct control. The trans-Saturnian planets, by their very nature, challenge ego's hegemony. When involved in the apparent either-or demand of the opposition, ego generally sides with the planet that seems to confirm ego's solidity and integrity: usually the planet closest to the Sun or the planet symbolizing gender-friendly factors promoting self-identification.

---

[6]As noted, the period was punctuated by an opposition from Saturn and Chiron over to Uranus and Pluto. Of course, the Vietnamese didn't *always* see themselves in the guise of Uranus-Pluto. It seems that they often saw themselves as embodiments of Saturn: people trying to maintain tradition social order. To them, the U.S. was a fine hook for the disruptive energies of Uranus-Pluto.
[7]I think I first heard of this principle in a lecture given by Robert Hand in Boston some decades back.
[8]Technically, Mercury is closer to the Sun than the Moon is; however, as one of the lights and as the most elemental of the archetypally feminine energies, the Moon generally seems gender-friendly to women and functions with close connections to the Sun.

Sometimes the gender-friendly outer planet will seem friendlier to ego than to a non-gender friendly inner planet. A man with an opposition from Uranus to either Venus or the Moon may play the role of Uranus, particularly if a woman seems intent on playing the role of Venus and/or the Moon. A woman with a Moon-Mercury opposition may well play the Lunar role and project Mercury onto a man.[8] We will find other exceptions as humans of varying capacities, tendencies, backgrounds, and habits respond to life's vicissitudes in multifarious ways. Despite the exceptions, the above-described patterns generally hold true. In cases where the person experiences an outer planet (Saturn, Uranus, Neptune, Pluto) as ego-friendly, some elements of that planetary energy will nevertheless arise through projection. We see this pattern with particular clarity during transits. For example, though a person in a position of authority has plenty of opportunities to play the role of Saturn, he or she will generally find that challenging transits from Saturn arise at least partly as projections involving apparently-external difficulties.

Consider, too, the example given above: when a man has a Moon-Uranus opposition, he may sometimes play the role of Uranus and project the Moon onto the woman closest to him, the former being more gender friendly and the latter symbolizing the feelings that ego generally takes to be part of itself. If the man has lost touch, even temporarily, with his lunar energies, the gender-friendly factor symbolized by Uranus will take on more prominence for him. He will then play the Uranian role and derive ego-satisfaction by projecting the Moon (feelings, security needs) onto women. This simply means that the man has a more conscious connection to Uranus-factors than to lunar ones at certain times (e.g. when he's in the woman's presence). As we have seen, he will value and, perhaps out of habit, identify with new ideas, sudden change, and the *puer* element in himself; he will reject his sensitivities.[9] Still, a challenging transit from Uranus will probably induce some forces of change to arise in the external world.

Though oppositions often suggest that ego has devalued one of the two planetary energies involved, the aspect can also suggest a hidden, inner compatibility. Planets in a standard opposition occupy signs of compatible elements, suggesting potential harmony and complementarity, at least between the energies symbolized by the opposed signs.[10] For example, though we may initially see

---

[9]As discussed in chapter II and IX, the fact that humans can sometimes see Uranus with the naked eye suggests that we can co-opt Uranus more easily than we can co-opt Neptune and Pluto. We can assimilate into ego's territory those characteristics associated with Uranus more easily than we can assimilate those characteristics associated with Neptune and Pluto. Similarly, the status quo functions of a collectivity can somewhat readily make use of Uranus (e.g. through various forms of new technology).

[10]Contrast this with the square, linking signs in incompatible elements (e.g. water and fire, as in squares from Scorpio to Leo). Also dissociate (out of sign) oppositions do not have this hidden quality, for they link signs in incompatible elements (e.g. Capricorn-Leo). Such aspects seem, on the one hand, less harmonious; on the other hand, because the modes differ, the planets may not create the kind of problematic tension we so often see with standard oppositions. Instead of flagrant conflict or projection, we often see a lack of coordination and a tendency to create life-rituals to link the two planets together (reflecting the hidden quincunx influence).

Aries and Libra as irreconcilable opposites, Aries having to do with self-focus and self-initiated action and Libra with cooperation and relationship, we don't have relationship without self-assertion and we don't have self-assertion without some kind of relationship, for self-assertion implies relationship of some sort. Even if the two planets in an opposition seem to present irreconcilable demands, the sign placements indicate a potential for harmony and clarity. Thus oppositions suggest not only a tendency to project, but also the potential for integration via objective understanding.

More generally, the opposition has some of the qualities of the Aries-Libra polarity,[11] for it demands careful weighing in connection to self-identification. When we weigh, we often use scales, and scales generally involve some sort of balancing. We can put a pound of wheat on one end of the scale, and a pound of something else on the other, but even if we have equal weight on each side, we don't necessarily have equal value. If I have two sacks of gold, I can use scales to tell me which I should take home, but if I have apples on one end and gold on the other, the scales will not tell me which to value more. Our evaluations don't have an absolute quality, but arise from particular situations: a pound of diamonds in the middle of the desert presumably has much less value than a pound of water. Similarly, in the evaluations we make regarding the energies symbolized in a horoscope, some of our assumptions may have discernible social causes.

When we go to the market and weigh rice, the scale has what Dane Rudhyar called a "socially accepted standard weight."[12] These scales enable us to assess the weight of something according to a socially accepted scale, and then to evaluate before purchasing. With oppositions, before we decide to accept one side and reject the other, we generally proceed by assumptions instead of objective assessment. We must find the value of each end, and to do that, we must pay attention to the counter-weight. If I have a Moon-Uranus opposition and I act like the embodiment of Uranus, I will probably do myself a lot of good by investigating my assumptions about freedom and feeling, for those assumptions affect my actions. With oppositions, we shouldn't start by weighing one end against another, but by weighing each end separately; we seek not some absolute value, but a more personal one: our own way of valuing the energy symbolized at each end of the aspect. Each end of the opposition plays a role in a person's life; if the person doesn't honor both ends, projection ensues.

When we have an opposition, we often weigh the devalued factor only in terms of the valued factor. So if a man with a Moon-Uranus opposition identifies with Uranus, he will weigh the Moon in terms of Uranus, seeing the Moon in terms of how well it satisfies or fails to satisfy Uranus' demands; if he identifies with the Moon, he will weigh Uranus by using lunar matters as the counter-weight. In general, we will use the valued factor as the counterweight by which to judge the devalued factor, as if the valued end had some sort of absolute value. If a person takes this approach, he or she will have a difficult time re-collecting the opposition, for the lunar element will have a hard time valuing the Uranian element and vice-versa.

---

[11] Libra, associated with the seventh sign, stands opposed to Aries, associated with the first sign and the Ascendant.
[12] Dane Rudhyar, *Astrological Signs: The Pulse of Life* (Boulder: Shambhala, 1978), 85.

Because the evaluations we make when using scales depend on what we use as a counterweight, any evaluation yields conclusions connected with underlying assumptions about how we should measure the world. These measurements reflect assumptions about what we take as "valuable" in the world; they constitute the counterweights that we use habitually. These assumptions alert us to the presence of Saturn, a planet symbolizing the way we "see and experience the universe as [we] have structured it,"[13] and, as the exalted ruler of Libra, a planet linked to any opposition. The way a person structures his world tells us, albeit indirectly, what that person accepts as real and valuable. Because of conclusions we have come to about ourselves and what we think "is possible" for us (or what we think "is good" for us), we reject parts of ourselves. We weigh parts of ourselves and find some parts unacceptable in relation to the human function in question. For example, if a person has Uranus opposed the Moon but trine Mercury, she may find Uranus quite acceptable, even integral, to her intellectual life while at the same time rejecting it within her emotional life. She may also find that intellectual understanding will provide a bridge toward an emotional (lunar) acceptance of Uranus.

If a person has a Moon-Mars opposition, two functions come to the fore: feeling and asserting. A person with this aspect will probably feel that self-assertion threatens emotionally secure relationships; she will probably find herself, more often than she wishes, with partners who behave in strikingly Mars-like ways when around her, particularly when she identifies with the lunar role. Yet when she has no-one to accept the projection, she may act in strikingly Mars-like ways (ways that may include a tendency to get headaches or fevers), particularly in relation to her own feeling nature, finding herself either angry at her feelings or simply feeling angry. The opposition gives us information about how the person will see the world in certain situations; but if we wish to be objective, we'll see this as a description arising from a habit of perception and behavior, not as a hard-and-fast, independent, or inherent "reality." Many people with challenging Moon-Mars aspects perceived the mother as angry, or as someone who had difficulty reconciling self-assertion with emotional connectedness, perhaps using one to escape from the other.

Many such problems reflect Saturn, for we experience Saturn, the exalted ruler of Libra and symbol of limitation and judgment, when we don't admit all of our capacities into our behavior, when we reject any planetary energy and experience it as belonging to someone or something else. We do this because of fear: we fear our own nature because we have decided that we "are" something else, something lacking the rejected quality. One might say, "I am not an angry person," and we will feel confirmed by our own behavior when we can project Mars onto people who serve as adequate hooks for that energy. The problem lies partly in how we have decided to perceive the situation—or, perhaps, how we find ourselves perceiving it, for the process often remains unconscious: we perceive the situation in terms of what we have decided we *are* instead of in terms of how we *feel*—or, if we do relate to how we feel, we often relate *only* to feelings we have habituated ourselves to feel, those with which we feel more comfortable. Because of habit arising from the

---

[13]Robert Hand, *Planets in Transit* (Atglen, PA: Whitford Press, 1975), 317.

aforementioned ideas, we actually feel only one end of the opposition. We see ourselves as manifestations of the non-projected planet and others in terms of the projected planet, for just as we carry and act out the former, so the other person carries and acts out the latter (usually in accordance with the football analogy described earlier).

Some oppositions split only in certain situations. Though Venus-Neptune oppositions will sometimes split, with the individual usually playing the role of Venus and projecting the role of Neptune, they also appear again and again in the horoscopes of people involved in "Neptunian" activities (e.g. dance, music, imaginative work generally: all the fine and projective arts as well as activities demanding compassion). In other words, though a person might experience a projection of Neptune in some situations, she will often find that in other situations she can bring the energies together fruitfully. Very often the person will find it easier to combine the planets via professional or vocational activities than in personal or intimate relationships, but even then it will likely reappear in intimate partnerships: the person will either project Neptune onto the partner or get into relationships characterized by Neptune (e.g. involving drug use, etc.) Similarly, a Jupiter-Uranus opposition may appear united in a person's progressive social vision yet produce disruption in the person's intimate relationships. A woman's Venus-Saturn opposition may emerge through her style in executive leadership, yet when in the presence of her intimate partner, the woman may experience Saturn largely as projection.[14]

Gender will also play a role. Consider the Moon-Uranus opposition in both men and women. We know that some men take well to lunar activities: they take well to the nurturing role, take pains to connect to their feelings and to relate to the world through empathetic response instead of through pre-conceived notions, fixed ideas, or a compulsive need to flee commitment. We wouldn't predict that such men will *always* play the Uranian role and project the lunar one. We could say something similar of men who have had early family environments that directly or indirectly encouraged them to see Uranus (change, rebellion, chaos) as an enemy;[15] though we might hypothesize that most men will usually project the Moon onto women and choose the Uranus-role for themselves, we should always test our hypotheses. In particular, if we make such hypotheses while doing a reading, we should always listen carefully to the client, using the hypothesis as a way to help both astrologer and client see more clearly.

Moon-Uranus oppositions in men's charts often give a mixed message: if we hypothesize that the man will identify with the planet closest to the Sun, then we will expect him to identify with the Moon, but if we hypothesize that he will identify with the gender-friendly planet, we would expect him to identify with Uranus. We shouldn't reject this mixed message in any misguided attempt to

---

[14]I have found in hundreds and hundred of cases that challenging aspects (and, even more predictably, missing elements) find more ready and helpful expression in professional and public work than in intimate situations. It often seems that what provides energy, drive, and creative vitality in the former can also provide disruption in the latter.

[15]Direct encouragement might involve a chaotic early family life. Indirect encouragement might arise through a strong parental emphasis on career and on responsibility.

"get the right answer," impress the client with our astrological acumen, or convince ourselves that "astrology works." Empirical evidence suggests, here as elsewhere, the mixedness of the message and of the man's experience. We will often find that the man with the Moon-Uranus opposition (or the Venus-Uranus opposition, or, though less reliably, the squares between these planets) will sometimes play the Lunar or Venusian role and sometimes the Uranian one: sometimes seeking security and finding himself in relationships with people who resist commitment, sometimes seeking the freedom of Uranus and finding himself in relationships with people who demand unexamined commitment from him. He may go through one relationship in which he plays the lunar rule and then one in which he plays the Uranian role; or he may play the lunar role for a time in one relationship and then opt for a more Uranian approach later on—or at the same time, in a different relationship. He may feel the contradiction within himself much of the time—not an unhealthy response, as it suggests that he recognizes an inner truth, however uncomfortable. The astrological material can help the person not only to see the pattern more clearly, but also to see how to work with it more effectively.

We might say similar things about other oppositions involving apparent contradictions. If a woman has a Mars-Neptune opposition and identifies with the gender-friendly planet, she will play the role of Neptune, suggesting compassion, openness, mediumship, and a tendency to play the victim or the weaver of dreams, the maker of alluring fantasies—manifestations considered archetypally feminine. Yet Mars has an easier time allying with ego than does Neptune, for Mars has much to do with the ways ego tries to get what it wants. Certainly Mars does not demand Neptune's sacrifice or a dissolving of ego, for he want to promote ego's interests, to act in behalf of those interests, and to battle with those who oppose them. Though prevailing social attitudes may tell the woman that she "is more suited" to Neptune, her survival instinct will tell her to honor Mars.

As a result of this ongoing conundrum, the woman may project the entire opposition onto men, coming into relationship with men who manifest the more problematic facets of the aspect (men given to dissipation, to confusion, self-aggrandizing martyrdom). Or, playing Mars-role, she may actively try to rescue men who play the Neptune-role, unconsciously seeking such men out, perhaps convincing herself that they "are inspired and misunderstood."[16] Or she may play the role of Neptune and feel that she needs to be saved by a strong-willed man (Mars). Or she may unite the two planets usefully: she may study dance, study or teach t'ai chi or yoga (activities that unite physical work with spiritual yearning or imagination), or she may work for an organization that helps others.

People with oppositions should strive to become aware of and accept their own conundrums, for those conundrums lie at the root of their adjustment. If they begin by recognizing and understanding what they accept in themselves, what they reject, and in what circumstances they do either, they can begin to re-collect their projections. This doesn't mean they will achieve immediate

---

[16] Men with Mars-Neptune aspects also fall into this trap, and maybe more readily; perhaps because of cultural conditioning, they will often take on the Mars-role, letting women take on the Neptunian one.

happiness, as no-one has discovered a way to make challenging aspects into harmonious ones. Such aspects, after all, point to inner complexities that the person needs to work out, initially through an effort to become more conscious, and then through a process of creative self-integration. This kind of work, though painful, seems healthier than blindly projecting one's own capacities, needs, and potentials onto others. Feeling the apparent contradiction within himself—knowing himself more accurately—he will see the world more accurately, even if (and perhaps *because*) he feels uneasy within himself.

To withdraw a projection indicated by an opposition aspect, one must cultivate or work toward the "objective awareness" astrologers often mention in connection with such aspects. One must cultivate objectivity about one's own awareness of the world, even about perception itself—not easy to do, as we generally assume that we already *have* such objectivity! If one can develop objectivity about oneself—beginning by seeing oneself as an object among other objects—then one can do the same about others. One must try to see oneself projecting parts of oneself onto the objects of the world: that kind of subjectivity enables one to see the world more objectively. In other words, one cultivates *objectivity* by seeing more clearly the projections that one has taken for the true *objects* of the world. And one sees, perhaps, that in order to see more objectively, one must first examine subjectivity.

To withdraw the projection to oneself does not necessarily mean that one will feel more comfortable or at ease. It doesn't even mean one will feel happier. One will simply feel more whole, more complete. To arrive at this completeness, one must acknowledge one's own suffering and the suffering of the world outside of oneself. Ultimately, it involves taking some *responsibility* for the one's own suffering and the suffering of the world; in daily life, it involves re-evaluating one's conclusions about oneself and the world.

A person struggling with an opposition will probably get hit upside the head by his projections time and time again. Curiously, this process brings a blessing, though probably a well-disguised one most of the time! Probably the pattern will repeat until the individual recognizes it both conceptually and non-conceptually (though concept helps, particularly at first), both energetically and empathetically. The recurrence can prod a person toward self-awareness, though sometimes it takes a lot of prodding! We might say that if a person wants to find satisfaction, he first must recognize, then welcome, the projected energy, find it within himself and willingly act through that energy in his close one-to-one encounters.

People will tend, opposition or not, and to a greater or lesser extent, to project Saturn into the world. Similarly with the Uranus, Neptune, and Pluto. What additional information can we gain when we see one of these planets in an *opposition*? First, the opposition indicates a more virulent, striking, personal matter, one stemming from particular qualities in one's own psychology, not merely patterns found in all (or at least *most*) people. Second, opposition-related projections generally arise in one-to-one relationships, even if also in one's relationship to society-in-general. Third, the person with such an aspect tends to see the projection more readily and to understand it more objectively; certainly he has more than enough opportunities to do so. He can see "his own stuff" more clearly because that stuff appears through the people with whom he comes into contact. The aspect-related projection describes not a general truth about human beings (as with outer planet issues), but an issue related to the individual's personal psychology and experience, an issue arising in specific situations. These situations present the person with opportunities to work directly with the projection by working with the people he finds as hooks *for* that projection.

Remember, finally, that astrological factors add up. If a man with a Moon-Uranus opposition happens to be a Cancer, with Venus and the Moon also in that sign, he will be that much more likely to play the lunar role and to experience Uranus as a projection—part of the time, at any rate. And if he *does* project the Moon onto women, we would do well to investigate how that projection relates to his basic Cancer energy. If he projects out everything lunar, he will project out creative potentials. If an Aries woman with a twelfth house Moon has the same aspect, she will be less likely to play the lunar role and project the Uranian one than will a Taurus woman with a Pisces Moon in the sixth opposed Uranus in the twelfth. So, as always, we must take all relevant astrological factors into consideration.

Interlude I: The Nature of Planets and Houses

If we are to know what aspects signify, we must know what the planets signify, for aspects consist of planets. Though they may symbolize much else besides, the planets symbolize the various psychological potentials of human beings. Taken together, the planetary energies give us a symbolic map of the human potential; when we describe planetary energies, we give a psychological portrait of human beings in general. Thus in an individual horoscope, the planets, through their positions and various interactions, offer a psychological portrait of the individual, complete with conflicts, conundrums, and creative possibility. The houses, and particularly the angles, provide the primary link to the external world, the primary doors through which the planetary energies emerge.

Of course, such an inner-outer dichotomy ultimately breaks down. A planet in aspect may arise through an apparently external situation, just as an astrological house can indicate something internal, external, or relational.[17] However, astrologers have traditionally connected the houses to the various things of the world (e.g. the first with appearance and the body, the second with money, the third with immediate environment, and so on), and the houses seem to retain this connection. So we can find some justification for saying that aspects between planets symbolize primarily *inner* energy configurations that connect to the outer world via the houses and angles, these providing a kind of terrestrial atmosphere in which the planets operate. The metaphor seems appropriate, for

---

[17]Robert Hand. See his discussion of houses in *Horoscope Symbols*.

the houses of a horoscope derive from the exact place of birth and thus have a connection to the earth itself. The aspects, on the other hand, remain the same all over the earth at any particular time. So on the one hand, we can find some truth in this inner-outer dichotomy; on the other hand, the distinctions between inner and outer worlds don't always hold up to scrutiny, as we have seen.

We should probably distinguish, here, between relative statements and ultimate ones. We can put into the first category the assertion that the planets symbolize potentials for behavior and the assertion that these potentials activate in the world when they find a door through which to enter, that door provided by the houses and angles. From that point of view, if the planets themselves symbolize inner potentials, so must the aspects that connect them. Thus when aspects seem to arise through some sort of external situation, when they arise through some sort of hook, they remain primarily internal or have their roots in the internal realm. Thus we can see how to begin work with them: not by obsessing about the external situation apparently indicated by an aspect, but by turning to the inner world. Aspects point to the kind of inner work a person has to do. Viewed this way, the external appearances of aspects qualify as projections.

In chapters XI and XII, we will look more at this inner-out dichotomy. In particular, we will investigate our dualistic assumptions, particularly the most basic one that has such a pervasive influence on our daily experience: that we can actually locate an external realm and an internal realm, that the two arise separate from one another. Of course, our astrological practices seem to suggest that "things are not so simple." Accepting that statement, though, we still have to admit that, at least from a relative point of view, we experience a me-over-here in some sort of set of relations to some sort of that-over-there. From that point of view, the houses have a clear but not exclusive relationship to an external realm, what in other contexts I have referred to as the extensional realm.

Interlude II: Lack of Oppositions

We can get a better understanding of the dynamic of oppositions by understanding what happens if a person doesn't have any in his birthchart. If a person's horoscope lacks oppositions, that person will often have difficulty recognizing projections *as* projections. He will not, we might say, "get the message" very readily or easily; and if he *does* get at least a glimmer of a message, he will generally not get it very accurately—or, he won't until he's done a great deal of work on himself–and perhaps not even then. Often such an individual will need first to be introduced to the idea of projection *per se*—at least of *personal* projection—because it seems that people without oppositions benefit from a conceptual understanding of projection and how it might manifest. Such a person will have to work harder to again objectivity in his relationships. By contrast, someone with at least one important opposition in his birthchart will generally get knocked around enough by his projections that he will have an easier time seeing projections at work, admitting to their power, and learning to work with them.

Of course, as in so many matters-astrological, we should remain wary of hard-and-fast statements. A person without oppositions *can* develop great objective awareness, great sophistication in dealing with his projections, though that sophistication will generally emerge more effectively in the person's professional work than in his personal life, so much so that in the professional life, the person may manifest the missing quality with great power. For one without oppositions, the objective awareness associated with oppositions may arise in professional dealings as a gift or unusual potential.[18] Carl Jung, to take a prominent example, lacked natal planet-to-planet oppositions, yet his work with projections was fundamental to what he offered to the world. Much of his later work—e.g. his alchemical studies and his work on the transference—explored projection either directly or by implication, and his work underlies much of the material in this book. (Notably, Alfred Adler also lacked oppositions, and Freud had only a dissociate opposition.[19]) Still, though someone who lacks oppositions may have gifts in dealing with projections as they arise in professional matters, he still may not see them clearly in his personal life—at least not without a good deal of effort. Generally he will need significant intellectual input before he can make progress, and learning about them will generally take him longer and occupy more of his time. Jung worked to refine his understanding of projections for some decades.

In his *Handbook for the Humanistic Astrologer*, Michael Meyer writes that a person without oppositions "needs to learn how to maintain an objective life perspective" and is "completely responsible for the maintenance of his own equilibrium." Meyer goes on to say that "this may place him in great control of his own destiny" but that it can also lead to a "disintegration of the personality."[20] My own observations support Meyer's. It seems that the person must take full responsibility for "the maintenance of [his] own equilibrium" precisely because he doesn't get the benefit of the straightforward feedback provided by projections involving opposition aspects. Without this precise feedback—without getting bonked on the head enough times—the person will have more difficulty getting the message. He will take his own version of the world as unquestionably real.

Of course, if someone lacking oppositions does *not* work on himself, he may fall victim to his projections. This observation may give us some insight into some of the policies of recent U.S. Presidents, for not only does George W. Bush lack oppositions, but Bill Clinton does as well—as does his former nemesis, Ken Starr—along with John F. Kennedy and Eisenhower. If we go back in time a bit, we could cite FDR, Harry Truman, and Abraham Lincoln. Starting with FDR, the United States had four no-opposition presidents in a row; more recently, we've had two more. This may account for some of our country's difficulties dealing with "opposition," for if the president acts on his own delusions, we can hardly expect good results in relations with other nations. The as-

---

[18] My studies have suggested that whatever is missing from a horoscope and whatever is empty in that horoscope—an element, a horoscope sector, a type of aspect—may prove a cross to bear in the personal life and a gift in the professional life. I have discussed these matters at length in an as-yet-unpublished manuscript that appeared, some years ago and in slightly different form, as a series of articles in *American Astrology* magazine.

[19] A dissociate opposition takes place from signs that do not oppose each other. We saw one such opposition in the horoscope of Alice B. Sheldon: she had her Sun in early Virgo and her Moon in late Aquarius, well-within the acceptable orb for an opposition, though Virgo and Aquarius do not oppose each other.

[20] Michael R. Meyer, *Handbook for the Humanistic Astrologer* (New York: Anchor Books, 1974), 161.

trological material may help to explain why Eisenhower and Kennedy catapulted the United States into Vietnam and why George W. Bush has catapulted us into all sorts of hot Middle Eastern water. It may help to explain why Truman dropped the bomb and why the fears of the Cold War became so exaggerated and solid in the minds of so many of these men. Most of them felt that they had sighted evil in the external world, but they seemed to have missed something within themselves. As for presidents "working on themselves," it seems that many people occupying the seats of power occupy themselves so much with what they take as *objectivity*, that they spend too little time asking whether their view of the world really qualifies as objective.

If a person has difficulty even *seeing* his own projections, he probably won't investigate them. He does not, we might say, get jolted upright by his projections; the projections arise, but he doesn't recognize them as projections and so doesn't see them as having any connection to his own psychology. He tends to regard them only as external problems. Without the kind of phenomenal-world feedback provided by oppositions, such a person must keep his own ship righted (as per Meyer, above), whereas a person with strong oppositions gets help from the people onto whom he casts his projections. Those people, not aligning perfectly with the person's projections, can wake him up. Without this feedback, the person lacking oppositions may lose the objectivity that oppositions can provide; he will more readily, and blindly, take his version of the world for the world itself, and thus may move further and further into fantasy. The person may feel in control of his own destiny (even to the point of becoming President of the United States) because he can get by, in some degree, without a great deal of reflection and without having his experience constantly wake him up.

People with important oppositions don't have this luxury (so to speak). They generally cannot function well in the world unless they reflect on the repeating experience brought to them via the opposition aspect. They must constantly stop to assess the meaning of experience; either that, or the projection will simply stand as an obstacle to overcome, impeding progress. People with important oppositions must develop more objectivity about the "objective" world if only because of the consequences of *not* doing so. But the *ob*jectivity in this case often involves becoming more *sub*jective, for to have objectivity about the objective world, one must plunge into oneself, to discover what one has rejected and ejected from oneself and how that ejected material has colored one's experience to an undue degree. Subjectivity, here, yields objectivity. By contrast, the person lacking oppositions will often take his subjectivity *for* objectivity: because the person doesn't find himself constantly prodded to reflect, he takes his subjective version as objective truth.

I should reiterate, here, that these problems arise most egregiously in people who not only lack oppositions but who are also not given to reflection or self-awareness. As we have seen above, we cannot discern a person's level of awareness through astrological factors alone. We could find many examples of reflective people who lacked oppositions (e.g. Jung and Adler). For such people, that which the horoscope lacks can arise as a creative gift, something one offers to the world; it seems that the person feels a lack of some sort, feels that he should cultivate something so he works, so he works to develop the missing energy—and, often, he works hard enough that the energy manifests through his vocation.

The Square

Aspects suggest praxes in relation to the planets involved. As we have seen, in working with an opposition, one should try to develop an objective awareness about the projections involved – about what one habitually projects, first rejecting specific psychic elements from consciousness and then experiencing those elements, vicariously, through events and people inhabiting a world that seems external to oneself. Sometimes the square functions in a way similar to the opposition: we sometimes project one end of the square out into the environment. Generally, though, the square brings a different dynamic.

Whereas the opposition symbolizes a need and a striving for objective awareness (an awareness about the objects of the world and their nature), the square symbolizes a propensity and need to build structures both psychological and situational. Because of this, the square often appears first either as an obstructive structure or situation in one's life or as an apparently intractable attitude within the psyche; and the two will reflect each other to such a degree that we can consider the former as the projected form of the latter; in any case, the person with a challenging square will generally get further if he includes the internal matters in his attempts to deal with the external challenges. Because of the square's connection to structure, when it appears as a projection, it will often appear as a whole, not split into a projected element and an element experienced as one's own. Thus, for example, a Moon-Saturn square in a man's chart will often arise as and through women (Moon) who seem to have Saturnian characteristics, whereas the opposition will often arise through projections in which the man plays the role of one planet or the other.[21]

As the presenting challenge of a square differs from that of the opposition, the two demand different praxes. Because the opposition involves role-playing, a person dealing with an opposition should strive to see the connection between the role that he projects and the role that he accepts; he will make progress if he sees the connection between the acceptance and the rejection. The square, on the other hand, tells us that the individual should develop a venue or structure through which to bring the involved planets into activity together.

We can see the structure-building energy of the square in the horoscopes of Thomas Mann and Henry Kissinger,[22] each of whom has a square from Saturn to Pluto, though in different signs, and with Mann's aspect having a much narrower orb. Despite the differences, both men involved themselves, not merely by theorizing or pondering, but in the primary activities of their lives, with the power (Pluto) of social structure (Saturn), or with the ways in which hidden power lurks in all sorts of status quo organizations and orientations. For Mann, this concern emerged through his published writing (Pluto in ninth) characterized by and sometimes explicitly based in a strong sense

---

[21]Of course, if, in a heterosexual relationship with a woman, the man plays the lunar role, he will find himself dealing with a woman who seems to have Saturnian qualities. But the projection of Saturn may also find its hook with men, particularly authority figures or older men, whereas the Moon-Saturn square as projection will generally finds its hook with the women in the man's life.

[22]See the horoscopes in the Supplementary Material at the end of the book.

of music (Taurus). Certainly his *Doctor Faustus* stands as an example of this connection. The aspect manifested slightly differently in *Death in Venice*, where an elderly scholar finds his reputation (Saturn) threatened by a forbidden, earth-bound obsession (Pluto in Taurus). Saturn in Aquarius suggests concerns with the structures of society; Pluto in Taurus suggests entrenched, hidden, and destructive power based in intransigent values and money. Saturn-Pluto also appears in Mann's *The Magic Mountain* and *Buddenbrooks*, both of which deal with the power of those in authority; though the power often remains hidden and behind the scenes, we see it move inexorably forward in both novels.

Kissinger's Saturn-Pluto square goes from Saturn retrograde in Libra in the fifth house to Pluto in Cancer in the first (though on the cusp of the second). Pluto in the first suggests powerful action; the influence of the second emerges through Kissinger's ongoing connection to financial elites, for whom he served as a combination spokesperson, ideologue, and power-broker. Saturn rules the eighth house, suggesting the money of others. In Libra, Saturn suggests that he structured his world, both mentally and situationally, around a socially-accepted standard weight: he defended the status quo arrangements, particularly those connected to the United States government, as his Saturn conjoins the United States Saturn; in the tenth house, the latter points to the way the United States tries to maintain an authoritative position among the "family of nations." Kissinger found himself inextricably bound with this drive for authority. Furthermore, his Pluto conjoins the United States Venus-Jupiter conjunction, an aspect that points not only to the United States' abundance (Jupiter) and good fortune (Venus and Jupiter) in maintaining (Cancer) the so-called "national security," but also, with its placement on the cusp of the eighth house, with others' values. Certainly Kissinger facilitated the United States attempt to secure wealth and thus find security by taking the values or resources (eighth) of others. With his Mars-Ascendant conjunction conjoining the U.S. Mars, Kissinger played a vital role in myriad U.S. aggressions; he thus taps into the U.S. tendency to act deceptively, a matter discussed in chapter X.

F. Lee Bailey's horoscope has a close square from his Gemini Sun in the third house over to his Mars-Jupiter conjunction in Virgo in the sixth. Bailey acted assertively, though some would say aggressively, with expansive confidence. In Virgo, Mars-Jupiter suggests services to others, which Bailey clearly performed, time and again defending people previously considered obviously guilty. With Jupiter ruling his ninth house (writing, legal philosophy) and Mars as the exalted ruler of his Midheaven, he combined writing, legal thinking, confidence, and the drive to serve. We can even detect principles (Jupiter) in his actions, though some will see only legal principles at work (and not, for example, moral ones), but I don't know enough about Bailey's inner world to comment on such a matter. In any case, all of these potentials connect to his Sun in Gemini in the third house: to his love of speech, of talk, of turning over facts, of engaging in repartee. In his legal work, he found the perfect venue, or structure, for these energies. This search for venue differs from what occurred with his Moon-Pluto opposition, for if we take the Moon in Capricorn in the tenth house as suggesting ambition and an ongoing connection between security and competence (i.e. he didn't feel secure unless he could demonstrate competence), then we can take Pluto as something he projected onto either the powers of the state or the dark qualities so many saw in the clients he defended, for often those people seemed threatening, unredeemed, and manipulative.

Though we will take a much longer look at the United States horoscope in chapter X, we can note, here, that it gives us another example of the venue-creating tendencies of the square and the very different dynamic of the opposition. Though the United States Mercury-Pluto opposition arises through situations in which the United States plays the role of Mercury in Cancer and projects Pluto onto other groups, the Mars-Neptune square arises either through the United States' own deceptive actions, or through the apparently deceptive actions of the purported enemy; and the Sun-Saturn square arises through the United States' authoritative stances, through the country's tendency to play the authority-role, and through what the United States perceives as the limitations (Saturn) of tradition-bound (Saturn again) societies in which family and blood-connections (Cancer) play dominant roles.[23] When Mars-Neptune arises as structure, the United States acts deceptively; when it arises as projection, the United States sees other nations or groups (e.g. Native Americans and communists from the Soviet Union, the so-called masters of deceit[24]) as acting deceitfully. When Sun-Saturn arises as structured activity, the United States tells other nations what to do; when it arises as projection, the United States sees other nations or groups as bogged down and limited by tradition or authoritarianism.

People generally work best with oppositions by developing objective awareness and accurate perception; people generally work best with squares by cultivating or developing activities or venues through which to bring the relevant energies into coordination.[25] With oppositions, we must *recognize* our own energies in the world; with squares, we must *utilize* our skills and strengths. With oppositions, we must recognize our own face *in* the world; with squares, we harness our potentials in order to change the face *of* our world. With the opposition, we recognize and gather; with the square, we harness and utilize.

People often utilize squares rather badly, at least early in life. For example, though a Mars-Neptune square can indicate great potential in any action demanding compassion, spiritual vision, or artistic inspiration, for most people it arises first as directionless action, deceptive action, self-deception, or as a tendency to send the troops off in the wrong direction. Though the aspect might point one toward a career in dance, yoga, social service, or theatre—anything that links one's vision

---

[23]This apparently simple phrase—*the United States sees*—doesn't seem simple at all upon closer examination. What, after all, do we mean when we say that a nation "sees"? I will return to this interesting question in chapter X.
[24]So called by J. Edgar Hoover in his *Masters of Deceit*.
[25]Sometimes one would give the same advice for working with a trine, though for different reasons. Trines often indicate laxness. The trine can point to arenas in which a person takes the path of least resistance, resting on whatever laurels one has available. If, therefore, a person finds a structure through which the trine can work creatively, he will act more productively. A person with a square can take the same approach, though for different reasons. Though someone with a trine won't suffer unduly if he doesn't create such a venue (except through what an economist might call an opportunity cost), someone with a square will generally find that unless he creates such a venue, the square will arise as situational blockages of all kinds.

or imagination to one's physical capabilities—it can also indicate tendencies to deceive oneself and others about one's intentions, or as a psychological tendency to avoid the structures and discipline necessary to unite one's will with one's vision. Neptune may vitiate Mars, so one may feel that one's will is sapped, that one cannot gather one's energy together. Most people find it difficult to remain a dreamer while fully engaged in self-directed, willful activity; but the aspect demands that the dream and the willful effort remain yoked together in order to accomplish the valuable work.

Squares tend to arise in at least two characteristic ways: creatively, through ventures or venues that constitute an energetic response enabling a person (or nation) to bring the two planetary energies together; or reactively, through external situations or challenges that reflect one's difficulty fully engaging one's own energy.[26] These external situations can arise at different times from the same square, particularly if the creative venue encompasses only a very limited amount of the aspect's potential. Thus with Thomas Mann's squares—Saturn squares Pluto, Venus, conjoining Pluto, squares Uranus—even if we posit that his writing served as a venue or conduit for his concerns about the social order, we should also acknowledge that in his non-professional life, the venue he developed did not seem to serve all that well. We can perhaps attribute this to Venus, which in conjoining Pluto participates in the square. Certainly Mann's taboo drives in matters of love or relationship ran up against the standards of the group (Saturn in Aquarius) or the status quo generally. Though Mann married, it seems quite clear that he desired men and thus found himself drawn to that which society had forbidden, suggesting Venus-Pluto. (I have read that when he lived in Pacific Palisades, he would go down to Muscle Beach and watch the men lift weights.) Because Venus has a fairly close square to Uranus, we would expect him to magnetize or feel drawn to (Venus) something considered non-status-quo (Uranus), for we can consider homosexuality as a Uranian activity when it runs counter to status-quo arrangements. To Uranus' penchant for the iconoclastic, Pluto adds the lure of the forbidden or taboo. In some ways, his marriage served as a façade or illusion: with Pisces on the seventh house cusp and Pisces-ruler Neptune in the eighth, Mann hid his honest yearnings as a reaction to others' values.

Though a square will usually arise either through organized actions in which the person, nation, or collectivity can engage both ends of the square, or through projections that include or express both ends of the square, it can split (as in Mann's case) in a manner similar to oppositions when the individual has a much more comfortable or socially-acceptable relationship with one planet than with another in some area of life (as in Mann's private life). This may occur when the square includes one inner or gender-friendly planet with an outer planet, or with some other planet that challenges ego. It may also occur if one's work or life situation encourages a more comfortable relationship with one planet than with another. Certainly this occurred in Mann's case, and it seems to have occurred with George Herbert Bush and Mitt Romney as well: each has a Sun-Uranus square; each has achieved a position of great social prominence allied with powerful forces in the prevail-

---

[26]Some decades back, Marc Edmund Jones wrote that the closest hard aspect in a horoscope has much to do with vocational direction. I have found this true with many, many clients. These observations reinforce the idea that squares need venue.

ing hierarchy; each has apparently found the Uranus energy incompatible with his drive for power within the prevailing hierarchy of the Republican Party; each has apparently projected Uranus onto leftists of various stripes.

Early-life patterns provide ready examples. A Moon-Saturn square will often arise, in one's first few years, through a mother (Moon) who is unable or unwilling (Saturn) to fully nurture the infant; the entire aspect will point to the child's experience of the mother—and, often, to some ongoing structure or situation in the mother's life. The infant clearly cannot yet create the venues necessary to bring the Moon and Saturn together creatively, so he experiences them together reactively.[27] Later, he will probably experience the square either as a projection onto women (women, for example, who doubt their own nurturing capacities or who lacked nurturance early in life), or as a subtle series of life-structures that serve as mechanisms helping the man to avoid looking at his own loneliness or sense of isolation, with the man playing the role of the Moon (emotions and security needs) and projecting Saturn into the world as forces resistant to his emotional fulfillment. However, these "forces" may appear through women who, seeming to embody the entire Moon-Saturn square, refuse or seem unable to offer emotional support.

Though a child will generally have difficulty finding or creating venues that might "house" the Moon-Saturn energies, an adult might do a better job. He might develop emotional independence, developing psychological structures and strength, realizing that beneath the suffering indicated by the aspect lurks a basic human wisdom: that in the last analysis, others will not nurture us, that one must learn to feed oneself, that each person exists alone and must not only recognize this aloneness but also find the path to wisdom that moves through it. At the same time, the person can develop external structures or venues, perhaps a vocation in which he can give emotional support to others through highly organized activity, perhaps through serving in an authority role, recognizing the necessary relationship between nurturing and structure—a relationship most parents recognize: that children generally don't get nurtured unless they have some structure or container, and that sometimes the structure actually seems to function as a source of nurturing support.

Squares may also arise when, because of economic or social circumstances, a person finds it difficult to act effectively for his or her own interests. If the square involves Saturn (as in the Moon-Saturn square just discussed), the person will quite possibly and habitually project Saturn into the environment (where it will appear as difficulties). However, an *entire* square may also appear as a projection: Moon-Saturn as women who seem restrictive, cold, or authoritarian; Sun or Mars-Saturn as men who seem to have similar dispositions; Mercury-Saturn as people or institutions with apparently rigid ideas or agendas; and so forth. Other squares may also arise through situations. The following examples illustrate some variations:

---

[27]These observations don't necessarily reflect on the mother's character. The mother may truly want to nurture her child, but her life circumstances may intrude. For example, she may have to work for a living. The aspect may also reflect the mother's own psychological state, which may be partly shaped by her relationship to her own mother.

- Mohandas Gandhi's square from a tenth house Leo Moon over to Jupiter and Pluto conjoined in Taurus in the seventh: an aspect projected, at least in part, onto the British Empire (because of Gandhi's opposition from Mars and Venus in Scorpio in the first over to Jupiter and Pluto in Taurus in the seventh) with its imperial ambitions mixed with social and financial power related to India (Jupiter-Pluto in Taurus). The square appeared creatively through Gandhi's way of putting his own personality on the line in dramatic moves involving public feeling and designed to increase the social influence of native peoples.

- Herman Melville's Neptune-Pluto square: projected, it appeared through numinous symbols such as the Great White Whale and through his ongoing concern with collective issues and trends (e.g. Melville's concern about the power of collective delusion); yet the aspect also appeared in the power (Pluto) of Melville's imagination (Neptune), and in the structures (square) he developed to communicate that powerful (Pluto) imaginative vision (Neptune).

- Jerry Rubin's square from his Cancer Sun over to Saturn in Aries on the cusp of the eighth house: an aspect projected, early on, onto the United States as an authoritarian system concerned with its own security (reflected in the U.S. square from the eighth house Cancer Sun up to Saturn in the tenth); late in life, after his Yippie days had passed, the aspect square arose through work involving feeding others and catering to their values.

- Bob Dylan's square from Mercury in Gemini on the seventh house cusp up to Neptune intercepted in the ninth house in Virgo lies on top of the U. S. Mars-Neptune square: to some extent, Dylan may have projected the aspect onto the United States, and he certainly spoke out against the United States' deceptive (Neptune) use of military power (Mars); yet it also appeared in his imagination, through a union of words (Mercury) and musical imagination (Neptune, particularly for someone with a strong Taurean emphasis)—songs that served as the venue for his imaginative mind.

- Hillary Clinton has a square from the Moon to Uranus. Sometimes the square appears in her own behavior: by achieving a position of power, she has done more to further women's freedom than many famous books have done. At various times in her life, though, the aspect has appeared through women younger and less encumbered than she by social sanctions like marriage and position. Sometimes the aspect has split, with Hillary playing the role of the Moon while her husband played the role of Uranus. Ms. Clinton also has a square from Mercury over to Saturn, and more loosely to Pluto, and Venus squares Pluto more closely. More than once, she found herself in the role of the jealous woman (Venus-Pluto, and with a Scorpio Sun). But Mercury-Saturn plays a particularly important role. Ms. Clinton thinks along organizational lines, not radical or progressive ones; when she uses her intellect, she usually does so in service to authoritarian regimes. After putting herself through the discipline needed to attain high positions (Saturn), she becomes more prone to project Moon-Uranus onto woman, for she takes on the role of *logos*, leaving *eros* to other women who come into her life (arriving there via a Leo husband who apparently likes their adulation).

- Ken Starr has a close square from Mars in Virgo down to Uranus in Gemini. Mr. Starr seems, at least at times, to have projected the aspect onto Bill Clinton, who is a pretty good hook for it, having Mars on his Ascendant and Uranus elevated in his ninth house conjoined his North Node. Some would perhaps say, though, that Starr played the role of Mars and projected Uranus onto Clinton, with Starr playing the role of assertive propriety, sometimes one of Mars in Virgo's less attractive manifestations. In his apparent sexual peccadilloes, Clinton served as a fine hook for an unaccepted Uranus. Starr played the role of a rule-keeper speaking with the voice of purported morality, as befits the conjunction between his Cancer Sun and Saturn, with the latter ruling his Capricorn Ascendant.[28] With such a strong Saturnian statement in his horoscope, he would have a strong tendency to project out the rebellious Mars-Uranus (or at least the Uranus part) and to condemn the activities it symbolizes even if those activities mirror unacknowledged tendencies in Starr himself.

- George Herbert Bush, whom Clinton followed into the White House, has a close square from his tenth house Gemini Sun to Uranus in Pisces in the seventh house. Uranus is also the focal planet of a loose yod, but because we find Uranus in the seventh house, we would expect Bush to project it onto others, particularly those who would rebel in any way against the status quo. But does Bush project the whole aspect, or just the Uranus part? Usually the latter, I think. Bush's Sun conjoins the United States Mars; his Moon conjoins the United States Saturn; the Sun and Midheaven trine both the Moon and Saturn (which conjoin each other in Libra). These aspects, along with the Sun's elevated position conjoined the Midheaven, brought some ease of function to the Sun as long as Bush played ball with those representing the U.S. power structure and as long as he aligned himself with the military (United States Mars). Understandably, he projected the Uranus on the descendant: anyone who upset the applecart, whether he call himself a radical or a Saddam Hussein, quickly became one of Bush's open enemies.

We can see from these examples that the square arises sometimes as a clear potential, sometimes as a feared potential in others, and sometimes as a mix, appearing now as one, now as the other. These examples also serve to reiterate the suggested praxis for the square: one should strive to develop a venue or structure through or within which one can harness both planets of the square into a single activity, moving them toward a single goal.

The Conjunction

Unless they occur in houses prone to projection (e.g. twelfth, seventh, eighth, even the tenth), conjunctions generally don't split like oppositions or demand venue like squares. However, much

---

[28]Starr's Sun-Saturn closely conjoins the U. S. Mercury in Cancer, the planet symbolizing the national popular opinion related to family values, the position suggesting that Americans like to see themselves as nice, insular, homemakers, people who tend to see any action threatening the home as immoral. (Starr's Moon also squares Saturn, though in a dissociate aspect, reiterating his conservatism in relation to "family values.") Starr's Sun-Saturn opposes the U.S. Pluto, suggesting that he will get caught up in any national obsession about taboos, sexual or otherwise.

depends on the person's relationship to the planet or planets in question. For example, a man with a Sun-Saturn conjunction in the twelfth house might project the entire aspect (Sun, Saturn, conjunction, twelfth, plus the sign involved) out onto people who in various ways undermine his progress in the world, often in ways that escape his observation. Sometimes such a conjunction can appear as people of authoritative power and confidence working in secrecy, or who help people who have suffered some defeat at the hands of the world, or who themselves have suffered that defeat, or people who work behind the scenes in some way. In other words, though the conjunction will usually appear as one's own capacity for disciplined creativity, and though the twelfth house has a documented connection to vocational work, it can sometimes appear in projected form. The placement in the twelfth suggests that the early life environment didn't encourage the expression of the Sun-Saturn energy.

But even if a conjunction occurs in a house not generally connected with projection, it can sometimes arise in projected form if the individual has for some reason rejected the energy. Sometimes we should at least ask whether a conjunction will end up as a projection at least some of the time. Consider the following possibilities:

- The conjunction falls in the seventh or twelfth house, houses that often indicate projection.
- The conjunction contains one more planets that raise difficult gender-issues: the so-called feminine planets for a man, the so-called masculine planets for a woman.
- The conjunction connects with other aspects, particularly an opposition in which the person will tend to play the role of the opposing planet (for example, in a woman's chart, an opposition between the Moon and a Mars-Uranus conjunction).
- More generally, when the conjunction presents energies that ego deems unacceptable.
- The conjunction contains two planets that work at apparent cross purposes to each other: Moon-Uranus; Mars-Neptune; sometimes Venus-Pluto; Sun-Venus, particularly in a man's chart; Saturn-Uranus, and so forth. In this case, we would look to see if the conjunction splits, with the person playing the role of one planet and projecting the other (not the usual manifestation, but a possible one).

In general, though, to decide whether a conjunction, or part of it, will end up as a projection, we must refer to related horoscope factors: sign position, house position, other aspects, and planetary compatibility. Gandhi's Jupiter-Pluto conjunction in the seventh house gives us a good example of how a conjunction may sometimes appear as a projection and sometimes as a consciously promulgated potential: as discussed above, sometimes it arose in projected form as the social and financial power of the British Empire, which makes sense considering its seventh house placement, suggesting "open enemies"; sometimes, though, it clearly appeared as a potential, for Gandhi quite consciously sought social (Jupiter) power (Pluto) in financial matters (Taurus), and he acted with what seemed immovable determination (Taurus again) in whatever work he undertook.

Chapter VI

Houses as Indicators of Projection

Any planet in any house can arise via projection at any time, as one level of house-symbolism tells us about external events.[1] In the traditional view, houses give us information about the life-areas in which the planetary capacities operate, and every house has a relational component that brings other people into the picture. We know that the seventh house has to do with one-to-one relationships with equals, and we also know that the seventh, whether as the house of marriage or of open enemies, contains information about the people with whom we will come into relationship as equals. The eleventh house tells us about one-to-many relationships and about the people we encounter in such relationships. Or, more precisely, these houses tell us about the individual's *version* of the people encountered in the relationship, or perhaps the individual's *experience* of those people, as distinguished from "the people themselves." The same principle holds for the other houses: for the sixth, which tells us about unequal relationships (master-servant; teacher-student; master-apprentice); for the eighth, which tells us about financial relations; for the tenth, which tells us about professional ones; for the fourth, which tells us about relationships in the home; and so forth. The symbolism of those houses includes people of various sorts, but the houses symbolize a person's *version* of those people rather than the people themselves.

Furthermore, because all of the houses tell us about relationships of some sort, we should see each house as symbolizing particular elements *of* those relationships. For example, though the sixth house tells us about unequal relationships, it also tells us about the inequality that we can find in most *any* relationship. If I decide to take guitar lessons, my teacher presumably knows more about

---

[1] Some of the material in this paragraph derives from Robert Hand's work. Many astrologers have obviously learned a lot from Mr. Hand, and I readily acknowledge even those borrowings that I have inadvertently omitted.

guitar-playing than I do, so the sixth house will give us information about that element or part of the relationship. We should distinguish that element or part from the relationship as a whole, for perhaps my guitar teacher wants to take cooking lessons from me (probably not a good idea, though she perhaps doesn't know that yet!), or perhaps she and I feel attracted to each other, so our relationship metamorphoses into a marriage (an as-equal relationship, at least in theory). In other words, we wouldn't say that the relationship "is unequal," for that attribution has little meaning outside of a rather narrow context. The teacher knows more about guitar-playing than I do, and insofar as she and I deal with guitar-playing (or cooking) via a teaching-relationship, the sixth house applies. However, if my teacher and I also refer to each other as "lovers," then in non-guitar-playing contexts, other houses have at least as much relevance: certainly the seventh, probably the eighth and first, and likely some others (such as the ninth if we like to travel together). Or, we might say, *all* the others, even if not to such a great extent, for the houses tell us, first and foremost, about a person's *approach* to discernible qualities or modalities of relationship. So though houses sometimes tell us about areas of activity or the arenas in which activity takes place, they also tell us about the above-mentioned modalities. Planets in houses tell us that a particular psychological component tends to express itself most directly in a specific arena or through a specific modality.

If we accept the premise that all of our experience qualifies as projection, or at least as partly mind-created, then we would see *every* house as a source or indicator of some projected material. I tend to think that such a view has merit, but if we adopt it here, we will veer toward statements about ultimate truths instead of the relative ones that arise in our experience day-to-day. In that day-to-day experience, some houses arise as more obvious, challenging, and discernible projections than do others. Also, if we accepted as a premise for this chapter the notion that all houses point to projections, we would lead ourselves into a discussion of all of the events that people experience in the various life-arenas symbolized in the horoscope, going from house-to-house to explain the panoply of human awareness and activity—obviously too big a task for one chapter! I will therefore concentrate on those houses that seem to produce projections that often hinder people's adjustment to experience in obvious and problematic ways. In this, I follow the approach of Marie Louise von Franz. In a passage quoted earlier, she says that in practice, we speak of projections only when they hinder a person's efforts to adjust to life, when they present obstacles of a sufficiently serious kind that the person can't see the way forward without additional insight. Though from an ultimate point of view we might see this as true for all of us all the time (for probably none of us has adjusted to life completely; for most or, probably, all of us, projections block the pathway to full adjustment, even if those projections seem opaque or seem like nothing other than the world itself), from a relative point of view, most of us adjust adequately much of the time. I will focus here on those projections that arise in the *rest* of the time.

I will therefore look first at projections related seventh, twelfth, and eighth houses, and then at the fourth, tenth and sixth. Not coincidentally, these houses begin at degree-measures from the Ascendant marking challenging aspects: 180 degrees (opposition; seventh house); 150 degrees (quincunx; sixth and eighth); 90 degrees (square; fourth and tenth); and 30 degrees (semi-sextile;

twelfth). We should remember, though, that the presence of factors already mentioned (gender-related projections; aspect-related projections) can indicate projections lurking in *any* house. Much depends, as always, on other factors in the horoscope.

The above-listed houses include all of the so-called water houses (fourth, eighth, and twelfth). We shouldn't feel surprised at this, given the general orientation of a culture in which myriad factors encourage us to deal with the world rationally, not emotionally; professionally, not empathetically; with attention to surface detail, not to hidden dynamics. Further, if we deal with our feelings, we often find ourselves out of step with professional demands (for I suspect that many, perhaps most, of us often feel like not going to work at all!) and in more direct contact with suffering and empathy. Our difficulties dealing with emotional demands seem particularly acute in the modern era. If, as I argued some years ago in *Astrology Beyond Ego*, we should direct much of our emotional energy to the living earth, with which most of us have less and less contact at least partly because of social factors and consequent environmental ones, then most of us will feel some dissatisfaction most of the time. On the one hand, practical demands often seem to dictate the ignoring of emotional needs; on the other, if some of our emotions find their most natural home in the natural world, then the ongoing destruction of the ecosystem will engender a painful emotional response.[2]

Despite these general patterns, house-based projections often have a distinctly personal feeling, for the houses in an individual horoscope derive from the particular time and place of the birth. The house-cusps change minute-by-minute, while the aspects remain in effect at least for some hours (aspects from the Moon), and sometimes for days, weeks, or months, depending on the aspecting-planets' rates of motion. Further (and as we will see) the projection of outer planets doesn't seem unique to any individual, for most humans apparently project those planets most of the time simply because ego wants stability and the outer planets threaten it. Something similar happens with Saturn: ego wants pleasure; Saturn generally doesn't offer it, at least not directly or obviously; most people therefore project Saturn a good deal of the time. Many (perhaps most) women (in our culture, at any rate, but apparently in many others as well) receive little encouragement to pursue iconoclastic activities, so they often project Uranus onto men. Many (perhaps most) men receive little encouragement to deal with their feelings; so they often project their lunar energies onto women. But though all people born on a specific day or time will have the same aspects, the houses in which those aspects fall give information unique to the individual. For example, projections involving the twelfth house often reflect specific factors in a person's early family life. Something similar might be said for projections involving the fourth house. Projections involving the seventh house reflect specific factors related to how a person asserts himself in the world, and eighth house projections often reflect a person's attitudes toward cultural taboos or socially-accepted values.

---

[2]Further, if, as I argued more recently in *The Machine Stops: The Mayan Long Count Through a Western Lens* (Tempe: American Federation of Astrologers, 2012), we live at the junction between two major aeons (at the end of the Mayan Long Count and the cusp between the Ages of Pisces and Aquarius), we can expect a considerable amount of social and cultural dislocation. How shall one find emotional security in connection to the living earth if that living earth may no longer support human life—or at least the life-approach commonly taken in the kinds of societies that humans have developed?

The Twelfth House

The traditional meanings associated with the twelfth house don't seem all that encouraging: hidden enemies, self-undoing, prisons, clandestine activities, hidden psychic factors, karma and self-undoing. Even if some of the negative elements seem to reflect cultural prejudices, the keywords don't provide much in the way of positive or hopeful prospects! And we can't really say that the traditional meanings are incorrect, for the empirical evidence surely suggests that the twelfth house presents real problems for millions of people: the house does seem to contain (so to speak) the hidden enemies of traditional astrological lore; it does have to do with "self-undoing"; in some cases, it has a clear connection to prisons, psychological impoverishment, and clandestine activities.

A more contemporary view of the twelfth house, backed by much empirical observation, suggests that this house contains the energy of early life defeats.[3] Twelfth house energies often emerge early in life and suffer some kind of defeat at the hands of the environment. The person therefore tends, because of painful personal experience, not to trust these energies, and even if we say that these energies, viewed differently, can emerge as potentials, they seem to come up at least partly as stumbling blocks in the continually-repeating short run. Furthermore, they seem to come up that way because we generally reject twelfth house energies and thus make them susceptible to projection. These hidden psychic functions, potentials in another guise, lie behind the difficult manifestations of this house. If we can bring them to the surface, we can mitigate this effect, so we should begin by trying to understand what the twelfth house represents.

If you are born within an hour or so after sunrise, you will have your natal Sun in the twelfth house, for the sun rises (so to speak) into that house. This connection between sunrise and the twelfth surely suggests that we should not consider the twelfth a malefic house, for the first hours after sunrise surely don't seem malefic. Many (perhaps most) people in our culture sleep through the twelfth house period of the day, particularly in summer (when the sun rises earlier), suggesting that perhaps we do not have intimate contact with the energies represented there; because many those people dream just before they wake up, we can see the connection between the twelfth house and sub-conscious energies that emerge into consciousness, for the twelfth lies above the horizon. The connection between the twelfth house and sunrise strongly suggests that the house contains enormous creative potential, often serving as a conduit through which non-conscious psychic elements emerge into the world. It seems fitting, then, that the Gaquelins found a close connection between the twelfth house and vocational eminence.[4]

The astronomical facts suggest a close connection between fresh, creative energy and vulnerability, for though the hours after sunrise contain the promise of the hours to follow, they also bring the ephemeral. Just as the dew that has formed on the grass during the night quickly disappears in the light of day or gets crushed by passersby, so planets in the twelfth house often get crushed or undermined early in life and thus bring setbacks and defeats later on.

---

[3] I think many astrologers have seen this connection. I may have come across it first in the writings of Robert Hand.
[4] See Michel Gauquelin, *Written in the Stars* (Northamptonshire, England: Aquarian Press, 1988).

When a person experiences early life defeats in relation to some of his potential, that person often learns to mistrust the potential. Thus the person often rejects twelfth house energies, relegating them to the unconscious—not the collective unconscious, which seems more closely connected to the 4th house and the nadir, but to the personal unconscious, what we might call the personal garbage heap, a collection of energies that the conscious personality has deemed unacceptable, unworthy, or counter-productive. Remaining unconscious, twelfth house energies readily arise as projections, appearing in the world as energies we mistrust or that undermine our efforts.

In order to understand the twelfth house, we should first understand the distinction between Freud's ideas about the unconscious and those developed later by his student, Carl Jung. The term "personal unconscious" derives from Jung and refers to psychic material that though once conscious has not remained so. The individual has repressed some material, finding it incompatible with the demands or habits of the conscious ego. In distinguishing between his ideas and those of Freud, Jung described Freud's view:

> In Freud's view, as most people know, the contents of the unconscious are reducible to infantile tendencies which are repressed because of their incompatible character. Repression is a process that begins in early childhood under the moral influence of the environment and continues throughout life. By means of analysis, the repressions are removed and the repressed wishes made conscious.
>
> According to this theory, the unconscious contains only those parts of the personality which could just as well be conscious, and have been repressed only through the process of education.[5]

Jung goes on to supplement this view of the unconscious, which he does not reject, with another view: the one that brings in the collective unconscious as an additional compensatory element. We will return to the collective unconscious later; here, we need only note the emphasis on repression, for though Jung tells us that repression cannot account for all of the material of the unconscious, it *can* account for some of it, what he refers to as "the most conspicuous"[6] elements. In other words, though we can surely find in the unconscious "allusions that go far beyond the personal sphere,"[7] we should not therefore ignore the personal contents of the personal unconscious. Jung's description of this, quoted at length here, has direct bearing on our understanding of the twelfth house:

> …we have to distinguish in the unconscious a layer which we may call the personal unconscious. The materials contained in this layer are of a personal nature in so far as they have the character partly of acquisitions derived from the individual's life and partly of psychological factors which could just as well be conscious. It can readily be understood that incompatible psychological elements are liable to repression and therefore become unconscious. But on the other hand this implies the possibility of making and

---

[5] C.G. Jung, "Relations Between the Ego and the Unconscious," *The Portable Jung* (New York: Penguin, 1971), 70-1.
[6] Jung, 71.
[7] Jung, 72.

keeping the repressed contents conscious once they have been recognized. We recognize them as personal contents because their effects, or their partial manifestation, or their source can be discovered in our personal past. They are the integral components of the personality, they belong to its inventory, and their loss to consciousness produces an inferiority in one aspect or another—an inferiority, moreover, that has the psychological character not so much of an organic lesion or an inborn defect as of a lack which gives rise to a feeling of moral resentment. The sense of moral inferiority always indicates that the missing element is something which, to judge by this feeling about it, really ought not be missing or which could be made conscious if only one took sufficient trouble. The moral inferiority does not come from a collision with the generally accepted and, in a sense, arbitrary moral law, but from the conflict with one's own self which, for reasons of psychic equilibrium, demands that the deficit be redressed. Whenever a sense of moral inferiority appears, it indicates not only a need to assimilate an unconscious component, but also the possibility of such assimilation.[8]

Note first of all Jung's emphasis on the personal history and his insistence that contents of the personal unconscious "belong to the inventory" of the personality. As noted, twelfth house energies often emerge early in life but suffer some sort of defeat in the environment; devalued, they retreat into the unconscious. That the twelfth house has a connection to sunrise suggests that its contents "belong to the inventory" of the personality; that the morning dew has a tentative quality and does not survive long after the sun's rays hit it suggests that the twelfth house has difficulty freeing itself from the dictates of unconscious tendencies or from personal material that comes into the light of day only with difficulty. We might say that twelfth house contents belong in the light of day but retain their allegiance to the night world and thus to psychological principles related to a hidden world that nonetheless appears all around us, for at night we can see the heavenly bodies that humans have for thousands of years taken as symbols of inner, or at least not generally observed, dynamics. Jung also speaks clearly about the sense of inferiority that accompanies contents of the personal unconscious not yet integrated into the personality, remarks that surely bring to mind the tentativeness and lack of confidence generally associated with twelfth house contents.

Furthermore, just as we can find in the personal history the "source" of the contents of the personal unconscious, so we usually find that the feeling of inferiority connected with twelfth house contents generally has a direct connection to early life events or situations. For example, many people with Saturn in the twelfth house did not find in the father a reliable model for taking one's place or position in the world, not necessarily because the father himself didn't have such a position or didn't have great capacity, though we sometimes see that kind of connection, but because the child, with the non-verbal understanding of children, somehow perceived a misalignment between the father's personality and his placement in the world: perhaps the father had gone into a kind of work not suited to his capacities; perhaps the father actively discouraged the child from accept-

---

[8]Jung, 80-81.

ing status-quo arrangements; or perhaps the father spent long periods away from home (perhaps because of a broken marriage; perhaps, too, because of the demands of work, as often occurs for people in the military). In any case, the child ends up with a hazy or unreliable parental model in areas related to Saturn.

Finally, Jung points to the possibility of reintegrating the repressed elements. (In this, the personal unconscious differs from the collective unconscious, for according to Jung the latter contains archetypal elements that the person cannot fully integrate.) The Gauquelins' work, with its indication of the twelfth house's importance to vocation, surely suggests the need to reintegrate that material and to offer it to the world. This seems particularly important when a person has a planet in the twelfth. The notion that one must offer twelfth house planets out to the world seems as relevant today as ever.

Twelfth house planets often seem like the idiot child who appears in many fairy tales. In these stories, the father or king has a dangerous and difficult task to perform, so he sends out his strongest son. That son invariably fails, so the father sends out the second son, who also fails. This leaves the father with only the son he considers an idiot, the son he has always undervalued and considered useless. The father hadn't intended to send him at all, but the son asks the father to let him go. The father does so, and this idiot son accomplishes the task, usually because of his humility and his direct connection to circumstances, like the naïve and newly-risen sun making direct contact with the world.[9] Similarly, though we don't trust twelfth house planets, we often find in them potentials to solve some of life's riddles; that such planets often play important roles in vocational endeavors surely speaks to their importance, not to their weakness, and reminds us that the undervalued may have great value indeed. As Yeats wrote,

> The best lack all conviction, while the worst
> Are full of passionate intensity.[10]

Some examples may illuminate the vocational potentials involved: Randy Newman, with his twelfth house Uranus, surely stands as a fine example of iconoclastic artistry; Ursula LeGuin, also with a twelfth house Uranus, wrote markedly political science fiction and fantasy, again and again taking stances against the prevailing status quo; Thomas Hardy, with his Moon in the twelfth in Cancer, wrote novels rich in redolent emotion and pathos in which the feminine often plays a dominant role; Gracie Slick's dramatic intensity on stage surely reflects her twelfth house Scorpio Sun; David Byrne's twelfth house Pluto appears in the power and universality of his music; Theodorus ("Theo") Van Gogh, with his Neptune in the twelfth, made a vocation out of selfless service, not only to his brother Vincent, but also to the many artists whose work he sold in Paris. The list could go

---

[9]The fairy tale also reminds us of Jung's discussion of the "inferior function," and though we might connect that function only to the astrological elements (for just as Jung posited four "functions," so astrologers posit four elements), it seems relevant to the twelfth house as well. As always, though, we should remain wary of attempts to graft the ideas of one system unreservedly onto the ideas of another.

[10]William Butler Yeats, "The Second Coming," *Selected Poems and Two Plays of William Butler Yeats*, (New York: MacMillan, 1962), 91.

on. This doesn't mean that every twelfth house planet manifests clearly in the vocation, but it surely suggests that we should not see such planets as weak. It also suggests that in seeking the vocational profile through a horoscope, we should always include the twelfth house in the analysis, starting with the hypothesis that planets there may sometimes play a dominant role in vocational activities.

In examining twelfth house placements, we would do well to examine a person's family-of-origin dynamics, for twelfth house planets usually tell us a lot about family taboos or unstated messages that the child absorbs.[11] For example, a twelfth house Mars often appears where a person experiences a family taboo—generally unstated, as a kind of family secret that even the family-members cannot articulate or remain only vaguely aware of—against her desire nature, her sexuality, her drive for personal distinction through action, or the simple drive to fulfill "needs." In such cases, a taboo of some sort stands in the way of the child fully identifying with his or her activity or desires—a phrase that suggests both the benefits and the drawbacks of such a placement. One learns to act tentatively or to subtly undermine one's effectiveness in the world, and Mars therefore often appears via projection.

A twelfth house Saturn often appears when a child experiences a taboo against ambition or against finding one's place in the world. Often the child experiences the father as a rather vague role model, someone who does not model for the child how one might find such a position. The resultant projection will often appear as people in authority who (or which, for in some sense they function as carriers of symbols, not fully as people) undermine or threaten the stability of one's life-structure or position in the community. Uranus in the twelfth often indicates a family taboo against freedom and will often appear through people who overstate their desire for freedom, perhaps mistaking it for latitude in action, or who seek freedom only *from* restriction and not *for* anything in particular. A twelfth house Neptune may represent a similar taboo against spirituality or dreaminess; often it will appear in the world through people who deceive, or who live dissipated lives, or even as purported or actual spiritual people. A twelfth house Venus suggests a taboo against beauty, against the joy of relating, of seduction, of beauty; it will sometimes arise through people who seem to manifest their social instincts with great ease.[12] A twelfth house Mercury suggests an early life environment that discouraged curiosity and natural intelligence; it also suggests a projection onto

---

[11] We will often find related themes in the horoscopes of siblings. However, sometimes an early life taboo gets lodged (so to speak) in only one child in the family, as if that child serves as a hidden scapegoat for some kind of family karma. Also, family dynamics may change over time, so what applies to one child may not apply to his or her siblings.

[12] From what I've seen, a twelfth house Venus is more obviously difficult for women than for men, while the situation with Mars is reversed. For men, Venus in the twelfth presents more subtle challenges related to self-value; for women, Mars in the twelfth presents more subtle challenges related to self-assertion. Whereas a man with a twelfth house Mars generally experiences the difficulties very early in life and in impossible-to-ignore ways, a woman may take some years even to recognize the challenges. We could say something similar about a twelfth house Venus, but with the gender-roles reversed—and with one addition: that Venus doesn't struggle against the demands of the twelfth as Mars generally does, for Venus finds some of her needs met by what the twelfth provides.

people considered intelligent, "clever," or "mercurial." A twelfth house Jupiter can suggest a taboo against becoming worldly and a longing to emulate successful, or at any rate "worldly," people.

Because the conscious personality will often reject the energies of a twelfth house planet, those energies will often appear through projection-hooks that manifest the planet's more problematic side. Thus someone with a twelfth house Mars may find himself continually running into people who seem aggressive, secretive, or subtly destructive, who seem self-serving in some way, unable to deal with their own will; the activities of these people, who serve as hooks for the projection, reflect the projector's rejection of energies that, in Jung's words, belong to the inventory of the conscious personality. On the plus side, someone with a twelfth house Mars may assert herself quite well when alone, perhaps through solitary artistic work or focused work on behalf of people defeated by the demands of society (e.g. people in prison, people in asylums or who cannot, for whatever reason, fend for themselves). Someone with a twelfth house Uranus may be continually confronted by people making questionable use of freedom, people who are destructively iconoclastic; yet the person with the twelfth house Uranus will often long to be similarly irresponsible, or to break out of ruts and act out either the positive or problematic aspects of the eternal *puer,* or to give active and creative expression to her own iconoclastic brilliance. Such a person may find much vocational power by applying Uranus' energy to concerns transcending his own interests.

Because the twelfth house planet works as a hidden enemy, the person will often undermine his own effectiveness through use of that planet or undermine the full manifestation of that planetary energy. Furthermore, people who serve as hooks for the projection, manifesting as the "hidden enemies" long associated with the twelfth, may work behind the scenes to retard or undermine one's progress. The person may feel that some sort of prison surrounds the twelfth house planet, disabling it from clear and confident expression. Those who serve as hooks for the projection may serve as helpful reminders; by relating to these people (though not necessarily harmoniously), one can often pick up the trail of the rejected potentials. By relating with twelfth house projections, we can "work on what has been spoiled." The commentary for the *I Ching* hexagram with this name reads, "WORK ON WHAT HAS BEEN SPOILED. Afterwards, there is order." Starting with stagnation, we move toward a new order; the twelfth house precedes the first just as all endings lead to beginnings. The text also reads, "It furthers one to cross the great water," a remark that suggests the twelfth house connection with sunrise, with movement, and with offering out to the greater world. The commentary says, "On going, one will have things to do," and, "That a new beginning follows every ending, is the course of heaven."[13] Translator and editor Richard Wilhelm comments,

> …something…spoiled imposes the task of working on it, with expectation of success. Through work on what has been spoiled, the world is set in order once more. But something must be undertaken.[14]

---

[13] Helmut Wilhelm and Cary F. Baynes, trans., *The I Ching, or Book of Changes* (Princeton: Princeton University Press, 1950). 476-77.
[14] Wilhelm and Baynes, 477.

The *undertaking* involves seeking out that which has *taken itself under* (so to speak): the rejected material that, taken into the personal unconscious, appears in the world as a projection. By working with that projection, we uncover "what has been spoiled" and so begin to re-dignify it. Like the idiot child, the rejected component can accomplish much benefit, not only for others, but for the conscious personality as well, for as Jung tells us, it "ought not be missing." The "inferiority" can disappear only if we "re-collect"[15] our potentials from the world of projection.

Seventh House

Projections involving the seventh house differ from those involving the twelfth in several important respects, most obviously that seventh house projections do not necessarily or usually involve repressed energies as we usually understand that term. Rather, seventh house projections arise as a result of habitual approaches to activity represented at the Ascendant, for the Ascendant's approach naturally gives rise to a seventh house approach in others—or, optimally, through one's approach to partnership.

Generally speaking, twelfth house energies have descended into the unconscious as a result of the interactions of the two surrounding houses. The first house and Ascendant symbolize a person's most natural way of interacting with the world; the eleventh house symbolizes a person's interactions with the larger society and the larger question of social values. As a result of the interactions between the individual and the larger world, one judges certain actions or approaches unacceptable, first in the eyes of others and then in oneself as one internalizes the externalized judgments. The seventh house, falling between the eighth and sixth, shows the result, in behavior and events, of the interaction between the values of others (eighth) and one's own personal integration (sixth). We can also see the seventh as arising from the fifth and sixth: in the former, one expresses oneself to the larger world; in the sixth, one receives and (hopefully) integrates some feedback and hones one's creative expression in order to meet the demands of that larger world. From that arises, optimally, clear relations with others. On the other hand, and as often happens, if the integration of the sixth gets short-circuited because of overweening influence of others' values (eighth), one will see the seventh house as something one seeks in external developments or people.

Seventh house energies reflect Ascendant energies. The Ascendant symbolizes a pattern of behavior that generates and seeks the pattern of behavior symbolized at the Descendant, for though the energies there seem opposed to those symbolized at the Ascendant, they also complement them. For example, Scorpio rising's intensity seeks, as natural complement, Taurus' earthiness and grounded stability; Capricorn's business-like approach generates and seeks Cancer's emotional sensitivity. We see in the Ascendant-Descendant connection a general principle of complementarity even if that complementarity often appears as opposition or conflict; thus the seventh house symbolizes not only marriage and partnership, but also "open enemies," for in dealing with a true enemy, we recognize some equality at work.

---

[15] Von Franz, *Projection and Re-collection in Jungian Psychology.*

The twelfth house contains (so to speak) hidden enemies, while the seventh contains open ones. The traditional keywords suggest the conclusion I offer above: that seventh house projections do not necessarily arise from repressed contents. Thus even if we agree with Jung that rejected energies arise as projections, we can also say that such a dynamic does not necessarily account for *all* projections, for some may arise from energies we ignore or for various reasons fail to acknowledge even if we don't repress them. Certainly the seventh house does not, by itself, symbolize energies rejected by the early environment and thus relegated by the conscious ego to some personal shadow-land. So what *does* the seventh house tell us about the dynamics of the psyche and their relation to experience?

If the twelfth house tells us about what the conscious personality has rejected, the seventh tells us about what it magnetizes or draws toward itself. Because opposites attract, energies related to the Descendant and seventh house will often appear, at least initially, as opposites in relation to the Ascendant. Any style of action symbolized at the Ascendant generates a characteristic response. In games like baseball or football, a certain style of offense will generate characteristic defensive postures; in international relations, aggressive posturing generates resentment, recalcitrance, or reasonable resistance; at your local bar, certain ways of attempting seduction yield responses that should come as no surprise; if I wander through my neighborhood at two in the morning shouting that everyone should get out into the street to play some volleyball, I shouldn't feel surprised if I get some distinctly non-playful responses from my neighbors.[16] The energies symbolized at the Descendant arise because of how we behave and because of the conscious emphases of the persona. Though we may sometimes ignore seventh house energies or demands, we don't do so because we lack awareness of them or because we find them unworthy—at least not always. We ignore them because we get caught up in our own behavior. Whereas we will often consciously *avoid* energies connected with the twelfth house, we will often *seek* energies associated with the seventh.

Still, though the seventh house doesn't tell us about material that we have found unworthy and relegated to the nether worlds, it *does* tell us about our own energy manifesting through others. The seventh house tells us not only what we will meet in as-equal relations of all kinds, but also how we need to approach such relations. To the extent that seventh house energies appear through others, we should hypothesize that we haven't fulfilled the demands or expressed the potentials of the horoscope. If you have Libra on the seventh house cusp, you should seek cooperation, equality, and proper or fair evaluation in all self-and-other dealings. Furthermore, you should take this approach *because* you have Aries rising—because, in other words, of your natural tendency to assert yourself straightforwardly.[17] If you have Pisces rising, Virgo will find its way into your one-to-one relationships. Perhaps you meet people whom you find overly critical or who demand precision; perhaps this occurs because of the tendency of a Pisces Ascendant toward precisely the opposite kind of behavior (though, again, much depends on the placements of the house rulers, particularly

---

[16]Obviously enough to some, I have borrowed some material from the movie "A Thousand Clowns."

[17]Much depends, of course, on the placement of natal Mars (by sign, house, and aspect) and other factors in the horoscope. A person with Aries rising and Mars in Pisces square Saturn in Gemini will express the Ascendant energy quite differently than will someone with Aries rising and Mars in Leo trine Jupiter in Sagittarius.

Neptune). Applying discriminating intelligence—intelligence we can call *critical* in the sense that we seek the truth about something[18]—we can find clarity in partnership.

We should probably distinguish, here, between unconscious psychic contents, as we usually understand that phrase, and psychic contents that simply remain non-conscious. The former phrase generally refers either to contents rejected by the conscious personality (what Jungians would call the contents of the personal unconscious) or contents that of their nature remain unconscious (what Jungians would call the contents of the collective unconscious). Contents of the personal unconscious remain unconscious as long as a specific sort of judgment, not necessarily consciously maintained, prevails in the conscious ego; contents of the collective unconscious remain unconscious because of something in their own nature, not because of any prevailing attitude held by ego. *Non*-conscious contents, on the other hand, remain non-conscious not because of any moral judgment, and certainly not because of anything in their nature. Rather, they remain non-conscious simply because conscious attention has been taken up (so to speak) by a prevailing habit of behavior. These energies do not generally get relegated to the unconscious, and unless other horoscope factors so indicate, will not find their ways into the complexes; they nonetheless arise through others in case after case.

An example might help to clarify the way non-conscious energies operate. If I have a habit of gazing, as I sally around the streets of my town, at young women whom I find attractive, I may not notice the skateboarder barreling down upon me in my blind spot. The skateboarder may knock me down or inadvertently knock me upside the head, but this does not occur because I have devalued skateboarders or found them unworthy of my attention. In fact, if gave the matter any serious thought, I might conclude that I should take up skateboarding myself, for if I did, I might more easily come into relationship with the aforementioned young ladies, particularly if they have emerged from the skateboarding generation (a vaguely-defined group, admittedly). In other words, I might conclude that I should cultivate some of the energy that, because I didn't notice it, has done me some harm. Doing so will perhaps encourage me to feel more spry—to feel, we might say, more complete, more capable of coming into relationship with what appears in my vision as I wander about enveloped in my habitual mode of behavior.

So though we might say that, at least from an ultimate point of view, all external activity in all life-arenas represent projections—so that we can see all of the houses as indicating projections of some sort—those houses do not necessarily represent repressed contents. Furthermore, insofar as the houses represent, with their ruling signs, *approaches* that one might take to certain life-activities, approaches emerging in one's own psyche, not all of the houses will contain energies properly referred to as conscious or unconscious.[19] Speaking more particularly of the seventh, we can say

---

[18] Literary criticism does not always involve evaluations of good or bad. Sometimes the literary critic wants to illuminate heretofore unnoticed qualities or elements in the literary work.

[19] Some do, of course, as we have seen in our discussion of the 12th, and any of them can, particularly if other horoscope factors suggest that they will. If the ruling planet of a house squares Pluto, or if that planet falls in the 12th, or if one of several other factors occurs, some unconscious elements could arise together with the house-energy.

that its contents appear as projections not because they have descended (so to speak) into the unconscious, but because of habits of attention. This house has to do with *otherness* in myriad forms; when we work with seventh house projections, we work with an ongoing source of misperception that we can usually discuss without referring to psychological theories dealing with the unconscious. At the seventh house level, we move toward clarity not so much by gaining clarity about the binding and blinding factors arising from the unconscious, but by developing an awareness of the peculiarities of any personal standpoint and giving in to the mystery of the world as it arises.

We often move in this direction through what we call *love*, for in dealing with what we love, we have a great motivation to see through self-deception. We all know that most of what we call *love* contains a hefty dose of infatuation and desire. Fascination with the loved-one often feels like falling under a spell, as so many songs suggest; the word *fascination* suggests something similar, for it initially meant to put something under a spell.[20] The root *fascinare* means *to bind* and emerged in the word *fascism*. As Joseph Shipley tells us, "Fasces came to imply union,"[21] which led to its adoption by the Fascist Party in Italy. Our fascinations bind us, and often we don't see clearly when under their spell. But as we work with them steadily, as in close love relationships or even relationships in which we find ourselves bound (the contractual partnerships associated with the seventh house), we begin to recognize what had heretofore escaped our attention: potentials that we had ignored; modes of behavior that feel completely appropriate for partnership, and which we must adopt if we wish the partnership to thrive. We might call this the crucible of relationship—or of love, union, marriage, and alliance generally, all symbolized, at least in part, in the seventh house.

Venus, the ruler of Libra, the seventh sign, and thus a natural ruler of the seventh house, has her exaltation in Pisces, a sign ruled by Neptune and associated with yearning, compassion, meshing, enmeshment, and self-deception. All of this reminds us that not all of our self-deceptions and mis-perceptions have to do with unconscious contents, at least not in ways that we can verify; some apparently come from our fascinations, beginning with the fascination that comes from getting "bound up" (so to speak) with our own point of view and what we feel drawn toward in the external world and what we hope to magnetize from it, so that though we may get driven about by unconscious elements, the projections themselves don't arise from them. In other words, while we may feel drawn to elements connected to unconscious material, what we magnetize doesn't *always* involve such material. Rather, we often magnetize material with a "charge" opposite to the one suggested by the Ascendant, the oppositeness having to do not only or even necessarily with gender but with energy that complements our most natural way of interacting with the world: with, in short, the sign opposed to the sign on the Ascendant. If we find and cultivate that energy in ourselves, we find that its fits quite nicely into what we might call our "relationship profile."

We can begin by considering these signs as opposites, for they seem to have opposite charges, but just as a battery cannot function without both a "positive" and a "negative" pole, so in the

---

[20] Glynnis Chantrell, *The Oxford Dictionary of Word Histories* (Oxford: Oxford University Press, 2002), 199.
[21] Joseph T. Shipley, *Dictionary of Word Origins* (New York: The Philosophical Library, 1945), 140.

relationships between opposing signs, the "opposite" signs must function together. Thus, as I have said in other publications, we should sometimes consider the zodiac as consisting of six bi-polar signs. Each has two names with the same referent but offering slightly different emphases: Ariba/Libries; Taurpeo/Scorpus; Geminarius/Sagini; Cancercorn/Capricance; Learius/Aquarleo; Visces/Pirgo. These names remind us that the opposite sign completes the original one. However, Ariba differs from Libries in that Ariba emphasizes Aries and doesn't relate to Libra as a personal potential; Libries takes the opposite approach. The practice has particular relevance to projections related to the seventh house, for though we generally relate more readily to the sign on the Ascendant and magnetize or draw into our world the sign on the Descendant, that sign arises as part of the double-sign, and thus as a hidden element in our own potential.[22]

At first, we refer to the manifestations of the opposite sign as "other" or "others." We wish to form some kind of relationship to "our other half." Though those representatives (so to speak) of our "other half" *do* qualify as selves in their own right, we can also see them as parts of ourselves that we have projected onto others at least partly because of our identification with the Ascendant-related energy. We may want to resolve this dilemma by saying that those others "really are" independent of our view or "really are" simply projection. However, the dilemma seems to arise because of the limits of our language, a language in which we do not have a word for "an element of experience that qualifies both as independent-with-its-own-integrity and a-projection-arising-because-my-fascination-with-myself." However, we do often refer to a person's partner-of-the-opposite-sex as his or her "other half." The phrase points us toward the six-sign zodiac.

The sign on the seventh house cusp represents a desire, a longing, and a demand. It arises as a desire or longing because most people want to come into partnership with people who have some connection to their seventh house. It arises as a demand because the sign on the cusp and any planets in the seventh house will tell us how we might best approach partnership, marriage, or any other as-equal relationship, how we might find and relate to the mysterious "other half." The natural pattern of behavior symbolized at the Ascendant generates what the person will see as relationship "needs" symbolized at the Descendant.

Traditionally, astrologers have seen the Ascendant as connected to appearance, persona, breathing, personal action, and simple presence; they have seen the seventh house as connected to marriage, partnership, and open enemies. We might find it equally useful to say that the Ascendant symbolizes what others most readily project onto us and that the Descendant symbolizes that which we most readily project onto others. The whole matter invites exploration.

What do we mean when we say that the Ascendant symbolizes "appearance"? It means that the Ascendant tells us much about how others will see us. Most everyone experiences himself as some-

---

[22]See Appendix: The Six Sign Zodiac.

thing solid; most everyone assumes that what others see in us results from "who we really are" in some sense, even if we don't have a clear referent for that phrase. It seems that the Ascendant tells us not only that we will behave and appear in ways resonant with the sign on the ascending angle, but also that that sign (and degree, and aspects, and ruling planet) will serve as a conduit for the other energies in the horoscope. We see this principle in action when we look at portraits done by excellent artists like Rembrandt and Van Gogh: the painter paints appearance, but the portrait offers much more than mere appearance. We could say, speaking metaphorically, that the portrait tells us about the "soul" of the person, something inside that emerges *through* appearance. From this point of view, the Ascendant sounds more like the place where a river emerges from a narrow gorge: enormous energy emerges into the world through fragile appearance.

When we consider all this, we won't consider the "oppositeness" of the Ascendant-Descendant combination as a simple matter. Aries may magnetize Libra, and we can describe the interaction to some extent. Forceful Aries magnetizes those who will cooperate; the desire nature drives outward toward the object of desire. But we have myriad types of Aries-Libra combinations, for each Aries Ascendant serves as the conduit for a different combination of energies symbolized elsewhere in the horoscope. Nevertheless, the ideas of complementarity and magnetization, particularly combined with the Six Sign Zodiac, give us a place to start in understanding projections involving the seventh house, for we seek at the Descendant that which complements how we do the seeking at the Ascendant.

In concluding, we should say a bit about the "open enemies" so often associated with the seventh house, for anyone who has studied many horoscopes along with their transits and progressions will attest that the seventh house often manifests as if this designation trumped all others. I found it amusing when one of my astrology students said, apparently not entirely in jest, 'Absolutely. And marriage is a social institution in which you sleep with the enemy!' Certainly many of us experience the seventh house as the residence of people who oppose us, not of people who complement us—or even compliment us!

Though we might say, accurately enough, that some of the perceptions here have a close connection to a language that distinguishes between *opposition* and *complementarity*, we should take a closer look. It might seem at first that if we experience the seventh house as the source of opposition, we have negativized the energies connected with that house. In some cases, this interpretation will prove accurate, and the astrological material will provide keys to self-understanding. (Perhaps the Ascendant-Descendant axis makes a close square to Mars, Saturn, Pluto, Neptune, or even Uranus; perhaps the ruler of the Descendant is in the twelfth house; perhaps that ruler receives challenging aspects; perhaps we find it in a purportedly "uncongenial" sign; and so forth.) In other cases, though, and perhaps in most, we simply fail to recognize the complementarity; we don't see that we actually *need* the complement, housed in the seventh, in order to move forward, whether that forward movement involves worldly success or increased awareness. In *Training the Mind*,

Chogyam Trungpa, a Tibetan lama who taught for many years in the United States and Europe, writes of the lojong saying, "Be grateful to everyone,"[23]

> [I]n a sense all the things taking place around our world, all the irritations and all the problems, are crucial. Without others we cannot attain enlightenment—in fact, we cannot even tread on the path. In other words, we could say that if there is no noise outside during our sitting meditation, we cannot develop mindfulness…If everything were lovey-dovey and jellyfishlike, there would be nothing to work with…Because of all these textures around us, we are enriched.[24]

And:

> The slogan "Be grateful to everyone" follows automatically once we drive all blames into one [the previous slogan].[25] We have a feeling that if others didn't exist to hassle us, we couldn't drive all blames into ourselves at all. All sentient beings, all people in the world, or most of them, have a problem in dealing with "myself." Without others, we would have no chance at all to develop beyond ego. So the idea here is to feel grateful that others are presenting us with tremendous obstacles—even threats or challenges. The point is to appreciate that. Without them, we could not follow the path at all.[26]

Aside from their obvious importance to our lives in general, Trungpa Rinpoche's remarks seem particularly relevant to any discussion of the "open enemies" element of the seventh house, for they emphasize the connection between one's personal path and one's relationship with others, between challenge and compassion, between "other" and the path beyond ego. From the astrological point of view, others, whether arising as enemies or lovers, arise as part of the personal path. Libra, the natural ruler of the seventh house, reminds us that any evaluation of anyone, whether as enemy or as lover, depends on the counter-weight we use in evaluating. The seventh house reminds us that we should step beyond personal reference points, so our counter-weight should consist not of personal elements alone, but of something that will help us do the stepping. The first step seems to involve

---

[23]The Lojong teachings, first developed by Atisha (982-1054 CE), served as an important part of the training in many Tibetan monasteries. Those teachings consist of many slogans, what we might call reminders, some of which deal with formal meditation, some of which deal with foundational principles, and some of which deal with post-meditation practice—with life in the world, life in a community or working with others. The sayings I have used belong to that third category. Several Tibetan teachers have offered commentaries on different Lojong texts (e.g. the one by Atisha, used here, and the one by Naropa). Interested readers can consult not only Chogyam Trungpa's *Training the Mind*, but also some of the CDs and DVDs available through Vajra Echoes (www.vajraechoes.com).
[24]Chogyam Trungpa, *Training the Mind* (Boston: Shambhala Publications, 1993), 48-9.
[25]Of this saying—*Drive All Blames Into One*—Trungpa Rinpoche says, in part, "Everything [our general approach to dealing with the world, apparently] is based on uptightness. We could blame the organization; we could blame the government; we could blame the police force; we could blame the weather; we could blame the food; we could blame the highways; we could blame our own motor-cars, our own clothes; we could blame an infinite variety of things. But it is we who are not letting go, not developing enough warmth and sympathy—which makes us problematic. So we cannot blame anybody." See page 43.
[26]Trungpa, 50.

questioning the solidity of our judgments (Libra, plus Saturn, Libra's exalted ruler), whether about ourselves or about others. Even the simple act of seeing involves some judgment, for we do not see everything accurately, and our judgments permeate our seeing. Our evaluations may seem to suggest that we have such-and-such qualities and that others have very different qualities. Let's let the jury remain out on the accuracy of that statement. Whatever judgments we make, we must learn to appreciate the world that we relate to as equals—to our other halves. We won't feel whole unless or until we do.

The Fourth and Tenth Houses

The fourth and tenth houses have a long-standing connection to the parents, though astrologers don't always agree about which house represents which parent. Though the traditional view connects the tenth to the father and the fourth to the mother—and understandably, with Saturn as the natural ruler of the former and the Moon as the natural ruler of the latter—Liz Greene seems to switch the assigned roles. That Ms. Greene gets demonstrably accurate results surely suggests that her approach has merit, but we don't need to opt for an either-or approach in these matters. The mother-father question doesn't deal with hard facts, after all, but with perceptions and experiences—inner matters that prove difficult to quantify or measure precisely.

To start, we can interest ourselves in the observation that these two houses arise in a person's experience as the parents at all. Whether we associate the fourth with the mother and the tenth with the father or the other way around, experience tells us that these two houses *do* arise as projections, most obviously so early in life, but also later on. Of course, they also arise as inner experiences, with the tenth having to do with vocational objectives—as both the inner approach to vocational objectives and the objective achievements or activities themselves—and the fourth with both private emotional states and their external manifestations. The houses do not necessarily tell us about the parents in themselves; they tell us about the child's experience *of* the parents (and similarly for the Moon and Saturn). We know this because not all children of the same parents have the same symbolism connected with these houses. We might initially explain this as the simple and obvious result of the parents' behavioral changes in the time between the birth of one child and then another; considering those changes, we would expect different children to experience the parents differently. However, the astrological material suggests something else in addition: that each child seems disposed to register certain elements of each parent's behavior and to ignore other elements. In other words, the axis tells us not only about external manifestation, which we can consider projections cast upon the parents early in life, but also about the inner dispositions or tendencies to experience the parents in one way and not another. The evidence strongly suggests that these houses tell us a lot about the relationship between inner and outer material in any projection.

Why do astrologers disagree about which parent to connect to which house? Skeptics might say that astrologers differ because their judgments have little connection to the world of experience and should be seen as arbitrary statements offered to the credulous. However, a more nuanced judgment suggests itself. We know that parents, in their various interactions, project various psychic energies onto each other, often with a connection to the anima and animus energies discussed earlier. If what I said above about energy-transfer has merit (e.g. in the football analogy), each parent will take on energy from the partner's unconscious; to a greater or lesser extent, each parent will behave in ways connected to the unconscious (anima or animus) of the other parent. If this occurs, we will find it useful to speak not about integral parents, but parents arising, for the child, in divided ways. It seems to me that the 10th house has a lot to do with what we can call the "unconscious mother" and that the 4th house has a lot to do with the conscious mother; we can reserve the assignments for the father.

When Liz Greene connects the tenth to the mother and the fourth to the father, her practice makes sense for the kind of analysis she does. Ms. Greene concerns herself largely, perhaps mostly, with unconscious elements. We know that children pick up or absorb the unconscious elements in the parents at least as readily as they pick up the conscious elements. If the father has affairs that neither the mother nor the child knows about consciously, the child (and, likely, the mother) knows, as we often say, "on some level." The child's knowledge needn't come from anything either parent says, and it needn't come from explicit actions. We might say that the child absorbs the knowledge but may not, for some years, articulate any specific conclusions. It seems that the tenth house represents unconscious elements of the mother that affect the child profoundly precisely *because* the child cannot, as a child or even later, articulate them clearly. The fourth house generally represents conscious and evident elements of the mother. For example, if someone has Virgo on the fourth house and Pisces on the tenth, the mother may appear quite critical or may always emphasize the practical at the expense of almost everything else. Likely, though, in ways that the child cannot see, she has strong Piscean leanings: perhaps she has poor boundaries with the child and others; perhaps she criticizes others because of frustrated or denied artistic capacities. The child sees the former but knows the latter only indirectly, probably via the unconscious. Further, the mother may project some of her own hidden life onto her husband, particularly if she hides the potentials even from herself.

With the father, the situation generally arises in the opposite way, with the tenth house more evident and the fourth house less so. If a child has Uranus in the tenth house in Capricorn, the father may appear iconoclastic; others may see him so, and the child will likely see some eccentricity. Cancer on the fourth, however, speaks to the father's not-very-evident security needs, or perhaps to his hidden capacity for nurturing others or providing a secure home. Much depends, obviously, on the disposition of the Moon both in the child's horoscope and in the father's. The father may project his lunar issues onto his wife just as the child projects his onto his mother.

If the fourth represents the unconscious father, it likely has a connection to the father's animus; if the tenth represents the unconscious mother, it likely has a connection to the mother's anima. Thus the two houses will sometimes tell us a lot about what the mother projects onto the father and vice-versa, about the father's version of the mother and the mother's version of the father. The so-called "real parents" don't appear here in unadulterated form, though we can probably discern at least *some*thing about those people by looking at the child's horoscope and making inferences.

Once a person gets beyond so-called "youth," the tenth may appear through projections involving vocation or through such pervasive institutions as government agencies, banks, and so forth; the fourth may appear either as the demands of earth or as people in one's own family, particularly if a person puts much energy into vocational matters. The former seems increasingly likely in a society that pays little attention to vocation (though much attention to career), the latter in a society that pays little attention to family (constantly reiterated political slogans notwithstanding).[27] We might say, of course, that our society pays *too much* attention to vocation, but we may confuse making money or performing jobs with vocation, forgetting that astrology dedicates different houses to these different functions. With the onset of ever-larger corporations, more and more people find themselves working only for "a living" and not out of any sense of joy or for any kind of creative fulfillment. In our universities, more and more students seem to take courses that will lead to "better jobs," not to kinds of work that express something deep within. All of this suggests that though the people at the top of the various hierarchies may have the freedom to seek vocations, most of the rest of us have a hard time managing that, at least on company time, and thus we may experience tenth house matters as projections rather more often than one might at first predict.

The strong collective assumptions regarding vocation and home also influence one's personal experience of the tenth-fourth axis. We know, for example, that various cultural factors encourage men to find their true vocation while women are encouraged to do anything but. Thus a woman with a loaded tenth house may have great difficulty getting untracked in her vocation, not simply because of external forces, daunting enough in themselves, but also because of inner attitudes. She may, however, feel drawn to men who exemplify her tenth house planets. Saturn presents the most cut-and-dried cases here, often manifesting as a rigid authority figure who seems to block the woman's progress or to whom the woman feels a magnetic tie, though other planets can sometimes prove just as difficult, perhaps in more subtle ways. A tenth house Saturn (or a fourth house one, for that matter) can reflect assumptions which an individual takes from childhood, but it's also true that women often find Saturn's obstacles insuperable while men often find them challenging. Similarly, a man with a strong fourth house may find it difficult—and again because of both daunting external challenges and unexamined assumptions—to give up career for activity in the home. He may find a home-based activity related to vocation, and thus may satisfy some fourth house demands, but some fourth house energies (e.g. Venus, Neptune, or the Moon there) do not, by themselves, prod a man outward. If such a man drives himself toward professional attainment, we may observe him experiencing the fourth house material through others.

It seems that in our society, the fourth house gets even shorter shrift than does the tenth. Though we might, at least in the United States, talk a lot about home and family, the overall trend

---

[27]Much evidence suggests that those who brought about universal public schooling did so at least partly to reduce the influence of the family. Clearly many of our other institutions serve the same function.

in our lives takes us away from both. Sitting Bull and other Native Americans noticed this a long time ago, and the so-called Industrial Revolution brought an overwhelming emphasis on activities that drew one away from home and impoverished its archetypal richness. In any case, if you work for a corporation, you have little say about where the corporation sends you; similarly for the military or other branch of government. Even those who work in education may have to travel far and wide just to find an opening. We may love to watch sitcoms about nuclear and quasi-insular families (starting with Rob and Laura, the Cleavers, or *Ozzie and Harriet,* and extending right through *All in the Family, Married with Children, the Simpsons,* and *Family Guy*), though fewer and fewer Americans experience that. We live in a land resplendent with broken homes, and even where the families remain insular, the children often not only leave the nest but also leave the town and state, and maybe even country, in order to satisfy tenth, sixth and second house needs.

Through all of this, the tenth and fourth will also arise in relationships, particularly relationships with people who carry the mark of one or both of our parents. As with the Moon and Saturn, these two houses don't seem to lose their archaic connections, so they appear in projected material related to those connections.

The Sixth and Eighth Houses

In the natural horoscope, the sixth and eighth houses begin 150 degrees from the Ascendant, in the western hemisphere, straddling the Descendant and seventh house. These facts suggest that the sixth and eighth arise largely through something considered as "other," that they lie slightly outside of a person's direct line of vision, and that they therefore represent matters not absolutely rejected but more simply disregarded. The seventh, lying directly across from the Ascendant, would seem to arise in one's line of sight, and thus we know it as the house of as-equal relationships of all sorts even if we also consider it a kind of "blind spot." But as we look out on the world, we have one area on which we gaze directly and areas to either side where objects take on less clear outlines.

We may have an easier time seeing how the eighth house will arise through projections, for it lies above the horizon, suggesting that we can see it clearly. Also, it has to do with the values of *others*. Further, it has a close connection to the evaluations of others, so we often experience it either through feedback coming from others (that necessarily includes their evaluations and values) or as things (objects, money, even property) owned by others. Though we can share in those resources, and though we can profit from others' evaluations, once we enter the eighth house, we know that we must deal as best we can with people other than ourselves. Planets in the eighth house often arise through situations in which one must adjust to the values, ideas, obsessions, or assumed regulations of others. Pluto in the eighth often proves particularly blind when it arises as a projection, for one must often deal with others who not only have power but also seem consumed by their obsessions and values. At the same time, Pluto in the eighth often suggests that, once one "re-collects" Pluto from the environment, one can work powerfully in, with, and through the values or evaluations of others. Saturn in the eighth often means that one structures one's world too readily around others' values and thus forgets about one's own values, value, and evaluation. Saturn in the eighth often indicates that one's work in the world involves the intelligent garnering and careful allocation of others' resources, money, or evaluations, and that one must act with discipline in order to bring about this more hopeful situation. Neptune in the 8th often indicates either over-idealization or obfuscation about others' values: as a personal trait, it often suggests that one doesn't take sufficient care with others' money or resources; as a projection, it often arises through people who act similarly. That position can also indicate a highly idealized view of personal transformation; people must ensure that they have a grounded approach.

Astrologers refer to the eighth as a house not only of others' values, but also of birth, death, sexuality, and transformation. It seems that if we fully accept the value of others (though not necessarily their evaluations, as one can find value in another person and still question his judgment), we necessarily undergo a death experience. Many of us (probably *most*, perhaps *all*) habitually consider ourselves as the most supremely valuable entities in the cosmos irrespective of our power to influence events; we stand at a perceptual center from which the world seems to radiate. In the eighth house, though, we must fully enter into the experience of others' value, letting go of self-insistence and widening our view. This in itself brings about transformation and seems like the seed of compassion just as it seems like the beginning of the inspiration to give oneself to helping others. We might say that the transformation comes from the experience of not holding back as we deal with the world.

Most of us resist that full giving-in, of course, so the eighth will often arise as a projection—or as a series of projections that we experience serially over time. We shouldn't, though, "give in" in the sense that we acquiesce to any demand, restriction, or difficulty that arises because of others' values. The eighth house has a close connection to the second, and the degree to which we give in, if we do at all, will depend on our development of self-value (second). On the most obvious level, this can have to do with money: if we have millions in the bank (second house) and we have Neptune in the eighth, we might feel willing to give someone money even if we doubt his ability to pay us back or even if we suspect deception. Less obviously, if we have a strong enough sense of personal value, we will feel more able to give ourselves fully to the value or values of others. The projections related to the 8th house test not only our personal value and groundedness (second); they also give us, though in a negativized form, messages about our own growth. An eighth house Saturn may *appear* through authority figures who refuse to recognize our importance to some course of action, but it may *indicate* a need for a disciplined program of transformation.

The sixth house also begins 150 degrees from the Ascendant in an equal house horoscope, but it lies beneath the horizon and thus indicates, at least in theory, something within a person instead of outside. The most pervasive projection involving the sixth house seems to consist of the body itself, or, more particularly, its need for maintenance. In other words, the sixth has to do with the body considered as other, considered as an ongoing agglomeration with which we must deal. The sixth house also arises through maintenance demands generally, perhaps in the work place but also more pervasively throughout the environment. More generally, sixth house projections arise through the demands that the world makes of us *and* the places in which such demands arise. For example, a sixth house Saturn may arise through difficulties with employers or employees, for the sixth has to do with unequal relationships, but it can also arise through the place(s) in which we deal with those people. If we consider the body, or the demands of work, or the demands of an employee, as obstacles to our full emergence into the world, we would do well to consider those difficulties as at least partly the result of projection related to the sixth.

Whereas the eighth house, lying as it does above the horizon and after the seventh (one-to-one, as-equal relationships), generally appears in the world through specific people, and despite the fact that the sixth can arise (as noted) through employers or employees, the sixth can also arise in rather hard-to-pin-down patterns of behavior that we see as necessary, that we experience as the palpable demands of the world, but that also represent our own attitudes toward personal maintenance. Planets in the 6th generally arise through more definite forms, though: Saturn there often appears as obdurate authorities; Uranus, though it generally indicates rebellious attitudes toward routine, can appear as rebellious people in the places where we perform routines; Mars can indicate physical inflammations even as it suggests anger at employees or employers, but as projection it would probably arise as the angry employees or employers themselves.

As noted above, though, the sixth house lies beneath the horizon and therefore seems more amenable to control; we more readily recognize it as an inner approach as much as an outer place, as something belonging to us even if we have alienated ourselves from it. Lying opposite the twelfth, it can provide a doorway to the hidden energies of that house. Our inner doubt appears in resistance to routine or in physical difficulties; the collective shadow convinces us that "work" and "routine" separate us from "freedom" and "joy." The more we make the sixth house our own, the more we experience the liberating qualities of doing what we think we must and finding in such activities the doorway to something beyond self-concern.

Chapter VII

Perception, Projection and the Signs

Character may seem inseparable from destiny, as Marc Edmund Jones suggested some decades ago, at least in part because a person's character—the effective, manifest result of his inner drives and tendencies—seeks, induces, or somehow gets drawn to certain types of experience. Though we often say that experience shapes a person's character, we could as easily say that a person's character shapes his experiences, or perhaps even that the character brings about, through a process of magnetization, experiences of a certain type. Furthermore, if what some call *destiny* seems either to lead us into the world of things and events or to consist *of* the things or events that arise around us, and if we must perceive these things and events in order to interact with them and (perhaps) find this destiny (if it exists), then character seems bound up with perception—with the filtering devices through which we experience the world in the first place.

Perception, after all, doesn't consist merely in the registering of self-evident external experience via a set of mechanical inner workings. Though we perhaps don't want to go so far as to say that the phenomenal world has no characteristics on its own, or that it has no characteristics that arise "independent of convention,"[1] we can at least admit that often different people who have witnessed "the same event" will give us not only different reports about what "really took place," but will also, even when agreeing about the so-called "facts," disagree about how to evaluate those so-called facts. On the one hand, a person with a character molded in a certain way (perhaps by culture-of-origin,

---

[1] The phrase comes from Jay L. Garfield's translation of Nagarjuna's *Mulamadhyamakakarika*. Many scholars consider Nagarjuna's treatise as the founding shastra (commentary on the sutras) of the Middle Way (Madyamika) Buddhist school. See Mr. Garfield's *The Fundamental Wisdom of the Middle Way* (New York: Oxford University Press, 1995), 101.

family-of-origin, economic factors, etc.) will pick out some things, events, or ideas as relevant, meaningful, or weighty, meanwhile ignoring material someone else will see as paramount; on the other hand, a piano falling from five stories up will kill a person, no matter how he or she perceives the world.

Because filtering devices, including but not limited to a person's predispositions, affect some of our perceptions, and because perceptions apparently have a close connection with "destiny," we would do well to investigate the filtering process. Though we could find as many different sets of "inner factors or predispositions" as we can find people on this planet, astrologers have isolated, with what seems a great deal of accuracy, the twelve character-types that we know as the twelve signs of the zodiac. Though many misunderstand the signs and what they represent (perhaps thinking that a person born "under" the sign of the Ram should necessarily undertake specific types of work and avoid others, or that such a person cannot manifest patience or act indirectly), we can still say, speaking metaphorically, that each sign has a characteristic way of perceiving the world, selecting some data and ignoring other data, emphasizing this and not that, and so forth.

The above doesn't refer only to a person's Sun-sign, for a person may have his Sun in Cancer and five planets in Gemini and so "behave more like a Gemini" than like a Cancer (a statement with some glittering generalizations that we will ignore for now). In discussing the signs, therefore, we will have to keep in mind that no description of the filters associated with any sign will tell us how any individual will perceive the world. The situation has some similarities to the situation described above about a person's cultural background: no description of any cultural biases will tell us how an individual will perceive or experience the world, even if that description gives us useful information relevant to that person's perception or experience. We encounter similar problems every time we apply broad generalizations to a specific person's behavior.

The sign-related factors affecting perception do not generally have to do with *unconscious contents* as we understand that term in the West, even though the individual does not usually have any clear awareness of the filtering that goes on. But the individual doesn't experience the sign-related filters as rejecting unacceptable material; that he doesn't notice something doesn't mean he has rejected it from consciousness any more than my failure to notice the roses indicates that I find roses unacceptable. We should consider the unnoticed material as *non*-conscious instead of *un*conscious, for the latter term often suggests material that the individual has, knowingly or not, dismissed from his awareness. Sign-related filtering seems much more like the filtering that takes place when a person habituates himself to a certain activity: he no longer thinks about the details or gives critical examination to the process. When we drive, we do so automatically. When a person has important planetary placements in a sign, he perceives through the filters that accompany that sign (so to speak), and he does that so often and in so many circumstances, probably ever since birth, that he takes the filtering devices for granted and the filtered perceptions for "reality."

Some would say that, as long as all goes well, we perhaps don't need to investigate such habitual processes. Even if we agree, we will probably admit that sometimes all does *not* go well. We see in professional sports that people who have mastered a certain activity (swinging a baseball bat, kicking a soccer ball, running) for years, decades, or an entire lifetime, at some point encounter difficulties or bad habits. At such points, people benefit from coaching, for the coach has an objective view that the athlete lacks. Just as people learn to run at a very early age and yet benefit from coaching in that area, so people influenced (so to speak) by certain signs of the zodiac from the moment of birth can gain a valuable perspective by seeing how the signs seem to color one's perception and experience of the world. These filtering devices do not seem to have the universal quality of archetypes and do not derive from unconscious contents as we usually understand that term. They have, rather, a distinctly personal coloring and cast a certain kind of light onto the world that the person experiences. Despite the personal nature of the contents involved in the process, the process itself seems universal, happening with everybody all the time. Though the dynamic differs in important ways from the projections we have discussed, it nevertheless leads to misinterpretations of the world.

All projections seem to involve perception: when we project, we perceive the world, or parts of it, in ways connected not only to the events themselves, and not only to the human perceptual apparatus and the conscious mind, but also to unconscious contents. Certainly projections affect how we perceive the world around us, and, as we have seen, we can describe these projections by looking at the factors in a person's horoscope. If Joe projects his Moon onto Sally, Joe will, for better or worse, perceive Sally as having some or all of the characteristics of his Moon, not necessarily because she possesses such characteristics to the degree that Joe thinks she does (though she will likely possess *some* of them, as she serves as the "hook" for Joe's projection), but because *Joe* possesses them but doesn't always know or see clearly that he does. Because he has rejected his own lunar energy, he perceives Sally as wrapped up in various overstatements of that lunar energy: as "too emotional, too dependent, too much involved with purely personal matters," and so forth.

We would say, in such a case, that Joe doesn't perceive Sally "as she really is." When we investigate our projections, we try to help ourselves to see the world "as it really is" and not merely "as we see it," for if there *is* a world "as it really is," that world would seem (theoretically, at any rate) to consist of facts independent of anyone's projections; and surely, in our everyday lives, we assume that we can locate some sort of "world as it really is," a world with an inner logic and structure independent of projection. We might say, then, that whatever prevents us from seeing the world "as it really is" constitutes a kind of projection that obscures our clear vision of that world. We do that in at least two ways: first by projecting unconscious contents into the environment; second by making assumptions about what is "really" out there, letting those assumptions cloud both perception and the evaluations we make about what we perceive.

Evaluation, after all, plays a role in most of our attempts to know the world. Even if we admit the possibility of "pure" perception in which a person registers the world accurately and to a reasonable degree of completeness, we will also have to admit that most of us most of the time either don't have those pure perceptions or don't register them when we do (for they seem to move very quickly). Further, even if we have momentary, pure perceptions, we generally cover them pretty quickly with conceptual overlays so thick that they obscure and even replace any pure perception we might have had. As a result, we find ourselves predisposed to perceive one element and not another; one element seems to rise readily into our vision of the world, while another element sinks into the depths or becomes obscure.

A person's version of the world seems to result not only from the projection-process we've been looking at—the projection of unconscious contents—but also from a series of conscious or semiconscious choices that a person makes, not necessarily or evidently in ways dictated by psychic material relegated to the unconscious. These choices influence perception—or what we might call our *cognizing* of the world—not because of what we explicitly reject from consciousness but because of how we shade or color conscious contents. Much of this sort of perceptual alteration seems closely related to the astrological signs.[2]

When we talk about projections arising from the signs, projections that we might more accurately refer to as *perceptual alterations*," we don't imply anything about projections as projec*tiles*[3] or about the unconscious mind projecting or casting forth a specific psychic content. Perceptual alterations based on sign-placements seem to result from dispositions so interwoven with moment-to-moment consciousness that one doesn't perceive them clearly. Considering their nature, we might want to distinguish them from projections of the usual type; hence my adoption of the term *perceptual alternations*, acceptable as long as we consider the relationship between perception and what we call *knowing* or *cognizing*. Though we generally think that we perceive first and come to know later, it seems that what we think we know shapes how we perceive. The resultant shading of the world seems not to contain projectile-like elements, but rather elements that seem to settle onto the world, giving that world a general coloring. Unlike projections arising from unconscious dispositions, these perceptual alterations arising from sign-placements seem to fall onto the world in general—and to fall so pervasively that the person doing the filtering doesn't consider that the filtered world may not correspond completely with the non-filtered one, for he takes the filtered world as *the* world. Generally he will not find himself pushed and prodded by (usually) unpleasant experience to question his version of the world,[4] nor will he continually find others questioning the accuracy of his perception of other people. In fact, others will generally see his perceptions as reasonable even if they don't necessarily agree with him about their significance. And, as noted, people around him will not feel as if he has launched projectiles at them.

If I have my Sun in Libra, I will often drop a subtle Libran dust onto the world. I will not as readily register that which does not resonate with the world I see through my filter, and I will gen-

---

[2]Not all of it, obviously. Some comes from cultural background, language, education and upbringing, and other factors.
[3]Marie Louise von Franz. See her *Projection and Recollection in Jungian Psychology*, 20-21.
[4]We will find exceptions to this. A person with a badly afflicted Sun in Leo, for example, may find himself constantly questioning his Leonine perception.

erally see non-Libran qualities as less important or worthy than Libran ones; I will evaluate Libran and non-Libran qualities from a Libran point of view.[5] If I project my Venus onto you, I will see *you* in Venusian terms; if I am a Libra, I will see the *world* in Libran terms. If I project my Venus onto you, I will unconsciously arrange for you to play the Venusian role and may experience you as a person concerned with aesthetics, beauty, and all things Venusian. I will have disowned some of the human potential astrologers call "Venus." If, on the other hand, I have my Sun in Libra, I will emphasize aesthetics, beauty, balance, justice, clear thinking, and so forth in a general and pervasive way, not because I have denied some part of myself, but because I have uncritically submitted to my Libran habit-patterns and ignored or never noticed my Libran filters. In both cases, I fail to distinguish my version of things from the things as they exist separate from my version, but the methods differ. In the latter case, I exercise the kind of creative spirit peculiar to Libra, but I may see it as the only creative spirit in town—and not really as a creative spirit at all, but as a descriptive mechanism that yields accurate results.

From a conventional point of view, such a shaping of perception will not appear pathological. Rather, it will seem sane in that the person connects to the world through such perceptions. We cannot always say this about the projections we've discussed in earlier chapters, for those projections often obstruct a person's adaptation to the world in more-or-less evident ways. Perceptual alterations involving signs generally seem to facilitate a person's adaptation to the world, at least as long as we retain a conventional understanding of "the world"; usually they don't seem like alterations at all. In fact, such alterations seem woven into the consensus views of "reality" as they appear throughout the world, for all people seem to accept that different people see things differently and don't see the differences as indicating pathology. These alterations don't serve as hindrances until a person wishes to register the world in a way distinct from consensus-reality. Though they will sometimes indicate or suggest obsessive concerns, sign-based perceptual habits generally integrate a person with consensus reality instead of setting him apart. They tell us how a given consciousness perceives the world, how a given consciousness colors the world, what selection a given consciousness will make when perceiving that world. For most people most of the time, these colorings, selections, and shapings so pervade our awareness that we take them for granted.

We come to know the world—or, to think that we do so—through our perceptions: through our senses, we seem to connect to the world outside of ourselves. In the West, we generally recognize five senses (sight, hearing, smelling, tasting, and touching); to those we can add mind, a sixth sense that plays an important role in Buddhist psychology. When Buddhists[6] discuss perceptions

---

[5] For example, Libra, a sign associated with judgments and evaluation, will often see Scorpio's version of the world as having less moral value and Virgo's as lacking aesthetic value.
[6] Those, at least, trained in the Tibetan Mahayana system. I am indebted, in what follows, to the writings of the Dzogchen Ponlop Rinpoche. See, in particular, *The Basic Journey* and his oral commentary on Lorik. These texts are available through Nalandabodhi International (www.nalandabodhi.org).

and the sense organs, they distinguish among the sense faculty, the sense organ, and the sense consciousness. The faculties are described as subtle forms that give to the organ its capacity to perceive. When the sense organ makes contact with the object of perception, a consciousness arises: the eye consciousness connected with the eye, the ear consciousness connected with the ear, and so on. When Buddhists speak of "consciousness," they generally mean the consciousness arising from the perception, so that whereas non-Buddhists might refer to *consciousness as a whole,* those schooled in the valid cognition teachings would speak of an ongoing coordination of these six consciousnesses, a coordination that seems, when unexamined, to be a single, continuous consciousness instead of five intermittent ones. Among its other functions, the mind consciousness coordinates the whole process.[7] Thus we experience continuity, an experience of ongoing consciousness that we take as centered in a self or ego.

We see similar notions in the Western tradition, though the terminology differs. Instead of *faculties,* we speak of the shift from a physical experience related to a perceptual organ to a non-physical experience, for the nerves run to the brain and the brain produces a mental event not equivalent to the physical processes that bring it about. Further, many Western psychologists will acknowledge that conceptual systems, language, and cultural factors each play a role in a person's attempt to know the world.

What we call "the external world," whether it exists as a thing in itself or not, arises for a person only via his awareness of it. We generally ignore this little bit of tautology. However, as Jung said, we have direct contact only with *psychic* experience and only indirect contact with the external world, a fact given much more weight in many other cultures than in our own. The valid cognition teachings distinguish between sense-direct valid cognition and mental-direct valid cognition, and between the latter and concept. In other words, they say that we can have a non-conceptual mental cognition. The teachings state that we first have a sense-direct valid cognition, then (directly afterward, but usually imperceptibly so) a mental direct valid cognition, neither of which involves conceptual grasping; concept arises only after that two-stage process. But even the sense-direct cognition has stages, beginning with the organ contacting the object, after which the eye faculty (often described as a subtle physical organ, perceivable only by the highly trained[8]) grasps the object; then emerges the sense-direct consciousness.

This explanation suggests a marked difference between a person's experience of the world and "the world itself." (It also suggests that when Buddhist teachers speak of "seeing the world as it is," the apparent simplicity of the statement masks something perhaps not so simple!) Even western studies of perception suggest that we should distinguish between *experience* of the world and a direct contact with, or knowing of, the external things themselves. Our means of contacting the world mediate our experience of it. Thus though we experience "form" in myriad ways (physical,

---

[7]Some Buddhist schools talk of eight consciousnesses instead of six. See below.
[8]I have always interpreted this "faculty" as an explanatory mechanism used to explain the mysterious process by which a physical impulse (associated with a physical organ) transforms into an apparently non-physical event (consciousness). However, the texts do not explain the matter this way.

auditory, olfactory, and so forth), the nature of that "form" often eludes us—and it may depend on the nature of the perceiving organs and the other matters connected to the receiving apparatus. On this point, Madyamikans, Jungians, and quantum physicists seem to agree.

In speaking of the development of ego, Buddhists refer to the five *skandhas*, or *aggregates*, starting with form and extending through consciousness.[9] In speaking of *form*, many teachers refer to the process just described, seeing our experience of form as connected with the dualistic fixation upon which ego depends and from which it arises. Chogyam Trungpa, Rinpoche writes:

> We could begin by discussing the origin of all psychological problems, the origin of neurotic mind. This is a tendency to identify oneself with desires and conflicts related to a world outside. And the question is immediately there as to whether such conflicts actually exist externally or whether they are internal. This uncertainty solidifies the whole sense that a problem of some kind exists. What is real? What is not real? That is always our biggest problem. It is ego's problem.[10]

Trungpa tells us that ego arises along with its projections, interdependently, each supporting the other in a process described by the eight consciousnesses: the eighth, an "unconscious ground" upon which the other seven arise; the seventh, sometimes described as the confused consciousness[11] or as the tendency to refer all experiences back to ego; then the six sense-consciousnesses, with sight developing last.[12] These consciousnesses have a close connection to form:

> These eight types of consciousness can be looked at as being on the level of the first of the five skandhas, form. They are the form of ego, the tangible aspect of it.[13]

As we have seen, this "form" includes all of our sensory experience. Chogyam Trungpa also tells us that before the creation of ego, we have a state of mind characterized by "openness, basic freedom, a spacious quality" in which we "just perceive the thing in the open ground," but that "immediately we panic and begin to rush about trying to add something to it, either trying to find a name for it or trying to find pigeon-holes in which we could locate and categorize it."[14] From a beginning in which we operate in open space, ego creates form-and-other, a basic duality that apparently precedes all later, conceptual realities.

After[15] the experience of form comes what Buddhist call "feeling," or "sensation," the second skandha. It develops from the basic dualism just described. One feels pleasure, or pain, or indif-

---

[9]Two of the best explanations of this subject come from Chogyam Trunpga, Rinpoche. See his *Glimpses of Abhidharma* and the chapter entitled "The Development of Ego" from *Cutting Through Spiritual Materialism*. See the bibliography and the next footnote.
[10]Chogyam Trungpa, *Glimpses of Abhidharma* (Boulder: Prajna Press, 1975), 7.
[11]Sometimes called the klesha consciousness. Klesha refers to emotional blockages of all sorts.
[12]Trungpa, *Glimpses of Abhidharma*, 8.
[13]Trungpa, 8.
[14]Chogyam Trungpa, *Cutting Through Spiritual Materialism* (Boulder: Shambhala, 1973), 122.
[15]Not all teachers describe the skandhas as a sequential process. In what follows, I follow the lead provided by Chogyam Trungpa's description in *Cutting Through Spiritual Materialism*. Some other Buddhist teachers speak of the skandhas not

ference. These primitive reactions arise in connection to the six consciousnesses just described; one experiences pleasure, pain, or indifference in connection to sight, to hearing, to tasting, to smelling, or to touch. From this comes what the Buddha called "mental fermentation," the birth of thought.[16]

Next comes perception, which arises initially without conceptual overlay and then develops into a perception mediated by concept. Buddhist texts have much to say about what distinguishes a valid cognition from an invalid one, but we can say that when concept intervenes, we generally don't have a valid knowing. We have, rather, imputation. Humans think, obviously, and though we shouldn't denigrate this ability (and the Buddhist teachings certainly don't), we should at least distinguish the conclusions we come to via thinking from the cognition we can have through direct contact with the world. In case after case, our *thinking* clouds our *knowing*. Thus many Buddhist teachers have distinguished not only between a direct understanding of the world and an indirect one, but also among direct *mental* valid cognition, direct *sensory* valid cognition, and *inferential* cognition. We don't need, here, to go into the particulars of those explanations, but only to note that our perception of the world has many facets and that when we perceive, we shouldn't assume that we've had a valid cognition. Quite likely, we've perceived according to concepts that have arisen from feeling. Buddhist teachings say that in order to perceive the world accurately, one must first tame the wildness of habitual mind, the thought-ferment that arises at least partly from *feeling* (the basic good-bad-indifferent setup mentioned above). And it helps to examine closely the means by which we do our perceiving.

In the final two skandhas, Concept and Consciousness, we develop conceptual schemes (Concept) to justify ego's expansion into new territory and develop an increasingly solid sense of ego, which the Buddhists consider a delusion. In the final stage (Consciousness[17]), we find ourselves engaged in the Six Realms of the World; that engagement will appear as an imprisonment, but the iconographic descriptions (e.g. The Tibetan Wheel of Life) tell us that we can awaken in any situation, in any state of mind.[18]

All of this has relevance to our discussion because it reinforces the notion that what we call "the world" or "reality" arises so closely interwoven with our various mental workings that we have a very difficult time separating them. By "mental workings," here, I mean not only, or even primarily, consciously-directed thinking, for the mind moves constantly, sometimes presenting gross-level thoughts, yet also keeping itself occupied with a constant undercurrent of unarticulated content. Though the perceptual issues that arise with the zodiac signs have to do with both types of mental

---

as a sequence but as a set of "aggregates" (one of body and four of mind). Most would consider this latter as the more traditional approach to the subject.

[16]Khai Thien, *Buddhist General Semantics* (New York: iUniverse, Inc., 2004), 63-64.

[17]Though we use the same English word to describe both, the consciousness of the 5th skandha differs from the consciousness associated with a sense organ.

[18]Readers can get more information about these matters through the many publications of Nithartha Institute. See www.nitartha.org.

operation, they have to do more with the latter than with the former. This doesn't mean that we should ignore those situations in which, acting quite consciously, a Cancer says, "I want to have a home" or a Virgo says, "I want to feel useful"; however, we should also consider the myriad untamed and unarticulated thoughts through which we shape the unstated assumptions we all make most of the time. We can undertake some taming by doing some articulating; the astrological language can help us in this process.

One final question before looking at the individual signs: do our perceptual overlays or filters actually add something to or subtract something from "reality," so that "reality" arises interwoven with our perception of it? Until or unless we know more about what we call "reality," we'll have difficulty saying whether people are adding to it or subtracting from it, so we'll have to leave the question unanswered. Nevertheless, it seems safe to say that sign-based projections represent assumptions a person makes about the world. These assumptions have to do with what a person considers important to, omnipresent in, or integrated into the world. They certainly deal with what draws a person's attention.[19]

A person strongly influenced (so to speak) by a certain sign (perhaps she has three or four planets in that sign; or perhaps she has one of the lights[20] there, or the ascendant or its ruler) will perceive the world at least partly in ways related to that sign. The person will take that perception as "reality" even though it seems colored by a number of assumptions that she has not made explicit. Someone strongly influenced by Capricorn will perceive the world quite differently than will someone strongly influenced by Libra or Aries. As a result of those habits of perception, a Capricorn will tend to act in the world differently than will a Libra or an Aries.

The sign-related factors involved here do not arise in a pure form. Every person's perception arises from an mixture of various psychological and energetic factors that we can identify in astrological terms. For example, even if your Sun is in Capricorn, your interpretation of the world will reflect other signs in addition to Capricorn. You may have Venus in Sagittarius, Mercury in Aquarius, the Moon in Gemini, and the ascendant in Leo. Also, the signs on the various house-cusps give information on how the person will perceive matters related to those houses. Sign-related perceptual overlays and filters become difficult to isolate or delineate if a horoscope has many planets in many different signs, and delineation related to perception becomes much easier (and, often, more important) when one or two signs dominate, or perhaps when one element dominates (for the different elements, too, register the world in different ways).

The world-descriptions offered by signs of the same element will coexist comfortably with one

---

[19]In this, sign-based projections have much to do with Saturn, the planet symbolizing the limits of conventional "reality." Saturn is also said to be the Lord of Karma, and the signs of the zodiac tell us about the sequential forms of that karma: as planets move from one sign to another, we witness the reaping and sewing of karma associated with those planets.
[20]The Sun or Moon.

another and may coalesce to form a rather pervasive world-view. By contrast, the world descriptions offered by signs of the same quality or modality (cardinal, fixed, mutable) will cause tension and so may appear as splits, though possibly creative ones, in attitude and behavior. These so-called afflictions can indicate marked creative ability partly because a person with many such differences will be forced, in adapting to the world, to bring together and coordinate different perceptions of the world. We might remember Marc Edmund Jones' description of the "bundle" personality, in which all the planets are within 60 degrees, as indicating a pragmatic approach to the world. If a person has all planets within 60 degrees, his perception of the world will show the influence of one or two signs. He may not so readily question his perception before acting on it. Thus the pragmatism. A person with planets in many different signs will find himself walking a different path.

So though we would not say that Joe's being a Scorpio indicates, by itself, that he will see the world in a certain way, particularly if other signs are strong in his horoscope, we could say that insofar as Joe acts or perceives through his Sun-sign energy, he will see the world through a Scorpionic filter. Furthermore, Joe will probably feel most complete when he acts and perceives at least somewhat through that Sun-sign energy. Other sign-energies will tell us how comfortable he feels doing that. Certainly if a person has several planets in a sign, the energy of that sign will color the person's view of the world. Further, if we assume an ongoing interaction between mind and phenomenon, then perhaps we should see perception as at least partly a creative act and not merely a reactive one. Perhaps we shouldn't feel surprised, then, when the world actually seems to behave differently for one person than it does for another: we shouldn't feel surprised when the world responds to a person according to the terms with which the person has described it.

On the other hand, a person may edit out anything not congruent with sign-energies that play important roles in his horoscope. A Capricorn may simply not perceive or register opportunities for relaxation and enjoyment; he may see events in terms of their practical potential rather than through their relational potential. The signs describe the kinds of filters a person interposes—or, that he finds interposed—between himself and the world. Furthermore, it seems that very few people perceive without filters of some kind and that they don't do any conscious or deliberate imposing. All of this suggests that if we wish to understand sign-based projections, we would do well to investigate our filters rather than (as with, say, projections involving the 12th house, or oppositions, or the outer planets) material we've rejected from consciousness.

For the purposes of efficiency, though, let's assume, at least in this chapter and for the sake of argument, that the signs do not alter the world itself but that they edit that world according to their various propensities. We can probably agree that in our daily activity we generally don't question the verifiability of the phenomenal world. We assume a world that arises with some qualities, things, and patterns that everyone sees the same way and that one can verify objectively. We can consider this as a relative, or conventional, truth, and it gives us a place to start. From this point of view, a person's Sun-sign will color that person's perception of the world; the Sun-sign would act as a kind of pervasive filtering device. A Libra would see the world in Libran terms simply because he has filtered out that which is not congruent with that perception and because his mode of perception predisposes him, for whatever reason, to register some elements and not others. Non-Libran characteristics will often remain "off the radar" for this person, not even appearing on his screen (so to speak), at least not clearly; and when they do appear, the Libra will generally not value them as highly as other material.

As noted above, we have to do, here, not with something we've rejected from ourselves, but with something we feel as integral to ourselves. If we wish improve our relationships, we should recognize early on that because of this inner sense, not everyone will color, filter, or perceive the same elements in the world in the same way. A highly emphasized sign in a horoscope, and particularly the sign containing the Sun, constitutes not so much a group of behavior motifs (though it will often indicate that, too) but a pattern or shaping of the world, a way of perceiving that shapes action.

Finally, we should remember that an outer planet in a sign colors the perception of an entire generation. For example, the Pluto-in-Leo generation looks at the world quite differently than does the Pluto-in-Cancer generation. Similarly for other outer planet sign placements. And these outer planet sign placements may harmonize or challenge natal propensities. Thus the Pluto-in-Leo generation's view challenges the perceptions that come most readily to Scorpio or Taurus; the Neptune-in-Libra generation's perception doesn't jive easily with that of the Neptune-in-Capricorn generation. Though each person's horoscope consists of many different sign-placements, we can benefit from isolating the filtering patterns common to each sign, even though in practice, a person's version of the world results from many such patterns interacting.

In considering the material to follow, combine it with matters already discussed, for sometimes a person will experience the sign-related energy via projection. For example, a man with an afflicted Moon in Cancer may see his partner as manifesting some of the more problematic perception-patterns associated with Cancer; a woman with her Sun in Capricorn may experience some of the problematic perception-patterns as arising through her husband.

Aries

Aries tends to perceive the world as a field for contesting, engaging, and even combatting, an arena in which one gets highly identified and focused in mental or physical activity, looking neither to the right nor to the left but acting one-pointedly. Aries wants to take on the world, to venture out into unknown parts of it, completely engaged in the pioneering spirit long associated with the sign. The world therefore appears, in subtle and not-so-subtle ways, as something Aries can take on, a place in which Aries will find physical, mental, and psychological tests and contests in which Aries can pioneer, can extend out or go forward one-pointedly. Because of this, Aries may sometimes see other people as contestants rather than allies, as obstacles instead of assistants, as elements to overcome or to challenge instead of elements to understand (unless the understanding has to do with the contesting). Sometimes Aries will see some part of the world as something with which to identify, for better or worse, and another part as an unknown in need of exploration.

In general, the world will appear as something to enter rather than something to observe, a place to act rather than a place to sit idly in contemplation; and if Aries *does* see the world as place for contemplation, he will want to be highly identified *with* that contemplation, often seeing the contemplation as a means to overcome something (e.g. habits, "worldliness," enemies inner or outer). He will often interpret the world through its challenges and difficulties rather than through its welcome-mats and harmonies. He will see the stadiums before he registers the grape arbors, the places of combat before the couches (unless the couches are places of challenge or combat).

Aries' strength lies in his ability to focus on and identify with a sequence of actions or ideas. Thus Aries' propensity for direct, physical action and for identification with ideas and intellectual positions that propel such action. In general, Aries will perceive the world quite readily and solidly as "other," and he will do this in a very direct, non-philosophical way. Not that Aries cannot engage in philosophy, but he prefers his philosophy active and engaged. All of this suggests that Aries registers the relative qualities of the world more readily than he registers the absolute qualities, for when viewed conventionally, the world arises as something distinct from consciousness. Ruled by Mars, Aries wants to "take on" that world, to engage it through action in which he identifies.

Yet as in so many cases, if one persists energetically in a certain direction, he finds himself in a place that seems the opposite of where he'd intended to go. Aries identifies with his action, and it turns out that if he does so energetically enough, he becomes one with that action and with the world in which he acts. We know that Aries can pioneer in psychic realms as well as in physical ones, and that if we pioneer far enough into the psyche, we begin to discover some curious things. For one thing, we discover that the world bears a curious relationship to the mind, the two seeming to reflect each other.[21] For another, we find, should we identify completely with what we do, that the distinction between internal and external dissolves. We get "into the zone."

Though under most circumstances Aries will deal with the world as an opponent, if he engages his warrior spirit, he finds his way beyond the assumptions that induce one to see the world in such oppositional terms. Much depends on what Aries perceives as the opponent: something in the world "out there," on the one hand; on the other, some element of self-deception, self-insistence, or self-blinding that he recognizes "in here." Ruled by Mars, Aries identifies with the act, whether coarse or subtle. We generally identify most readily with our bodies; our bodies act in the world. Aries tends to see the world as a place for embodied action; Aries sees the world in terms of its relationship to the acting agent or in terms how much it invites one's activity (again, either physical or psychic). Identification suggests dualism, at least at first; but full identification with one's acts leads to a kind of "pure act"—one of Thomas Aquinas' definitions of God. Full identification leads beyond dualism.

---

[21] As we will see in a future chapter, this realization has much to do with Pluto, the planet some people hold as the exalted ruler of Aries. As ruler of Scorpio, Pluto rules over the time of year in which organic life dies and renews the soil. In Aries, organic life arises again from that soil. Because Pluto has to do with both death and rebirth, many astrologers feel that Pluto should have some connection to Aries.

In seeing the world as an arena for contest, Aries may select out from the world those elements with which one might contest (as distinguished, say, from those with which one might exist in a peaceful or restful harmony) or those elements that invite one's direct action or conquest (as distinguished from elements that invite a laissez faire attitude). Thus Aries' love for humans (damsels not excluded) either in distress or in any situation in which Aries might do some saving. If one wants to act, one must find arenas in which action will seem necessary.

Aries clearly has a close connection with warriorship, both enlightened and not-so-enlightened. Warriors often act kindly. The codes of chivalry stipulate that they should. But chivalry arises from the idea that "I" will affect others by my actions, and this remains true whether the warrior-in-question decides to fly jets, promote programs in urban renewal, develop low cost housing initiatives, or fight for the legalization of midwifery; whether the warrior fights city hall or fights invading armies; whether he or she blindly tries to "take that hill" or tries to prevent mining companies from blowing the top off of it.

Taurus

Taurus tends to perceive the world as a place that gives rise to or contains enduring value or values that might be preserved and augmented by husbanding in harmony with apparently natural or unavoidable processes that, once in motion, go forward on their own, without human intervention: processes like the growth of a tree or the accumulation of interest. Taurus wants to invest in the augmentation processes of the world; she tends to see the world as a place that one might enrich or in which one might gather riches, a place in which to enrich oneself, psychologically or financially, through what one husbands. Thus, Taurus tends to see the world in terms of its natural productive capacities, though Taurus will welcome industrial or financial productive capacities as long as they augment via processes that mimic the natural.[22]

In seeing the world as the ground to plant a tree, grow crops, or organize a factory, Taurus may select from the world those elements that either support or undermine stability and that make growth possible. Taurus' love of stability stems from Taurus' connection to natural growth-processes: an uprooted tree does not grow; nor does a tree planted in soil without the necessary nutrients (Taurean richness). Thus Taurus, in its love of stability, has a strong sense of place not only as a value in itself, but also because an enriched place produces further riches. (Thus the Moon's exaltation in Taurus.) Money gathers interest or augments through wise investment; properly cultivated soil gets richer through generations.

Taurus seems to magnetize the world's natural capacities for ecological or industrial richness,

---

[22]Capricorn also perceives the world in terms of productive capacity (see below). However, Capricorn, being a cardinal sign, emphasizes the individual's contribution to productivity, particularly through an executive mentality, whereas Taurus will emphasize the harnessing of productive capacity per se. Capricorn will tend to say, "I must act; I must organize; I must execute." Taurus will tend to say, "Will direct action increase natural production? What must be done in order to increase the available abundance?" Though both might say, "I must produce," Capricorn will tend to accent "I" where Taurus will accent "produce."

to perceive those capacities more readily than other signs. This doesn't mean that Taureans can do nothing but plant flourishing gardens or invest money. As a counselor, Taurus can magnetize the client's richness; as a movie director, Taurus can magnetize the actors' abilities; as a movie producer, Taurus can magnetize the money needed to produce the movie in the first place; as a musician, or any other kind of artist, Venus-ruled Taurus can magnetize the natural beauty of the world. In general, Taurus perceives the world in terms of what one can magnetize.

Taurus also tends to see the world in and through its concreteness and in its fruitfulness. When Taurus uses abstractions, she prefers them to adhere closely to the concrete: if Taurus thinks that a piece of land "is good," she probably means that it will yield something of value or that it pleases the senses. Though both Taurus and Aries tend to see the world as *other*, Taurus will not see the world as a place for combat or a place that by nature encourages pointed engagements; rather, Taurus will see the world as a place in which all things can increase in whatever value or potential lies within them. Because many things flourish when we let them alone, Taurus will often do precisely that, perceiving most readily those relationships that can produce abundance, growth, and beauty on their own (rather than, as with Aries, relationships that encourage direct engagement).[23] Taurus perceives relationships in terms of their value and richness, whether from the soil, an institution, or a person, and whether the richness manifests financially, aesthetically, or interpersonally. Taurus perceives in terms of the potential for augmentation, whether monetary, intimate, or artistic. Whereas Aries will most readily perceive elements in the world that encourage pioneering, Taurus will most readily perceive those elements connected with settled increase. Thus the great human civilizations first appeared during the Age of Taurus, characterized by agricultural surpluses and settled abundance.

Hidden within all this appears one of Taurus' main conundrums: how will a person involve herself in practical and gainful activity focusing on production (organic, monetary, artistic) and yet discover rich relations with others, finding value in the moment instead of seeing the moment as a time in which to work for augmented value? Also, Taurus often wants to act productively yet wants to remain settled; hence Taurus' love for things like property and bank accounts, which can increase in value while Taurus sits back and eats grapes! We can see the solution to the conundrum (if conundrums have solutions) by noting how Taurus attunes to the inner value of things, assuming that something with inherent value should naturally increase. Thus a valuable stock will increase in value, likewise a valuable piece of land, a valuable musical instrument, a work of art, a good seed, a valuable relationship, and so forth. However, Taurus develops most fully when engaged with items she sees as valuable because they naturally increase in value, or with things that have value and thus increase in value (not necessarily monetary).

---

[23]Aries seeks relationships that bring engagement. These tend to be shorter-lived than relationships that enrich. I can engage my enemy, but if I kill him, the relationship ends. On the other hand, I can try to come to some mutually enhancing connection with the person I have called my enemy. At its best, Aries destroys what needs destroying; at its best, Taurus brings stability to that which needs stability.

Taurus sometimes tends to hold onto valued items, even as they increase in value, thinking in terms of future value instead of present enjoyment. We see, again, Taurus' need to find a balance between productivity and enjoyment, between the abstracted future and the lived present, between the transcendent value of earth and the social values derived from that earth. Like Buddha, one of the most famous Taureans, Taurus must find value in the moment, for Buddha's meditation practice not only brings benefit in the future, but also in the transient moment – and unless one finds the latter, one will not experience the former, for some future benefits do not accrue unless momentary benefit inheres.

We see, in all this, the major perceptual difference between Taurus and Aries: for Aries, the world arises as a field in which one might act on immediate concerns; for Taurus, the world arises as a field in which one might plant. Whereas Aries selects from the perceptual field those arenas that invite immediate action and that promise immediate results; Taurus selects from the perceptual field materials or gardens that promise development, not necessarily sudden or immediate, of the richness inherent in a situation. For Aries, the world appears as a place for immediate action; for Taurus, the world appears as a place for enhanced growth. Taurus may assert herself, but only if that assertion enhances production in some way.

Not that Taurus doesn't recognize an enemy when he sees one, but his response will differ from Aries'. While Aries will assume that enemies must be confronted, Taurus will tend to think that they need to be controlled if they are to produce. Thus Taurus rules both bankers (control of monetary value[24]) and farmers (control of living and organic value), and particularly people who organize seed-banks. Taurus doesn't assume that enemies must be manipulated (though Scorpio[25] may!); rather, Taurus will seek to control enemies or allies through wealth, richness, and abundance. Sometimes Taurus will see this wealth and abundance in monetary terms; sometimes Taurus will see it in non-monetary terms, perhaps as human warmth and closeness, perhaps as the kind of value Buddha emphasized by pointing to the earth as witness to the truth of his teachings. Surely Taurus often finds wealth, abundance, and earthy value in the sensual. In general, whereas Aries acts on the world, Taurus offers inducements *to* the world.

Taurus generally sees the world as a sensual place. Taurus will see the arbors instead of the battlefields, the solid looking home instead of the racetracks (unless Taurus can, without undue effort, make some money at those racetracks). Taurus readily takes in the beautiful and aesthetically pleasing, seeing the world as a place to develop and enjoy lush beauty; she will feel drawn to lushness as a value and will want to embody it.

In some cases, Taurus will interpret the world in economic terms: one person with important Taurus placements tells me that even at a very young age he wondered how various institutions made enough money to survive; he wondered where all the money came from and how the compa-

---

[24] If a state cannot control the value of money to some extent, money quickly loses its value. The post-WWI situation in Germany serves as a ready example.
[25] We can see Taurus and Scorpio as the two parts of the same bi-polar sign. See the Appendix.

nies were maintained. In looking at a beautifully landscaped group of office buildings, he would be drawn to the lushness of the lawns, but his mind would turn quickly to financial questions, seeing the buildings in financial terms. All this before the age of ten! Later, he studied so-called primitive tribes and questions related to productivity: how did they find enough food or avoid depleting the soil or destroying the local environment?

While Venus, planet of love and relationship, rules Taurus, Taurus' connection to Venus has more to do with beauty than with relationship per se. Taurus perceives and relates to the world through its beauty and bounty, and she perceives and relates to others in terms of her own beauty and bounty. Contrast this with Libra, also Venus-ruled, a sign that emphasizes ideas and social exchange. Whereas Libra seeks relationship as a kind of social sanction, Taurus seeks relationships that increase in value and richness.

Gemini

As we might expect, Gemini tends to see the world in two very different but complimentary ways. First, he[26] will see the world as a place inviting curiosity, adaptability, and the gathering of information. Second, he will tend to see the world as a place for the play of communication and the communication of play. Gemini tends to see dualistically and conceptually, so he may often divide the world up into the light and the dark, the acceptable and the unacceptable; but many Geminis prefer not to look very deeply at the dark or unacceptable, so dark or unacceptable elements will often arise as projections, as something shadowy, something resistant to one's play—as, we might say, a dark twin.

Gemini sees the world not only as information or as a series of social interactions, but as a multifarious network that invites communication. Gemini sees the world as a realm that welcomes and requires communication, a realm that fulfills itself *through* communication and consists primarily *of* communication. (Compare this with Taurus, who doesn't always see much need for verbal communication. You certainly don't need to talk to get fruit trees to grow! Besides, she may feel that a person should recognize value without being harangued about the matter. Though Taurus and Gemini may both sometimes hang out chatting with people at coffee-houses, Gemini will hang out there for the play of communication itself, whereas Taurus will be occupied with more practical and/or aesthetic matters. Gemini will communicate in order to communicate; Taurus will often want some more earthy justification.) Seeing the world this way, Gemini may select from experience those elements that welcome curiosity or block its expression. Not only does Gemini magnetize multifariousness, but he sees the world in terms of that quality (and not, as with Taurus, in terms of its productive potential).

Gemini's curiosity does not necessarily, or even usually, make him an intellectual or a scholar.

---

[26]Though I have adopted the masculine pronouns for the "masculine" signs (air and fire) and the feminine for the "feminine" signs (earth and water), I don't see either as quite appropriate for a sign ruled by a hermaphroditic deity. However, I can see no mellifluous alternative, and when dealing with Gemini, one should surely opt for mellifluousness in language!

Gemini doesn't direct his curiosity only, or even most readily, to matters related to disciplined intellect, but rather to matters of communication and interaction per se. He doesn't always seek merely to know, but also to *communicate*, to build bridges of symbols that symbols use to go from one person to another or from one level of expression to another. Gemini concerns himself with the movement of information, whether in the form of ideas, symbols, people, or vehicles. An intellectual puts information together and finds a pattern; Gemini doesn't necessarily or usually do that. He generally doesn't seek order or system, but simply "the thousand and one things"; he will register most readily not the pattern formed by quanta, but the multifariousness of the quanta themselves. Curiouser and curiouser![27]

However, if we see Gemini as a mere dilettante, we miss the ways in which Gemini develops spiritually through knowledge and communication. Spiritual development doesn't necessarily require abstraction or intellectual patterning; it takes place in the moment, within the multifarious dualities of experience. The twins speak to this duality: the light twin has to do with the perceiving consciousness, the dark twin with the "dark" matter of the external world or the unconscious. One of Gemini's conundrums arises because whereas Gemini takes a great interest in the world itself, he will often find himself so entranced by his own curiosity that he won't look deeply into his relationship with what he perceives. Gemini finds his truth about the world through interacting with it. But whereas Aries interacts with the world in terms of its challenges and its invitations for pioneering, and Taurus in terms of its richness and productive potential (its natural value and seed-value), Gemini interacts with the world in terms of the mental and social stimulation it offers—and he prefers both types! He sees the world in terms of information, not in terms of a philosopher's meaning.

Because Gemini puts such an emphasis on concept and mental stimulation, he finds himself involved with labels, what some Buddhist teachings call "isolates" (because the label isolates the item or category from everything other than that item or category). Ruled by Mercury, Gemini too often takes the label for the thing-itself or fails to see what happens when we label the items of experience. We *all* do this, of course, whether we have planets in Gemini or not, but Gemini, with its love for the verbal, does so perhaps more readily and impulsively than other signs, and each of us has Gemini somewhere in his horoscope. The tendency to label, so ready at hand for all of us, runs right into Gemini's greatest gift. We see, here, one of Gemini's conundrums. It leads to another: how to see and revel in the information-quanta presented by the world, how to interpret that quanta through a labeling processes that to Gemini seems the essence of understanding, yet to see the relationship between the label, or the labeling process altogether, and what we perhaps too facilely call "reality."

Gemini will tend to see as good or acceptable that which stimulates or enlivens, and as bad or unacceptable that which brings torpor and fails to stimulate. These interpretations arise at the conceptual level of perception, not at the immediate level, but Gemini will have a hard time seeing

---

[27]See the second chapter of Lewis Carroll's *Alice's Adventures in Wonderland*.

through them because the seeing-through doesn't seem to provide much stimulation. Gemini often perceives the world in terms of a kind of stagnation-stimulation spectrum.

Gemini, the first of the "human" signs, has to do with something essential to our humanity: our ability to communicate with verbal symbols, to abstract from experience, and to pass information from person-to-person or generation-to-generation. Gemini tends to perceive the world in terms of its communicable symbols, whether these arise in a social setting, a scientific journal, a novel, or in legal jurisprudence. Gemini perceives the world as a field of communicative, interactive activity. Whereas Taurus will more readily perceive that which yields value, Gemini more readily perceives that which invites communication and conceptualization. To Gemini, symbols and signs drive the world, and Gemini will tend to assume that people's development cannot be separated from their ideas and the ways those ideas get transmitted.

Cancer

Cancer tends to perceive the world in terms of the security it provides—or that it doesn't provide. Cancer also perceives the world in terms of its life-giving properties, its capacity for bringing organic life into being, its propensities and opportunities for nurturing and belonging, perceiving security as necessary to this process. It tends to perceive the world in terms of the organic processes that create the "sub-lunar realm" (organic life on earth) and through the kinds of relatedness that promote or threaten belonging.

Because Cancer sees the world in terms of security, she will also see the world in terms of its lack of security; so Cancer often perceives the world in terms of its threats: threats to the security that Cancer values; threats to nurturing, home, emotional safety, and intimacy; threats to self-esteem or cherished self-image; threats to personal sensitivities; threats to all that Cancer perceives as vulnerable. Cancer will see these threats more readily than do other signs[28] because Cancer seeks to protect that which she sees as needing protection; Cancer will often see the threats more readily than she will see world-elements not related to the security-spectrum.

Cancer's spirituality often grows out of these concerns: seeking security and realizing that the world provides no ultimate security and very little of the relative kind, Cancer often seeks a security not of this world—that is, either a security of the imagination or of the spirit, or perhaps what some might call *soul security*. The security of the imagination can mean that Cancer wants a security not generally found in our lives, a security in and of the imagination; it may also mean that Cancer seeks an imaginary safety in a world that rarely provides the genuine item. This soul security finds

---

[28]To some extent, all the cardinal signs see the world in terms of threats—or at least in terms of obstacles or challenges. This is because the cardinal signs seek to act; they seek to change the world in some way through direct activity. Aries often sees the world as a place to battle and assert oneself, so Aries sees the world in terms of those who stand opposed to one's assertions. Cancer often sees the world as a place to find security, whether emotional or situational, so Cancer sees the world in terms of those who threaten that security. Libra often seeks relationship, so Libra sees the world in terms of forces that obstruct one's effort to find or maintain that relationship. Capricorn often seeks the fulfillment of ambition and social advantage in a hierarchical world, so Capricorn often sees the world in terms of those who block that ambition.

its home in devotional practices of various kinds and in any spiritual practices that recognize and speak to the most personal elements of a person's experience. Cancer sees the world through a very personal lens, seeing most readily those elements related to personal emotions, sensitivities, and experiences. Cancer may generalize her experience, assuming that all people experience as she does, yet she often creates problems when she lives through such abstractions, doing better when she remains alive within the direct experience and sensation.

As the most fertile and organically fruitful sign in the zodiac, and as the primary sign of motherhood, Cancer rules over all wombs, including the earth itself. Cancer seeks to develop physical, situational, or emotional containers in which nurturing can take place or flourish, and Cancer sees the world in terms of how it supports or threatens the creation or maintenance of such containers, whether that containment relates to the nurturing of children, the maintaining of a secure relationship, or the stewardship of the natural world. In registering and relating to the feeling-qualities of the world, Cancer sees that world as a place governed and sustained by people's most intimate feelings, sensitivities, and vulnerabilities. (It seems that Cancerian women will more often feel linked to the sensitivities that need protection and that Cancerian men will as often feel linked to actions that protect. Thus U.S. President George W. Bush, for better or worse, saw himself as the protector of certain alleged freedoms. Thus, too, the United States itself, its Sun conjoined Bush's, advertises itself as the protector of alleged freedoms. Both President and country interpret the world in terms of its threats.) In perceiving a world governed by feeling, Cancer generally selects from experience those qualities that encourage or block emotional connection (and thus security) and ignores those apparently governed by the isolated intellect. On the other hand, as Cancer approaches experience, the mothering qualities of the world often emerge even if sometimes under threat.

What moves Cancer to action? Threat, at least sometimes: mothers, even if passive at one moment, become highly active if something threatens their children. But we should probably speak of the perception of threat, rather than the threat itself. Caught up in her own emotions, Cancer may fail to distinguish nuances in this area. Seeking security, Cancer always registers the possibility of threat. We see this process at work in political figures as apparently different as George W. Bush, Henry Cabot Lodge, and Nelson Rockefeller. Each of these men drew inspiration from a perception of threat. Bush perceives as threats all manner of Middle Easterners; Lodge perceived as threats anyone he perceived as aligned with Communism (e.g. in Vietnam); Rockefeller apparently perceived as threats those who stood against the power of wealth.

Leo

Leo tends to perceive the world as a place in which one might dramatize oneself or create one's personal kingdom. (Contrast this with Cancer, who tends to see the world as a place in which one might make oneself secure, often by remaining private.) Leo tends to perceive most readily those elements of experience that encourage his dramatic and self-aggrandizing qualities. In seeking creative social outlets, Leo may select from experience those qualities that encourage or discourage the recognition and presentation of a personal point of view or a personal dramatization. On the other hand, Leo may find that the world presents itself through opportunities for self-dramatization or obstacles to such. Surely the melancholy Jacques, from Shakespeare's *As You Like It*, had some Leo in him; otherwise, he wouldn't have perceived the world as a stage!

Leo sees himself as standing at center-stage; he will often perceive others as revolving around him. He tends to see the social in terms of its relationship with his own personality; thus, he tends to see it as peripheral, and he relates to it in terms of how much it notices or fails to notice him. Though Leo certainly notices others, he generally does so in the manner of a king noticing his subjects: they come within his circle and thus have relevance. He does not necessarily seek authority in the bureaucratic sense (as might Capricorn, for example); rather, he generally thinks that he should have authority because of the radiance of his being rather than because of his organizational capacities or his hard work. Or he may prefer the role of a royal figure-head, letting others do the bureaucratic and organizational work.[29] But because he stands on a stage, Leo will see the world in terms of how readily it recognizes him or his deeds. At the center stands Leo with his personal dramatism; at the periphery waits the rest of the world, properly observant or deferential (even if hierarchical roles seem to indicate something else).[30]

To some extent, of course, everyone perceives the world from such a vantage. But for Leo, this mode of perception predominates. Leo, a fixed sign, gets more fixed in the center-periphery mode of perception, for better or worse. As noted, as the sign of royalty, Leo will often perceive the world in ruler-subject terms, generally with Leo itself as the former and the rest of the world as the latter, for kings have realms in ways that wanderers do not. (Of course, if the person projects that Leo Sun onto others, he will see others as playing the Leo role.) Light and radiance come from the center, and others bask in it. Leo still sees the world primarily as "other." He does not see himself as the creator of the world itself, but simply as the one who does the most vibrant creating within that ongoing world. With his regal nature, Leo perceives the world in terms of enticements, supports, or encouragements to that regality. Leo perceives in terms of this kind of subtle valuation.

---

[29]Much here depends on the entire horoscope. A Leo with a strong Saturn can make a fine organizer, even a fine prime minister. Thus Winston Churchill with his final degree Leo Moon and Sun-Saturn sextile. The latter—plus the fact that the solar arc Moon remained in Virgo from the age of six months to roughly his thirtieth birthday—suggests organizational capacity; the Leo Moon itself providing dramatism. Thus, too, Benjamin Disraeli, also with a late Leo Moon. From its natal position at 27 Leo 55, the solar arc Moon moved into Virgo around Disraeli's second birthday and remained there for the next thirty years. Add to this his Mercury-Saturn square, with Saturn exalted in Libra and dispositing Mercury in Capricorn. Thus too Margaret Thatcher, her Moon in the final degrees of Leo (Do we detect a pattern here?), just over five degrees from the 3 Virgo 51 Midheaven, moving via solar arc into Virgo before Ms. Thatcher was two, and Saturn within two degrees of her Scorpio Ascendant, sextile Jupiter and trine Pluto.

[30]To some extent, these tendencies seem to characterize the Pluto-in-Leo generation, certainly a group with a flair for the dramatic. Pluto suggests deeply seated complexes; that generation seems driven by what we might call a primitive dramatism complex, an assumption that the individual's creative radiance is what really counts—and, for some, that the transformation of the self is what really counts, a transformation arising from an awareness of the connection between the unconscious and the visible powers of the world. Other generations have not shared this notion. For example, the Pluto-in-Cancer generation seems obsessed with security in all its forms, no doubt partly because of the threats to world security (WWI, National Socialism) that arose during Pluto's movement through Cancer.

Leo also sees the world as a place in need of light—or of enlightenment: Carl Jung, with his Leo Sun, shed light on unconscious processes; Oscar Wilde, with his Leo Moon, shed light on the social foibles of his day (though, with that Moon in the twelfth house, his dramatic light-shedding led him to prison). Leo radiates; the world reacts to that radiation. Like Aries, Leo wants to affect the world through his individuality; but Aries, the cardinal sign, does so directly, through action, whereas Leo, the fixed sign, does so by remaining faithful to his own consciousness and his own self-valuation. He may affect the world by remaining where he is, the effect arising from firm confidence. In radiating confidence, he brings out this quality in others. In ruling, he can encourage others to rule their lives more fully. He sees the world as a place in which all of this might happen.

The sordid, the squalid, the shadowy, the deceitful, the untrustworthy threaten Leo's regality. If Leo notices these, he will generally perceive them in terms of his own dignity, seeing them as elements needing enlightening. We can see some judgment involved, here, but it does not result from careful weighing; Leo judges by making the same kinds of assumptions that kings do, assuming the subservience of a world of subjects. On the other hand, a more enlightened Leo views others as an enlightened king would: as elements under his care, elements he might help toward more consciousness and self-awareness. As long as Leo can see past personal self-centeredness, he perceives the world in terms of its capacity for wakefulness, either about personal matters or collective ones. Consider Gandhi: with a Leo Moon in his 10th house trine his 6th house Neptune and ruling the midheaven, he publicly dramatized issues related to India's security (Cancer midheaven) and the insecurity that threatened it (Neptune square midheaven), yet he also seemed committed to personal wakefulness.[31] Consider Chogyam Trungpa (Leo Moon), who brought the authentic lineage of Tibetan Buddhism to the West and who had great concern about awakening his students and bringing about a more enlightened society (Sun in Aquarius).[32] Both of these men remind us that if Leo perceives the world in terms of a ruler-subject relationship, he must ensure that he rules with wakefulness, compassion, and a sense of community.

Leo's perception harmonizes well with Aries': both see the world in terms of action, though Aries' action moves in a single direction, like an arrow, and Leo's moves in all directions, like radiation. Leo's perception harmonizes less well with Taurus', for whereas Leo puts self-creativity at the center, Taurus sees creation in the natural processes of earth itself; where Leo sees the world surrounding the self, Taurus sees the self as growing from the natural world. More generally, Leo, in seeing the world bathed in light, must cultivate an appreciation for the shadows, for that which does not arise in reference to his own self-will, and for the larger body-social without which personal dramatization cannot occur. For Leo, shadows arise in the guise of the other three fixed signs: the psychological underworld symbolized by Scorpio; the natural fruitfulness of the world symbolized by Taurus; human society, in which lie abundant shadowy projections, symbolized by Aquarius.

---

[31] Uranus at the Midheaven suggests the way Gandhi always upset the status quo. His Scorpio-Pluto elements point to the self-control that characterized both his public and his private life.

[32] See Chogyam Trungpa, *Shambhala: the Sacred Path of the Warrior* (Boston: Shambhala, 1988).

Virgo:

Like the other earth and water signs, but perhaps more urgently than any of them, Virgo needs a better press agent. Many books seem to suggest that Virgo might make a good secretary, servant, bed-maker, or housekeeper, but little else. How, then, to explain the curious number of Hollywood sex-symbols who have had strong Virgo placements? Consider Sophia Loren, Sean Connery, Madonna (Virgo Moon on the Ascendant), and Gina Lollobrigida. Or how to explain Goethe, or Memphis Slim, or Peter Sellers, Jimmy Rodgers, Leo Tolstoy, Arnold Schonberg, Cannonball Adderley, B.B. King, Hank Williams, or Greta Garbo?

None of these people seem like secretarial types (if such a type exists), yet we suspect that the secretary label came from somewhere. Virgo *does* tend to perceive the world as a place in which one might do useful work and to relate to the practical and down-to-earth qualities of life. In seeking to serve, Virgo may select from experience those areas that welcome one's assistance, intelligence, or practical acumen. In connection with this, Virgo may find that the world manifests in terms of practical need. The world will seem to demand Virgo's service more than her passion, her practical intellect more than her vision, her skill with details rather than her grace in the dance, unless the grace in dancing results from detailed application. Admittedly, Virgo can dance dramatically, but she generally does so after much perfecting of technique and much attention to detail. (Madonna seems a good example, here.) At the center of Virgo's mandala we find often find the goddess of demand. She demands efficiency; she insists that one must serve, on one level or another, a vision belonging to someone else, for better or worse. This somewhat resembles Taurus' tendency to see the world as a place in which production (natural or otherwise) takes place, but Virgo puts more emphasis on the individual's relation to the process of production rather than to the production itself as naturally occurring. Virgo perceives the world in terms of its invitation to create or participate in efficient processes through the application of discriminating intelligence, and though she wants to get things done, she puts more emphasis on their getting done *properly*. Taurus would just as soon sit back and watch production happen; Virgo's antennae locate ways to participate in and refine any productive ritual or process.

We might say, not entirely facetiously, that Taurus will gravitate toward stocks that augment by themselves, while Virgo prefers day-trading. Taurus plants his fruit trees and goes at leisure to pick the fruit; Virgo relates to the pruning, culling, and perfecting in the orchard. Taurus wants to take in as much of life as possible; Virgo wants to select from the available material the most useful elements in order to serve whatever higher good Virgo has in mind—if, that is, Virgo hasn't forgotten to keep the higher good in mind. Unfortunately, she often does precisely that, for she often gets caught up in the thousand-and-one-things of the world, especially the ones associated with task-orientation. Taurus perceives a good, verdant, and fruitful earth; Virgo espies places to plant and actively maintain the perfect garden.

Virgo relates to the periphery of her mandala in terms of how that periphery relates to the assumed demand to serve. Because Virgo wants to serve and has skill in doing so, she will tend to perceive the world in terms the master-servant relationship—that is, in terms of inequality. This can mean that Virgo readily sees opportunity to serve whenever that service promotes a "higher good" as understood either by Virgo or (just as likely) someone else. It can also mean that Virgo becomes obsessed by her own lack of position in a hierarchical world. Like Capricorn and Taurus, the other two earth signs, Virgo perceives the world in terms of its hierarchies, but whereas Taurus generally relates most readily to the natural hierarchies of the world (the order of nature) and Capricorn to the human or social ones, Virgo does best to connect one to the other—and she does this because such harmony promotes efficiency in task-orientation.

However, some Virgos in our highly technical society focus purely on the question of efficiency and ignore the natural world, thus creating a barren kind of efficiency, generally offered in service to someone else's vision; not surprisingly, therefore, astrologers categorize Virgo as a "barren" sign. As mutable sign, Virgo must, to ensure its own health, pay attention to process instead of result. In particular, Virgo must seek purity of motive and method. As an earth sign, Virgo must involve the natural world in some way: if she leaves out of her calculations the demands of natural hierarchies, she will see the world merely in terms of task-orientation, of the number of details needing coordination, the number of jobs demanding completion, the number of imperfections crying out for perfecting, fields of unrefinement in need of refinement. But she must relate not only to this kind of calculated efficiency, but to the vision behind the process: Virgo must ask why she does what she does, not merely *how* she does it.

As noted, Virgo often prefers to serve someone else's vision. Virgo's critical intelligence must come into play here lest Virgo end up serving an unworthy vision. Perceiving the world in terms of its opportunities for service, Virgo may forget to look at the world in terms of values. Or, seeing the world in terms of its efficiency, Virgo may forget to see in terms of motive. Why, Virgo must ask, should one act efficiently or promote efficiency in *this* case? What does the efficiency serve?

In the end, Virgo perceives—or should perceive—not only in terms of practical efficiency, but also in terms of inner motive. And Virgo may quite readily discern the primary impurity in all motivation: ego-clinging. Virgo will want to keep her own motives pure, to release ego-clinging; and to Virgo, this often means putting oneself second to others. Yet this brings us to one of Virgo's main conundrums: if a worker works for someone else, he will often (as Karl Marx noted) lose his motivation and thus not act efficiently. Virgo will readily perceive the inequalities in the world, but insofar as Virgo looks to the motive, she looks inward. Thus the more subtle conundrum: how to use those gifts that encourage one to turn outward, yet respond to those demands that one look inward to the purity of one's motive?

So Virgo looks simultaneously at both external function and internal motive. This can unfortunately generate Virgo's oft-reported criticism. It arises not merely from impatience in the face of external inefficiency, but because Virgo sees clearly into the motives, finding there an upsetting impurity. Virgo's sharp criticism results, often, because Virgo too often doesn't acknowledge, even to herself, what she knows about what goes on beneath the surface, in workers' hearts.[33] However, when given a choice between seeing the world in terms of motive and seeing the world in terms of external efficiency, Virgo generally chooses the latter. In capitalistic western cultures, Virgo tends (often because of education) to look first at practical efficiency and only secondarily at motive. Thus the need to cultivate the latter tendency: a habit of perception in which one looks within.

Virgo often perceives the world in terms of sickness and health. Purity (e.g. in food) assists health; impurity generally does the opposite. Virgo may sometimes see only sickness or that which causes it, and the sickness may be physical or moral. Thus, Virgo will often see the impurities that make one sick but not as readily see those elements that promote good health. The corrective measures usually come from one's connection to the heaven principle as one's motivation, for Virgo must find a purity of motive, whether generated by personal determination or connection to the critically-tested vision of someone else.

In other words, Virgo should strive to see the world in terms of Heaven-Earth-and-Man, not as a set of abstract principles, but as a working basis for activity and as a guide. Too often she emphasizes the latter two at the expense of the former. She will see opportunities for practical efficiency, but she will not as readily see the vision that lies behind that practical efficiency. This reflects her tendency to act for someone else's vision, to perceive the world in someone else's terms. So she will often perceive the world not in terms of how it encourages vision, but in terms of how it promotes efficiency (or doesn't). Yet when aligned properly to Heaven, Virgo will perceive not so much the external world or the internal world as distinct areas, but their ongoing relationship arising through work and the offering of service.

Libra

Libra tends to perceive the world as a place in which one finds partnership and balance, or some combination of partnership and balance (balanced partnership, a balance between partnership and independence), a place in which to manifest a socially verified beauty or magnetism and where balance and beauty bring benefit. Libra relates to the social and graceful qualities of the world. In seeking relationship and partnership, Libra will often select from experience those qualities or elements that seem to promise those, and Libra seems to magnetize or attract those elements that promise partnership or contact. With Saturn as its exalted ruler, Libra will often perceive the world in terms of how it harmonizes with what Dane Rudhyar once called a "socially accepted standard weight,"[34] with how much or how readily it ensures lasting form.

---

[33] The criticism may also reflect Virgo's failure to cultivate Pisces, Virgo's polar opposite. Just as Taurus and Scorpio form one bi-polar sign, so with Virgo and Pisces. In each bipolar sign, one end serves as an antidote for the excesses, lacks, and neuroses of the other end. Thus Pisces' openness to unconscious influence, along with Pisces watery gentleness, serves as an antidote for Virgo's excessive criticism. Virgo may criticize excessively; Visces (or Pirgo, if you wish) will recognize that our intellectual understanding of truth, our intellectual accuracy, needs to be tempered, refined, harmonized, and made more effective by sympathy, artistry, and a sense of unity.
[34] Dane Rudhyar, *Astrological Signs: The Pulse of Life* (Boulder: Shambhala, 1978), 85.

Libra generally perceives the world in aesthetic terms. Aesthetics generally involves standards of some sort. Some philosophers would say that aesthetics has to do with how we decide what "is beautiful" and what "is not beautiful," and Libra certainly gets involved in that sort of evaluation. Libra selects from experience those elements that lend themselves to such evaluation. That Libra has so much to do with "socially-accepted standard weight" suggests that the ideas underlying any experience of and decisions about "the beautiful" depend on social values that we often do not see clearly and may not see at all. We often take these values for granted, assuming that our evaluations arise from objective seeing instead of social shaping.

We should not assume from this that Libra wants only to have things "be beautiful." Libra will apply these principles of balance and aesthetics to legal matters as readily as to artistic ones, to larger social structures as readily as to relationships, to poetry as readily as to parties, to philosophy as readily as to pulchritude. Of course, Libra will often see and evaluate law, social structure, and social gatherings in artistic terms, seeking a truth that yields beauty and thus has truth.

Libra generally sees the world in terms of standards and sometimes considers those standards as part of the world itself rather than as something applied by the evaluator. To avoid getting frozen in this kind of perception, Libra must constantly investigate the mystery of standards: where do they come from, why do we hold them, and on what do we base them? Libra receives praise for purported objectivity, coolness of judgment, perhaps more so when no-one asks about the counterweight on the scales. In any case, scales yield only relative values, not absolute ones. Libra, perhaps more than other signs, needs to see the difference between the two, for he may take the former for the latter. Because Libra has such a strong connection to the "socially standardized weight" and so readily sees "truth" in social terms, he must strive for objectivity regarding social values.

But because Libra, in orienting toward the external world, often sees that world through a series of implicit or (often) explicit standards, Libra encounters many pitfalls on the path toward objectivity. Of course, all signs make evaluations and apply standards: we all see the world in terms of the categories we apply to it. However, Libra's path to truth lies in the standards themselves. (By contrast, Gemini's lies through the dualistic fixation that underlies curiosity, Virgo's lies through the demand for perfection, Leo's through the ongoing self-concern that Leo so much takes for granted.) So, Libra's conundrum: how to find one's way toward truth by applying standards that themselves become the obstacles to finding one's way toward truth? If Libra ignores the standards, he ignores his potential for evaluation, yet to see the world only through those standards makes evaluation empty. Like the other air signs, through its connection to the mental function, Libra encounters obstacles bound up in conceptualization.

But how does Libra perceive? What conceptual underpinnings shape Libra's perception? Concepts related to value, it seems. Yet Libra's values differ from Taurus', for Libra values social grace and standards implied by social structure and socially-conditioned evaluation, while Taurus values what we might call "natural" values, values implied by and in natural processes. Libra's social values impinge upon and shape Libra's perception, not peripherally but pervasively, so much so that Libra has generally has a difficult time perceiving truths not socially conditioned and may twist perceptions to fit socially-conditioned assumptions.

For example, Libra will readily perceive in terms of such abstractions as justice, beauty, balance, fairness, social appropriateness, politeness, decency, harmony, order, and so forth. Libra will often perceive in terms of whether a person, situation, or process achieves a certain standard in any of these areas. Social appropriateness tends to play an important role in all this, though different Librans will interpret this term differently. Gandhi, for example, with his Libra Sun and Libra Ascendant, linked social appropriateness with justice; he understood "appropriateness" in political terms and against a background of social injustice. Oscar Wilde, with his twelfth house Libra Moon, did not think in political terms as often as in social ones, applying his verbal scalpel to social foibles. To another Libra, social appropriateness might have to do with "acting nicely" or cultivating social graces. The number of social reformers with strong Libra placements reminds of us Libra's ongoing relationship to the "socially accepted standard weight" and of Libra's tendency to perceive the world in terms of that standard.

Libra's association with sunset (suggested by Libra's glyph) points to the importance, for him, of seeing unconscious elements at work in daily life, particularly in connection with social taboos taken as universal laws. Libra has a pervasive affinity with the socially acceptable, and because every society has not only a series of social taboos but also a marked way of shaping the world as a whole, Libra will often fail to investigate the social values that dictate the taboos and do the shaping. Saturn's connection to Libra and to social control suggests Libra's affinity with the processes of social control that generate taboos—and Libra's love of limits and bounded or choreographed movement. On the other hand, Libra has a well-documented desire to find inner truth and inner value. Though Libra wants to act in a socially acceptable manner and to cultivate grace and adornment, Libra also wants to balance internal and external demands. We shouldn't mistake the behavior for the motivation. Libra perceives the world in terms of relationships, including the relationship between the hidden and the manifest. So we would say that Libra has the capacity to step beyond socially-defined points of view but often fails to do so with sufficient strength (suggesting Saturn's continuing connection to matters-Libran).

Libra readily perceives underlying aesthetic form, not only in artistic work, but in social situations generally. And, as noted, Libra perceives in terms of relationships, in terms of human connections within social constructs and in terms of social value (e.g. relationship). When Libra labels the world, the labels generally have to do with social construct: approving labels go to those elements that either harmonize with the prevailing aesthetic order or with those abstract principles that Libra has weighed and found beneficial. Because Libra perceives according to relationship, he will not readily register opportunities for solitude. Because Libra not only perceives according to social standard-weights but also seeks balanced and detached judgment, Libra experiences a final conundrum: How will one achieve a balanced and detached judgment within social situations if the social situation in which one judges constantly influences the evaluations one makes? The resolution to the conundrum involves Libra's ability to weigh another pair of elements: conscious and unconscious, light and dark—the issues of sunset.

Scorpio

Scorpio tends to perceive the world as a crucible of sexual, financial, or political power-dynamics. Scorpio perceives most readily those elements of the world that promise transformative power and intensity. In perceiving and seeking power or its lack, Scorpio may select from experience those qualities or elements that enable one to bring about fundamental change or that present only intransigence (though the latter often suggests projection at work); when looking at the world, Scorpio readily perceives those hidden elements that promise power as well as the obstacles that inhibit its manifestation or development.

Scorpio seems to have a way of magnetizing or attracting those elements of life that come charged with the power of the underworld. Because Scorpio seeks transformation and change, and because these processes require some degree or power and control, she most readily perceives those elements that promise such power and control or that demonstrate it in others. When looking within, Scorpio perceives quite readily those elements that promote or prevent change. When looking at others and desiring some control over them, Scorpio readily perceives or intuits those unconscious processes that enable or eviscerate such control.

Above all, Scorpio perceives the world as a process of perpetual birth and death. Seeing an infant, Scorpio may perceive it as part of a process leading to death, as part of the financial order, or as a being manifesting through its transformations; Scorpio will perceive death and rebirth in every moment of the infant's existence. She may often perceive the surface world as a simulacrum: she will see it in terms of what lies within it, in a hidden realm fecund with the powers of transformation.

Scorpio readily perceives sexual dynamics and possibilities (or, as above, blockages) within the immediate environment (and will often interpret blockages in sexual or financial terms). However, though many astrologers make much of Scorpio's emphasis on sexuality, this emphasis sometimes masks deeper concerns about hidden power dynamics including but not limited to sexual ones. Scorpio readily perceives the world as a place in which change and struggle takes place constantly, in which birth and death follow one upon each other in every moment. In our culture, we have very few situations that encourage this view of the world, and many that block it. Those wanting to experience death and rebirth in the moment won't find any more ready arena than the sexual one, so they turn to that arena readily enough, partly because it promises transformation, partly because it opens the door to the hidden realm mentioned above, and partly because it brings a momentary experience of powerlessness. In a society in which transformative experiences received greater social or institutional sanction, Scorpio would quite possibly perceive—and behave—very differently.

Gandhi provides a good example of some of Scorpio's perception patterns. He had three first house Scorpio planets (Mercury, Venus, and Mars). Two of these planets (Venus and Mars) opposed a Jupiter-Pluto conjunction in Taurus in the seventh house. Though with his Libra Sun and Ascendant Gandhi saw the world in terms of justice, he also saw it in terms of sexual and power dynamics, the former as something to be controlled, as per his 1st house Scorpio planets, the latter as something to be engaged, as per his seventh house conjunction involving Pluto. Gandhi perceived not only in terms of justice, but also in terms of power and control; he had a great desire to control elements in his world that he could control (as in his great, some would say compulsive or obsessive, concern about bodily functions). Yet at the same time, he directed his transformational drive out into the world. The transformative energies emerged through his own actions (Scorpio and the 1st house); the objects of his work were Taurean in nature (financial issues and open enemies).

Gandhi's "open enemies" (seventh house) arose as entrenched financial interests (Taurus), plutocratic interests related to power (Pluto) and those promoting political or imperial expansion (Jupiter). The Scorpio and Taurus planets form, with Gandhi's Leo Moon in the tenth house, a powerful t-square. The Leo Moon in the tenth emerged as public dramatism. The empty leg of this t-square falls in the fourth house, symbolizing homeland. Thus, dramatic public expressions aimed at transforming entrenched financial interests that controlled his homeland as part of the British Empire's global expansion. Gandhi's perception thus reflects not only Scorpio, but the rest of his t-square as well; however, the primary perception involved control and transformation, for Ghandi's drive to control his body and impulses, sexual and otherwise, had an intimate connection to his political work.

We can see, through all this, that to get a complete picture of a person's perception, we must consider the entire birth chart, yet that certain signs clearly stand out. In Gandhi's case, we find the initial perception colored partly by his Libra Sun and Ascendant (perceiving in terms of justice and balance), partly by his Scorpio planets (perceiving power dynamics related to transformation), and partly in terms of his Leo Moon (he saw the world as a place in which one should dramatize one's feelings through public work: Moon rules Midheaven and in the tenth). Gandhi's seventh house gives us more specific information about how he viewed partners and open enemies: Aries on the cusp tells us that he picked up quickly on others' aggression; Taurus planets in that house tell us that he saw this aggression as part of a larger financial pattern.

Negatively, of course, Scorpio creates ceaseless and senseless power struggles out of small disagreements. First she perceives the world as redolent with power dynamics; then she acts on behalf of some conclusion not warranted by the available facts. We see one example in the famous Scorpio jealousy (not necessarily sexual); we see numerous others in Dostoyevsky's *The Underground Man*—and, of course, in *Crime and Punishment*. However, Dostoyevsky also shows us how obsession can lead to spiritual insight or emancipation (as with Raskolnikov in *Crime and Punishment*).

Sagittarius

Sagittarius tends to perceive the world as a field in which one seeks meaning and as a place for the manifestation of principles. Sagittarius often perceives the principles at play in that world more readily than he registers the people influenced by those principles. Sagittarius relates most readily to those elements of the world that promise to teach or that expand one's vision beyond the demands of immediate circumstance. In seeking education in the broader sense, Sagittarius may select from experience elements that promote a broader and more inclusive view. Also, Sagittarius often seems to create learning experiences from nothing, to find opportunities where none seem to have existed before. Sometimes Sagittarius will speak of abstractions as if they had the same kind of existence as tangible objects or beings.

Sagittarius (through Jupiter, his ruler) tends to perceive the world as a place into which one might expand through what one decides to see as principled behavior. Sagittarius often sees the world as being full of material (territory, ideas, information) that one might encompass or through which one might find meaning and attain fulfillment. Sagittarius can misperceive the world by ignoring or failing to look carefully at details: in seeing the world as a stage for the playing-out of principles, he will often perceive the principles instead of the actual activity, mistaking one for the other, or seeing only the principles and not the people—a kind of Platonism run wild! The people of the United States (Sagittarius Ascendant), when caught up in the developed national zeitgeist, tend to see the rest of the world much as the colonists saw what they called the "New World": as a place in which to expand via the principles of religion and philosophy, however naïve. Yet the United States does not readily see the sensitivities, needs, and wisdom of the people over whom those principles would hold sway.[35]

For Sagittarius, the world becomes the place in which purportedly principled expansion takes place and in which one can promulgate one's principles or try to further one's interests (financial, intellectual, territorial), for better or worse. Sagittarius generally does not perceive the world as a place ruled by hidden emotional dynamics or intrigues (Scorpio), nor as a place to manifest aesthetic notions or create beauty (Libra). Rather, he perceives the world as a place inhabited (so to speak) by purportedly self-evident principles (the above-mentioned abstractions).

Perhaps more than for most signs, the world for Sagittarius arises as an open field waiting to be sewn, though often with ideas instead of seeds. At the same time, Sagittarius will often perceive the world as a place in which principles and meaning play active roles. As a result, someone strongly Sagittarian will, in acting on that world, do so via principles, for better or worse, and whether or not those principles seem self-evident to others. For example, when we look at the activities of the United States, the idea of *freedom*, however understood by the United States' leaders at any particular time, seems to play an active role, for better or worse.

---

[35]As we will see, the United States, with its Sun in Cancer, also sees the world as a place in which to ensure one's security. That the ruler of the Sagittarius Ascendant (Jupiter) conjoins (albeit loosely) the Cancer Sun in the eighth house tells us that the United States will perceive that expansion via principles will always be linked to security, so the United States constantly expands in order to secure (so to speak) its security. The eighth house enters the picture as well: the United States finds its security through taking the resources of others. In fact, others are often perceived according to how willingly they offer up their resources to the United States' effort to find security. See chapter X.

Sagittarius tends to perceive the world as a place inviting a quest for larger vision or larger truth subjectively perceived. He tends to perceive the world romantically, in terms of its horizons instead of what lies directly in front of him. Like the knights in old romances, Sagittarius tends to see present circumstances in terms of what they might lead to or what they symbolize, and he will want those circumstances to lead to expanded vision, encompassing understanding, or territorial aggrandizement. Like Scorpio, Sagittarius often perceives events in terms of their meaning; however, unlike Scorpio, Sagittarius doesn't search for *hidden* meaning or power, but for what he takes as evident generalities and movements. Sagittarius will often perceive abstractions, such as *ethics*, as embedded in tangible situations.

For Sagittarius, patterns predominate; they precede, and even give birth to, particulars or details. Such patterns also inhere in those details, giving them meaning not only on their own but in relation to the pattern. Sagittarius wants to expand (via Jupiter), not only or primarily by garnering physical territory, but by establishing ideological territory first and foremost. In the end, Sagittarius perceives the world in terms of "truth"—in terms of the abstraction itself, which Sagittarius often claims works within the extensional realm.

Capricorn

Capricorn tends to perceive the world as a place to exercise ambition or ability. She will select from the world elements that invite or offer opportunities for definitive, organizational leadership, or that offer opportunities to climb, generally on steps provided by the existing social order, to a position of relative prominence. Capricorn relates most readily to those elements of experience most closely related to hierarchy or social ordering. In fact, Capricorn tends to see the world in hierarchical terms: either Capricorn will register the existing social hierarchies and learn to work with them, or Capricorn will simply see the *good* as hierarchical in nature, as something one should value in terms of how much social sanction it garners. In seeking accomplishment in the broadest sense, Capricorn may select from experience elements that aid one in the drive *for* accomplishment, particularly elements connected with larger social organization. On the other hand, Capricorn seems to create a need for hierarchically based creative enterprise; sometimes Capricorn will create the hierarchies themselves, often through projects that flourish *through* such structures and that encourage one's capacities to direct social enterprise.

Capricorn perceives the world as a place to demonstrate competence and ability. He will perceive most readily elements related to his and others' ability to do this. He will not only perceive the hierarchical qualities in any situation, but he will often perceive others in terms of their competence within such a structure or their competence in relation to his own development. Thus Capricorn often perceives things and people in their relationship to purportedly more important ends (rather than, for example, seeing relationships as ends in themselves). Capricorn tends to perceive means in terms of the ends toward which they lead. We might call this a habit of perception related to accomplishment. Though some have described Capricorn as an amoral sign, we might more accurately describe it as a sign that sees the world in terms of means, a sign that does not as readily register abstract, purportedly moral, qualities that others might attribute to those means and ends. None of this means that Capricorn cannot make moral judgments, but he often connects value-judgment to effectiveness. To say that Capricorn imposes concepts upon the world does not mean that she does so more readily than do other signs. Rather, Capricorn, as a cardinal earth sign (and thus a sign associated with tangible acts) does so in a more evident way, a way more directly related to and reflected in concrete action and accomplishment.

Compare, for example, Capricorn and Scorpio. Both perceive the world in terms of its alteration: Capricorn wants to bring about change through his own external accomplishment, Scorpio through his own internal power; Capricorn tends to define his change in external terms, not the internal ones so important to Scorpio. Scorpio tends to work from the inside out, Capricorn from the outside in. Not that Capricorn sees only external developments and Scorpio only internal ones, for Capricorn can make acute psychological evaluations just as Scorpio can make astute political ones. Capricorn finds personal meaning by achieving ends he has set out to achieve, with achievement often preceding meaning; she doesn't need meaning in order to achieve, for Capricorn will discover the meaning *in* the achievement. She tends to see achievement in external terms, though we could find many exceptions.

Thus, the world appears as a place not to apply principles, as with Sagittarius, but to apply organizational notions. Both Sagittarius and Capricorn concern themselves with the external world; but Capricorn orients himself through actions she sees as directly practical, just as Sagittarius orients himself through application of principle. As a cardinal sign, Capricorn tends to focus on relative truth, on the immediately presenting situation as a path to approach ultimate truth. Capricorn will certainly want to bring about change, but he will give greater emphasis to his capacity for initiation within a given social framework. Whereas Sagittarius will often perceive the world as a place in which to go on a quest for truth, Capricorn will generally perceive the world as a place in which to *express* truth through tangible action within the mentioned frameworks.

Whereas Aries (the first cardinal sign) perceives the world in terms of his own individual capacities for action, and whereas Cancer (the second) perceives the world in terms of her personal search for security, and whereas Libra (the third) perceives the world in terms his personal search for recognized partnership, Capricorn sees the world in terms of what she might accomplish in it—and in terms of what others might accomplish, though Capricorn often gravitates toward the forefront simply because, perceiving the world as she does, she can often develop and uncover useful organizational possibilities that others either ignore or simply miss.

Some will take this to mean that Capricorn doesn't readily register opportunities for play or recreation. However, most Capricorns will disagree. Surely the number of apparently playful Capricorns argues for some different interpretation. However, Capricorn often plays in different arenas than do the other signs, and others will not readily see him as playing. Capricorn often finds play within the structure or ambition that he chooses and within which he may (perhaps too often, some will say) isolate herself. Where others work as a prelude to play or so that they can play later, Capricorn plays while he works; whereas most of us don't easily keep our balance in high places, mountain goats gambol playfully about there. Further, whereas others must find a balance between work-time and play-time, Capricorn must find a balance between work-orientation and play-orientation within one activity.

The fish-element of the goatfish reminds us of Capricorn's need to find deep grounding for his earthy efforts. Whereas Libra, the previous cardinal sign, makes judgments involving a socially-accepted standard weight, Capricorn, also ruled by Saturn, makes judgments involving reference-points in the depths. Thus we should say not only that Capricorn sees life in terms of its externally-defined organizational capacities and demands, but also that Capricorn seeks some sort of ultimate fulcrum-point from which to move the world both practically and spiritually. However, most humans find those depths rather murky, so Capricorn must take care not to fool herself.

Aquarius

Aquarius tends to perceive the world as a place in which one might improve social conditions and that invites group activity. At the same time, Aquarius tends to see the world in terms of how much or little it manifests or harmonizes with his ideas about the preferred social order. Aquarius relates most readily to groups and to the ideas that govern the groups' movements. In perceiving the world as a place in which one might make a contribution to society, Aquarius may select from experience elements apparently related to larger social or group developments. On the other hand, Aquarius often seems to magnetize the ideas that make manifest the need for change and development; paradoxically, he prefers structures that will last. In his search for progressive change, he wants one structure to replace another, not to eliminate structure altogether—though Uranus, one of Aquarius' ruling planets, may disagree about this.

The preceding reflects Aquarius' dual rulership. Uranus promotes in Aquarius a drive for change, a desire for the new and groundbreaking, a tendency to love the progressive or revolutionary. But Saturn asks Aquarius to relate always and constantly to structure, to the organizational ground from which and in which change occurs. This often brings Aquarius into relationship with those involved in organizations of some sort, and often with the holders of traditions—or, some will say, with those who maintain remnants from the past. Thus Aquarius wants to change structures, not run away from them; to change or revolutionize society, not run off to the woods and commune with the nature deities.

Consider Thoreau. With Aquarius rising, he acted as a social critic and took stances related to the status quo, perceiving the world in terms of social relations. But with his Cancer Sun and Moon, he saw the world not as a place to make social improvements but, as he once wrote, as a place to live; he acted in order to achieve his own security, moving to Walden and making himself at home in a semi-isolation he apparently found somewhat congenial (Cancer Moon trines Saturn; Saturn squares Midheaven-Nadir axis; Saturn rules the twelfth house of retreat and isolation, and co-rules the Aquarius Ascendant). As befits someone with Aquarius rising and Uranus in Sagittarius in the tenth, he promulgated his ideas in the abstract and often perceived the world in terms of social principles; but as befits someone with such a strong emphasis on Cancer, he perceived the world partly in terms of the security it offered. Even in isolation, though he remained fully engaged with the society from which he had isolated himself.

Aquarius may want to cultivate the new and groundbreaking; however, because of Saturn's influence, he will also perceive the world as an arena for tangible application of for his new and groundbreaking programs or ideas. He may read or write revolutionary tracts, but he generally will want to change social structures instead of changing himself by solitary retreat. At the same time, the dual rulership suggests that Aquarius has ambivalent feelings about change and revolution.

Because both Saturn and Uranus rule Aquarius, Aquarius may perceive the world quite differently at different times; but because so many situations remind us of the borderline between Saturn and Uranus, Aquarius will often perceive the world in terms of this borderline – that is, in terms of the relationship between freedom and order, between the new and the traditional, between the progressive and the conservative, between the revolutionary and the orderly, between innovative and standard approaches. Thus he will often perceive social developments in terms of how readily, often, or pervasively they inhibit individual freedom; similarly, he may perceive the world in terms of the ongoing threats to the established order, or about the relationship between order on the one hand and new intellectual developments on the other. Sometimes he will have a reputation for progressive thinking and action even if a sober examination reveals his love for the established order. Consider, in this regard, Franklin D. Roosevelt and Abraham Lincoln. Other notable Aquarians serve as reminders of the same Saturn-Uranus connection: Ayn Rand, Sir Thomas More, Charles Dickens, Norman Mailer, and even Charles Lindberg.

These days, Aquarians often throw their lot in with those who demand more freedom; certainly they do this in the popular mind, if not so consistently in world itself! Those who do that throwing will often perceive the world in terms of its restrictions: Saturn will appear as a projection, often as some element in the social order that restricts. Yet politicians like Lincoln and Roosevelt in the above list, though they have a reputation as reformers, reformed in order to preserve the existing order instead of to establish a new one.

Among the signs with two rulers (a traditional one and a newer one),[36] Aquarius seems to have the most openly antagonistic pair. For example, while Scorpio's two rulers (Mars and Pluto) can work together through empowered action in which one's unconscious drives are in harmony with one's conscious predispositions, and while Virgo's two rulers (Mercury and Chiron) can work together through an intelligent and useful understanding of how to heal whatever wounds present themselves, and whereas Pisces two rulers (Jupiter and Neptune: see below) can work together through a union of social-conceptual and emotional-mystical understandings of spirituality, Aquarius' two rulers seem at first to stand for opposed principles.

---

[36]Scorpio, Aquarius, Pisces. Those who use Transpluto and connect him with Taurus will include that sign in the group.

We find this antagonism reflected in the Greek creation myth. We have looked at it already, but we can briefly review. Uranus, Saturn's father, tries to bury his children back into the mother (Gaia). The children, particularly Saturn, take a dim view of this and, with the help of the mother, fashion a sickle that Saturn uses to castrate his father. We might point to one meaning among many: that the demands of structure, responsibility, and ongoing restriction will seem to take away the life-giving power of a person's genius if that person doesn't cultivate a healthy respect for form, karma, and the vehicles through which creativity must manifest. We could also interpret the myth to mean that if we don't find forms for our creative inspirations—and particularly if we resist the effort needed to find those forms—then we lose the life-giving power of the creativity. As the son of Uranus, Saturn seems to represent the natural result of Uranus' gifts: the forms through which we express creative ideas. Uranus, however, resists the process represented by his son. We might say that he resists the karmic process altogether, preferring to remain ensconced in the cocoon of his ideas.

Though we will look at the Saturn-Uranus relationship in chapter VIII, we should say a bit more here about how Aquarius' paired rulers influence Aquarius' perspective (including in that phrase the collective habits of perception appearing as we enter the Aquarian Age). When Aquarius sees the world through Saturnian eyes, he will often experience the Uranus element as a projection, and when he experiences the world through Uranian eyes, he will often experience Saturn as a projection. We shouldn't attach a positive value to Uranus and a negative one to Saturn, as they form a potentially-complementary pair that we can see at work in situations ranging from the personal to the political. For example, the Confederate States had a strong Uranian element in that they wanted to break away from the established order, though they also had a strong Saturnian element in that they wanted to maintain the rigid hierarchies of the slave-system. Lincoln had his Sun in Aquarius, Uranus in the twelfth house, and Saturn conjoined Neptune on his Sagittarius Ascendant. With Sagittarius rising, he saw the world in terms of principle; with Saturn and Neptune conjoining that ascendant, his principles were aligned with the prevailing order, an order that (some would say) he idealized (Neptune). With Uranus in the twelfth house, he found himself battling those who wanted to break with the established order (i.e. the Confederates). Some might see Lincoln as clearly Uranian in his desire to free the slaves, but he said at one point that his primary goal was to preserve the union and that if he could have preserved the union without freeing the slaves, he would have done so. Like many Aquarians, he saw the world sometimes in Saturnian, and sometimes in Uranian terms.

Franklin D. Roosevelt, another "progressive" American president, had the Sun, Mercury and Venus all in Aquarius, Uranus conjoining his Virgo Ascendant,[37] and the rest of the planets between Saturn in Taurus at the cusp of the ninth and the Moon in Cancer in the tenth house. In many ways, Roosevelt undertook more clear-cut reforms than did Lincoln. Unlike Lincoln, who for the most part emphasized preservation of the status quo, Roosevelt authored progressive programs, perhaps because he had no choice, despite the objections of those representing his 8th

---

[37] January 30, 1892 8 PM. (Stephen Erlewine, *Circle Book of Charts*. (Tempe: American Federation of Astrologers, 1982), 78.) Soft data. Most estimates range from 8-8:45 PM. See Erlewine's notes on his sources.

house Saturn in Taurus, a position suggesting limits coming from others' values, likely manifesting as others' objections to his programs, no doubt because they were deemed "too progressive." But in true Aquarian fashion, Roosevelt put his progressive ideas (Uranus) into a form (Saturn) that has endured for several decades, and he did so in order to preserve the basic economic form of the United States. Furthermore, his actions in land reclamation and international affairs often seem decidedly Saturnian. In the former, he continually aligned himself with corporate interests; in the latter, he augmented the power of the military, refused peace overtures from Japan, and seemed bent on making the United States the major power in the Pacific.[38]

As a fixed air sign, Aquarius emphasizes fixed ideas. Often these fixed ideas have to do with social well-being. Sometimes, we might say, these fixed ideas produce fortunate results; sometimes they prove instrumental in the producing works of genius (as with James Joyce[39]). Just as often, the ideas may seem markedly reactionary (as with Ayn Rand and Ronald Reagan). But in all cases, the Aquarian perceives a social world in which ideas play a major role.

Pisces

Pisces tends to perceive the world as a place inviting compassion, as a place in which individual entities are moved by larger forces or energies (spiritual, military, economic). These forces and energies may have no relation to the prevailing social order. Rather, Pisces often perceives them as spiritual or quasi-spiritual, as emerging from or expressing some more pervasive, encompassing, or permeating truth. Pisces relates most readily to those elements in experience that promise spiritual illumination or reward, emotional merging, or idealistic yearning. In seeming to absorb collective energies, Pisces may edit out the mundane. On the other hand, Pisces will often seem to magnetize energies that some will call "spiritual" and which others will call "delusional"; to others, she may seem at times oblivious to the difference.

Because Pisces sees the world as inviting compassion, she will readily perceive the suffering of that world. She will perceive most readily those elements that don't hang together, that have difficulty standing up to the harshness of the world, that seem to have absorbed poison, that seem driven by visions and not practicalities. Pisces tends to perceive the world both as a vale of tears and as a seedbed of spiritual possibilities and actualities; and sometimes she will see the world as a place in which the spiritual possibilities arise out of compassion.

Some will say that Pisces more readily perceives absolute truths than do the other signs, and this

---

[38]Roosevelt's connection to aggressive U.S. imperialism appears in the connections between his horoscope and that of the United States: Roosevelt's Moon in Cancer conjoins the United States' Venus-Jupiter conjunction; his Mars conjoins the United States' Mars. As the U.S. Ascendant ruler, Jupiter plays a major role in U.S. imperialism, generally driven by various factors connected expansion and arising from notions about security. The U.S. seventh house Mars tells us much about U.S. ongoing belligerence and the way the U.S. almost always perceives others as the aggressor. See chapter X.
[39]Notably, Joyce's works have a markedly Saturnian quality. *Ulysses* has an extremely tight structure (so much so that Joyce once said, if I recall correctly, that he had perhaps imposed too much order on the work). His startlingly revolutionary (Uranus) approach to literature emerged through time-tested forms (Saturn).

because Pisces, the most absorptive sign of the zodiac, might seem to have fewer or thinner filters than the other signs. Pisces still has her filters, of course, as she filters out the simple, mundane elements of the world and prefers to see possibilities for the absolute. In other words, though Pisceans perceive through a more subtle—some will call it more *pervasive*; others will see it as more fuzzy or *delusional*—dualism than that of other signs, they see through a dualism nonetheless: on one side Pisces perceives purported absolutes; on the other side, she perceives what we call the relative, even when perhaps subsumed into the absolute. And though Pisces might often see them as meshing with one another, and though she will say that even within simple, personal neurosis lie enlightened possibilities, she will still tend to edit out one end or the other.

We can get a sense of how Pisces influences perception by looking at the prevailing view of the Christian churches (developed during the Age of Pisces), a view in which the world seemed a "vale of tears," a place where people work through suffering toward their own salvation, a fallen world in need of redemption. The Christian churches have maintained a strong devotional emphasis, reflecting Pisces' nature as a mutable water sign that sees emotion as a path toward another level of consciousness or awareness. Pisces perceives the world in terms of how well it facilitates this change, this movement toward encompassing emotional acceptance.

As we have approached the end of the Piscean era, we have seen philosophical and scientific trends that move us beyond Pisces' subtle dualism. We have heard quantum theorists telling us that we cannot do objective experiments on the world; we have read Nietzsche's injunction to step "beyond good and evil"; we have read in Jung that whatever one rejects from the self appears in the world as an event; we have heard much talk (as here) of projection.[40] But still we see the subtle dualism of Pisces, a dualism perhaps based in what seems a primitive tendency in the human psyche to divide that which ego finds acceptable from that which ego does not find acceptable. Despite its alleged spiritual leanings, Pisces seems as enmeshed in that dualism as any other sign, often using "spiritual" leanings to solidify ego.

Ego may want what it calls "spiritual growth"; it wants to grow beyond itself. Herein we find Pisces' subtle dualism: ego's desire for spiritual things, for spiritual energy, for energy that dissolves ego itself. Pisces must face this paradox, as must we all. We all have Neptune and Pisces in the horoscope: we desire spiritual things (so-called) even though merely having the desire may separate us from the spiritual; ego sometimes wants that which dissolves ego. Too, when Pisces perceives the world, she sees suffering, and Pisces apparently distinguishes that from not-suffering. Further, Pisces will often differentiate between the apparently conceptual and the apparently non-conceptual. This subtle dualism seems to reflect Pisces' two rulers, for Jupiter has to do with concept and Neptune with absorptive emotion.

---

[40] We have perhaps not heard of the Tibetan distinction between relative truth and absolute truth (Tb: kundzop and dondam; kundzop means "all dressed up," presumably with our concepts and delusions, among other things). When people do not examine their experience, or when they do so without the necessary tools or discipline, they experience relative truth; when they cut through delusion, they experience absolute truth. Some Tibetan texts describe absolute truth as that which the enlightened person experiences.

We find this last dualism expressed historically. On the one hand, throughout the first approximately 1600 years of the Christian era, devotion played a primary role in the religious life in the Christian countries. But with the dawn of what we call the Reformation, the scientific view began to encroach on areas previously felt as belonging more properly to religion or spirituality. Eventually, scientists seemed to take over religion's ground, so that we find quantum theorists seeming to speak of absolute truths and social critics speak of science as a religion. Jung felt that the shift in view arose when the equinoctial point reached the point in the constellation Pisces where the two fishes join:

> The northerly, or easterly, fish, which the spring-point entered at about the beginning of our era, is joined to the southerly, or westerly, fish by the so-called commissure. This consists of a band of faint stars forming the middle sector of the constellation, and the spring-point gradually moved along its southern edge. The point where the ecliptic intersects with the meridian at the tail of the second fish coincides roughly with the sixteenth century, the time of the Reformation, which as we know is so extraordinarily important for the history of Western symbols. Since then the spring-point has moved along the southern edge of the second fish, and will enter Aquarius in the course of the third millennium. Astrologically interpreted, the designation of Christ as one of the fishes identifies him with the first fish, the vertical one. Christ is followed by the Antichrist, at the end of time. The beginning of the enantiodromia would fall, logically, midway between the two fishes. We have seen that this is so. The time of the Renaissance begins in the immediate vicinity of the second fish, and with it comes that spirit which culminates in the modern age.[41]

Astrologers recognize that the slightly later (1781) discovery of Uranus ushered in a period of significant scientific and technical development, as well as important revolutions in politics. Next came the discovery of Neptune, and the first discovery led inevitably to the latter, as astronomers measured perturbations in Uranus' orbit and hypothesized that they were caused by a more distant planet. This hypothesis catalyzed and directed the search that culminated in the discovery of Neptune in 1846. We find several significant developments marking the period: the development of anesthesia; the height of the whaling trade; *The Communist Manifesto* (Marx) and *The Condition of the Working Class in England* (Engels). New ideas related to individualism (Uranus) led to new ideas about collectivization in society (Neptune). Science began to take the place of religion as it received the sanction of national organizations (e.g. The Smithsonian) and national publications (e.g. *Scientific American*).[42]

---

[41] C.G. Jung, *Aion* (Princeton: Princeton University Press, 1959), 93-94

[42] A full discussion of Piscean dualism in the historical record would take us too far afield. To some extent, Virgo represents the shadow-side of Pisces, for where Pisces often wants absorption (as a fish gets absorbed in water), Virgo wants a careful analysis of particulars with an eye toward use value. To some extent, too, Uranus may represent the shadow side, for Uranus brings a premonition of—and to some extent sets up the conditions for—the shift into the Age of Aquarius. Virgo's desire for ritual counter-balances Pisces' yearning for absolutes. Uranus' insight counter-balances any over-statement of emotion, spiritual or otherwise.

These dualisms tell us much about Pisces and Piscean perception. Pisces will generally side with the emotional instead of the rational, the boundariless instead of the bounded. However, in doing so, she inevitably invites the opposites and perceives them as part of her world. Moreover, she often experiences them as obstacles to some kind of not-entirely-defined spiritual growth. Though we can clearly find exceptions to this (Einstein, for example), Pisces often perceives the world through this kind of subtle dualism, even though Pisces may insist that she sees in all-encompassing terms.

Chapter VIII

The Foci of Security: Saturn and the Moon

Much projection apparently arises from our desire for situational or psychological security. Because ego seeks security, it will often exclude from its experience whatever threatens that security: in seeking to preserve situational security (e.g. of the home, in the job), we attempt to exclude items from the extensional world that seem threatening or that we classify as enemies or obstacles; in seeking to preserve psychological security, we attempt to exclude elements from the intensional world,[1] the world of mind and its concepts, psychic elements interpreted as threatening to our self-conception or our feeling of safety. Ego seeks security, and we could even say that security-seeking seems like a necessary condition for any definition of ego, perhaps even a *sufficient* one. Seeking security and thus excluding items from its inventory of the acceptable, ego anchors itself in the world by relating to its projections. The search for internal security, a state of mind in which one feels comfortable and ensconced, finds its mirror-image in an extensional realm populated to an extraordinary extent by the myriad hooks for ego's projections.

Such a remark makes no claim about the nature of the extensional realm *per se*, a matter about which we should withhold judgment, for though whatever ego excludes from its inventory arises as projection, it does not necessarily follow that everything in the extensional realm qualifies as

---

[1] As far as I know, the terms *extensional* and *intensional* come from S.I. Hayakawa's *Language in Thought and Action*. *Extensional* refers to what we can verify as going out outside of our heads; *intensional* refers to what we can verify as going on inside of our heads (e.g. thinking, evaluating). As we will have seen and will see, the boundaries between these sometimes seem rather porous. Nevertheless, in the world of consensus reality in which we all make our deals and walk about, the distinction seems an important one. We generally take the truck barreling down the pot-holed post-road as part of the extensional world and my infatuation with Pretty Polly as part of the intensional world.

projection. If we posit a pervasive and intimate connection between mind and world, we should also withhold judgment about the nature of either until we feel we understand both; in particular, we should first attempt to map the strange and mysterious territory we call *mind*. Of course, that a conclusion "does not necessarily follow" does not mean that we should reject it!

Security and Its Discontents I: The Big Daddy

What does ego value and think that it needs? Security, to begin with, whether emotional or situational: ego wants to feel secure not only in an inner realm where feelings develop and shift in a fairly predictable pattern, but also in its connection to the external world, where it finds security in a series of structured relations—the realms of Moon and Saturn respectively. Ego engages in a constant search for both types of security, though the search takes place so automatically that ego doesn't generally have a sense of engaging in a search at all. Just as a tornado doesn't search for things to destroy, its destruction and its movement toward items in our world seeming like expressions of the tornado's nature, so ego doesn't necessarily make a consciously-directed search for items that provide security. Security-seeking and ego-maintenance seem inseparable. Further, though ego seems like a solid thing, we would do better to see it as a process, as something one *does* instead of what one "is," as a verb instead of a noun. We might say something similar about the astrological planets: they symbolize types of actions. The Moon and Saturn symbolize actions crucial to ego-formation and ego-maintenance, yet those actions seem to take place automatically, and in a realm difficult to discern clearly.[2]

We can describe the process of ego formation and maintenance by referring to the planets out to and including Saturn.[3] The Sun symbolizes the basic experience of centrality and radiant power that seems so intrinsic to us moment-to-moment; but the Sun's light blinds, and when we emerge from the blinding light of self-referencing, we find ourselves somewhat bewildered. From that bewilderment comes our tendency to separate ourselves from the world around us via habit patterns taken from childhood, habitual emotional reactions, and a habitual sense of body (the Moon). Having separated ourselves from the world around us, we evaluate that world (Venus, ruler of Libra, sign of the scales), apparently automatically and perhaps instinctively, on a very primitive level, finding some elements welcoming, some threatening, and some neutral. We then actively perceive the world according to that basic dualism, our perception influenced pervasively by our ideas about the world and by the symbolic systems we use to describe it (Mercury); once we think we perceive things accurately, or once we think that we know it at least on a rudimentary level, we act (Mars) on what we think we know. We then we develop intellectual justifications and schemes to buttress the whole process (Jupiter, through its connection to philosophy and religion).

---

[2]In our astrological tradition, we consider the Moon and the Sun as planets, though we give them a special designation within that class (as "the Lights").
[3]See *Astrology Beyond Ego* (American Federation of Astrologers, 2010), particularly chapter two and the Appendix. My descriptions here owe a great deal to the teachings of various Tibetan masters, particularly Chogyam Trungpa. (See the bibliography.)

The final stage in this process has a close connection to Saturn. We might say, speaking colloquially (and quoting Edward Albee) that at this stage of ego development, we move "bag and baggage into our own fantasy worlds" and begin "playing variations on our own distortions."[4] Having developed intellectual justifications to convince ourselves of the solidity of ego, we build worlds; we begin to live in realms. The "realms" consist not only, or even primarily, of the various situations in which we find ourselves, or of the various courses of action that we undertake or commitments we make, but also, and more importantly, of the various decisions we make about who we "are," and thus of our characteristic types of mental patterning.[5] From these ideas about ourselves—often consisting of a phalanx of self-limiting is-propositions that we make about ourselves and the world—further structures develop.[6]

These structures arise from fear, so we find ourselves enmeshed in the realm of Saturn, who rules both structure and fear. Astrologers should know, in a way that non-astrologers perhaps don't, that self-limiting structures and fear occupy two sides of the same coin. Thus Robert Hand wrote, decades back, that Saturn "represents the way you see and experience the universe as you have structured it,"[7] a matter we will explore below. Thus we associate Saturn with political and economic structures, and we often say that we fear them, little recognizing that we perhaps fear them not only because they threaten ego's hegemony, but also because the fearsome appearance we see in such structures arises at least partly from their genesis in our own fears—in other words, that they arise as collective projections of human beings' Saturn-energies.

These social and intellectual structures, though arising from fear (Saturn), serve as opportunities as well as limitations. This means, on one level, that every social form or niche, ranging from language to lucre to job to genre in creative work, provides not only a venue through which one can act on and in the world, but also a set of restrictions upon that action. Thus if you take it into your head to devote yourself to novel writing, you will probably not satisfy your political ambitions.[8] In addition, the novel form itself limits, as do the forms of the political world. A form serves as a venue precisely *because* it limits. We can shout our anguish or exultation to the seven winds, but the shouts probably don't qualify as artistic creations until we modulate them into and through a form or set of forms. In the end, Saturn symbolizes many basic formal structures of human existence,

---

[4] *Who's Afraid of Virginia Woolf?* George says this to Martha.
[5] This stage has a fairly close correspondence to the Tibetan notion of the "six realms," depicted in the largest section of the Tibetan Wheel of Life iconography.
[6] Thus a person might say, "I am a depressed person." Insofar as the person takes such an assertion to heart, he limits himself, not only because he encourages himself to keep acting or thinking in a certain way, but also because the assertion, particularly when constantly reiterated, limits his vision of the possible. Similarly for other such statements: I am a moral person; I am a great lover; I am attractive to the opposite sex; I am lovable; I am shy; etc.
[7] Robert Hand, *Planets in Transit* (Atglen, PA: Whitford Press, 1976), 317.
[8] Norman Mailer fans can feel free to object, here! I do not know if Mr. Mailer intended to continue his writing had he won the mayoralty of New York City. Because he did not win the election, we will perhaps never know. Shelley told us that poets were the unacknowledged legislators of the world, but, unacknowledged as they remain, they never have to spend their time in committee meetings!

beginning with the skeleton and ending with our so-called allotment of three-score years and ten: the former prevents us from flying but serves as the vehicle for all creative action; the latter, even if it runs to six-score years and a dozen, reminds us of life's inherent limitations and prods us to give form to our potentials before time runs out.

Saturn symbolizes ego insofar as ego maintains its position and attempts to secure its hegemony by cementing itself into social positions and identifying with social function. Thus it has to do with "social security" not only because Saturn rules old age, but also because Saturn seeks security through the various functions, niches, positions, posturings, and productions of the social world. That world goes a long way toward structuring our ideas and insisting on one set of evaluations instead of another. Its influence, though pervasive, generally remains shadowy, just as Saturn remains in Tartarus. And just as free creative insight (Uranus) brings limitation and form (Saturn) into existence, so limitation and form bring into existence not only the psychological complexes and the deep unconscious (Pluto), but also our spiritual or artistic yearnings (Neptune) and our search for some compensation through social expansion (Jupiter).[9]

Having apparently solidified its position through connection to social forms, the developed illusion that we call "ego" attempts to block out the vaster world that arises beyond its domains. Just as Heisenberg's Uncertainty Principle tells us that the more one knows about a particle's position, the less one knows about its momentum, so in ego's realm the more ego concerns itself with its position and its security, the less it will develop an awareness of what lies beyond. This does not mean that *any* position one takes comes at the expense of one's spiritual development, for if one can function without attachment, one can maintain one's awareness in *any* position, as the Dalai Lama and many other Tibetan tulkus have demonstrated. However, if one ensconces oneself within the walls, structures, and limitations of ego, whether manifested in mental patterns or the patterns of extensional living, one may miss an important paradox: that the world "beyond ego's domains" has its locus right within the ego-process itself. Just as Milarepa once said that ultimate truth arises between every two thoughts, so our capacity for wakefulness takes place right within the processes that blind us—which we can see if we look directly at the blinding processes themselves.

From ego's point of view, security means survival, whether psychic or physical: ego wants to survive, not only through the physical body, but psychologically, through a secure sense of identity that it constantly props up through the drives symbolized by the inner planets: through emotional patterning and connection to the body (Moon); through a sense of centralized identity and radiation (Sun); through thoughts and ideas (Mercury); through values and magnetism (Venus); through action and identification (Mars); through social connectedness on various levels (Jupiter); and through a developed sense of what one "is" (Saturn) either psychologically or socio-culturally, matters discussed above. Because it thinks in terms of security and stability, ego also thinks in

---

[9]This sentence traces the mythic genealogy of Uranus and his various sons.

terms of threats *to* that security and stability. Ego therefore finds itself driven about and ruled by the dichotomy mentioned above: hope and fear, hoping for security and fearing its disruption.[10]

Further, ego seeks security by encasing itself in personal or social cocoons to such an extent that ego seems inseparable from the cocoon.[11] The ingredients of the cocoons vary from person to person, and the security that results includes not only the kinds of emotional security we associate with Cancer and the Moon, but also the security we think we get from having an apparently solid, structured, dependable, continuous, and largely knowable personal identity through which we enmesh ourselves into social scaffolding and that we hope links us to others in a reliable way, even as the personal identity itself seems to precipitate at least partly from the social web. Of course, we never actually find the security we seek, at least not in pure form, so the search for it goes on and on through innumerable twists and turns. Ego never quite gets what it wants, for the security ego seeks consists of stasis in a world characterized by mutability. Thus ego's effort proves futile in both extensional and intensional realms.[12]

Ego therefore finds itself constantly trying to maintain security and thus ensuring that the security will slip away, for the search for security seems pretty much synonymous with the fear of losing it. Thus ego has an ambivalent relationship to change, for on the one hand ego entertains itself by engaging constantly changing stimuli to mask its essential loneliness and to keep itself entertained,[13] while on the other hand it fears any change that undermines security, however delusory. This constantly changing stimulation with which ego entertains itself shields a person from the more basic insecurities that lie beneath the phantasmagoria. For some people (e.g. those we could call "adventurers"), ego maintains itself through engaging in external change, even though ego wants some degree of stability in what we might call its own self-perception; for others, the entertainment arises largely in the mind. In the end, ego thinks and perceives in terms of its attachments; it wants to have fixed reference points. Furthermore, ego generally convinces itself that it *has* this reference point and that the reference point has inherent reliability. We see mirrored in this search for entertainment the problematic elements of Jupiter and Uranus, for Jupiter has much to do with the search for joyful connections to the larger social world, while Uranus has much to do with our desire to escape from the world of experienced limitation into the world of ideas both disembodied and potent.

---

[10]Many astrologers see Jupiter as an exalted ruler of Cancer. Certainly Jupiter has much to do with hope (hence its position as the greater benefic). Hope and security go together. Saturn, symbol of fear, rules Capricorn, Cancer's polar opposite, yet he rules another kind of security, as noted above. The Cancer-Moon type of fear may seem more evident to us day-to-day than does the Capricorn-Saturn type, for, as already noted, Saturn dwells in the underworld.

[11]These ideas in these paragraphs owe a great deal to the various writings of Chogyam Trungpa.

[12]I more or less stole this idea from Gautama Buddha, whose first noble truth tells us that life is characterized by suffering (or, as Chogyam Trungpa sometimes put it, by ongoing anxiety), and whose second noble truth tells us that this suffering arises because we develop attachments in a world that changes constantly. It may be worth noting that he referred to these as *noble truths*, not as *unfortunate facts of life*.

[13]I have derived from Chogyam Trungpa the idea about using entertainment to keep ourselves distracted from our own pain.

Though any planet can serve the needs of ego by aiding ego's effort to maintain security in one of the ways described above, two planets hold a particularly important place, standing at the beginning and the end of the process:[14] the Moon and Saturn, the planetary system's two primary symbols of security. These bodies have various astronomical and symbolic connections. Most obvious among the former are the similar periodicities: that Saturn takes about 29.5 years to move through the zodiac while the Moon has a synodic cycle of about the same number of days. The most obvious symbolic connections have to do with astrological dignities: the Moon and Saturn rule Cancer and Capricorn respectively, signs that oppose one another. They therefore have their dignities in each other's detriment. They also have their exaltations in signs that quincunx each other but that both have Venus as ruler (Libra and Taurus respectively), this last suggesting that both have to do with value, love, relationship, and connections with others. The symbolic connections suggest a functional relationship that we can see more clearly if we consider the Moon and Saturn in relation to ego development and security-seeking. Because so many projections arise as reactions to either the Moon or Saturn, we should investigate those symbols carefully.

Security and Its Discontents II: Ego and the Moon

The Moon symbolizes ego's search for security through emotional patterning and in those situations (e.g. home, at least in theory) that seem to promote, preserve, and safeguard such patterning; through its connection with feeding and nurture, the Moon has much to do with organic growth in the sub-lunar realm. The Moon also symbolizes the search for safety and protection, psychological or situational, to underlie ego's various activities and enterprises. This kind of security has much to do with one's search for roots (emotional or situational), whether through having property, by developing a web of personal connections, or by finding an inner security through habitual, apparently safe, and possibly-blinding emotional patterns. Thus the Moon has to do with such basic "needs" as food and shelter as well as with feelings, because we can "feel at home" with our feelings even if we don't have an actual home, and the actual home feels secure only insofar as it supports the "feeling at home" provided by habitual patterns of feeling-response.

Gurdjieff is reported to have said that "the Moon is eating you."[15] I take him to have meant, at

---

[14] If we wish to state how a particular planet serves in the process of ego-formation and ego-maintenance, we can use this phrasing: X (one of the planets) *represents ego insofar as ego maintains itself by X1* (an activity, assumption, or emphasis associated with that planet). Thus, Mars represents ego insofar as ego maintains itself by physical and psychological self-identification, particularly through physical or mental action in which one has a particular effect on the external world. Venus represents ego insofar as ego maintains itself through personal adornment, personal appearance, relationship, or a sense of either personal or extra-personal value. Mercury represents ego insofar as ego maintains itself through ideas, opinions, speech, and the labeling process. (Obviously enough, the labeling process also enables us to function in world of ordinary experience. Nevertheless, it seems that, both beneath and side-by-side with this practical orientation, the labeling process serves to anchor us in our version of the world.) Jupiter represents ego insofar as ego maintains itself through expansion and general social influence, through expanding intellectual territory (extending Mercury's function) or philosophical conviction, and through ongoing hope. The Sun represents ego insofar as ego maintains itself through a sense of personal creativity or centrality, through a sense of personal authenticity.

[15] The quotation comes via Ouspensky, I think.

least in part, that habitual patterns taken from childhood (the Moon) devour a person's creative spirit and his drive to become individuated, to accomplish what Gurdjieff called "being human." In what seems like a similar vein, Erich Neumann writes of a cycle perpetuated by the "emotional-dynamic" components of the psyche that have an organic root in

> [t]he most primitive parts of the brain, namely the medullary region and the thalamus. Since these centers are linked up with the sympathetic nervous system, the emotional components are always intimately associated with unconscious contents. Hence the vicious circle we are constantly coming up against: unconscious contents release emotions, and emotions in their turn activate unconscious contents.[16]

We see in such descriptions the blinding power of energies that astrologers associate with the Moon. These ideas have some similarities with the Shambhala teachings of Tibetan Meditation Master Chogyam Trungpa, in which he describes the way that we wrap ourselves up in habitual responses that inhibit a fresh and open response to experience:

> The way of cowardice is to embed ourselves in this cocoon, in which we perpetuate our habitual patterns. When we are constantly recreating our basic patterns of behavior and thought, we never have to leap into fresh air or onto fresh ground.

The cocoon, says Trungpa, is "comfortable and sleepy"; in it, we feel that spring cleaning is "too much work, too much trouble." We would "prefer to go back to sleep."[17] These remarks seem connected to the Moon, symbol of protection (like the cocoon) and of emotional habituation.

The Moon offers us a paradox: on the one hand, it seeks security; on the other hand, the Moon-ruled flow of feeling changes constantly, going through phases and never appearing the same from one day to the next. Though the pattern remains, within it we experience constant change. Ego goes through phases based on emotional patterning. Though ego appears solid, unchanging, and unitary, closer inspection reveals nothing reliable except ongoing self-deception. Ego must do constant self-maintenance, a process that, in a way ego seldom notices, develops into an end in itself: we take the maintenance process as ego itself and we experience the effort as psychological equilibrium.[18] The Moon's symbolism suggests that we develop attachment to the process of emotional

---

[16] Erich Neumann, *The Origins and History of Consciousness* (Princeton: Princeton University Press, 1954), 330.

[17] Chogyam Trungpa, *Shambhala: The Sacred Path of the Warrior* (Boston: Shambhala, 1988), 60-61.

[18] We can see this process writ large in the United States, a country with its Sun in Moon-ruled Cancer: the ongoing obsession with security eats up huge chunks of the available national resources and national budget; it often appears as an end in itself. The Cancer Sun suggests that many citizens confuse the drive for national security with the drive for national identity, and in its foreign dealings, the United States often presents itself in security-oriented terms, dealing with other nations in varying ways depending on how they seem to affect United States' security. Throughout its history, the United States has enjoyed more security than almost any other nation on the planet, yet it constantly attempts to secure that security (so to speak), protecting itself against threats that either don't exist or that have arisen because of the over-stated security-seeking.

patterning. But if we can see this process clearly, the capacity to wake up appears within the blinding process itself; if we examine habitual patterns, we uncover the capacity to wake up by accepting the inherent impermanence that imbues all of our experience. By looking right at habitual patterns instead of ignoring them, we find something less claustrophobic and more awake. Because the Moon can illuminate, in many spiritual traditions it stands as a symbol for illumination.

Nevertheless, in its more problematic manifestations, the Moon encourages us to build a cocoon in which we respond not to the world itself but to our own protective devices, our habitual patterns. Through those patterns, we half-consciously seek security. The Moon symbolizes ego insofar as ego maintains and occupies itself, or finds itself occupied *by*, the kind of security-seeking described here. The process takes place in at least three ways: ego maintains a *physical* environment in which one no longer preoccupies oneself with worry about "primary needs"; ego maintains a *psychological* environment in which one doesn't need to question the security purportedly provided by habit patterns taken from childhood (patterns closely connected to the cocoon-making described above); and ego tries to maintain a relational environment that makes the psychological maintenance easier. Even if we achieve security about primary needs, we generally find ourselves seeking psychological security, the sense of being secure in our patterns of response, which we take as something solid; and many of us tell ourselves that the proper relational environment will help us maintain psychological security and vice-versa.

The Moon symbolizes how we most readily and immediately respond to the world around us. This response generally takes place automatically, before concept gets involved (though not much before, so that we often take our concept *for* the response), though the Moon will readily incorporate conceptual input into the emotional response.[19] Because the pattern repeats and repeats (a process we can discern as the transiting Moon moves through the birth horoscope), we identify with it, taking it as something solid and reliable and as a basis for what we call *identity*. That the Moon also symbolizes nurturing suggests that we constantly feed ourselves by remaining in this pattern. And yet it also seems that if we stay there, claustrophobia sets in: the Moon feeds off of us. In any case, the Moon symbolizes ego insofar as ego maintains itself through a constant and patterned set of emotional responses whose initial impulses arise before concept gets involved but that we then shape by our concepts. Our responses shape our view of ourselves, of the world, and of the interaction between the two.

Security and Its Discontents III: Saturn and Ego

Saturn, the so-called "greater malefic," represents ego insofar as ego maintains itself through worldly position, social assumption, and a general sense of limitation often expressed through structured ideas about oneself or the world. We express these ideas through language, of course, often by using phrases such as "I am X" ("I am a good person"; "I am a depressed person"; "I am a

---

[19]Our language distinguishes between concept and feeling even though the two often (perhaps usually) arise together. Most of our "feelings" contain a hefty dose of labeling and concept; most of our concepts have more than a little attendant feeling.

lawyer"; "I am a loving person"; "I am quite bitchy," "I am a great lover," "I am an occultist," "I am kind and compassionate," and so on) or "A is B" ("Life is tough"; "Life is full of love"; "There is no way to do X"; "Society is Y"). The first type of statement tells us what one thinks about oneself; the second type tells us what one thinks about the world. If we look closely, we will see the constrictive nature of such judgments, for none of them takes into consideration the vast variety of experience, and each presents the world in two-valued terms.[20] We will also see their function in our ongoing effort to secure ourselves, however painfully, in the world. When we establish some kind of social identity, we often use similar statements to refer to this identity: we say, "I am a social worker," "I am the President of the United States," "I am an astrologer," and so forth. These statements—and the social positions from which we derive them—further buttress ego. When we offer limiting propositions about the world, we limit our ideas about what qualifies as *possible* and what does not.

We seek Saturn's type of security through structure. We build structures, including the intellectual ones just described, which develop from Mercury's initial labeling and Jupiter's further abstraction-creation, structures through which we can protect ourselves and through which we can feel "established" as specific something-or-others in a social context and in a world we have convinced ourselves that we understand. Whereas the Moon has a close connection to the survival instinct in relation to feeding,[21] Saturn symbolizes that instinct as transformed by social custom: survival through social and intellectual integration. A person establishes himself socially by adopting a role (*I am a teacher; I am a lawyer; I am the President of the United States*) and psychologically by adopting a certain description, however multifaceted, of himself (*I am a kind person. I am a selfish person. I am an ambitious person. I am a fearful person. I am not the kind of person who does X. I am the kind of person who does Y. I am not a joiner. I am a leader, not a follower. I am a coffee-person. I am meek and mild but a terror on the highway.*). He establishes intellectual security via propositions about the world (*Life is hard. Emotionalism is good. Rational thinking is good. Joe is an idiot. It is good to be stable. It is bad to let others manipulate you. This world is a vale of tears and full of sorrow. Life is good.*).[22]

Whereas with the Moon we make assumptions based on habitual feeling-patterns, through Saturn we come to certain conclusions about the way life allegedly *is* or the way we allegedly *are*—and these conclusions function as assumptions that we cease to question. Once I have decided who I "am," I will have decided what I "am not," thus relegating various energies to the world outside of myself instead of accepting them as potentials—a process with obvious importance to any discus-

---

[20] If I say, "Life is tough," I suggest only one alternative, that life "is not tough." Of course, such a construction also fails to clarify what "toughness" refers to when applied to "life."

[21] The Moon doesn't symbolize survival per se. A person survives because of many different activities. Mars has to do with the active and direct procurement of necessity; Moon has to do with feeding; Mercury has to do with the mental operations that facilitate, among other things, Mars' activities.

[22] We can note, here, two types of "to be" usage: the is-of-identity and the is-of-predication. In the former, we use nouns: *I am an accountant; I am an undertaker; I am the ruler of an evil empire.* In the latter, we use adjectives: *I am kind; I am beautiful and graceful; I am ungainly but genuine.*

sion of projection. From our assumptions, we build a seemingly solid world in which we have a seemingly reliable place and in which we know what "is part of us" and what "is not," a judgment made on the surface of things, generally driven by social custom or personal fear instead of by knowledge arising from deep introspection. Such judgments bring us to the roots of projection, for they play an important role in the repression of psychic contents. As Ms. von Franz writes,

> According to Jung, all psychic contents of which we are not yet conscious appear in projected form as the supposed properties of outer objects. Projection, from this point of view, is a displacement, occurring unintentionally and unconsciously, that is, without being noticed, of a subjective psychic content onto an outer object.[23]

We might consider judgments that separate conscious contents from unconscious ones as conclusions that have developed from assumptions through patterned behavior. If we maintain our conclusions and assumptions for enough time (decades, perhaps), we may cease to investigate or question them, considering them as self-evident truths. Just as all arguments arise from assumptions of some sort, so with all world-structures. The assumptions about world-structures get cast onto a larger screen, but they result from an analogous process. Both sorts of assumptions serve to limit us even when—and probably *especially* when—we remain unaware of them; they serve as the foundations for whatever structures we choose to build in our lives, ranging from career choice to choice of marriage-partner to choices regarding life-style (etc.). We may see these structures as inherently limiting, but though structures *do* limit (my skeleton, for example, apparently prevents me from flying), they also facilitate creative work (my skeleton will also, people say, serve me well should I decide to learn to tango).[24]

This last sentence suggests the creative function of Saturn, for all creative work manifests in some form, and though astrologers seem fond of referring to Uranus as the "planet of genius," Saturn appears in anything that we refer to as a "work of genius." Insofar as we refer to *works*, we refer to form; insofar as we refer to form, we refer to Saturn. Saturn symbolizes the structures, ranging from intellectual to skeletal, that underlie our attempts to understand the world, and, as far as we know, the world itself. He rules all scaffolding as well as the structuring material that goes onto the scaffolds, material ranging from cement to bedrock to assumptions to regulations to laws to propositions to aesthetic forms to girders. The intellectual structures arise in the mind via assumptions, but we generally don't maintain a very precise awareness of those assumptions or where they came from. They function, rather, in a shadowy realm, embedded within social and intellectual structure, just as the mythical Saturn in Tartarus remained Lord of this World. Satan/Saturn still apparently performs that function, so we often refer to him as "The Lord of this World."

Someone might say, of course, "But I *am* a lawyer," or, "I *am* good and decent," or, "I *am* the

---

[23] Marie Louise von Franz, "Projection," in *Psychotherapy* (Boston: Shambhala, 1993), 257.
[24] We can see this pattern—conclusions about reality resulting from assumptions—in entire cultures, for each culture functions according to a set of assumptions and resulting habit patterns; working in tandem, those two processes influence how most people in that culture see "truth" and has much to do with their patterns of projection.

leader of the free world." But the process through which one arrives at such conclusions involves the kind of self-limiting propositions-structures mentioned above. Such structures limit because when we think in terms of is-propositions and the sorts of abstractions that drive such remarks, we reject much data about the world and about ourselves, for not only do such propositions encourage us to perceive the world in two-values, they also encourage us to ignore much important data. After all, a person "is" much more than any label we apply to him, certainly much more complex and intriguing than the proposition "I am a lawyer" suggests. Putting aside the question of whether a person can ever "be" a category or a role, we should consider that the inner processes of one lawyer differ from those of every other lawyer. We do ourselves a disservice if we begin to see the world through the lens provided by such limiting abstractions. Saturn limits not only because abstractions limit the amount of information we include in our understanding of ourselves and the world, but also because, having first limited ourselves in the labeling process itself, we then limit what we perceive.

Using general semantics terminology, we would say that this kind of thought-structure, one I connect largely to the Saturn-function, generally does not, in its descriptions of people and the world, provide very accurate or helpful maps of the territory in question (the actual people and situations with which we must deal). Furthermore, if someone "is" something – if Joe "is" emotional, or if he "is" a bastard—then he will remain in that straightjacket, for that's what he "is." When we ask how Saturn manifests in the mind on a moment-to-moment basis, we can see that these kinds of thoughts play an important role. And, often, we find the is-propositions linked to should-propositions: *I am a bad student; I should be a better one.* Such self-limiting propositions, particularly the ones structured around "is," play an important role in projection, for as we say what we "are," we build a wall between what we "are" and what we "are not," not only in the extensional realm, but in the intensional one as well. Intensional notions about who or what we "are" have much to do with what we reject from our self-conception, what we experience as projection, and what we assume we "are not."

Of course, someone might say, "But we *have* to use labels, after all. We can't avoid doing so." True enough: we must have the Saturn function in some form. Not only does the world apparently depend upon and arise from structure, but creative work does as well, for we work with Saturn whenever we create structure or see the creative possibilities in existing ones (novels, poems, hip-hop routines). However, if we don't strive for more awareness about this shadowy function, we find ourselves beset by projections created by Saturn. That the myth has Saturn relegated to Tartarus tells us that we generally relegate this function (the limiting function, as described) to a shadowy realm of the mind; however, that we so often refer to Saturn as "lord of this world" reminds us that when we relegate automatically and blindly, we will look into the world and see Saturn on all sides and deal with our own limitations via their projected appearance. It seems, though, that if we look more carefully at Saturn, we find the way toward wakefulness. Some ancient gnostic writings describe Satanael as Jesus' twin brother, suggesting that structure and wakefulness come from the same source. Though we have deeply ingrained habits in how we structure our "reality"—in what we decide to accept and what to reject, and in all matters related to evaluation, habits reflecting Saturn's exaltation in Libra—we also have the ability to shed light on such processes. The Sun, after all, rules the sign opposite Saturn's traditional "day sign" (Aquarius), suggesting that we *can* shed light on the Saturn process and see how it affects the sense of self with which it has such a close relationship.[25]

Like the Moon, Saturn symbolizes psychological processes that lie at the root of the projection process. Seeking both emotional and situational security, we reject anything that threatens either. But just as projections arise at least in part because of the Moon and Saturn, so the Moon and Saturn can arise *as* projections. We have already seen the Moon's close connection to projections related to a man's anima, and Saturn, with his connection to the father lineages, surely has a connection to a woman's animus. However, Saturn also appears as projections with no necessary or primary connection to gender. Those projections include the world of rigid authority figures and rigidly organized situations, and though one can see that men occupy most of the authority positions in those situations, men must cope with these projections just as women do, though perhaps they adopt different strategies as they do so. All humans, regardless of gender, experience fear; all of us communicate through language structures; all of us apparently need to contract in order to generate forms, and it seems that we must focus attention in order to create.

The people or situations that arise as Saturn-projections inform us that we consider some actions, attitudes, and approaches to life as acceptable and some as unacceptable. As a result of Saturn's weighing and judging, we project out whatever does not fit into the way we structure not only our psychological and social world, but also how we think about "reality." Within these arenas, we find Saturn's shadowy judgment-function constantly at work. The things we refer to as *structures* thus bear the mark of Saturn, which, like the other planets, symbolizes a certain type or class of action, for like the other planets, Saturn symbolizes something we *do* rather than simply what we *encounter*. Though we have discussed these already, we should probably look more carefully into at least five types of structuring activity:[26]

- First, and perhaps most obviously, we structure the external spaces in which we live our lives. We put one object here and another there; we create various physical structures and encase them in larger matrixes (buildings and roads within cities, for example) within which millions of human beings work, live, and grow. Despite the great variety visible in each, every culture has a characteristic way of doing this: most of us know immediately if we've entered a space orientation emerging from a culture different from our own. Most Anglo-Americans

---

[25]That Uranus now shares rulership of that old day-rulership surely suggests that in the modern era, people have developed publicly-available tools to undertake the necessary examination and bring forth the necessary insight.
[26]As noted earlier, some of this phrasing about structuring one's world comes from Robert Hand, though I take responsibility for the elaborations on that term.

know, for example, when they've entered, say, a Japanese space, a Chinese space, a Native American space, and so forth. This examination will often tell us quite a lot about the people who inhabit those spaces, but we may have more difficulty examining our *own* space, cultural or personal, in a helpful way. Because we have created that space from habitual patterns of thinking and emotional response, we have difficulty seeing that space as other than "reality." (Here again we see the astronomical situation reflected in our lives: we do not see Saturn easily; though he hides in plain sight, one must know where to look.)

- Second, we structure the world through time-measurement. Obviously enough, people in so-called "developed" countries do a lot of what we call "scheduling"; they structure the way they work with time: one person says he has a full schedule; another sees her schedule as rigid; a third person feels panic if he departs from his. If you go to a traditional Catholic monastery, you'll see yet a different way to structure time. The time-measurements themselves qualify as structures, but humans invent and maintain those measurements, deciding to structure their lives according to them. Some people divide the day into twenty four hours, the year into twelve months, and the century into a hundred years; the Maya worked more closely with the Moon and a 360-day approximate year, adding the *tzolkin* (often called the Sacred Calendar), the cycle of Venus, and many other measurements; many Chinese and Tibetan people use a sixty year calendar; and the Jewish calendar divides time differently than does the Gregorian. Despite the differences, all humans apparently share this propensity to structure time and to integrate the measurements into social custom.[27]

- Third, we structure our world by deciding what "is real" and what "is not real." A person who believes that ghosts "are real" structures her world differently than does someone who evaluates as "psychotic" anyone who "believes in the supernatural." (The person who claims to see ghosts will probably see them as quite *natural*, of course.) Someone who believes in an omnipotent spirit has adopted a different reality-structure than someone who sees such a belief as arrant foolishness. Much evidence suggests that a person's belief-structure has a profound influence on how that person perceives the world. Some (e.g. those who wrote or compiled the *Tibetan Book of the Dead*) will say apply this statement to the after-death realm as well. We have all sorts of metaphysical is-propositions that reflect, reiterate, and reify what we think we know about reality. One person says, "Death is not the end." Another says that there "is" a Heaven, or a God, or a Redeemer; a third will say that only oblivion follows death; a forth believes in holy war or that "God" has instructed him to invade another country; yet another says that world we see "is not real." And so forth. (From this point of view, Saturn doesn't symbolize death itself, but a set of assumptions we make *about* death—about the structures and limits of human existence. The abstracting process lurks in all such no-

---

[27]In *Technics and Civilization* (New York: Harcourt, Brace, and World, Inc., 1934) Lewis Mumford describes the mechanical clock as "a piece of power-machinery" whose "product" is seconds and minutes (15). He also feels that though it found its first significant use in the Catholic monasteries of the pre-Renaissance period, we should consider the clock as the "key-machine of the modern industrial age."

tions, for if death "is" the Grim Reaper—if we accept that as an identity-relation—we will probably fail to understand, or take in, something about death, having mistaken our ideas about the world for the world itself—assuming that the latter exists![28]). We limit our understanding at least partly via the structure of our propositions.

- Fourth, a related point: we structure our world according to the self-limiting is-propositions and should-propositions already discussed. If I categorize myself as "a brilliant philosopher," that proposition ('I am a brilliant X') will probably play an important role in the ways I choose, not always or even usually consciously, to structure my world, and therefore in the way I interpret "reality" and relate with other people. We structure our reality at least partly via language, perceiving the world in terms not only of the categories provided by the language we speak, but also in terms of the various interconnections provided by that language's grammar and syntax, what we might call the *structure* of the language. Thus the linguist Edward Sapir wrote in 1929,

  > Human beings do not live in the objective world alone, nor alone in the world of social activity as ordinarily understood, but are very much at the mercy of the particular language which has become the medium of expression for their society. It is quite an illusion to imagine that one adjusts to reality essentially without the use of language and that language is merely an incidental means of solving specific problems of communication or reflection. The fact of the matter is that the 'real world' is to a large extent unconsciously built up on the language habits of the group.[29]

  This doesn't mean that language determines consciousness or that consciousness "is entirely determined" by language. It means only that language plays a role as a structuring principal that, though visible in everyday life, nonetheless operates beneath the surface (Saturn's Tartarus), hiding in plain sight.

- Fifth, and most intimately, we structure our world as a result of our physical limitations; or, we might say, those limitations serve as filters through which we perceive the world. A bird probably sees quite a different world than we see; similarly for a horse, for the horse's eyes do not look straight ahead. Certainly a blind person's experience differs a good deal from mine, and if I had the ability to project my consciousness into another kind of creature, I surely would have a differently-structured experience. As infants, our physical limitations influenced us pervasively. As we grow, the skeleton develops and supports not only our living organs, but our myriad creative activities. The skeleton supports life but also establishes what appear as limits. From the skeletal structure arise many of the other structures mentioned above.

---

[28]See chapters XI and XII.
[29]Edward Sapir, "The Status of Linguistics as a Science," first published in Language, 5 (1929: 207-214. My copy comes from *Selected Writings in Language, Culture, and Personality*, by Edward Sapir, published by 1963 by the University of California Press in Berkeley, California, and later (2012) re-issued by Forgotten Books.

Like the other structures in the list, the skeleton operates beneath the surface. In speaking of the skeleton, we can take this remark quite literally, but in each of the other structuring processes, we see the creation of structures and forms that, though in many ways completely evident to our senses or awareness, nonetheless escape our notice constantly. This hidden quality—what I have called *hiding in plain sight*—reminds us of Saturn's home in Tartarus. Though Lord of this World, Saturn moves through the shadows, far from the Sun's light, at the edge of an outer darkness; he symbolizes processes that, through clearly apparent in external phenomena, usually escape our notice.

Though we can see many of the extensional results of inner structuring processes (results such as buildings, borderlines, bosses, beggars, bustling cities, street-grids, houses, hell-fire sermons, and hierarchies), the processes themselves remain in the shadows. We do not, therefore, come to a proper understanding of those extensional results, for we don't see their connection to inner workings. We see clearly how we structure physical space, whether in our homes or in society-at-large; we remain more-or-less constantly aware of our time-structures; we can bring our ideas about reality easily to mind; we make use of the structure of language every time we speak, listen, think, or write; and we surely can get a sense of our skeletons whenever we take a moment to come out of our thoughts and into our bodies. In most cases, though, we don't register either the connection between one structure and another or see the pervasive influence of the structuring principle. Our awareness of these matters remains shadowy and uncertain; we seldom see them as the ways we structure our world at all, but rather as a set of givens, as elements we take as part of reality itself. That we engage in structuring constantly doesn't mean we see it *as* structuring, or as limiting, or as form-giving. That we don't notice such structuring processes suggests that they will, to use Ms. Von Franz's phrasing, "appear in projected form as the supposed properties of outer objects."[30]

Most people project Saturn into the world at least some of the time, and probably most of us project at least some Saturnian elements most of the time. Because so many millions of people do this so constantly, Saturn marks the collective projection in a profound way; though that collective projection will appear differently in different cultures, those varied forms have common characteristics, for Saturn consistently arises as the set of limitations that have gained currency in a status quo and that reflect culture-wide assumptions about value and purpose—and about the nature of reality. These assumptions lie at the root of most social structures, for it seems that social structures arise from unexamined ideas about the purpose of human life, the purpose of society, or some other collectively-held assumption. Just as on an individual level Saturn symbolizes decided-upon limits that come to define an individual's life, on a collective level projected Saturn arises as generally-accepted limiting factors and structuring factors of all sorts (social, political, psychological, "natural") that some people use creatively and others less creatively.

In general, people "negativize" Saturn, so we find ourselves confronting problematic structures; we generally conclude that the problems and negative elements exist in the structures and limitations themselves, not in the psyche. Thus we find what people have found for thousands of years:

---

[30]Von Franz, *Psychotherapy*, 257.

purportedly-problematic structures on all sides. Government hierarchies, military orders, financial institutions that devour poor nations—entities such as these seem like the order of the day. However, because of the genesis of such projections, we shouldn't assume that *all* structures *must* do harm. If we look honestly at our world, we will see that many structures serve as vehicles or venues through which people do creative work, and even the ones that seem harmful have at least the *potential* to bring benefit. In the former class we can include the sonnet, the rap song, the sonata, the haiku, the novel, the astrological birth horoscope, the thirty-two bar song-form; in the latter, we can include the World Bank.[31]

Saturn stands as the antithesis to the Moon, Jupiter, and Neptune. (Astrologers say that the Moon rules Cancer and that Jupiter and Neptune have their exaltation there, opposite Saturn-ruled Capricorn.) As the antithesis to the Moon, Saturn emphasizes roles and niches (structural elements) instead of the feeling that we bring *to* those roles and niches; whereas Saturn throws his lot in with socially defined roles and venues, the Moon, with its emphasis on biological necessity, symbolizes that which resists socially defined roles, as well as that which underlies them and makes them possible. We could also say that Saturn emphasizes limitation on feeling (by duty, for example) rather than enrichment *by* or *of* feeling. As the antithesis to Jupiter through expansive social participation, Saturn symbolizes crystallization through the establishment *of* social position. As the antithesis to Neptune, a planet symbolizing the yearning for absolute truth beyond structure, Saturn symbolizes the cleaving to relative truth and the structures that seem to embody it. Also, Neptune symbolizes yearning for what of its nature we cannot grasp, while Saturn symbolizes engaging with what we *can* seem to grasp or what seems to have grasped *us*. Whereas Neptune symbolizes the deceptions that prompt and arise from our quest for ultimate truth, Saturn symbolizes the deceptions that prompt and arise from our acceptance of relative truth. Typically, Saturn appears as the opposite or foil of any planet he encounters, acting within the realm of activity symbolized by that planet, but he does so more obviously with Cancer's various rulers.

Saturn stands at the borderline between those planets that ego can co-opt more or less easily and those that ego can co-opt only partly, or with great difficulty, or perhaps not at all. Though sometimes we can convince ourselves that we can coopt the outer planets with our fear, generally our attempts to do so do not end well. Compare, for example, the relationship between Saturn and Mars, a planet within Saturn's orbit, and Saturn and Neptune, a planet outside of that orbit. The ego-structure or socially-derived identity (connected to Saturn) can generally identify with action (Mars), with *doing*, and thus does not generally find itself prompted to reflection when acting as or through Mars. Mars serves ego because ego wants to act, to have potency in a relational world, to defend itself against attack, and to identify with its own body and (purportedly) self-willed activity. When we find ourselves completely identified with what we do, whether intellectually or physi-

---

[31]Some weeks before I wrote this, the World Bank issued a report on climate change verifying the warnings of countless reputable scientists and challenging the recalcitrance of the dominant nations to facilitate necessary changes. So far, though, the First World powers have not changed course in any notable way.

cally, we generally don't reflect. Mars, with his emphasis on action, pretty much takes the external world as it appears.

Neptune, on the other hand, presents the ego-structure with an ineffable world to which ego has trouble connecting, a world where solidity deceives—a world of ideals and yearnings instead of deals and earnings! Though we can maintain some simulacrum of self-identity by living within a kind of delusion, we have difficulty maintaining that self-identity if our sense of reality constantly dissolves in front of us. (Think of Alice wandering in Wonderland: her wanderings certainly caused her to do some wondering about identity; or consider the characters in Stanislaw Lem's *Solaris*, who seem to have even deeper problems.) Ego wants a solidity that Neptune constantly dissolves. However, Neptune's exaltation in Cancer reminds us that we can relax and rest right within our habitual patterns, in the midst of ordinary life and feeling; that exaltation reminds us that we will find "spirituality" within the most ordinary patterns of life.

What occurs at the borderline, the ring-pass-not symbolized by Saturn, and what does that borderline consist of? Many things, but let's focus on two: the limiting identifications discussed above, and fear. Identifications and fears represent two stages of Saturn's process. We see ourselves as such-and-such, and the world as such-and-such, with the seeing interwoven with fear. Fear apparently generates the desire for structures and identifications. Because of fear, it seems, we try to fix ourselves in an ever-changing world, a world that seems to undermine our security at every point. We want to see the world as solid and reliable because seeing it that way seems to provide a measure of security within the social realm. We accept and constantly re-iterate the world's is-ness: we not only accept the world as a solid and reliable something-or-other or as a somewhat trustworthy place where effects follow from appropriate causes, all of which seems to make it trustworthy and somewhat predictable, but also as a place where the objects of the world go through changes purportedly distinct from the workings of the observing consciousness: a world of external objects independent of mind.[32] Seeing the world that way, we often investigate the behavior of that world. We then label the world and its contents in such a way as to exclude (Saturn as limiter) other possibilities.[33]

We can see in our linguistic habits this tendency to crystallize the phenomenal world. For example, we often describe the world in terms of its attributes and in terms of its "is-ness." We say, "Johnny is a good boy," or, "Johnny is certainly a scoundrel of the worst sort." Or we say, "That *is* the White House," or "The things that make up objects *are* atoms." The verb *to be,* which I link to

---

[32]Many astrologers call Saturn the Lord of Karma, which seems appropriate as far as it goes, though it doesn't go far. The entire horoscope symbolizes one's karma. However, insofar as Saturn symbolizes reaping, grim or otherwise, we can see him as connected to the formal—or structural—results of previous thought-structures and rigidity.

[33]If we sought the "nature," we might ask whether certain appearances arose because of causes independent of mind, or causes having something to do with mind. I have heard Tibetan lamas say that the world arises as it does for us because of the way we label it. These teachings come from very old teachings on Madhyamaka and Valid Cognition in India many centuries ago.

Saturn, provides a ready linguistic tool that we can use to convince ourselves that the world has the verifiable solidity we attribute to it. From those convictions, expressed in language, actions follow. More generally, we convince ourselves (through this labeling process) that the world *is* as we have decided it *must* be; and we've decided that it must *be* as it *is* because we have told ourselves that that it "*is* what it *is*." We also conclude that the world is *not* what it is *not*: we offer propositions like, "The world is composed of matter, not spirit" (or the other way around). Having succeeded in seeing the world in terms of *is-ness*, we make attributions and take those attributions as essential qualities of the world itself. Described this way, the process seems circular; language often works that way, for we define words in terms of other words.[34]

Thus ego, at least partly through the use of language, sees itself as something solid in relation to a world of purportedly verifiable solidities. This kind of perception, which we can see as a structure through which we experience the world, buttresses ego's sense of security. Ego finds its position in the world both psychologically (in terms of is-ness) and behaviorally (in terms of attributions, as when one says, "I am such-and-such" and "that thingamabob over there is such and such"). Astrologically, this kind of intellectual crystallization, having to do with Saturn, stands opposed to the organic world symbolized by the Moon and may—or may not—complement it.

From this linguistic and perceptual structuring, we build various other Saturn-ruled structures. Each person structures his world in the ways described above: he structures his living space; he structures his world according to time (so that he perhaps has what we call a "schedule" or what we call "no schedule"); he structures his world according to social position; he structures his world according to various viewpoints to which he holds tightly. All of this structuring arises from the security-drive and reflects the basic fear that external and internal "things" don't have the reliability we attribute to them. If you see someone constantly working, linguistically or otherwise, to maintain some kind of security, you might conclude that he fears the *lack* of that security. It seems that most humans go through this process.

Saturn symbolizes both fear and structure. As Lord of Boundaries, he symbolizes the boundaries between ego and everything that lies beyond—or that lies be*neath*. He symbolizes the boundary between ego and what ego fears: anything that ego cannot co-opt or control, anything that threatens the structures that seem to ensure security. Throughout human development, Homo sapiens' ability to categorize and label has played a crucial role not only in the building of culture, but in

---

[34]This argument draws from both the Buddhist Madhyamaka and General Semantics—and it takes as its foil the world suggested by Aristotelian logic (a thing is what it is; a thing cannot be both itself and not itself; etc.). It also has a close connection to the arguments presented in *Saving the Appearances: A Study in Idolatry* by Owen Barfield (Middletown, CT: Wesleyan University Press, 1966). Mr. Barfield sees science as a form of idolatry insofar as (or when) it takes the representations (e.g. scientific "laws" and equations) as the reality that those representations merely represent. Alfred Korzybski described General Semantics as a "non-Aristotelian" discipline.

[35]I have called the world of mind unverifiable because we have difficulty measuring its workings; even if we consider the external world as ultimately unverifiable, we will admit that, at least from a relative point of view, we can measure many of its parts. On the other hand, as Jung pointed out, though we have only indirect access (through our senses) to the

survival *per se*. At the same time, Saturn symbolizes the apparent boundary between a purportedly verifiable world (e.g. matter, things with qualities) and a not-so-verifiable world (e.g. of mind).[35] Here, though, we see the origin of the notion that Saturn functions as trickster, for he tricks us into thinking that this boundary "really exists" and provides a truth we can purportedly rely upon. In building the barrier between the world of mind and the world of objects, though, Saturn gives birth to projection, for the world of objects consists at least partly—some would say entirely, but let's put that question aside again, at least for now—of our projections.

Saturn arises sometimes as bounded social situations or positions and sometimes as bounded intellectual positions (as just described) and sometimes as highly structured actions designated for accomplishment, these three categories reflecting Aquarius, Libra, and Capricorn, Saturn's traditional dignities. Ego uses boundaries and social structures to protect itself, preferring to remain shielded, sheltered, or otherwise protected from fear, for fear brings pain that ego prefers to avoid. Fear undermines security because fear reminds ego of the illusory or dressed-up nature of ego's cherished (and purported) security. By maintaining both physical and intellectual structures, ego finds and maintains provisional protection from fear. Or so it seems at first.

Saturn symbolizes not only fear, but also the various structures we use to shield ourselves from that fear, structures that we can consider as projections *of* the fear, as outer representations of the unacknowledged. This occurs because of the same dynamic discussed in earlier chapters: whatever we don't acknowledge as part of the self appears in the world as an event, or as a person or persons, or as institutions or institutional structures, the latter two having a close relation to Saturn, particularly when he appears via collective projection. Another of Saturn's tricksters manifests here, for Saturn tricks us into thinking that his structures provide security; he tricks us into experiencing this fear as solid and real, into considering it as reasonable because embodied in structures recognized by purportedly reasonable people. Feeling limited, we feel fear: because life itself has a limit (death) that we don't wish to confront, fear lurks in the shadows constantly; because within socially-delimited living we experience all sorts of other limitations, Saturn appears, though veiled, in the events of the world. But because we don't like such feelings, we get Saturn to retreat into the unconscious. From there, he tricks us into thinking that he's really departed; he does this while he appears in his favorite disguise: as the world's limitations.

The Saturnian forms of our world seem pervasive as we move into the Age of Aquarius, still partly ruled by Saturn. Those forms range from oppressive governments to ambition to hierarchies to pervasive collective structural assumptions about development, economics, and social organization. We can interpret them as projections. In doing so, we remind ourselves that the structural elements of the extensional realm (governments, social structures, economic demands) have psychological roots. We can see them as collective projections (or as one large, coordinated collective projection) connected with the psychological processes symbolized by Saturn. The root cause:

---

external world, we have direct access to the internal one, however much we obstruct that access by constant reification and habitual modes of thought.

humans do not like to acknowledge fear or negativity, so fear becomes unconscious; becoming unconscious, it becomes prone to projection and thus "appears in the world" as groups of events. Once we have projected Saturn into the world, we usually project the outer planets as well, for if we don't look carefully at fear, we won't look carefully at those destabilizing elements that lie beyond. We will discuss these matters more fully in chapter IX.

Saturn and the Shadow

Saturn has a close relationship to what Jungians call the Shadow, a term we can consider as having both personal and collective referents. Jung describes the former as "the dark characteristics… inferiorities…that have an *emotional* nature, a kind of autonomy, and accordingly an obsessive or, better, possessive quality."[36] Jung notes that though "with insight and good will, the shadow can to some extent be assimilated into the conscious personality," certain of its features

> …offer the most obstinate resistance to moral control and prove almost impossible to influence. These resistances are usually bound up with projections, which are not recognized as such, and their recognition is a moral achievement beyond the ordinary. While some traits peculiar to the shadow can be recognized without too much difficulty as one's own personal qualities, in this case both insight and good will are unavailing because the cause of the emotion appears to lie, beyond all possibility of doubt, in the other person. No matter how obvious it may be to the neutral observer that it is a matter of projections, there is little hope that the subject will perceive this himself. He must be convinced that he throws a very long shadow before he is willing to withdraw his emotionally-toned projections from their object.[37]

In his Foreword to Eric Neumann's *Depth Psychology and a New Ethic*, Gerhard Adler describes the shadow as the evil within oneself, one's "own 'dark,' inferior personality" that often gets projected onto another person, which he describes as "one way of satisfying the well-known need to find a scapegoat for one's own shortcomings." He adds, in a sentence that leads us to a discussion of the collective shadow (a main concern, as we will see, of Neumann's book),

> As a result, we have split the world into "good" and "bad," superior and inferior nations, races, or individuals, with catastrophic results.[38]

I said above that Saturn has a close relationship to the shadow, but this doesn't mean that we should equate the two. If the Jungian shadow contains or houses psychic elements found incompatible with the conscious persona, then other planets certainly play a role in the formation and maintenance (so to speak) of the shadow, and any planet may contribute at least occasionally. In order to understand how Saturn fits into the Jungian schema, we should review the major terms Jungians use to discuss that schema.

---

[36] C.G. Jung, *Aion* (Princeton: Princeton University Press, 1959), 8.
[37] Jung, 9.
[38] Gerhard Adler, Forward to Erich Neumann, *Depth Psychology and a New Ethic* (Boston: Shambhala, 1990), 8.

When Jungians refer to the *persona*, they mean the psychic and behavioral qualities that appear on the surface and constitute an adaptation to collective values. Eric Neumann refers to the persona as the "façade personality," which he says "represents a considerable achievement on the part of conscience," for "without its aid, morality and convention, the social life of the community and the ethical ordering of society would never have been possible in the first place." He describes it as "…what one passes for and what one appears to be, in contrast to one's real individual nature," a psychic system that "corresponds to one's adaptation to the requirements of the age, of one's personal environment, and of the community."[39] He describes it further as

> …the cloak and the shell, the armor and the uniform, behind which and within which the individual conceals himself—from himself, often enough, as well as from the world. It is the self-control which hides what is uncontrolled and uncontrollable, the acceptable façade behind which the dark and strange, eccentric, secret and uncanny side of our nature remains invisible.[40]

The term *shadow*, by contrast, refers to psychic and behavioral qualities deemed (by the ego, though the deeming doesn't always, or even generally, seem conscious) unacceptable, unworthy, and even taboo. Neumann writes:

> The shadow is the other side. It is the expression of our own imperfection and earthliness, the negative which is incompatible with the absolute values; it is our inferior corporeality in contradistinction to the absoluteness and eternity of a soul which 'does not belong to this world.' But it can also appear in the opposite capacity as "spirit," for instance when the conscious mind only [sic] recognizes the material values of this life. The shadow represents the uniqueness and transitoriness of our nature; it is our own state of limitation and subjection to the conditions of space and time. At the same time, however, it forms a part of the nuclear structure of our individuality.[41]

Saturn clearly has a close relationship with both the persona and the shadow; in some sense he seems to form the borderline between the two. Because of his connection with the status quo, Saturn has a connection to the persona; because he has so much to do with evaluation (via his exaltation in Libra), he represents the boundary between what we see as in accordance with the socially accepted standard weight[42] and what we see as unacceptable according to social standards. Further, because he has so much to do with the way we structure our lives, not only in our thinking but in our behavior, he has much to do with what we present to the social world with its emphasis on consensus reality and its panoply of behavioral and psychological restrictions. The persona, after all, arises in a social context, finding its place in the world via some markedly Saturnian elements such as time, schedule, profession, and formal adaptation. On the other hand, Saturn's relation to

---

[39]Neumann, *Depth Psychology and a New Ethic*, 37.
[40]Neumann, 38.
[41]Neumann, 40.
[42]Dane Rudhyar. He applies this phrase to Libra. See *The Pulse of Life*, 85.

the underworld—for after Jupiter dethroned him as king of the gods, Saturn made his home in Tartarus—Saturn has a close connection to psychic elements relegated to the nether world. Because Saturn has to do with judgment, he has to do with the process by which we judge psychological or behavioral elements as inferior.

Saturn as shadow and boundary-keeper engenders not only social participation and expansion, but also our yearning for what of its very nature remains ungraspable, and the complexes and taboo elements of the unconscious; thus we have Saturn with his three sons, for Jupiter symbolizes participation and expansion, Neptune has to do with the ungraspable, and Pluto with complexes and taboos. It seems that though some Jungians posit a *persona* and a *shadow* as distinct elements, the two often seem to arise together as inseparable sides of the same coin. The persona not only arises from and through Saturn's forms, but it also takes its shape from the kinds of judgments Saturn makes. Those same judgments form the boundaries within which shadow-elements reside and fester. These patterns reflect Saturn's astrological connections to the Ascendant: as ruler of Libra, the sign opposing the Ascendant in the natural horoscope, Saturn symbolizes the "other half" of the Ascendant, the series of socially-validated values and judgments, and thus limitations, that do so much to define the persona, for things receive their definition through their connection to external and opposing elements. As the ruler of Capricorn and the tenth house of the natural horoscope, Saturn also has much to do with a person's drive to externalize inner energies into the world of social demand via a professional or public persona. Thus Saturn tells us much about the forces shaping the persona (seventh house) and the structures adopted by the persona as vehicles for social expression (tenth).

However, though Saturn symbolizes the boundaries and judgments that give birth to persona and shadow, he does not seem a sufficient symbol for the *contents* of either. The Ascendant certainly has much to do with the persona's more obvious qualities, particularly when we consider aspects to that point, along with the Ascendant ruler with its position and aspects. The Midheaven also plays a role in those processes, for it symbolizes venues through which we participate in society; along with its aspects and related astrological factors, it tells us how we participate in the social world via position and role. Thus we can see two personae, one emphasizing direct, personal contact with the world, the other symbolizing a person's professional personality. That the Ascendant squares the Midheaven in the natural horoscope suggests that many people—and perhaps all of us in the "natural" state so few of us experience anymore—experience a potentially-creative tension between those two gateways; many of us act quite differently in public than in non-professional encounters.[43]

The contents of the shadow appear not only through Saturn (and his sign and house position

---

[43]The two angles opposing the Ascendant and Midheaven—the Descendant and Nadir respectively—may arise as projections when one identifies with the activities suggested by Ascendant and Midheaven, and vice-versa. The Descendant, as we have seen, arises as partners, lovers, and open enemies, so we have a rather easy time seeing its connection to projection. The nadir, with its close connection to home, arises through projections relating to unacknowledged factors in the family of origin or at the root of our social participation.

along with his aspects), but through a variety of horoscope factors. Those factors obviously include the outer planets, but, somewhat less obviously, they can include the symbolism of any planet either with afflictive aspects (e.g. to Saturn and the outer planets) or with some other astrologically-indicated difficulty (such as the ones described in other chapters). Instead of functioning as a receptacle for the contents of either psychic system (the persona and the shadow), Saturn functions as the guardian at the gate who has a big say in determining what moves through the personae directly out into the world and what moves into the shadow—and thus, of course, indirectly out into the world via projection.

Before leaving this subject, we should distinguish between Jungian notions about the shadow and about the complexes, for we often find the outer planets, especially Pluto, connected to the latter. Jung describes complexes as "nodal points" in the psyche, and he distinguishes between two types: complexes that the ego splits off via repression, and complexes that "have never been conscious before" because they "grow out of the unconscious and invade the conscious mind with their weird and unassailable convictions and impulses."[44] Jung did not see the latter, which we might call complexes *per se*, as pathological; rather, he saw them as part of the structure of the psyche. However, he recognized that they can arise in pathological ways when they "undergo a specific transformation and coloration by being drawn into an area of individual conflict."[45] The complex per se partly consists of a "problem which no longer represents solely [a person's] personal conflict but gives expression to a conflict that it has been incumbent on man to suffer and solve from time immemorial."[46]

The complexes have a clear connection to what astrologers understand as Pluto, and Jung's descriptions of them often sound much like astrologers' descriptions of that planet. Like Pluto, a complex reaches down into the primordial depths of the psyche; like Pluto, a complex contains enormous and fruitful creative energy; like Pluto, a complex can do much harm if it gets "swollen and overgrown by too much personal material"[47]; like Pluto, the complexes contain greatly concentrated psychic energies; and like Pluto-related patterns such as we find in the plutonium bomb, complexes can increase in power via a kind of chain-reaction, magnetically drawing psychic energy to themselves and developing into powerful nodal centers independent of the conscious personality. Anyone who has tried to deal with Pluto, whether as a natal planet or via transit or progression, will see the similarity; astronomically a double body, Pluto seems an apt symbol for psychic process in which separate power-centers develop and conflict with each other.

---

[44]C.G. Jung, *Psychology and Religion*, paragraph 11, qtd. in Jolande Jacobi, *Complex, Archetype, Symbol in the Psychology of C.G. Jung* (Princeton: Princeton University Press, 1959), 22.
[45]Jacobi 25-6.
[46]Jacobi, 26.
[47]Jacobi, 27.

Just as Saturn symbolizes the processes that give birth to the shadow (and persona), so Pluto symbolizes processes that gives rise to the complex. Also, just as Saturn does not necessarily symbolize the contents of the shadow, so Pluto does not necessarily symbolize the contents of the complexes. To explain this distinction, we can use the mother and the father complex, which Jung often used to illustrate the functioning of complexes in the psyche. Pluto participates in such complexes because, as part of what Jung called the "structure of the psyche,"[48] he symbolizes the processes by which powerful nodal points develop and draw energy to themselves. But a person can have a mother-complex or a father-complex even if Pluto doesn't contact, say, the Moon, the Sun, Saturn, or any other "parental indicator" in the horoscope. The complex will have a Plutonian flavor to it even if the contents of the complex seem more connected to other astrological factors. Though planets *do* symbolize things in the world or psyche, primarily they symbolize processes. Pluto may arise via projection as a ruthless dictator, but he arises first in the psyche as the drive for transformation that necessitates a giving up of reference-points as a starting point.

As Jung's writings on pre-WWII Germany suggest, collective projections and developments have archetypal qualities best expressed not through simple description but through mythological references. Thus in 1936 he wrote, speaking of the Norse god Wotan and his connection to developments in Germany:

> …what is more than curious—indeed, piquant to a degree—is that an ancient god of storm and frenzy, the long quiescent Wotan, should awake, like an extinct volcano, to new activity, in a civilized country that had long been supposed to have outgrown the Middle Ages. We have seen him come to life in the German Youth Movement, and right at the beginning the blood of several sheep was shed in honor of his resurrection. Armed with rucksack and lute, blond youths, and sometimes girls as well, were to be seen as restless wanderers on every road from the North Cape to Sicily, faithful votaries of the roving god. Later, towards the end of the Weimar Republic, the wandering role was taken over by the thousands of unemployed, who were to be met with everywhere on their aimless journeys. By 1933, they wandered no longer, but marched in their hundreds of thousands. The Hitler movement literally brought the whole of Germany to its feet…and produced the spectacle of a nation migrating from one place to another. Wotan the wanderer was on the move.[49]

We see Pluto, discovered in 1930, lurking in Jung's description and on the move during Hitler's rise to power and the other events Jung describes. In other words, we see in the collective events

---

[48] Jacobi, 25.

[49] C.G. Jung, "Wotan," *Essays on Contemporary Events* (London: Ark Paperbacks, 1946), 11. This material also has a close connection to the material discussed in chapter XII, where I suggest that we see Pluto as a "higher vibration" of Mercury. Wotan seems to have a close connection to both planets, but we know him as the god lurking behind Wednesday (Wotan's Day), which the French call Mercredi (Mercury's Day). Jung had, I think unknowingly, made a similar connection, for the Mercurius he discusses in his alchemical writings seems as much like Pluto as like Mercury. The events Jung discusses in connection to Wotan seem to have the mark of Pluto—and not surprisingly, as the Nazi movement arose around the time that Percival Lowell discovered Pluto.

the constellation and projection of an archetype and the shrouded presence of the underworld ruler, who when he went among men always wore a helmet that made him invisible. In this case, of course, Pluto marks not only the process—a complex with archetypal contents appearing as projection—but also the contents of the projection itself.

Saturn's symbolism contains much that seems ambivalent, for on the one hand he has a close connection to how a person behaves in a creative connection to the status quo, and on the other to the restrictions that a person feels in a reactive connection to that status quo. As a symbol of self-judgment arising through a series of self-limiting is-propositions and should-propositions, Saturn certainly symbolizes something we *do* in addition to something that we *have*. On the other hand, Saturn also symbolizes the results (karma), often experienced via projection, of the self-limiting propositions just mentioned: authority figures or anyone else who restricts a person's creative freedom and expansion; figures reinforcing, even if unwittingly, a person's sense of unworthiness; figures representing the projected versions of psychic contents deemed unworthy. So Saturn arises as a projection in two ways: directly via contents that bear the mark of Saturn himself; indirectly via contents that arise because of Saturn's evaluative and limit-setting functions, even if the contents themselves don't seem marked by Saturn.

These remarks should remind us that the terms *persona* and *shadow* refer not only, or even primarily, to things, but to functions, and thus to verbs. The shadow as a psychic *realm* (so to speak) comes about because a person has engaged in what we might call *shadow-making*: making judgments that relegate material to the shadows. (Shadows come about, after all, only through the relationship of matter, apparently either physical or psychic, to the light either of the sun or of awareness.) The persona as an expressive conduit functions via a process of judgment (i.e. we relegate some materials to the shadows) through which one adjusts to the demands of the status quo and channels some psychic and behavioral elements into the external world as a façade-personality.[50] Thus just as the shadow (as a realm) results because people *shadow* (as a verb: people reject psychic elements), so the persona (as a thing) results because people *persona* (as a verb: people present some behavioral and psychic elements). The functions seem more important; we think of the shadow and the persona as *things* only because we don't see the *functions* clearly, missing the fact that they go on constantly, so close to us that they get into our blind spot.[51] Saturn symbolizes both the function and the thing, and as always, because he moves out on the borders of what the conscious ego can see without special aids, most of us have only a dim awareness of how the *thing* masquerades for the *function*—or that with sufficient insight (Uranus), compassion and willingness to let go of reference points (Neptune), and a close connection to the projective power of mind (Pluto), we can begin to cast light into the darkness.

---

[50] I have borrowed the phrase from Erich Neumann.
[51] Buddhist texts suggest something similar about ego: that though it appears as a thing, we should probably considering it as a function, as an ongoing and habitual pattern of mind that, via meditation and disciplined analysis, one can begin to cut through. The process begins with an attempt to see clearly what one has heretofore not seen clearly.

Saturn and the Moon

We often build structures to blind us to our ongoing feeling of insecurity; the security-needs of the Moon become cemented into the fear-based structures associated with Saturn, as most of us structure our world as we do because of the dictates of our fears. On the other hand, when the Moon and Saturn act creatively together, we can develop disciplines and commitments that enable us to look more closely at habitual mind and the ways that we perpetuate our insecurity precisely when we think we do the opposite. Teachers in various spiritual disciplines have used the Moon as a symbol of illumination, even though it also symbolizes blinding habit patterns taken from childhood. It seems that we find the bridge between those two, which seem to lie on the opposite sides of a chasm, when we realize that spiritual disciplines (Saturn) must begin with the most ordinary elements of human awareness (Moon), about which we must take a nurturing attitude first and foremost (the Moon again).

We know that Saturn and the Moon maintain an intimate relationship in any astrology chart, even when they're not in aspect. This ongoing relationship is suggested by the fact that the secondary progressed Moon more or less keeps pace with transiting Saturn as the two go through the signs and houses of a horoscope.[52] The pacing is not exact: the Secondary Progressed Moon moves about 1 degree more per year than does transiting Saturn.[53] Thus though the natal relationship changes, it does so quite slowly. So, we want to look at two facts: first, that they move more-or-less in pace with each other; second, that they don't move *exactly* in pace with each other.

The first fact suggests what I mention above: the ongoing relationship between emotional reaction and either the reality principle or one's general connection to social norms. The second suggests that our feelings slowly disengage from social norms, so that as we age, we find ourselves able to make clearer distinctions between the two. We can also distinguish between feeling per se and the fear that we build on top of feeling by maintaining Saturn-based structures that seem to protect us but that also seem to make our fears into something solid and impenetrable (with the structures as projected versions of the fears). If we can do this, we will find ourselves less prone to move into relationships simply in order to allay our fear of being or alone or because we blindly follow social convention. We can discover a sense of feeling-connection independent of fear or habit.

---

[52] The Moon's synodical cycle (from one conjunction with the Sun to the next) is 29.53 days, while Saturn takes about the same number of years to go through the zodiac. Thus the progressed Moon and Saturn more or less "keep pace" with each other during an individual's life.

[53] Two examples. Kevin Costner (January 18, 1955; 9:40 PM; Lynwood, CA) has his natal Moon at 4+ Sagittarius and his natal Saturn at 19+ Scorpio, a separation of about 15 degrees. On May 24, 2005, with Costner just over 50 years old, his secondary progressed Moon had moved to 11+ Libra and transiting Saturn to 23+ Cancer, a separation of 78 degrees (Moon 78 degrees ahead of Saturn). The separation has expanded by 63 degrees (78-15 = 63) in 50 years, just over a degree per year. George Bush (July 6, 1946; 7:26 AM New Haven, CT) has his natal Moon at 16+ Libra and his natal Saturn at 26+ Cancer, a difference of 82 degrees, with Moon ahead of Saturn. By May 24, 2005, the secondary progressed Moon had reached 7+ Sagittarius, with transiting Saturn at 23+ Cancer, a separation of 134 degrees. The separation has grown by 52 degrees in 59 years, about a degree/year.

That Saturn and the Moon rule polar opposite signs (and thus have their detriments in each other's dignity) suggests that they complement each other even as they often seem antithetical. Saturnian issues will always have a relationship with lunar ones. For example, we see millions of people establishing positions in hierarchies (Saturn) so that they can maintain their homes (Moon). We also see millions of cases in which a person's ambition or responsibility draws him away from home; and we see people developing wisdom by adopting disciplines (Saturn) that enable a more effective examination of lunar processes (feeling; habitual mind; nurturing tendencies).[54] That Cancer and Capricorn oppose one another suggests that we can attain objectivity about the connection between feeling and fear, but that to do so we must remain willing to look into our projections, for when we play the lunar role, we will tend to project Saturn, and vice-versa.

Saturn and the Moon symbolize two of the main cogs of ego's somewhat predictable but shadowy development. They symbolize the beginning and the end of the ego-process, two of the main ways in which we solidify our sense of self and inhibit our access to our full potential: emotional habit patterns and fixed ideas about ourselves and about the world in which we live.[55] Because they have so much to do with ego, and because we so seldom look at the process of ego-creation, Saturn and the Moon have much to do with projection. Projections of the Moon arise very early in life, projected onto the mother as nurturer. The Moon continues as a projection onto all that mothers and protects. Saturn arises early in life through the parental law-giver (generally the father) and the life-organization provided by both parents and by society, in the home and beyond; later, Saturn appears as real or imagined rules of all sort (e.g. scientific laws, the laws of the land and those who enforce them; "authority figures" of all types; a wide variety of 'should' propositions and 'is' propositions).[56]

Early in life, it seems that we experience the Moon almost entirely through the nurturing parent (generally the mother) and Saturn almost entirely through the structuring parent (generally the father, but also through the early-life structure altogether).[57] As the child grows, he or she slowly withdraws these projections, feeling his or her own feelings, developing his or her own sense of limits (part of which psychologists call "internalizing"), developing concepts about how the world works. But whereas we can connect directly and empathetically to the lunar principle (as feelings), we often connect only indirectly with Saturn. People learn many rules and limits through contact with or by confronting the outside world, initially represented by the parents, so they often ex-

---

[54] For example, the Dalai Lama, with his Moon-Saturn opposition, has undergone great trials to maintain a home for his people. And he has maintained an awareness about the nature of the Saturn projection (saying, for example, that he feels grateful to the Chinese for giving him an opportunity to practice patience).

[55] Buddhists will recognize the similarity, here, to what Buddhists texts refer to as emotional blockages (klesha) and incorrect views about reality (*avidya*).

[56] One's notion of "mother country," particularly in the modern age, arises from both Saturn and the Moon (as well as other planets). Here, the collective mother becomes bureaucratized; "mother" becomes a hierarchy. This suggests that though we have the ability to differentiate objectively between Saturn and the Moon, we do not always put that ability to use.

[57] It seems that more mothers take on the Saturn-role than fathers do the lunar one, at least very early in life. Fathers cannot nurse children, whereas mothers can easily set limits, though they probably do harm when they combine the two principles unwisely, for example by deliberately setting *limits on nurturance*.

perience Saturn through external situations that bear his mark. Thus people tend to see Saturn as arising outside.

Furthermore, because we will not always feel threatened by feeling (because feeling does not always *feel* bad or threatening), we will not automatically reject the Moon. Rather, we often make use of lunar energy to weave a cocoon around ourselves, and whereas some cocoons promote the process of personal or even spiritual development (as with spiritual retreats), many of them inhibit as much as they enhance. In that, at least, humans differ from caterpillars, whether of the smoking variety or not. (Notably, the smoking caterpillar apparently sees his cocoon-phase as immensely valuable).[58] Though we can certainly build Saturnian cocoons—as when a person structures his world through work or an intellectual edifice, either of which can shut him off from the living world of feeling—Saturn more often arises externally as evident restriction and internally as fear and self-limiting notions. Because ego prefers to feel neither, it will somewhat automatically reject Saturn as an internal process. Saturn then appears through projections that seem to shield us from our fear by encouraging us to see limitation as arising from an external situation. Thus Saturn arises as the rules and regulations of society and as a series of notions that we experience as external demand even if they arise first in the mind (e.g. commitments, time-sense, and all sorts of ideas about how things "are"). We experience that society as inherently limit*ed* and limit*ing*.

When operating within their designated social roles, people feel provisionally protected from unnamed threat, external or otherwise; because they have not faced the fear directly, that fear (Saturn) appears on the outside. (Thus Saturn appears *as* projections in addition to serving as boundary-keeper who ensures that projection takes place.) People experience this externalized Saturn as, at least in part, the given social order; and because everyone projects Saturn much of the time, Saturn arises as a collective projection visible to just about everyone: as the status quo, the embodiment and crystallization of a set of beliefs (not all of which consist of conscious ideas) held by the people who find provisional contentment within that social order (i.e. the majority; what Neumann calls "the mass"). We experience Saturn as boundaries in general, for people deem boundaries some sort of protection from external threat even though the presence of boundaries sometimes seems to bring the threats into existence in the first place.

Interestingly, both the Moon and Saturn have to do with protection (and thus with boundaries, and thus with projection). Lunar protection arises as the drive to protect that to which one has an emotional connection. Saturnian protection often arises as systems such as those connected with "law and order" even when laws seem to engender as much disorder as order (for to one who adheres to rules, rebels and outcasts appear as projections related to the astrological Uranus).[59] The Moon responds to fear because the Moon realizes that the environment itself can kill; thus people formed into kinship groups in order to find protection and ensure survival and to find some protec-

---

[58]See Lewis Carroll's *Alice's Adventures in Wonderland*, chapter V.
[59]Hence astrologers say that Saturn rules the skin. But the barrier often consists of language structures as well. Our enemies have an intimate connection to our labeling systems.

tion against predators. Saturn's predators arise because of the workings of conceptual frameworks: we conceive the enemy *as* enemy and we have ideas about him (e.g. we say, "He is the enemy"), so that he becomes an enemy not necessarily because of his character, but because of our concepts (interacting, no doubt, with some of his own, for, like us, he has Saturn operating). More generally, we see the world arising beyond the walls or limits of the self, and we deal with the world at that Saturnian barrier.[59] Saturn's enemies arise because of the ways people have ordered societies—that is, because of their ideas. The Moon's enemies seem less reactionary, for many of them existed long before humans did, and certainly long before humans devised social orders.

Because ego will almost always opt for security, even if only psychological (as a revolutionary may feel psychologically secure in rebellion), it will attempt to create stasis of some sort if in doing so it can ignore or deny that everything from our state of mind to the phenomenal world itself changes constantly, right before our eyes. Ego has a hard time finding any security in change, so it attempts to solidify itself and the world via conceptual imposition—and by solidifying itself *in* the world via socially-validated position or in some other way (Saturn). With concept, ego draws a map, labeling various elements of the world, thereby creating the illusion of stasis and verifiability even though the mental map doesn't correspond very well with the territory (for the labels remain the same as the world does the opposite).

We can see the second of these Saturnian solidifications quite easily: we refer to ourselves as "I" or by name. We then create various labels for the world and come to various decisions about how that world functions and about what it "is"; we decide that it, too, is something fixed and solid, something with a fixed is-ness independent of the observer.[60] The intellectually and emotionally fixated ego wants to relate to a stabilized world. These internal and external processes of crystallization reflect Saturn, the Lord of Form and the Lord of Is-ness. When Saturn runs the show (and as a trickster, he seems inordinately fond of shows), people create forms of all sorts—vocational forms, ideational forms (reflecting Aquarius, one of Saturn's traditional dignities), physical forms, and the bureaucracy of ego—and they convince themselves that all of this has the aforementioned independent is-ness, a verifiability somehow separate from the one doing the verifying. Thus Saturn rules a psychological territory created by ideas and assumptions with a close connection to traditional scientific views bearing the stamp of Newtonian physics and maintaining a pervasive influence on the collective, despite the challenges from quantum theory. (See chapters XI and XII.)

Saturn thus plays an integral role in the human image-making process, not only because he has so much to do with mental formations, but also because, standing at the border of the unseen world yet devoted to form, he has a penchant for giving form to the formless. I have referred to Saturn as the bureaucracy of ego, and this bureaucracy seems closely connected to the functions I have just described. Some decades ago, Erich Neumann spoke of related matters in *The Origins and History of Consciousness*:

---

[60]These ideas have a close connection to general semantics, developed by Alfred Korzybski. Korzybski often pointed out that we can use language to make distinctions about the world that may not arise in the world itself.

> Ego consciousness is a sense organ which perceives the world and the unconscious by means of images, but this image-forming capacity is itself a psychic product, not a quality of the world. Image formation alone makes perception and assimilation possible.... The psychic world of images is a synthesis of experiences of the inner and outer world, as any symbol will show.[61]

I don't mean to suggest that we don't find any expression of Saturn apart from language or the way we describe our experience. Nevertheless, if we wish to see Saturn in action—if we wish to see Saturn as something we *do* instead of merely as something with which we have to deal—we should look steadily at our symbol-making proclivity (or, perhaps, instinct), especially as it appears in language, for the process of crystallization apparently has an ongoing relationship with how we conceptualize experience. This doesn't mean that all karma arises because of the way we use language, but even those Saturn-elements *not* apparently or immediately connected to language arise in experience that we quickly subject to the limits of language, beginning with labeling and extending through various levels of evaluation.[62]

Saturn, Uranus and the Borderline

We have just said that Saturn represents processes that remain largely unconscious. Certainly we have heard hundreds of times that the outer planets also represent unconscious energies, and at various points in our lives, we surely experience these planets as projections. It seems that the more readily we can see the planet with the naked eye, the more readily we can bring the symbolized energy into clear focus for the conscious mind. Thus though we can all experience our emotions and our "need" for emotional security (Moon), we have more difficulty getting a clear sense of how we structure our world (Saturn).[63] We can experience emotion directly, but we have to step back from the welter of direct experience to get a sense of Saturn's structures. Those structures therefore usually operate at the horizon of consciousness even though they create both consciousness and horizon. If we cannot see the planet with the naked eye, we need some special tool or technique in order to get this focus. We may take this as a metaphor: to understand the psychological energies represented by the outer planets, we need some special tool or technique. Some use astrology; others use psychology; others use meditation, contemplation, or psychotropic breath-work; and so forth.

Over the centuries, astrologers have grouped the planets in various ways. Since the discovery of Uranus in 1781, astrologers have distinguished between the traditional planets (the planets out to and including Saturn—and including the Sun and Moon) and the trans-Saturnians. Planets in the first group have arisen as part of human consciousness for millennia; planets in the latter

---

[61]Neumann, *The Origins and History of Consciousness*, 294.
[62]Students of general semantics will recognize, here, the influence of Korzybski's *Structural Differential*. Buddhist students will recognize the influence of the Madhyamaka, the Yogachara, and the teachings on Valid Cognition.
[63]Because of its proximity to the Sun, humans generally have difficulty seeing Mercury. Thus we have difficulty getting perspective on the ongoing playful, trickster quality of words and communication.

group have not so arisen, though we may find enclaves in which people worked actively with the energies symbolized by those planets.[64] Astrologers have generally held that the traditional planets symbolize elements of the traditional understanding of human psychology and that the latter symbolize human beings' drive for personal transformation or psychological development beyond the psychological status quo. This doesn't mean that before Uranus' discovery no-one developed psychologically, for some people who lived centuries ago clearly experienced that drive; some groups (e.g. Buddhists in monasteries, Christian contemplatives, Sufi groups) developed techniques for engaging the trans-Saturnian energies. However, the discovery of each new planet symbolized the availability to the collective of the human capacity symbolized *by* the planet.

When someone discovers a new planet, people must take responsibility to make that planetary energy part of their ongoing awareness—and if they don't, the planet will appear as a projection. However, because these planets represent energies that generally arise outside the status quo of ego, demanding changes that ego doesn't want to countenance and that the status quo resists, and because people require special tools, techniques, or insights to work with those energies effectively, most people find themselves confronting the outer planets as projections instead of as potentials. As we will see in the next chapter, people find themselves confronting a collective situation, describable in terms of the projected versions of the outer planets, that differs markedly from the one current before the planet's discovery.

To understand this process, we can return to an idea mentioned above: that we can divide planets not only as most astrologers do (planets out to an including Saturn, on the one hand; the trans-Saturnians, on the other) but also in terms of whether we categorize the planet as "readily visible" to the naked eye. Of course "readily visible" suggests a somewhat inexact boundary, for a person in one place (e.g. away from cities, perhaps in the mountains) may see Saturn rather easily if he knows where to look, whereas a person someplace else (e.g. the Los Angeles basin) may not see him at all. Still, most people would describe the Sun, Moon, Venus, and Mars as "readily visible," Mercury, Jupiter, Saturn and Uranus as "visible, but not readily," and Chiron, Neptune, Pluto, the asteroids, and the trans-Plutonians as "not visible at all" with the naked eye.[65] Of course,

---

[64]Of course, nowadays in our large cities and areas near them, people cannot see Saturn at all due to air pollution. This may suggest that as human societies developed new technologies (particularly electricity and other conveniences that light up the night), people lose their conscious awareness of the Saturn function. Perhaps modern man "takes Saturn for granted," assuming the necessity for a wide variety of social forms but not carefully examining their effects; people may conclude that in the present social structure (which I describe at length in *The Machine Stops*), we see the only remaining possibility for social ordering. Though we may say that in the modern era people have more awareness of the outer planets (not surprisingly, as people in former eras had no awareness of them at all!), we still can't see them unless we use a new technology (Uranus). Curiously, even as we perhaps too often ignore Saturn or take him for granted, many people in the modern era see the importance of transpersonal growth symbolized by the trans-Saturnians (with Saturn functioning as discipline). Thus far, though, the trans-Saturnians seem to arise collectively as a series of problems, however much they may tell us much about the psychic development of many individuals. See chapter IX.

[65]This division somewhat closely parallels the traditional one simply because the discovery of Uranus, the first trans-Saturnian planet, ushered in a period of technological advancement that made possible the discovery of Neptune, Pluto and Chiron. We know that the telescope was invented previous to Uranus' discovery, making it possible to look much

people eons ago saw both Jupiter and Saturn and recorded their movements but did not see Uranus or record *his* movements, accounting for the generally accepted divisions; still, if we consider the planets in terms of their "ready visibility," we can learn a lot about how these planets function in the human consciousness, for though we can all see Jupiter and Saturn in the sky, most of us don't know either where or when to look, particularly for Saturn, and so don't register these planets readily. This suggests that people don't have a clear sense of why they operate as they do in the larger society, and, more specifically, that they remain unaware of how collective assumptions (Saturn) serve to shape our thinking.[66]

Considering the category of "ready visibility," we might say that Saturn and Uranus together constitute a borderline, not merely for the reasons stated, but because the status quo (Saturn) of a society does much to determine what new developments (Uranus) will take place there. That humans can see Uranus with the naked eye (when he opposes the sun) suggests that Uranus functions sometimes as part of the conscious mind and sometimes as part of the unconscious mind; that most of the time most people *don't* see him (for if they did, people wouldn't for so many eons have considered Saturn as the outermost planet) suggests that Uranus will generally arise as a projection. We have already seen how he arises in gender-related projections; more generally, he arises as sudden threats to the stability and imagined integrity of ego (sometimes in the form of *insights*); in the collective, he manifests as movements challenging status quo arrangements. To Saturn's gamut of is-propositions and should-propositions, Uranus brings information suggesting that many of those propositions don't hold up, at least not in all circumstances. First and foremost, Uranus' very presence demonstrated that Saturn was no longer the outermost planet; the energy that arose with Uranus' discovery challenged the idea that people should be content with the given social order. From there, the dominoes began to fall, and it sometimes seems that as quickly as Saturn props them up, Uranus knocks them down. Together, these two planets symbolize the development of reflective, two-way consciousness.[67]

Notably and as noted, we can see Uranus (more readily, that is) along with Chiron, Neptune, and Pluto, if we have the appropriate tool, and Uranus' discovery punctuated a period of technological development, the results of which enabled us to see the outer planets more readily. When we understand *tool* symbolically, it can refer to psychological tools with which we can work more effectively with outer planet energies. In this, too, we stand at the Saturn-Uranus border, for the tools current in any particular society reflect the use of Saturn *in* that society. Furthermore, any group has its ideas and assumptions about what people consider normal and what people consider abnormal or unacceptable. In our day-to-day consciousness, our ideas about normalcy create our ideas about the non-normal. Yet according to the Greek myth, our ideas about the normal (Saturn)

---

farther into the heavens; however, after Uranus' discovery, these abilities took a quantum leap forward.
[66]People in modern cities probably can't see either of these planets with the naked eye most of the time. This may suggest that as we plunge further toward megalopolis-dominated culture, we may have increasing difficulty attaining perspective on the symbolized functions.
[67]See Neumann, 295.

should derive from our insight into the nature of the world in which we find ourselves (Uranus as creator sky-god, Saturn's father). Because of fear, however, Saturn comes to rule the world—for a time gaining the title of King of the Gods, and in the Christian tradition as Lord of this World—so we experience Uranus (rebellion, insight, iconoclastic actions and thoughts) as a reaction to the status quo.

In his encounter with Satan, Jesus recognizes him—his twin brother, according to some gnostic teachings—as Lord of this World. Satan's hegemony, like that of Kronos/Saturn in Greek and Roman myth, didn't last. In the Greek tradition, it ended when Zeus deposed his father Kronos (just as Saturn had in some sense deposed *his* father); in western history, Uranus' discovery ushered in a period in which revolutionary fervor, psychological insight, spiritual yearning, and the human drive for evolutionary growth challenged Saturn's hegemony. Because Saturn has such deep roots in the human psyche, we shouldn't expect that the forces of change will rout the old structures—at least not soon! Nevertheless, it seems that human beings must awaken to new potentials and to find new modes of social integration. The old, dysfunctional family of Greek myth must find ways to harness the disparate potentials of the family members, thereby achieving the full human potential both for individuals and for the societies in which they live.

Part of the problem surely lies in our lack of understanding of Saturn. Astrologers consider him a symbol of the status quo, whether psychologically or socially, despite the fact that in both the Greek and Christian myths, he initially plays the role of rebel. The Greek Kronos rebelled against his father and temporarily took over as ruler of the gods. In both myths, he ends up with power over an underworld, and in both cases he ends up getting overthrown by a relative: Saturn by his son Jupiter, Satan by his twin brother Jesus, with Jupiter and Jesus each garnering a reputation as a bringer of hope to a purportedly darkened world. Despite the fact that Saturn ends up ruling a domain, he seems to have within him some revolutionary fervor, no doubt an inheritance from his father. These mythic stories remind us that over five thousand years ago, society developed with powerful Saturnian elements yet served revolutionary and creative purposes even while ushering in all manner of problems that have remained with us ever since. Though humans broke free of many Neolithic limitations, they also established equally limited social structures that simultaneously empowered and disempowered. (See my *The Machine Stops*.[68]) When those societies developed in the Middle East, and as others followed in all parts of the world, humans found themselves exercising all manner of potentials that had remained dormant during previous eons. For good or ill, potentials manifested in durable forms, a pattern evident in both the Greek myth, where Saturn's act brings ideas (Uranus) into the realm of tangible action, and in the Biblical one, where Adam and Eve must deal with time, suffering, and duality—for one interpretation of the Biblical myth goes like this: Satan gets Adam and Eve to rebel against Yahweh by getting them to buy into a dualistic consensus reality consisting of good and evil (as in the "tree of the knowledge of" those twin notions); once they rebel at Saturn/Satan's instigation, they find themselves imprisoned in a world of dualities such as self-and-other and life-and-death.

---

[68] The American Federation of Astrologers, 2012.

It seems that we find a similar process in the workings of mind that take place, automatically and in a way we apparently take for granted, in the process of ego-formation as described in the Buddhist Abhidharma.[69] In *Glimpses of Abhidharma*, Chogyam Trungpa discusses "the basic ground" that is "the source of confusion and also the source of liberation," which he describes as "that energy which happens constantly, which sparks out and then goes back to its basic nature, like clouds…emerging from and disappearing back into the sky." From that develops the "eighth consciousness," which Trungpa describes as "ego's type of ground":

> …the eighth consciousness arises when the energy which flashes out of the basic ground brings about a sort of blinding effect, bewilderment. That bewilderment becomes the eighth consciousness, the basic ground of ego…If the energy were to go along with its own process of speed, there would be no panic. It is like driving a car fast; if you go along with the speed, you are able to maneuver accordingly. But if you suddenly panic with the thought that you have been going too fast without realizing it, you jam on the brakes and probably have an accident. Something suddenly freezes and brings the bewilderment of not knowing how to conduct the situation. Then actually the situation takes you over. Rather than just being completely one with the projection, the projection takes you over. Then the unexpected power of the projection comes back to you as your own doing, which creates extremely powerful and impressive bewilderment. That bewilderment acts as the basic ground, the secondary basic ground of ego, away from the primary basic ground.
>
> So ego is the ultimate relative, the source of all the relative concepts in the whole samsaric world.[70]

Out of the potential for non-dualistic understanding, apparently, comes dualism, ego along with it, and we have what we call "the world." Astrologers see that world as Saturn's realm, one ruled by fear, limitation, and conceptual impositions arising as reactions to a more encompassing brilliance.

Before moving across the borderline from fear and limitation to something more open and encompassing, we should take a final look at Jung's ideas about the shadow. The term refers to a function that humans can bring to consciousness. Many of Jung's descriptions of the Shadow link that concept to his ideas about the anima and animus. Jung saw all three as archetypal forms, but he saw the Shadow as the "easiest to experience,"

> The shadow is a moral problem that challenges the whole ego personality, for no one can become conscious of the shadow without considerable moral effort. To be-

---

[69] Buddhists refer to the Abhidharma as one of the three "baskets" that make up the Tripitaka, the corpus of Buddhist teachings. The Abhidharma deals with the psychological background to the process of ego-formation and the revelations of egolessness.
[70] Chogyam Trungpa, *Glimpses of Abhidharma*, 9.

come conscious of it involves recognizing the dark aspects of the personality as present and real. This act is the essential condition for any kind of self-knowledge, and it therefore, as a rule, meets with considerable resistance.[71]

This "moral problem" seems more like a process than like a solid thing (and we could say the same for the anima, and the animus). The process takes place in our evaluating and distinguishing. As Chogyam Trungpa says, "You cannot have criteria, notions of comparison, without ego."[72] If in dealing with the shadow we deal with psychic elements deemed negative, the shadow must involve evaluation, criteria, and comparison, for what Jung calls the "dark elements" of the personality seem dark because of evaluation. In speaking of the shadow, Jung speaks of its "*emotional* nature" and of its connection to areas of the psyche where "adaptation is weakest" and where we find "a certain degree of inferiority and the existence of a lower level of personality."[73] This suggests that we should not consider the shadow as inherently negative, but only as negative in the evaluation of the conscious ego and persona. Jung felt that "with insight and good will, the shadow can to some extent be assimilated into the conscious personality," but that the shadow has "certain features which offer the most obstinate resistance to moral control and prove almost impossible to influence." The obstinate features surely reflect not only Saturn's deep roots in the psychic system, but also the outer planet projections that we all experience. Our deeply-rooted patterns of evaluation and judgment prove obstinate enough in themselves; to that obstinacy we add the projected outer planets, negativized through the same pattern of evaluation and judgment.

Thus the *contents* of the shadow appear not only in Saturn (along with his sign and house positions and aspects), but also in other horoscope factors prone to projection. Some such factors seem connected with the anima and animus, of course, but others seem connected to the shadow and to the complexes. Jung wrote, in a passage we have seen before,

> While some traits peculiar to the shadow can be recognized without too much difficulty as one's own personal qualities, in this case both insight and good will are unavailing because the cause of the emotion appears to lie, beyond all possibility of doubt, in the other person. No matter how obvious it may be to the neutral observer that it is a matter of projections, there is little hope that the subject will perceive this himself. He must be convinced that he throws a very long shadow before he is willing to withdraw his emotionally toned projections from their object.[74]

Jung felt that projections arising from the shadow involved figures of the same sex, not figures of the opposite sex (as happens with projections involving anima and animus). We should therefore resist the temptation to see Saturn, a predominately male figure in myth, in all of the shadow's contents. Rather, Saturn has to do primarily with the processes by which we support our notions of

---

[71] C.G. Jung, *Aion*, 8.
[72] Chogyam Trungpa, *Glimpses of Abhidharma*, 9.
[73] C.G. Jung, *Aion*, 9.
[74] C.G. Jung, *Aion*, 9.

inferiority, strength, acceptability, and unacceptability. Certainly some projections bring Saturn as content, but others seem to bring other planetary energies into the fold. Even in these latter cases, Saturn represents processes by which we accept or reject facets of the total psyche—and thus the processes by which we give birth to projection. Unless he manifests as spiritual discipline, Saturn generally lurks in those automatic turnings-away from brilliance of the basic ground.

We can acknowledge, then, that when a person projects Saturn, he will often find himself in conflict with difficult, even intransigent situations or authority figures, or with people who in some way represent the law-giving father. Such projections represent the person's fear, and the particulars of Saturn's function in the birthchart (sign and house position, aspects, etc.) tell us where that fear will most likely surface as judgment, evaluation, and dualistic thinking. However, Saturn-projections also arise through institutions. This observation leads us into the subject of collective projections, for we can summarize many of the world's difficulties, now and for the past two centuries, by describing the projections of Saturn and the outer planets, with some admixture of Jupiter and Mars. And to this subject we turn next.

Chapter IX

Collective Projections

Viewed through an astrological lens, the collective situation takes on a curious appearance, as it seems congruent, in ways both disturbing and haunting, with the energy-pattern described by the outermost planets: an ever-expanding (Jupiter) yet restrictive social ordering (Saturn), through the use of new technologies (Uranus), foments illusion on a grand scale (Neptune) and thus disempowers the people even as it gives ever more power to forces that do the disempowering, using the means of plutocratic domination (Pluto). That the external situation arises as a series of increasingly obdurate problems bearing the marks of the outer planets suggests a widespread rejection of those outer-planet energies, as if millions of people "negativize" the energies-in-question and then project that negativized energy into the world. That the collective situation has reached a point of crisis, and that all efforts of political entities seem unavailing, even counterproductive, suggests that we need a new praxis. If we look at matters through the aforementioned astrological lens, we can get a hint of what such a praxis might look like. That the projected planetary energies also symbolize the human capacity for evolutionary psychological and spiritual development suggests that the collective situation represents our rejected human potential gone awry.

For many centuries at least, humans have noticed a curious connection between mind and "external reality." We find, for example, Hindu teachings on *maya*, a term they applied to the world around us and that also means *illusion*. Sometimes *maya* referred to creating illusions to dupe one's enemy as part of an effective military strategy; thus it referred to "deceit, fraud, any act of trickery or magic, a diplomatic feat."[1] However, the term came to refer not merely to deceit practiced by one

---

[1] Heinrich Zimmer, *Philosophies of India* (New York: The World Publishing Company, 1951), 122.

human on another, but to deceit practiced by the gods—and to the ongoing deceit that characterizes humans' relations with their environment, both allegedly-physical and psychological. According to Heinrich Zimmer, author of the classic *Philosophies of India*,

> Maya denotes the unsubstantial, phenomenal characteristics of the observed and manipulated world, as well as of the mind itself – the conscious and even subconscious stratifications and powers of the personality.[2]

This doesn't mean, however, that we should consider *maya* and *illusion* as synonyms, or that we should consider the world and the personality as "devoid of all reality whatsoever."[3] The word also refers to an autonomous power connected to humans' attempts to understand the world in which we find ourselves, to the

> …basic problem in the mind of men when they start philosophizing and before they reduce their aspirations to questions of methodology and the criticism of their own mental and sensual faculties. "All this around me, and my own being": that is the net of entanglement called maya, the world creative power. Maya manifests its force through the rolling universe and evolving forms of individuals. To understand that secret, to know how it works, and to transcend, if possible, its cosmic spell—breaking outward through the layers of tangible and visible appearance, and simultaneously inward through all the intellectual and emotional stratifications of the psyche—this is the pursuit conceived by Indian philosophy to be the primary, and finally undeniable, human task.[4]

We find somewhat similar ideas annunciated in the Buddhist tradition, particularly as expounded in India in what scholars refer to as the Yogachara, or Mind-Only Teachings. These teachings speak of the world as imaginary in the sense that appearances arise as they do because of the habit patterns of mind. To find reality, one must cut through those habit patterns. At the same time, though one interprets phenomena as external and independent of mind, one would perceive more correctly if one perceived them as mind, not as opposed to the external phenomena, but as their hidden nature. The Madhyamaka ("Middle Way") teachings speak of relative truth and absolute truth; the Tibetan term for the former, *kundzop*, translates roughly as "all dressed up." The teachings tell us that though the relative world that we experience moment-to-moment (*kundzop*) has its own integrity and coherence and thus qualifies as a "truth," it doesn't qualify as final or absolute. Rather, if we perceive kundzop correctly, we will experience it as ultimate truth (Tib. *dondam*). The world we experience moment-to-moment appears "dressed up" with, among other things, our conceptual impositions and habitual modes of reacting. All of this might sound a bit like Bishop Berkeley on a bender, but if we watch our minds carefully, we realize that everything we think that we know about "the external world" emerges first in the mind.

Many centuries after the development of the Yogachara and Madhyamaka, and even more

---

[2]Zimmer 19.
[3]Zimmer 19.
[4]Zimmer, 27.

centuries after the writing of the Hindu Vedanta, Carl Jung noted that though we often find it completely normal and natural to consider the mind as an epiphenomenon of matter, we have direct access to mind and only indirect access (via the senses and the mind) to the material world. Considering this, Jung found it strange that so many people saw matter as primary and mind as secondary. Erich Neumann, following up on ideas first sketched by Jung, devoted a whole book (*Depth Psychology and a New Ethic*) to a discussion of the relationship between the unconscious and the collective. Writing in the shadows engendered by World War II, Neumann spoke of "the shadow side of the human race" towering over us all, "darkening the sky with its death-rays and its atom-bombers."[5] Central to these difficulties, he wrote, was the problem of evil:

> The problem of evil is one of the most central problems of modern man. No appeal to old values and ideals can shield us from the recognition that we live in a world in which evil in man is emerging from the depths on a gigantic scale and confronting us all, without exception, with the question, "How are we to deal with this evil?"[6]

In our relativistic age, we may feel uncomfortable with Neumann's concentration on "evil," perhaps feeling that it contains unwarranted references to moral standards no longer applicable. But say what we will about our purported advances in self-understanding, old ways and notions persist, affecting not only our conscious attitudes but our unconscious predispositions. Thus we should heed what Neumann says about the connection between the Jungian shadow and what arises in the collective:

> …This reality of evil by which the individual is possessed is not derived simply from his personal reality; it is also, at the same time, the individual expression of a collective situation. Similarly, the creative energies of his unconscious, with their hints of new possibilities, are not simply his own energies but also the individual form taken by the creative side of the collective—that is, universal human—unconscious.[7]

And:

> The future of the collective lives in the present of the individual, hard-pressed as he is by his problems – which can, in fact, be regarded as the organs of the collective. The sensitive, psychically disturbed and creative people are always the forerunners.…The connection between the problems of the individual and those of the collective is far closer than is generally realized.[8]

Later, Neumann discusses the connection between, on the one hand, the suppression and re-pression of psychic contents, and on the other, the collective malaise. The first step involves inner dynamics, for "[psychic] contents which are capable of becoming conscious but whose access to

---

[5] Erich Neumann, *Depth Psychology and a New Ethic* (Boston: Shambhala, 1990), 20.
[6] Neumann, 25.
[7] Neumann, 29.
[8] Neumann, 30, 31.

consciousness has been blocked become evil and destructive."[9] From that dynamic arises the "projection of the shadow":

> The shadow, which is in conflict with the acknowledged values, cannot be accepted as a negative part of one's own psyche and is therefore projected—that is, it is transferred to the outside world and experienced as an outside object. It is combatted, punished, exterminated as "the alien out there" instead of being dealt with as "one's own inner problem."[10]

We will see in chapter X that collectivities (e.g. countries) readily project the national shadow; the process seems similar to the ancient custom of scapegoating, though not so formalized, and in contemporary nations it often proves much harder to discern. In this chapter, however, we have to do not with the shadow of a nation or specific collectivity with its own peculiar psychology, but with the creation of a collectively relevant external situation that arises as a series of collective projections transcending national boundaries: projections, generated by millions of people in every nation or collectivity, of individual shadow-contents held in common, material that people find unacceptable or as coming from beyond the pale.

Insofar as the outer planets symbolize unconscious factors, we can see why they would appear as *individual* projections. And insofar as these planets symbolize gender-related material—Uranus generally appearing as a masculine energy, Neptune and Pluto as feminine energies, at least in western culture during the post-Renaissance era—we can see why they would arise as individual projections related to gender. More generally, though, outer planets energies end up as projections because they challenge ego's hegemony, thereby inviting ego to reject them—or, we might say, to *eject* them into what we call the outer world. It seems that the operation we see on an individual level also occurs on the collective one, or that we can consider the external problem as the individual problem writ large: the rejection of the energy results in a projection of that energy into the external world as a series of events, whether personal or collective in orientation. In other words, our concern here has to do not with whether or how a planet presents challenges specific to gender or within particular human relations, but with the challenges a planet presents to the process of ego maintenance altogether for all humans. Because most people project these energies most of the time, they will arise not only as personal projections, but also as collective ones.

Dane Rudhyar wrote many years ago that the outer planets represent unconscious factors, and astrologers have by and large accepted his judgment. However, the outer planets don't seem to remain unconscious for all people at all times. A person involved in revolutionary activity will sometimes make conscious use of the energy astrologers refer to as "Uranus";[11] an actress will some-

---

[9]Neumann, 49.
[10]Neumann, 50.
[11]In revolutionary movements, revolutionaries generally take on the role of Uranus and project Saturn onto the forces

times make conscious use of the energy we call "Neptune"; a person involved in psychology, high finance, or with some underground organization will make some conscious use of the energy we call "Pluto." For many centuries, people involved in spiritual disciplines have made conscious use of all three planets, with Uranus arising as insight, Neptune as compassion, and Pluto as the drive to transform oneself by dying to an old sense of self and experiencing rebirth with an empowered awareness. Throughout the spiritual process, Saturn arises as discipline, consciously undertaken. We can see from these descriptions that the outer planets can participate in conscious activities, at least for some people some of the time; the degree to which they do so depends on factors in a person's natal horoscope and in the person's level of awareness.

If we consider the outer planets as representative of the collective unconscious, we might speculate that this participation occurs (*when* it does, of course) because certain types of action put us more readily and evidently in contact with archetypal qualities. Notably, however, activities associated with the outer planets encourage a person to step beyond a purely personal reference-point: into the larger political world, into the world of imagination, or into the development of power that dwarfs the individual will. Though the ego often, if left unchecked, attempts to get what it can out of these activities, the activities themselves draw ego in a different direction. In any case, if we posit that human actions express archetypal energies, we can add that some activities provide more convenient outlets for the outer-planet energies than do others, even within the lives of specific individuals. Thomas Jefferson probably found a more ready outlet for Uranus in his political activities and jottings that does an employee of government bureaucracy.[12]

Though ego can sometimes participate in activities symbolized by the outer planets, it still projects the outer planets most of the time. Apparently this occurs because no matter what activity a person undertakes, ego wants a security and stability (Moon and Saturn respectively, as we have seen in the previous chapter) seldom on offer from the outer planets, for those planets constantly challenge whatever security ego wants to claim. Whereas the inner planets symbolize factors that ego generally uses to express and delineate itself and thus find anchor in society, the outer planets symbolize factors that generally challenge, undermine, and uproot ego's hegemony. Though ego can sometimes use outer planet energies to buttress its position, those energies don't lend themselves easily to the process. Each outer planet symbolizes a different type of change, and ego, preferring stasis to alteration, finds it difficult to co-opt, encompass or enlist any of them for any length

---

attempting to maintain the old order. However, insofar as they devalue Saturn (preferring Uranus), it represents an inner energy that will eventually surface, probably in more virulent form. This partly explains the dynamic of so many revolutions, for Uranian movements often lead to Saturnian reversals. The history books call these reversals "counter-revolutions"; counter-revolutionary forces attempt to reinstate an order even more repressive than the "old order." Saturn and Uranus rule Aquarius, a fixed air sign having to do with larger social groupings. Small wonder, then, that when humans have difficulty making helpful progressive change, the main problems arise from their own fixed ideas. In the Greek creation myth examined in earlier chapters, Uranus gives birth to Saturn, the pattern of so many human revolutions.

[12]Like many "progressive thinkers," Jefferson apparently had more difficulty integrating Uranus into his personal life than into his writings. When one of his slaves escaped to the north, Jefferson reportedly had her caught and, playing a role redolent with Saturnian judgment, beat her badly once she had been returned.

of time, with the degree of difficulty symbolized by the planet's distance from the Sun.

When ego rejects these outer planet energies, they fall into the unconscious, from which realm (so to speak) they arise as projections. If we posit that this process of rejection and projection takes place in the vast majority of human beings, we can expect the pattern of collective projection sketched earlier. Thus the creation of the external problematique fits into the general pattern we have traced for the individual: humans generally project what they reject; they experience their own psychic potential as people, events, and developments in the world that seems to lie outside. Though we cannot depend on ego to project inner planet energies, we can generally depend on ego to project the outer ones. Thus most people, in projecting those planets, create and shape the collective projection—what we call "the world around us."

One more point before proceeding: though in discussing these matters we must resort to language, we should remain wary of the biases of the one in use here. In the English language, we can speak of an external world and an internal world; in doing so, one might feel prompted to ask, "Well, is the external world real or not? Does it exist on its own or only in connection to the unconscious mind?" Let's put off any in-depth discussion of these questions, at least for now, noting only that the shape of the questions may confuse us more than any answer will, for the questions suggests two-valued orientations (real vs. not real; arising on its own vs. arising in connection with something else), whereas the world apparently arises in multiple values. We can, at least for now, content ourselves by saying, "Well, what can we verify about the world that seems external to us?"

The Collective Projection: How It Appears; How to Work With It

Because Saturn and the outer planets usually remain unconscious for the vast majority of people, those planets generally arise through projection. Because so many people project the same planetary energies into the world, those people experience similar, or at least congruent, projections. Thus millions of people agree on the basic characteristics of the collective situation. It seems that Shakespeare's Prospero had it right when he said that we "are such stuff as dreams are made of."[13] Quite likely, too, his remarks about "the baseless fabric of this vision" have much merit, for the world may qualify as a "vision" as much as it qualifies as a bunch of non-visionary and merely-physical items. It seems made of mind-stuff as much as of the non-mind-stuff many scientists often talk about. Many people, from Buddha to Jung and including many in between, have spoken to this notion, as we will see. From an astrological point of view, the projection consists first of the detritus of Saturn: a series of status-quo structures that not only limit but that also provide venues through which humans can express their creative potentials. We can say this, it seems, about any society: it limits expression even as it provides opportunity, and if it didn't do the former, it wouldn't do the latter, for the opportunities themselves qualify as limitations (reflecting, perhaps, another bias of our language).

---

[13] The Tempest. Act IV, Scene I.

Beyond the gates of the ordered town in which we pursue social ends, though, the rebels, radicals, and iconoclasts remain at work, their objections lobbed like mortar shells over the wall, capsules of ideas about the delimiting function of the status quo. Some of these ideas prove quite useful to those in power, as any new idea will. The first civilizations, not exactly models of democratic functioning and certainly not recognizing the rights of the individual, surely arose from ideas, first and foremost. Hierarchical forces (Saturn) control the brilliance and invention (Uranus) even if that brilliance and invention claims that it holds no brief for the hierarchy. The hierarchy uses the ideas to foment illusion (Neptune), and thus to disempower (Pluto) the collective. Lost in all this is the curious fact that the ideas predate the hierarchies—and that the ideas actually brought the hierarchies into existence. Uranus fathers Saturn, after all; ideas give rise to forms (no doubt due, at least in part, to Gaia's earthy influence).

Astrologers know that the same planetary energies can arise in quite a different way: as disciplines undertaken to release the human potential for insight that in turn gives birth to compassion and creative vision; these in turn can yield great transformative power to millions of people. If the ideas hadn't led to forms, the ideas would have disappeared; humans retained those ideas only because people had developed structures—language primary among them, but also including social structures of various kinds—to enable the ideas to endure. Just as many spiritual teachers point to the primordial quality of wisdom and insight, so they ask their students to engage in disciplines or vehicles to carry the wisdom forward. Among the various structures and disciplines (Saturn) that yield such insights (Uranus) and that give birth to visionary and artistic power (Neptune and Pluto), astrology, connected with all of the outer planets but particularly Pluto, holds an important position, for within its symbolic vocabulary we find the basic assumption mentioned at the beginning of this book: that its symbols tell us not only, or even primarily, about external events, but about internal developments and potentials—and astrological methodology arises, as a matter of course, from the assumption that external and internal mirror each other. This mirroring takes place not only within the experience of each individual, but also within the collective.

One might object, here, by saying that the world arises in the same way for everyone because that's the way the world *is*: everyone sees the same world because that world "is real" or "is all there is to see." But even if we say that the world "is merely matter existing outside of the mind," the form of the proposition itself, with high-level abstractions to either side of the is-of-identity, suggests the workings of Saturn and thus of limitation. We can consider as a conventional truth that the phenomenal world has its own logic and structure, and that this structure appears constantly, and for most observers unstintingly, in the experience of most people on the planet (plus, it seems, the lions and tigers and bears, oh my). Nevertheless, when we realize that the world arises in ways we can describe so precisely by referring to the outer planets, planets that refer to psychological functions, we might wonder why this occurs. That it does so suggests that we should step beyond the dualism inherent in questions such as, "Is the world real, or does it arise from mind?" We could probably answer both questions in the affirmative, but we would probably do better to think in terms of both/and instead of either/or, concluding that the question itself probably qualifies as a false dilemma typical of the world ruled by Saturn. If we begin to step beyond facile dualisms, we can begin to reconnect to experience more precisely and openly.[14]

Collective Developments and the Discovery of New Planets

The astrological symbolism can help us to sort out and describe this ongoing projection. This projection changes in dramatic ways when new planets appear, just as it did when Pluto appeared, and, before that, when Neptune and Uranus appeared. If we look at the historical developments taking place around the discovery of each of the four newest additions (Uranus, Neptune, Pluto, and Chiron) to the astrological vocabulary, we can begin to get a sense of the components of the overall collective projection.[15] We will see at work here a basic principle of historical astrology: events in the collective at the time of the discovery of planet or other important astronomical body tell us a lot about the nature of the planet. We might say that people, not having integrated the energy symbolized by the planet, project it into the environment as events. We might also say that the evolutionary demands of human awareness lie behind both the events and the discovery. Both versions probably give us partial truths.

The collective projections of Uranus have drawn the attention of many historians, for those projections usually disrupt delimited routines. We find good examples of such projections right around the time of Uranus' discovery, when the collective teemed with Uranian activities. The American Revolution ended in October 1781, just months after the March 1781 discovery of Uranus. A few years earlier, Jefferson and others had issued the Declaration of Independence. A few years later (in 1789), the French Revolution broke out. In October 1781, Holy Roman Emperor Joseph II issued his *Edict of Tolerance,* introducing many organizational reforms in monasteries and loosening ties between those institutions and Rome. The period also brought marked technical innovations, particularly in two inventions by James Watt: the steam operated flour mill and the double-acting rotary steam engine (an improvement on his 1765 invention), technical developments that could have alleviated many Saturnian difficulties had not the powers of Saturn co-opted those developments for the advantage of those with power in political and economic hierarchies. Saturn's tendency to co-opt Uranus' inventiveness to Saturn's limited purpose appeared throughout the period. Lewis Mumford tells us that "the noisy clank of Watt's original engine was maintained, against his own desire to do away with it, as a pleasing mark of power and efficiency" and that the factory chimney, "whose pall of smoke increased the number of and thickness of natural fogs," shutting off "still more sunlight," an emblem of a crude and imperfect technics, "became the boasted symbol of prosperity" and that the "concentration of paleotechnic industry added to the evils of the process itself."[16]

Some lesser-known but equally-significant developments also deserve mention. Dutch plant

---

[14] I have borrowed the term conventional truth (i.e. kundzop; see above) from the Buddhist tradition.
[15] As I write this, astronomers have just recognized a body that they have named Eris. I have not investigated its effects enough to make definitive statements about it at this time.
[16] Lewis Mumford, *Technics and Civilization* (New York: Harcourt, Brace & World, Inc., 1934), 168.

pathologist Jan Ingenhousz established some of the principles later called *photosynthesis*, continuing some of the 1774 work of Joseph Priestley involving the "improvement" of air by the introduction of plants, which Priestley said produced "dephilogisticated air," later called *oxygen*. In 1781, Kant published his *Critique of Pure Reason*, a work that served as a foundation for much later philosophical criticism and that opened avenues of inquiry (at least for the Western world) about the relationship between intellectual categories and valid understanding. Kant also insisted that human beings should be treated as ends, not means, though he did so during a period when precisely the opposite occurred: when "mechanical industry had begun to treat the worker as a means…to cheaper mechanical production," when human beings "were dealt with in the same spirit of brutality as the landscape," as "a resource to be exploited."[17] The period also brought the flowering of Mozart's music, plus important advances in the understanding of electricity, medicine, and technology. The year of Uranus' discovery also witnessed the founding of Los Angeles, a quintessentially modern city that developed from ideas instead of natural causes.[18]

Though the discovery of Uranus ushered in a period of pervasive technical progress, that technical progress took place, and received its impetus from, a climate of ideas:

> In the eighteenth century the notion of Progress had been elevated into a cardinal doctrine of the educated classes. Man, according to the philosophers and rationalists, was climbing steadily out of the mire of superstition, ignorance, savagery, into a world that was to become ever more polished, humane, and rational—the world of the Paris salons before the hailstorm of revolution broke the windowpanes and drove the talkers to the cellars…In the nature of progress, the world would go on forever and forever in the same direction, becoming more humane, more comfortable, more peaceful, more smooth to travel in, and above all, much more rich.[19]

The dark elements of the picture may seem more evident to us now than they did to the people of the time. Mumford writes that the picture of persistent, straight-line, uniform progress "had all the parochialism of the eighteenth century," and that

> …despite Rousseau's passionate conviction that the advance in the arts and sciences had depraved morals, the advocates of Progress regarded their own period—which was in fact a low one measured by almost any standard except scientific thought and raw energy—as the natural peak of humanity's ascent to date.[20]

---

[17]Mumford, 172.
[18]Los Angeles grew from an amalgam of forces, certainly including massive publicity and public fraud regarding water rights. The Los Angeles area doesn't seem the ideal place to build a city, for it lacks water. To have a city, the city's promulgators had to get water from someplace. The getting-process involved deception on a massive scale and couldn't have taken place without the technical improvements coincident with the discovery of Uranus. Though we generally consider Los Angeles a Neptunian sort of place (and small wonder, considering the water-problems that have beset it), it also bears the clear mark of Uranus.
[19]Mumford, 182.
[20]Mumford, 182.

Thus we see around Uranus' discovery a pattern similar to the one we will see around Neptune's, Pluto's, and Chiron's: a problematic use and manifestation of the planetary energy in the public sphere running parallel with more positive developments in work and thought that didn't have sufficient effect on that public sphere to stem the problematic tide. In Uranus' case, we see a problematic use of the new and groundbreaking, for just as new technical developments led to much social and environmental degradation, so ideas of freedom in both new and old worlds led to terror and destruction (as witness the destruction of native peoples in the Americas and the piles of corpses resulting from the French Revolution). The assumption reigned that new developments clearly brought only improvements—this despite the evidence. But just as perturbations in Uranus' orbit led to the discovery of Neptune, so the perturbations in the social order of the late 18th century ushered in illusions related to "progress" and its attendant convictions. The new technical developments may have brought enormously increased efficiency in production, but they also brought about a starvation of life. Such ideas about "the new" have remained in circulation, with equally problematic results in millions of cases.[21]

Several themes emerge from the period around Neptune's discovery on September 23, 1846. The first involves, not surprisingly, deception and subterfuge.[22] On completely specious grounds, the United States invaded Mexico, purportedly because Mexican troops had entered United States territory, but really in order to gain more territory to "expand the area of freedom"—that is, to increase the land below the Mason Dixon Line, where people could own slaves. (With Neptune in the ninth house and closely square Mars, the United States has a habit of using deception to get into wars; the deception generally involves an overly idealized national vision. We see more national deception with the annexation of Oregon in 1846 and Texas in 1845.[23]) The war also brought the first amphibious military (Neptune) assault with General Winfield Scott's landing in Vera Cruz.

The idea of Manifest Destiny, circulated widely in the United States beginning in the 1840s, surely qualifies as a manifest deception, promulgated on a wide scale and still affecting us today. The term, first used in 1845 by John O'Sullivan, a lawyer, literary critic, and publisher, among other activities and vocations, serviced to justify policies in which millions died. O'Sullivan himself seemed blind to the idea's effects or to its moral implications. Starting off as a non-violent idealist, he soon came to seem like an embodiment of the United States' Mars-Neptune square. Richard Barnet (*The Rockets' Red Glare*) describes him:

---

[21]The phrase "starvation of life" comes from Mumford (182). We might note some similarities to our current period, as we move into the Age of Aquarius, ruled by Uranus and Saturn. We see all around us a "starvation of life," now on a grander scale than at the end of the 18th century, for humans have, with the aid of their various inventions and mechanical devices, impoverished three of the main sources of life-giving energy: the soil, the air, and the water (particularly, but not only, that in the oceans).

[22]I have taken much factual material from James Trager's *The People's Chronology* (New York: Henry Holt and Company, 1992). See 434ff.

[23]See chapter X.

A romantic visionary who believed that the United States was destined to expand across the continent not by force of arms but because its freedoms would attract all the peoples of North America. The United States would "never be the forcible subjugator of other countries." But he soon came to believe that arms could be of considerable help. He became a soldier of fortune in Cuba, recruiting a private army to liberate the island when President Polk balked at sending in the marines.[24]

Not surprisingly in a country with Neptune in its ninth house, many people took these remarks as prophecy. Neptune, bringer of idealism mixed with deception and only the most tenuous grasp of consensus reality, seems redolent throughout.[25]

The second theme concerns leveling and dissolving barriers. The former emerged most clearly in literature, most evidently with Marx and Engels' *Communist Manifesto*, published in 1847 and Engels' *The Condition of the Working Class in England*. In 1845, in a different work, Marx had opined that "religion is the opium of the people," reiterating the connection between deception and mass-movements—and reminding us of Neptune's connection to drugs and addiction, though Marx spoke metaphorically. Both works argued against the class system, as did Frederich Douglas' journal *North Star*, which began publication in 1847. Further still, free trade acts and lower tariffs had a leveling effect in international relations. They also led to increased trade, generally over water (Neptune), greatly facilitated by the launch of the first clipper ship in 1847. We also see lowered barriers of another sort in the development of modern anesthesiology by William Thomas Green Morton in Boston and in the discovery of ether in 1842. The development of the telegraph, with the first telegraphic message sent in 1846, lowered the barrier of space in human communication; as one of the first electronic media, it also led to the lowering of standards in our evaluation of communication.[26] At present, we find ourselves deluged, appropriate for matters-Neptunian, by ever newer electronic media that serve to delude more than to enlighten. Shades of Uranus and Neptune indeed!

During the same period, Russell Alfred Wallace's insect studies in South American and Asia ran parallel to the work of Charles Darwin; both leveled the distinctions between humans and other animals, showing that all creatures evolved and that ideas about human specialness or precedence

---

[24]Richard Barnet, *The Rockets' Red Glare: War, Politics and the American Presidency* (New York: Simon and Schuster, 1990), 99. These ideas remain with us, as we can see in the pronouncements, after 9/11, of George Bush, Colin Powell, and others, that other nations' anger at the United States resulted because other peoples envied U.S. freedom. The connection to military expansion points to factors unique to the United States with its square from Mars in Gemini in the seventh house up to Neptune in Virgo in the ninth house. The aspect suggests mass delusions effecting military action. We might see this as a collective tendency connected to the Long Count horoscope with its Mars-Neptune conjunction in Scorpio (see *The Machine Stops*); however, some nations seem particularly prone to act out that aspect.

[25]We obviously cannot credit O'Sullivan with inventing the idea that the new nation had some sort of destiny granted by god. Movements west, and the slaughter of native people, had gone one for centuries already. O'Sullivan seems to have grabbed an idea already in the air and given it a ringing title. We should not underestimate the importance of such actions, of course, but O'Sullivan seemed swept up in an already-dominant zeitgeist.

[26]We can consider Thoreau as one of the first critics of this new media. He attempted to disillusion people regarding its effects: on finding out that distant places could now communicate, he said, 'I wonder what Texas has to say to Baltimore?'

rested on untenable assumptions. The cannibalism of the Donner Party struck a resonant chord, surely suggesting to many that humans remained capable, despite our "moral standards," of bestial behavior. Surely, too, inventions like the powered sewing machine made possible further regimentation of human beings, further inequality in labor (reflecting Virgo, polar opposite to Neptune-ruled Pisces). Neptunian idealism seems redolent in the Crystal Palace Exhibition of 1851, in which Uranian inventions and the doctrine of progress received social sanction in the country where they had thus far worked the most mischief.

In general, the period brought an emphasis on the masses, evident not only in the writings of Marx and Engels, but also in the famines that swept Ireland and Europe. Two and a half million people died in Europe in 1843; the famine did not go away, as we can see from the Irish Potato Famine a few years later (1846). In Europe, the masses rose up, sometimes because of the famine, sometimes because of the influence of The Communist Manifesto. Across the ocean, the California Gold Rush of 1849, following the 1848 discovery of gold in that state, certainly qualified as a mass movement—and probably a mass delusion, somewhat akin to the Mexican War. After the war, the American masses elected General Zachary Taylor, lead general in the conflict, as President of the United States, pointing to the country's Mars-Neptune issues. The development in 1847 of the first covered shopping arcade points to another Neptune trend: the development of mass delusion connected to mass-produced items of all sorts.

Neptunian problems, like Uranian ones, remain with us today, for clearly we have not integrated Neptune even yet. The unintegrated version still appears in the collective as mass delusions and mass enthusiasms, particularly those that lead the masses into the mass sacrifices we call "wars." Neptune also appears in forces that level distinctions, and through widespread idealism, particularly of the sort not closely connected to reality. Neptune appears in drug use and in the movie industry, in the artistic inspirations of many and the delusions of many more. The collective projections arise because humans have a hard time integrating Neptune into their lives in constructive ways. After all, Neptune dissolves solidity, including the one we call ego, and lowers boundaries, particularly the one we so assiduously maintain between the conscious mind and the unconscious.

The period[27] around Pluto's discovery in 1929 brought the stock market crash, Hitler's rise to power, Stalin's pogroms, the widespread persecution of Jews by the Nazis, the United States refusal to give Jews safe haven in the United States,[28] Gandhi's "fast unto death" undertaken to

---

[27] I have taken much factual material from James Trager's *The People's Chronology* (New York: Henry Holt and Company, 1992). See pp. 786ff.

[28] Though Hitler has received, and rightly enough, the brunt of the blame for the Holocaust, the United States took little action to save Jewish lives. Howard Zinn tells us (*Failure to Quit*, (Boston: South End Press, 2002, 83) that in January 1934 a resolution was introduced into the U.S. Senate expressing "surprise and pain" at "what the Germans were doing, and asking for a restoration of Jewish rights." However, the State Department "used its influence to get the resolution buried in committee."

dramatize the British colonial government's treatment of the "untouchables", and the granting of Nobel Prizes to several important figures in quantum research. The period also witnessed the publication of many important works speaking to plutonic concerns (as long as we take those concerns to include my contention that Pluto has to do with the connection between mind and phenomena): Richard Wilhelm's translation of *The Book of the Golden Flower*; Carl Jung's important psychological introduction to that text as well as his *Modern Man in Search of a Soul*[29]; Alfred Korzybski's *Science and Sanity*. We will look at several of these works again in chapters XI and XII, where we will concern ourselves with the projection-making factor in the human psyche. Here, we concern ourselves with the collective manifestations of Pluto and what they tell us about individual psychology.

One theme has to do with the totalitarian impulse, particularly seen from a psychological vantage (i.e. as a projection). The actions of Hitler and Stalin clearly exemplify this theme, as do the forces against which Gandhi pitted himself in non-violent resisistance: the forces of the British Empire, based in plutocratic demands of power and money, precisely the forces that Gandhi confronted. As a series of collective projections, Pluto appeared as totalitarianism driven by financial concerns and characterized by pervasive brutality.

A second theme has to do with transcending or penetrating two-valued or dualistic thinking, and it has a close but hidden connection to the first. (We would hardly expect the ruler of the underworld to make his connections clear!)[30] This theme appears in the writings of Alfred Korzybski and Jung around that period, as it appears in the quantum theorists winning Nobel Prizes. In different ways, the investigations done in general semantics, psychology, and physics all speak to the connection between perception and mind, between intensional and extensional realms, between the unconscious mind and the phenomenal world, the field in which collective projections arise. Thus Korzybski alerted us to the way our language, arising as it does from a two-valued orientation, predisposes us to see not the world in itself, but our linguistically-mediated version. Writing around the same time, Jung told us that that whatever we reject from conscious awareness appears in the world as an event. If enough people do this, a collective projection arises: a panoply of events and developments that people take as components of the external situation. Thus Jung wrote of the period after World War I that he had "noticed peculiar disturbances in the unconscious" of his German patients, and that "this condition was by no means a purely Teutonic phenomenon," as "the onslaught of primitive forces was more or less universal."[31] These forces, emerging from within, led to disastrous consequences. Thus Jung, looking back in 1946, wrote,

> In Hitler, every German should have seen his own shadow, his own worst danger. It

---

[29]During the same period, Jung plunged into his studies on alchemy, studies that played a major role in both of these works and that led to *Psychology and Alchemy*, published in 1944.
[30]We may say, "Well, are the planets mere projections or are they really there?" But the way we frame the question shapes the way we might answer it. A different framing would prompt a different perspective. The "to be" form in the question suggests that it reflects a Saturnian approach to the problem.
[31]C.G. Jung, *Essays on Contemporary Events* (London: Ark Paperbacks, 1946), 2.

is everybody's allotted fate to become conscious of and learn to deal with this shadow… The world will never reach a state of order until this truth is generally recognized.[32]

In 1936, in an essay entitled *Wotan*,[33] Jung wrote,

> …what is more than curious…is that an ancient god of storm and frenzy, the long quiescent Wotan, should awake, like an extinct volcano, to new activity, in a civilized country that had long been supposed to have outgrown the Middle Ages. We have seen him come to life in the German Youth Movement, and right at the beginning the blood of several sheep was shed in honor of his resurrection. Armed with rucksack and lute, blond youths, and sometimes girls as well, were to be seen as restless wanderers on every road from the North Cape to Sicily, faithful votaries of the roving god. Later, towards the end of the Weimar Republic, the wandering role was taken over by the thousands of unemployed, who were to be met everywhere on their aimless journeys. By 1933 they wandered no longer, but marched in their hundreds of thousands. The Hitler movement literally brought the whole of Germany to its feet, from five-year-olds to veterans, and produced the spectacle of a nation migrating from one place to another. Wotan the wanderer was on the move.[34]

And:

> Wotan is a restless wanderer who creates unrest and stirs up strife, now here, now there, and works magic…I venture the heretical suggestion that the unfathomable depths of Wotan's character explain more of National Socialism than all three reasonable factors [economic, political, and psychological] put together.…Perhaps we may sum up this general phenomenon as *Ergriffenheit*—a state of being seized or possessed. The term postulates not only an Ergriffener (one who is seized) but also an Ergreifer (one who seizes). Wotan is an Ergreifer of men. And unless one wishes to deify Hitler—which has indeed actually happened—this is really the only explanation.[35]

Thus we see a link between Wotan and possession, the latter concept clearly connected with Pluto, not only in myth, where Hades/Pluto abducts Persephone, but also psychologically, visible in all Pluto-related obsessions and compulsions. Later in the same essay, drawing from Martin Ninck's *Woden und germanischer Schicksalsglaube*, Jung notes the same connection:

> The Romans identified Wotan with Mercury, but his character does not really cor-

---

[32] Jung, 6.
[33] Wotan seems closely related to Mercury and Hermes, as Jung notes in the essay. We might at first think that we shouldn't associate him with Pluto. However, Pluto and Mercury have a close connection, a matter I discuss in chapter XI and that Jung, though using a different vocabulary, apparently noticed in his writings on Mercurius' function in alchemy. That Jung's interpretation of Wotan connects that figure to the astrological Pluto (and Mercury) appears clearly in some of the quotations to follow.
[34] Jung, 12.
[35] Jung, 11-12.

respond to any Roman or Greek god, although there are certain resemblances. He is a wanderer like Mercury, for instance, rules over the dead like Pluto and Kronos, and is connected with Dionysus by his emotional frenzy, particular in his mantic aspect.[36]

Further in the same essay, Jung notes that it "was not in Wotan's nature to linger on and show signs of old age," but that he "simply disappeared when the times turned against him, and remained invisible for more than a thousand years, working anonymously and indirectly."[37] We see clearly the connection to Hades/Pluto, who often wore a helmet that made him invisible, though he remained at work in the world. Thus Jung, as if he had read the astrological runes, had noted that the projection of Pluto appeared in egregious form right around the time of Pluto's discovery.

Meanwhile, several important quantum theorists received Nobel Prizes for work with important psychological implications, for in suggesting that humans cannot do an objective experiment on phenomena—because the act of observation alters the thing observed—Heisenberg and others seem to describe one of Pluto's manifestations. For Pluto symbolizes not only the human capacity to transform our psychological orientation, it also symbolizes something integral to our experience: that we do not always deal with an objectively real world, and that perhaps we never do, for apparently mind in some sense alters the world it observes. Thus just as Jung saw that the unconscious material in and from millions of individuals had a close, and perhaps even causal, relationship with collective events, so Heisenberg noted an inescapable connection between mind and phenomena, between observer and observed. Both men would agree that the alteration does not result from conscious attention; Jung and others have suggested that we take the quantum world as a metaphor for the unconscious. We see the mark of Pluto on all these discussions, for not only does Pluto, ruler of the underworld, have a close connection to the complexes of the unconscious, he (or she, if you prefer, for female deities have more often ruled the underworld than have male ones), consists of two bodies revolving around a gravitational center belonging to neither, just as mind and phenomena seem to do.

A third theme has to do with the power of something small to bring about enormous change. Surely we see this theme emerge in Gandhi's actions; just as surely, we see it in Hitler's, for otherwise we would have difficulty explaining how a social misfit and nonentity could serve as an agent for such destruction tendencies. As a result of Hitler's actions, too, we find a further chain reaction, for surely Hitler's obsessions prompted others, some of them German scientists who defected, to create the atomic bomb, a weapon that works by controlled chain reaction. From the earlier uranium-based weapons developed later plutonium-based ones. Pluto works by chain reaction, whether through a Gandhi, a Hitler, or a series of atomic nuclei. Further, and certainly more creatively (i.e. less reactively), we see the same principle at work in the influence of the work of such people as Jung, Gandhi, Heisenberg, and Korzybski. In remarks that I take as the *raison d'etre* for this chapter, Jung suggested a path to healing the collective, pointing to what astrologers will recognize as the Plutonic imperative:

---

[36] Jung, 19.
[37] Jung, 20.

> All beginnings are small. Therefore we must not mind doing tedious but conscientious work on obscure individuals, even though the goal towards which we strive seems unattainably far off. But one goal we can attain, and that is to develop and bring to maturity individual personalities.[38]

Further, Jung linked the demands of individual psychology to the workings of what may at first appear as collective inevitabilities:

> As I have said, the uprush of mass instincts was symptomatic of a compensatory move of the unconscious. Such a move was possible because the conscious state of the people had become estranged from the natural laws of human existence. Thanks to industrialization, large portions of the population were uprooted and were herded together in large centres. This new form of existence—with its mass psychology and social dependence on the fluctuation of markets and wages—produced an individual who was unstable, insecure, and suggestible.[39]

And:

> As I have already told you, the tide that rose in the unconscious after the first World War was reflected in individual dreams, in the form of collective , mythological symbols which expressed primitivity, violence, cruelty: in short, all the powers of darkness. When such symbols occur in a large number of individuals and are not understood, they begin to draw these individuals together as if by magnetic force, and thus a mob is formed. Its leader will soon be found in the individual who has the least resistance, the least sense of responsibility and, because of his inferiority, the greatest will to power. He will let loose everything that is ready to burst forth, and the mob will follow with the irresistible force of an avalanche.[40]

The plutocratic domination that we see around us now tells us quite clearly that humans still project Pluto into the environment. We could say the same for the continued insistence, on the part of one government after another, on accessing power from underworld realms, whether considered literally as oil deposits or symbolically as hidden financial reserves. At the time of Pluto's discovery, Jung wrote not only that every good quality has its bad side and that "nothing that is good can come into the world without directly producing a corresponding evil," remarks suggesting Pluto's insistence on non-duality, but also that we "can no longer get along unless we give our best attention to the ways of the psyche."[41] Those words seem just as true now as when he wrote them.

---

[38] Jung, 41.
[39] Jung, 5.
[40] Jung, 3.
[41] Jung, "The Spiritual Problem of Modern Man," in *Modern Man in Search of a Soul* (New York: Harcourt Brace Jovanovich, 1933), 199, 201.

We come, finally, to Chiron, discovered in 1977 by Charles Kowal.[42] Chiron, sometimes called a comet and sometimes a minor planet,[43] orbits mostly between Saturn and Uranus, sometimes coming closer to Earth than Saturn, sometimes venturing farther out than Uranus, all of which seems appropriate, as he is the grandson of the latter and the son of the former, and thus half-brother to Jupiter, Pluto, and Neptune. He thus has membership in the rather dysfunctional family so central to Greek mythology.

As always occurs with the discovery of a new planet important to astrologers, the events taking place around the discovery period give us clues to the planet's nature and function. Furthermore, they constitute the first collective projection of the planetary energy. At first the projected energy appears more clearly than the psychological demands, for most people haven't yet learned how to work effectively with the energy-in-question. In the 1970's, many social agencies spoke to the importance of preventative solutions to medical crises instead of simply reactive ones. Scientists began to speak in similar terms about the environment as a whole. *The Limits to Growth*, first published in 1972, aimed to

> …improve our mental models of long-term, global problems by combining the large amount of information that is already in human minds and in written records with the new information-processing tools that mankind's increasing knowledge has produced….[44]

Though the authors admitted that their model, like any model, was imperfect, oversimplified, and unfinished, they nevertheless felt confident enough to state, among other conclusions, that,

> [i]f present growth trends in world population, industrialization, pollution, food production, and resource depletion continue unchanged, the limits to growth on this planet will be reached sometime within the next one hundred years. The most probable result will be a rather sudden and uncontrollable decline in both population and industrial capacity.[45]

They saw it as quite possible "to alter these growth trends and to establish a condition of ecological and economic stability that is sustainable far into the future," but that "the vast majority of policymakers seems to be actively pursuing goals that are inconsistent with these results."[46]

Around the same time, the United States government gave clear, if unwitting, support to that last sentence: it drastically increased oil imports, particularly late in the decade, not only accelerating the development of what we now call climate change, but also sowing the seeds of future

---

[42]According to Richard Nolle (*Chiron: The New Planet in Your Horoscope*. Tempe: AFA, 1997. See chapter 1.), Koval discovered Chiron around 10 AM on November 1, 1977 in Pasadena, California.
[43]And sometimes an asteroid, though it orbit falls nowhere near the asteroid belt.
[44]Donella H. Meadows, Dennis L. Meadows, Jorgen Randers, William W. Behrens III, *The Limits to Growth* (New York: New American Library, 1972), 26.
[45]*The Limits to Growth*, 29.
[46]*The Limits to Growth*, 29.

military conflict that would further exacerbate social and ecological problems in both rich and poor nations, in both the aggressor and the aggressed-upon. Events all over the world suggested that leaders either refused to take the advice offered in *The Limits to Growth* or remained ignorant about the problems discussed there. Oil began to flow from Alaska's Prudhoe Bay, the largest source of domestic petroleum. Retail terrorism took place in all sort of places, ranging from Washington DC to the Middle East; Genetech started the first commercial gene-splicing program.[47] Though on the one hand the period brought some attempts to heal old wounds (e.g. Carter's pardoning of United States draft resisters, and the release of 100,000 prisoners from Chinese jails), it also brought its share of new wounds, particularly via new ritualistic behaviors (e.g. the importance of oil to the United States social ritual and thus new policies regarding oil-rich nations). The establishment of a U.S. Department of Energy seems a perfect example of the latter, as the DOE virtually ensured that the United States would make decisions about energy that had nothing to do with environmental health.

As an individual projection, Chiron appears as people involved with healing, personal or planetary, and particularly when those people work through institutions. While some would say that we shouldn't argue too vociferously against the medical establishment, some social critics have felt that the proliferation of hospitals and other organizations connected with "Health, Education, and Welfare" does not indicate an improvement in health, but rather a deterioration. Notable among these critics stands Ivan Illich, who in his *DeSchooling Society*, first published a few years before Chiron's discovery, argued that in the modern, bureaucratized state,

> [h]ealth, learning, dignity, independence, and creative endeavor are defined as little more than the performance of the institutions which claim to serve these ends….I will show that the institutionalization of values leads inevitably to physical pollution, social polarization, and psychological impotence: three dimensions in a process of global degradation and modernized misery. I will explain how this process of degradation is accelerated when nonmaterial needs are transformed into demands for commodities; when health, education, personal mobility, welfare, or psychological healing are defined as the result of services or "treatments."[48]

A projected Chiron appears problematically not only as planetary illness, but also as figures or institutions who or that purportedly help to ensure health, provide education (Chiron's exaltation in Sagittarius), and provide for the welfare of people. The proliferation of such institutions suggests that, as Illich claims, people have given up their own capacities to self-healing, self-education, and self-maintenance; Illich's book pointed to the need for change.

Illich (unwittingly, I think) reminds us of Chiron's connection to shamanism, for one didn't take on the role of shaman until he or she could heal him or herself. Admittedly, Chiron himself

---

[47]Another interesting development, not directly related to this study: 1976 saw the first use of word processors and fax machines. These seem related to Chiron through his connection to Virgo (work; subservience; efficiency).
[48]Ivan Illich, *Deschooling Society* (New York: Marion Boyars, 1971), 1.

doesn't fit all the criteria for shamanism, for he had teachers (most notably Asclepius, often referred to as the father of Greek medicine, as well as Apollo), and he couldn't cure the most serious of his own wounds, giving up his immortality after Hercules wounded him with one of Chiron's own poisoned arrows. Going to the underworld, he released Prometheus, who brought fire (civilization; social wisdom) to human beings. Like other spiritual teachers, Chiron suffered death. However, he transmitted his wisdom to the future. His wounds transformed into future benefit. That Chiron healed others but could not heal himself suggests that if we engage in the transformative path just to make our own pain go away, we will end up disappointed. We must begin by going *into* that pain, not *away* from it—and by extending out to others. By facing our woundedness, by descending into our own shadow-side (the underworld), we release our new light to the world, prompting the next step in the transformative process.

The industrial processes that have led to the planetary wound have resulted, at least in part, from a collective effort to get away from suffering. This collective avoidance has ensured that we meet the wound in the collective. Yet the personal process demanded by Chiron—the acknowledgment of our own wounds along with our capacity to heal ourselves—has a close connection to collective events. Erich Neumann speaks to the intimate connection between the search for wholeness, one's personal connection to the shadow elements of the personality, and the development of what we might call symbolic infection:

> The ethical aim of being "non-infectious" may appear to have a purely negative content. This negative limitation, however, is compensated by the principle of wholeness in the personality, the effects of which extend far beyond ethics and the problem of evil….
>
> In the final analysis, it is once again the psychology of the scapegoat which provides us with a general category that also includes this type of infection of one's immediate personal environment. It is a fact…that, owing to the primary unconscious identity of groups, the transmission and reception of psychological contents to and from the environment is both possible and of frequent occurrence.[49]

That Chiron spends most of his time between Saturn and Uranus, his orbit taking him sometimes inside the orbit of Saturn and sometimes outside the orbit of Uranus, suggests that Chiron shows us how to move from fear to insight, from the personal realm to the transpersonal realm—and that our connection to personal wounds brings us to the borderline across which "infection" gets transmitted. Chiron symbolizes not only the bridge between personal and collective, and thus the bridge over which such infection crosses, but also the bridge for a more positive kind of infection, a kind of sympathetic response similar to what we see with musical harmonics. In the more positive type of infection, we transmit the openness, compassion, and transformative power symbolized by the three outermost planets. Having developed confidence and perspective (Jupiter, ruler of Sagittarius, the sign of the centaur), we move from being imprisoned within our own fears (inside the orbit of Saturn) to a state in which our insight (Uranus) leads us to feel natural com-

---

[49]Neumann, *Depth Psychology and a New Ethic*, 103.

passion (Uranus leading to Neptune) and inspires us to bring about fundamental change (Pluto).

During the period around Chiron's birth, many reputable scientists recognized and began to speak out about deeply rooted environmental problems and a realization that the solution to these problems must extend beyond the cosmetic to the systemic. For example, during the late 1970s, scientists recognized and began to write about the hole in the ozone, a problem clearly emerging from deeply-rooted social imbalances. Considered as projections, these developments tell us that most of us haven't engaged the wounded healer as part of our personal potential. On the other hand, that period brought many spiritual teachers from India, China, Tibet, and Japan to the western world, suggesting that the wounds, both planetary and personal, drew the healers. Not having found the inner guru, yet feeling the need to heal, people magnetized, it seems, external ones.

In these dynamics we can see Chiron and his family lineage. Saturn symbolizes the social order; Uranus symbolizes the need for change. The need for all of us to move from Saturn to Uranus, via Chiron orbiting between them, emerges through a collective, or planetary, wound. Perhaps we can see the period's emphasis on healers and teachers as a response to the developing planetary crisis, for the planetary wound resulted largely from the activities of people in the western hemisphere, people to whom the teachers came. We can see quite clearly how a problem such as ozone depletion develops from fundamental imbalances in social structures; at the same time, we can see an intimate connection between problematic social structure and inner difficulties, between imbalances in the body social and imbalances in the way we structure our personal lives. Jung said that the gods come to us through our wounds, not merely because of them, so it seems incumbent upon us to look carefully at the wounds before we insist that Health, Education, and Welfare provide us with doctors.

The Pattern of Human Potential: What to Cultivate

Before looking more in depth at the world situation resulting from the collective projection of our planets, we should look again at the pattern of human potential, the energy that in projected form arises as the world the *world problematique*.[50] Once we look at that potential, and then at the way it arises in negativized form, we can suggest a praxis that can at least partly recollect the projection—or so we can hope.

As we have seen, the inner planets symbolize potentials to which people generally retain a conscious connection. Admittedly, we can point to some exceptions: men often project the Moon, and even Venus, onto women; women often project the Sun and Mars onto men. These mythic figures, however, do not rule underworlds the way Saturn and Pluto do; nor do they rule an elemental realm the way Neptune does; nor, finally, do they, like Uranus, rule the realm of ideas from which forms emanate. Though the inner planets may, for this individual or that, remain unaccessed, we shouldn't conclude that they represent energies inherently difficult to access. Men may project the Moon onto women, but the sub-lunar realm surrounds us on all sides, even on the inside, for our

---

[50] The term comes from Tielhard de Chardin.

bodies surely form part of that realm. Men may project Venus onto women, but those men surely can access their own value-structure and aesthetic sensibilities. Women may project Mars onto men, yet women surely feel anger, and even in the face of abundant social conditioning driving them in other directions, they can develop a sense of conscious, creative identity (the Sun).

The outer planets and Saturn present quite a different sort of problem. The mythological background and astronomical position of these planetary figures suggest that people will have significant difficulty accessing them. This difficulty does not mean that people *cannot* access these energies, but it surely suggests that the symbolized potentials tend to sink into the unconscious. That humans have discovered the planets in outer space, however, suggests that people can find the planetary energies in inner space as human potentials. But what do the planets tell us about the human potential?

Chiron tells us that we have the capacity to work with the woundedness that seems inherent in our nature. We die, after all, and before we die, we go through great suffering. By refusing to acknowledge that, we ensure the projection of Chiron into the environment. Because our sense of woundedness strikes to the core of our nature and has so much to do with the body, the projection of Chiron understandably has much to do with the earth itself, where we see the wound quite clearly. Just as Chiron comes from (so to speak) Saturn and a partly-human woman (Philyra, the daughter of Saturn's brother Oceanus), so the wound results from the ongoing relationship between human beings' god-like capacities and their inescapable physical existence. Though all animals die, humans *know* that they will die; they have an *idea* about death that they carry with them. Saturn, ruler of social forms, has a child by his niece, so we also have a sense of violation: that the social forms humans have created (Saturn) have in some sense violated the natural order; thus we see wounds in the eco-system. Surely the late 1970s marked a time when that violation of the social order began to appear in the collective, marked by (among other things) global warming, the closely-related depletion of non-renewable resources, and the endemic conflict that makes humans seem incapable of solving the problems besetting them. At the same time, that Chiron may have come from outside of the solar system suggests that we have potentials that come from beyond the prevailing understanding of human potential.[51]

As a potential, Chiron serves as a bridge from Saturn to Uranus. That he comes closer to earth than Saturn suggests the connection between woundedness and human-created structures such as our various social orders and our languages, the former serving unsuccessfully as attempts to shield us from our suffering, the latter serving unsuccessfully in our various attempts to fully understand the world in which we live. As ruler of Virgo, Chiron has much to do with the development of social rituals through which we deepen the wound and reiterate our blindness. However, if we look

---

[51] The forms mentioned in this paragraph seem to have a close connection to the subject-matter of my previous book, *The Machine Stops*, where I use astrological symbology (in connection with the Mayan Long Count) to trace a cycle of human development that began in the 4th millennium BC and reaches its culmination in our own era. We generally call that cycle of development "civilization."

at the wound directly, we can stop thinking that the benefits of the social order will somehow free us from our suffering. Accepting our suffering, we can see our social forms as avenues for human creativity—and surely they qualify as that, as witness the enormous creative output of the 4th millennium BC, an output no less impressive even if it included many problematic elements.

Chiron reminds us that Buddha, in giving us his Four Noble Truths, including "The Truth of Suffering," referred to them as *noble* truths, not as unfortunate facts of life! In other words, we shouldn't shirk them or the responsibility that they bring. They open us to the realm beyond fear. Perhaps Jung meant something similar when he made his remark about the gods coming to us through our wounds.

According to Buddha, we suffer because of attachment—the realm, at least partly—of Saturn, for Saturn symbolizes the ways that ego tries to maintain itself via social attachment and the identification with social forms. As I have said above and will explain more below (in Chapter XI), Saturn appears in our speech largely through the verbs *to be* and *should*, and thus in every statement we make about what we *are* and what we *should be*: I *am* a teacher and *should be* a good one (or should be quarterback for the New England Patriots, or a wandering sage, etc.); I *am* a dishwasher but I *should be* a pool shark (or a corporate CEO, a leader of the free world, etc.). Every time we describe what we *are* by referring to a social category, we express our attachment to external social forms; every time we say that we *should be* something else because of socially-conditioned evaluations or language-forms, we express our attachment to internalized social dictates.

As we have seen, Saturn hides in plain sight. We can see our suffering, but we generally don't do so. We speak our language constantly, yet we remain largely unaware of the limitations it brings; we deal with social forms every day, yet we generally don't see the subtle ways they condition even our rebellious urges (for most rebellions just drive us toward new iterations of old structures). But just as these same external forms can serve as vehicles for human intelligence, ingenuity, and creative inspiration, so Saturn, the capacity for discipline, can serve as a vehicle for human awakening. The discipline-in-question involves Chiron, for it often involves looking directly at our woundedness. A connection to that woundedness opens us to the trans-Uranians, bodies we cannot see without technical aids, for Chiron travels not only beyond Saturn, but beyond Uranus as well. Though in the mythic tale insight leads to form (Uranus fathers Saturn), a pattern we can see in the world around us every day, on the developmental path, disciplines (Saturn) that open us to our woundedness (Chiron) open us also not only to insight (Uranus), but also to compassion (Neptune). We can all experience this pattern as soon as we undertake the disciplines laid out by a guide (Saturn leading to Chiron).[52]

From discipline comes insight into the world of limitation. Though in his negative manifesta-

---

[52] Chiron symbolizes the guru insofar as the guru exposes us to our woundedness and shows us how to move from fear to insight. However, a guru can manifest as any of the planets, alone or in combination.

tions Uranus often arises as at attempt to escape into the realm of ideas and thus to disconnect from ordinary life in which those ideas would purportedly manifest, in his positive manifestations he sheds light on the limitation itself and thus shows us that greater possibilities exist. (Also, of course, we perhaps wouldn't take on spiritual discipline without pre-existing insight into our situation, so in that sense Uranus leads to Saturn as in the mythic tale, for insight reveals limitation.) Furthermore, though we say, accurately enough, that insight arises from discipline, we shouldn't say that discipline *causes* insight or brings it into being. Saturn, after all, doesn't bring Uranus into existence, for Uranus existed before Saturn did! Discipline, rather, helps us to uncover the insight that seems part of each human's birthright. We know Uranus as the great sky god, after all, not as someone created by anyone. Similarly, Buddhists speak of *prajna*[53] not as something *caused* but as something *self-existent*, as already present, waiting to be uncovered; they refer to our basic nature as a jewel covered by many layers of mud. Other traditions have similar notions.

One of Uranus' insights has to do with the commonality of human suffering and limitation (Saturn). Once a person relates to his own wounds and sees the patterns through which they arise, he will perhaps realize that the same patterns take place in all other humans. We see here a hint of the leveling process that we associate with Neptune; we also see the arising of compassion. These connections reflect the historical fact that perturbations in Uranus' orbit led astronomers to look for another planet – and, eventually, to discover Neptune. What starts as a recognition or insight (Uranus) can develop into a vast feeling that envelops one's experience, as seems to have occurred for the great spiritual teachers in all traditions. Of course, for this envelopment to occur, one must give up reference points; one must realize that such a development happens *to* one more than that one causes it to happen (causality being, it seems, one of the reference points that goes by the boards!). Or, we might say, the process happens simply because we have the relevant seeds within us; given the proper conditions, they grow.

Astrologers connect Neptune to dreams, imagination, deception, idealism, and obfuscation. It clearly has a close connection to dance, theatre, and all the fine and projective arts, just as it has a close connection to alcoholism, hallucinogenic and addictive drugs, and any substance that we use to either confuse us about the world we live in or show us that the boundaries that we think exist—between self and other, conscious and unconscious, good and evil, personal and collective—don't have the solidity we attribute to them. All of these attributions have close inter-connections, obviously, and all reflect Neptune's affinity for, first, yearning for what of its very nature lies beyond the reach of ego, and second, a realm of experience in which logic fails us and where we will have difficulty telling accurate insight from complete self-deception. In short, Neptune opens us to vast truths while at the same time dissolving such boundaries as the one between truth and delusion!

---

[53]Some will translate this Sanskrit word as wisdom. The great scholar Herbert Guenther, translator of many Tibetan and Sanskrit texts, translated it as "discriminating insight born from wisdom." His definition suggests Uranus' relationship to the two planets adjacent to it in the solar system: Saturn, symbol of worldly wisdom developed through suffering; Neptune, symbol of compassion and selflessness, quite a different sort of wisdom, yet one we discover by dealing with suffering (for Saturn fathers Neptune).

As a symbol for the human capacity to dissolve boundaries, Neptune has a close connection to non-personal love and compassion, neither of which arise without a dissolving of boundaries between self and other. Neptune also has to do with the power of imagination; it thus has a connection to all of those symbol-systems and activities that offer glimpses of vaster truths, and to works of imagination that take us beyond our sense of limitation. Further still, Neptune has to do with the dissolving of self into more encompassing realities; it thus has to do with deception (for surely we have all known people who seemed to deceive themselves about that kind of dissolving!) and with the ability to let go of narrow concerns. Neptune's trident pierces through the three poisons that lie at the root of all processes of attachment: passion, aggression, and ignorance.

Again, though, as we dissolve coherence, we open ourselves to the possibility of self-deception, for we dissolve our reference points. Thus, as we have seen, Neptune has a close connection to such highly deceptive ideas as Manifest Destiny, on the one hand, and to ideals such as "love thy neighbor as thyself" on the other. Our yearning for an ideal world lies as much behind the former as the latter. It seems that Neptune symbolizes the elements of the spiritual instinct that have to do with yearning, devotion, longing, and letting go. Though in projected form Neptune often emerges as extensional elements that deceive in order to achieve selfish ends, we shouldn't conclude from this that Neptune qualifies as a malefic energy. Even potentially positive qualities can emerge via projection, and Neptune, through its connection to the matters mentioned above, clearly symbolizes many positive qualities. However, they generally will not seem positive to ego, for ego doesn't wish to let go and doesn't wish to dissolve boundaries. The kind of yearning ego engages in generally has to do not with a world of benefit available for all, but with a world of benefit for ego itself. Thus the tendency to project Neptune into the environment.

As I write this, Pluto remains the final firmly established planet—and this remains paradoxically true, partly because clearly other bodies orbit outside of Pluto's range, and just as clearly, many astronomers have decided not to label Pluto as a planet at all! All of this seems quite appropriate for Pluto, a double-body having to do with fusion, power, death, transformation, and the roots of projection. Seeking power and fusion, Pluto will gladly fuse notions such as "Pluto is a planet" and "Pluto is not a planet," thus stepping beyond the blindness of two-valued thinking. Pluto suggests that if we concern ourselves with such labelling, we miss the doorway to deeper truths.

Though will discuss Pluto more fully in the next chapter, we should note, here, his connection to language forms and transformative change. I often tell clients undergoing Pluto transits to "watch your language" and to eschew the verb "to be" (as in "Pluto is not a planet" or "I am a bad person") and to use operational statements in all descriptions of intensional and extensional realms. Operational language makes it easier to distinguish between those two realms—particularly important, in another Plutonian paradox, when one's experience fuses them. If I say, "Dick Cheney is a tyrant," I confuse an extensional situation with an intensional one; if I say, "I categorize the man as a tyrant," I recognize my part in the evaluation, for, as a concept, tyrant-ness belongs to the intensional realm. I err if I think I can see it in the extensional realm, though I may wish to show how my intensional map ("I categorize Dick Cheney as an X") lines up with an extensional situation (Dick Cheney doing what he does in various places outside of my mind).[54]

Pluto fuses intellect and feeling. He symbolizes the human capacity for transformation that takes place when we cut through dualistic frameworks and cut to the root of those structural elements that promote dualism. Whereas Neptune encourages idealism and arises from feeling, and whereas Uranus encourages insight and arises from ideas, Pluto fuses all such processes, recognizing that many such distinctions arise from our symbol-systems instead of from the world itself. Just as in the quantum realm, where notions of mass and energy dissolve, so in Pluto's realm many of our cherished frameworks and standpoints dissolve. From both realms emerge enormous power: from the fusion of mass and energy we can get the plutonium bomb or the ability to transform the world around us; from the fusion of frameworks and standpoints we can set of a chain-reaction of intensional and extensional change, transforming both at the same time.

Though we will always have a hard time describing this potential and process in words (for after all, Pluto fuses words with their referents; thus Pluto has a close connection to magic in its myriad forms, for in magic, the symbol has extensional power), we find some excellent attempts in literature, some "raids on the unspeakable"[55] that may yield some understanding in us. For example, in *The Woman at Otowi Crossing*, Frank Waters describes the transformative experience of his main character as she encounters, from one side, the teachings of native shamans from the kiva societies of the nearby pueblo, and, from the other, the workings of the scientists on Black Mesa, developing the atomic bomb. Fyodor Dostoyevsky provides us with numerous examples, particularly in *The Idiot* and *Crime and Punishment*. One could also consult some of the late poems of Wallace Stevens such as "The Course of a Particular" and "The Snow Man."

The human potentials symbolized by the outer planets have close interconnections—hardly surprising, considering the family connections we find in the inter-related mythic stories. Uranus, the idea, fathers the whole brood. Saturn, his son, tries to get rid of all of his children, a group that includes Jupiter, Neptune, and Pluto. Apparently the social and psychological status quos (Saturn) don't take kindly to our attempts to learn too much (Jupiter), to dissolve reference points (Neptune) or to transform the very structures upon which the status quo takes it rather questionable stand (Pluto).[56] In this somewhat dysfunctional mythic family, one which has a tendency to get rid

---

[54]If I speak this way, I also help myself to recognize that Dick Cheney can never qualify as a category (tyrant). I may examine his actions, evaluate them, and come to some conclusion. Perhaps a million people will accept my conclusion and find value in my evaluation, but it still remains an evaluation. See the following chapters for more on this.
[55]Thomas Merton's phrase, I believe.
[56]Saturn's attempt to devour Jupiter seems particularly relevant to 21st century United States, for our government seems particularly intent to squelch the activities of people like Bradley Manning and Julian Asange, people who in Jupiterian fashion want to spread knowledge and information and give perspective.

of children (or at least attempt to do so), Neptune and Pluto have a particular close relationship in meaning and function, suggested by the fact that their orbits interweave.[57]

Both Neptune and Pluto urge us to step beyond reference points. Neptune accomplishes this by dissolving coherence, Pluto by a process that, unifying emotion with the rational mind, radically undermines any attempt to take a simplistic stand on any idea. On the problematic side, Neptune symbolizes deception, while Pluto symbolizes the empowerment of that deception in order to disempower the masses (Neptune); on the more hopeful side, Neptune symbolizes compassion and imagination, while Pluto symbolizes the empowering of both or either. Pluto's penetration of Neptune's orbit coincided with the penetration (Pluto) of the human immune system (Neptune partly rules the white blood cells) by the HIV virus connected to the AIDS (Aides, Hades, Pluto) epidemic during Pluto's most recent transit through Scorpio, her dignity. The event gave humans advance warning, generally unheeded, that the collective immune system was breaking down and that the planet as a whole could no longer tolerate the empowered delusions manifest in rampant industrialism and plutocratic delusion. That penetration also suggested that people often need to transform their connection to understandings mediated by symbol systems before they can move to understandings not mediated by such systems.

That Pluto penetrates Neptune's orbit suggests that sometimes we need a probing understanding in order to free our compassion from delusion. In a world in which Neptunian delusion, in union with Uranian technology, has well-nigh deluged the civilized world—and the non-civilized world as well, as witness the melting ice-caps and permafrost—the twenty year fecundation (Rudhyar's term) sounded a clear warning on a collective level. But the penetration symbolized empowerment as long as, or if-and-only-if, humans could find their way to the penetrating understanding symbolized by Pluto. As we will see, Pluto has much to do with communication and symbol systems; as we have seen, Pluto's discovery coincided with major developments involving the relation between those symbol-systems and the so-called "real world," developments suggesting that the distinctions we generally make between mind and world, idea and feeling, self and other, and even good and evil, don't hold up to scrutiny. Thus Jung wrote at the time that every good that comes into the world does so accompanied by a corresponding evil—and that we should consider this as a manifestation of a psychological law.

The potentials symbolized by Neptune and Pluto both have to do with non-dualism, but the approaches differ. In their highest manifestations, they appear as compassion and empowered knowledge not defined by concept; as imagination and power, as boundarilessness and penetrating power, as the enveloping nature of higher truth and its transformative drive. When we look into the world and see empowered delusion, we can usefully consider events as projections of these basic human

---

[57]In some sense, the family has two interwoven subgroups, one consisting of Saturn, Chiron, and Uranus (for Chiron, as we have seen, comes closer to earth than Saturn and ventures father than Uranus, thus tying those two antagonists together through the medium of our wounds), the other consisting of Jupiter, Neptune and Pluto (for the reasons presently under discussion).

capacities; however, if we don't let go of the Janus-like reference points of individual ego and social identification, we will find it difficult to consider them as empty forms created by our refusal to accept our full human potential.

Praxis: Joining Self and World

The praxis begins when we consider that everything that we take as "reality," but particularly the collective situation, consists at least partly of projections, and that all of it comes to consciousness only through the mind.[58] In accepting these, we discover a venue through which to work with our experience: we begin, as Ms. Von Franz suggests in her discussion of individual projection, by calling the habitual, collective representations into question.[59] Of course, we may find this much easier when dealing with individual projections: we will probably find it easier to see our own anger in others than to see our feeling of powerlessness writ large as the inappropriate uses of power by the rich and powerful! So we start by working on our own projections, not only because we can work more effectively at that level, but also because by doing so, we empower ourselves to work effectively on collective matters.

It seems that all transpersonal work—as, for example, any attempt to ease collective suffering—must have a view, a path, and a fruition. It also seems that the fruition always retains a close connection to the view, for we reach fruition when we actualize the view.[60] In this case, we begin with the view that the *world problematique* arises from the negativized and acted out version of the human potential described above. But that view, at the outset, remains simply a concept, a view about the world, not yet a lived experience. To make it a lived experience, we start with our own projections; once we call into question our own solidified views and versions of what constitutes "reality" in situations that affect us directly, we can extend our view to situations in which we see ourselves in a peripheral role (i.e. in relation to the collective).

In other words, we ask first to what extent the world we experience exists independently of our experience of it—particularly situations where strong emotion comes into play, when a person comes to some sort of decision about how the world, or some element of it, "really is." First we see our own potential projected into and onto others; later, we begin to see the full human potential—ours allied with everyone else's—projected into the collective. If the ideas presented in this book have merit, the world before us represents, at least in part, our human potential gone awry in billions of individual cases, those billions of cases, taken together, forming the *projection we call the world,* as distinguished from *the world itself.* The prevailing social order, mechanical as it seems and complete with scientific explanations that offer us the world as *other*, often promulgates the

---

[58]I don't claim that it *is* a projection. But if we simply consider it so—for the sake, we might say, of furthering our understanding—we gain much insight. If we rest content with the is-proposition (X is a *projection*, for example) we too-readily accept the limitations of a Saturnian structure.

[59]Von Franz, *Projection and Re-collection in Jungian Psychology*, 9-19.

[60]My approach here owes a great deal to the teachings of many Tibetan lamas.

[61]The word *real* itself perhaps induces us to accept Saturn's truth, as that word comes from roots meaning '"relating to

illusion, inducing us to take that illusion as ultimately real.[61] Though Saturn leads to Pluto in the journey out from the Sun—and in myth, where Saturn is Pluto's father—on the return journey of renewal, the process starts with Pluto, at least as far as we know at this point in human development, for Pluto symbolizes death and transformation, an end-point possibly followed by a "turning about in the deepest seat of consciousness."[62]

To the ancients, Saturn represented the outermost planet, the "ring pass not," the ultimate truth, the end of the known. Saturn symbolizes the way we structure reality *and* the structure of what we take *for* reality. As we have seen, to understand Saturn, we must understand the way we structure our reality, which means, in turn, that we must understand the structural assumptions that we apply to our world. Some of these assumptions come from our early family life, of course, but many also come from the larger social structure and thus transcend purely personal matters. The social structures in which we live have arisen from numerous assumptions, taken as accurate conclusions but never closely examined, about what humans need for their development. Foremost among these structures we find language, even if most people take it for granted and don't consider it an intellectual structure at all. The conclusion seems strange, for as we have seen, as the structure of a language seems to have much to do with the kinds of thoughts one thinks and the kinds of conclusions one finds valid. Thus Edward Sapir wrote in 1928 (shortly before the discovery of Pluto),

> Human beings do not live in the objective world alone, nor alone in the world of social activity as ordinarily understood, but are very much at the mercy of the particular language which has become the medium of expression for their society. It is quite an illusion to imagine that one adjusts to reality essentially without the use of language and that language is merely an incidental means of solving specific problems of communication or reflection. The fact of the matter is that the 'real world' is to a large extent unconsciously built up on the language habits of the group. No two languages are ever sufficiently similar to be considered as representing the same social reality. The worlds in which different societies live are distinct worlds, not merely the same world with dif-

---

things, especially real property" (*Oxford Dictionary of Word Histories*, page 419). Of course, our understanding of the word would then hinge on our understanding of "things." In Buddhist logic, the term translated as *thing* refers to that which can perform a function, and many teachers do not regard composite items such as human beings and boulders as things but as groups of "partless particles," the latter being regarded as things in some non-Mahayana schools of thought. The English word *thing* comes from Germanic roots meaning meeting as well as "matter," "concern," and "inanimate object," a curious collection suggesting connections (meetings) to both the extensional and intensional realms (inanimate objects and concerns respectively). (See *Oxford Dictionary of Word Histories*, p. 510.) Of course, as long as we deal with language alone in these matters, we will end up going in circles, for we must define words in terms of other words. A language constitutes a limited system by which we try to refer to an apparently unlimited world. With that remark, I return, not entirely satisfied, to our discussion!

[62]Lama Anagarika Govinda, *Foundations of Tibetan Mysticism* (New York: Samuel Weiser, 1960), 77-80. Lama Govinda attributes the phrase to the Lankavatara Sutra.

[63]Edward Sapir, "The Status of Linguistics as a Science," *Selected Writings in Language, Culture, and Personality* (Berkeley:

ferent labels attached.[63]

Not only did written language make "western civilization" possible, and not only does it continue to underlie all of our social structuring, so much so that without it our entire social structure would quickly collapse, all from a very ordinary point of view, but different languages offer us different assumptions about the structure of reality. Within all this, we discern Saturn, hiding in plain sight.

We also find Saturn lurking about in our dualistic notions about mind and world. Even today, many people hold to the notion that physical reality constitutes an absolute truth as a solid something-or-other not connected with mind. Thus "matter" arises external to mind, though "mater," as in "Great Mother," suggests a psychological energy. The assumption about matter's independence from mind lies at the root of much traditional Western science and technology. I don't claim that we should reject the assumption entirely, for it has given rise to a technical skills and scientific insight that have led to verifiable consequences of all sorts. However, we should recognize the truths of science as merely conventional truths for the most part.[64] That the resulting technology "works" suggests that we have a truth: it works in a world with its own consistency and structure, and for most of us constitutes that which we cannot get beyond most of the time. We generally conclude, at least when working on practical matters, "This is the way things are," the verb *to be* telling us that Saturn lurks within our assertions and that our assertions probably represent a limited view.

Perceiving the world that way, we create various verbal, technical, and emotional structures, attempting to deal effectively with that reality. If, by contrast, a person holds firmly to some set of Christian beliefs, seeing *those* beliefs as connected to "the way things are," he might structure his world around monastic life, seeing "this world" as of paltry importance in connection to some other realm. Science, however, has apparently taken its place as our modern religion, complete with its set of beliefs and assumptions. The traditional scientific view gives us a kind of security, and we fear developments that threaten it. Seen from this vantage, our relative truth, or at least our clinging to it, reflects our fear. And as we know, many traditional scientific views no longer hold the hegemonic position they once held in our thought; from the quantum point of view, the traditional view, often connected with Newton's laws, represents a special case within the larger truth provided by quantum theory.

Saturn, however, symbolizes not only our fears, but also the potency of disciplines necessary to

---

University of California Press, 1963), 162.

[64]As in some other sections, I have borrowed here from the Buddhist tradition, here particularly that part of it known as Madhyamaka, generally translated as "The Middle Way." Madyamakan texts distinguish between absolute truth (Tb. *dondam*) and relative, or conventional, truth (Tb. *kundzop*). We can also borrow from the terminology of general semantics, for many general semanticists would say that our technology "works" because the symbolic maps that humans use to create that technology have the same structure as the territory the symbols map in the world of conventional truth. Much of our mathematical theory and structure seems to have a structure very close to that of the phenomenal world (and similarly for the system we call *astrology*). Thus we can use mathematical equations to measure that world accurately—and in myriad ways. I leave it to my reader to decide whether our mathematics has the same structure as the world because of some genius in human devising, or because both the mathematics and the world arise from the same source—or for some other reason.

Your Hidden Face: Projection in the Horoscope

face those fears. If we discipline ourselves to face our fears, insight (Uranus) arises about those fears' nature and genesis. From that develops a sense of compassion (Neptune), for we empathize with others, seeing ourselves all crowded into the same boat. At that point, we may yearn (Neptune) for some way to transform not only, or even mainly, our life-situation, but our view or perception of the world altogether (Pluto). Or perhaps we feel motivated by compassion (Neptune) to bring about change (Pluto) that will alleviate suffering; and perhaps we see the need for insight (Uranus) in order to bring about substantial (Saturn) change (Pluto, Saturn's son).

Some philosophers have said that for human beings, the death-and-rebirth process happens as it does because people's habitual patterns of response become so frozen that the awareness cannot develop further in a particular body. Thus the person dies but the mind promulgates forward into a new form. Perhaps human society, taken as an aggregate, has reached the point where habit patterns have crystallized to such an extent that the present form must die in order for human evolution to go forward.[65] Certainly the astrological symbolism suggests that after idealism and delusion comes the stage of death-and-transformation (Pluto). We cannot avoid that final stage, it seems, but, perhaps fortunately for us, Pluto's symbolism has several levels. Pluto symbolizes not only death-and-rebirth, but also the intelligence to penetrate through the dualistic fixation. After we experience Pluto as death, we can experience Pluto as power emerging from new understanding—from standing under the world, in some sense, to see how it operates.

———

Even if we keep the mind out of things (so to speak), we will probably admit that the problems of the world seem increasingly, if not unsolvable then at least resistant to any of the solutions proposed thus far by world-leaders. Those problems[66] will probably remain unsolved as long as we regard them as purely external sets of difficulties. We might, on the other hand, refrain from concluding that these problems "are" either purely external or purely internal. In other words, we might keep *to be* forms out our descriptions of the situation, for just as the structure of traditional scientific views seems second nature to millions, so millions of people take certain language-conceptual structures for granted, limiting their thinking and adaptability as a result. We habitually refer to problems as either external or internal, as if only those two possibilities exist, as if those possibilities "are" mutually exclusive, and as if we know precisely what *internal* and *external* refer to.

A new approach, one without what we might call *the is-ness of things*, reflects Pluto. Pluto symbolizes fusion processes and power: the power of fusion, the fusion of external and internal

---

[65]See *The Machine Stops* (Lyons), published in 2012 by AFA.
[66]A high level abstraction, admittedly. However, consider the multitude of problems that we sum up as "global warming." If we deal with this problem as purely a set of external issues, we will never solve it. To solve the problem, we must find its roots in our assumptions about ourselves and the societies we wish to live in. That, however, would provide subject matter for a set of books, so let's put it aside for now.
[67]I owe a debt, here and elsewhere, to the purveyors of e-prime. Interested readers can either google that term or pick up one of the anthologies of e-prime published by the International Society for General Semantics, beginning with the first

leading to power, the power *of* that fusion.[67] An active Pluto indicates that someone or something *seeks* power or has gotten involved *with* power in some way. Power means change: physicists define power as a function of change, according to the equation P = WT, where W = Work and T = Time. Thus by definition, Power is the rate at which we do work, the rate at which we bring about change. Pluto has to do with approaches to change that include not merely external dynamics, but also the relationship between external dynamics and internal ones: the work takes place *within* and *without* simultaneously. Pluto has much to do with depth psychology, with the psychological complexes and the shadowy elements of the psyche, not only with the personal shadow but with what Eric Neumann refers to as the "archetypal shadow,"[68] and also with complexes and psychic taboos, all of which appear as projections; and when they appear as collective projections, we have the *world problematique*. As a double planet (Pluto and Charon) with what seems like dual sexuality (for in the Greek and Roman pantheons, male deities ruled the underworld, whereas in many other cultures, female deities held that position), Pluto asks us to fuse not only gender-based dualities, but also external and internal realms, reminding us that when we do so, we will often release tremendous power that we should learn how to work with. The rise of Hitler and Stalin so close to the year of Pluto's discovery surely reminds us of the enormous power lying coiled in the underworld.

Perceptual processes provide a doorway to that those realms. In our perception, our unconscious contents and assumptions about the world work perpetual mischief, so much so that for myriad reasons, many of which have a close connection to conceptual structures, we may not perceive the world accurately at all. These difficulties accord with Pluto, for unlike the other planets in the system, Pluto consists of two bodies of comparable size rotating around a common center. Though some astronomers categorize Charon as one of Pluto's moons (the largest of four), others refer to the Pluto-Charon system as a "binary system" because the barycenter (center of gravity) does not lie within either of the individual bodies.[69] The astronomical situation resonates nicely with the understanding of the perception-dynamic articulated here: Pluto-Charon symbolizes new developments and capacities related to perception, with Pluto symbolizing the power and Charon, on whose boat souls crossed the River Styx to the underworld, telling us of the road *to* that power, the power residing within the apparent polarity of perceiver and perceived. The center of gravity—the place from which to perceive accurately—doesn't lie in either the projector or the projection, in either the perceiver or the perceived, in either the mind or the world. We won't find the truth if we say that the phenomenal world "is real" or that it "is not real," for such a dualistic framework will yield only obfuscation, even if (and perhaps *because*) our symbol-systems reflect and reinforce such a view.

Some astronomers now say that Pluto "isn't a planet" at all, and considering the previous discussion, we shouldn't find this surprising. When dealing with Pluto, we should remain skeptical of all is-propositions, knowing that they will not lead us to the truth. It doesn't matter whether Pluto "is" a standard planet or "is" a dwarf planet or "is" some numbered object in the Kuiper Belt. We

---

of the series: *To Be or Not: An E-Prime Anthology*.
[68]Erich Neumann, *Depth Psychology and a New Ethic*, 138.
[69]Wikipedia, among other sources.

should ask, rather, what Pluto symbolizes in our experience and what evolutionary capacity arises once we engage with that capacity. What *happens* when we deal with the energy we label as *Pluto*?

On a collective level, the capacities symbolized by Pluto appear as a series of projections, generally of a problematic nature due to the "negativizing" process described in earlier chapters: people do not value Pluto; they negativize that energy in themselves, rejecting it and relegating it to the unconscious. It therefore appears in the world as events, institutions, and larger social patterns bearing the mark of Pluto: as plutocratic movements of all sorts; as plutonium in the hands of terrorizing groups or governments (e.g. the United States); as people seeking or wielding a dark and primitive kind of power and control. Pluto symbolizes the taboo, the unacceptable, that which lies "beyond the pale."

If a person has been tricked by Saturn into thinking that the external world exists apart from any person's observation or perception of it, Pluto will generally appear as *external* power, particularly if the person has Pluto prominently placed in the natal horoscope.[70] If the person sees through Saturn's trick—sees through the assumptions of consensus reality, created, as described above, from fear and doubt—Pluto can arise as a drive to re-envision the world.[71] If the present argument has merit, we can work most effectively with the external world by looking not only outward, but inward at the same time. This doesn't mean that we reject Saturn, for we continue to take him seriously, knowing that projections can kill, sometimes by the millions. Thus we take Saturn in great earnest and turn to Pluto in order to deal with him. If we simply turn inward and ignore the external world, we fall victim to another dualism and thus to a resultant set of projections. Pluto wants to fuse dualisms in order to release their transformative power. Because most iterations of self-identify arise from or depend on either subtle or gross dualisms, Pluto threatens the core of self-identity.

We obviously haven't, in this discussion, fully encompassed Pluto yet, and we probably won't do so in the remaining chapters either! The next chapter includes much material on Pluto's role in the relations among countries. The last two chapters of the book will look at questions specifically related to language and to what we will, for now, euphemistically call "truth."

---

[70]Many power-wielders of the 20th century certainly had Pluto prominently placed. Astrologers seem fond of pointing to Hitler, and certainly his Pluto qualifies as "prominently placed," but we should also include the following: Stalin (Pluto in Taurus, ruling the Midheaven, opposing Venus, sextiling the Capricorn Ascendant); Woodrow Wilson (Pluto in Taurus, squaring the Moon, the Midheaven ruler); Franklin Roosevelt (Pluto in Taurus, squaring Mercury, the Ascendant ruler); Winston Churchill (Pluto in Taurus as the focal planet of a yod and loosely opposing Mercury). We could cite many others.

[71]Again we could point to many examples, including the following world-re-perceivers: Herman Melville (Pluto in Pisces conjoining Saturn and square the Uranus-Neptune conjunction); Karl Marx, Queen Victoria, Walt Whitman, Henry David Thoreau and others had the same aspects, sometimes linked to other planets); Goethe (Pluto in Sagittarius square a Sun-Midheaven conjunction); Thomas Jefferson (Pluto in Scorpio in a loose conjunction with the Midheaven, in a close square with Mars and a looser opposition with Venus).

Chapter X

Projection and United States Foreign Policy

In discussing the projections of nation states and other collectivities, I will often use phrases like, "The country never seems to acknowledge…" even though "the country" doesn't have a precise referent. In many cases, it refers to the country as an entity that acts in "the community of nations"; however, it can also refer to the people in the country, even though those people will obviously not all agree about any of the nation's policies or initiatives. Though some of the symbols in a nation's horoscope do have more specific referents (Mercury symbolizing the press, tenth house planets symbolizing approaches taken by the head of state, etc.), the referent for the horoscope as a whole seems much vaguer. In the material that follows, I use phrases like "the country" or "the United States" fully aware of this problem. We can say, for example, that the United States sees Iran as a hostile nation even though we could find millions of people—perhaps even a majority of U.S. citizens—who do not see Iran in that light at all. The United States has not yet acknowledged that the government lied as a prelude to the 2003 invasion of Iraq, yet millions of people in the United States have made precisely that acknowledgment over and over. For the sake of style, though, I do not enter these qualifiers for every statement I make about a collectivity. In using the phrase "the U.S.," I generally mean the nation as an active agent in international affairs. When I mean something different, I will try to make the difference clear.

As we have seen, projections pervade the experience of most, and probably all, human beings, permeating not only our intimate relationships, but our more casual ones as well, and many of our assumptions and interpretations of myriad elements of experience. As we have also seen, individuals can work to recall their projections, to *re-collect* them: to *collect again*, to bring back from the environment elements connected to the psyche. If people do this, they can see the world and themselves more accurately and eliminate or reduce unnecessary conflict arising from misperception and inaccurate fixation. If people develop greater awareness, they can do a better job penetrating their projections, taking more responsibility for what goes on in their lives. Perhaps people can never re-collect *all* of their projections, but they can certainly re-collect some of them. Doing so seems an integral part of any "spiritual" development.

When we turn to international affairs, we find, unfortunately for the world at large, that nation states generally develop less of this kind of awareness than do individuals. History teaches that they develop very little of it at all. Certainly nation-states, lacking a conscious and integral point of orientation, don't seem to have the capacity that individuals do for reflection and personal scrutiny. Thus nation-states generally do not (and probably *can*not) work on themselves in the way individuals do, for to do so would require an unprecedented degree of common commitment on the part of the nation's people. Though we can perhaps envision, in some ideal world, such extraordinary unity of view arising spontaneously or at the instigation of a leader of great vision who could encourage people to take on a unitary commitment, in the world as we know it, that sort of unofficial view never seems to occur. Further, in those rare instances when millions of people unite to achieve a common goal, that goal generally has to do with external situations or institutions, not with the *national awareness*, assuming that such a thing exists. So whereas an individual can work to understand his own psychological workings, a nation cannot seem to do so, lacking a center from which to organize such an effort.

The historical evidence shows quite clearly that nation states tend to manifest what we might call the least enlightened possibilities suggested by the national horoscope. We could cite many examples of this, but because the United States' behavior with other nations provides such excellent support for this proposition, and because the United States has wrought such havoc in the world-at-large by failing to recognize its projections, I will start with a discussion of that horoscope.

The United States Natal Horoscope[1]

The United States' horoscope contains three important and stressful aspects that tell us much about the country's self-perception, delusions, and relations with other nations. To those three, we can add Uranus' placement near the descendent of the horoscope, a placement suggesting that, for all of the United States' claims about valuing freedom, it actually rejects progressive movements wherever they turn up, often using its financial clout and military might to subvert them. So we

---

[1] I use the "Rudhyar chart" for the United States: July 4, 1776, 5:13:55 pm, Philadelphia. This doesn't mean I reject all other horoscopes. Jim Lewis got positive results working with a chart for the onset of the Revolutionary War, for example. Similarly, some astrologers have worked effectively with the horoscope for the signing of the U.S. Constitution. I see no contradiction here. The different horoscopes measure different aspects of the nation. We can see a parallel in the way some astrologers have worked effectively with "conception" horoscopes. That they do so does not indicate that time-of-birth horoscopes have no validity. Further, an astrologer can cast a chart for a specific event in a person's life and have much to say about the patterns developing from that event.

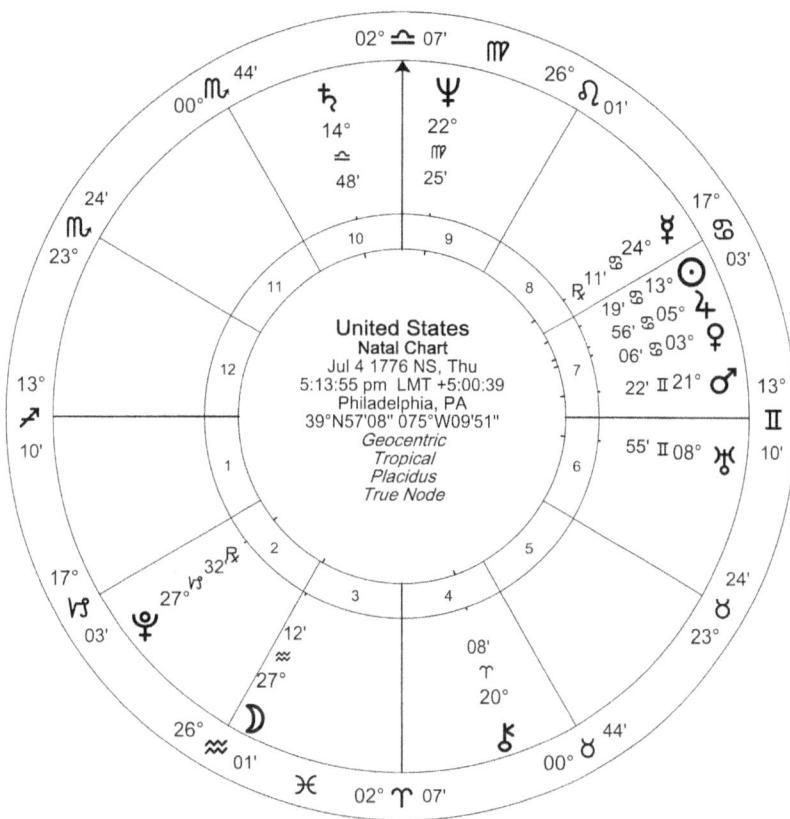

have, in all, four astrological factors to discuss, each of which plays an important role in the pattern of projection that has characterized U.S. history:

1. The opposition from Mercury in Cancer in the eighth over to Pluto in Capricorn in the second.

2. Uranus at 8 Gemini, opposed to the Sagittarius Ascendant. Also important here: the Sagittarius Ascendant itself.

3. The square from Mars in Gemini in the 7th up to Neptune in Virgo in the ninth.

4. The square from the eighth house Cancer Sun up to natal Saturn in Libra in the tenth.

Mercury in Cancer Opposition Pluto in Capricorn

As we have seen in the discussion of aspects, a person with an opposition generally plays the role of the planet closest to the Sun and projects onto others the planet farther from the Sun. (Though gender-related factors will often give a different message, those don't come into play in the activities of nations.[2]) We would therefore expect the United States to play the role of Mercury in Cancer and to project Pluto in Capricorn onto other nations or groups. The historical record certainly suggests that this occurs, as the United States has seen one nation or group after another as plutonian threats.

The pattern appeared even before the United States declared itself a nation, as the invading Europeans saw the native people as dark, savage, primitive, and cruel, despite the sophistication of many native civilizations and the marked primitive savagery—characterized by historian Michael Rogin as a drive for "primitive accumulation"—of the Europeans. Later, with the institution of the slave trade, African slaves served nicely as a hook for the United States' projection. Later still, the Soviet Union did yeoman service in that role, and once the Soviet Union fell apart, various Middle Eastern groups and leaders served equally well. Even a cursory examination of the rhetoric used to describe these different peoples and nations, all generally deemed enemies no matter what their intentions, shows the pervasive power of the projection.

Meanwhile, the people of the United States by-and-large have seen themselves as merely seeking security. Mercury in a nation's horoscope symbolizes not only the popular press, but also the way the people think about themselves. Mercury in Cancer suggests that millions of people in this country tend to see themselves merely as home-oriented folk seeking security and safety, tendencies reiterated by the Cancer Sun. (See below.) Those people tend to see themselves as under threat by various plutonic others: by people who seem mysterious, who seem to carry a kind of primitive aura and who seem obsessed with destruction. Meanwhile the popular press (Mercury in Cancer) constantly reiterates the Cancer theme: that the people remain concerned about a security deemed under threat from dark forces. Meanwhile, too, the plutocrats maintain their control over that popular press (Mercury-Pluto opposition) to an astonishing degree.

As I write this, transiting Saturn has moved from a square to natal Mercury toward the final phase of his square to natal Pluto. These transits, in effect for many months now, have coincided with the various Occupy movements. In those movements, people have spoken repeatedly about the effect of the wealthy one percent on the rest of us—on, more particularly, our home-based personal security. The evidence suggests that the people in the Occupy movement have recognized what those in the political class have not: that the enemy lies within, that Pluto has to do primarily with the plutocratic class in the United States. In astrological terms, we would say the Occupiers have recognized that though the United States habitually projects Pluto onto other nations and goes to war with them, the home-grown plutocrats have acted as enemies of a different sort. Whether the Occupy movement achieves it goals or not, its various pronouncements seem like a sign of health, indications that the Occupiers have seen through the projection and wish to recall it.

---

[2]Different astrologers have seen different nations as "ruled" by, as somehow characterized by, specific signs, which they consider to have gender. Similarly, and as we have seen, astrologers often see planets as having gender, though those astrologers don't necessarily agree on the particulars. Here, of course, we have two planets of rather ambiguous gender. In mythology, Mercury qualifies as neither male nor female, and as we have seen in earlier chapters, Pluto sometimes takes a masculine role and sometimes a feminine one.

The historical record supports the claim strongly suggested by both the Mercury-Pluto opposition in the "money" houses (the eighth and the second) and the Sun in the eighth (with Venus and Jupiter on the cusp): that the United States enriches itself at the expense of other nations or groups, for the U.S. took, first and foremost, land and resources belonging to Indians; later, the economy of the South depended on the value, in the form of people, stolen from Africa; later still, particularly after the dawn of the 20th century, the United States tried to take what it wanted, whether from the Philippines, Cuba, or, with the expansion of the industrial and wartime economy, the oil-rich Middle East. Because the expansion has generally involved money (Jupiter, ruler of Sagittarius Ascendant, on the cusp of the eighth, and conjoined Venus, Midheaven ruler and the planet most evidently connected with value, with the Sun and Mercury also in that house[3]), the drive for economic control, such as what we still see in U.S. involvement (to use a euphemism) in Central and South America, also fits this pattern. The square from the eighth house Cancer Sun up to Saturn in the tenth in Libra points to the myriad contributions of the executive branch of the government in these matters: an attempt to give order to the world in order to ensure more effective rapacity.

In a nation's chart, the planet closest to the Sun will appear as part of the focus of national identity, while the planet farthest from the Sun will arise through groups that seem to oppose the nation's purported "interests," groups that draw the country's attention, or that end up as the focus of its aggression. The only planetary opposition in the United States horoscope is the one from Mercury, retrograde at 24+ Cancer in the eighth house, over to Pluto, retrograde at 27+ Capricorn in the second. Hypothesizing that the United States will see itself in the role of Mercury, we would expect Americans to perceive themselves as home-owners and family people concerned with security (Cancer), as people who communicate about their feelings, who talk about their homes, their families, and "family values" (Mercury in the eighth, a house connected with values).[4] The symbolism suggests that Americans like to see themselves—and, with the help of the press (Mercury) generally *do* see themselves—as people primarily concerned with security, not necessarily or usually in any aggressive sense but out of a concern for life, out of a concern for safety and a desire to protect their children (Cancer). Three other Cancer planets—the Sun, Venus (the Midheaven ruler), and Jupiter (the Ascendant ruler)—reiterate these tendencies, though as ruler of the ascen-

---

[3]As the natural ruler of the second house, the house associated with one's own values and finances, Venus clearly has a lot to do with money. In the United States' horoscope, the interconnections between the second house and the eighth, most evident in the Mercury-Pluto opposition but also via Venus (the natural ruler of the second house on the cusp of the eighth), points to the myriad ways in which the United States' wealth has always derived from "the values of others" (eighth house).

[4]The eighth house symbolizes the values of others. The afflicted planets there (Sun and Mercury) suggest that notions related to family values don't really sit as comfortably with Americans as we might think. This might account for the way the United States has traditionally disrupted the family values of others, starting with Native Americans and extending through African and Vietnamese villages, the former in order to take people as slaves, the latter as part of an unprovoked invasion driven by financial obsessions (second and eighth houses). Numerous other examples could be cited.

dant and indicator of expansion, Jupiter participates in the imperialistic aggression that has for so long purportedly served "national security interests."[5]

Cancer certainly suggests security; the Sun in Cancer suggests a national identity rooted in security-orientation and in a search for a safe home-ground; Mercury there suggests identity-issues supported by ideas (and, as noted, by the press). The eighth house suggests that the United States will find this security by incorporating, or simply taking, the values or goods of others. With a Sagittarius ascendant and ruling Jupiter in the eighth, the United States expands (Jupiter) driven by ideologies (Sagittarius; also Mercury and, perhaps most importantly, Neptune in the ninth house, discussed below) supporting a domination of others' resources (eighth house). Thus the United States finds its security (Cancer) rooted in eighth house concerns (the finances and resources of others), but furthers its purposes via a constant reiteration of purported principles (Sagittarius) and often confuses security-needs (Cancer) with a desire for affluence (Venus-Jupiter).

The eighth house suggests that much of the U.S. identity-structure (Sun, ascendant ruler Jupiter) comes from the resources of others. American family life, with its ongoing (and some would say rather myopic) affluence, depends on the wealth that the United States has derived from foreign sources. And, of course, right from the beginning, the European invaders took their home ground from Native Americans, taking what those people valued (e.g. the land) and building purportedly secure homes there, apparently without much concern for the securities of the people they displaced (Native Americans), or, later, stole (Africans) or dominated (e.g. people in oil- or mineral-rich nations). No nation on earth has such a far-flung economic empire. The coffee that Americans[6] drink in the morning comes from places where the U.S. has achieved economic, and often military, hegemony; similarly for car-tires, computers, bicycles, televisions, and many other possessions. The U.S. depends on other nations for the oil that powers cars and heats homes; Americans can purchase everything relatively cheaply because labor in third world countries costs so much less than does American labor. All of this reflects the eighth house: the money or values of others. "Free Trade" agreements, encouraged by the U.S. government, make the taking all that much easier.

But it often seems that, remaining blind to the source of its wealth, the U.S. at a certain point considers the wealth of others as its own, and from that stolen wealth Americans derive a certain view of themselves. Further, because of that wealth, Americans become very concerned with "national security," an appropriate term for a country with the Sun and three other planets in Cancer, particularly when that security (Cancer) is so bound up with the values and goods of others (eighth house) and thus quite vulnerable. The U.S. has gained control over these resources largely through expansion (Sagittarius rising; Jupiter in the eighth) rooted in a quasi-religious ideology (Sagittarius;

---

[5] Though this phrase has come into wide use only in the past few decades, we can see the centuries-long aggression against Native Americans as serving "national security interests." Certainly Americans often saw native peoples as threats to their security—and, obviously, vice-versa.

[6] I use this term well-aware that people in Mexico, Canada, Guatemala, and other nations in the Western Hemisphere could also go by the same title. Here, obviously enough, I intend the word as a synonym for "citizens of the United States."

Neptune in the ninth)—not "democracy" so much as "free enterprise," which came to mean the right to achieve economic domination over others.

The Sun and other important planets in the eighth house suggest that the American "creative spirit"—the creative spirit of a people constantly seeking security—arises through this acquisitive process, this *enterprise* (for the word comes from roots meaning "to take"[7]). Jupiter and Venus, the two benefics, suggest that Americans have generally seen this process as good and healthy (though, as noted, the 2012 transits from Saturn seem to have brought more awareness and self-criticism); the conjunction between the Ascendant ruler and the Midheaven ruler suggests that Americans experience good fortune and plenty by engaging in such acquisitive activities. U.S. leaders continually portray the U.S. as the harbinger, bringer, promulgator, and transmitter of freedom, of uplifted or civilized values—convictions suggested by the Venus-Jupiter conjunction. However, though Venus-Jupiter may confer luck or abundance, it does not seem to confer honesty, particularly in a country with a Mars-Neptune square. Other nations will probably not put such a positive spin on U.S. actions—and if we look at the situation from an astrological perspective, we would probably conclude that the United States' enterprises have less to do with bringing freedom than with taking things from other people. That both the eighth house Sun and the eighth house Mercury receive challenging aspects suggests that the U.S. will make a not-entirely-altruistic use of others' resources, money, or energy.

The United States takes what doesn't belong to it even as government rhetoric attempts to convince the people (and members of the government itself!) that this taking will benefit the people deprived of what belongs to them. It may seem obvious enough to an objective observer that the people being deprived *don't* benefit, but if the eighth house planets get bound up in projections, the United States (people or government) will have a hard time attaining objectivity. When, as in the United States horoscope, the planets receive hard aspects,[8] we would expect projections and lack of objectivity regarding eighth house matters.

The Mercury-Pluto opposition suggests that something in the American psyche rejects the Pluto energy and will see it more readily in other nations than in the United States itself—and this despite the fact that Pluto plays such a prominent role in the horoscope, and thus in the United States' psyche. Though most nations see the United States as the world's major plutonic power (in more ways than one, certainly), Americans have throughout their history seen others as the carriers of a dark, threatening, destructive power. Though the U.S. has harnessed underworld gods (e.g. via the plutonium research and extensive mining operations), Americans generally see others as the carriers of this underworld energy. Pluto in the second house suggests that the U.S. derives money from power and power from money, acquiring and maintaining wealth through financial means con-

---

[7] Joseph T. Shipley, *Dictionary of Word Origins* (New York: The Philosophical Library, 1945), 345.
[8] Squares and oppositions.

nected with underworld powers, and that its plutonic elites shape the financial structure of the nation and the course of public opinion (Mercury). Yet Americans have constantly had great concern with others, seen as threatening, who live on land enriched by those same underworld gods (e.g. oil in the Middle East, uranium in lands once owned and later granted to the Native Americans).

Most obviously, the United States harbors most of the world's plutonium-based weapons. Further, U.S. weapons of all stripes, clearly linked to plutocratic concerns, provide the power that the United States brings to bear in order to protect its wealth. Other nations see the United States as the world's power-broker, and the U.S. does an ongoing and manipulative trade in arms, most obviously to Israel but to other nations as well, so that even its enemies (e.g. Iraq) have guns made in the United States, a fact reflecting both the U.S. seventh house Mars (see below) and its Pluto. Thus, the U.S. gets wealth (second) from power (Pluto) and power from wealth. The U.S. deals with the world through that power and wealth, killing or having clients kill thousands upon thousands in order to further national designs. Small wonder that most of the world sees the U.S. as a terrorist state. Yet though the U.S. terrorizes others, it sees terrorists as the enemy. From a psychological point of view, the nation's virulent fear and hatred of terrorists strongly suggests unacknowledged terrorists within—terrorists including not only various white supremacist groups but also the government itself. Not liking to see itself in the Plutonic role, the U.S. projects Pluto onto other nations or groups.

During the last decades of the 20th century and the first decade of the 21st, the United States has hung it Pluto-projection[9] most often onto the so-called Arab Terrorist groups and Iraq, with the focus now (2012) perhaps shifting to Iran and Pakistan. United States' pronouncements about all these groups or nations sound remarkably similar, as the government lumps them together as enemies and threats to national security. For the past decade, the U.S. has fought a war against "insurgents," "terrorists," and "Taliban" throughout the Afghan countryside, allegedly to root out terrorist groups, more likely to gain some degree of control over resources (eighth). This war—essentially, a war against the country's own projections—quickly extended to other parts of the Middle East and has affected millions of ordinary people in that part of the world, people who most likely just want to live their lives and raise their families and who have no important connection with terrorist activities. But the U.S. identifies itself with Cancerian security and so doesn't see Cancer qualities in others. If those others merely want to raise their families and farm their land, the U.S. doesn't notice; and those people, the hooks for the U.S. projection, have projec*tiles* aimed at them constantly. In the often-myopic vision perpetuated with particular strength inside the Beltway, those people appear Plutonic and the U.S. sees itself as acting accordingly. Just as in Vietnam, U.S. soldiers often couldn't distinguish between peasant farmers and Viet Cong, so in Afghanistan, Pakistan, and other places, the U.S. can't seem to distinguish terrorists from people who want most of all just to defend—and live in!—their homes.[10]

---

[9]See earlier remarks on projections and hooks.
[10]In the Middle East, the U.S. projection of Pluto seems to have effected a fusion (typical for Pluto), as U.S. attacks have surely turned many farmers into at least terrorist sympathizers. The longer the United States occupies a country, the more

In disowning its Pluto and projecting it onto others, the U.S. sees those people largely through a Plutonic lens. They then appear, particularly in the plutocrat dominated mainstream media (Mercury opposed Pluto), as darkly secretive people harboring and supporting terrorists, or as terrorists themselves. And yet, as noted, most of the world sees the United States as the major terrorist power. If we define terrorism as the threatening of civilians in order to gain political or economic ends (a phrase I think I've borrowed from Noam Chomsky[11]), we would quite appropriately refer to the attack on the World Trade Center as "terrorism"; however, using the same definition, we would also describe United States-sponsored actions in Central America, South America, the Middle East, and elsewhere as terrorist acts, though of the wholesale variety instead of the retail type practiced by official "enemies." Surely civilians in those places suffer enormously because of the United States' pursuit of political and economic aims or its attempts to protect the "national interests."

"Terrorists," and even the Taliban or Saddam Hussein, serve as perfect hooks for a projection of Pluto. As we have seen in previous chapters, if the hook for one's projections has some characteristics associated with the projected planet, then the projector (in this case the United States) will have difficulty seeing through the projections, for they will seem to accord well with "reality." Because the projected-upon groups in the Middle East (and elsewhere) sometimes terrorize people, they serve quite well as hooks. Thus they make it that much easier for the U.S. to ignore the plutonic elements in the national psychology and evident in the nation's history. Further, if the theories presented in this book have merit, then U.S. projections contribute to the egregious behavior of the people on whom the U.S. casts the projection. If we use again the football analogy from earlier chapter, we would say that the United States has handed to alleged terrorists its own Pluto-energy. As a result, with both their own Pluto-football and that of the U.S., those people will act in increasingly Plutonic ways.[12]

In a relationship with many similarities to its relationship with American Indians, the United States treats most Arabs and other Middle Easterners (and, it seems, dark-skinned people generally) as not-quite-human; the United States takes what belongs to them and kills them when they resist. We might say of the United States' relation to such groups what Michael Paul Rogin says of the invading Europeans' relation with American Indians: that it "belongs to the pathology of human development,"[13] for it arises from fantasies and unresolved psychic contents in the invaders and demonstrates the "triumph of the death instinct—the murderous rage at any phenomenon with a life of its own." This holds true even though, as Rogin says about that earlier era, the work "was not the work of paranoids and social madmen, but of a consensus of almost all of our leading political

---

the term terrorist-farmers seems appropriate.

[11] I acknowledge the influence of Noam Chomsky on this and other passages in this section.

[12] It seems that this kind of shift clearly occurs rather often in international affairs. If you take away a person's home because you consider him unworthy, you reduce his options: you can in some sense turn him into your projection. That this occurs so often in international affairs strongly suggests that it also occurs in interpersonal ones.

[13] Michael Paul Rogin, *Fathers and Children: Andrew Jackson and the Subjugation of the American Indian* (New York: Vintage Books, 1976), 9.

and intellectual figures" and that the sources of white expansion "seem straightforward."[14] Further, it seems evident that more-recent U.S. invasions obviously bring up the underworld demons in the invaded people, particularly if the invader remains blind to the consequences of his actions and threatens the lives and well-being of those who serve as hooks for the projections. Those perpetrated upon, weaker in conventional military strength, take a plutonic approach to power: acting in secret, hatching plots, performing terrorist acts, and so forth. At the same time, an account of United States' secret and underhanded actions would take up some volumes and would include many actions presented by government as appropriate and necessary.

We will look, below, at the synastry between the United States and Iraq, an examination that will show us how each nation projects its own negative qualities onto the other, resulting in stagnation and warfare, a situation that provides a graphic illustration of Ms. von Franz's principle that being hit by someone else's projection feels like getting hit by a projec*tile*. That so many peoples in the world have been hit by American-made projectiles should tell us something, at least; that all wars seem to involve projectile-sending surely suggests something about the psychological roots of such conflicts. But before going into the facts on the ground, we should ask ourselves why the U.S. remains so blind to its projection of Pluto. Why, with the facts easily available, do so many people in this country remain so steadfastly in the dark? To answer this question, we need to look more carefully at Mercury in the U.S. horoscope.

In a nation's horoscope, Mercury rules the press, communications, the postal and telephone services, transportation of all sorts, the content of national opinion and its means of promulgation, as well as worries or cares of the population-at-large (Mercury having much to do with anxiety or nervousness). The third house in a nation's horoscope (a house always connected with Mercury, and in the United States horoscope the location of the Moon, dispositor of Mercury and the other Cancer planets) has to do with means of movement (rails, roads, etc.), with travel and communication within a nation's borders (hence, again, the domestic press and all means of moving information from one place to another) as well as neighboring nations. Here we should look carefully at matters concerning national opinion (already discussed), the press—and, interestingly enough given post 9-11 anthrax scares, even the post office.

We have already seen that the voice of national opinion in the U.S. keeps telling us about security, about the family—about what we might call nationalism with a national security spin. That voice of national opinion has been strongly influenced by plutocrats (Pluto). Obviously enough, plutocrats—dominant financial interests and power-brokers—control the major media outlets in this country; accordingly, the press pretty much parrots the ideas of the people with money. Little serious dissent surfaces in those major outlets, either now or in the past.[15] The flame of patriotic

---

[14]Rogin, 11.
[15]The periods leading up to WWI and both Gulf Wars, and the periods following the latter, provide excellent examples. Some will see the Vietnam period as an exception, but even there the press went along with government propaganda for many years, and very few newspapers questioned the basic government version of the situation: that the problems in Vietnam amounted to a Civil War; that we were battling the expansionist communist surge.

fervor gets fanned as much as the power-brokers deem necessary. Thus Chomsky writes, of the Creel Commission and other efforts, that

> ….during the First World War, American historians offered themselves to President Woodrow Wilson to carry out a task that they called "historical engineering," meaning designing the facts of history so that they would serve state policy…Shortly after that, American journalists like Walter Lippman, the famous American journalist, said in 1921 that the art of democracy requires what he called "manufacture of consent," what the public relations industry calls "engineering of consent…The idea was that in a state in which the government can't control the people by force it had better control what they think.[16]

As for the post office, a mover of information and thus under the influence of Mercury, it had to deal with anthrax-threats initially announced by law enforcement as from domestic sources, though very quickly the press launched the idea that the anthrax had possibly come from bin Laden or other "terrorists." One congressman even said that though he knew there was no good evidence to support his conclusion, he nonetheless felt that the anthrax problem was connected with terrorists from overseas, bin Laden in particular. (Pluto-driven obsessions do not require evidence.) The astrological evidence suggests that it has come from the United States: natal Pluto lies in the second house, the house of the country's own values, not the house of others' values. Thus, the astrological factors suggest that the anthrax threat seems to have arisen at home, as later evidence suggested.

Mercury's opposition to Pluto certainly suggests the control of media and public opinion by plutonic powers. We see, here, the disturbing connection between the so-called freedom of speech about which Americans so proudly proclaim—represented by Aquarius on the third house cusp, and by the Moon, dispositor of Mercury and other Cancer planets, in the third house in Aquarius—and the entrenched financial interests that simply don't allow certain information to appear in their publications, or who marginalize (to borrow Chomsky's term) everything that suggests another vantage or framing of that information. The whole process remains largely hidden from public view (Pluto), though available to those who wish either to dig beneath the surface or draw simple inferences from the obvious: the horoscope has both Mercury and Pluto in retrograde motion and Mercury in the eighth; Pluto rules the twelfth house (secrets), and Cancer has a well-deserved reputation for reticence. Thus most citizens remain dutifully unaware of what controls public opinion or even that that anyone does so. (These factors describe the situation that has prevailed until recently; however, with Pluto transiting through Capricorn and Uranus through Aries, and with Saturn having transited recently through a square to both Mercury and Pluto, we have seen and will see much heretofore largely-unacknowledged material coming to the surface. Wikileaks seems a harbinger of things to come.)

Noam Chomsky gives an example of the control of media by powerful interests. He notes that

---

[16]Noam Chomsky, interviewed by David Barsamian, *Stenographers to Power* (Monroe, ME: Common Courage Press, 1992), 5.

back in 1990 and 1991, on the eve of the Gulf War, Iraq proposed bringing into possible peace negotiations matters related to nuclear proliferation and offered

> …to withdraw from Kuwait but in the context of a settlement of regional strategic issues, including the banning of weapons of mass destruction. That position was recognized as "serious" and "negotiable" by State Department Middle East experts. Independently of this, that happened to be the position of about two-thirds of the American public according to the final polls that were taken before the war—a couple of days before.
>
> We do not know whether these Iraqi proposals were indeed serious and negotiable as State Department officials concluded. The reason we don't know is that they were rejected out of hand by the United States. They were suppressed to nearly a hundred percent efficiency by the media. There were a few leaks here and there. And they've been effectively removed from history.[17]

As a result of the plutocratic mass media, the U.S. saw Hussein only as an unreasonable terrorist who listened to no-one. That these characteristics appear even more clearly in U.S. behavior points to the projection onto Hussein of specific elements of the United States' own psychology. The U.S. tended to see him as concerned only with power, as a cruel tyrant who would sacrifice any number of people in order to gain his own ends. And, of course, Hussein served nicely as a hook for U.S. projections precisely because of his cruelty and of the way he killed so many people in order to maintain his power—precisely because, like any terrorist,[18] he sacrificed civilians in order to gain political, ideological, or financial ends.[19] That he served so nicely as a hook tells us why the United States people have had such a difficult time seeing through the projection—and why they've had such difficulty seeing the United States' role clearly. Understandably enough, one might say, considering the influence of the plutocratic press.[20]

The last few sentences of Chomsky's remarks relate to the control of the media by American power-brokers. "Public opinion" falls under Pluto's control (i.e. Pluto opposes Mercury). Noel Tyl connects Pluto to "world perspective," an accurate delineation as far as it goes. But Pluto's symbolism also includes various other matters: power, power related to money, hidden power brokered in back rooms, and all sorts of financially motivated and supported manipulations. Pluto in the second house of the U.S. horoscope suggests that the entire U.S. economy and value system serve

---

[17]Noam Chomsky, *Prospects for Peace in the Middle East* (http://www.chomsky.info/talks/20010304.htm).

[18]If we label Hussein as a terrorist, we reject the U. S. government's own definition of terrorism. In the 2002 Report on Terrorism issued by the state department, our government says quite explicitly that terrorists operate outside the purview of nation states. The definition, convenient enough for U.S. policy-ends, has implications not apparently considered by those who offered it.

[19]This sentence owes much to Chomsky's definition of the term.

[20]Domestic plutocratic powers have much to gain if the United States dominates Iraq, for if the United States controls Iraq it accomplishes two ends: it gets cheaper oil, and it gains access to "free markets" for U.S. corporations (i.e. plutocrats).

such interests. Pluto's opposition to Mercury symbolizes the control of the U.S. media and public opinion by such interests. The factors enumerated above suggest that the process remains hidden, though we can see the results quite clearly[21]: a tightly-controlled description of international affairs, a description that passes for "world perspective" but which is really the "plutonic perspective," the perspective offered by plutocrats, a perspective tightly controlled and with enormous controlling power.

Further Evidence

Both U.S. attacks on Iraq correlated with important developments involving the Mercury-Pluto opposition. The first attack took place on January 17, 1991. Saturn conjoined the U.S. Pluto on January 16, having opposed Mercury on December 18, 1990. Furthermore, a lunar eclipse occurred on January 15 at 25 Capricorn 20, just a few degrees from conjoining Pluto and a bit over a degree from opposing Mercury.[22] Mars served as a trigger: retrograde during the entire troop-buildup in Saudi Arabia, he turned direct on New Years Day at 27 Taurus 45, directly square the United States Moon (27 Aquarius 12), so the U.S. people found themselves in a fighting mood, ready to defend the country against alleged threats; that natal Mars squares natal Neptune warns us to watch for deception in the works. With natal Mars in the seventh house, the transit brought yet another iteration of the nation's tendency to see others as threats even as the United States threatens them and to go to war based on a series of deceptions (natal Mars-Neptune). Transiting Neptune opposed the U.S. Sun on December 10 (1990) and squared the U.S. Saturn on January 19, aspects suggesting deception emanating from the ruling hierarchy and in service to the reigning U.S. ideology (natal Neptune in the ninth house), leading to military aggression (natal Neptune square natal Mars); Mars, in the seventh house and disposited by Mercury, suggests that due to the machinations of the plutocratic press, the citizenry registered the deception as coming from somewhere else (Iraq, suspected of all sorts of hidden and deceptive tactics).[22] Chiron also participated, having turned retrograde in early November 1990 very close to an opposition to U.S. Pluto and moving back to conjoin U.S. Mercury on January 16.

The United States launched Gulf War II, the actual invasion of Iraq, on March 19, 2003, with transiting Saturn conjoining the U.S. seventh house Mars,"[23] triggering the habitual projection of

---

[21]Pluto rules the twelfth, a house connected with secrets even though it lies above the horizon, suggesting that we can see the secret material in behavior.

[22]The U. S. Sun-Saturn square points to the national security (Cancer) bureaucracy (Saturn) that so often serves as the expressive arm of the country. Richard Barnet writes (*Intervention and Revolution*, p.29):
"Classic theories of economic imperialism, which view the state as an agent of the most powerful domestic economic interests, underestimate the independent role of the national-security bureaucracy which in the United States has taken on a life and movement of its own." Any transit, progression, or direction involving Mars or Neptune brings to the fore the tendency, mentioned above, to act deceptively on behalf of a deceptive national ideology or vision (Neptune in the ninth househ) and to see others as the aggressors even when objective observers see the U.S. as the aggressor (Mars in the seventh house). Any transit, progression, or direction involving the Sun-Saturn square brings the national security structure into the picture, along with the United States' ongoing insistence on playing the authority-role (Saturn in the tenth house) in all relations involving the values of others (Sun in the eighth house).

[23]Saturn had separated from the exact conjunction by about a degree, having made a station within a degree of natal Mars

Mars (seventh house) onto other nations or groups. Thus the U.S. insisted on seeing Iraq as the threat, the potential aggressor even though the U.S. initiated the attacks and Iraq never threatened the U.S., continuing the pattern discussed above. Transiting Pluto remained in the U.S. first house (powerful action; action driven by plutocratic concerns even as we projected Pluto onto Iraq).[24]

Despite the importance of Saturn's transit, solar arc directions played the dominant role during this second attack.[25] Six months before the attack, as the build-up to invasion was taking place, largely through the auspices of the plutonic press (Mercury opposed Pluto), the solar arc Ascendant opposed the U.S. Pluto, activating the Mercury-Pluto opposition. Also, at the time of the invasion, solar arc Pluto had moved to within about half a degree of a square with the U.S. Ascendant from the ninth house. Other solar arc directions provided background: the solar arc Moon approached Saturn, while solar arc Saturn separated from its square to the U.S. Moon in late Aquarius; solar arc Uranus opposed natal Mercury, activating the Mercury-Pluto opposition. This last aspect reminds of the tremendous resistance to the war evident in one of the most extensive anti-war movements this country has seen, a movement not well-reported in the "major media," but which included people from all economic groups and which demonstrated a profound split in the American public, suggested by, among other factors, the activated Mercury-Pluto opposition and the very different emphases of the Aquarius Moon's two rulers (Saturn and Uranus). Because all transits, progressions, and directions bring relevant natal factors forward, we find the influence of the U.S. natal chart in these solar arc directions:

- Pluto's solar arc direction brings forward the natal Mercury-Pluto opposition: hence the influence of the press and the activation of the country's tendency to project Pluto onto others while seeing itself as a nice, family-oriented, security-seeking bunch of emotional and vulnerable home-owners. According to the Bush and cohorts, Iraq presented a direct threat to the United States.[26]

---

in late February. The symbolism of the conjunction suggests cold, cruel anger related to "open enemies" (seventh house). Note the interaction between the Mars-Neptune square and the Sun-Saturn square, one similar to the interaction that triggered the invasion of Mexico in 1846.

[24]Also, significantly, Jupiter (expansion) was on George Bush II's Ascendant: he felt in need to of some personal expansion, some personal self-expression.

[25]That is, directions as distinguished from transits. Transits measure the actual movements of planets in the sky. If we have a good enough telescope and know where to look, we can see the transiting planets. Solar arc directions, on the other hand, do not reflect astronomical realities. Each year, we move each planet by the "solar arc," the distance the sun moves in a day. As this distance averages about a degree, the solar arc positions for the tenth year will be about ten degrees in advance of the natal positions. However, the measure diverges from the degree/year measure as one goes on in years; for a country born in 1776, the two measures will differ a good deal by the end of the 20th century.

[26]Each of the three challenging aspects from solar arc Pluto to the U.S. Ascendant have led to what we might call international assertions on the part of the U.S. The 1823 square from the third house brought the Monroe Doctrine, in which the U.S. asserted its exclusive rights in the Western Hemisphere (over, notably, millions of native peoples who had not given their consent); the opposition in 1915 brought World War I and the plutocratic press's drive to get the U.S. involved; the 2003 square from the ninth house found U.S. troops making "long journeys over water" to fight a battle with important ideological roots back in 1823.

- The Sagittarius Ascendant again appears through the desire to expand. Solar arc Pluto's square to that Ascendant thus indicates a powerful desire to expand, but also a tendency to see plutonic forces as enemies (due to the natal Mercury-Pluto opposition). Also, the U.S. press, nominally free even if surreptitiously controlled, constantly points out the problems with government control of the press in enemy countries. The solar arc Ascendant also opposed natal Pluto, reiterating the importance of these matters.

- Thus as the U.S. projects Pluto *onto* Iraq, the U.S. exerts power *over* Iraq in an effort to expand the national sphere of influence through taking control of others' values (e.g. oil). Because the aspect from solar arc Pluto is a square, U.S. actions affect the extensional situation in structural ways. Thus, we see a change of government in Iraq. Because the square comes from the ninth house, we find ourselves exerting power—and battling with our projections—after a "long journey over water."

- Throughout, we see the influence of Pluto and the difficult square: a use of power many find inappropriate, driven by unconscious impulses and obsessions. And the U.S. doesn't take responsibility for its own power or its own destructiveness, seeing Pluto only in Iraq and not at home.

- The horoscopes for both Iraq and Saddam Hussein also have oppositions running from the third decanate of Cancer to the third decanate of Capricorn: Hussein has Jupiter at 26 Capricorn and Pluto at 26 Cancer; Iraq has Saturn at 28 Capricorn and Pluto at 23 Cancer. Clearly the United States has found some hooks for its projections: when it looks toward its Pluto, it sees Saddam Hussein's Jupiter and thus fears Hussein's alleged expansionism (conveniently ignoring the home-grown version); it also sees Iraq's Saturn and its alleged intransigence, along with Iraq's long tradition and infrastructure. (See below.)

All of this combined with the 2004-2005 opposition from transiting Pluto to natal Mars and the closely coinciding square from transiting Pluto to natal Neptune. Pluto-Mars combinations suggest ruthless power just as the Pluto-Sagittarius combination, via the square from solar arc Pluto to the Sagittarius Ascendant, suggests ruthless expansion. Thus, ruthless power used in service to a ruthless expansion, all in the name of security (Cancer) based on the acquisition of the resources, values, and properties of others.

With the opposition from transiting Pluto to natal Mars, as with so many oppositions, a split occurred. Here, however, we have the joining of two planets that the U.S. typically projects onto others. As a result, the different parties took on now one role, now another: the U.S. sometimes played the role of Pluto, acting powerfully against an open enemy (Mars in the seventh house); sometimes, the U.S. played the role of Mars (military aggression), attacking an enemy characterized as Plutonic; sometimes the whole aspect appeared in projected form: as Hussein and Iraq purportedly marshaling hidden power as an open enemy. Many in the United States would probably have said, as the invasion began, that the United States was using its military (Mars) against the forces of darkness (Hussein, Iraq, terrorists in general); I suspect that many people in Iraq felt themselves invaded by the plutonic (wealthy and with a lot of plutonium available) barbarians. In any case, when you start a war against your own projections, you cannot win, for even if you *seem* to win, you find later that you have somehow metamorphosed into the enemy, or something very much like him. Besides, we know that Pluto constantly metamorphoses into other forms: the U.S. will always think that it has terrorists to fight, though the projection falls on different groups as the decades pass.

United States Uranus Near the Natal Descendant

The United States has a reputation, at least within its own borders, as a supporter, promulgator, and defender of freedom. Its third president, Thomas Jefferson, once said that a country will remain healthy if it has a revolution every generation (or something to that effect). Indeed, with the national Moon in Aquarius, partly ruled by Uranus, the people in the United States like to see themselves as freedom loving and progressive. Furthermore, with its Uranus near an angle and its Sagittarius Ascendant, the United States indeed has a connection to freedom and to principles. However, we get a different view when we include other factors in the analysis. For example, the opposition from Mercury, dispositor of the Cancer Moon, to Pluto suggests what we have discussed above: an insistence on security and a tendency to remain blind to some of the darker elements in the national character. Further, though Uranus does conjoin an angle, it conjoins the *Descendant*, suggesting that the United States will project Uranus onto others, which seems to have occurred again and again in international relations even if in the United States people have more freedoms than do the people in most other countries.

Certainly the U.S. generally does not take progressive stances in its dealings with other nations, and it almost always fears revolutionaries, leftists, and alleged upsetters of international apple-carts. In other words, despite its self-congratulatory self-image as the purveyor of freedom throughout the world, despite the national folklore in which the country promulgates and defends freedom, despite a Declaration of Independence that talks about the right of people to revolt against tyranny, and despite a Bill of Rights that purportedly enshrines human freedom and dignity and protects them against all incursions—despite all that, the United States generally finds freedomfighters threatening. Some of this ambivalence reflects Aquarius' dual rulership: partly ruled by Saturn, the eleventh sign doesn't always align itself with progressives. In the U.S. horoscope, Saturn, exalted by sign, dignified by house position, and with close aspects to both the Sun and Ascendant, seems to dominate the country's public behavior much more than Uranus does. Though as a representative of the Shadow, Saturn doesn't appear readily in the consciousness of individual Americans, replaced there by the aforementioned ideas related to freedom, its position in the horoscope doesn't suggest a proneness to projection. Though it generally doesn't appear in Americans' self-evaluations, it appears quite clearly in national ambitions; so does the projection of Uranus.

The projection of Uranus first appeared in dealings with the American Indians even before the U.S. birthday, for Indians' exercise of freedom appeared as a threat to the expanding nation (Sagittarius Ascendant), not only because Indian groups resented the invaders' territorial incursions, but also because native control of land stood in the way of economic and political expansion. The vast tracts of available land in the so-called New World lured many thousands of people from Europe, for in America they could advance more quickly from servitude, indentured or otherwise, to prosperity. Though Indians sometimes represented Pluto in the national consciousness, sometimes they represented Uranus as well, for they rebelled against the advancing materialistic tide that would within centuries sweep over the entire continent. Historian Carl Degler sees this materialism as a formative principle in the development of the American nation:

> The relative ease with which wealth could be accumulated stimulated a materialistic drive among even those in the lower ranks of society who would probably never live on Beacon Hill or lower Broadway.... Even the usually sanguine and democratic [French-American writer and author of *Letter from an American Farmer* in 1787] Crevecoeur was disturbed by the obvious scramble for money among individuals....The ambitious American, intent on his own success, Crevecoeur sadly noted, was harsh and even fraudulent in his dealings with...new arrivals. The American, he wrote, appears "litigious, overbearing, purse-proud." After 1740, when the wars with the French provided wider and more frequent opportunities for the piling up of wealth and the perpetrating of highly profitable, if dubious, commercial deals, colonial incomes and avarice scaled new heights. While British and colonial soldiers and seamen were dying fighting the French and Indians in the forests of the West and on the high seas, other colonials were lucratively trading with the enemy.[27]

The Indians, not prone to accumulate wealth and without the emphasis on monetary systems that we see in the invaders, surely seemed like rebels, ready to stand by their own freedom instead of giving in to the "advance of civilization."

Furthermore, the Alien and Sedition Acts of 1798 and 1795 made it a crime to publish "false, scandalous, and malicious writing" against the government or some government officials.[28] Directly partly against those (like Jefferson) advocating states' rights, and partly against those fomenting what some saw as revolutionary tendencies in the young republic, the Acts generated enormous opposition but remained in effect. Even though this legislation inspired a pointed response from Jefferson and a more careful defining of freedom of the press in the United States,[29] we can see the effects of such laws even today as dissidents find themselves hounded by federal agents, thrown in jail, and in some cases killed. In general, anyone who has spoken out against the expansionist empire (Sagittarius rising), and even many who have spoken in favor of it (e.g. Jefferson) have found themselves in the crosshairs (the crosshairs themselves suggesting Mars in the seventh house; see below). Thus Saddam Hussein became an enemy not when he killed untold thousands of Kurds, for he did that with complete U.S. complicity and support, but when he threatened to upset the

---

[27] Carl N. Degler, *Out of Our Past: The Forces That Shaped Modern America* (New York: Harper and Row, 1984), 48- 9.
[28] See section 2 of the Sedition Act of 1798.
[29] Degler, 71.

status quo that the United States wanted to maintain in the Middle East. Thus Ho Chi Minh appeared as an enemy no matter how many times he professed his respect for the Declaration of Independence and his admiration for those who had put their signatures on it. These examples support the hypothesis given above: that the projection of Pluto gets mixed with the projection of Uranus (and of Mars, as noted): the hooks for these projections seem to the U.S. not only as dark and threatening (Pluto), but also as progressive or revolutionary.

The U.S. Sagittarius Ascendant symbolizes the way the United States most naturally enters into relations with others; the polar opposite descendant gives us information about both alliances and open enemies. Throughout its history, in ways completely evident to any objective observer, the United States has expanded its horizons constantly; rampant expansionism characterized the colonists' behavior even before the onset of nationhood. The United States has remained bent on ideology-driven expansion, and with Jupiter, ruler of that Ascendant, conjoining Venus, ruler of the Libra Midheaven, on the cusp of the eighth house and in Cancer, the expansionism purportedly supports security via the securing of other nations' or peoples' resources, as noted. And once we arrive at Cancer, we find ourselves working with the U.S. Saturn, who squares the U.S. Cancer Sun. Thus the United States, despite the promulgated rhetoric about progressive ideas and freedom, aligns itself with any status quo that enables or empowers the taking of others' resources as the national life-blood.

Uranus' position near the Descendant but in the sixth suggests that when the United States attempts to expand, ideologically or militarily, it will find itself opposed (Descendant: open enemies) by people who seem unequal (sixth house), certainly in military strength, but also in moral quality as the U.S. evaluates such matters. The Sagittarius Ascendant symbolizes the United States' conviction that the country acts on principles; combined with Neptune in the ninth house it symbolizes the conviction that the U.S. occupies the highest moral ground available, a pattern traceable throughout this country's history but which reached a nodal point in the mid-19th century with the promulgation of the notion of Manifest Destiny. For example, in 1846, Thomas Gilpin, friend to Andrew Jackson, wrote that the *"untransacted* destiny of the American people" is

> ...to subdue the continent—to rush over this vast field to the Pacific Ocean—animate the many hundred millions of its people, and to cheer them upward...to regenerate superannuated nations—...to cause a stagnant people to be reborn—...to shed a new and resplendent glory upon mankind—to unite the world in one social family—to dissolve the spell of tyranny and exalt charity—to absolve the curse that weighs down humanity, and to shed blessings around the world.[30]

Though Manifest Destiny seems connected most obviously to natal Neptune in the ninth (see below), it also has a close connection to the Sagittarius ascendant and Uranus. The people who found

---

[30] Qtd. in Henry Nash Smith's *Virgin Land* (NYC, 1950, p. 40; then qtd. in Rogin, page 296. Gilpin spoke these words in 1846, the year of Neptune's discovery. In the U.S. ninth house, Neptune suggests a deceptive national vision. See next section for a further discussion.

themselves in the path of Manifest Destiny, however allegedly unequal, always seemed to hold to the iconoclastic idea that they should remain masters of their own destinies and owners of their own land—that they should remain free agents (Uranus). We can trace these patterns through the historical record. For example, one of the less-advertised parts of the so-called Monroe Doctrine states that the United States will not support revolutionary movements until those movements established themselves as duly-constituted ruling establishments. A hundred and eighty years later, the U.S. invaded Iraq not because Iraq had broken any law or acted in any way that the U.S. hadn't already (and, of course, the U.S. had provided Saddam Hussein with the arms he needed to slaughter his own people), but because Hussein had gotten out of line, had gotten too big for his warlordly britches. Something similar had occurred some decades earlier in Iran, when Mohammed Mosaddegh had tried to nationalize the oil industry, an attempt deemed unacceptable by the U.S. (and by Great Britain, as Churchill urged the U.S. to get involved), a nation that sees other nations' resources as its own. With the two benefics, rulers of the Ascendant and Midheaven,[31] in Cancer and the eighth house, the United States sees moral and material benefic accruing when we use other nations' materials to ensure the security (Cancer) of the American people.

So whereas in relation to the Mercury-Pluto opposition, the United States plays the role of Mercury and thus sees itself as composed of people concerned with their security and their homes, not as a rapacious country with an increasingly plutonic government and enough plutonium stockpiled to destroy the world several times over, in relation to the opposition from Uranus to the Ascendant, the United States plays the role of the Sagittarius Ascendant, advocating principles of various sorts and allegedly expressing those principles through expansion and the expression of good will, the while continually opposed by so-called insurgents or revolutionaries who resist U.S. efforts at purportedly beneficent domination. It may seem strange that a country born from a revolution, particularly one that inspired so many important statements about human rights, would project Uranus onto others. It would probably come as news to many U.S. citizens that this occurs at all, for the U.S. Aquarius Moon tells us that the people see themselves as progressive thinkers.[32] The Aquarius Moon in the third house disposits Mercury in Cancer and thus tells us a lot about how Mercury expresses itself: through convictions about social good. This last phrase reflects Aquarius, a sign with a reputation for progressive thinking but that often expresses itself through restriction and recalcitrance.

The Mars-Neptune Square

As the closest hard aspect in the horoscope, the Mars-Neptune square points directly to the United States' vocational drives. Unfortunately, it generally arises as a combination of deception

---

[31]Jupiter rules the U.S. Sagittarius Ascendant; Venus rules the United States' Libra Midheaven.

[32]This doesn't contradict what I said above about Mercury in Cancer. The Aquarius Moon disposits Mercury in Cancer, so the country's behavior combines both symbols: we see first that people see themselves as nice homemakers concerned about home and family; then we see that those people see themselves as progressive thinkers concerned with general social well-being. (Perhaps worth noting: the horoscope usually given for Nazi Germany has the Sun in Aquarius in the tenth conjoined Saturn and Mercury.)

and aggression in the United States' various military ventures, and as a series of projections in which the U.S., despite its aggressive proclivities, somehow manages to see other peoples and nations as the aggressors and threats (Mars in the seventh house). The aspect points directly to the aggression that, coupled with a series of lies and deceptions related to national vision (Neptune in the ninth house) have characterized the United States' actions right from the beginning. Certainly other nations and groups have "seemed profoundly impressed with the idea that Americans were an ambitious and encroaching people,"[33] suggesting not only the Sagittarius Ascendant but also Neptune in the ninth house (national vision). Certainly the Indians learned this, and though many Americans have seen the conquest as not only inevitable, but also necessary for the cause of some vaguely understood "progress" and some even less understood sense of "manifest destiny," the real principles seem "as old, in human affairs, as the Roman sack of Carthage." In the conquest of the Indians as in virtually every other conflict into which the U.S. has entered, we see the national tendency "to transform our crimes into mythical triumphs of virtue," even though "some crimes are so immense that not even time and the human imagination can work such a metamorphosis upon them."[34]

Obviously enough, the United States generally goes to war because of a set of falsehoods. We can cite two types of falsehood, one that Americans have blithely told to themselves and having to do with motives, and one that Americans have equally blithely told to others and having to do with events and extensional causes. Both appear clearly in the historical record. Most recently, the U.S. invaded Iraq after telling a series of egregious lies about the weapons of mass destruction that obviously no longer existed. Earlier, we find similar lies preceding the invasion of Afghanistan, the attack on Iraq in 1991, the invasion of Vietnam, and even the Pacific theatre of the Second World War. To get into the World War I, the government had to create a special commission (the Creel Commission) to convince the American people to enter; somewhat like Lyndon Johnson many decades later, Woodrow Wilson campaigned as the candidate of peace even as he actively planned to go to war. To the above list we can add the numerous incursions and proxy-wars in Central and South America, the related drugs-for-arms swaps of the Reagan years, the so-called War on Drugs (in which, an increasing amount of evidence suggests, the CIA worked actively with one drug-lord after another), the invasion of Mexico (1846; see below), in addition to the series of lies told during the centuries-long decimation of American Indian tribes. The pattern appears clearly when we consider that since the final defeat of organized native resistance in 1890, the United States has sent its military to intervene in over 150 situations (some involving domestic unrest or labor disputes), the actions ranging from bombing runs to advisorships to full-scale invasions.

Despite all those interventions, most Americans apparently see themselves as supporting a fight (Mars) for a righteous national vision (Neptune in the ninth house), whether that vision expresses itself through the Monroe Doctrine, the later Truman Doctrine, ideas like Manifest Destiny, the so-called Reagan Doctrine, Bush I's "new world order," the so-called neo-liberal reforms that have

---

[33] Samuel Flagg Bemis, qtd. in T.D. Allman, *Unmanifest Destiny* (New York: Dial Press, 1984), 263.
[34] Allman, 263.

traumatized the world, or the unquestioned economic doctrine dictating that one can sell anything (e.g. weapons, "advisors," or "economic assistance") to anyone regardless of the short and long term harm that results. Whether going into war itself or doing so by proxy, the United States generally offers some sort of lie before entering, offers further lies during the conflict, and later never admits to the truth of what has gone on.

Neptune in Virgo suggests deceptions having to do with inequality, and the pattern appears clearly throughout U.S. history. Americans may see their nation as welcoming the poor and indigent, but more often the military goes off to slaughter poor and innocent people in all corners of the world. Writing in the 1980s, T.D. Allman summarized the pattern and states its importance:

> Our attempt to resolve the unresolvable contradiction between the ideology of liberty and the reality of force is one of the great themes linking the crises of our distant past with the crises of today, and tomorrow. One result is that in the Mississippi Valley or El Salvador, in the nineteenth century or today, we Americans often find ourselves fighting two separate wars.
>
> The first war is the one that makes the headlines and produces the body counts. It unfolds in the jungles of Indochina, or in the mountains of Central America, or at Tippecanoe or along the Little Big Horn. The second war unfolds at closer quarters. But it, too, is a war for "freedom," in this case the struggle to free the American mind from any sense of its own contradictions.
>
> El Salvador, as much as any incident in our history, provides a paradigm of those twin struggles. On the ground there, one war unfolds in a straightforward manner; it is a campaign to kill all those we oppose, conducted with unspeakable barbarism. The second war is more complicated. It consists of the perpetual American struggle to convince ourselves that even when we support terror and pursue a policy of mass slaughter, "It is not our power but our will and character that is being tested," as President Nixon said when he invaded Cambodia in 1970. Our attempts to transmute our crimes against others into triumphs of American virtue in large part explains why the reports from places like San Salvador or Saigon and the reports from Washington so often seem as though they are describing completely different conflicts, as though they flow from completely different, and fundamentally antagonistic, realities.[35]

Furthermore, the U.S. generally sees others as the aggressor (Mars in the seventh house). The pattern repeats, as easily visible in Vietnam as in Iraq—or in any of a number of Hollywood productions:

> Even now the prevailing image of the Indian, in our popular culture, is the same as it was in the nineteenth century. The Indian is the aggressor who surrounds the wagon train, who scalps innocent women and children, who attacks the frontier outpost of

---

[35]Allman, 265.

civilization. Will the aggressors triumph? Or will the Americans successfully defend themselves?[36]

If the brutality claimed for the Indians suggests Pluto, the fact that they get depicted as the aggressors against security (Cancer) and civilization (Saturn) surely suggests a projected seventh house Mars. That they seem like the dark twin of the civilized encroachers surely reflects a projected Gemini. That Americans see such enemies as deceitful and subtle, whether in the guise of Communist "masters of deceit" or in purported Indian trickery and lies, surely suggests the projected Mars-Neptune. That the encroachers see their own actions as allied to an enlightened principle or as service to humanity even if an objective observer will see only the promulgation of inequality surely suggests the square to Neptune in Virgo in the ninth house. That the "news from Central America or Southeast Asia is always the news of death" while the headlines from Washington "are always the headlines of liberty"[37] suggests not only the projection of Pluto or the control of the press by plutonic elements, but also the projection of Mars-Neptune.

In the previous section, I saw Manifest Destiny as connected to the Sagittarius Ascendant, for the Ascendant symbolizes an entity's most natural mode of expression and Sagittarius suggests expansion based on stated principles. Neptune in the ninth house presents a closely related group of symbols, for the ninth house in a nation's horoscope has to do with the nation's self-promotion, its habits in international relations, and the view or philosophy that drives public expression (tenth house); Neptune's close square with Mars in the seventh house brings additional material to the table. Though the Sagittarius Ascendant by itself does not suggest deception, with ruling Jupiter in the eighth house, it certainly suggests that the United States will speak of principles as it takes the resources of others to ensure domestic affluence. Neptune in the ninth house, on the other hand, strongly points to deception in the national ideology, while the connection to Mars tells us of the connection between that ideology and the military.

Insofar as it served as an inspiration to expansion and the taking of others' resources, Manifest Destiny certainly appears in Ascendant-related behavior, but insofar as it involves actual deceptive ideologies connected to military aggression, it appears through Mars-Neptune. Again, we can cite many examples in which the United States claimed that it sought only the expansion of freedom when it really sought a war that would empower the aforementioned taking: most obviously, we have the invasion of Mexico in 1846, usually called the Mexican War; more generally, we have a series of American presidents justifying U.S. military aggression by referring to abstractions like freedom and democracy. In this latter group we can include tableaux like the one in which Richard Nixon justifies the bombing of Cambodia as a test of the country's moral character or the one in which Woodrow Wilson sets out to "make the world safe for democracy."

---

[36]Allman, 265.
[37]Allman, 266.

The term itself—Manifest Destiny—suggests not only that everyone should see find certain guiding principles *evident* and *clear,* but also that everyone should see the process as *inexorable.* We see here one of the many deceptions associated with the term, for clearly not all nations or people could see anything destined or manifest in the process. It they had, they presumably would not have fought so hard against it. But more importantly, the process clearly did not lead to democracy, as so many claimed, but to hegemony. Here we find a second deception—and this part may, indeed, qualify as manifest to other nations. The deception relates to the American people and government officials who promulgated the idea, for clearly the officials wanted to advance the cause of American business, not to bring freedom to people halfway across the world (or, as it turns out, just down the isthmus). Finally, we find racist ideas permeating both the idea and the resulting praxis. Journalist John L. O'Sullivan, who coined the term in an article published in the summer of 1845, speaking of the invasion Mexico that serves as such a quintessential example of both idea and praxis, wrote,

> The Mexican race now see, in the fate of the aborigines of the north, their own inevitable destiny. They must amalgamate and be lost, in the superior vigor of the Anglo-Saxon race, or they must inevitably perish.[38]

To see such a deeply racist policy as democratic seems like the greatest deception of all. It reminds us of Neptune's position in Virgo, a sign associated with service and inequality in its various forms.[39] In another context, O'Sullivan opined that U.S. dominance of the North American continent would take place

> ... without the agency of our government, without responsibility of our people—in the natural flow of events, the spontaneous working of principles, and the adaptation of the tendencies and wants of the human race to the elemental circumstances in the midst of which they find themselves placed.[40]

It seems, then, that the expansion would take place without the involvement of the military at all. Believing this, one would certainly conclude that any aggression must come from others, from those who for some reason obstruct the "spontaneous working of principles." Thus the projection of aggression (Mars in the seventh house) has a clear connection to Manifest Destiny.

A third deception, ongoing for many decades, has to do with the land itself and demonstrates a similar link.[41] Once the U.S. had the lands acquired through the Louisiana Purchase, many felt that the country had acquired a vast piece of useless real estate. People didn't automatically flock there;

---

[38] Qtd. in Rogin, 309.
[39] This doesn't mean that someone with planets in Virgo will believe in inequality more than someone with planets in Libra or any other sign. Virgo's connection to inequality shows up as often in apprenticeship relations or the desire to serve others as it does it any desire to lord it over others. Virgo seems at least as likely to play the role of servant as to play the role of master, as likely to perform compassionate service as to get involved in unenlightened despotism.
[40] Qtd. in Allman, 282-3.
[41] I have borrowed liberally, in this section, from Marc Reisner's *Cadillac Desert* (New York: Penguin, 1986).

they needed convincing. Many movements arose, in full flower during the last six decades of the 19th century, to convince people to move west of the Mississippi, to the lands then (and sometimes now) referred to as the Great American Desert, so-called because so much of that land gets such scant rainfall, certainly not enough to grow crops without irrigation (which in many places turns the soil alkaline). Government and commercial enterprises combined to make that area appear as something quite different. The process shows us both Mercury-Pluto and Mars-Neptune in action. The railroads served as prime movers. The government gave large land-grants to the railroad companies; those companies sold those lands to settlers. Of course, they had to lure prospective settlers into those areas, and to do that, the railroad spokespeople had to concoct descriptions of the land and weather markedly at odds with reality. To do this well, the concoctors brought in some homespun scientific theories (Neptune in the ninth house). One of these, current for many years in America and taken seriously by many thousands, held that rainfall would follow the plow: that if people worked the land, rainfall would increase and remain plentiful. A closely related theory held that if farmers planted trees in one part of their land, the trees would bring increased rainfall. (In some places, therefore, to purchase land, one had to agree to devote some of that land to trees.) The railroads, owning their own newspapers and conveniently neglecting to mention their ties with the land-sales companies they owned, offered some startling descriptions of the land in the Great American Desert. For example, the Rock Island Railroad's gazette described Kansas as "the garden spot of the world" a place that "would grow anything that any other country will grow, and with less work." Further, the gazette held that "it rains here more than in any other place, and at just the right time." Another publication claimed that the Laramie Plains of Wyoming were "as ready today for the plow and spade as the fertile prairies of Illinois."[42] Some publications also claimed important health benefits for Kansas and beyond.

The publicity blitz went as far eastward as Europe, and it had enormous influence in the eastern states of the country. It reminds us that powerful interests (Pluto) have for quite some time controlled much that passes for communication (Mercury) in this country. Further, the publicity had as a primary aim the transformation (Pluto) of opinion (Mercury) by claiming that people would find easier security and affluence if they moved west than if they stayed on their holdings in the east.

William Gilpin, later the first governor of the Territory of Colorado, epitomizes much that went awry in that expansionist era, for though a 20th century historian once described his science as "a priori, deduced, generalized, falsely systematized, and therefore wrong,"[43] he and others like him had enormous influence. Marc Reisner writes,

> Imagining himself in space, Gilpin saw the North American continent as a "vast amphitheater, opening toward heaven"—an enormous continent-wide bowl formed by the Rockies and Appalachian ridges which was ready, as far as Gilpin was concerned, "to receive and fuse harmoniously whatever enters within its rim. A capitalist-

---

[42]Reisner, 38.
[43]Reisner, 40.

expansionist mystic as only the nineteenth century could offer up, Gilpin thundered to a meeting of the Fenian Brotherhood in Denver, "What an immense geography has been revealed! What infinite hives of population and laboratories of industry have been set in motion ... North America is known to our own people. Its concave form and homogeneous structure are revealed."[44]

He envisioned 1,310,000,000 people fitting comfortably into his "bowl," and though not nearly that number came, many thousands did, beginning the settling of a land where one could not grow crops without irrigation, a place subject to crippling droughts, with vast tracts of land that no amount of irrigation could transform. (Add to that the fact that in many sections, irrigation would work only for a limited time, for it would bring salts up from the underlying clay, eventually killing whatever one planted there.)

Though capitalistic control of public opinion reflects the U.S. Mercury-Pluto, capitalists sought that control at least partly because of the larger vision of Manifest Destiny. If one took it as obvious that the Europeans should and would spread over the continent, attempting to reproduce there the brand of civilization found in Europe, one had to concoct stories, however false, to make that land seem amenable to such plans. So Manifest Destiny had delusion at its core not only in the ways it ignored the rights of people with just claim to the land, and not only because of its underlying racism, but because of the way it required a falsification regarding the very land that people were manifestly destined to inhabit. And, as noted above, because the theory (euphemistically so-called) held that the process would take place on its own as a working out of self-evident principles, without the need for aggression or even government intervention, it invited people to see anyone who objected to it as either obstructionist (as people saw John Wesley Powell) or aggressive (as people saw Indians, Mexicans, and the British[45]).

United States' Mars and Uranus

Though Mars and Uranus in the U.S. chart don't oppose any planets, they both lie close to the seventh house cusp,[46] with Mars formally in the seventh and Uranus in the sixth but within six degrees of the descending angle. We would hypothesize, then, that both will emerge as projections:

---

[44] Reisner, 40.

[45] The British enter the picture in this way: the British government found itself engaged in a dispute with the U.S. over boundaries in Oregon. Fear of British aggression abounded, surely augmented by British actions, for though the British never threatened invasion, apparently preferring negotiation to armed conflict, the British government ordered the arming of ships of war right about the time that the U.S. invaded Mexico. The U.S. government got the message: negotiate in Oregon, or face a foe consisting not of innocent and unarmed farmers in Mexico, but of British ships of war. Polk, in direct contradiction to his campaign promises, accepted British proposals for boundaries in Oregon, giving us the border we recognize today, though it took some years to work out all the details. The territories garnered north of the Mason Dixon Line would convince northern politicians that north-south relations would not alter greatly as a result of territorial expansion in the south. See the discussion of the Mexican War below.

[46] These remarks would hold true for any of the Sagittarius rising horoscopes currently in use. Though my remarks refer specifically to the Rudhyar chart (which I feel has been verified by recent events: see above), they would be accurate in any

that the United States will see aggression as arising in others instead of ourselves, and that the United States will mistrust revolutionary groups or groups willing to upset whatever apple-carts the U.S. sees as economically vital.

As noted above, it might seem strange, at first, that the United States would project Uranus. Wasn't this nation, after all, born from a revolution? Doesn't our Declaration of Independence talk about freedom, rights, and human dignity, Uranian matters all? True enough, and not surprising, considering the Aquarius Moon (co-ruled by Uranus). However, the Saturnian elements in Aquarius came to the fore very early in U.S. history. Even as the Founding Fathers talked of dispensing liberty to the whole world, they exempted some rather large groups (e.g. women, Africans, Native Americans) from that dispensation. Furthermore, Uranus appeared in projected form very early on. For example, throughout the United States, people saw the Indian uprisings of Tecumseh[47] as led and inspired by British interests bent on disrupting the established order in the United States. Similarly, in the same era, Andrew Jackson invaded Florida (at that time a colony of Spain) because he and others feared that the Spanish, Indians, and displaced Africans down there would threaten the established order. Apparently many people saw as Jackson did, for they elected him president twice (or three times, if you count 1824).

We may think, today, that, considering much-discussed emphasis on freedom and what people believe about the Monroe Doctrine, that the United States must have played a significant role in all Latin American freedom movements. Yet in its early years as today, United States stood almost completely apart from, and in many cases against, those movements:

> No American Lafayettes or Kosciuskos had fought alongside O'Higgins or Bolivar. No U.S. fleet had sailed to the rescue of the Latin Americans, the way a French fleet had sailed to our assistance—and thus assured our ultimate victory over the British—at Yorktown. Instead we maintained full diplomatic relations with Spain, and recognized the Latin American states only after the battles were won.
>
> This point is absolutely critical to any understanding of the Latin American reaction to our periodic pretensions that we Americans, going back to the time of Monroe, have always been the great champions of liberty in the western hemisphere.[48]

Speaking of the period around the Monroe Doctrine, T.D. Allman writes that expediency, "for neither the first nor last time, also played a very important role in an American decision to spurn the appeals of those fighting for their liberty."[49] The United States hoped to purchase Florida; to aid Latin American countries in their efforts to gain freedom from Spain would surely have incurred

---

case. Mars will be in the seventh house for almost any Sagittarius rising horoscope (and any of the ones currently in use), and seventh house planets are often projected onto "open enemies." Uranus is also in the seventh house in the Lynes chart (7+ Sagittarius rising) and is still within orb of an opposition to the Descendant of the Rudhyar chart.

[47]The following version of the period around the Monroe Doctrine owes much to T.D. Allman's *Unmanifest Destiny*.
[48]Allman, 123.
[49]Allman, 123.

Spain's displeasure; the United States could not, therefore, see its way to giving aid to anyone until Spain had ceded Florida—and even after that, the United States gave no aid at all, partly because it didn't have the wherewithal, partly out of disinclination.

As for the Monroe Doctrine itself, such as it was, Monroe issued it largely to discourage Britain. He apparently didn't so much want to encourage freedom, much less revolution, in the New World, as to ensure that British influence in Canada, the Caribbean, or the high seas would not surround the new republic. Britain, here, arises as a disruptive force—as an odd kind of Uranus in the United States' crosshairs, rather than in the Saturnian role we might expect of a nation steeped in royal and imperial traditions. In short, the United States greatly feared that Great Britain would obstruct the new country's expansion by holding on to Oregon just as it had done in Canada, hindering the United States' efforts to fulfill its purported national destiny. Appearing as disruptive Uranus opposing U.S. expansion (Sagittarius Ascendant), even Saturnian Britain served as a hook for the U.S. Uranus-projection (combined, of course, with Mars).

Further, the United States coveted the vast territory of Mexico, now free from Spain, and didn't want the British to lay any claims there. For the British would surely prove more difficult to deal with than the fledgling nation south of the Rio Grande. We can see this fear clearly articulated in Vice-President Adams' diary, where he mused that a system of independent Latin American republics, "protected by the guarantee of Great Britain," would establish, as Allman puts it, "a far stronger barrier to our national expansion than the Spanish had in Florida," given the comparatively enormous power of Britain at the time.

Allman summarizes this alternative view of the Monroe Doctrine as follows:

> Thus, to all our other illusions about the "Monroe Doctrine" must be added a culminating one: it was our own national ambitions in North America, not some philanthropic urge to help the Latin Americans, and our own quite justified sense of vulnerability to British power, not some threat of the European powers' harming our neighbors, that produced the document later revered as the "Monroe Doctrine."[50]

In other words, Monroe and other United States officials acted as they did "only because the United States—not Latin America—faced a serious challenge from the opposite side of the Atlantic."[51]

In fact, as Allman notes, just a few months before Monroe issued the document that bears his name, British Foreign Secretary George Canning sent a message to Washington, offering five points that, taken in sum, sound rather like what Monroe said later. Canning proposed, in effect, that other countries leave burgeoning Latin American republics alone. He added that Britain "could not see any portion of them transferred to any other Power, with indifference," even though Britain did not "aim at the possession of any portion of them ourselves."[52] Thus we can see the Monroe Doctrine as a Saturnian document recommending the maintaining of the status quo and opening opportuni-

---
[50]Allman, 128.
[51]Allman, 128.
[52]Qtd. in Allman, 129.

ties for future U.S. expansion, not a Uranian statement encouraging revolution, for the document interpreted any non-status quo movements as dangerous. Insofar as Britain appeared to threaten that status quo, it took on the guise of Uranus and Mars. (By 1823, most of Latin America had attained nominal freedom from Europe already, though domestic situations remained difficult.)

Thus we have the United States playing a role suited to its Sun-Saturn square from Cancer in the eighth house to Libra in the tenth: insisting on status quo arrangements in order to preserve national security via others' resources and seeing any revolutionary developments (Uranus) or groups as adversarial or undesirable. The pattern has permeated United States history: others threaten revolution or progressive movements threaten U.S. hegemony; the U.S. objects, finding hooks in any nations or groups (Cuba, El Salvador, Native Americans, etc.) who object. Because the U.S. had advanced inexorably into lands occupied by others, those others have defended themselves; in so doing, they have served as hooks for the seventh house Mars (another example of the energy-transfer resulting from projections).

Astrologers often refer to the seventh house as the domicile of marriage and "open enemies." In a nation's horoscope, planets there will arise through other nations, or at least through the country's relations with those other nations. Mars there surely suggests relations characterized by violence, usually because Mars appears as the aggression of those other nations, not that of the United States (which, as noted makes pronouncements about peace, principled order, and liberty). Thus the United States' Saturnian leadership (Saturn in the tenth house), while speaking of justice and fairness (Libra) and concerned with "national security" (Cancer Sun), sees other countries as aggressors—this, no matter what the evidence suggests and no matter if other countries see us in the same light. We will see this quite clearly in our relationship with Iraq (below), but we can see it quite clearly in Ronald Reagan's remarks about El Salvador's purported threat even as we decimated that country; we can see it in the invaders' relations with Native Americans (almost always portrayed as threatening and bloodthirsty savages even as they died by the millions), with Mexico at the time of the Mexican War (which started as a result of United States' deceptive claims about Mexican incursions), and certainly with Vietnam during the entire period of that war.

The United States sees threats everywhere, it seems, and it attacks those purported threats, using as justification ideas about the nation's benevolence. We see this tendency reflected in the square from Mars in the seventh house (projection of aggression onto "open enemies") and Neptune in the ninth (delusions and self-deceptions arising from over-idealization regarding the national mission or the national philosophy: ideas related, for example, to Manifest Destiny, still alive in diplomatic circles). Thus the U.S. attacks people, blaming them the while, while professing compassionate motivation and a desire to bring freedom to them. (Of course, Neptune has much to do with oil, so while the U.S. preaches compassion, it now seems that we seek oil to foment delusion.)[53]

---

[53]During the occupation of Iraq, transiting Pluto opposed Mars and squared Neptune, provoking this aspect and bringing up all manner of problem related to it. Pluto's connection to the underworld and Neptune's to oil surely tells us something about the United States' real motivation for invading Iraq. As Noam Chomsky once asked, can we imagine

The Sun-Saturn Square

The Sun-Saturn square points to the United States' desire for authority, and to its tendency to establish (Saturn) that authority by taking the values or resources of others (Sun in eighth house) as a way to ensure its own security (Cancer, plus Saturn).[54] In international matters, the U.S. has generally seen itself as the final arbiter in legal matters, for the United States generally accepts only those international laws that it wishes to accept, an attitude epitomized by Ronald Reagan's claim that the international court had no jurisdiction in U.S. relations with Nicaragua.[55] The United States takes this approach to protect the twin securities of the Cancer Sun and the tenth house Saturn, satisfying the security needs of the former by establishing the structures associated with the latter; these structures enable the United States to take others' resources (eighth house) in order to maintain the "security" associated with the affluent lifestyle enjoyed by millions of its people. And, of course, the United States expects people to obey its Saturnian authority (Saturn in the tenth house). The affluence of the American lifestyle seems connected to the Venus-Jupiter conjunction in Cancer at the cusp of the eighth house and square the Libra Midheaven (ruled by Venus, with Saturn exalted there). When the United States government speaks of "security," it often means that it desires to sustain and maintain this affluence. Thus the constant effort to maintain low oil prices in this country, prices clearly not necessarily for security *per se,* but deemed important for the *affluent* security (Venus-Jupiter in Cancer) so long in vogue. The square indicates structures, whether organizational or psychological, linking the twin securities; small wonder that so many in the United States see them as inseparable. Though the Sun-Saturn square arises as projection through traditional (Saturn) agrarian (Cancer) people who wish to continue to live as they have for centuries (at least!), it also arises as the deeply entrenched set of attitudes and practices that virtually ensure that the United States will project Uranus and Pluto onto other nations. If we posit a nation steeped in concerns about its own security and that assumes an ongoing and benevolent connection between that security and domestic authority regimes that seem to ensure it, we should hardly feel surprised when that nation sees all transformative (Pluto) or progressive (Uranus) forces as completely unacceptable (thus ensuring their projection onto other nations or groups).

The Sun-Saturn square, uniting as it does two astrological symbols closely connected with the father lineages (three, if we include the tenth house, traditionally associated with the father), tells us much about how the U.S. expresses its organized energy in the world. It appeared very early in

---

the U.S. invading Iraq if that country's main export had been pickles? Transiting Pluto's 2008-2009 square of the United States Midheaven nadir axis brought yet another iteration of the Pluto-projection.

[54] Whereas the Moon and Cancer have to do with emotional security, Saturn generally symbolizes one's efforts to build structures that will ensure stability (often another kind of security, after all). Thus Saturn's association with ambition and career, as with authority hierarchies in general, not merely as a means to establish a reliable self-identity, but as a means to secure the nation in the world community. As Lord of Boundaries, Saturn looks to the relationship between external situations and the maintenance of one's own situation; Saturn's approach to security generally involves walls and positions rather than feelings. In the tenth house, Saturn tells us much about the United States' approach to public persona (whereas the Sagittarius Ascendant tells us much about how the United States acts).

[55] http://www.wsws.org/articles/2010/jan2010/twih-j18.shtml

the paternalistic approach to American Indians, evident in documents too numerous to count and epitomized in the following example from Martin Van Buren, Andrew Jackson's secretary of state and the eighth president of the United States. He wrote,

> ...we are as a nation responsible *in foro conscientiae* to the opinions of the great family of nations, as it involves the course we have pursued and shall pursue toward a people comparatively weak, upon whom we were perhaps in the beginning unjustifiable aggressors, but of whom, in the progress of time and events, we have become the guardians, and, as we hope, the benefactors.[56]

Whatever D.H. Lawrence might have said about the American Indian as the inner double of the invading Europeans,[57] Indians found themselves cast in the role of children, despite their many thousands of years of sophisticated civilized living. Though the insistence on seeing the Indian as a barbarian seems to point to the projection of Pluto (which itself gives a paradox, for with Pluto in Capricorn, these "barbarians" had a long past of organized living, as have virtually all U.S. enemies[58]), the gravitation of the U.S. government toward the father role points to the Sun-Saturn square.

The Sun-Saturn square didn't seem to function any more honestly or nobly then than it does now. In *Fathers and Children: Andrew Jackson and the Subjugation of the American Indian*, in a passage worth quoting at length as it sounds as if the author had in mind many of the astrological factors discussed in this chapter, Michael Gilbert Rogin writes:

> Indian dispossession, as experienced by the whites who justified it and carried it out, belongs to the pathology of human development. Indians remained, in the white fantasy, in the earliest period of childhood, unseparated from "the exuberant bosom of the common mother." They were at once symbols of a lost childhood bliss and, as bad children, repositories of murderous, negative fantasies....
>
> Expansion, whites agreed, inevitably devoured Indians; only paternal governmental supervision could save the tribes from extinction. Paternalism, however, met white needs better than Indian ones. The new American world undermined the authority provided by history, tradition, family connection, and the other ties of old European existence. Political authority, as Locke demonstrated...must derive from interactions among free men, not from paternal relations. But Indians were not liberal men. The paternal authority repressed out of liberal politics returned in Indian paternalism.
>
> This paternalism was badly contaminated by the destructive maturing process from which it grew. It required children to have no independence or life of their own ... In

---

[56] *Annual Report of the Secretary of War*. 1831. Qtd. in Rogin, p.4.
[57] See Rogin p.5. Also see D.H. Lawrence's *Studies in Classic American Literature*, first published in 1923, particularly the first chapter.
[58] Indigenous peoples generally stand in the way of capitalistic expansion and resist the world ruled by capitalist assumptions. Rebelling forcefully against the prevailing order, they become excellent hooks for both Uranus and Mars.

their paternalism toward Indians, white policy-makers indulged primitive longings to wield total power. They sought to regain the primal infant-mother connection from a position of domination instead of dependence....

The mature white father reconciled himself to Indian destruction and took no responsibility for it. Benevolence and greed, power and helplessness were irrevocably split in this figure. The failure to achieve an integrated paternal figure who could accept responsibility for his actions recalls the failure to integrate childhood experience into the adult world. Such splits in the ego characterize schizoid personalities; and the inability to tolerate separation, the longing to return to an ego less "dual unity" stage, is a source of schizophrenia. There may have been madness in American Indian policy, but it did not drive the country mad.[59]

The pressure resulting from the unintegrated, quasi-schizoid approach, Rogin argues, found release in westward expansion, a process symbolized by the idealistic Neptune in the ninth house in combination with Mars, the expansionism of Sagittarius, the paternalism of Sun-Saturn, and the dark obsessions possible with Pluto, for despite the pious language of Indian removal, one could "hear the hum of destruction underneath."[60]

Of the three hard aspects discussed in this chapter, two have very narrow orbs of aspect, with the Mars-Neptune square as the closest hard aspect and the Sun-Saturn square following close behind. The narrowness of the orb tells us much about the importance of the aspect, as does Saturn's close aspect to the Sun and exaltation in Libra in the tenth house. Some decades back, Marc Edmund Jones wrote that the closest hard aspect points toward the vocation, to which I would add that *all* close squares add important information, for the square symbolizes the need to build structures, venues, and vehicles to put apparently disparate energies to use. Once united in a common purpose through the structure or venue, the disparate energies can accomplish much.

In the U.S. horoscope, the two squares surely tell us a lot about how the U.S. has manifested in the world: constantly as an aggressor inspired by fantasies not only of military omnipotence (Mars-Neptune), but also of benevolence and what passes as "destiny"; just as constantly as the presiding authority figure, one with authority not only over his own territory, but over whatever in others' territories he might covet, with Neptune in the ninth house telling him that even in his authoritative aggression and incessant robbery, the great white father serves a higher cause. The present retrograde movement of secondary progressed Mars, which will take it through a conjunction to Saturn and a square to the Sun, will hopefully bring about a re-evaluation of the behavior indicated by both aspects. This must remain a hope, however, as previous challenging transits, directions, and progressions have failed to bring about such a change.

---

[59] Rogin, 9-10.
[60] I have loosely followed Rogin's argument, here, but the quotation, offered in Rogin's text, comes from D.H. Lawrence's *Studies in Classic American Literature* (p. 93 of the 1953 edition). As Marc Reisner shows (*Cadillac Desert: The American West and Its Disappearing Water*), the destructive hum had pronounced effects on the environment as well.

Saturn rules the United States second house and disposits Pluto, so the authority-regime has a financial emphasis. The U.S. uses business (Saturn, plus Pluto in Capricorn) to ensure emotional security (Sun in Cancer); it extends its authority in order to secure financial well-being. Saturn's connection with Pluto symbolizes the connection between plutocratic control and the authority system.

As noted, the Mars-Neptune square suggests aggression in service of either idealism or delusion. In an individual, we might hope for the former; with a nation, we would fear the latter. Neptune in the ninth house suggests that the delusional national view or philosophy manifests in ideas like Manifest Destiny. Neptune's connection with Mars also reminds us about how easy it is for the United States to see its aggression in an idealistic light, with the ruling class offering boilerplate platitudes about freedom and benevolence while promulgating something rather different. Neptune in the ninth house suggests a delusional national philosophy. Virgo suggests inequality, that the national philosophy has a powerful racist element. Fortunately, Virgo also suggests the precise examination and attention to details that can help people see through the delusion. In a person's horoscope, we would have some reason to expect at least some personal re-examination. Unfortunately, nations generally seem to express the meanest qualities of the national horoscope.

That the Mars-Neptune square is the closest hard aspect in the chart suggests that it will find its way into the national vocation. Problematically, this suggests the kind of blind, delusional aggression we see promulgated by the U.S. government and characterizing so much of U.S. history. The closeness of the Sun-Saturn square suggests the interconnections between this delusional aggression and the national authority system that facilitates the taking of others' resources. Though Mars-Neptune could suggest the kind of compassionate action we see undertaken by numerous United States citizens in all sorts of situations, in government actions it manifests quite differently.

Case Study 1: The Invasion of Mexico

Among the numerous available examples of projection at work in the United States, the invasion of Mexico, known in the history books as the Mexican War of 1846, stands out, not only because it launched the first formally-declared attempt to augment the empire's territory,[61] but also because the transiting and progressed factors for that event show quite clearly how some of the challenging aspects of the U.S. horoscope interact when they appear via projection. Not coincidentally, the war began shortly after Johann Galle discovered Neptune on September 23, 1846 and about a year after John O'Sullivan clarified the racist elements in the unofficial U.S. policy (as in the quotation given above). Ideas about Manifest Destiny ruled the ideological roost, at least partly because of what some interpreted as "destiny" denied, for though ideas about destined expansion had occupied an important place in the national ideology since at least the second decade of the 19th century, the new nation had thus far failed to add anything to its territory except Florida. And to get Florida, it had to cede Texas to Mexico, an action that various politicians blamed on each other, but that, the

---

[61] The U.S. did not consider its ongoing slaughter of the Indians as war in the proper sense.

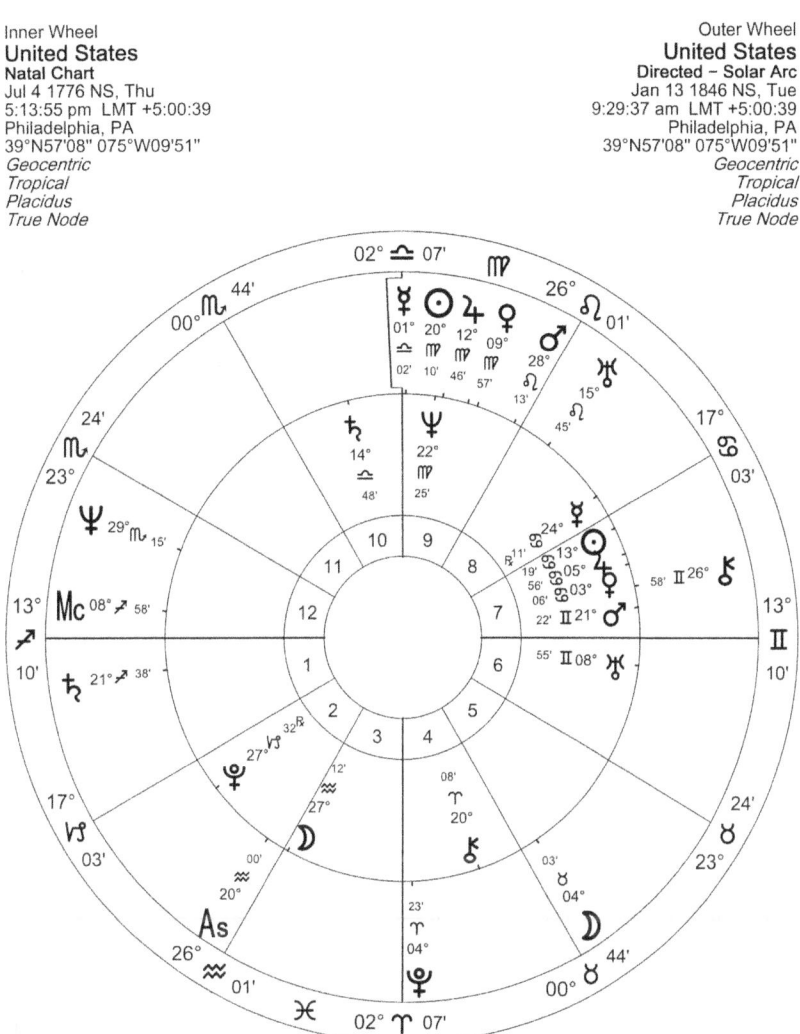

record seems to show, most of them accepted at the time, only later to repudiate their own actions when those actions seemed at odds with the prevailing ideology.[62]

    The war began with an apparently innocuous skirmish along the Mexican border. Though much evidence suggests that the United States played the aggressor role, President Polk took the event as evidence of needless aggression by Mexico. Many historians have found Polk's claims spurious, partly because of the ongoing territorial disputes in the area (for historians disagree about whether the territory occupied by the Mexican army really belonged to the United States), and partly because they feel, not unreasonably, that Polk actually *wanted* a war and did what he could to bring

---

[62]See Rogin, chapter 10.

one about. Polk and others, including Andrew Jackson, wanted to "expand the area of freedom," by which they meant the area below the Mason Dixon Line, which they could form into slave states and thus maintain some degree of parity with the industrial north. And so the war began, though it quickly turned into an invasion of Mexico that included artillery bombardments of cities and the slaughter of untold thousands of Mexican citizens. The United States forces, led by Generals Zachary Taylor and Winfield Scott, made a long march to Mexico City. They met with little resistance, and most U.S. losses took the form of desertions, as many of Taylor's forces drifted away into the deserts of Mexico, apparently unwilling to risk their lives in the military venture.

The transits, progressions, and, especially, directions, illuminate the workings of the various aspects discussed above, but particularly the Sun-Saturn square and the Mars-Neptune square (not surprisingly, considering the recent discovery of Neptune). As the war-frenzy mounted in the U.S., solar arc Saturn opposed natal Mars (October 4, 1845). During the invasion, solar arc Saturn squared natal Neptune (October 29, 1846). Aspects from the solar arc Sun closely followed, with the solar arc Sun squaring Mars and conjoining Neptune before the war concluded (April 11, 1847 and May 4, 1848, respectively).[63] Thus the war brought together the U.S. propensity to project Mars onto others—to see others as the aggressors even in situations in which the U.S. clearly played that role—and its tendency to welcome its own distortions of the actual situation, distortions serving the national ideology even as they do violence to the truth and encourage violence toward official enemies. The directed planets—the Sun and Saturn—symbolize the national tendency to take on the authority role in service to national security, a tendency very much in evidence both before and during the war. This may seem surprising, as no reasonable observer could see Mexico as a threat to the United States. This did not prevent unreasonable ones from seeing threats everywhere. In addition, many within the U.S. saw the union as threatened from *within* because of the division between north and south. Leaders, apparently acting largely unconsciously, projected this threat out so that Great Britain appeared as an active threat to U.S. interests. Thus Andrew Jackson's assertion that events in adjacent countries "appeared to threaten not merely economic and strategic interests but also the security of democracy."[64] Historian Albert Weinberg explains in *Manifest Destiny*, that Jackson's conception of an "extension of the area of freedom"

> ...became general as an ideal of preventing absolutistic Europe from lessening the

---

[63] Every major war in which the United States has engaged coincides with at least one solar arc direction from the four astrological factors I've discussed in this chapter (Mercury-Pluto, Uranus, Sun-Saturn, Mars-Neptune). Some powerful corroborating transits mark the beginning of the invasion of Mexico: at 24 Aries, Pluto squares Mercury and closes in on a square to its own natal position; at 27 and 29 Aquarius respectively, Neptune and Saturn still conjoin the U.S. Moon, having recently conjoined on that position as part of a three-series of conjunctions (April 4, 1848, 27 Aquarius 18; September 5, 1846, 26 Aquarius 20; December 11, 1846, 25 Aquarius 42). At 25 Gemini 02, Mars has recently conjoined his natal position and squared natal Neptune; Uranus at 12 Arie s01 squares the U.S. Sun and opposes the U.S. Saturn, setting off the projection of Uranus discussed above and "explaining" the perceived threats to national security based in others' resources (natal Sun in Cancer in the eighth house).

[64] Qtd. in Allman, 271.

> area open to American democracy; extension of the area of "freedom" was the defiant answer to extension of the area of "absolutism" [Europe, according to Jackson]⁶⁵

Thus, as occurred in a later period, the U.S. saw itself as fighting another system of government; as one senator put it back around 1850, it all came down to "a question of two great systems."⁶⁶

U.S. leaders decided to see Britain as plotting against the U.S., even though the British government actively pursued negotiation. We see, here, the projected Pluto, for Britain purportedly worked in an underhanded way. T.D. Allman writes that, far from plotting to undermine the American democracy or take territory "destined" for the United States, "from Canning's time onward it was much more British policy to appease than to contain the territorial ambitions of the United States—as the events of the 1840s would reveal most dramatically." He adds,

> Not that these mild truths would have been acknowledged by Americans at the time. By the election year of 1844 [when Polk, a dark-horse candidate advocating war, was elected] the United States was in the grip of a war fever not witnessed since 1812—and seized of a virulent Anglophobia such as this nation would never experience again.⁶⁷

To achieve the balance between slave and free states purportedly needed to maintain national unity, particularly given the ongoing negotiations with Britain about the Pacific Northwest (territory which would metamorphose into non-slave states), Polk and others saw the need to gather as much southern territory as possible. So, Allman tells us:

> In 1846, for no morally or strategically justifiable reason, the United States attacked a foreign nation, overthrew its government, devastated its lands, terrorized its people and, in this case, stole nearly a million square miles of its national territory.⁶⁸

He adds, in words that alert us to the astrological patterns under discussion here,

> Yet, as Weinberg demonstrates, this was not how many Americans saw things. In fact, President Jackson's view of the British and Mexican "threat" was identical to President Reagan's view of the Soviet and Central American "threat."⁶⁹

Case Study 2: Iraq, Afghanistan, and 9/11

After hearing Allman's remarks about the similarities between the Jackson-Polk era (1830s and 1840s) and the Reagan era a century and a half later, and particularly his description of the Mexican war as one that terrorized people, devastated lands, and overthrew governments, we should

---
⁶⁵Qtd. in Allman, 271.
⁶⁶Qtd. in Allman, 271.
⁶⁷Allman, 271.
⁶⁸Allman, 270.
⁶⁹Allman, 270.

consider more recent events marked by transits and directions of some of the same planets activated during the earlier period. The patterns suggest similarities regarding the nation's karmic pattern, mixed with some important differences, though the differences seem connected more to the lands invaded than to the mindset of the invader:

- Solar arc Midheaven opposition natal Saturn: March 27, 2003, having squared the natal Sun on October 7, 2001
- Solar arc Pluto square Ascendant from the ninth house: October 14, 2003
- Solar arc Mercury square Ascendant from the third house: February 12, 2007
- Solar arc Uranus conjunct Pluto: October 10, 2006
- Solar arc Uranus opposition Mercury: June 11, 2003
- Solar arc Mars sesquiquadrate Neptune: March 15, 2004
- Solar arc Ascendant conjunct natal Jupiter: April 12, 2005
- All solar arc planets sesquiquadrate natal positions: March 4, 2003
- Transiting Saturn stationary direct square U.S. Neptune and conjunct U.S. Mars: February 22, 2003
- Transiting Mars conjunct U.S. Ascendant: February 6, 2003; opposition Mars: February 19, 2003; square Neptune: February 20, 2003; square Midheaven/IC: March 7, 2003; opposition Sun: March 25, 2003; square Saturn: March 27, 2003; opposition Mercury and conjunct Pluto: April 2003.

Further, during the occupation, Saturn transited through Cancer, making aspects to all planets in cardinal signs in the U.S. horoscope: Venus, Jupiter, the Sun, Saturn, Mercury, and Pluto; in the eighth house, Saturn brought up questions related to others' values. (Certainly the Iraqi people did not value the U.S. occupation.) Finally, secondary progressed Mars moved into its retrograde station just as the invasion of Iraq began.

Since 1776, solar arc Pluto has squared the U.S. Ascendant twice and opposed it once. The first square, coming from solar arc Pluto in the third house, brought the Monroe Doctrine, a statement about U.S. relations with neighbors (third house). The opposition (1915) coincided with WWI: solar arc Pluto came to the U.S. Descendant, so the war seem to involve people "over there" ("open enemies"), though due to Woodrow Wilson's machinations and his new propaganda machine (Mercury-Pluto), the U.S. shortly found itself fully involved.[70] The 2003 square, from the ninth house, involved the "long journeys over water" (ninth) that the U.S. military had to make to

---

[70]Some would say that J.P. Morgan's extensive loans to Great Britain also played a role. This doesn't seem surprising, considering Pluto's connection with money (second house, opposed Mercury in the eighth house).

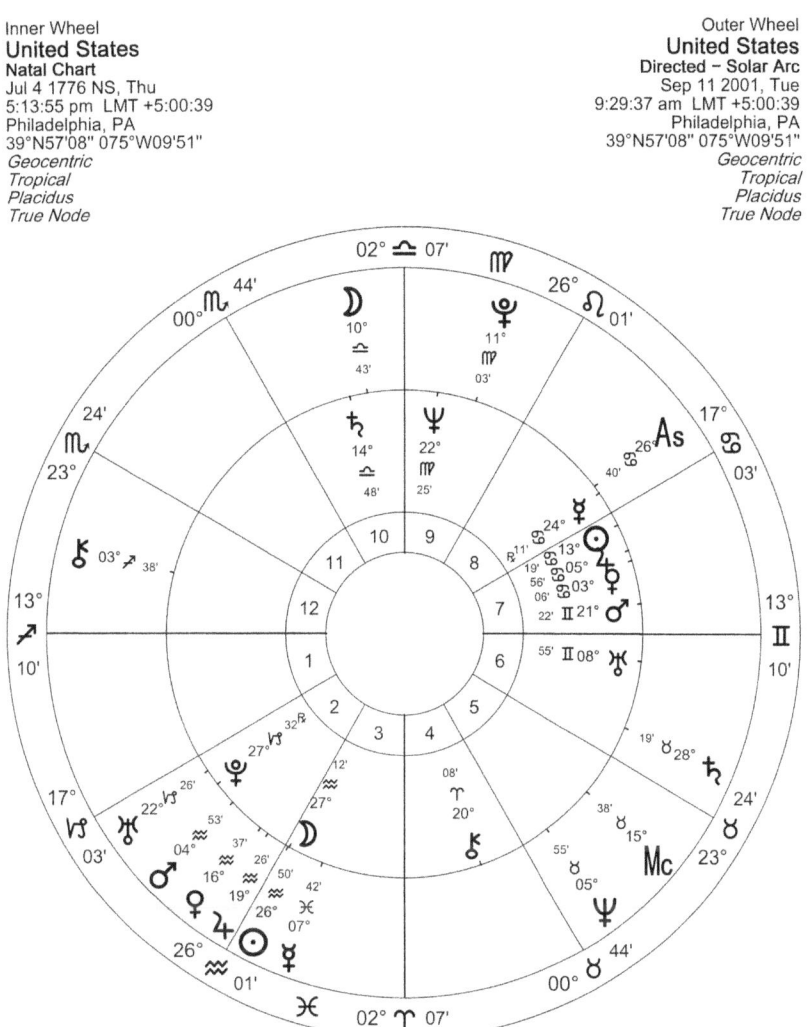

effect an invasion of Iraq; it also brought the national ideology to bear in unfortunate ways. With Neptune in the ninth house, the U.S. sense of "destiny" has often involved foreign nations, but the aspect manifested even more literally in 2003.

Solar arc Uranus' opposition to Mercury arose through the extensive anti-war demonstrations that took place in the United States, with the demonstrators finding themselves taken as enemies, corralled and jailed in many cases, always seen as an enemy of expansionist enterprises. Solar arc Uranus' conjunction with Pluto combined two planets generally projected: many (e.g. those in

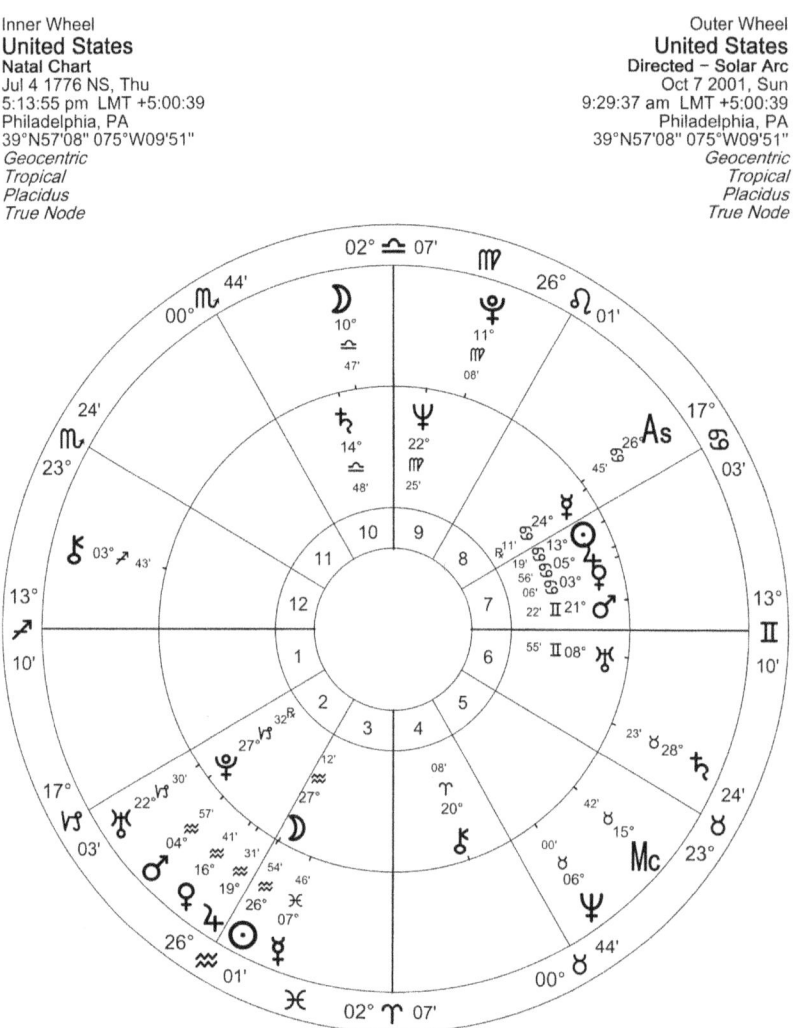

the inner circles of government, those influenced by the plutocratic press) took those who rebelled against U.S. plans as people influenced by terrorist elements, not so much in the United States as in Iraq, where people disrupted U.S. plans with such tactics as they found useful against a vastly superior military force. The solar arc directions of the Midheaven to the Sun-Saturn square formed a t-square, with the solar arc Midheaven opposing Saturn and the solar arc IC conjoining it, having squared the Sun just a bit earlier. These directions activated the authoritative streak in the national psyche; more particularly, they brought to the surface the ongoing connection between authority and others' resources.

This connection to others' resources developed into an ongoing problem as transiting Saturn moved into Cancer and through the U.S. eighth house. That transit almost always brings difficulties and limitations related to others' values, so though the U.S. government seemed at pains to show that Iraqi citizens applauded U.S. "liberation," events quickly demonstrated that the vast majority of Iraqis did no such thing. By 2005, transiting Pluto had reached its opposition to natal Mars and its square to natal Neptune: the projection of Pluto onto others gained public attention as the public press spoke endlessly of Iraqi "insurgents" and of Al Qaida influence in Iraq, forces purportedly using deceptive aggression. As Pluto has moved into Capricorn, we have seen some of the karmic results of these events; at the time, we saw flagrant projections, first of Mars, later of the entire t-square (transiting Pluto plus natal Mars-Neptune).[71] That t-square had its empty leg in the third house of the U.S. horoscope, suggesting that the solution lay in accurate fact-finding. Unfortunately, with its Mercury under the control of Pluto, its Sagittarius Ascendant, and its Neptune in the ninth connected with Mars, the U.S. government has generally proved deficient in that activity.

Notably, in 2003, all solar arc planets made sesquiquadrate[72] aspects to their own positions. Astrologers see the sesquiquadrate (sometimes called the sesquisquare: an aspect of 135 degrees) as an indication of too much impetuosity; the upper sesquiquadrate has an eighth house emphasis and thus involves the values, resources, or monies of others. Notably, too, in sesquiquadrating his own position, Mars also sesquiquadrates natal Neptune (March 15, 2004), producing a back-to-back sesquiquadrate formation with its focus on solar arc Mars, suggesting present opportunities for, or insistence on, assertion or aggression. Of the sesquisquare, Bil Tierney says that it deals with "the consequences...of a lack of composure and self-restraint in interpersonal situations" and that the individual "tends to react irrationally or act immoderately at the expense of others." It "tends toward extremism," he says, and "temporarily stuns, shocks, or jolts our sensibilities and/or those of others we confront."[73] The connections seem clear.

Additional Note on 9/11

On September 11, 2001, Pluto at 12 Sagittarius 38 hovered close to the U.S. Ascendant, while Saturn, at 14 Gemini 41 lay on the U.S. Descendant and thus very close to the U.S. Mars-Uranus midpoint. Though for an individual such aspects could suggest the acceptance of stern feedback as an impetus toward new ways of acting, the United States experienced much of the aspect as a projection, with a harsh judgment (Saturn) emerging from open enemies (seventh house), attacking the "twin towers" (Gemini) in New York; the Sagittarius Ascendant appears indirectly, via the words "world trade," for Sagittarius has to do with long journeys and foreign places, and its ruler,

---

[71]The term "insurgents," so much promulgated by the plutocratic press, seems an odd one. Many people so designated did not see themselves as insurgents at all, apparently because they did not see the imposed government as a legitimate one. Lacking a legitimate government, one has nothing against which to insurge.

[72]Because solar arc directions move about a degree each year, solar arc planets make their first sesquiquadrate aspect to natal positions around 135 years after the birthdate and the second such aspect 225 years after the birthdate. In this case, the aspects came due 227 years after the birthdate (1776 + 227 = 2003).

[73]Bil Tierney, *Dynamics of Aspect Analysis: New Perceptions in Astrology* (Reno: CRCS, 2983), 32.

Jupiter (on the cusp of the eighth house) with the values of others. U.S. insistence on expanding into the world via principles that exonerated the taking of others' resources seems to have acted as a motivation for those who attacked (opposed) the twin-towers (Pluto on the ascendant opposing the Gemini Descendant[74]). When the attacks occurred, transiting Jupiter had reached 11 Cancer, approaching a conjunction to the natal Sun and a square to natal Saturn, important because as ruler of the Sagittarius Ascendant (expansion), Jupiter's conjunction with the Sun suggests a new period of expansion, which the attacks certainly initiated, via a new authoritarianism (Saturn). The attack itself surely reflects the long-standing anger resulting from the centuries-long expansion (Jupiter) that has taken others' resources (Sun in the eighth house) and ignored others' religious and financial values.

An Astro*Carto*Graphy map for the event shows the Saturn line going right through lower Manhattan Island. To some, this will indicate that the attack came from forces in the U.S. government hierarchy (Saturn), but though some will see such a view as not unreasonable, Saturn on the descendant points to open enemies. If we posit that the attack came from within, we would seek something involving the twelfth house, hidden enemies. Interestingly, we have such a symbol, as Pluto rules that twelfth house, so the hidden power system in the U.S. could easily have planted explosives underneath the World Trade Center, as some have suggested (as in the film *Loose Change*). I wouldn't discount this interpretation, though I think it more likely that Saturn's position on the descendant suggests the open enemies who did the attacking, while Pluto on the ascendant ushers in a new period of power, executed via secret (twelfth house) channels, once again launched against the national projection of Pluto. This interpretation also points to the financial ruin that followed upon this new period of power, as the wars in the Middle East have surely undermined the financial power and security of the United States.[75]

We have seen that Pluto often arises partly or entirely as a projection, as it does here. Even though Pluto's transit of the ascendant ushered in the new period of expansive (Sagittarius) and underhanded (influence of twelfth house) power (Pluto), it also arose at least partly through the people who attacked the World Trade Center. Say what we will about the ways the U.S. provoked the attack or the ways in which the U.S. "intelligence" refused to see it coming, despite available evidence, we still must interpret the attack as a plutonic enterprise, and the people who flew the planes on 9-11 certainly qualified as plutonic operatives. Saturn-Pluto stands as a nice symbol for old and festering resentments finally emerging into the open; that the aspect falls on the horizontal

---

[74]Despite its placement by transit on the Ascendant, Pluto, opposite Mercury in the birth horoscope, seems to arise, here as throughout U.S. history, at least partly via projection.

[75]In the years leading up to 9/11, Pluto made its way through the U.S. twelfth house, the house of secrets and hidden enemies. It would make sense, therefore, that government agents worked in secret to present something later (the events of 9-11) to the public, and that the presentation would take place as Pluto came over the Ascendant. Of course, it would also make sense that the "hidden enemies" gaining power during the twelfth house transit served as the hook for U.S. projections: foreign operatives planning and executing the plans of 9-11. Because of the U.S. tendency to project Pluto onto others, I find this second explanation a bit more convincing, though one might also argue that secret operatives in this country (e.g. CIA employees) served as hooks for the projections coming from the U.S. public.

axis of the horoscope speaks volumes about the astrological message to the U.S. about dealing with the national projection pattern. The opposition arose through a series of events: not only the attack on the World Trade Center, but also the subsequent bombing of Afghanistan, anthrax-related incidents in this country, the wholesale altering of the United States' position in the world, and the institution of a quasi-police-state at home. The opposition presents a paradox, for though we might expect the United States to play the role of Saturn, as it does so readily and so often, in this case Saturn appears on the Descendant, on the cusp of the house of "open enemies" and "the other" in general. Further, though with Pluto on the Ascendant we would expect the U.S. to take on the plutonic and plutocratic role, and though other nations surely saw the U.S. as doing precisely that, the U.S. tends to project that energy onto others and so experienced Pluto as people from foreign countries (Sagittarius) with hidden power (Pluto) attacking a symbol of financial dominance (World Trade Center). So as the U.S. took on the role of the authoritative power (Saturn-Pluto) and played it to the hilt, it also projected the entire aspect onto others (e.g. onto "terrorists" who represented traditional values and the structural securities of their own regions).

Whatever person or group organized and carried out the attacks on the World Trade Center served as an excellent hook for the projection of both Saturn and Pluto, making the projection difficult to recognize and re-collect. Millions in the U.S. readily took the projection for a simple reality and not a complex problem requiring something other than a merely externalized response. No national re-examination took place; very few discussions of causes took place in any U.S. media outlet. Yet any situation involving projection involves, as Ms. Von Franz points out, a need for a moral re-examination. Indeed, the U.S. didn't seem to go through any of the stages necessary for the withdrawal of projections: considered as a whole, the country didn't separate the facts of the extensional situations from the country's ideas about it; it didn't undergo any moral evaluation; it didn't consider any elements of the situation as illusory or as connected as much with the perceiver as with the perceived; and it certainly didn't ask any serious questions about the psychic factors involved. Instead, the U.S. apparently remained in the state of primitive identification, considering the perception as identical to the extensional events.

If we label the attackers as "Islamic Fundamentalists," or something of that order, they serve as perfect hooks for the projection of Pluto, a planet associated with fanaticism, religious or otherwise, and with a close connection to power arising from hidden places (and most Middle Eastern places will seem, to the U.S., as hidden and shadowy). But what makes the situation particularly difficult is that these so-called fundamentalists will also cast themselves in the role of Saturn: they will see themselves as the protectors of tradition, the keepers of a traditional order. If we then turn to the Taliban, the "open enemies" attacked in Afghanistan, we again see both Saturn and Pluto: they provide a strict set of rules and regulations; they limit artistic expression; they have taken bureaucratic control in Afghanistan; and they seem involved, even if only in a supporting role, in some activities not unreasonably labeled "terrorist." However, if they quite reasonably cast themselves in the role of Saturn (for they had bureaucratic power in Afghanistan), they would find a perfect hook for transiting Pluto in the plutocratic power attacking their country. (Also, because the U.S. Saturn squares the Cancer Sun, we would also expect some connection, in the projections cast upon the Taliban, to agriculture. The Taliban limited, some would say nearly eliminated, the growth of opium poppies, replacing those poppies with food-crops. Thus they brought some benefit to the country via both Saturnian limitation and Cancerian fruitfulness.)

We can see quite clearly that the events of 9/11 did not bring about national soul-searching in the U.S. Rather, the nation expressed itself via its Ascendant and related factors: it expanded its influence; it attacked others (Mars in the seventh house) after "long journeys over water" (Neptune in the ninth house); it saw the Taliban, a group concerned with domestic matters, as the aggressor and thus sent the U.S. military to attack them; and it took on the role of international authority, losing much self-respect in the world in the process (transiting Saturn in the eighth house). When projections alleviate life in what ego takes as a positive way, one will not feel the need for reflection; with its military might yielding apparent success in defeating projections, the U.S. did not at first feel the need for reflection. Even at this writing in 2012, the U.S. has still not admitted to any significant wrongdoing. Expansion (Sagittarius Ascendant) again served to keep the national psychosis at bay.

As noted briefly above, the U.S. Mars-Neptune square also came into play during the 2003 invasion of Iraq and its aftermath: transiting Pluto first contacted the square in January 2004; it didn't leave the relevant degrees until October 2005. If, furthermore, we allow some orb of aspect both entering and (to a lesser extent) when leaving, we would see Pluto as affecting Mars-Neptune in the run-up to the war, in the initial invasion, and in the first few years of the invasion-occupation. During the first year of the invasion, SP Mars turned retrograde, strongly indicating that the United States would find itself stuck in the sand as a result of its own deceptions.[76]

In opposing Mars, transiting Pluto squared natal Neptune, thus forming a t-square to the latter. PlutoNeptune empowers illusion. It can also empower inspiration, or compassion; but neither seemed evident in the invasion, unless by "inspiration" we understand the inspiration to enforce U.S. will on others. Pluto empowers the delusions related to national ideology (natal Neptune in the ninth) and to inequality (Virgo). The square suggests difficulty in making headway, particularly considering secondary progressed Mars' retrograde turn. Mars suggests aggression not only from the U.S. (military action), but also from others (e.g. so-called "insurgents" in Iraq). The t-square suggests great challenges in dealing with the prevailing national delusions no matter how much evidence came to the fore. Unfortunately, the transit brought challenges by *empowering* the delusion.[77]

---

[76] A discussion of Mars' retrograde, and Mars' entrance, decades back, into the "shadow of the retrograde" would take us too far afield. Suffice it to say that Mars' retrograde motion will take Mars back over positions it passed in direct motion back in the 1970s during, among other developments, the hostage crisis in Iran. During his retrograde, secondary progressed Mars will pass back over natal Saturn and square to the natal Sun. These developments do not bode well for the United States, suggesting as they do a lack of success in military ventures, conflict with other nations over resources, and a reaping of karma over past deceptions (Neptune) stemming from an insistent sense of national destiny (Neptune in the ninth house). Mars retrograde also suggests aggression turned inward; we see, as one of its manifestations, the turning of the power of the authority state against people within the U.S. (I've borrowed the phrase "stuck in the sand" from Christopher Hitchens' Harpers article with that title (http://harpers.org/archive/1991/01/0000414).

[77] The same aspects coincided with the flooding of New Orleans during and after Hurricane Katrina. Transiting Pluto em-

The astrological material suggested a resolution to this rather unsettling difficulty. The t-square "emptied" into the third house.[78] This house symbolizes neighbors, siblings, and one's daily round of activity, the ordinary as distinguished from the philosophical. We find emphasized, here, the need to treat other countries as neighbors or siblings with common interests, as people with whom we could establish straightforward communication, not merely as enemies or people who do not measure up to the morals and principles purportedly held by the U.S. The configuration also suggested that the U.S. can find solutions in neighborhoods, in local control (e.g. local control of education, but also such things as solar power, which takes people off the central grid, enables them to power their homes *from* their homes, and helps to reduce the so-called dependency on foreign oil as a cause of Middle East difficulties). Obviously, these potential solutions never got a fair hearing, for transiting Pluto brings the natal Mercury-Pluto aspect into play, suggesting control of the press by plutocrats who seek solutions in power dynamics instead of neighborly connections or cooperation.

The third house also suggests the use of mind to gather facts. The ninth house, by contrast, suggests mind directed by principles and abstractions. The ninth starts from abstractions and applies these abstractions to particular situations, overlaying the latter with the former. The ninth house has a natural affinity with Sagittarius (the ninth sign) and with deductive thinking. The third house has much more to do with inductive thinking: with reasoning from facts toward conclusions. The United States' primary delusions arise from its tendency to abstract before gathering facts, from its tendency to see the world in terms of abstractions that may have little relation to the actual situation. Pluto's transit square natal Neptune brought this difficulty to the surface, as the government and millions of Americans refused to look at the facts, preferring to remain with principles related to U.S. "benevolence," "security," and expansion, principles annunciated or assumed in the documents enumerated above.

Though the t-square suggested that the U.S. could find balance by simply looking at the facts, by reasoning inductively (third house) instead of deductively (ninth house), the U.S. could never take that simple step. Thus T.D. Allman ponders in another context, "Would our leaders be able to differentiate between simplistic doctrines and the manifold complexities of the world? Would they be able to distinguish between reality and fantasy?"[79] Because the U.S. seldom if ever makes that distinction, it promulgates delusions like the ones that did such harm in 2003 and the years following. The U.S. horoscope suggests that the country acts (Mars) on its delusions (Neptune), bringing the military (Mars) to bear, attacking alleged enemies, seeing aggression in others and only benevolence at home. Mr. Allman describes the pattern:

---

powers the lord of the waters, altering structures of all sorts, overwhelming those structures and opening the doorways (so to speak) to inundation. The horoscopic factors suggest what many leftist commentators have suggested: a connection between the lack of government response in New Orleans and the invasion of Iraq.

[78]We could see a t-square as like a three-legged table; it needs the fourth leg, symbolized at the point opposite to the focal planet. For the t-square in question, this point—the so-called "karmic degree"—is at 22+ Pisces in the third house.

[79]Allman, 99.

A history of conquest, oppression and massacre is easy enough to relate. But how does one come to grips with the progression through time and across foreign lands of an illusion, a fantasy, a kind of hallucination?[80]

---

[80]Allman, 98.

Chapter XI

Perception and "Reality"

(Along with Some Remarks About Pluto as a "Higher Vibration" of Mercury)

Pluto plays an important role whenever projections dominate the personal or public spheres—which means pretty much all the time. In order to understand Pluto's role in projective reality (a term we will examine), we should begin with Pluto itself, investigating its function both in our personal lives and in the life of the collective. In the latter, Pluto gives us continual examples of the energy of collective projections, for when millions reject Pluto as a personal potential, the energy arises in problematic form in events that influence all of us. As discussed in chapter IX, the potent developments around the time of Pluto's discovery gave humanity its first collective insight into the planet's nature.

When astrologers discuss Pluto, they generally talk about power: power struggles, the doings of totalitarian governments, the clandestine doings of capitalistic "democracies"; persons or groups having power over others; a person being in the grip (under the influence or *power*) of a neurosis, complex, delusion, or conviction. Some astrologers will also point to Pluto's cathartic effects, or connect Pluto to death and rebirth processes, clearly an area of power, or with the dredging up of powerful complexes. Most will speak with some foreboding of Pluto's influence, and not surprisingly, considering Pluto's connection with the taboo. In part, Pluto symbolizes that which people have rejected and considered unacceptable, for both quasi-instinctual reasons, as seems the case with the incest taboo, and socially conditioned ones, as in the taboo against prostitution and (among some groups) homosexuality. We might do better not to call these last two *taboos* at all, as they seem to represent social prejudices instead of the biological facts apparently connected to the incest taboo; however, both come at least partly under the auspices of Pluto, the former because Pluto represents a non-conscious power-drive that transcends the personal, the latter because Pluto, as the son of Saturn, symbolizes behaviors considered taboo because of some sanction from a hierarchical power-system. Prohibitions against homosexuality clearly arise not from an instinctual reaction to the behavior (for if it did, all societies would have opposed it, and they haven't), but because of the idea-structures (Saturn) of people living within social structures (Saturn) that in turn encourage the types of idea-structure in evidence—ongoing feedback loops. In general, of course, Pluto has a close connection to all taboos involving sexuality and power.

Some astrologers also see in Pluto a symbol for a kind of fate that manifests with an implacable insistence in both the apparently external world of objects and the seemingly internal world of thoughts and feelings. The decrees of the Lord of the Underworld have always been taken as irrevocable, so that the world seems like a stage on which the fates of individuals go through motions some take as predestined or preordained, as if we all find ourselves in some sort of Thomas Hardy novel.[1] Then, too, Pluto seems to hold some sort of hidden truth, a truth that one purportedly should not, or dare not, speak, even if one could, perhaps because one has concluded that this truth holds great power to do harm if it gets into the wrong hands. (The knowledge of plutonium comes to mind, as do the teachings of some spiritual traditions.) In any case, one generally finds it difficult to describe this hidden truth in words, perhaps because the notion that it "is" a truth arises from linguistic habits that Pluto seems to undermine.

Of Pluto's purportedly hidden (purported) truth, we can say that it appears quite clearly in the world around us. We can see death and rebirth all around us all the time—or, we can see what we *describe* as birth and death. We may take the death-and-rebirth process as a merely external phenomenon instead of as a metaphor or reflection of the mind. Here, perhaps, we find why Pluto's "truth" remains "hidden": we find it difficult to see because we keep looking for something external rather than internal, something thing-like instead of process-like, something we feel we can grasp instead of something that grasps us—as some will say fate does. Thus we may say that the truth "is withheld," "is secret," but perhaps because of social habit, not because of *its* nature but because of *our* habits. Perhaps we have developed those habits because the truths we wish to keep hidden threaten ego's hegemony—or its very existence, for ego seems to depend on its own hegemony!

Astrologers generally interpret Pluto as a planet associated with emotion, particularly with emotional complexes, emotional upheaval, and emotional power-struggle. Pluto rules Scorpio, a water sign associated with depth of feeling and a tendency to interpret all situations in terms of the emotional power involved. When Pluto comes calling, we generally see examples of this powerful emotional upheaval. The connection between Pluto and emotion seems arrived at both inductively and deductively: inductively because it seems supported by evidence; deductively because it follows from certain premises about Pluto itself, premises drawn from Pluto's mythic relationship with the

---

[1]Hardy had Pluto conjoined his Midheaven in the tenth house, so it appeared in his public presentation (his writing).

underworld and the figures that rise up from it, a relationship we will examine in due course.

Much evidence suggests a connection between Pluto and rape, assault, power-struggle, plutonium, suicide, and self-destructive tendencies. These and other connections suggest that we not take Pluto lightly. Pluto can bring a kind of emotional intensity that many people find difficult to deal with, intensity that seems to burst its socially-defined containers and wreak havoc on the local or non-local territory. On the historical stage, Pluto arises, accompanied by other planetary energies, as plague, mass destruction, deadly viruses, and famine, to take just a few examples. We can see plutonic issues on both the collective stage and the personal one, and though the results on the latter achieve less historical notoriety, they often prove equally debilitating for those involved. All of that notwithstanding, if we restrict ourselves to saying that Pluto deals with forbidden emotions or fate, we won't necessarily know how to deal effectively with what arises; and if we simply say that Pluto brings "transformation" without speaking of the component parts of that transformation or how to bring it about, we don't help ourselves very much. As we will see, by providing a different analysis of the Pluto-problem, we open the door to alternative praxes. Within experiences associated with Pluto we can find keys to understanding Pluto's nature and thus to enhancing our lives.

We have already looked at the events taking place back at the time of Pluto's discovery, finding in that material some important keys to Pluto's meaning.[2] Many astrologers quite rightly point to Hitler's rise to power as appropriate to Pluto's symbolism, indicating Pluto's connection to totalitarian governments and the ruthless subjugation of one group of people by another. When death seems to stalk the world, we generally find Pluto active in one way or another, perhaps through transit to a nation's birth-chart, or perhaps through a strong natal (or transiting) Pluto in an important leader's birth chart, perhaps in some other way. As an example of the first, consider solar arc Pluto's late 1940s conjunction of the United States Sun in Cancer and square to Saturn in Libra in the tenth house, a movement coincident with the development of the CIA and an often ruthless national drive toward international power, supported in part by the power of the atomic bomb and in part by equally-Plutonic secret agencies, quintessentially Plutonic devices.[3] Transiting Pluto's movement through the same area of the zodiac in the mid-to-late 1920s brought tremendous expansion of plutocratic elements in the United States economy and led inexorably to the crash of 1929, a development correlated with Percival Lowell's discovery of Pluto.

Consider, as an example of the connection between Pluto as a personal challenge and Pluto as a collective concern, transiting Pluto's opposition to Woodrow Wilson's Capricorn Sun and Pluto's

---

[2] As noted in chapter IX, the principle at work here is well-known to many astrologers: important events in the collective at the time of a planet's discovery hold a key to unlocking that planet's meaning. The metaphor—"holding a key"—seems important: by examining those events, we can unlock heretofore hidden meanings.

[3] The atomic bomb reflects Pluto not only because bomb-makers eventually saw plutonium as a substance of choice in bomb-making, but also because the bomb brings about enormous change from a very small amount of material, and because the destruction involves chain-reactions.

movement through Cancer altogether. The former brought Wilson much power and notoriety, but it also brought him into conflict with the international community (transiting Pluto in ninth, moving toward Wilson's Saturn and Midheaven) in the struggle over the League of Nations.[4] On a collective level, Pluto's entire transit through Cancer saw the death of old assumptions about security, and the rebirth of what seems a more destructive approach to the whole matter. Security became subject to power and collective ideas or assumptions; the underworld arose as a threat, embodied most obviously in people like Hitler, Stalin, and Mussolini, less obviously in people like Woodrow Wilson, Churchill, and Franklin D. Roosevelt.

More recently, solar arc Pluto's square of the United States' Ascendant[5] in mid-Sagittarius, along with transiting Pluto's opposition, from the first house (actions initiated) to the United States seventh house (open enemies) Mars, coincided with this country's 2003 invasion and occupation of Iraq, allegedly because Iraq had weapons of mass destruction (marked by Pluto, lord of mass destruction). But quite clearly the United States had at least as many plutonian qualities in play as did Iraq, for the U.S., sitting on mountains of plutonium and destructive weaponry, made a rather evident play for more power in the Middle East.[6] That transiting Pluto formed an opposition to the U.S. Mars suggests that one of the planets would arise as a projection: either the U.S. didn't see its own aggression (Mars), and therefore saw aggression only in others (Iraq, "terrorists," carrying the projection of natal Mars in the seventh); or the U.S. didn't see itself as a terrorist state, and thus saw terrorists lurking in all sorts of places. In this latter case, the United States would play the role of Mars (military action), seeing itself as in combat with Pluto-like others. The United States' deceptions entered the picture through its ninth house Neptune, square natal Mars and thus the apex planet for a t-square formed by transiting Pluto.

Furthermore, many problematic power-figures of recent history had Pluto afflictions. Consider Hitler with his Moon-Pluto quincunx, or Napoleon with his square of Pluto to the Ascendant. Richard Nixon's prominent tenth house Pluto opposed his Mars and Mercury, while Dwight Eisenhower, who helped bring Nixon to the forefront of American politics (and who was certainly not known, in the Third World, as kind, grandfatherly Ike) had Neptune and Pluto conjoined at his Midheaven,[7] an aspect suggesting self-deception concerning the use of public power as well as a connection to

---

[4]Woodrow Wilson: b. 12/28/1856 in Staunton, VA, probably at or around 11:45 AM.
[5]I am using the so-called Rudhyar chart for the United States.
[6]All three of the movements of solar arc Pluto to the U.S. Ascendant—1823, 1813, 2003—brought evident power plays connected to financial interests (Pluto in the U.S. second house). See chapter X.
[7]Each person's horoscope has important, non-Plutonic factors in play, particularly Saturnian ones. Of course, the presence of a strong Saturn plus a strong Pluto doesn't, by itself, demonstrate ruthlessness; much depends on other horoscope factors and the person's level of awareness, particularly about projection – an awareness not generally evident in so-called world leaders. The level-of-awareness will not appear in the horoscope. Still, a strong Saturn plus a strong Pluto will sometimes indicate that a person will have to deal with positions (Saturn) of power (Pluto), sometimes by being in one of those positions. Eisenhower's Neptune perhaps gave Eisenhower a rather idealistic or self-deceptive view of the power he wielded. The midheaven, a Saturnian position, suggests public display. Pluto, again, symbolizes power. Idealistic public power, then, possibly used deceptively, the deception directed both at others and at oneself.

power (Pluto) supported by collective emotion (Neptune). Each of these people accomplished a great deal of work (i.e. brought about great change) in a short period of time.[8] All of them exerted enormous influence over large masses of people, generally with not-very-favorable results.

Hitler provokes particular interest here not only because he came into power around the time of Pluto's discovery, but also because his activity seems to carry so much negatively plutonic energy. Hitler facilitated a ruthless totalitarian militarism through tremendous aggression and widespread scapegoating. He oppressed *through* power, was apparently obsessed and possessed *by* power, and functioned as a lens through which the power of the Germanic myth showed its destructive side to the world. The coincidence of dates is impressive: Pluto was discovered on February 18, 1930. In September of that year, the National Socialist party won over 6 million votes in the German election, up from 800,000 in 1928; the party won 107 seats in the Reichstag, a gain of 95. (Hitler was prevented from taking his seat because he was an Austrian: Saturn was in his third house, conjoining his Moon in Capricorn. He didn't become dictator until 1933, when Saturn finally crossed his nadir and began to move upward toward his Midheaven. Jupiter had conjoined his Midheaven in 1931, however, so he had already been in a position of prominence.)[9]

In the United States, the period after Pluto's discovery brought an exponential increase in the power of the U.S. military-industrial complex, the latter being a set of social forms linking collective wealth and government power. When discovered, Pluto was transiting the U.S. eighth house (the money of others, collective wealth), in the U.S. Sun-sign (Cancer), in a loose conjunction with that Sun, almost exactly conjoined the U.S. Sun-Mercury midpoint, loosely square Saturn and moving toward an opposition with natal Pluto in late Capricorn. Though Hitler has received the brunt of the blame for the Holocaust, the United States took little action to save Jewish lives and after WWII began to broker its own power in the world, as noted above. Howard Zinn tells us that in January, 1934, with Hitler well-ensconced as dictator and his campaign against the Jews gathering steam, the United States deliberately abstained from action: though "a resolution was introduced into the Senate expressing 'surprise and pain' at what the Germans were doing and asking for a restoration of Jewish rights," the State Department "used its influence to get the resolution buried in committee."[10]

Thus Hitler became a projection of Pluto for the United States. He served as a perfect hook, for he willingly slaughtered millions of people. However, viewed from a psychological point of view, he represented the unacknowledged power-drive in the national psyche. Appearing in the eighth house (values of others), Pluto arose through Hitler's values, through the dark shadows that gathered in Europe, while in the United States, people apparently felt absolved of any wrongdoing. Once Hitler disappeared from the international scene, the plutonic elements in the United States

---

[8] Physicists define power as the rate at which one does work, and they define work as a function of change.
[9] Dates and background information from *The People's Chronology* by James Trager (New York: Henry Holt and Company, 1994). Information comes from the relevant dates. (The book is an extensive chronology of world-events.)
[10] Howard Zinn, *Failure to Quit* (Boston: South End Press, 2002), 83.

rose to the surface in ways both evident (as in the bombing of Japan) and more shrouded (as in the Truman Doctrine).

The life of another markedly plutonian figure, Mahatma Gandhi, shows that Pluto doesn't always bring negative results. In 1932, Gandhi began his "fast unto death" to "protest the British government's treatment of India's lowest caste 'untouchables', whom he calls *harijans*—'God's children.'" These events reflect Pluto in several ways. First and most obviously, Gandhi saw the transformative power lying dormant in what many people considered taboo (i.e. in the harijans). Second, Gandhi insistently brought their plight to the attention of the collective (Pluto's dredging action). Third, Gandhi used methods we would certainly call "plutonic": he said he would fast "unto death"; and he demonstrated how even one person, acting with enough concentrated energy could bring about enormous change by setting off a chain reaction of awareness. A final detail: Gandhi, with his seventh house Pluto, decided to confront those with power (the seventh house symbolizing "open enemies"). His Mars-Pluto opposition suggests the possibility of Gandhi getting assaulted by others, and as we know, precisely that occurred. As with the plutonium bomb, Gandhi's methods demonstrated that something very small could, via chain reaction and once a "critical mass" arose, undermine the power of even the world's most powerful empire.

Much evidence suggests that though collectivities will generally make the worst possible use of Pluto, individuals can, through a process of personal transformation, make more positive use of the same energy. The process apparently involves seeing both oneself and the world in a new way, not so as to separate oneself from the world, but so as to work more powerfully *in* it, riding the Pluto dynamic in order to help others. Gandhi's life also reminds us that Pluto desires power and control both externally and internally. Gandhi exerted a rigid control over his body, had great interest in internal workings such as bowel movements, and did not allow himself what we, perhaps simplistically, call personal freedoms. Though we can see quite clearly the links between Pluto and people like Hitler, Stalin, Roosevelt, Eisenhower or Gandhi, we should remember that Pluto symbolizes a psychological dynamic as well as a political one, something internal as well as external; something that properly belongs neither to the internal realm nor to the external one, if for no other reason than that Pluto symbolizes the fusion of duality.

One might object that these events could not possibly reflect Pluto's discovery, that people had acted in this way before. But a planet's discovery suggests not that energy didn't exist before, and not that people with special gifts or training cannot recognize it and work effectively with it (as Gandhi had done, following the example of people trained in his tradition, and as people in monasteries or spiritual retreat had demonstrated for centuries), but that the planet's energy appears clearly in the collective. For individuals, the newly discovered planet suggests that a psychological dynamic heretofore manifest only in special enclaves or situations now arises as the responsibility of every individual.

How shall we describe that dynamic? To answer that question, we can turn to two fields of investigation active at the time of Pluto's discovery: the work of quantum theorists, and Jung's work in alchemy and analytical psychology.

Collective Events and Mind

The year 1930 did not bring significant breakthroughs in the development of quantum theory. In fact, most of the major discoveries had already been made in the 1920s: in 1926, Erwin Schrodinger, extending the theories of French physicist Louis-Victor de Broglie, applied wave theory to quantum mechanics. In the same year, Paul Dirac advanced a formal theory that would "hereafter govern the study of submicroscopic phenomena."[11] In 1927, Heisenberg announced his Uncertainty Principle, in which he suggested that the process of observation affects the thing observed. During the same period, Dirac announced that classical physics exists as a "special case" within quantum theory. In 1927, Max Born and others offered what became known as the "Copenhagen Interpretation" of quantum theory (see below). However, though the work was done earlier, these men achieved world-wide recognition only after Pluto had been discovered: Nobel Prizes were awarded to Heisenberg in 1932, to Schrodinger and Dirac in 1933. (Max Born didn't get his until 1954, though Heisenberg felt that he should have shared the 1932 award with him.) The first textbook presenting quantum theory from the perspective of the uncertainty principle (Herman Weyl's *Theory of Groups and Quantum Mechanics*) appeared in 1928 and was translated into English in 1931, dates straddling the Pluto's discovery-date.

What did these people announce to the world around that time? Heisenberg stated that the more we know about an elementary particle's position, the less we can know about its momentum and vice-versa (or, that one cannot observe light as both a wave and a particle simultaneously), not because of the limitations of our instruments, but because of the effect of the observer on the system under observation and because of nature of the material (for lack of a better term) in that system, for the act of observation apparently affects the material being observed, so much so that the experimenter cannot separate them, and therefore cannot do an objective experiment on the "external world". Scientists might offer a physiological explanation for this:

> We can only [sic] see things by looking at them, which involves bouncing photons of light off them and into our eyes. A photon doesn't disturb an object like a house very much, so we don't expect the house to be affected by looking at it. For an electron, though, things are rather different. To start with, an electron is so small we have to use electromagnetic energy with a short wavelength in order to see it (with the aid of experimental apparatus) at all.[12]

In fact,

> ...if an electron is in an atom, the very act of observing it may knock it out of the atom altogether.[13]

Heisenberg was clear on the implications of his conclusion. "We cannot," he said, "know, as

---

[11]Trager, 776.
[12]John Gribben, *In Search of Schrodinger's Cat* (New York: Bantam Books, 1984), 156.
[13]Gribben, 157.

a matter of principle, the present in all its details" because "the more accurately we know the position of a particle, the less accurately we know its momentum, and vice-versa."[14] All of this, of course, assuming the particle-nature of the phenomenon in question—that is, assuming that what we observe "is composed" of particles, of things that are thing-like instead of idea-like; however, sometimes light behaves like a wave, and when scientists do experiments designed to measure these waves, they do not measure the behavior associated with particles. John Gribben explains:

> The questions we ask [at the quantum level] are highly colored by our everyday experience, so that we seek properties like "momentum" and "wavelength," and we get "answers" that we interpret in terms of those properties. The experiments are rooted in classical physics, even though we know that classical physics does not work as a description of atomic processes. In addition, we have to interfere with the atomic processes in order to observe them at all, and, said Bohr, that means that it is meaningless to ask what the atoms are doing when we are not looking at them. All that we can do, as Born explained, is to calculate the probability that a particular experiment will come up with a particular result.[15]

Heisenberg published his ideas in 1927. He explained uncertainty by describing electrons, as in the passage above about a photon (light particles) bouncing off other electrons (or houses, skyscrapers, etc.). However, it turns out that "what the uncertainty principle tells us is that, according to the fundamental equation of quantum mechanics, there is no such thing as an electron that possesses both a precise momentum and a precise position."[16] This seems to suggest that electrons don't exist in the way we normally assume that they exist; it also seems to suggest, as electrons purportedly function as one of the fundamental parts of the external world generally, that the external world doesn't exist in the way we generally assume that it exists. Further, it seems to suggest that the world arises as it does because of our observations—our experiments, for Heisenberg—in which we approach the world via our conceptual frameworks (Saturn). Pluto transforms this, inviting us to look into the empty space between observer and observed, symbolized by the space between Pluto and Charon.

According to quantum theory, the uncertainty principle doesn't reflect the limitations of our instruments; if we search for the reason why we cannot ascertain some qualities via experiment, we would not conclude that the problem lies with our inadequate instruments, or that if we only had better instruments, we could simultaneously measure the position and momentum of a sub-atomic particle. Rather, the uncertainty apparently arises as "a fundamental truth about the nature of the universe."[17] Apparently, according to quantum theory, we cannot facilely separate or distinguish mind-stuff from non-mind stuff; mental events and what we think of as the external events of the phenomenal world do not seem clearly distinct. All of this, at least, from the perspective of quantum theory.

---

[14]Qtd. in Gribben, 156, 157.
[15]Gribben, 120-121.
[16]Gribben 157.
[17]See Gribben, 119-120.

Pluto suggests, and constantly reminds us, that we should take these principles as descriptions, not only of the sub-microscopic world of elementary particles, but also of our social relations and of the unconscious mind, of mind and world generally. We tend to think, as we go about our daily business, which we generally do without analyzing experience *per se*, that there is some sort of external world that we observe from some sort of central headquarters, and that the former goes its way independent of the latter, with the latter merely recording, either accurately or not, what goes on in the former. But quantum theory generally, and the Uncertainty Principle in particular – not to mention the Buddhist Yogachara and Madyamika[18]—seem to suggest that the act of observation doesn't seem neutral, but interactive and transformative (Pluto). Mind interacts with world, possibly to such an extent that we should remain wary of any hypothesis or assumption that separates them in the first place. In saying that we cannot know the present in all its details, Heisenberg apparently referred primarily to the quantum world. For "quantum world," read "unconscious"; for "unconscious," read "projections, personal and otherwise."

These questions recall our earlier discussion about whether projection involves merely misperceiving the world or whether it involves an actual change in that purportedly external and independent world. When we project onto an object some of the contents of the unconscious, we observe not the object itself, but our own version of it. We should at least admit the possibility that, on the object-level as well as the sub-microscopic one, we alter the observed world itself. This flies in the face of many theories of projection, for those theories either assume that the projecting person doesn't do any altering, or leave the entire matter undiscussed. If we assume that the projecting person doesn't do any altering, we apparently assume that the "object itself" exists as an objective something-or-other in itself, apart from anyone's perception of it. This assumption develops from a more encompassing assumption: that an objective world of some sort exists as an assemblage of objective something-or-others including the observed object. Such assumptions underlie most scientific work, particularly that undertaken before the so-called quantum revolution. After noting that science "requires a kind of faith" but that, unlike most religion, it introduces its basic assumptions "surreptitiously," E. Alan Wallace describes some of the most basic assumptions underlying traditional scientific investigation:

> The universe as it exists apart from human perceptions and conceptions can be known by means of scientific methods; although the world exists independently of our concepts, its components and laws can be grasped by concepts; although science repeatedly abandons its earlier theories, it is progressing steadily toward a correct representation of the universe.[19]

---

[18] We might add, here, the views of Sapir and Whorf. As we have seen in an earlier chapter, Sapir felt that our conceptual impositions, inherent to the language we speak, affect the way we experience the world. Whorf's studies of Native American languages suggest a similar conclusion. (A student of linguistics once told me that the Sapir-Whorf hypothesis "has been disproven." The statement, with *to be* lurking within it, suggests a Saturnian thinking-structure of which we should perhaps remain wary. In any case, the "proofs" that I have seen—"proofs" that the hypothesis "isn't true" or has no value—speak to claims that, to my knowledge, neither Sapir nor Whorf make.) See below.

[19] E. Alan Wallace, *Choosing Reality: A Buddhist View of Physics and the Mind* (Boulder: Snow Lion Press, 1996), 12.

We may think, at first glance, that stacks of data support such assumptions, but first-glance-observation has a well-deserved reputation for inaccuracy, particularly when collective assumptions affect, or even condition, that glance. Further, quantum theorists consider the traditional scientific model as a special case arising within quantum theory, which they consider more encompassing. Someone from a different culture—especially someone whose language has no close relation to our own—would perhaps start from different assumptions. (Consider Indians of the Great Plains praying to the buffalo before a hunt.) Finally, we should admit that we haven't examined our first-glance-observations very seriously, perhaps because we suspect or fear, in some region of the unconscious, that if we did so, we would discover something rather shocking, something ego would find threatening in the extreme, something best left unexamined just as we may prefer to leave psychological complexes unexamined. Ego depends on duality; it takes the external world as a reference point through which ego can anchor itself—or, at least, through which it can feel anchored, apparently depending on its projections for ballast.

But what if we *do* alter the object by observing it? One might, at least for sub-microscopic phenomena, offer the somewhat mechanical interpretation sketched above: photons bounce off sub-atomic particles and change or move those particles in some way. But as noted above, classical physics does not serve well as a descriptive mechanism for the quantum world, so perhaps we should not take the physical model (photons bouncing against this and that) literally. We might take it, instead, as a somewhat flawed model for processes largely or partly psychic, taking physical-psychic as another dualism arising possibly as a delusion—and reflecting our language-structure, of course. Some quantum theorists tell us that an electron doesn't really act like an object, that it merely has "a tendency to exist." But whether we take the process as mechanical or not, we can quite easily come up with examples of projections altering the object in the macroscopic world: when X looks lustfully at Y, Y reacts, changing in some way; when X looks suspiciously at Y, Y reacts, changing in some way. When we observe, we apparently don't always do so neutrally, so much so that perhaps we shouldn't we speak of "observing" at all, for much that we call *observation* probably qualifies as *evaluation*, however shadowy. In observing, it seems, we apparently alter the object's behavior in some way. Or, so we might hypothesize.

If the observation-evaluation carries with it sufficient unacknowledged and unconscious psychic material, significant alterations might occur in the observed person. Again borrowing terminology from Marie Louise von Franz, we could say that when one gets hit with a projection, it feels like getting hit with a projec*tile*. We can feel this particularly during intense emotional interactions. We might again offer a mechanical explanation, but because the projectile (the observation-projection) does not seem to have a physical form that we can measure with contemporary technology, we should probably not settle for an explanation offered in purely physiological terms. Consider the situation described above. The physical model suggests that any alterations must be the result of the photons and electrons involved. But one wonders whether the photons involved in lustful looks have different properties than those involved in suspicious ones. Still, even on this simple level, we observe alterations in the "observed objects"—in other words, we see the mind-phenomena interaction even on this evident level, working with what we call composite objects involved in human interaction and not with the sub-atomic interactions observed by physicists.

I don't mean to suggest, here, that these simple examples should convince everyone that projections alter the observed world. In the end, we may find ourselves dealing, here, with a pervasive and remarkably subtle process not fully describable or understandable with our current symbol systems. The examples merely suggest that in some cases we alter the world by observing it and by how we observe or perceive it—and that we can notice ourselves doing this if we look carefully enough; we therefore might well suspect that a similar process goes on in ways we do *not* observe. In order to clarify our understanding, we can turn to theories of language—or, theories that relate language to consciousness or awareness. We could find many such (as in the Buddhist Madyamika), but let's start with a more home-grown one already mentioned.

Writing a few years after Pluto's discovery on the differences between the Hopi language and what he calls Standard European Language (SEL), Benjamin Lee Whorf calls attention to the (in his opinion resultant) differences in world view between Hopi and European/American culture:

> I find it gratuitous to assume that a Hopi who knows only the Hopi language and the cultural ideas of his own society has the same notions, often supposed to be intuitions, of time and space that we have, and that are generally assumed to be universal. In particular, he has no general notion or intuition of TIME as a smooth flowing continuum in which everything in the universe proceeds at an equal rate, out of a future, through a present, into a past, or, in which, to reverse the picture, the observer is being carried in the stream of duration continuously away from a past and into a future.[20]

Whorf then speaks of "the metaphysics underlying our own language, thinking, and culture" (though he distinguishes the popular view from the view arising from "modern science"). This metaphysics, he says,

> …imposes upon the universe two great COSMIC FORMS, space and time; static, three-dimensional infinite space, and kinetic one-dimensional uniformly and perpetually flowing time—two utterly separate and unconnected aspects of reality (according to this familiar way of thinking). The flowing realm of time is, in turn, the subject of a threefold division: past, present, and future.[21]

He then points out that "Hopi metaphysics has its own cosmic forms comparable to these in scale and scope" and goes on to describe them—"MANIFESTED and MANIFESTING"—and to show how they have their root in language, particularly in verbs that according to Whorf point, in

---

[20]Benjamin Lee Whorf, *Language, Thought, and Reality: Selected Writings of Benjamin Lee Whorf* (Cambridge: Massachusetts Institute of Technology Press, 1956), 57.
[21]Whorf, 59.

different ways (ways not easily describable in our language), to the borderline between these two (i.e. between "manifested" and "manifesting"). According to Whorf, these linguistic habits – habitual tendencies perhaps created and certainly maintained by language—determine what a Hopi takes as "reality." According to Whorf, Hopi metaphysics includes the idea that what we would call the subjective realm (included in "MANIFESTING") has an ongoing and pervasive influence on what he calls the MANIFESTED. Of the MANIFESTING, Whorf says,

> This realm of the subjective or of the process of manifestation, as distinguished from the objective, the result of this universal process, includes also—on its border but still pertaining to its own realm—an aspect of existence that we include in our present time. It is that which is beginning to emerge into manifestation; that is, something which is beginning to be done, like going to sleep or starting to write, but it is not yet in full operation.[22]

Whorf's investigations suggest two conclusions relevant to our discussion: first, different languages produce different perceptions of what we might facilely call "reality"; second, some of these perceptions can include the notion that mind somehow alters what we take as external phenomena.

To say that we alter the world constantly simply by observing it, labeling it, or coming to conclusions about it may seem to suggest that mind occupies a primary position and the world a secondary one. We may be tempted to say that what we think of as world-stuff we should more properly think of as mind-stuff. We may find this idea attractive, but the astronomical facts and psychological meanings of Pluto suggest another interpretation. As we have seen, Pluto has a companion body: Charon. Some astronomers have referred to Pluto as a double planet: two bodies rotate around a common center where we observe no physical body.[23] The astronomical situation stands as an apt symbol for mind and phenomena rotating (symbolically speaking) around a common center where we don't find anything definite, where we find space and possibility. Just as quantum theorists see light as both wave and particle, so we can see world and mind as simultaneously the same and different. The empty center between Pluto and Charon suggests a mystery, empty space, generally not brought to consciousness—for we have to do, here, with underworld figures—in the relationship between mind and phenomena.

---

[22]Whorf, 60.

[23]Though most scientists will agree about the astronomical facts, they will not all agree on how to categorize Pluto and Charon. Some will say that Pluto is the planet and that Charon the Moon—and that, therefore, one should not speak of these bodies a double-planet. Nevertheless, some scientists have preferred to "think of Pluto/Charon as a double planet rather than a planet and a moon" (seds.lpl.Arizona.edu/nineplanets/nineplanets/pluto.html). All agree that Charon is "the largest moon with respect to its primary planet in the solar system (a distinction once held by Earth's Moon)." (Ibid). Of course, with the discovery of new planet-like bodies orbiting outside of Pluto, some astronomers have said that Pluto doesn't qualify as a planet at all. In what some will take as insouciant effrontery, I have sometimes suggested that astrologers should opt for the term "astrologically relevant mineral agglomeration orbiting Old Sol [ARMAOOL]," but "planet" certainly seems to trip off the tongue more lightly, pleasing Hamlet, the old god at the center of the turning cosmos. I should add that the astronomical similarities between Pluto and Earth (both with large moons and interestingly-placed barycenters) suggests the importance of Pluto to human evolution.

Thus the astrological Pluto directs us toward foundational processes underlying projection: the observing mind and the observed phenomena "are" not really one and "are" not really two; they rotate around a common center, go through an ongoing dance, and remain constantly in relationship. To find out more about that relationship, we can look more carefully at phenomena or at mind, or we can look at the empty space between them. If we look carefully at this empty space, we can learn a lot about our perception of the world altogether. I take Pluto's message—or, perhaps, demand—as something like the following: we must investigate this emptiness, this relationship between what we call mind and what we call phenomena; we must see how we participate in what we take as subject-object relations, what we call "human experience." Milarepa's remark about absolute truth arising in the space between two thoughts also seems relevant here.

As we have seen, from the quantum point of view, light (metaphorically, the "observable") "is" neither a wave nor a particle, just as, in the example used above, the woman upon whom the man looks lustfully "is" likely "neither one thing nor another."[24] Some scientists tell us that, depending on how we observe it, light actually *becomes* either one or the other.[25] If we take this metaphorically, it would seem that the world around us "is neither one thing nor the other," but that we shape it into a more-or-less specific conglomeration of "something or others" through observing it. After all, if light itself, necessary for all visual observation, arises as a specific something-or-other only because of how we observe it, we can probably say something similar about what light sheds itself *on*, what we call "the world," whether we limit that world to Schrodinger's Cat, or whether we include paramecium, electrons, quarks, and lions and tigers, and bears, oh my! We can put this in Plutonian terms: observation has *power*; it does work; it has effects; it affects the observed.

We should tread carefully here. We can start by observing that Pluto has to do with the power to affect phenomena, whether the effects result from a plutonium bomb or a penetrating awareness. We may say that the power resides primarily in the mind and that the results—the acts of dictators, their armies, and other elements of the phantasmagoria—qualify as effects resulting from mind. Perhaps such a causal model explains something of what goes on. However, in giving primacy to mind, such a view seems to relegate the phenomenal world, dictators' armies and all, to a less powerful realm, considering them a group of effects instead of causes. Such a view doesn't accord with the experience of most people, as phenomena certainly seem to have the power to create effects. Nevertheless, we seem to have direct access to mind and only indirect access to the world with its dictators, with the access coming through the mind. From a pragmatic point of view, then, and no matter what we say about how things "really are," we probably do well to begin our work with the mind instead of with the world, even as we do what we must regarding dictators, armies, and what Lao Tzu called "the thousand and one things."

---

[24]Male observers-interpreters-projectors would probably do well to remember that!
[25]See Gribben, 203ff.

I suspect that most of us will probably fall quite readily into a causal model, concluding that if we can locate a connection between mind and phenomena, mind must do the altering. We may think that what we observe (some particular something-or-other) "is what it is" before we alter it by observing it. In other words, we may think that what we observe has its particular form and that the form changes because someone or group of someones observes it. This version suggests that the observer somehow has power over the world, as if we all practice psycho-kinesis on an ongoing basis, altering the world by observing it. Perhaps this occurs, and we might find comfort in the power such a view affords us. However, such a view may tell us more about our assumptions than about the phenomenal world itself. Such a view distinguishes between the object and the observation, instead of suggesting that they could arise together, in dependence on each other. Perhaps the observer and the observed come together and give birth to something, belonging to neither, in the empty space between them. Such a process would mirror the relationship between Pluto and Charon; it would also accord with the nature of the underworld, wherefrom phenomena arise, and with Pluto, lord of death and rebirth, for with the death of our ideas about ourselves may come a new understanding of the way we experience the world. As we go along, we give continual rebirth to the world, or, as one Buddhist teacher once said, "Samsara begins now."[26]

Though we might say, adopting an ultimate point of view, that no causal relationship pertains—in other words, that events arise from the interaction of observer and observed, not because the observer does any causing—from the standpoint of the observer, observation seems like a cause that has an effect on the phenomenal world. The "Copenhagen Interpretation" of quantum theory seems to deal with related conundrums. It was first offered in 1927, as a synthesis of much experimental data gathered by quantum theorists, by Neils Bohr in lecture in Como, Italy. *In Search of Schrodinger's Cat*, John Gribben offers this interpretation:

> He [Bohr] pointed out that whereas in classical physics we imagine a system of interacting particles to function, like clockwork, regardless of whether or not they are observed, in quantum physics the observer interacts with the system to such an extent that the system cannot be thought of as having independent existence. By choosing to measure position precisely, we force a particle to develop more uncertainty in its momentum, and vice-versa; by choosing to measure wave properties, we eliminate particle features, and no experiment reveals both particle and wave aspects at the same time, and so on....
>
> ...Today, the key features of the Copenhagen interpretation can be more easily explained, and understood, in terms of what happens when a scientist makes an experimental observation. First, we have to accept that the very act of observing a thing changes it, and that we, the observers, are in a very real sense part of the experiment—there is no clockwork that ticks away regardless of whether we look at it or not. Sec-

---

[26]In Buddhist philosophy, *samsara* refers to the realm driven by delusion and characterized by suffering and confusion—what we generally call "the real world."

ondly, all we know about are the results of experiments. We can look at an atom and see an electron in energy state A, then look again and see an electron in energy state B. We guess that the electron jumped from A to B, perhaps because we looked at it. In fact, we cannot even say for sure that this is the same electron, and we cannot make any statement about what it was doing when we were not looking it...

This is the really fundamental feature of the quantum world. It is interesting that there are limits to our knowledge of what an electron is doing when we *are* looking at it, but it is absolutely mind-blowing to discover that we have no idea at all what it is doing when we are not looking at it.[27]

The connection to Pluto-Charon seems evident, but what has all this to do with our everyday lives? Though we might grant, at least for the sake of argument and speaking from an ultimate point of view, that quantum theory (the Copenhagen Interpretation in particular) offers an accurate description of the world in which we live, how does this view connect to our attempts to live our lives moment-to-moment, crisis-to-crisis, or opportunity-to-opportunity? I might say (and, admittedly, usually *do* say) that the coffee cup on the table in front of me in this coffee-shop does not go through major alterations as a result of my observing it, and I would bet my life savings (such as they are) that if I walk away for a moment, the coffee cup will, in the interim, act just as it does now (unless some dastardly being decides to act on it), preventing my much-needed caffeine concoction from spilling onto the not-entirely-clean wooden floor, waiting for me to return and feed what I call "my addiction" once again. How shall we bridge the gap between these quantum and Pluto-related truths and our experience, between truths apparently connected to ultimate questions and truths apparently connected to relative ones? Jung's investigations into alchemy, extending from his analytical psychology, suggest some answers.

Around the time of Pluto's discovery, Swiss psychologist Carl Jung offered ideas similar to those of the quantum physicists. In *Modern Man in Search of a Soul*, most notably in the chapter entitled "The Spiritual Problem of Modern Man," Jung notes that the external world is intimately interwoven with psychic processes. For example:

>...the psyche is not always and everywhere to be found on the inner side. It is to be found on the outside in whole races or periods of history which take no account of psychic life as such....Whenever there is an established external form, be it ritual or spiritual, by which all the yearnings and hopes of the soul are adequately expressed - as for example in some living religion—then we may say that the psyche is outside....[28]

In response to the events of the late 1920s and early 1930s, Jung said succinctly and clearly that

---

[27] Gribben 160-161.
[28] Carl Jung, *Modern Man in Search of a Soul* (New York: Harcourt Brace Jovanovich, 1933), 200-201, 203.

"we can no longer get along unless we give our best attention to the ways of the psyche."[29] Though each culture, he said, gives birth to its "destructive opposite,"

> ...no culture or civilization before our own was ever forced to take these psychic undercurrents in deadly earnest. Psychic life always found expression in a metaphysical system of some sort. But the conscious, modern man can no longer refrain from acknowledging the might of psychic forces. This distinguishes our time from all others. We can no longer deny that the dark stirrings of the unconscious are effective powers—that psychic forces exist which cannot, for the present at least, be fitted in with our rational world order...
>
> The revolution in our conscious outlook, brought about by the catastrophic results of... [World War I] shows itself in our inner life by the shattering of our faith in ourselves and our own worth. We used to regard foreigners—the other side—as political and moral reprobates; but the modern man is forced to recognize that he is politically and morally just like anyone else. Whereas I formerly believed it to be my bounden duty to call other persons to order, I now admit that I need calling to order myself.[30]

Whether he was conscious of it or not, Jung offers us here an interpretation of the importance of Pluto, discovered as Jung was writing his book (*Modern Man in Search of a Soul*, published in 1933) and of "collective projections" as described above (see chapter IX). As we've seen, the discovery of a new planet suggests that human beings must now take the energy of the new planet as a set of individual demands that we ignore at our peril, not only individually, taking the planetary energy as a component of psychological development, but also in the collective, where that energy arises as a conundrum that all humans must investigate. The power of the collective projection tells everyone that if we remain content to project that energy into the world, the results can threaten us all.

Each person must, therefore, take personal responsibility for the energy symbolized by a new planet. If individuals do not do so—if enough people refuse the call—the resultant collective projection will lurch out of control. Thus what Jung wrote in 1932 speaks to Pluto run amok:

> ...[t]he gigantic catastrophes that threaten us today are not elemental happenings of a physical or biological order, but psychic events. To a quite terrifying degree, we are threatened by wars and revolutions which are nothing other than psychic epidemics. At any moment several millions of human beings may be smitten with a new madness, and then we shall have another world war or devastating revolution. Instead of being at the mercy of wild beasts, earthquakes, landslides, and inundations, modern man is battered by elemental forces of his own psyche. This is the World Power that exceeds all other powers on earth.[31]

---

[29] Jung, 201.
[30] Jung, 203.
[31] C.G. Jung, *Essays on Contemporary Events* (London: Ark Paperbacks, 1946), 82. (The quoted material comes from the epilogue, taken from a lecture given in 1932 to the Austrian Kulturbund in Vienna.)

That Jung's words have a contemporary ring tells us that humans have apparently not dealt all that well with Pluto even to this day.

If we put together the ideas of Jung with those of Heisenberg, we might conclude that, because of the power of mind, each person must work diligently on his or her own unconscious, recognizing the connection between unconscious contents and the situations, personal or collective, that one confronts. Possibly Pluto's discovery presented a demand for a kind of collective alchemy through which people address apparently external issues at least partly by looking more carefully at momentary experience, the empty space mentioned above that presents itself constantly and in which arise both what we call problems and what we call potentials. Perhaps humans will always resist Pluto, for Pluto demands that we give up ego's hold not merely philosophically or intellectually, but immediately, within momentary experience, in our perceptions, concepts, and emotional confusion. Certainly the present resistance of external events, many carrying the mark of Pluto, to facile or externally oriented solutions suggests that we need a new approach to collective problems. Such a solution must include the potentials symbolized by Pluto.[32]

In looking at the world-scene in 1930, Jung apparently perceived a similar demand. He recognized that "the upheaval in the world and the upheaval in consciousness are the same."[33] This recognition reflects Pluto in at least two ways. First, Jung saw clearly the rise of what astrologers might call "negative plutonic manifestations" in the world: ruthless totalitarian powers on the rise. Second, he recognized that such problems would resist solutions that didn't take account of the psyche. He recognized the presence of the psyche in the problem itself, just as quantum theorists saw the observer in the material observed, and thus concluded that we must include in our solutions an understanding of that psyche. People will not solve "external problems" if they fail to recognize such problems as psychic disturbances. If the root of the problem pointed down to the psyche, then people had to pay attention to that psyche, whatever its nature or extent, just as quantum theorists had to take the observer or experimenter into account.

Around 1930, Jung was making his first significant forays into alchemical ideas. Having had a series of dreams beginning in 1925 that seemed to point him in that direction, in 1928 Jung encountered Richard Wilhelm's translation of *The Secret of the Golden Flower*, an ancient Chinese alchemical text. In 1929, he wrote an introduction to that text, and in 1930, an obituary for Richard Wilhelm, writings that, along with a seminar given in 1929, gave us what Joseph Campbell calls the first "intimations...of his pre-occupation with alchemy." According to Campbell (in his introduction to *The Portable Jung*), it was through this book that

> ...light on the nature of European as well as far Eastern alchemy came to him. "Grounded in the natural philosophy of the Middle Ages, alchemy formed a bridge,"

---

[32] Quite likely the solutions must also include the potentials (and must address the challenges) symbolized by the newly-designated bodies beyond Pluto. However, I have not investigated the manifestations of those bodies enough to feel confident in making definite assertions about them.
[33] C.G. Jung, *Modern Man in Search of a Soul*, 201.

he found, "on the one hand into the past, to Gnosticism, and on the other into the future, to the modern psychology of the unconscious." Moreover, in European thought alchemy represented a balancing tradition to what Jung had always felt to be an excessively masculine, patriarchal emphasis in the usually accepted forms of the Jewish and Christian faiths, since in philosophical alchemy the feminine principle plays a no less important part than the masculine.[34]

Alchemy reflects Pluto in several ways. Through the alchemical process one transforms excrement or lead into gold: one transforms psychological darkness into the living plant of consciousness, something dead (lead) into something living. Metaphorically, alchemy involves a transformation from death to rebirth. Second, the process involves a constant confrontation with one's projections—or, more precisely, with the projection process *per se*. The alchemical texts that Jung references speak quite definitely of a close connection between mind and matter:

> The spiritual constitution of man in the pre-modern cycles of culture was such that each physical perception had simultaneously a psychic component which 'animated' it, adding a 'significance' to the bare image and at the same time a special and potent emotional tone.[35]

Jung himself wrote of the alchemical process that

> [t]he real nature of matter was unknown to the alchemist: he knew it only in hints. In seeking to explore it he projected the unconscious into the darkness of matter in order to illuminate it. In order to explain the mystery of matter he projected yet another mystery—his own unknown psychic background—into what was to be explained: Obscurum per obscurius, ignotum per ignotius! This procedure was not, of course, intentional; it was an involuntary occurrence.[36]

And he quotes an older text called the *Novum lumen*:

> To cause things hidden in the shadow to appear, and to take away the shadow from them, this is permitted to the intelligent philosopher by God through nature....All these things happen, and the eyes of the common men do not see them, but the eyes of the understanding [*intellectus*] and of the imagination perceive them [*percipiunt*] with true and truest vision [*visu*].[37]

Jung later quotes this passage from the *Tractatus Aristotelis*:

> The serpent is more cunning than all the beasts of the earth: under the beauty of her skin she shows a harmless face, and she forms herself in the manner of a *materia*

---

[34]Joseph Campbell. "Editor's Introduction" to *The Portable Jung* (New York: Viking Press, 1971), xxiv.
[35]C.G. Jung, *Psychology and Alchemy* (Princeton: Princeton University Press, 1953), 242. (The book appeared in Germany in 1944. Jung quotes, here, from Evola's *La tradizione ermetica*.)
[36]Jung, *Psychology and Alchemy*, 244-245.
[37]Jung, *Psychology and Alchemy*, 250.

hypostatica, through illusion, when immersed in water. There she gathers together the virtues from the earth, which is her body. Because she is very thirsty she drinks immoderately and becomes drunken, and she causes the nature wherewith she is united to vanish.[38]

Jung adds that the serpent is Mercurius "who as the fundamental substance (*hypostatica*) forms himself in the water and swallows the nature to which he is joined...Matter is thus formed through illusion, which is necessarily that of the alchemist. This illusion might well be the *vera imaginatio* possessed of 'informing' power."[39] Thus what we call matter appears through the workings of the mind; it does not function as a given something-or-other outside of the mind, that the mind merely observes. Thus Mercurius seems to have a close connection to the astrological Pluto—as does the astrological Mercury, as we will see below.[40]

Mercurius symbolizes both the material worked on and the solvent that does the work, as both the world "external" to the observer and the observer himself. The whole process involves an investigation of perception itself, an investigation of how we attempt to "know" the "knowable", how we attempt, as Buddhist teachers have said, to "see things as they are." Throughout his discussion, Jung has in mind the idea of "active imagination": "*vera imaginatio* possessed of 'informing' power," a process he attributes to alchemists, a version of which he often recommended to his clients. The secret of "the art," it seems, both to Jung and to the ancient alchemists, lies hidden in the human mind—or, Jung felt, in the unconscious. That the mind has an "informing" power, not just a power related to recording or mere observing, points to the active role played by the mind in all perception. At the same time, if unconscious contents appear, via projection, in the material world, then we can understand why Jung says that for the alchemist, "the one primarily in need of redemption is not man, but the deity who is lost and sleeping in matter."[41]

Pluto functions as a messenger from the unconscious, more particularly from the psychological complexes that most psychologists will recognize as having such a pervasive influence on perception. Pluto's constant presence reminds us that "active imagination" goes on all the time as a constantly-functioning but hidden power. Because projection seems such an integral part of our world, Jung wrote that "strictly speaking, projection is never made; it happens, it is simply there. In the darkness of anything external to me I find, without recognizing it as such, an interior or psychic life that is my own."[42] From such a vantage, it seems, we constantly re-invent the world, constantly seeing our *image* of the world instead of the world itself, not merely because of the limitations of our sense-organs, but because of the power of unconscious contents. Jung's practice thus takes a

---

[38] Jung, *Psychology and Alchemy*, 252.
[39] Jung, *Psychology and Alchemy*, 252.
[40] We've seen this connection before: in Europe in the years between the world wars, Jung saw Wotan, connected to our Wednesday, at work; in French, Mercredi means "Wednesday." Thus the connection between Mercury and Pluto, discovered as Jung made his observations.
[41] Jung, *Psychology and Alchemy*, 312.
[42] Jung, *Psychology and Alchemy*, 245.

very natural process—for it seems that human beings project constantly and quite "naturally"—and makes some of it perceptible to the conscious attention.

We may tend to dismiss the investigations of the alchemists. After all, how could any intelligent person claim to change lead into gold (despite the fact that radioactive substances change their nature constantly)? However, the ideas of the alchemists foreshadowed those of the quantum physicists, who assert that the mind affects the material world, at least on a sub-atomic—metaphorically: unconscious—level. Alchemists, working in laboratories as did the physicists of the early 20th century, made discoveries that seemed to them relevant to the world outside of the laboratory, at least symbolically (for many alchemists acknowledged that they did not seek the same gold as most people sought). In their treatises, many alchemists apparently assume that there exists a power, residing at least partly in the human mind, to transform symbolic lead into symbolic gold. Of course, many of those alchemists apparently understood their process as involving a kind of meditation, and meditation has not become part of the methodology of most quantum theorists—though some of them, admittedly, sometimes sound rather like contemplatives.

Though many scholars see chemistry as an advance on alchemy, the while admitting that the latter at least paved the way for the former, we might suggest that the opposite view has as much merit. Alchemists seemed to anticipate many discoveries of quantum mechanics. According to Paracelsus, the "prime material," that which the alchemist strives to transform, "is a great secret having nothing in common with the elements" and "fills the entire region aetherea, and is the mother of the elements and all created things."[43] Paracelsus felt that this "material" came from the deity; however, without engaging in any religious or doctrinal discussions, we should note that it sounds a lot like the Buddhist notion of space, the fifth element in most Tibetan systems, or the *alaya* (sometimes called the "storehouse consciousness"). In any case, as Jung notes, the alchemists "came to project even the highest value—God—into matter," a notion that brings us back to Pluto, for Pluto unites the apparently high with the apparently low, insisting always that to find what we call "spirit," we must work through what we call "matter."

We should not underestimate the importance of these mysteries. Jung wrote,

> With the highest value thus safely embedded in matter, a starting point was given for the development of genuine chemistry on the one hand and of the most recent philosophical materialism on the other, with all the psychological consequences that necessarily ensue when the picture of the world is shifted 180 degrees. However remote alchemy may seem to us today, we should not underestimate its cultural importance for the Middle Ages. Today is the child of the Middle Ages and it cannot disown its parents.[44]

When Jung spoke of the "psychological consequences that necessarily ensue" from the 180 degree

---

[43]Jung, *Psychology and Alchemy*, 320-1.
[44]Jung, *Psychology and Alchemy*, 323.

shift, he surely had in mind, at least in part, the destructive events of the 1930s and thereafter. The 180 degree shift has taken us into a world in which, despite the warnings of quantum theorists and experimentalists, we by and large have bifurcated our world into an external world apparently going its own way and an internal world, also going its own way and with little connection to external matter. We have already looked at the consequences for ourselves and for the world at large. But the substance "that harbors the divine secret" apparently exists "everywhere, including the human body" and "can be had for the asking and can be found anywhere, even in the most loathsome filth."[45]

Pluto has to do with the power of perception, with the power of the unconscious, with the power of active imagination, an ongoing activity that we can put to work not only to benefit ourselves, but also to benefit others and the world in general. We can speak of redeeming the world, but we first must recognize (to *know again*) that the world we wish to redeem has an ongoing, generally hidden, apparently pervasive, and certainly implacable connection to the mind of the observer. This truth applies equally to the quantum world and to the world of events. Jesus, the one who would purportedly redeem world from its sins, continually put the responsibility onto people to take up their burden. His death on a dualistic cross seems to suggest dying to a simplistic dualism; his rebirth seems to suggest that humans have the potential to overcome even the most opaque of those dualisms.

With a proper understanding of Neptune, a planet associated with imagination and apparent deception, we can do the Plutonic work more quickly. Uranus gives us the insight to begin, Saturn gives us the discipline and the social forms that both give us a reason to proceed and the *methods* to do the proceeding. Pluto reminds us that constant change, transformation, and death-rebirth characterize our world; he also reminds us that our conceptual frameworks, risen from fear, appear in the world as events. He reminds us, finally, that we have work to do.

Some might point out that I'm quoting from a text (*Psychology and Alchemy*) published over a decade after Pluto's discovery and thus not relevant to the energy of Pluto. However, with all things-Plutonic a chain reaction occurs. For Jung, the process can be traced back to 1916, when he first began to work with active imagination as part of his own work of self-discovery. The process was catalyzed just before 1930 when Jung read Wilhelm's translation of *The Secret of the Golden Flower*, for the ideas in this book dovetailed nicely with Jung's own. As we have seen, Jung was writing *Modern Man in Search of a Soul* during that period, articulating the close relationship between mind and world. Thus the period around Pluto's discovery proved a seed-time for Jung in the investigations that astrologers will recognize as relevant to the outermost planet discovered up to that time, and that even non-astrologers will recognize as a seed-time for our understanding of the hidden relations between what we call *mind* and what we call *matter*.

---

[45] Jung, *Psychology and Alchemy*, 313.

Jung seemed concerned, in *Modern Man in Search of a Soul*, with the rise of National Socialism in Germany, for though he doesn't mention Hitler by name, both in that book and in other writings he speaks clearly to the threat looming over Europe, a threat he saw as inextricably connected to the human psyche. As we have seen, Jung felt that in the modern age, people "can no longer get along unless we give our best attention to the ways of the psyche,"[46] presumably because if we don't, the projected psychic contents will endanger us all. He went so far as to claim that "[t]he upheaval of our world and the upheaval in consciousness is one and the same,"[47] suggesting that what according to the quantum physicists operates at the subatomic level also operates quite observably on the interpersonal and collective levels as well, always with roots in the unconscious. Astrologers will probably find this less surprising than most, for they recognize as part of their standard practice that external phenomena (the planets' positions and angular relationships) give us information about psychological states. They also know that the three planets associated with the unconscious also reflect, via their sign positions and aspects, observable collective trends.[48]

Perception and Transformation

One of the goals of any spiritual path must have to do with enabling students to experience the world accurately. If we don't experience the world accurately, if we rest content with our delusions, if we remain content with only our own version of things, we proceed in ignorance. The accuracy-in-question apparently does not depend on philosophical view. Rather, it has much to do with immediate perception, an ongoing process in which habit patterns intervene constantly in present experience, though we generally remain largely unaware that such interventions occur. Thus, clear perception plays an important role in any spiritual journey or spiritual path, playing the role of a *necessary* condition even if not a *sufficient* one.

We might wish that one astrological symbol would equate with the perceptual process, but as we have seen in the chapters of this book, all parts of the horoscope participate to a greater or lesser extent, with different symbols playing dominant roles in for different people at different times. As we have seen, important signs in a person's horoscope tend to influence the person's perception pervasively; planets in opposition aspects, or with strong gender orientation, or placed in certain houses, will all influence a person's perception, either continually, as with natal planets, or for a certain period of time, as with planets in time-analysis. Despite all this, it seems that the symbolism of Mercury and Pluto speak poignantly to elements in the perceptual process that arise for all of us.

---

[46]Jung, *Modern Man in Search of a Soul*, 201.
[47]Jung, *Modern Man in Search of a Soul*, 211.
[48]The first of these, Uranus, was discovered at the time of the French Revolution, a period which Jung was as transitional as regards the collective interest in psychic matters. "There can be no doubt," he writes, that from the beginning of the nineteenth century—from the memorable years of the French Revolution onwards—man has given a more and more prominent place to the psyche...." (*Modern Man in Search of a Soul*, 209). Uranus has a close astrological affinity with Pluto, it being the exalted ruler of Scorpio, the sign of Pluto's dignity, and an occult ruler of Aries, according to some the sign of Pluto's exaltation. We see this affinity in the link between uranium and plutonium.

Mercury does not symbolize the perceptive organs *per se*; nor does Mercury seem to deal with the objects of perception. Rather, Mercury symbolizes the way humans sort and categorize the results of their contact with the world, seeking a concept-based order instead of what we might call the natural order of the world itself. It also symbolizes the amoral curiosity that impels us to investigate the world in the first place. In this sense, Mercury symbolizes not only the way we sort information, but also the motive behind the sorting. Thus Mercury's role as a trickster, for our ideas about the world imbue the perceptual process, clouding it, making accurate-seeing or accurate-experiencing difficult to come by.

Buddhist teachings talk about five sense-organs: the five recognized in the west (i.e. sight, hearing, touch, smell and taste) plus a sixth one known as *mind*. "Mind" orders the other five senses into some kind of rudimentary order. *Yid*, the Tibetan term for this aspect of mind, signifies

> ...mental sensitivity. It is associated with the heart and is a kind of balancing factor which acts as a switchboard in relation to the other five sense consciousness. When you see a sight and you hear a sound at the same time, the sight and sound are synchronized to constitute aspects of a single event by the sixth sense. It does a kind of automatic synchronization job, or automatic computerization of the whole process of sense experience. You can see, smell, hear, taste and feel all at the same time and all of those inputs are coherently workable. They make sense to you because of *yid*.[49]

This doesn't mean that Mercury symbolizes what Buddhists understand as *yid*, but it clearly suggests a close connection between the two, for they symbolize similar functions. Astrologers have often linked Mercury to the "lower mind", the mind that takes information from the world and then sorts and labels it—functions distinct from those of the "higher mind," symbolized by Jupiter, that sifts meanings from that information, that develops meaning from the raw material of "lower mind" (for we probably should not assume that information itself contains meaning). Mythologically, Mercury functions as the messenger of the gods; experientially, Mercury brings messages from phenomenal world, not via direct contact, but via mind. Each of us *does something* after we make direct contact with the world. Contact becomes experience largely through Mercury, and this seems closely aligned to *yid*.[50]

This interpretation of Mercury's function doesn't diverge from that offered by other reputable astrologers. Robert Hand, one of the most articulate of these, writes,

> [Mercury] creates the relationship between subject and object that is necessary in order for consciousness to exist.[51]

In other words, Mercury does not symbolize the subject-object relationship per se, but only the re-

---

[49] Chogyam Trungpa, *Garuda IV: The Foundations of Mindfulness* (Boulder: Vajradhatu, 1976), 20.
[50] In the Buddhist system, yid, mind as the sixth sense consciousness, does not have direct access to the phenomenal world.
[51] Robert Hand, *Horoscope Symbols* (Rockport: Para Research, 1981), 55.

lationship "necessary for consciousness to exist." Human consciousness seems intimately connected to the use of symbols and rudimentary concepts (most of which we express through, or even derive from, symbols) in order to mediate between sense organs and awareness; perhaps we should see symbols as necessary to that awareness. If we take the first five sense consciousness as representing our connection to objects, then the sixth sense consciousness seems to create a relationship between object and subject. Somehow we seem to take something (e.g. an object) not part of consciousness and incorporate it into awareness, transforming something external and physical into something internal and not physical.[52] One energy becomes translated into an energy the other can understand. Mercury seems connected to this translating function.

This might seem a simple, automatic matter; but spiritual teachers would not place such an emphasis on perception if we could not penetrate it with awareness. Many spiritual teachings seem designed to prod students to question some of their assumptions about the way the world appears, suggesting that students needn't, and shouldn't, accept that appearance on its own terms. As Hermes, Mercury has functioned as a trickster from way back, and the same could be said for the way we take our moment-to-moment perceptions as accurate and unadulterated representations of the world in which we find ourselves. We take *interpretation* for *reality*, and so find that we have deceived ourselves. But before we can question our perceptions and assumptions, we first must know what influences them. Thus we find ourselves looking at the underworld, among other matters.

As Hermes, Mercury serves as psychopomp, guiding souls through the underworld; psychologically, he mediates not only between object and mind, but also, in company with Pluto, between conscious and unconscious mind, between the connections that we think we understand and those that operate beneath the surface, affecting all that goes on outside of the underworld. We can interpret these connections to mean that Mercury—our active intelligence, our curiosity, and our ability to label the world—can serve as initial guide in our attempts to understand the unconscious mind and its effects on our perception of the world. Certainly curiosity can help us to shed light on that underworld and on its dynamics, and so can help us to find our way through the hidden realm that appears before us all the time; we could not begin to understand those dynamics if we could not apply our conceptualizing abilities. (No evidence that I know of suggests that creatures unable to categorize have developed any inkling even that an unconscious mind exists, let alone any understanding of its function.) On the other hand, the connections-in-question should remind us that we must keep constant watch on Mercury, as we would with anyone known for playing tricks. Seeing might "be believing," but if our beliefs influence what we see, then we should probably look more carefully.

We could also say that our intelligence guides us through *this* world, and that *this* world seems co-extensive with the unconscious to the degree that the unconscious controls perception. In other

---

[52]Some may object by claiming that the internal event—the awareness—is also a physical event, probably one connected to the nerves. But an impulse along a nerve does not seem to have an equivalence relationship to the mental event even if that impulse makes the event possible.

words, when we experience "this" world, we experience the world as mediated by mind—and, most importantly, by mind under the influence of unconscious and non-conscious factors. If this occurs constantly, we will have a hard time distinguishing not only between "the world" and our perception of it, but also between that world and the unconscious elements arising within it. The two arise fused together—and so we find ourselves looking at one of Pluto's function as a result of having engaged Mercury. If we get too solidified in our ideas about these matters, we solidify perception and get tricked. If we investigate the trick, looking into things to see the hidden dynamics, we can begin to question the solidity. If we can get beyond the duality of real-vs.-illusion, we can take the first step toward transforming the phenomenal world.

This interpretation of Mercury-Pluto and the relationship between perception and power may seem far-fetched, the stuff of science fiction or the result of uncritical speculation. But though it doesn't accord with the mechanical world view, derived from Newton, that so dominates our everyday experience, it accords quite nicely not only with quantum theory, particularly the Copenhagen Interpretation, but also with Jung's tested practices in analytical psychology and with some theories about mind developed many centuries past, seasoned with contemporary terminology. If the "objective world" doesn't qualify as *objective* at all, but rather as a world peopled by our projections, then the "ordinary" world through which we move every day seems difficult to distinguish from the underworld. Insofar as we experience the compulsions of the unconscious as unpleasant, we might agree with Mephistopheles, who in Christopher Marlowe's Dr. Faustus equates our world with the underworld.[53] If we take our projections for accurate versions of "reality," then our ordinary world would indeed qualify as the underworld, for our projections come from the unconscious. Mercury, symbolizing the most ordinary function of mind (though not less mysterious for its ordinariness), guides us through a world we could categorize as "neither one thing nor another," but certainly peopled, colored, and pervasively influenced by unconscious contents (Pluto).

We solidify many of our projections by labelling them, for labels reflect the functions of both Mercury and Pluto, working in tandem. Mercury labels the world, but that "world" and the labels affixed to it carry the underworld with them. If we take the world that we label as "the real world," we freeze both the world and our perception of it; like Mephistopheles, we find ourselves in a hell, or at least a purgatory, of our own making. If we take the world as at least partly an underworld, we will investigate further, using Mercury (curiosity) either to find a way back to the surface or to live in the world with active interest and active intelligence. Some say that hell is cold, and the unconscious can freeze the world if we get caught in our own versions of "how things are"; however,

---

[53]The exact quote, from scene III, spoken by Mephistopheles in Faustus' study:
Why, this is hell, nor am I out of it:
Thinkst thou that I who saw the face of God
And tasted the eternal joys of heaven
Am not tormented with ten thousand hells
In being deprived of everlasting bliss?
The lines seem to me to accord quitely nicely with the experience of people when tormented by projection, as long as we consider "God" as referring to clear seeing and "bliss" as referring to the feeling arising from such clarity.

the unconscious can also transform that world. Or, we might say, it does so constantly, though we generally don't see the process clearly.

Saturn—sometimes known as Satan—tells us what the world "is" and creates consensus reality. If we close down as a result of our acceptance of that world, we see why Saturn has a reputation as the Greater Malefic. On the other hand, if we remain open about the nature of Saturn's world/underworld, we invite ourselves to investigate, to get beneath the surface by examining the surface insistently—for, after all, surface/beneath-the-surface seems like another dualism created by Saturn but not accepted by Pluto, for whom the contents of the surface world seem to, at the very least, arise imbued with unconscious material. We can learn to live happily in the underworld as long as we see that we've seldom experienced anything else, and that even our notions of happiness and unhappiness reflect a dualistic bias (possibly driven by language, as suggested earlier).

Pluto symbolizes a kind of ongoing "active imagination." Though I do not use this term in the formal Jungian sense, some of the cautions explained by Marie Louise von Franz about that practice apply here as well as in formal counseling. In words that remind us of Pluto's connection with magic, destructive or otherwise, Ms. Von Franz writes that "such misuse of the imagination is very dangerous" and that it can be very attractive "to people with schizoid tendencies." It "by no means gets them out of their mess," she says, "but on the contrary makes them vulnerable to psychosis." Pluto, as astrologers know, can produce tremendous inflation *and* tremendous depression; in some cases, a client may not benefit from being told about the aspects of Pluto's power under discussion here. Some people, after all, will do better to work simply and directly with consensus reality. I would say, really, that we all should start by dealing squarely with consensus reality. Pluto may yield the riches of the underworld in the form of insight, but we can easily get overwhelmed if we don't have our feet planted firmly on Saturnian earth! As always, Pluto offers a paradox: while on the one hand perception can have a transformative effect on both inner and outer worlds, it seems to produce benefit only when we don't seek any power.

Nevertheless, what we generally call "perception" or "our experience of the world," seems colored, shaped, and brought into existence by the dictates of unconscious factors—and we would do well to keep this in mind as much as possible. Pluto symbolizes our capacity to recognize this coloring, shaping, and bringing into existence, thereby attaining insight into the perceptual process and a more accurate connection to the phenomenal world altogether. Pluto thus functions as a higher vibration of Mercury, giving us new information about the nature of perception, intelligence, and communication, whether between self and other, or between self and the world as a whole.

As a symbol for the "lower mind," Mercury generally takes the world as it appears, creating categories or symbols in response to that world. Jupiter, generally held to symbolize the "higher mind," often arises simply as a tendency to form higher mental categories; as a symbol for the philosophical mind, Jupiter can surely indicate a broadened understanding, though he usually needs reminding that "victory is an illusion of philosophers and fools."[54] Pluto also has a close connection

---

[54]William Faulkner, *The Sound and the Fury*. Quentin Compson quotes his father as saying that "…no battle is ever won,"

with the mind and mental functions, though not as either "higher" or "lower," even if as lord of the underworld he seems lower than Mercury, who mediates between worlds, and even if as lord of the night sky, resplendent symbol of the underworld, he seems higher than Jupiter. Pluto symbolizes the fusion between mind and phenomena and our ability to see the fusing as it occurs moment-to-moment in our most ordinary mental processes, driven by forces about which we generally remain unconscious. From the world we get ongoing, though cryptic, messages; these often arise through gaps in our ongoing habitual awareness. We might call these gaps "little deaths," a term once applied to the orgasm, when the conceptual mind ceases, at least momentarily, to operate, leaving us at one with our experience and thus experiencing at-one-ment. This seems connected to what Milarepa said about non-conceptual wisdom arising between one thought and another. Pluto affects all of our communications, for any communication involves us in the same truth: that what we take as "other" appears to us as it does because of something extremely close to home, so close that the world may not qualify as "other" at all, just as Charon, part of the double planet we call "Pluto," may not qualify as "other" than Pluto. Pluto tells us that mind and phenomena rotate around a common center where we find nothing.[55]

Jung felt that some unconscious contents would never be incorporated into consciousness. In particular, he felt this about some elements or qualities of the collective unconscious, some of which he felt could split off and arise as autonomous personalities.[56] Much in the manner of medieval alchemists, he associated the unconscious with matter; we cast our projections into the world of matter, whether the matter that we refer to as "humans and their institutions," the night sky, or something else. (Of course, if we can't incorporate all unconscious elements—all matter—then some will continue to appear as the various elements of the material world, but we should perhaps put such metaphysical speculations to the side!) In any case, the world around us seems peopled with archetypes and shadows—or with shadowy archetypes. Thus the world, as Jung put it, can take on a darker cast, seeming more threatening; the darker realms of mind become the realms of the world. Yet we have the ability to shed light on these matters (so to speak).

Around Pluto's discovery, Jung wrote that "today we can no longer get along unless we give our best attention to the ways of the psyche." [57] Two things are worth noting, both having to do with Mercury and Pluto. First, to "give our best attention," we must engage the Mercury function. Second, "the ways of the psyche" seems to refer, at least in part, to Pluto. A few pages later, Jung spoke

---

that "they are not even fought," and that the battlefield "only reveals to man his own folly and despair, and victory is an illusion of philosophers and fools." See *The Faulkner Reader* (New York: Random House, 1953), page 59.

[55]Students of Buddhism may wish to equate this "nothing" with emptiness (Skt. shunyata). I don't necessarily disagree, though I remain wary of any attempts to find one-to-one correspondences between one system and another. Some measurements of vacuums indicate that vacuums, purportedly empty, have infinite amounts of energy, suggesting that nothing (e.g. emptiness, shunyata) is something.

[56]See, for example, Jung's discussion of this matter in his commentary to Richard Wilhelm's *The Secret of the Golden Flower* (page 112 of the Harvest Book version published by Harcourt Brace & World, 1962).

[57]Jung, *Modern Man in Search of a Soul*, 201.

of the need to "take these psychic undercurrents in deadly earnest."[58] If the *taking* and the *earnestness* suggest Mercury, the deadliness seems Plutonic, raising the stakes to life-and-death levels—not the death of the body, and not only the death of the ego, but death on a mass scale in the collective: the storm that became World War II in Jung's time, climate change and other developments likely causing millions of deaths in our own. We know about the intimate link between the world and the unconscious precisely because we have engaged Mercury: curious, we have considered, labelled, and looked into the Pluto-dynamic, seeing mind and world circle constantly around empty space.

Thus the world that we experience day-to-day and moment-to-moment arises imbued with underworld elements, at least insofar as that world consists of projections from the unconscious. It seems that with the discovery of Pluto, humans have at least partly overthrown Saturn as Lord of this World—or, that we *must*. Though as we have seen, Saturn still has enormous influence on the way people structure their world, his three sons have taken over some of his prerogatives and rule as a triumvirate. The ancient Greeks recognized Jupiter's importance, and not surprisingly for a culture with such an emphasis on abstraction, connected in obvious ways with Jupiter; our ability to abstract has given us extraordinary control over phenomena. But Neptune has, unbeknownst to most, also exerted great influence, as anyone who pays attention to deception can see; surely human beings have created the world they have at least partly out of yearning and self-deception. Finally came Pluto, who rules via the projective quality of mind, as unconscious elements arrive from the hidden realms, passing through the membrane made permeable by Neptune, to people the world with shadows. The world we experience seems ruled by Jupiter and Saturn insofar as it results from hope and fear; however, it also seems ruled by Neptune and Pluto insofar as it results from delusion and projection. Saturn's inability to devour his sons suggests that however much humans insist on status-quo reality, others truths will gain entrance into human society and the human mind—and that we should consider this a natural process.

Mercury/Hermes, the active and curious intellect, serves as a guide through these realms, particularly Pluto's. Through active perception of duality, through active curiosity and interest, we discern (Mercury) Pluto moving through this realm; if in our curiosity we refrain from making judgments or creating solid versions of "reality", accepting the creative and destructive elements equally (reflecting Mercury's hermaphroditism and Pluto's tendency toward fusion) we move intelligently (Gemini) and skillfully (Virgo) through the "common" world, the realm we think we know and understand.

In much astrological treatment of Mercury, we find a deeply imbedded dualism. It has been said, for example, that in Mercury's glyph the cross represents the mind's reaction to immediate circumstances, while the semi-circle represents mind's reaction to inspiration, thus nicely separating immediate circumstances from inspiration, as if one could not derive the latter from the former. And apparently many earlier astrologers assumed that we should see the inspiration as much preferable, or "higher," than the circumstances. However, it seems that immediate circumstances provide

---

[58] Jung, *Modern Man in Search of a Soul*, 203.

as much inspiration as one could want, for they inspire us to look more curiously at experience; by working with earth, limitation, and a firm sense of form, we find the path leading to an understanding of mind and its projections. Mercury's glyph seems to represent the creation of wholeness out of duality and the resultant awakening to something beyond that insular wholeness. The glyph also provides a warning, as it might suggest that perception (semi-circle: receptivity) arises separate from the material world (cross), separated by the insular completeness which we call ego or the self (circle).

By contrast, Pluto's glyph suggests that perception actually joins heaven and earth, that perception or receptivity links the body to spirit and that our sense of completion, or self, or spirit, arises from an open perception of phenomena. In other words, whereas Mercury's glyph separates the cross from the semi-circle.;Pluto's glyph connects them. Mercury's glyph suggests a path in which if we have a sense of place, simple and unadorned (circle) we can investigate or develop curiosity about the relationship between matter and receptivity. Pluto's glyph adds to this that the receptivity itself—perception—constitutes the bridge between matter and spirit, between limitation and completeness. That we connect Pluto with power surely suggests that we can access power by investigating the ways in which perception links the material and non-material realms.

Pluto, planet of the underworld whose glyph suggests the birth of wholeness out of perception—reminds us that "heaven" and "earth" (or underworld) arise together in each act (power). They reflect each other, just as the figures of the zodiac in the heavens reflect the dynamics both of the unconscious mind and of the world of ordinary reality. Pluto functions as a higher octave of Mercury in that *he* (or *she*, for, like Mercury, Pluto seems to have hermaphroditic qualities) takes us beyond the dualism that Mercury so often revels in. Pluto takes us "beyond" by urging us to investigate hidden factors at work in the world we experience immediately, moment-to-moment. Such an investigation yields power, not *over* external phenomena, but *through* a willingness to give up the desire for power as it arises, immediately. After all, *immediately* derives from roots meaning "with nothing in between,"[59] in this case in terms not only of time, but also of psychological events. The path begins right here, immediately. To get beyond, we give up trying to go beyond the immediate.

Neither Pluto nor any other planet symbolizes perception itself. Rather Pluto symbolizes something about the nature of our world, those functions or operations in that world that seem vital to all of us these days, processes through which the perceptions of the world, at least by human beings, have an ongoing and intimate connection to the apparently-external world perceived. Pluto has to do with death because ego holds onto its dualism for dear life, maintaining the illusion by constantly re-fortifying its projections, sensing that it cannot exist without them. Pluto has to do with rebirth because apparently a new kind of life and awareness awaits the person willing to go through the death, willing to give up the dualistic fixation. This death occurs in the moment and can happen again and again, not as a single release from the phenomenal world. Pluto's discovery indicated that human beings had to confront, grapple with, and penetrate this truth about our world—or, we

---

[59]Shipley 187.

might say, the discovery indicated that we ignore that truth at our grave peril. Subsequent events, right up to the present, seem to suggest the same conclusion.

This truth—this fact of life—had found expression in many spiritual teachings throughout many centuries, yet until the last several decades, it did not find its way out of the secret enclaves in which these teachings arose. It remained more-or-less secret knowledge, even if it awaited rediscovery by anyone willing to look directly at immediate experience. Certainly this truth occupied an important position in the Buddhist teachings, as we can see from the following Zen story, taken from the Mumonkan, a series of koans given to students as part of their training:

> The wind was flapping a temple flag. Two monks were arguing about it. One said the flag was moving; the other said the wind was moving. Arguing back and forth they could come to no agreement. The Sixth Patriarch said, 'It is neither the wind nor the flag that is moving. It is your mind that is moving.' The two monks were struck with awe.[60]

Perhaps we should feel similarly.

---

[60]Zenkei Shibayama, *Zen Comments on the Mumonkan* (New York: Harper and Row, 1974), 209.

Chapter XII

Truth-Seeking 101: An Epilogue of Sorts

Truth? There is no truth, only subjective perceptions related to conceptual schemes.—Professor Raymond G. Mckelvey to an Occidental College Political Science Class

Nothing happens.—XVI Gyalwang Karmapa

What's happening?—Various and sundry hippies, ex-hippies, beatniks, ex-beatniks, etc.

Full disclosure: though I have repeated Professor Mckelvey's remark many times over the years, in the process almost convincing myself that I actually took a class from the man during my halcyon days at Occidental College (long before Barry Obama used it as a way-station on his way to the White House), I never even met the man and didn't take a single political science class at the excellent but smog-beset institution at which he presided. Yet I have noticed that, perhaps because I have related the incident so often in circumstances ranging from parties with n'er-do-wells to the writing classes I have taught for over two decades at a not-entirely-reputable state university at the foot of the Rocky Mountains, I can see Professor Mckelvey in my mind's eye intoning the quoted words in a manner both dignified and urbane. The event, reported to me by a fellow student who *had* taken a class from the notoriously theatrical professor, often takes on the status of fact in what I perhaps-over-simplistically call "my memory."

As regards the Karmapa's remark, which he offered in Tibetan, I can neither vouch for the accuracy of the translation nor claim that I have a full understanding of the meaning, though I *can* vouch for the fact that I've seen the words on scores of bumper stickers. Some readers might wish to point out that, the Karmapa's remark notwithstanding, quite a lot surely *seems* to happen, constantly and all over the place. This rather pervasive *seeming* may lead us to conclude that the

Karmapa's remark, made shortly before his death in Zion, Illinois over three decades ago, warrants further pondering. Surely the Karmapa could see that a whole lot of stuff seemed to go on and on and on, and I can personally report having seen the Karmapa himself moving among some of those goings-on, actually seeming to qualify as one *of* those goings-on. A full exploration of the Karmapa's probably-intended meaning would take us on a rather long tour through the Buddhist Madhyamaka, a subject in which the Karmapa qualified as an expert, where we would find texts that distinguish clearly between relative truth and absolute truth, matters touched on earlier in this book. I suspect that the Karmapa would have wanted to at least loosen the tight hold we had on our ideas about "reality." I suspect, further, that he would have said that if one looks closely, insistently, and steadily at what appears to happen, the solidity of the happening seems to dissolve like the goings-on of dreams.

If you ponder these matters, you may feel a tad uncertain about how to respond when one of the aforementioned hippies (etc.) greets you with the question quoted above. If, further, someone who knows you more-than-passingly asks, "What's happening in your relationship, friend?" you might feel even less certain how to respond—though this astrologer tentatively recommends that you say, at least as a provocative conversation-starter, "Projections, friend. Lots of projections." If you ask one of the people in the relationship, he or she will perhaps give you one version of what allegedly happens, but if you ask the other person, you may come away wondering if the people have the same referent for "our relationship." Of course, that different people have different versions of events doesn't, by itself, mean that nothing happens, but it might at least induce one to say, when asked about what allegedly is happening, "Well, in truth, I have no idea." That might bring you full circle back to Professor McKelvey and the remark he may or may not have made.

In the much-maligned sixties, many of us spoke a lot about going to "happenings." The term seemed to refer to some sort of grouping of human entities having at least some vague sense of purpose (including "having a good time," a high-level abstraction with no precise referent, it seems). Most of us didn't doubt that such happenings really happened; most of the time, we didn't consider them as illusions, and we would have perhaps looked skeptically on the Karmapa's remark even though we "knew" that Tibetan high lamas had great wisdom and spiritual insight, and even though, had the Karmapa ever shown up any place nearby, his showing-up would have constituted a "happening" of the most worthy sort even if, and perhaps because, most of us had rather different notions about "spiritual things" than the Karmapa did.

No doubt most of us would have projected a whole lot of psychic material onto him, for I think we had all sorts of high expectations of "holy men," particularly those from India or Tibet.[1] In do-

---

[1] During that period, the Karmapa could have qualified as either Indian (for he lived in India) or Tibetan (for he had been born in Tibet). Hopefully I and my friends, having eschewed all "to be" forms, wouldn't have asked, "Are you Indian, or are you Tibetan?"

ing so, we would, I think, have failed to see him accurately, for we would have seen, primarily and probably blindingly, our version of him, that version consisting of a curiously American amalgam of delusion, grandeur, homespun intelligence, and miscellaneous notions imbibed in school. We would, I think, have already come to all sorts of conclusions about "Tibetan High Lamas," and we would have seen him in light of those conclusions, saying that such personages "are" what we take them to be. Perhaps, in all that, we would have projected onto him our capacity for spiritual development (a term I will not try to define here), for as self-respecting hippies and such, though we saw ourselves as concerned with "spirituality," most of us probably hadn't done much walking on any spiritual path worthy of the name.

Though we observers would have certainly said of such goings-on that "something was really happening," I somehow doubt that his experience amongst us would have induced the Karmapa to say, "Well, lads and lassies, it appears that I was wrong. Everything *does* happen," though he perhaps would have taken a moment or two to deal with our confusion. I have a feeling that he would have said, perhaps following a lead provided by Nagarjuna, whom we have briefly discussed, that such goings-on qualified as "relative truths," as having existence only insofar as they were in accord with convention, but that they had no existence independent of the causes and conditions that had brought them into apparent existence (and that, quite possibly, lent them what form they posess). I also have a feeling that some sort of something did "happen," even if only on the level of relative truth, in events like that, but with projections running amok, most of us probably had not-entirely-accurate notions about *what*. In all that, I suspect that most of us would have generated much confusion, often mistaking an inner world with an outer one, much as we do in our relations with each other, doing a lot more *concluding* than *knowing*. But what do I know?

I don't know whether readers of astrology books like this one come looking for statements about "truth" or "reality," at least of the ultimate sort. I suspect that most of us come to astrology and books about it with questions about less encompassing matters. We want to know whether a certain relationship will "work," or whether such-and-such a date "is good for a wedding," or whether we should quit our present job and take up free-lance online embezzlement, or whether the United States really will throw intelligence and human decency to the winds yet again and invade whatever Middle Eastern country has remained untouched by our policies or soldiers (if any such countries still exist). Sometimes we may ask the astrologer to tell us whether we will ever find love, or whether we will always be poor, or whether we should go back to school in a subject allegedly more practical than philosophy or literature.

Sometimes, though, our search for answers to even the most straightforward questions can lead us into some curious ponderings. If I ask whether a certain relationship "will work," I should probably look into the projections that the people in that relationship seem likely to cast upon one another. Will those people go on projecting? What will they project? What psychological dynamics can we see at work in those projections? Even if someone asks whether she should get married, the answer will often, or perhaps *should* often, include an exploration of the projections at work between the people. If someone asks whether she should unceremoniously quit one job and take up the aforementioned freelance work, she would do well to investigate the projections at work in the workplace.

I don't mean that the astrologer should never give a simple answer to a client's question. Sometimes the simpler answer may produce more benefit, and if someone asks the astrologer to come up with a date for a wedding, the astrologer might want to refrain from discoursing on projection-related material (as it usually has to do with *whether* people should get married, not with *when* they should). Even if the astrologer has concerns about truth and long-term consequences, he or she should consider acquiescing to the client's wishes in such questions, answering the questions the clients asks instead of telling the client what questions *to* ask. A waitress serving you a steak may have concerns about your cholesterol level, and she may have done much study about such matters, but you may not feel appreciative if she chooses that moment to lecture you on your dietary habits. Quite possibly she will forfeit her tip is she gets too insistent. Just as possibly, an astrologer's insistence on going into the *whether* when the client has asked about the *when* may cause the client to leave the building like Elvis, forfeiting the perhaps-considerable benefit of the astrologer's conclusions about matters not involving hidden psychological dynamics.

On the other hand, the astrologer should probably remember that insofar as we consider astrology as a language—with the signs often functioning as modifiers, the planets as verbs, and the houses as nouns—we might do well to investigate its inner workings, for if we remain blind to the assumptions lying behind any language, we can lead ourselves astray. The English language contains modifiers, nouns, and verbs, and we may assume, if we speak that language, not only that all languages must have them—or that astrology must, if we consider it a language—but also that the world to which language purportedly refers contains qualities, actions, and things, that a close examination will reveal things with qualities, and that further examination will reveal those things-with-qualities taking actions of various kinds. (Not to belabor a point related to Saturn, but we might also assume that because the language has the verb "to be," the world must contain identity relations of some sort, relations about which we can say that X "is" a Y.[2]

Among its other possible uses, astrology functions as a labeling system. As practiced in the West, it generally uses labels analogous to those commonly used in the languages that Benjamin Lee Whorf called SAE (Standard Average European),[3] which might remind us of the possible limitations of the system. It might also remind us that if we delve into the astrology of China, or of India, or of Tibet, or of any culture using a vastly different language from our own, we might find different notions at work. We tend to get answers suited to or shaped by the questions we ask. Thus astrologers working with the Vedic system may give different answers than will astrologers work-

---

[2]John is a third-rate and rich lawyer. Bill is a dignified idiot. Sally is a neglected sage. Astrologers are cool.
[3]Benjamin Lee Whorf, *Language, Thought, and Reality* (Cambridge: The MIT Press, 1956), 138.

ing in the "Western" system. Those considering astrological "wisdom" should keep these points in mind, for just as in the sciences we find different theories offered to account for the same data, so in considering the accurate inferences derived from astrological data, we can come up with more than one theory to account for what we see.

In the astrology generally practiced in this country, with its connection to the assumptions generated by psychological theories current in "our culture," the symbols can often tell us about projection. Using astrological methods, we can more readily see projection at work, finding much empirical data to support our conclusions. Good enough so far, as long as we realize that the methods themselves, like other scientific methods, encourage us to see this pattern and not that, this fact and not that, this characteristic and not that—and to see characteristics in the first place!

"Spiritual teachers" in various traditions have called their students' attention to the connection between mind and phenomena, between what we think about the world (or ourselves) and the world as it exists beyond our ideas about it (assuming we can locate such an item). I can offer no final statements on these matters, but I do think that astrology can aid us in our exploration of the relevant territories. Though the set of techniques, notions, and labels we call *astrology* will always remain somewhat like the finger pointing at the Moon (to use a Zen analogy) and seems rather unlike the Moon itself, it can have value insofar as it helps us to know where to look for important revelations such as those involving the mind-phenomena connection, or if it reminds us where to recover such revelations again once we've misplaced them among the thousand-and-one items of daily life.

Interestingly, in the Zen analogy of the finger and the Moon, the Moon appears as it does because of its relationship with the sun. We wouldn't see the moon at all if the sun's light didn't shine on it, and we see only the part of the moon that receives the sun's light. What we see hinges on relationship and vantage, with vantage as another kind of relationship. In the material discussed above, I have tried to provide different vantages from which we might view the relationship between our awareness of the world and the world itself; I have also suggested that "the world itself" may qualify as a verbal fiction, though we'd probably do well to withhold judgment on that, even here at the end of the book! In any case, we generally contact that "world itself" only via such equipment as we have available: senses, mind, and symbol systems.

In *Choosing Reality*, B. Alan Wallace writes, "Experiment does not inform us of the ontological status, or intrinsic nature, of microobjects as they exist apart from measurement."[4] In our scientific tradition, scientists generally do their experiments on material purportedly outside of their minds. However, any meditator, any psychologist, or anyone willing to look carefully at his or her mind can equally qualify as an experimenter, though the material upon which one experiments seems

---

[4] B. Alan Wallace, *Choosing Reality: A Buddhist View of Physics and the Mind* (Boulder: Snow Lion, 1996), 76.

to reside inside the cranium, or at least inside the mind, rather than outside. In other words, we can understand *experiment* not only as something that scientists do in the laboratory, but also as something that people can do—and that some people have already done – as they work with on themselves. If we persist in such experiments, we may find ourselves in the position of scientists as described by Wallace:

> Given one system of measurement, results are produced that suggest the presence of a wave phenomenon; given another system, the "same" measured object seems to be a particle. In the absence of any system of measurement, we have no evidence of waves, particles, potentia, or anything else. We may conclude, according to the above principle, that an electron existing as an independent entity is in principle unknowable; therefore this independent entity does not exist as a potentiality, for it does not exist at all.[5]

Science having apparently taken the place of religion for many in our culture, we shouldn't feel surprised that scientists like the ones Wallace describes sometimes offer us assertions not only about the nature of the world in which we find ourselves, but about our own nature as well. Though we can acknowledge the importance of our scientific tradition and the insights it has offered so many people for so long, we probably do well to remind ourselves, as Wallace reminds us, to remain skeptical about the belief "that our physical theories represent the world as it exists independently of our means of observation and conceptualization, that is, that they reflect objective reality."[6]

I don't claim, here, that we should all go in for deep pondering about the nature of reality or the relationship between mind and phenomena. Admittedly, as I say early in this book, the astrological methodology can lead us into such pondering, for the methods astrologers have used for centuries seem to assume some sort of mysterious connection between worlds "inner" and "outer," often pointing to dimensions of experience not readily acknowledged. However, we should perhaps begin, in considering these matters, with an instrumentalist approach, asking of our methodology not necessarily that it provide us with answers to the riddles of the cosmos, but that it serve "as an effective leading principle for a more inclusive range of inquiries" than many other methods, and that it supply "a method of analysis and representation that makes possible more precise and detailed inferences" than other methods.[7]

The inferences, here, have to do with relationship, whether between people, between countries, or between any person and "the world in general." Those inferences can help us to make more accurate distinctions between what goes on in the mind and what goes on in the world. Most human beings have seen this distinction as an important one, and many societies have provided not-so-comfortable retreats for some of the people who cannot or will not make the relevant distinctions.

---

[5]Wallace, 87.
[6]Wallace, 87
[7]Wallace, 99. (Wallace does not, of course, have astrology in mind here. He has in mind scientific theories as most people understand that term.)

Even if, from what we might call an "ultimate" point of view, mind and phenomena often seem to arise together, in the day-to-day world in which most of us live most of the time, we assume the world to have some objectivity, and in most of our dealings, we get good results if we rely on that assumption.

On the other hand, I suspect that most readers have found themselves in situations where the most practical approach even to mundane matters has to do with looking first at one's own mind, finding the source of projections in ongoing psychological habit patterns. Most of us habitually exclude some material from conscious awareness and thus experience that material embodied in various apparently-external forms—usually people or groups—that resist our efforts to find resolution, peace of mind, or clarity. Think what we will about philosophical matters that seem abstruse or abstract, most of us want to have a clear understanding of the happenings in our lives. Hopefully the material in this book will help us to have such an understanding at least some of the time. Having said that, I leave my readers to their own explorations.

FINIS

Appendix I

Polarity Therapy: The Six Sign Zodiac

The seventh house cusp symbolizes not only what a person will tend to project onto others, but also what a person should, can, and often *will* cultivate or bring to relationship. The person with Taurus rising may wish to approach life with simple, earthy good will, but he should recognize the power of relationships to transform, for he has Scorpio on the descendant and should bring Scorpio's transformative quality to his relationships. If the descendant indicates an energy that a person readily projects onto others, the person must possess that energy already, even if unconsciously. Similarly, but less obviously, a person will need to cultivate the energy of any sign opposite any of his planets, though some of these signs (e.g. the ones opposite his Sun and Moon) will have more weight in the analysis.[1]

If we doubt that opposite signs can arise together, as two sides of bi-polar units, we need only consider the astrological ages. In the Age of Pisces, which began around 0 CE and the impending conclusion of which seems evident in our own era, both Pisces and Virgo arise in critical ways. Pisces arises clearly enough in the name of Jesus, in all the fish symbolism prevalent in the Middle East around the time of his birth, and in the devotion and emotion-based religions that have arisen

---

[1] In astrological matters dealing with oppositions and the seventh house, opposites function as complements. The word opposite has, of course, different meanings depending on context, a statement that holds true in astrology as it does in the world-at-large. Astrologers often say that adjacent signs "are opposites"; they say something similar about signs 180 degrees apart in the zodiac, and sometimes something similar about signs 90, or even 150, degrees apart. This last may seem a bit odd, but signs 150 degrees apart degrees apart seem to share very little, coming from elements held incompatible and in different modes. Virgo, a mutable earth sign, quincunxes Aries, a cardinal fire sign. Astrologers have seen fire and earth as incompatible elements. Signs in squares come from the same modality; signs in oppositions come from elements held compatible.

in the past two thousand years. Virgo appears in the myriad difficulties related to purity that beset the contemporary world, in the dominant religions' emphasis on a kind of moral purity that often does violence to people's inclinations, and the pervasive wage-slavery that has spread over the globe. And, of course, Jesus purportedly had a virgin for a mother.

Analogous patterns appear in the other Ages: in each case the sign ruling the era provides what we might call the dominant symbolism and the opposite sign provides an energy that, in a slightly more subtle way, seems equally pervasive in the activities characterizing the period.[2] This hardly seems surprising, of course, as astrologers measure these Ages by the precession of the spring equinoctial point backwards through the signs. The autumn equinoctial point will therefore fall in the sign opposite the one that lends its name to the period.

A planet tenanting a sign generally gives a person a kind of bias toward that sign; he will likely have a clear and evident relationship to that sign, seeing it as something that he should cultivate, unless gender-related matters intrude, as discussed earlier in the book. A person with an opposition will usually gravitate toward the planet-plus-sign closer to the sun; he will usually project the other planet-plus-sign onto others, as also discussed earlier. However, the person will want to recognize that other planet and sign as part of his own potential, as something he should cultivate from within. This may prove more challenging with opposition aspects than otherwise, but any planet in any sign will find the opposite sign as the natural area of completion. A similar principle applies to opposing houses.

Many astrologers recommend that during challenging transits, particularly from the outer planets, a person can deal with the challenges of the transiting planet if he cultivates the energy of the sign opposite the sign ruled by the transiting planet.[3] For example, someone receiving a transit from Pluto will do well to cultivate Taurus, while someone receiving a transit from Saturn will do well to cultivate Cancer, not as an energy coming from outside of himself, but as an inner potential. A person in the midst of a difficult transit from Pluto can cultivate groundedness by hanging out with "grounded people," but he will do better to find that groundedness within himself, whether he has natal planets in Taurus or not. If he experiences Taurus through others—and this may well occur, as we often magnetize that which we should cultivate within—he should consider it as a projection of inner capacities.

We can say of all opposites that they depend on each other. My ideas about bigness depend on my ideas about smallness; my ideas about joy depend on my ideas about sorrow; my ideas about wealth depend on my ideas about its lack. Furthermore, night depends on day, just as *east* depends on *west* and *up* depends on *down*. Such terms take their meanings from the context given by the opposite; in a very real sense, such opposites arise together, with one extreme more evident than the other.[4]

---

[2] I trace this pattern in *The Machine Stops* (AFA, 2012). See chapter I.
[3] Decades ago, I heard Antero Alli speak of this principle. I think it may have come originally from Marc Edmund Jones.
[4] Perhaps worth noting here: words, like astrological signs, can have a number of opposites. What shall we consider as the opposite of ordinary? extraordinary? strange? unusual? bizarre? Similarly, what shall we consider the "opposite" of Leo?

Something similar applies to signs located a hundred and eighty degrees from each other. Pisces' oceanic awareness takes its meaning from a sense that one could also opt for a precise awareness of detail (Virgo). Leo's emphasis on self takes its meaning from ideas about social awareness (Aquarius). Scorpio's intense emotionalism takes its meaning from our notion of steady grounding in the ordinary world. A concern with general principles, such as we often find with Sagittarius, takes on meaning when we connect it with the particular facts and the fact-gathering that gives rise to generalities, for generality and specificity depend on each other for their meanings.

We can see, then, not only that opposite signs clearly arise together in visible events such as the ones characterizing an aeon, but also that the meaning of any sign depends on and cannot arise without a consideration of the meaning of its polar opposite. So both in the evident world of events and in the world of our conceptions and ideas, opposites arise together. We find them linked, like partners in a marriage in which the partners find themselves joined together for life. Or, we might say, the situation seems somewhat like married people who have children: even if the partners separate, they will always have a link. Like men and women, opposite signs join and produce evident results in the world.

A zodiac consisting of six bi-polar signs emphasizes these kinds of polarity. It also interprets signs not merely as indicators of characteristic behaviors, but as capacities for the cultivation of that which promotes growth and awareness. Just as the polarities in our ideas (e.g. good-bad, tall-short, war-peace) point to some of the basic parameters through which we organize experience, so the six bi-polar signs symbolize six pathways through which we not only organize our ideas about the world, but also through which we can gain greater awareness by engaging groups of potentials that through their interrelationships promote development.

As we have seen, we often simply project one end of a pair onto other people, experiencing ourselves through the signs in which we have planets, or, with opposition aspects, the planet-sign energy with which we identify, for any of the reasons given in earlier chapters. If we can find the complementarity between the pairs, and if we can recognize that both ends belong to us, we can put ourselves in harmony with natural processes. In psychological terms, this often means to withdraw projections from the environment whenever those projections hinder adjustment to the world.

In any consideration of polarities, we should consider that energy naturally generates, turns into, and uncovers its opposite. We see this principle at work in the *I Ching*, the Chinese *Book of Changes*, in which the hexagrams depict human life as the interaction between yin and yang lines, and in which a strong movement toward either yin or yang results in a change in polarity.[5] We can see a similar movement in the signs. For example, a strong curiosity about the world seems to

---

Shall we point to Aquarius? Scorpio? Capricorn? Pisces? All can claim to have qualities "completely opposite" those of Leo. The difficulty arises, I think, because just as *ordinary*, as an abstraction, has no single and definite meaning, so with each sign, for each one functions as a high level abstraction with no single and definite meaning. Also, just as *ordinary* and other terms for qualities function as modifiers, so with the signs.
[5] A strong yin line turns into a yang line; a strong yang line turns into a yin line.

generate a philosophical outlook (Gemini-Saggitarius), a powerful emotionalism seems to generate a strong desire for grounding and a connection to earth (Scorpio-Taurus), impetuous self-assertion (Aries) leads one necessarily into connection with others (Aries-Libra).

And so we have the six bi-polar signs, offered here not only as a heuristic device one can use in dealing with all opposition-based projections and all polarities in the horoscope, but also as a description of the way energies arise in ourselves and in the world around us. Each sign has two names, depending on which end of the polarity receives initial emphasis:

Ariba, Libries

Taurpeo, Scorpus

Geminarius, Saggini

Cancercorn, Capricance

Learius, Aquarleo

Visces, Pirgo

Ariba-Libries: Independence and Interdependence

Independence implies and generates relationship, and vice-versa. Not only does independent action automatically lead one into relationship of some sort, so relationship requires individual initiative to exist at all. If one doesn't act in such a way as to move away from home ground, pioneering into the world, one initiates no relationship. If I act, I move into a territory called "otherness." If I find myself in relationship, I must have taken some sort of action, however subtle or automatic.

Astrologers often connect Aries to pioneering. Pioneers always seem to encounter others; at the very least, they encounter environmental factors and come into relationship with them. Problems arise, however, if the pioneers, in coming into relationship with others, forget to leave their home-ground, instead carrying with them home-ground-based patterns of behavior not appropriate to the organized life they encounter, seeing their own actions and those of others through the limiting lens of their own background.[6] Seeking, even if unconsciously, to recreate the family-of-origin, they create one difficulty after another.

Libra, as we have seen, has much to do with cultural norms and standards, and these often limit independence; the individual who initiates runs smack dab into such norms as limiting factors. However, the vast majority of human activities have, for millennia, taken place largely within social settings, those settings serving as the arenas within which people act. Pioneering may seem different, but even pioneers act within social constructs, many of which they carry with them; in addition, the very notion of pioneering implies a social situation from which one has departed. Many of the pioneers we know about have attempted to impose their own constructs onto the

---

[6]Readers will note, here, the suggestions of Cancer and Capricorn (Cancercorn/Capricance), the two signs that square the signs of Ariba/Libries. Bi-polar signs often generate challenges related to the bi-polar sign ninety degrees away.

people they encounter. Remaining blind to the presence of these norms in their own minds, such pioneers end up searching for an Eldorado that looks remarkably like Seville, running roughshod over the locals in the process.

The above describes Aries without a proper understanding and awareness of Libra. How about the reverse? What occurs when we simply accept social values without asking, "But what have these values and norms to do with me and what I wish to accomplish?" In theory, social norms exist to promote individual growth, but if people consider the norms as ends instead of as means, the norms hinder the individual more than help him.

If Aries sees Libra as part of him, he will see more clearly how to work constructively and creatively with whatever social norms and values he encounters, either within himself or in the world he encounters; if Libra sees Aries as part of him, he will not accept social codes blindly, but will have some at-least-partial enlightened-self-interest, asking that the norms and codes serve him, not the other way around. If people reject one side of the bipolar sign, it will arise as projection; if people see more clearly not only that action brings one into relationship, but that any relationship worth the name consists of individuals, the strength of this bipolar sign will manifest clearly.

Taurpeo-Scorpus: Values of Self and Other

Via their connections to the second and eighth houses, Taurus and Scorpio have connections to one's own money or values (Taurus) and the values or money of others (Scorpio). Also: Taurus revels in sensuality, Scorpio in sexuality; Taurus considers the fruitful present, Scorpio considers the need to live transformatively. But these notions bear careful consideration. First, the value of my money has an intimate connection to the values or valuations of others, as any banker or stockbroker knows; the worth of my bank account depends on the valuation of currencies and a host of other economic matters that I neither create nor control. Second, sensuality and sexuality mix inextricably. Third, the fruitful present has its fruitfulness because of transformation; the fruitful plum tree in my back yard bears fruit because it goes through changes constantly.

An over-emphasized Scorpio may act ruthlessly, giving too little attention either to the lush beauty of the world or the full valuation of other people. Also, if we want to walk the transformative path so often associated with Scorpio, we must first stabilize the mind and develop some love for the present moment, when all transformation occurs. The Buddha's enlightenment, which according to the traditional story took place on the full moon in May, with the Sun in Taurus and the Moon in Scorpio, gives us a good symbolic rendering of this point. The Buddha sat still beneath a tree, a Taurean approach surely, and achieved enlightenment, a full transformation of his outlook. He then pointed to the earth as a witness to his awakening.

Buddha also discovered that he couldn't make full progress on the path if he maintained an ascetic attitude or followed the ascetic path (one suggesting Scorpio's love of obsessive thinking). He first had to treat himself well: instead of fasting, he decided to feed himself; instead of mortifying the flesh, he took up a comfortable posture. He sat with Taurean firmness, rooted to the ground beneath a Taurean tree, and a serpent (Scorpio) came to protect him as he approached awakening. Taurus generates Scorpio, surely, and in every in-depth transformation, we find a Taurean element. But Scorpio also generates Taurus, for awakening enables one to appreciate the fruitful moment more completely, as many awakened people have reported in various traditions. The whole idea of transformation seems to arise from our notions of ordinariness. Feeling ourselves ordinary, we may wish to transform ourselves. That transformation makes us extra-ordinary; Taurus and Scorpio remain joined.

Finally, if we take Taurus as a symbol of the earth, and as a fixed earth sign Taurus fills the bill better than any other sign (with the possible exception of Cancer), and Scorpio as a symbol of the unconscious, with ruling Pluto as Lord of the underworld, then we find ourselves back to the Jungian notion that the unconscious had a close connection to the material world altogether, not only in alchemy where alchemists "project even the highest value—God—into matter,"[7] but also because, as Marie Louise von Franz writes,

> our division into material versus mental, that which is observable from the outside versus that which is perceivable from the inside, is only a subjectively valid separation, only a limited polarization that our structure of consciousness imposes on us but that actually does not correspond to the wholeness of reality…it is rather to be suspected that these two poles actually constitute a unitary reality.[8]

Thus the psychological concerns that play such an important role for so many Scorpios, and the material concerns that play a similar role for so many Taureans, may have much in common. Just as an alchemist projects God into matter (much, it seems, as God purportedly projected himself into the material world), so a person may project his various complexes onto whoever serves as an appropriate hook.

In general, the richness of earth fructifies the transformations that we refer to as the organic world, and the richness of the unconscious fructifies the transformations we call "spiritual growth," a growth that takes the physical body as a necessary element, as Buddhists, alchemists, and others have seemed aware. More particularly, we see the Taurus-Scorpio connection in the Egyptian death-cults, groups believing that the deceased rides on a barque over the waters of the underworld, taking many worldly possessions on the journey.

Geminarius-Sagini: Facts and Meaning

Astrologers know Gemini as a sign concerned with particulars and curiosity, a sign that revels in the world's multifariousness. Sagittarius, by contrast, has less concern with particulars than with the patterns formed *by* those particulars, with the meaning that humans might derive from data, and with the purpose that serves as guiding force for naturally-curious human beings. Gemini likes the "thousand and one things"; Sagittarius likes to derive principles to unite them. For details on

---
[7]Jung, *Psychology and Alchemy*, 323.
[8]Marie von Franz, *Psyche and Matter* (Boston: Shambhala, 1992), 11.

Gemini, read Allen Ginsberg's poetry, or Walt Whitman's. If you want to see a Gemini cultivating some Sagittarian sagesse, read William Butler Yeats or Thomas Mann. If you want to see a Sagittarian find a symbol in even the most common occurrence, consult Mr. William Blake. Of course, as mutable signs, Gemini and Sagittarius may sometimes seem to act similarly. Both may forget to wash the dishes, for example. However, they do so for different reasons: Gemini does so because his mind is all flummoxed and fascinated by the multifarious interesting-ness of "le monde," whereas Sagittarius, though hardly appearing flummoxed, gets lost in principles and pronouncements. Leave the dishes to the earth and water signs!

Sagittarius quests for meaning, taking part in quests composed of one particular after another. Gemini, then, seems part of the quest. (See *The Grail Legend*, by Marie Louise von Franz and Emma Jung, for more about quests.) This bipolar sign asks us to use information wisely, to recognize that we have no wisdom without information, but that human beings seem to have a natural gift and propensity for symbolization and meaning-making. If we divorce philosophy from the thousand-and-one-things, we have empty abstractions; if we find no meaning in the particulars of life, we end up lost in the tall weeds. But this bi-polar sign reminds us to consider homo-sapiens not as the tool-making creature, but as the symbol-making one.

Gemini brings joy to the whole process. The joy comes not from the meanings we derive from our curiosity, but from the joy we take in the curiosity itself. To Gemini, the world seems a curious place, with lots of curious creatures in it! At the same time, humans *do* seem to have this propensity not simply to revel in their wondrous curiosity, but to reflect on it, to ask what the things indicate, dictate, or "mean." This relationship appears in human behavior pretty much as far back as we can trace it, perhaps for as long as humans have looked out upon the world with interest, speculating as they did so.

We might say that Gemini revels in experience and Sagittarius in meaning, but this oversimplifies. What we call *experience* seems to include meaning. Neither end of this bipolar sign tells us about the direct contact of our senses with the world; both ends remind us of how our experience of those thousand-and-one (or more!) things comes to us imbued with symbolization, language premier among them. We can, on the one hand, channel Allen Ginsberg, the Gemini poet who, on returning from India and responding to a question about what he remembered, raised a whimsical finger skyward and intoned, "Particulars!" Or we can channel William Blake, a goodly Sagittarius, who described the rising sun in richly symbolic terms, seeing the symbol as equal to the event, insofar as he saw fit to separate them. Or we can remember Mr. Ginsberg, sitting on many a college campus, drone box in his lap, singing Blake's *Songs of Innocence and Songs of Experience* in the real and symbolic sunshine.

A final note or two, and perhaps a return to whimsicality. We know Bob Dylan as a Gemini with his Sun conjoined Jupiter, ruler of Sagittarius. We also know that he wrote a fine song about Billy the Kid (for the movie *Pat Garrett and Billy the Kid*, in which Mr. Dylan played an interesting role) and that in another song, he wrote, with what degree of sincerity we don't know, that though he might have looked like Robert Ford, he *felt* just like Jessie James. In yet another song, he wrote that to live outside the law, one must be honest. We can perhaps take honesty as deriving from Sagittarian principles, but to live outside the law suggests that though one may or may not break the laws, one certainly lives beyond their vantage. Outsiders purportedly live by some sort of truth we can interpret as connected to Sagittarian principles such as those practiced by Mr. James (who apparently had Jupiter on his ascendant); also, outsiders often have in them a considerable portion of Gemini's playfulness and curiosity—and, at least for those outsiders also called outlaws, Gemini's reputation for trickery.

But enough of that. Let's on to the next bipolar sign.

Cancercorn-Capricance: Home and Away

Astrologers associate Cancer with the nurturance, feeling, and home, and Capricorn with vocation, ambition, and career. Cancer symbolizes our private emotional conditions, Capricorn our public actional ones. On another level, Cancer symbolizes our emotional connection with the organic world as a whole, a connection manifesting most clearly through feelings of empathy and sympathy, while Capricorn has more to do with our practical connection with the inorganic world, a connection manifesting most clearly in a drive toward accomplishment or a sense of mission. Cancer has a close connection to the mother complex of symbols, with the giving and taking of life itself; Capricorn has a close connection to the father complex of symbols, with the taking of one's place in the structures and hierarchies of society.

In the industrial and post-industrial phrases of our civilization, we find a pattern perhaps endemic to civilization itself: a divorce between home and away, between private and public lives. The more recent phases of our so-called civilization have witnessed a more egregious separation, one that resulted at least partly from the machinations of industrialists in a series of initiatives evident at least as early as 1800 and that reached a crescendo (if initiatives do that) in the early 20th century. Thus John Taylor Gatto writes, speaking of Ellwood P. Cubberly's *Public Education*, that the early 20th century saw industrialists engaged in social engineering that would break up the home and create what industrialists wanted. Cubberly wanted "a new lengthening of the period of dependence" (a section-title in his book) for children, feeling that such a development would further the "coming of the factory system." All of this meant depriving children of what Gatto calls "the training and education that farm and village life once gave." With the breakdown of home and village industries, Gatto writes,

> [T]he passing of chores, and the extinction of the apprenticeship system by large scale production with its extreme division of labor (and the "all conquering march of machinery"), an army of workers has arisen, says Cubberly, who know nothing.[9]

---

[9] John Taylor Gatto, *The Underground History of American Education* (New York: Oxford Village Press, 2006), 39. Mr. Gatto received teacher of the year awards in both the New York City and New York State public schools. He then left teaching and began writing books critiquing (to use a mild term) the public school system.

Gatto also cites Arthur Calhoun's 1919 Social History of the Family," which, he says, "notified the nation's academics what was happening": that

> ...the child was passing from its family "into the custody of community experts." He [Calhoun] offered a significant forecast, that in time we could expect to sese public education "designed to check the mating of the unfit."[10]

Social engineering 101, it seems, based on the attack of the home (Cancer) by the industrial hierarchy (Capricorn)

In many societies someone, generally the male, must leave home in order to procure some of the necessities for survival. Among some people native to this continent, the buffalo provided not only meat to eat, but also bones for various utensils and hide for tepees. The connection between the home and the world beyond it remained clear, concrete, and intimate, not nearly so abstract as the one we witness in our societies, where people go off to what we call jobs in order to make money to put in banks wherefrom they can later withdraw it and give it to stores, mortgage companies, and hot-dog vendors at the ball game, procuring both necessities and the amenities that we apparently see as vital. For a Lakota, everything in the home came in a concrete way from excursions away from home (particularly the hunt), and the periodic moving of the home often took place because of considerations related to hunting.

For non-Lakotas, though, important questions remain. Do we feel at home in our work? Do we even own our homes, or does the bank still have the best financial claim thereto? Can I call my home "mine" in the same sense that Sitting Bull could call *his* home his (before the onslaught of invaders who apparently gave less consideration to home-ground than Sitting Bull did)? In procuring the items needed for his home, Sitting Bull and his associates didn't need to work for anyone else and didn't need to have a bank account or get a permit to locate a tepee; and though he perhaps taxed himself in the hunt, no-one leveed taxes *on* him!

The divorce so many people feel from their work seems typical in our society, but we needn't take the situation as unalterable. We feel the connection between Cancer and Capricorn every time we develop an emotional connection to the work we do, every time we bring home the real or metaphorical bacon, every time we write a novel (or astrology book, if you please) in our home garret before sending our work out to meet the big, bad world of critics and the big, kind one of open-hearted readers, every time we leave home to do something we find meaningful, every time family-of-origin matters influence a person's public work, and every time a person realizes that fulfillment in doing the work he must do enriches his sense of being at home with himself wherever he happens to dwell.

We can add a few words about the Moon and Saturn, the traditional rulers of Cancer and Capricorn respectively. The Moon rules the sub-lunar realm of organic life, while Saturn, sometimes called the Lord of this World, rules both the non-organic structures of society as well as the

---

[10] Gatto, 39.

structural elements within living things (e.g. skeletons). That last phrase suggests an intimate connection between the two rulers, suggesting as it does not only that Saturn often has a connection to the organic world, but that the organic world arises as it does because of structures, considered either as elements we can see with the naked eye or as structural elements within cells, molecules, atoms, or what have you.

The Moon presents cyclic patterns: blood circulates through the body, breath comes in and goes out, the tides do likewise, the seasons turn and turn. Saturn presents an apparently non-cyclic set of patterns: when one ascends a mountain or gambols about on the precipices like a Capricornian mountain goat, the patterns seem linear, and similarly for a person setting out on a mission, whether to convert Sitting Bull to Christianity or to write a novel or to feed the hungry. Yet people setting out on missions generally find that the blood circulates more rapidly, the breath manifests more fully, and the seasons come and go in a rhythm apparently exalted. For better or worse, such mission-goers bring their roots with them, even if invisibly or unconsciously.

Learius-Aquarleo: Self-Creation and Group-Amelioration?

In using "amelioration," I fall prey to one of the many pro-Aquarius prejudices abounding in the contemporary astrological press (if such a thing exists!): that Aquarius always promotes progressive causes, always wants to ameliorate the social situation. But Aquarius has two sides, one ruled by Uranus and one ruled by Saturn. In discussing Learius/Aquarleo, then, we find ourselves dealing with two polarities: one between the two ends of the Learius/Aquarleo, one within Aquarius itself, another kind of bipolar sign, as suggested not only by its two rulers, but also by its dualistic glyph.[11]

We have discussed Aquarius' inner polarity already. It often manifests in an Aquarian's connection to the body social, a connection often characterized on the one hand by progressive views and on the other by a non-progressive set of activities. Aquarius generally has a respect for social form, and though he might want to reform it, he usually doesn't want to eradicate it. Often he will reinstitute old forms in a new way, or he may manifest progressive thinking in some areas and remarkably reactionary thinking in others. Franklin D. Roosevelt seems an apt example here, as he adopted policies (e.g. unemployment insurance, social security) that many see as intrinsic to any progressive society, yet he needed considerable prodding before he took his leftward turn, for, coming from the patrician class, he seemed temperamentally inclined toward the needs of the rich. Further, his international policies, particularly toward Japan, hardly seem progressive, at least seen in the rear-view mirror.

Leo, of course, has a reputation for overweening concern with the self at the expense of the body social. Or, we might say, Leo wants to participate in the body social only insofar as others recognize him either as leader or as center of attention. By itself, Leo would seem to have little patience with Aquarius' concerns with social well-being. However, any social progression worthy of the name

---

[11] Four signs have glyphs we could see as mirror-image symbols: Gemini, Cancer, Aquarius, Pisces. Each sign has an evident inner polarity, Aquarius most evidently, because of the marked differences between its rulers.

must include attention to the individual. As an air sign, Aquarius tends to see social questions in the abstract, as ideas; Aquarius tends to forget that all societies consist primarily of people. Though Leo puts his attention on the individual and Aquarius on the group, they arise together in a simple experience that everyone has: that one's sense of individuality arises largely as a social construct, so that self-interest in one society may look rather different than self-interest in another society.

Learius/Aquarleo continues the process begin in Cancercorn/Capricance. While the latter deals with the relationship between private and public identities, between emotion and mission, between isolation and vocation, the former deals with the relationship between the voyage of self-discovery and the social groups and constructs through which that voyage moves and winds. The groups not only serve as the environment in which self-awareness arises, but they also have a lot to do with the kinds of self-awareness that arise there.

Leo symbolizes the re-discovery of the self, but as we have seen in Ariba/Libries, that development implies and implicates *other* (other people, the world of law and regulation, everything experienced as something a person encounters). Ariba/Libras emphasizes one-to-one encounters. Learius/Aquarleo emphasizes one-to-many encounters. This fifth bipolar sign seems less concerned with marriage than with the relationship between individual and group. Whereas Ariba/Libries will often emphasize marriage between individuals, Learius/Aquarleo will often emphasize the individual's non-intimate interconnections with the group.

Leo wants to take center stage, of course. The presence of a stage implies the presence of a group of observers. Leo tends toward self-involvement but needs to develop self-confidence and creative élan without arrogance. Aquarius, by contrast, puts his attention on the theatre house in which someone puts a stage, on the social reality of such a stage-setting, and on the social values either implied by the setting itself or expressed in the performance.

In theory, society exists to promote individual self-awareness, but individual self-awareness also has a causal relationship to social grouping. Of course, self-awareness must also include an awareness of unconscious contents. Learius/Aquarleo tends to ignore the unconscious or to underestimate its importance, the Leo side ignoring the myriad ways in which unconscious contents influence awareness and performance, the Aquarius side ignoring the myriad ways in which those contents pervade social form and function. Yet as a fixed pair, this bipolar sign must always deal with unconscious contents (as fixity, whether in counseling, meditation, or self-examination, often brings unconscious material to the surface). But though Taurpeo/Scorpus, the bipolar sign squaring Learius/Aquarleo, will often welcome unconscious contents and feel the need to dig into them, Learius/Aquarleo often resists them. The king presiding over his court does not wish to concern himself with what goes on beneath the castle. Water sinks into earth; fire and air move over the surface.

However, that we ignore unconscious contents does not mean that they go away or have no influence. Ignoring them may actually increase their power, corroborating evidence for which comes from uncountable social situations in which concern with the visible predisposes both rulers and ruled to ignore the not-visible. Yet both self and society consist partly, and perhaps largely, of unconscious contents; both individual and group have shadow-elements, as we have seen. If individual or group ignore these facts, development easily leads to over-inflation, while work for social benefit can easily generate demagoguery. Such concerns should concern us as we enter an Age ruled by this bipolar sign.

Visces-Pirgo: Compassionate Service, or the Deluge of Particulars?

Astrologers have long connected Virgo with work and service and Pisces with selflessness and compassionate openness. Though these designations oversimplify the energy of this final bipolar sign, we can all agree (I hope) that compassionate service and selfless work have much to recommend them. On the other hand, work or service without vision degenerates into drudgery or worse, while vision without the tools to bring it into the tangible world quickly devolves into illusion.

Those we label as compassionate people usually put their compassion to work. This suggests that Virgo and Pisces naturally arise together. (And, as noted, we see the two arise together in the activities characterizing the Age of Pisces/Virgo, perhaps more properly called the Age of Pirgo.) Some astrologers say, with some truth, that Virgo often misses the forest for the trees, getting too involved in the thousand-and-one tasks and practical details of the world and missing the larger living whole that encompasses those thousand-and-one tasks and details. Thus Virgo's need for, and tendency to gravitate toward, Pisces. On the other hand, it often seems that involvement in the details awakens one to the larger pattern. Thus John Taylor Gatto, mentioned in the previous section in another context, worked for years as a teacher, finding that his work alerted him to the larger patterns and awakened his compassion. Thus Gandhi's service led him to a more encompassing social conscience motivated by concern. Just as one can see universal patterns in a drop of water, so one can see in any service-work the more encompassing patterns of our world. And, of course, if one works in a service capacity, one finds one's compassion arising naturally.

We have heard, even if not always from reliable sources, that the path to hell is paved with good intentions. Pisceans lacking practicality will willingly provide the macadam for such a path. Further, Pisces, purveyor of all sorts of good intentions arising from a deeply-felt sense of the unity of all life, may yet live in a kind of hell if she finds no way to offer her gifts to others; your local Piscean may all too easily promote a kind of directionless compassion, drifting without any need for accomplishment. Surely we have all seen Pisceans swimming about aimlessly in the swirling seas of their own feelings, with no sense of how to swim to the shore towns in which those feelings might take root and do work beneficial to all. In the end, Pisces wants compassionate service and doesn't want, despite whatever habits she has, to emphasize only the motive.

I have said in other places that Virgo symbolizes our need, through tangible practice or even ritual, to unite heaven, earth, and man. Though to some extent we could say the same of all mutable signs, as the earth sign of that group, Virgo wants to find a practical manifestation of the principles. With her tendency to see only the trees, Virgo often forgets about the heaven principle. Left to only Virgo-oriented devices, she may seek only down-to-earth work, organizing the particulars of life for any vision on offer. In our society, with so many people cut off not only from the source of life and more-or-less forced to drink impure water (suggesting a problematic Virgo-Pisces connection, as does the impurity of the oceans), with people working in offices hundreds of feet above the life-giving earth, Virgo may often lose its connection to the earth-principle as well, leaving only the *man* principle, doing barren work without vision or life-sustaining energy. Thus Virgo can often end up pursing a series of meaningless tasks.

We can see, then, that Virgo and Pisces need each other. Virgo needs Pisces lest Virgo end up in the mentioned lifeless tasks; Pisces needs Virgo lest Pisces end up with directionless vision. The compassionate work of many church groups, or any work motivated by a coherent vision, can help alleviate the former type of problem; rituals connected with spiritual practice will often address the latter.

Do they arise together, though, in the activities of individuals? The waters gathering in the earth promote the harvest half a year later, and similarly for the life-giving richness of the earth, which reaches a peak before the planting season. Service work can generate despair if one serves a barren master, or wisdom if one serves something or someone worth serving. The oceanic depths of the human imagination, present in rituals of all sorts, come to fruition through human practical ingenuity, the types ranging from lama dances in Tibetan monasteries to the ritualistic behavior of your local novelist, writing at the same time every day and using techniques passed down through generations of artists. Oceanic feeling finds its fullest life in specific techniques.

The mutable signs, sometimes called "common" signs, all have to do with moving from one level or type of activity to another. Visces/Pirgo has to do with the finding of the profound within the mundane, and considering this activity as a path toward emancipation of some sort. Notable here: when we speak of finding the profound within the mundane, we don't mean that we bring the profound into the mundane from some outside point, but that the profound exists within the mundane right from the start. Within such experiences, we find the meaning of this final bi-polar sign.

Appendix II

Horoscope Data

Chapter II
   Emily Dickinson, December 10, 1830, 5:00 AM LMT, Amherst, MA[1]

Chapter III
   William Butler Yeats, June 13, 1865 NS, 10:40 PM LMT, Dublin, Ireland

Chapter IV
   Alice B. Sheldon (James T. Tiptree, Jr.), August 24, 1915, no time available, Chicago Illinois

Chapter V
   F. Lee Bailey, June 10, 1933, 2 AM EDT, Waltham, MA[2]
   Thomas Mann, June 6, 1875, 10:15 am LMT, Lubek, Germany
   Henry Kissinger, May 27, 1923, 5:30 AM MET, Fuerth, Bayern, Germany
   C.G. Jung, July 26, 1875, 7:29 PM LMT, Kesswil, Switzerland[3] (Rodden C)
   Alfred Adler, Feb. 7, 1870, 2:00 PM LMT, Vienna, Austria (Rodden DD)
   Mohandas Gandhi, October 2, 1869 NS, 7:11:48 AM (-4:38:24), Porbandar, India
   Herman Melville, August 1, 1819, 11:30 pm LMT, New York City (Rodden A)
   Jerry Rubin, July 14, 1938, 10:34 AM EST, Cincinnati, OH

[1] As I say in the text, I've taken this time from Habegger's biography. Other charts I've seen for Dickenson use the same time.
[2] The time sounds rounded off to me. However, I've worked a bit on this horoscope and it seems fairly accurate, as far as I have seen. I have not, however, done a formal rectification of it.
[3] This seems the usual horoscope for Jung. On astrodatabank.com, a note indicates that this time has been arrived at via rectification.

Bob Dylan, May 24, 1941, 9:05 PM CST, Duluth, MN (Rodden A)
Hillary Clinton, October 26, 1947, 8:00 PM ?? CST Chicago, IL[4]
Ken Starr, July 21, 1946, 6:45 pm CST, Vernon TX (Rodden AA)
George Herbert Bush, June 12, 1924, 10:30 AM EDT, Milton, MA

Chapter X

United States/Rudhyar: July 4, 1776 NS, 5:13:55 pm LMT, Philadelphia
Invasion of Mexico: January 13, 1846, noon, Charleston, SC
World Trade Center Attack: September 11, 2001, first plane strikes first tower, 8:46 am
Afghanistan War: October 7, 2001, noon, Kabul, Afghanistan
Iraq War: March 19, 2003, noon, Baghdad, Iraq

Chapter XI

Adolf Hitler, April 20, 1889 NS, 6:30 pm, 0:52:08, Branau am Inn, Austria

---

[4]People have suggested different birth times for Hillary Clinton; anything before about 10 pm has the Moon still in Pisces and square Uranus; earlier times yield a closer square.
[5]I have also seen a horoscope cast for noon; it has 24 Pisces 22 Ascendant.

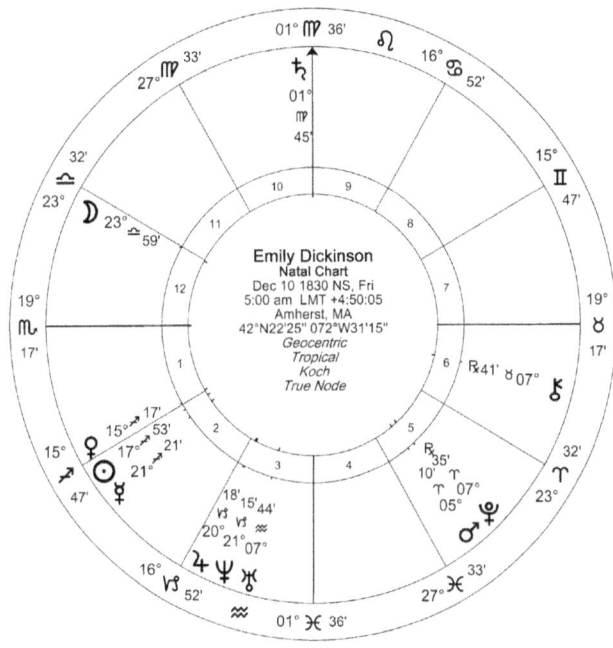

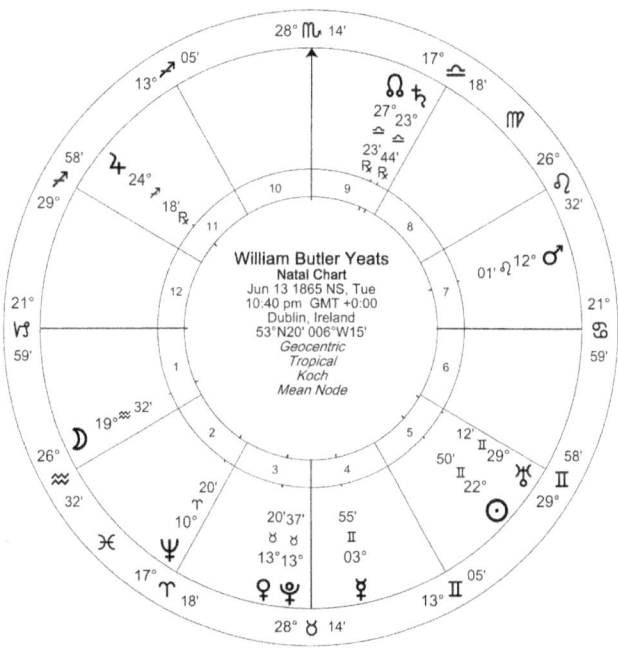

Your Hidden Face: Projection in the Horoscope

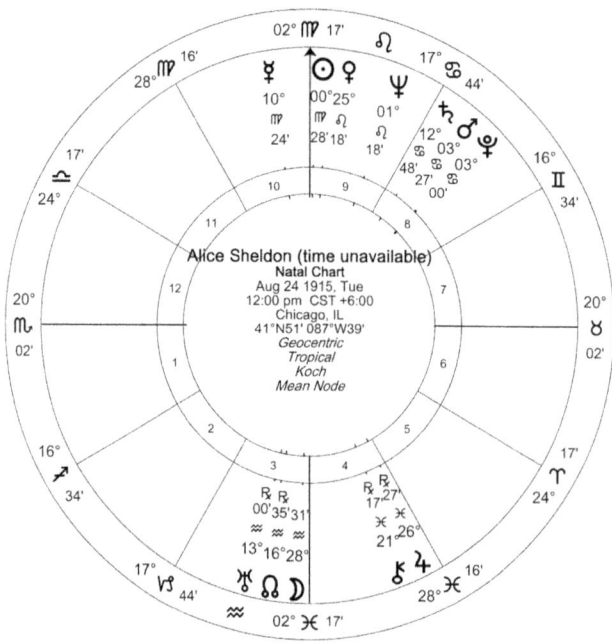

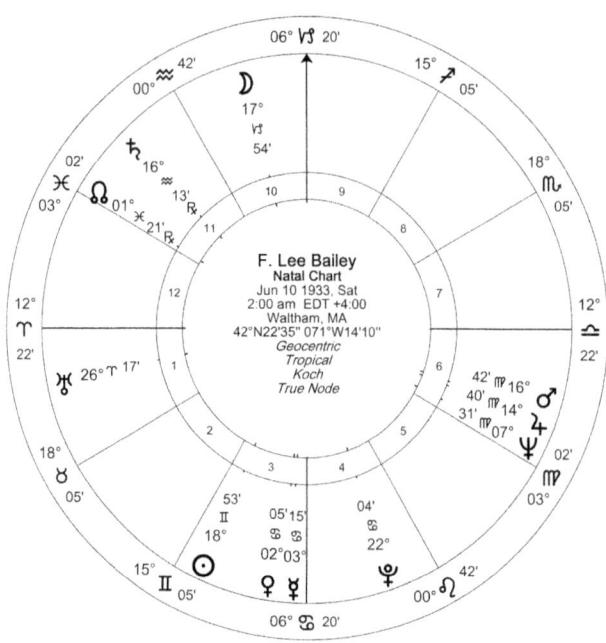

Appendix II, Chart Data

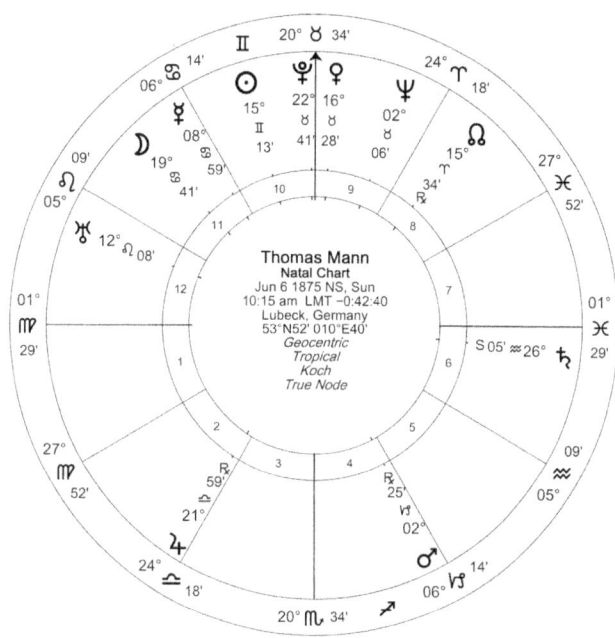

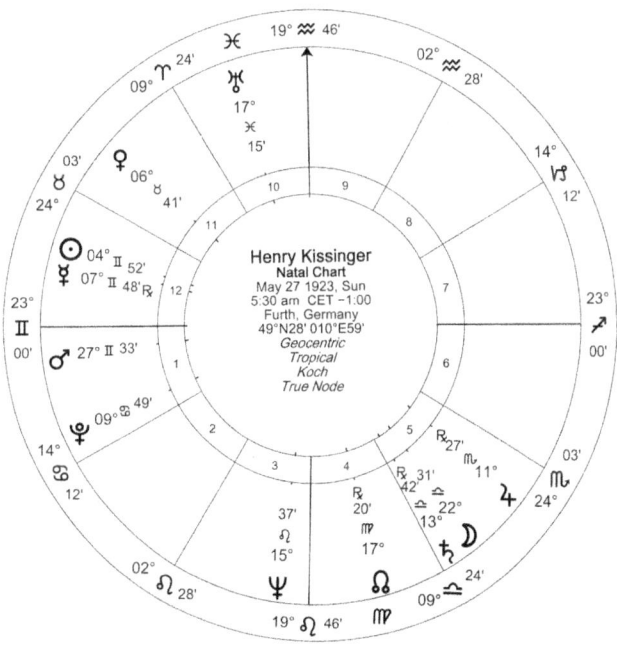

Your Hidden Face: Projection in the Horoscope

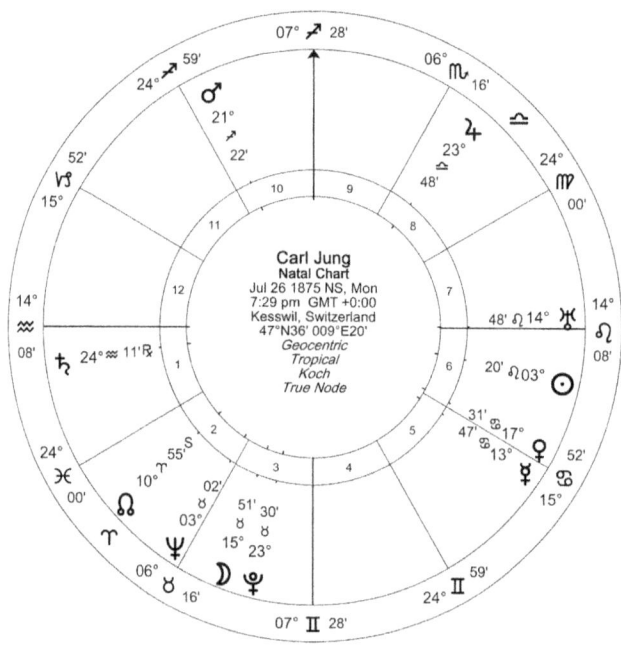

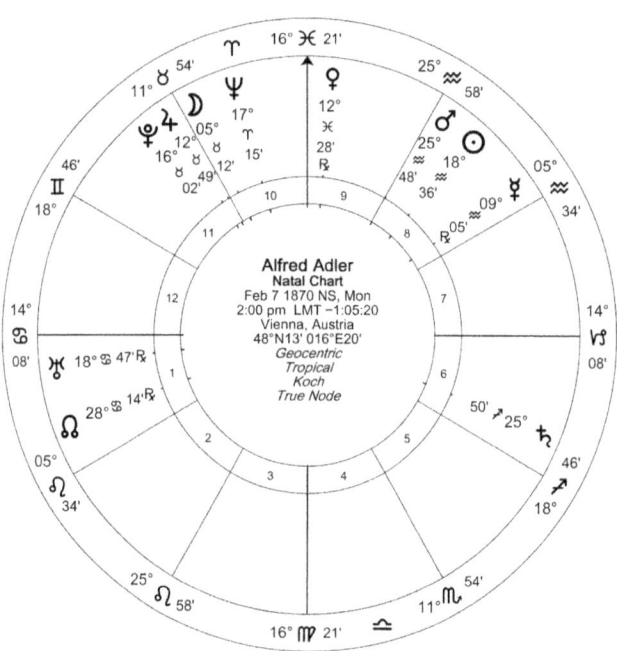

Appendix II, Chart Data

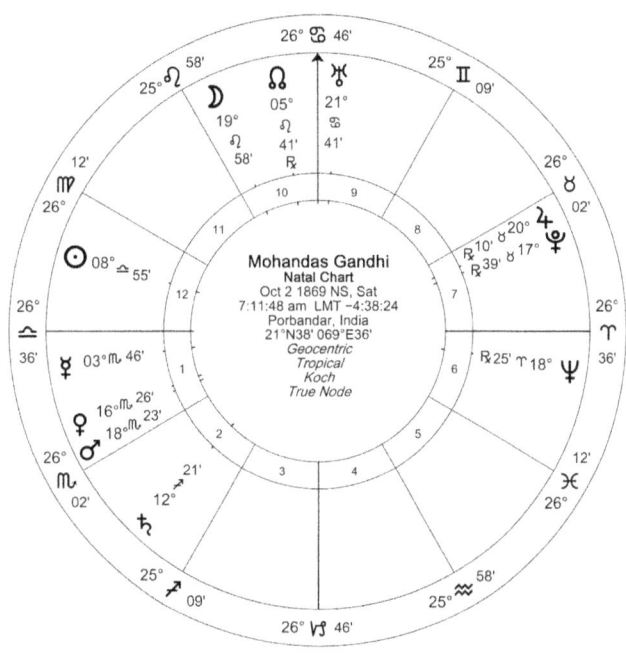

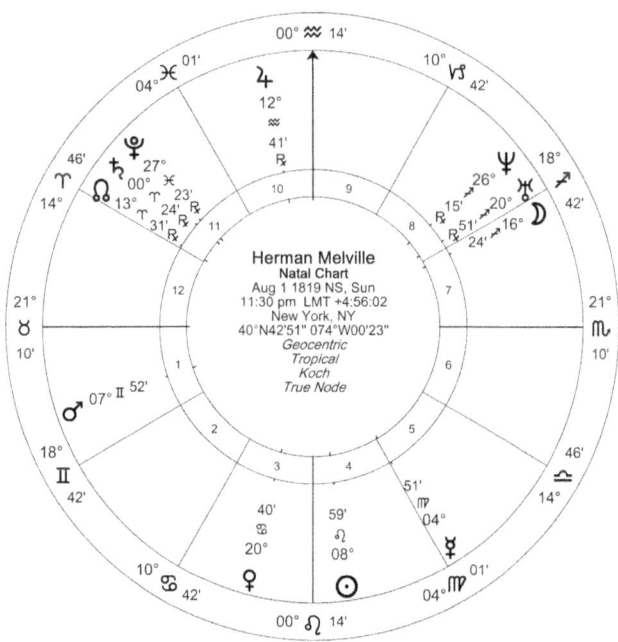

Your Hidden Face: Projection in the Horoscope

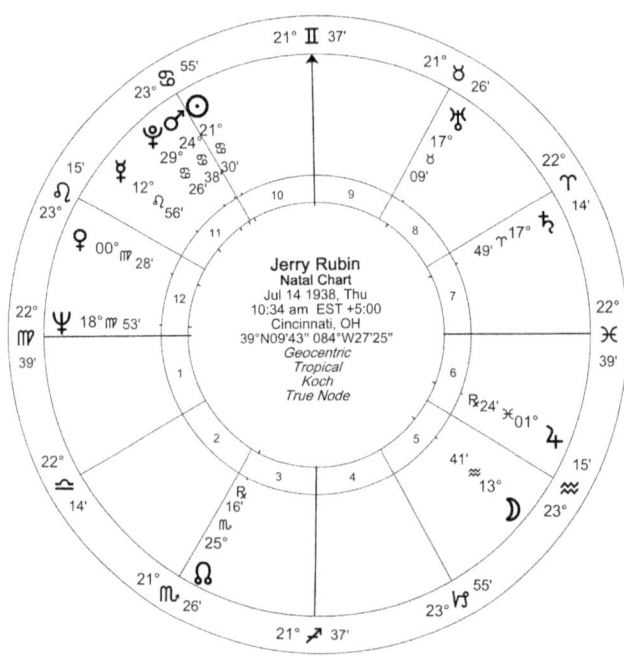

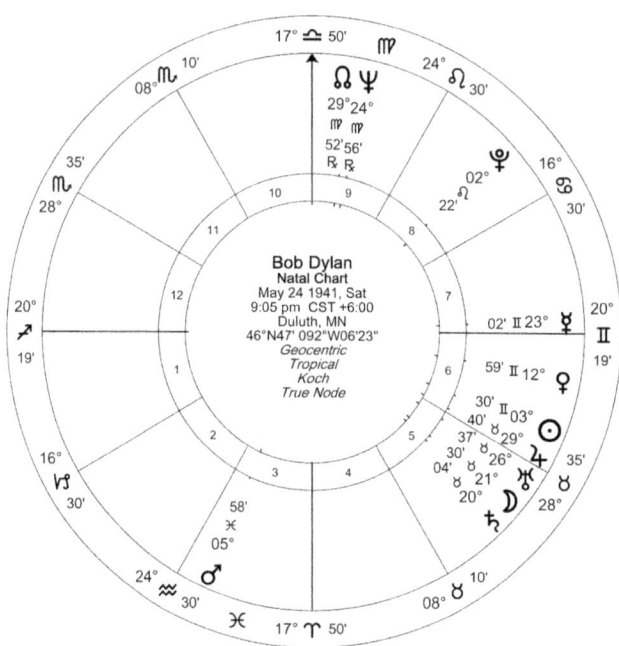

Appendix II, Chart Data

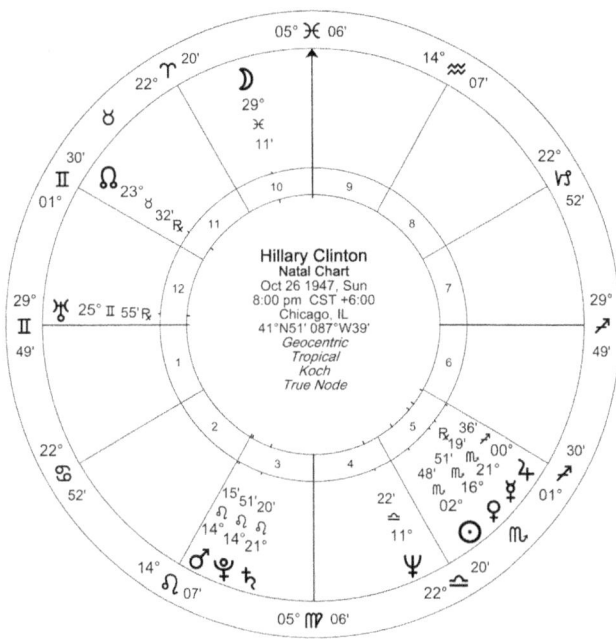

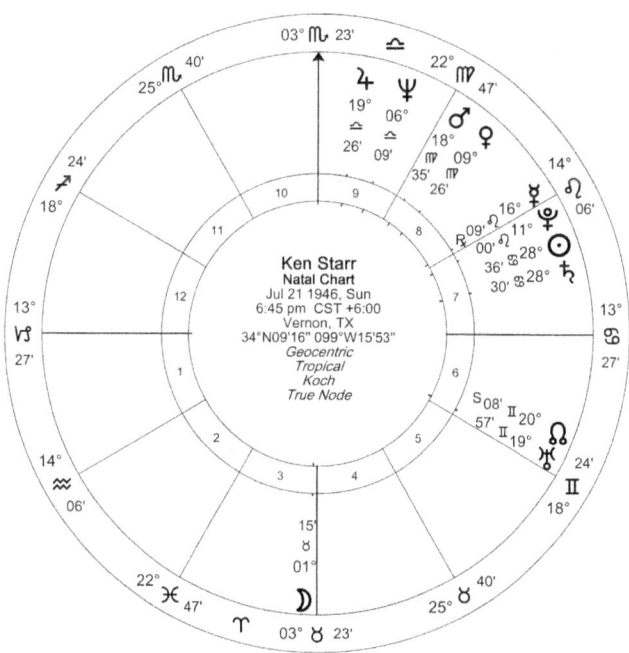

Your Hidden Face: Projection in the Horoscope

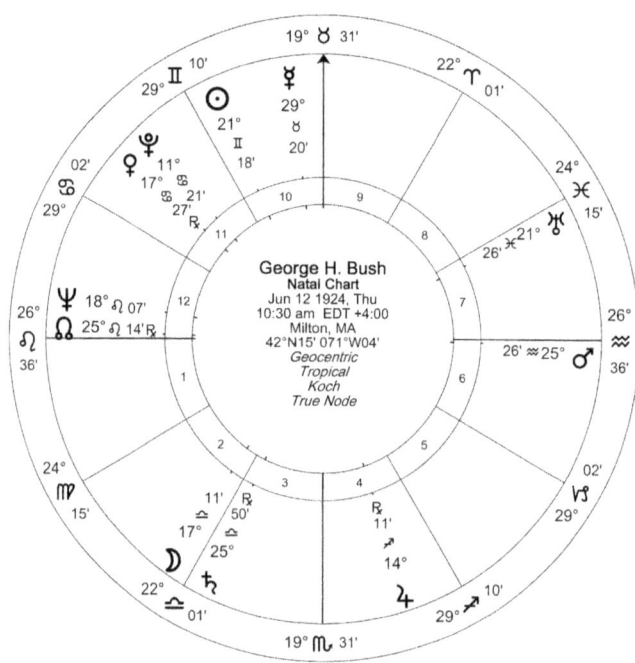

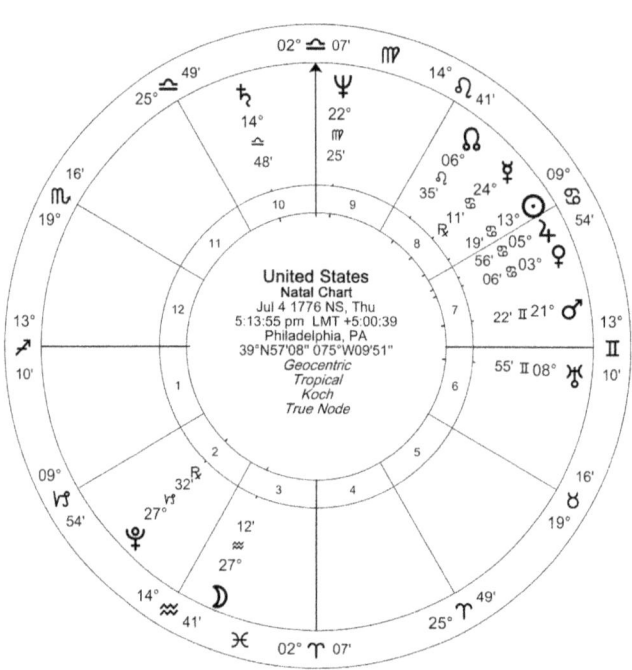

Appendix II, Chart Data

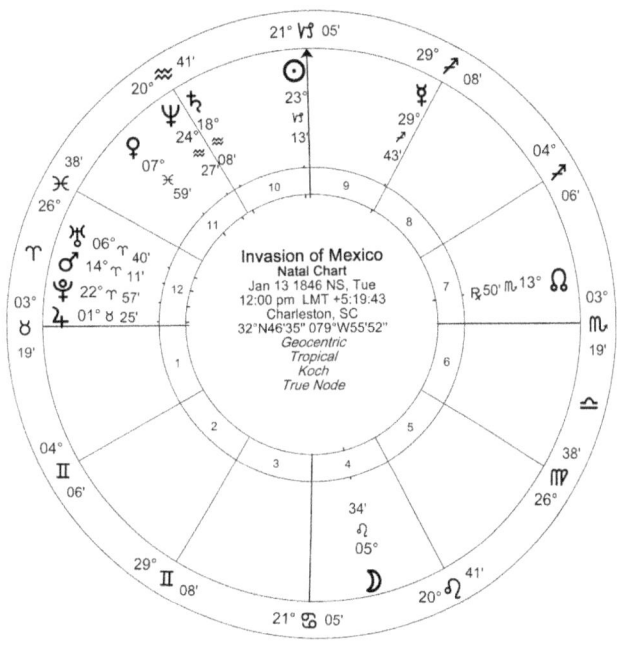

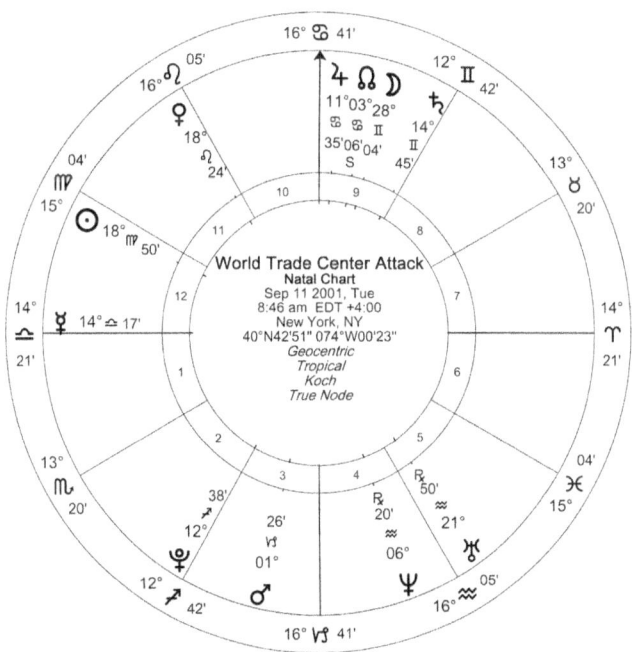

Your Hidden Face: Projection in the Horoscope

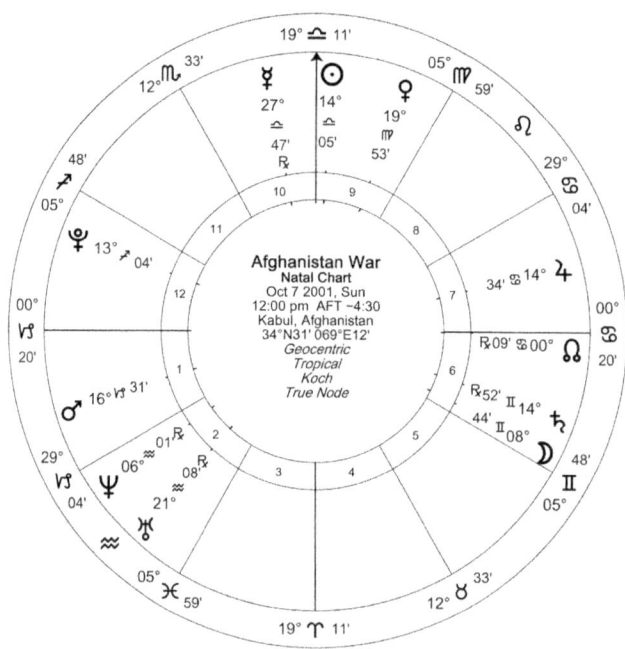

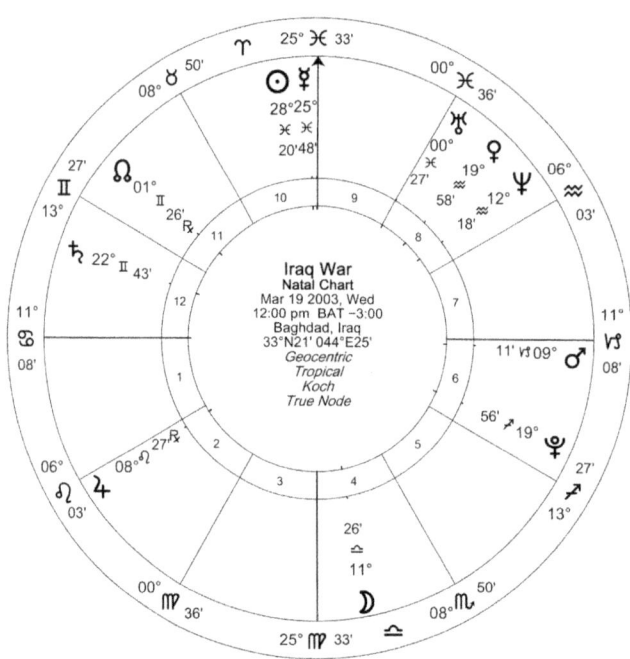

Appendix II, Chart Data

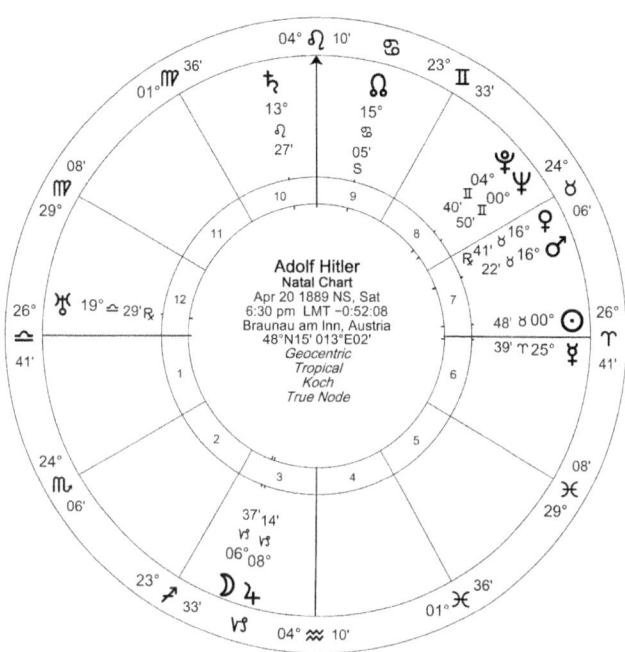

Your Hidden Face: Projection in the Horoscope

Inner Wheel
United States
Natal Chart
Jul 4 1776 NS, Thu
5:13:55 pm LMT +5:00:39
Philadelphia, PA
39°N57'08" 075°W09'51"
*Geocentric
Tropical
Placidus
True Node*

Outer Wheel
United States
Directed – Solar Arc
Jan 13 1846 NS, Tue
9:29:37 am LMT +5:00:39
Philadelphia, PA
39°N57'08" 075°W09'51"
*Geocentric
Tropical
Placidus
True Node*

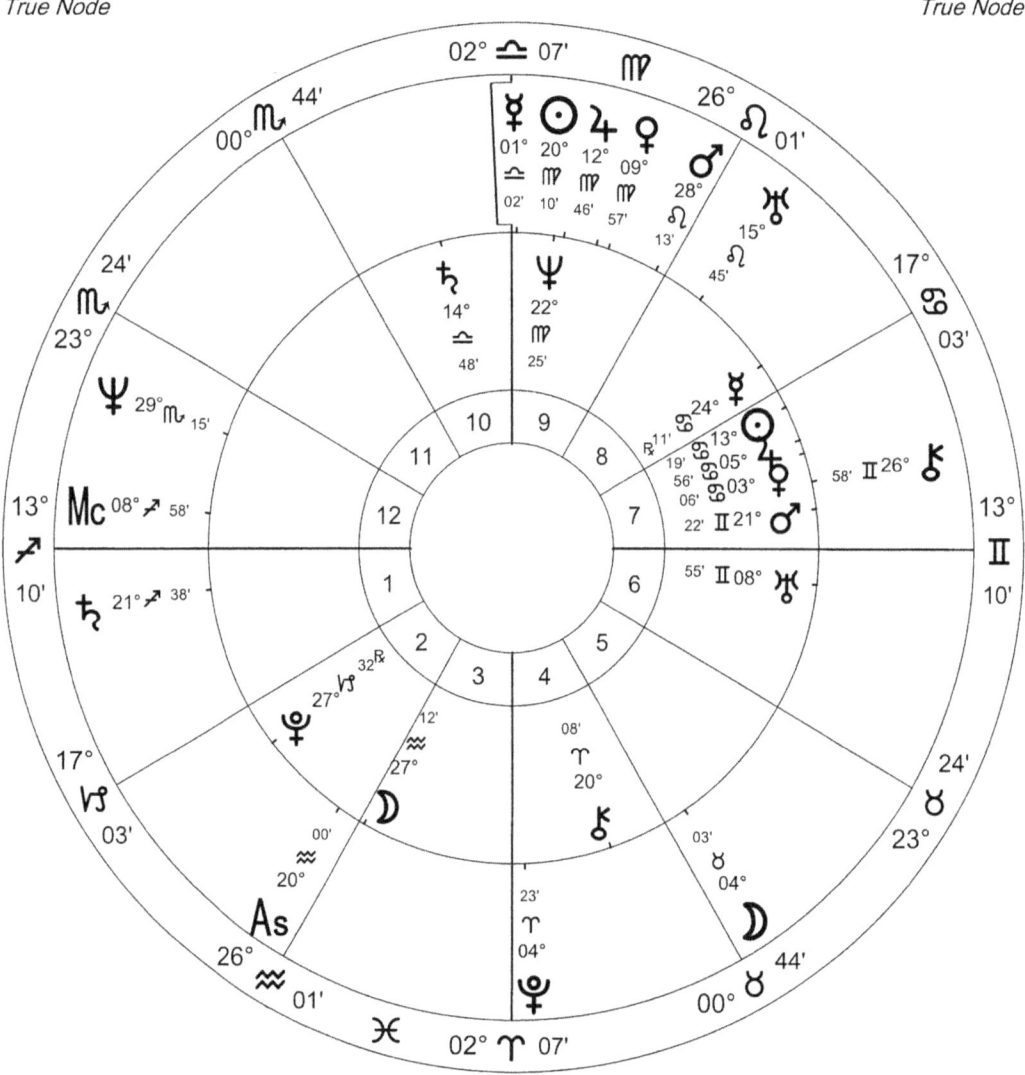

Appendix II, Chart Data

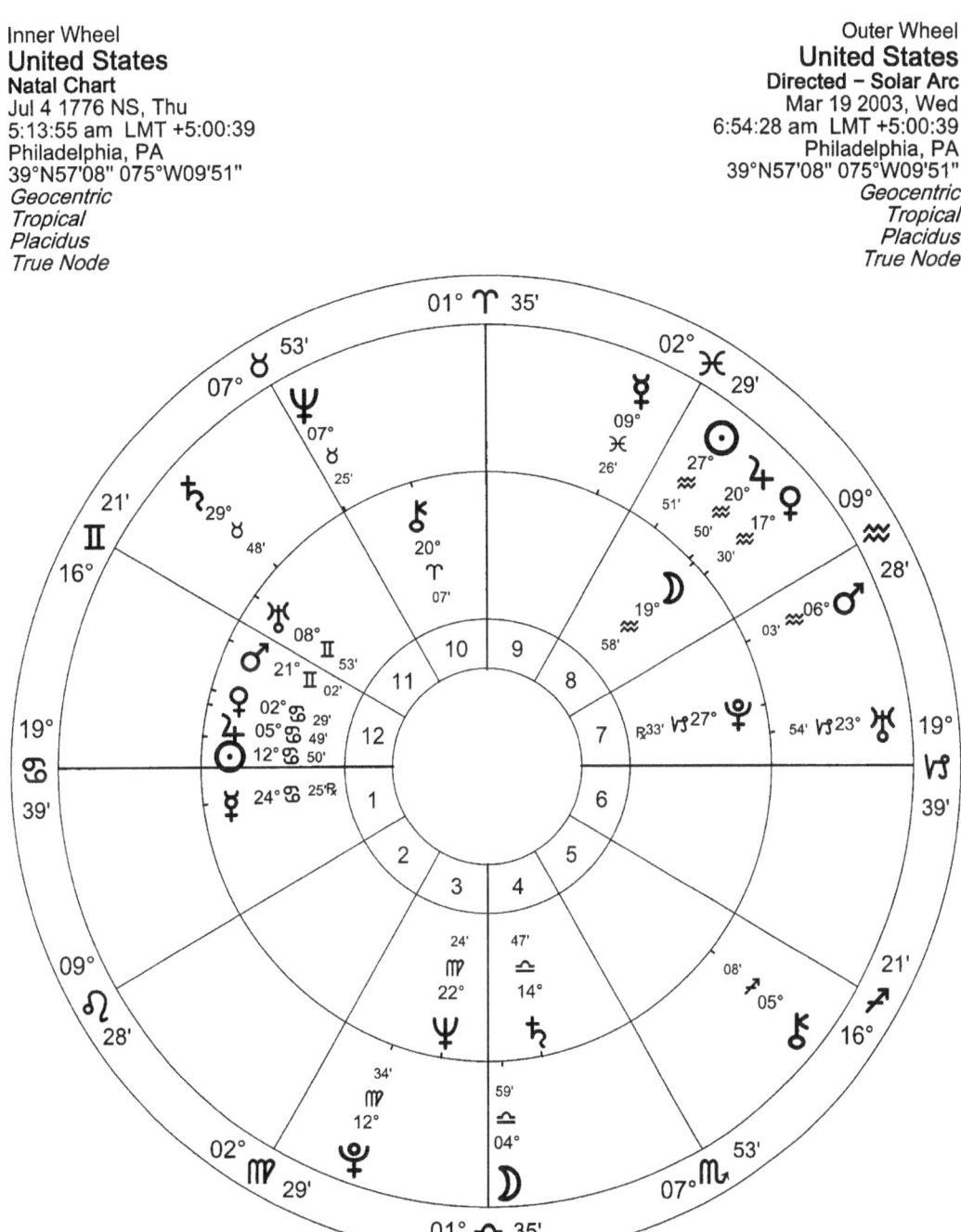

Bibliography

A Thousand Clowns. By Herb Gardener. Directed by Fred Coe. Hollywood: United Artists, 1965. DVD.

Adler, Gerhard. "Foreword" to Erich Neumann's *Depth Psychology and a New Ethic*. Boston: Shambhala, 1990.

Albee, Edward. *Who's Afraid of Virginia Woolf?* New York: Pocket Books, 1963.

Allman, T.D. *Unmanifest Destiny*. New York: Dial Press, 1984.

Barfield, Owen. *Saving the Appearances*. Middletown CT: Wesleyan University Press, 1988.

Barnet, Richard. *Intervention and Revolution*. New York: Meridian, 1972.

_____. *The Rocket's Red Glare: War, Politics, and the American Presidency*. New York: Simon and Schuster, 1990.

Barsamian, David, editor and interviewer. *Stenographers to Power*. Monroe, ME: Common Courage Press, 1992.

Bourland, D. David and Paul Dennithorne Johnston, editors. *To Be or Not: An E-Prime Anthology*. San Francisco: International Society for General Semantics, 1991.

Campbell, Joseph. Editor's Introduction, *The Portable Jung*. New York: Viking Press, 1971.

Carroll, Lewis. *Alice's Adventures in Wonderland and Through the Looking Glass*. New York: Oxford University Press, 1998.

Chantrell, Glynnis, ed. *The Oxford Dictionary of Word Histories*. Oxford: Oxford University Press, 2002.

Chomsky, Noam. "Prospects for Peace in the Middle East." www.chomskhy.info/talks/20010304.htm 2001.

Freud, Sigmund. *The Freud Reader*. New York: WW. Norton and Company, 1989.

Garfield, Jay. *The Fundamental Wisdom of the Middle Way*. New York: Oxford University Press, 1995.

Gatto, John Taylor. *The Underground History of American Education*. New York: Oxford Village Press, 2006.

Gauquelin, Michel. *Written in the Stars*. Northamptonshire, England: Aquarian Press, 1988.
Gould, Stephen Jay. *The Mismeasure of Man*. New York: W.W. Norton and Company, 1981.
Govinda, Lama Anagarika. *Foundations of Tibetan Mysticism*. New York: Samuel Weiser, 1960.
Greene, Liz. *The Inner Planets*. York Beach, ME: Samuel Weiser, 1983.
Grossinger. Richard. *The Night Sky*. New York: Random House, 1983.
Guenther, Herbert V. and Chogyam Trungpa. T*he Dawn of Tantra*. Boulder: Shambhala, 1975.
Habegger, Alfred. *My Wars are Laid Away in Books: The Life of Emily Dickenson*. New York: Modern Library, 2002.
Hand, Robert. *Horoscope Symbols*. Rockport: Para Research, 1981.
_____. *Planets in Transit*. Atglen, PA: Whitford Press, 1976.
Hayakawa, Samuel I. *Language in Thought and Action*. New York: Harcourt, Brace and Company, 1940.
Hollard, Dorothy C. and Margaret A. Eisenhart. "Moments of Discontent: University Women and the Gender Status Quo." In *Schooling the Symbolic Animal: Social and Cultural Dimensions of Education*, ed. By Levinson Bradley, A.U., Kathryn M. Borman, Margaret Eisenhart, Michele Foster, Amy E. Fox, and Margaret Sutton. New York: Rowman and Littlefield Publishers, Inc., 2000.
Illich, Ivan. *Deschooling Society*. New York: Marion Boyars, 1971,
Jacobi, Jolande. *Complex, Archetype, Symbol in the Psychology of C.G. Jung*. Princeton: Princeton University Press, 1959.
Johnson, Wendell. *People in Quandaries: The Semantics of Personal Adjustment*. New York: Harper and Brothers Publishers, 1946.
Jung, C.G. Aion. Princeton: Princeton University Press, 1959.
_____. *Answer to Job*. Princeton: Princeton University Press, 1958.
_____. "General Aspects of Dream Psychology," *Collected Works, 8*. Princeton: Princeton University Press, 1969.
_____. *Essays on Contemporary Events*. London: Ark Paperbacks, 1946.
_____. *Modern Man in Search of a Soul*. New York: Harcourt Brace Jovanovich, 1933.
_____. *Psychology and Alchemy*. Princeton: Princeton University Press, 1953.
_____. *Psychology and Religion*. New Haven: Yale University Press, 1938.
_____. "Psychological Commentary," *The Secret of the Golden Flower*, edited and translated by Richard Wilhelm. New York: Harcourt, Brace & World, 1962.
_____. "Relations Between the Ego and the Unconscious," *The Portable Jung*. New York: Penguin, 1971.
Jung, Emma. *Anima and Animus: Two Essays by Emma Jung*. Dallas: Spring Publications, 1957.
Jung, Emma and Marie Louise von Franz. *The Grail Legend*. Princeton: Princeton University Press, 1998.
Kerouac, Jack. *On the Road*. New York: Penguin, 1998.

Kodish, Bruce and Susan Presby. *Drive Yourself Sane: Using the Uncommon Sense of General Semantics.* Pasadena: Extensional Publishing, 2001.

Korzybski, Alfred. *Science and Sanity.* Englewood: Institute of General Semantics, 1933.

Lawrence, D.H. *Sons and Lovers.* New York: Viking, 1968.

Lem, Stanislaw. *Solaris.* New York: Berkley Medallion Books, 1971.

Lyons, Tim. *Astrology Beyond Ego.* Tempe: American Federation of Astrologers, 2011.

_____. *The Machine Stops.* Tempe: American Federation of Astrologers, 2012.

Marley, Bob. "Redemption Song," from *Legend: The Best of Bob Marley and the Wailers.* New York: Island Records, 2002.

Meadows, Donella H., Dennis L. Meadows, Jorgen Randers, William W. Behrens III. *The Limits to Growth.* New York: New American Library, 1972.

Meyer, Michael. *Handbook for the Humanistic Astrologer.* New York: Anchor Books, 1974.

Mumford, Lewis. *Technics and Civilization.* New York: Harcourt, Brace, and World, 1934.

Neumann, Erich. *Depth Psychology and a New Ethic.* Boston: Shambhala, 1990.

_____. *The Great Mother.* Princeton: Princeton University Press, 1963.

_____. *The Origins of and History of Consciousness.* Princeton: Princeton University Press, 1954.

Nolle, Richard. *Chiron: The New Planet in Your Horoscope.* Tempe: American Federation of Astrologers, 1997.

Percy, Marge. *He, She, and It.* New York: Fawcett Crest, 1991.

Phillips, Julie, James T. Tiptree, Jr.: *The Double Life of Alice Sheldon.* New York: Saint Martin's Press, 2006.

Ponlop Rinpoche, The Dzogchen. The Dzogchen, *Lorik Oral Commentary.* Seattle: Nitartha Institute, 1996.

_____. *The Basic Journey.* Seattle: Nalandabodhi, 2002.

Reisner, Mark. *Cadillac Desert: The American West and Its Disappearing Water.* New York: Penguin, 1986.

Rodden, Lois. *Astrodatabank Collection.* www.astro.com/astro-databank/Main-Page.

Rogin, Michael. *Fathers and Children: Andrew Jackson and the Subjugation of the American Indian.* New York: Vintage Books, 1976.

Rudhyar, Dane. *The Astrological Signs: The Pulse of Life.* Boulder: Shambhala, 1978.

_____. *The Astrology of Personality.* New York: Doubleday, 1970.

Sapir, Edward. *Selected Writings in Language, Culture, and Personality.* Berkeley: University of California Press, 1963.

Shibayama, Zenkei. *Zen Comments on the Mumonkan.* New York: Harper and Row, 1974.

Shipley, Joseph T. *Dictionary of Word Origins.* New York: The Philosophical Library, 1945.

Simmonite, W.J. *Arcana of Astrology.* North Hollywood: Symbols and Signs, 1979.

Stevens, Wallace. *The Palm at the End of the Mind.* New York: Vintage Books, 1990.

Thien, Khai. *Buddhist General Semantics.* New York: iUniverse, Inc., 2004.

Tierney, Bil. *Dynamics of Aspect Analysis*. Reno: CRCS, 1983.

Thompson, Judith Jarvis. *The Realm of Rights*. Cambridge: Harvard University Press, 1990.

Trager, James. *The People's Chronology*. New York: Henry Holt and Company, 1992.

Trungpa, Chogyam. *Cutting Through Spiritual Materialism*. Boulder: Shambhala, 1973.

_____. *Garuda IV: The Foundations of Mindfulness*. Boulder: Vajradhatu, 1976.

_____. *Glimpses of Abhidharma*. Boulder: Prajna Press, 1975.

_____. *The Myth of Freedom*. Boston: Shambhala, 2005.

_____. *Shambhala: The Sacred Path of the Warrior*. Boston: Shambhala, 1988.

_____. *Training the Mind*. Boston: Shambhala, 1993.

Tyl, Noel. *Astrology: Mundane, Astral, Occult*. St. Paul: Llewellyn, 1977.

United States Department of State. 2002 Report on Terrorism. Washington: Government Printing Office, 2003.

Von Franz, Marie Louise. *The Puer Aeternus*. Sigo Press, 1981 (no place given).

_____. *Projection and Recollection in Jungian Psychology*. London: Open Court Press, 1980.

_____. *Psychotherapy*. Boston: Shambhala, 1993.

_____. *Psyche and Matter*. Boston: Shambhala, 1992.

Waley, Arthur. *The Way and Its Power: A Study of the Tao Te Ching and Its Place in Chinese Though*t. New York: Grove Press, 1958.

Walker, Barbara. *The Woman's Encyclopedia of Myths and Secrets*. San Francisco: HarperSanFrancisco, 1983.

Wallace, B. Alan.*Choosing Reality*. Boulder: Snow Lion Publications, 2003.

Waters, Frank. *The Man Who Killed the Deer*. New York: Washington Square Press, 1942.

_____. Waters, Frank. *The Woman at Otowi Crossing*. Athens, OH: Swallow Press, 1987.

Whorf, Benjamin Lee. *Language, Thought, and Reality: Selected Writings of Benjamin Lee Whorf*. Cambridge: Massachusetts Institute of Technology, 1956.

Wilhelm, Helmut and Cary F. Baynes (trans.). *The I Ching, or Book of Changes*. Princeton: Princeton University Press, 1950.

Yeats, William Butler. *Selected Poems and Two Plays by William Butler Yeats*. New York: MacMillan, 1962

Zimmer, Heinrich. *Philosophies of India*. New York: The World Publishing Company, 1951,

Zinn, Howard. *Failure to Quit*. Boston: South End Press, 2002.

Index

Adler, Gerhard, 226
Afghanistan, 309
Ages, astrological, 357
Aggression, 94
Alaya
Alchemy
Ali, Antero, 89
Alice in Wonderland, 223
Angry, anger, 6
Anima, 34, 65
Anima, and tenth house, 164
Animus, 34
Animus, and fourth house, 164
Aquarius, 24
Aquarleo, 160
Aquinas, Thomas, 180
Archaic identity, 4
Ariba, 160
Aries, 24
Aspect, 125
Astro*Carto*Graphy, 314
Astrology Beyond Ego, 75
Bailey, F. Lee, 140
Blake, William, 363
Born, Max, 325
Bowles, Samuel, 48
Browning, Elizabeth Barrett, 50
Buddha, 361
Buddhism, 174
Bush, George W., 187
Bush, George Herbert, 145
Byrne, David, 153
Campbell, Joseph, 335
Cancer, 24
Cancercorn, 160
Capricance, 160

Capricorn
Character, 169
Cheney, Dick, 266
Churchill, Winston, 293, 322
Clinton, Hillary, 144
Cocoon, 213
Cognition, valid, 176
Collectivities, 127
Complex, psychological, 229
Complex, and Pluto, 229
Conjunction, 125
Copenhagen, Interpretation (of quantum theory), 325
Counter-revolution, 247
Creative, creativity, 45
Creel Commission, 294
Cronus, 110
Dalai Lama, 210
de Broglie, Louis Victor, 325
Depression, 9
Destiny, 169
Dickens, Charles, 201
Dickinson, Emily, 48
Dirac, Paul, 325
Doctor Faustus, 343
Dostoyevsky, Fyodr, 196, 267
Dylan, Bob, 144, 363
Earth, 29
Eden, Garden of, 34
Ego, 9
Ego formation, 208
Egolessness
Einstein, Alfred, 206
Eisenhower, Dwight, 322
Eliot, Thomas Stearns, 17
Experiment, 353

Fascination, 159
Fascism, 159
Fate, 320
Faulkner, William, 46, 344
Faust, 37
Fear, 33
Filtering, 170
Football, Uranian, 44
Football analogy, 44
Form, 29, 72
Form, Saturnian, 72
Form, lunar, 72
Form
Freedom, 32
Freud, Sigmund, 1
Gaia, 29
Gandhi, Mohandas, 144, 196
Gatto, John Taylor, 364, 365
Gauquelin, Michel, 150
Geminarius, 160
Gemini, 24
Gender, 23
Ginsberg, Allen, 363
Glyph, Mars, 106
Glyph, Pluto
Glyph, Venus, 106
Goethe, 37
Great American Desert
Greene, Liz, 111, 164
Habegger, Alfred
Hand, Robert, 126
Hardy, Thomas, 153
Heisenberg, Werner, 14, 257, 326
Hera,
Hitler, Adolf, 322
Ho Chi Minh, 292
Homosexuality, 319
Hook, 5
House, 126

House, eighth,
House, fourth,
House, second,
House, seventh,
House, sixth,
House, tenth,
House, twelfth,
Hussein, Saddam,
Infidelity, Uranus and,
Illich, Ivan, 260
Industrial Revolution, 166
Integration, 9
Iraq,
Islamic Fundamentalists, 315
Jackson, Andrew, 292
Jones, Marc Edmund, 178
Joyce, James, 203
Jung, Carl, 1, 333
Jung, Emma, 363
Jupiter, 23
Karmapa,
Karmic situation, 32
Karmic principle, 29
Kerouac, Jack,
Kissinger, Henry, 139
Korzybski, Alfred, 68
Lakota, 365
Lao Tzu, 331
Learius, 160
LeGuin, Ursula, 153
Lem, Stanislaw, 223
Leo, 24
Libra
Libries, 160
Limits to Growth, The, 259
Lincoln, Abraham, 201
Lindberg, Charles, 201
Loose Change, 314
Lunacy, 61

Lyons, Tim, 75
Mailer, Norman, 201
Manas, 61
Manifest Destiny, 252, 292
Mann, Thomas, 139, 363
Marlowe, Christopher, 343
Mars, 23
Mars, projection of, 93
Meaning
Melville, Herman, 144
Mephistopheles, 343
Mercury, 23
Mexico, invasion of, 294
Meyer, Michael, 137
Midlife, 46
Milarepa, 210
Mind, 61, 341
Mind, universal, 39
Modern Man in Search of a Soul, 335
Moon, 12, 23
Moon, ego and, 208
Moon, mother and
Moon, security and, 208
Moral integration, 9
More, Sir Thomas, 201
Mother, 66
Mussolini, Benito, 322
Myth, 42
Myth, Greek creation, 45
Napoleon, 322
Native American, 75
Negative, negativize, 8, 89
Neptune, 23
Neptune, discovery of, 252
Neumann, Eric, 226
Newman, Randy, 153
No one knows,
Non-conscious, 158, 170
Non-dualism, 77

Objectivity, 138
Opposites, 358
Opposition, 125
Oppositions, and U.S. presidents, 137
Ouranus, 29
Pallas Athena, 111
Perception, 2, 169
Persona, as function, 231
Persona, 231
Pirgo, 160
Pisces,
Planets, outermost, 128
Planets, categories of, 238
Pluto, 23, 319
Pluto, and emotion, 320
Pluto, discovery of, 254
Polk, James, 308
Projectile, 7
Projection, 1
Projection, five stages in the withdrawing of, 18
Projections, collective, 243
Projections, wandering of, 90
Prostitution, 319
Psychotic, 5
Pueblo Indians, 96
Puer aeternus, 11
Quantum theory, 14
Quantum mechanics, 326
Rand, Ayn, 201
Reagan, Ronald, 203
Reality, 4
Relationship, 63
Relationships, intimate, 24
Revolution, 247
Roosevelt, Franklin D., 201, 322, 366
Rubin, Jerry, 144
Sagini, 160
Sagittarius,

Sane, sanity, 5, 90
Sapir, Edward, 270
Saturn, 23
Saturn, creative work and, 217
Saturn, ego and, 208
Saturn, language and, 249
Saturn, security and, 208
Schrodinger, Erwin, 325
Scorpio, 24
Scorpus, 160
Security, 9, 25
Security, psychological, 207
Security, situational, 207
Security needs, 12
Self-acceptance, 75
Sense organs, 174
September 11, 2011, 309
Shadow, as function, 231
Shadow, the, 226
Shadow, Saturn and, 228
Shamanism, 260
Shibayama, Zenkei
Should's, 79
Signs, 169
Signs, bi-polar, 160
Simmonite, W.J., 87
Sitting Bull, 365
Six-sign-zodiac, 160, 357
Slick, Gracie, 153
Social roles, 42
Solar child, 89
Sound and the Fury, The, 46
Square, 125
Stalin, Joseph, 322
Starr, Kenneth, 145
Stevens, Wallace, 267
Sub-lunar realm, 30
Subjectivity, 138
Sun, 23

Sun, projection of, 87
Taurpeo, 160
Taurus, 24
Thoreau, Henry David, 200
Transference, 1
Unconscious, personal, 151
Unconscious, collective, 151
Unconscious, unconscious mind, 1
United States, 127
United States, horoscope of, 276
United States, people of, 275
Uranus, 10, 12, 23, 25
Uranus, discovery of, 250
Van Gogh, Vincent, 153
Venus, 23
Venus, projection of, 99
Vietnam, 128
Violence, 94
Virgo,
Visces, 160
Von Franz, Marie Louise, 1
Wallace, E. Alan, 327
War, with Mexico, 252
Waters, Frank, 96, 267
Weyl, Herman, 325
Whitman, Walt, 363
Whorf, Benjamin Lee,
Wilhelm, Richard, 335
Wilson, Woodrow, 322
World Trade Center, 314
Wotan, 256
Yeats, William Butler, 153, 363
Yid, 341
Yogachara, 66
Zen,
Zeus, 111

www.ingramcontent.com/pod-product-compliance
Lightning Source LLC
Chambersburg PA
CBHW081157230426

43666CB00016B/2840